Lecture Notes in Computer Scie

T0237853

Commenced Publication in 1973
Founding and Former Series Editors:
Gerhard Goos, Juris Hartmanis, and Jan van Leeuwen

Valérie Issarny   Richard Schantz (Eds.)

Middleware 2008

ACM/IFIP/USENIX
9th International Middleware Conference
Leuven, Belgium, December 1-5, 2008
Proceedings

 Springer

Volume Editors

Valérie Issarny
INRIA Rocquencourt
Domaine de Voluceau, 78153 Le Chesnay CEDEX, France
E-mail: Valerie.issarny@inria.fr

Richard Schantz
BBN Technologies
10 Moulton Street, Cambridge, MA 02138, USA
E-mail: schantz@bbn.com

Library of Congress Control Number: 2008940422

CR Subject Classification (1998): C.2.4, D.4, C.2, D.1.3, D.3.2, D.2, H.2, H.4

LNCS Sublibrary: SL 2 – Programming and Software Engineering

ISSN   0302-9743
ISBN-10   3-540-89855-7 Springer Berlin Heidelberg New York
ISBN-13   978-3-540-89855-9 Springer Berlin Heidelberg New York

Springer is a part of Springer Science+Business Media

springer.com

© IFIP International Federation for Information Processing, Hofstrasse 3, A-2361 Laxenburg, Austria 2008
Printed in Germany

Typesetting: Camera-ready by author, data conversion by Scientific Publishing Services, Chennai, India
Printed on acid-free paper   SPIN: 12581047   06/3180   5 4 3 2 1 0

Preface

This volume contains the proceedings of the International Middleware Conference, held in Leuven, Belgium during December 1–4, 2008. This year marked the ninth rendition of this annual conference in its current format initially adopted in 1998, aspiring to serve as the premier venue focusing exclusively on important middleware results. A lot has happened over the intervening 10-year span. Middleware has become pervasive in an increasingly interconnected world, with its concepts now securely embedded in the notional architectures driving forward the information age. The conference continues to be a focal point for important new initiatives and results for new generations of middleware. With each succeeding year, it has become an even more competitive publishing venue, further extending its selectivity this year as well. Of the 117 submissions, only 21 were able to receive acceptance invitations, for an acceptance rate of less than 18%. Competitive indeed. Additionally, these submissions continue to come from all over the globe, spanning authors from 23 countries. A truly world-wide endeavor.

But other things have also changed as we turn the corner on the first decade of this conference. In many ways, middleware has achieved significant success where it really counts: in terms of technical innovations, advanced capabilities, successful ideas, and fielded systems which permeate society, industry, government, and academia. With this success comes maturity. Many of the themes which kicked off the focus on these intermediary technologies have long since transitioned, and with each new middleware conference, the field takes on a slightly different view from earlier. This year, the topics were a bit more diverse, and represent a blend of maturing themes and new areas of focus for the conference. Accepted papers in this proceedings volume fall roughly under four categories: four papers concerned with platforms extended to new capabilities (e.g., mobility, off-line operation), six papers concerned with advanced software engineering focusing on specific system properties, five papers focusing on overall system management techniques, and six papers concerned with components and system algorithms and properties. Notably, new avenues of investigation are coupled with application initiatives and focused properties in deriving new uses and more detailed scenarios of operation. And more attention is now focused on keeping systems running or running correctly, in place of merely creating the system; moreover, focus is shifting to managing resources of the "virtual" variety, in addition to real and countable ones. Those are all measures of maturing, but they also leave wide open-space for another wave of innovation. In seeking these new tributaries from the earlier basics, we are in fact laying a foundation for new generations of middleware pursuits.

The proceedings contain 21 papers covering a wide-range of recent research. Each paper submitted to Middleware 2008 was reviewed by a minimum of three members of the Program Committee (PC), with many having four PC member reviewers. After initial reviews were posted, papers with multiple positive reviews were subject to interactive conferencing among the reviewers and PC Chairs to debate the pros and cons of each and to allow discussion of differing viewpoints among reviewers. From these, a more manageable set was selected, discussed and debated among the entire PC to arrive at the final program. New to this conference was a shepherding process for a number of papers which were conditionally accepted pending changes suggested and requested by reviewers toward an improved quality of the submission. From this extensive and interactive, multi-pass process, we believe the proceedings capture the best of the submissions and provide the reader with the highest quality, most readable results. We hope you agree. The PC Co-chairs thank each and every one of the 47 members of the PC for putting forth the timely and extra effort involved with this process; as a result of their diligence these results are available to all.

In addition to the regular papers in the proceedings, this year we introduced a separate industry track, with its own call for papers, and its own mini-PC. It was our intent to provide an avenue for papers better suited to industry concerns and perspectives than to more traditional research papers. These additional papers are made available separately. The industry track session, along with continuing venues for a Work in Progress (WiP) session providing an early look at emerging new research, keynote speakers, panel and demos and posters sessions, complemented by two days of workshops, and the third annual Doctoral Symposium, round out the program for Middleware 2008.

We hope you share our enthusiasm for the results. In closing we would also like to express our deepest gratitude to the General Conference Chairs, Wouter Joosen and Yolande Berbers, the Special Session Chairs, Fred Douglis, Cecilia Mascolo and Bert Lagaisse, the Publicity Co-chairs, Michael Atighetchi and Sonia Ben Mokhtar, and to Richard van de Stadt and Davy Preuveneers for help with online tools for the conference and program selection process, each contributing significantly to a successful conference.

September 2008   Valérie Issarny
                                                        Rick Schantz

Organization

Middleware 2008 was organized under the auspices of IFIP TC6WG6.1 (International Federation for Information Processing, Technical Committee 6 [Communication Systems],Working Group 6.1 [Architecture and Protocols for Computer Networks]).

Executive Committee

Conference Chairs	Wouter Joosen (K.U.Leuven, Belgium)
	Yolande Berbers (K.U.Leuven, Belgium)
Program Chairs	Valérie Issarny (INRIA, France)
	Rick Schantz (BBN Technologies, USA)
Workshops and Tutorials Chairs	Frank Eliassen (University of Oslo, Norway)
	Hans-Arno Jacobsen (University of Toronto, Canada)
Industry Chair	Fred Douglis (IBM, USA)
Work In Progress Chair	Cecilia Mascolo (University of Cambridge, UK)
Publicity Chairs	Michael Atighetchi (BBN Technologies, USA)
	Sonia Ben Mokhtar (UCL, UK)
Posters and Demos Chair	Bert Lagaisse (K.U.Leuven, Belgium)
Doctoral Symposium Chair	Sam Michiels (K.U.Leuven, Belgium)
Corporate Support Chair	Katrien Janssens (K.U.Leuven, Belgium)
Local Arrangements Chair	Davy Preuveneers (K.U.Leuven, Belgium)

Steering Committee

Gordon Blair (Chair)	Lancaster University, UK
Jan De Meer	SmartSpaceLab, Germany
Peter Honeyman	CITI, University of Michigan, USA
Hans-Arno Jacobsen	University of Toronto, Canada
Elie Najm	ENST, France
Gustavo Alonso	ETH Zurich, Switzerland
Jean-Bernard Stefani	INRIA, France
Maarten van Steen	Vrije Universiteit Amsterdam, The Netherlands
Shanika Karunasekera	University of Melbourne, Australia
Renato Cerqueira	PUC-RIO, Brazil
Nalini Venkatasubramanian	UC Irvine, USA

Program Committee

Gustavo Alonso	ETH Zurich, Switzerland
Christiana Amza	University of Toronto, Canada

Jean Bacon	University of Cambridge, UK
Dave Bakken	Washington State University, USA
Guruduth Banavar	IBM Research, India
Alberto Bartoli	University of Trieste, Italy
Christian Becker	Universität Mannheim, Germany
Gordon Blair	Lancaster University, UK
Roy H Campbell	University of Illinois at UC, USA
Renato Cerqueira	PUC-Rio, Brazil
Angelo Corsaro	PrismTech, USA
Paolo Costa	Vrije Universiteit Amsterdam, The Netherlands
Geoff Coulson	Lancaster University, UK
Jan De Meer	SmartSpaceLab, Germany
Fred Douglis	IBM T.J. Watson Research Center, USA
Naranker Dulay	Imperial College London, UK
Frank Eliassen	University of Oslo, Norway
Markus Endler	PUC-Rio, Brazil
Pascal Felber	University of Neuchatel, Switzerland
Paulo Ferreira	INESC ID / Technical University of Lisbon, Portugal
Nikolaos Georgantas	INRIA, France
Chris Gill	Washington University, USA
Paul Grace	Lancaster University, UK
Indranil Gupta	University of Illinois at UC, USA
Qi Han	Colorado School of Mines, USA
Peter Honeyman	CITI, University of Michigan, USA
Gang Huang	Peking University, China
Shanika Karunasekera	University of Melbourne, Australia
Bettina Kemme	McGill University, Canada
Fabio Kon	University of Sao Paulo, Brazil
Doug Lea	Oswego State University, USA
Rodger Lea	University of British Columbia, Canada
Mark Linderman	Air Force Research Laboratory, USA
Joe Loyall	BBN Technologies, USA
Cecilia Mascolo	University of Cambridge, UK
Satoshi Matsuoka	Tokyo Institute of Technology, Japan
Elie Najm	ENST Paris, France
Bala Natarajan	Symantec Corp., India
Gian Pietro Picco	University of Trento, Italy
Alexander Reinefeld	Zuse Institute Berlin, Germany
Luis Rodrigues	INESC-ID/IST, Portugal
Antony Rowstron	Microsoft Research, UK
Douglas C. Schmidt	Vanderbilt University, USA
Jean-Bernard Stefani	INRIA, France
Gautam Thaker	Lockheed Martin Adv. Tech. Labs, USA
Peter Triantafillou	University of Patras, Greece
Apostolos Zarras	University of Ioannina, Greece

Referees

Artur Andrzejak
Juliana França Santos Aquino
Mikael Beauvois
Pedro Brandao
Raphael de Camargo
Roy Campbell
Nuno Carvalho
Matteo Ceriotti
Lipo Chan
Sand Correa
Julien Delange
UmaMaheswari Devi
Ioanna Dionysiou
Kevin Dorow
Partha Dutta
David Eyers
Fabiano Cutigi Ferrari
Bruce Fields
José Viterbo Filho
Alessandro Garcia
Joanna Geibig
Harald Gjermundrod
Rick Grandy
Stefan Guna
Manish Gupta
Sebastian Gutierrez-Nolasco
Irfan Hamid
Aaron Harwood
Loren Hoffman
Mikael Högqvist
Jose Mocito
Amadeu Andrade Barbosa Júnior
Kalapriya Kannan
Manos Kapritsos

Bjoern Kolbeck
João Leitão
Renato Maia
Marcelo Andrade da Gama Malcher
Alan Marchiori
Naoya Maruyama
Giuliano Mega
Luca Mottola
Nanjangud C. Narendra
Anh Tuan Nguyen
Sebastian Gutierrez Nolasco
Lakshmish Ramaswamy
Rajiv Ramdhany
Imran Rao
Valeria Q. Reis
Etienne Rivière
Liliana Rosa
Romain Rouvoy
Giovanni Russello
Richard Süselbeck
Gregor Schiele
Florian Schintke
Thorsten Schütt
Rudrapatna K. Shyamasundar
Amirhosein Taherkordi
Francois Taiani
Verena Tuttlies
Zografoula Vagena
Luis Vargas
Luis Veiga
Akshat Verma
Eiko Yoneki
Chenfeng Vincent Zhou

Sponsoring Institutions

 International Federation for Information Processing
http://www.ifip.org

 Association for Computing Machinery
http://www.acm.org

 Advanced Computing Systems Association
http://www.usenix.org

 Katholieke Universiteit Leuven
http://www.kuleuven.be

 Interdisciplinary Institute for Broadband Technology
http://www.ibbt.be

Corporate Sponsors

 BBN Technologies
http://www.bbn.com

 Google
http://www.google.com

International Business Machines Corporation
http://www.ibm.com

Table of Contents

Platforms

Software Engineering

System Management

Components and System Algorithms and Properties

Adaptive Content-Based Routing in General Overlay Topologies

Guoli Li, Vinod Muthusamy, and Hans-Arno Jacobsen

University of Toronto
gli@cs.toronto.edu, {vinod,jacobsen}@eecg.toronto.edu
http://padres.msrg.toronto.edu

Abstract. This paper develops content-based publish/subscribe algorithms to support general overlay topologies, as opposed to traditional acyclic or tree-based topologies. Among other benefits, publication routes can adapt to dynamic conditions by choosing among alternate routing paths, and composite events can be detected at optimal points in the network. The algorithms are implemented in the PADRES publish/subscribe system and evaluated in a controlled local environment and a wide-area PlanetLab deployment. Atomic subscription notification delivery time improves by 20% in a well connected network, and composite subscriptions can be processed with 80% less network traffic and notifications delivered with about half the end to end delay.

1 Introduction

Publish/subscribe (pub/sub) is a powerful messaging paradigm that maintains a clean decoupling of data sources and sinks [3,4,5,8,14,24,31,34]. Interoperating through simple publish and subscribe invocations is especially useful for the development of large, distributed, loosely coupled systems. While there are many applications based on group communication and topic-based pub/sub protocols such as information dissemination [17,22], a large variety of emerging applications benefit from the expressiveness, filtering, distributed event correlation, and complex event processing capabilities of content-based pub/sub. These applications include RSS feed filtering [31], stock-market monitoring engines [33], system and network management and monitoring [7,20], algorithmic trading with complex event processing [10,29], business process execution [32], business activity monitoring [7] and workflow management [5]. Typically, content-based pub/sub systems are built as application-level overlays of content-based pub/sub brokers, with publishing data sources and subscribing data sinks connecting to the broker overlay as clients. In pub/sub systems, event *filtering* is supported by atomic subscriptions, whereas composite subscriptions are used by more sophisticated pub/sub applications to *correlate* events from distributed sources [5,7,14,29]. To support the class of applications above, this paper considers both atomic and composite subscriptions.

Most existing pub/sub systems [5,8,19,23] are based on an acyclic overlay broker network. With only one path between any pair of brokers or clients, content-based routing is greatly simplified. Despite this success, an acyclic overlay offers

V. Issarny and R. Schantz (Eds.): Middleware 2008, LNCS 5346, pp. 1–21, 2008.

limited flexibility to accommodate changing network conditions, is not robust with respect to broker failures, and introduces complexities for supporting other protocols, such as failure recovery. For example, since only one path exists between any pair of clients, an acyclic overlay cannot accommodate routing around congested, overloaded, or failed brokers. Furthermore, because acyclic networks are more vulnerable to partitions, failure recovery is more expensive and topology reconfiguration can be complex since their repair actions must maintain the acyclic property of the overlay [27]. Maintaining the acyclic property is difficult since a broker often only knows about its direct neighbors and not the entire topology.

However, supporting general overlay topologies requires changes to the standard content-based routing protocols in order to avoid routing messages in cycles. Consider a topology graph $G = (V, E)$ with vertices V and edges E. Broadcasting a single message in G will generate $\frac{|E| - |V|}{|E|}\%$ of redundant messages. For instance, in a 500 broker topology with an average connectivity of 10 neighbors, a single advertisement induces 2500 messages, 80% of which must be discarded.

This paper focuses on enabling content-based routing in cyclic overlays. Supporting such general overlays affords great flexibility for selecting an optimal routing path based on some optimality criteria or utility function, something not possible in acyclic overlays, where at most one path exists between any data source and sink pair. A novel dynamic routing algorithm takes advantage of this capability to route publications based on changing overlay-link statistics. The flexibility of a cyclic overlay is further exploited by a new composite event detection algorithm that efficiently correlates events from distributed data sources with the objective of reducing the dissemination of unnecessary messages and minimizing the notification delay. By allowing for general overlay topologies, the content-based pub/sub protocols in this paper also provide a foundation for potentially simplifying the support of other features such as failure recovery, load balancing, path reservation, or splitting message streams across multiple paths.

To address the above problems, this paper makes the following contributions. First, Section 3 develops significant extensions to standard content-based routing protocols to enable message routing in general overlay topologies. The design preserves the original simple publish and subscribe interface to clients, and does not require changes to a broker's internal message matching algorithm, allowing the approach to be easily integrated into existing systems. The solution applies to advertisement-based and to subscription-based routing, and exploits redundant routing paths so that publications can be routed to subscribers more optimally, for example, based on assessing load conditions on links. An interesting byproduct of the algorithm is that message routing can be significantly improved by performing matching only once per message, as opposed to existing approaches that match messages at each broker in the overlay. Second, Section 4 presents a novel dynamic routing algorithm for handling composite subscriptions in cyclic overlays. The algorithm is fully distributed, and seeks to minimize the message delay and network traffic by continually adjusting composite subscription propagation paths based on the publication traffic and the overlay network load distribution. Third, Section 4 also develops a cost model that is used by the composite subscription routing algorithm to dynamically optimize the placement of composite subscription *join points*, where publications are filtered and correlated. Finally, in Section 5, implementations of the protocols are experimentally evaluated on various topologies in a controlled local network environment and in a wide-area PlanetLab deployment.

2   Related Work

Content-based Pub/Sub: Most pub/sub systems assume an acyclic overlay network. REBECA [8] explores advanced routing algorithms based on an acyclic broker overlay network, and JEDI [5] uses a hierarchical overlay for event dispatching. SIENA [4], however, proposes a routing protocol for general overlay networks, using reverse path forwarding to detect and discard duplicate messages. In this solution, any advertisement, subscription or publication message may be duplicated. As well, routing path adaptations to changing network conditions and the implications for composite event detection are not addressed.

There have been attempts to build content-based pub/sub systems over group multicast primitives such as IP multicast [6]. To appreciate the challenge in doing so, consider a scenario with N subscribers. In a content-based system, each message may be delivered to any subset of these subscribers, resulting in 2^N "groups". It is infeasible to manage such exponentially increasing numbers of groups, and the algorithms seek to construct a limited number of groups such that the number of groups any given message must be sent to is minimized and the precision of each group is maximized (i.e., minimize the number of group members that are not interested in events sent to that group). This is an NP-complete problem [2], but there have been attempts to develop heuristics to construct such groups [23,30]. To avoid these complexities more recent content-based routing algorithms [4,5], as well as the algorithms in this paper, have abandoned the notion of groups and rely on an overlay topology that performs filtering and routing based on message content.

The expressiveness and filtering capabilities of content-based routing comes at the price of larger routing table state. Techniques such as subscription covering [4], merging [13,19] and summarization [34] reduce broker routing state, message traffic and matching overhead, and are orthogonal to the routing protocols in this paper.

There have been a number of content-based pub/sub systems that exploit the properties of distributed hash tables (DHT) to achieve reliability. Hermes [28] builds an acyclic routing overlay over the underlying DHT topology but does not consider alternate publication routing paths as in this paper. Other approaches [3,9,21], construct distributed indexes to perform pub/sub matching. This paper, on the other hand, assumes a more traditional dedicated broker network model, one benefit of which is the lack of additional network and computation overhead associated with searching a distributed index to perform pub/sub matching. The model in this paper can achieve lower delivery latencies when there are no failures, but still use alternate paths for publication routing in case of congestion or failure. Admittedly, the DHT protocols, designed for more hostile network, tend to be more fault-tolerant than the algorithms in this paper which assume a more reliable, dedicated broker network.

Pub/Sub systems have been developed for even more adverse environments such as mobile ad-hoc networks (MANET). These networks as inherently cyclic but the protocols [12,26] require periodic refreshing of state among brokers due to the unreliability of nodes and links, an overhead that is not required by the work in this paper. As well, MANET brokers can exploit wireless broadcast channels to optimize message forwarding. For example, brokers in ODMRP [12] do not maintain forwarding tables, but only record if they lie on the path between sources and sinks in a given group. Brokers simply broadcast messages to their neighbours (discarding duplicates) until the message reaches the destinations. The protocols in this paper, on the other hand, cannot rely on broadcast transmission and also explicitly attempt to avoid duplicate message delivery. As well, ODMRP does not support the more complex content-based semantics.

Composite Subscriptions: A *composite subscription* correlates publications over time, and describes a complex event pattern. Supporting an expressive subscription language and determining the location of composite event detection in a distributed environment are difficult problems. CEA [29] proposes a Core Composite Event Language to express concurrent event patterns. The CEA language is compiled into an automata for distributed event detection supporting regular expression-type patterns. CEA employs polices to ensure that mobile event detectors are located at favorable locations, such as close to event sources. However, CEA's distribution polices do not consider the alternate paths and the dynamic load characteristics of the overlay network.

One of the key challenges in supporting composite subscriptions in a distributed pub/sub system is determining how the subscription should be decomposed and where in the network event collection and correlation should occur. While this problem is similar to query plan optimization in distributed DBMS [25] and distributed stream processing [11], data in a relation or a stream have a known schema which simplifies matching and routing. Moreover, a database query is evaluated once against existing data, while a subscription is evaluated against publications over time. This may result in different optimization strategies and cost models. In the IFLOW [11] distributed stream processing engine, a set of operators are installed in the network to process streams. IFLOW nodes are organized in a cluster hierarchy, with nodes higher in the hierarchy assigned more responsibility, whereas in our approach, brokers have equal responsibility.

3   Routing in General Overlays

The work in this paper builds on the PADRES distributed, content-based pub/sub middleware platform. PADRES uses advertisement-based routing adapted from SIENA [4] and REBECA [8]. Each broker records its overlay neighbors in an

Overlay Routing Tables (ORT), and advertisements are broadcast through the network forming an advertisement tree. Advertisements are stored in the Subscription Routing Table (SRT) which is logically a list of [advertisement,last hop] tuples. Subscriptions are propagated in reverse direction along the advertisement trees, and are stored in the Publication Routing Table (PRT), which is logically a list of [subscription,last hop] tuples, and is used to route publications. If a publication matches a subscription in the PRT, it is forwarded to the last hop broker of that subscription until it reaches the subscriber.

Each PADRES broker consists of an input queue, a rule-based matching engine, and a set of output queues. The matching engine takes messages from the input queue and routes them to the proper output queues after matching the message content against the SRT and PRT. An output queue represents a destination which could be a broker, a client, a database or a JMS broker.

3.1 Challenges

Cycles in the network introduce misleading message routing paths and redundant traffic. In the network in Fig. 1(a), advertisements Adv_1 and Adv_2 are broadcast and form two advertisement trees. Since brokers discard duplicate advertisements, the trees shown in Fig. 1(a) may vary based on relative message delays. Now, a subscription Sub_1 matching

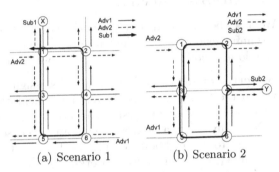

(a) Scenario 1   (b) Scenario 2

Fig. 1. Cyclic routing of subscriptions

both Adv_1 and Adv_2 arriving at Broker 1 from Broker X is forwarded both towards Broker 6 along the Adv_1 tree, and towards Adv_2. Unfortunately, at Broker 6, Sub_1 matches Adv_2 and is routed back to Broker 1, forming a cycle.

Another scenario of a subscription cycle is shown in Fig. 1(b), where Broker 4, forwards Sub_2 to Brokers 6 and 2, following the paths built by Adv_1 and Adv_2, respectively. However instead of stopping at Brokers 5 and 1, the two copies of Sub_2 continue to be routed unnecessarily. The duplicate subscriptions are not detected until they arrive at the same broker, say Broker 3.

Subscription cycles not only cause redundant subscription messages, they can cause publications to be routed indefinitely in cycles as they keep switching among matching subscription routing paths.

In summary, cycles in the overlay lead to duplicate advertisements, subscriptions or publications, a problem that is exacerbated in well-connected networks with many redundant paths. However, since there are relatively few advertisements, detecting and discarding advertisements is advantageous, provided subsequent cyclic routing of subscriptions and publications can be prevented.

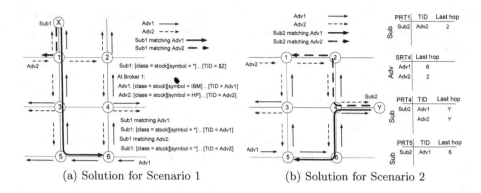

(a) Solution for Scenario 1   (b) Solution for Scenario 2

Fig. 2. TID-based subscription routing

3.2   TID-Based Routing

We describe extensions to the standard content-based routing using Fig. 2(a) as a running example. These extensions are contained within the routing protocol and do not modify the interface to the pub/sub clients.

Advertisement: Each advertisement is assigned a unique *tree identifier* (TID) within the broker network. In our implementation we use message identifiers, which are unique in our system, as TIDs.

Normally, when a broker receives an advertisement, it broadcasts the advertisement to its neighbors and inserts the advertisement in its subscription routing table (SRT). For cyclic networks, we extend this behavior such that brokers discard duplicate advertisements upon receipt, so each advertisement forms a spanning advertisement tree distinguished by TID. As we will see, our approach only requires such duplicate detection for advertisements, which we expect to have fewer of than subscriptions and publications.

Subscription: When a broker receives a subscription from a subscriber, it adds an existential predicate [TID, =, $Z] that uses a variable binding mechanism.[1] If the subscription matches an advertisement in the SRT, the advertisement's TID is bound to the variable $Z. For example, in Fig. 2(a), Sub_1 is matched by both Adv_1 and Adv_2 at Broker 1. A copy of Sub_1 with TID bound to Adv_1 is forwarded to Broker 6 and another copy bound to Adv_2 is forwarded toward the publisher. In our implementation, the TID attribute may have a set of values associated with it so that only one copy of the subscription is forwarded if subscriptions with different TIDs have the same next hop.

A subscription with a bound TID value only propagates along the corresponding advertisement tree. Therefore, when a broker receives a subscription with a bound TID value, it can forward the subscription without matching the subscription against all the advertisements in the SRT. As a result, subscription

---

[1] The predicate tests whether a message contains a *TID* attribute, in which case the value is bound to the variable in the subscription. Otherwise, the predicate is false.

forwarding is greatly sped up by the use of TIDs, by matching subscriptions against advertisements only once.

Subscriptions set up paths for routing publications. We extend the publication routing table (PRT) to a list of [subscription, {TID, last hop of subscription}], such as PRT_4 in Fig. 2(b). Since a subscription may arrive at a broker via different paths labeled by TIDs, the PRT records the TID and the last hop broker of the incoming subscription. A subscription not in the PRT is inserted; otherwise the existing record is updated with the new {TID, last hop of subscription} pair.

A subscription matching multiple advertisements may be bound to several TIDs, and will form alternate routing paths for publications if the subscription with different TIDs has different last hops. For instance in Fig. 3, Sub matches both Adv_1 and Adv_2 at Broker 1, and is assigned two TIDs in PRT_1 with different last hops. Copies of subscriptions with different TIDs propagate along their corresponding advertisement trees and these paths may diverge and reconverge at a broker due to intersections among the advertisement

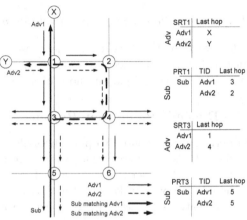

Fig. 3. Multiple publication routing paths

trees. Thus, a broker may receive multiple copies of a subscription with different TIDs. These are not, however, duplicate messages as they correspond to different paths, and are stored in the PRT as potential routing path alternatives for publications.

Alternative paths for publication routing are maintained in PRTs as subscription routing paths with different TIDs and destinations. More alternate paths are available if publishers' advertisement spaces overlap or subscribers are interested in similar publications, which is often the case for many applications with long-tailed workloads. Our approach takes advantage of this and uses multiple paths available at the subscription level.

Subscription covering, merging, and summarization optimizations [4,13,19,34] eliminate redundant subscriptions and result in smaller routing tables. These optimizations can be applied among subscriptions with the same TID.

Publication: When a broker receives a publication from a publisher, the publication is assigned an identifier equal to the TID of its associated advertisement. From this point, the publication is propagated along the paths set up by matching subscriptions with the same TID without matching the content of the publication at each broker. This simple and fast *fixed publication routing* algorithm is enabled by the use of TIDs. Alternatively, the *dynamic publication routing* algorithm described in Section 3.3 exploits alternate paths.

Notice that with the TID extensions, subscriptions form a directed, cycle-free graph between publishers and their potentially interested subscribers, so publications are never forwarded in a cyclic manner. In the directed graph, there may be multiple paths between any pair of brokers depending on how subscriptions are routed along multiple advertisement trees. In fixed publication routing, brokers do not need to detect duplicate publications and, consequently, no bandwidth is wasted due to redundant publication traffic.

Property 1. *No broker receives duplicate publication messages.*[2]

It follows from Property 1 that no subscriber receives duplicate publications, since a subscriber connects to exactly one broker, brokers forward a publication at most once over a link, and no broker receives duplicate publications.

3.3   Dynamic Publication Routing

Subscriptions are routed to publishers along advertisement trees. If the advertisement trees of different data sources intersect, multiple publication routing paths to a subscriber result. In Fig. 3, *Sub* is forwarded to Broker 1 over two paths (Path 1 via Brokers 5, 3 and 1, and Path 2 via Brokers 5, 3, 4, 2 and 1). Publications of Adv_1 take the path through Broker 3, while publications of Adv_2 take the path through Broker 2 in the fixed routing approach. However, if the TID of a publication could be adapted in transit, a better path may be chosen. A publication of Adv_2 arriving at Broker 1, could be routed to Broker 3 by changing its TID to Adv_1 instead of being routed to Broker 2.

A routing algorithm is required to determine the "best" path, based on metrics such as the fewest hops or the shortest end to end delay. While similar to the routing problem in IP networks, those solutions cannot be applied to pub/sub systems directly. In address-based routing, the shortest path can be calculated based on a global topology graph, such as with link state routing [18], whereas our brokers are only aware of their overlay neighbors, a property we wish to retain for scalability and manageability. More importantly, IP networks can rely on the clustering of addresses; all nodes in a part of the network may have the same network mask, and can be represented by a single routing table entry. In content-based pub/sub, however, nodes' addresses (i.e., their subscription), may not be clustered. This makes global optimizations infeasible, and instead we use a decentralized solution based on local link status information.

In the *dynamic publication routing* (DPR) algorithm, a broker forwards a message through the link with minimal cost, using the heuristic that this link is also on the minimum cost path to the destination. To dynamically select paths while network traffic loads or topologies change, each broker maintains a *Link Status Table* (LST). For example, to minimize the delay cost, the LST can store the link utilization ratio of each neighbor, and update the ratio whenever messages

---

[2] The proof is presented in [15].

are sent or received over the link. The link utilization ratio is $U = \frac{r_{output}}{r_{sending}}$, where r_{output} is the rate of messages entering the output queue corresponding to the link, and $r_{sending}$ is the rate of messages sent on that link. The link utilization ratio captures the queueing delay of a link. Other costs can also be modeled in the LST but are not considered in this paper.

When a broker receives a publication, for each matching subscription that may come from multiple links with different TIDs, it selects the link with minimal latency, and assigns the corresponding TID to the publication. The algorithm ensures that, for one subscription with different TIDs, each representing a path from a publisher to the subscriber, only one publication is forwarded to one of the potential neighbors. Also, only one copy of the publication is forwarded to a neighbor if several matching subscriptions come from the same last hop. For example, in Fig. 3 PRT_1 shows that publications matching Sub have two available paths, through Broker 2 or 3. Consulting the LST, the broker will forward the publication to the destination with minimal delay, say Broker 3.

When a broker fails or a link is overloaded, the broker's neighbors detect the failure or congestion as a result of messages queueing up in the corresponding output queue, which cause the link utilization ratio to increase. Consequently, publications will be routed around the failed or congested broker. While this approach tries to use as many available paths as possible to route messages around failures and congestions, it cannot guarantee delivery, such as in the case of a network partition, until the failures have been repaired by a separate module. Guaranteed delivery is out of the scope of this paper.

Modifying a publication p's TID in transit seems to change the set of subscribers notified of this publication, but this is not the case. Intuitively, the algorithm works because for any given subscription s_i from a subscriber S that matches p, p's TID is only changed to an advertisement's TID that also matches s_i. That means p will be delivered to S by "borrowing" branches of another advertisement tree. The DPR algorithm is formalized in Algorithm 1 and its correctness is established by Property 2.

Property 2. *Changing a publication p's TID while in transit will not change the set of notified subscribers N.*[3]

Our solution exhibits several useful properties. First, it retains the pub/sub client interface. No changes to the pub/sub matching algorithm are required, since TID attributes are matched just like any other attributes. Second, with the TID attribute, optimizations can be performed at each broker to speed up and simplify subscription and publication propagation. For example, subscriptions are matched only once while forwarded to publishers. Third, our approach generates duplicate messages only when broadcasting advertisements; subscription and publication forwarding do not create redundant traffic. Fourth, subscriptions may determine multiple routing paths for publications. The DPR algorithm can route publications around failed or congested brokers, making the system more robust to broker failures and dynamic network traffic. Moreover, the DPR

---

[3] The proof is presented in [15].

Algorithm 1. Dynamic Publication Routing

Require: An incoming publication $p(c, TID_p)$
Ensure: forwardMsgs: A set of publications with destinations and updated TIDs
1. forwardMsgs = $\emptyset$
2. S = $\{s_i | p$ matches s_i in the PRT$\}$
3. **for** $s_i \in$ S **do**
4. $\wp = \{[TID_j, LastHop_j] | [s_i, TID_j, LastHop_j] \in$ PRT$\}$
5.   Find m such that link utilization ratio of destination $LastHop_m$ is minimal in $\wp$
6.   nextHop = $LastHop_m$
7.   **if** p'.content$\neq$ content and p'.nextHop $\neq$ nextHop,$p' \in$ forwardMsgs **then**
8. p.TID = TID_m
9. p.nextHop = nextHop
10.   forwardMsgs = forwardMsgs.add(p)
11.   **end if**
12. **end for**
13. **return** forwardMsgs

---

algorithm selects efficient routes based on network conditions to minimize notification delay. This is useful in applications with quality of service constraints.

4   Composite Subscription Routing

PADRES supports an expressive subscription language that can specify constraints on a publication's content and correlate publications in a distributed environment. A composite subscription consists of a Boolean function over atomic subscriptions. For example, the following subscription detects when Yahoo's stock opens at less than 22, and Microsoft's at greater than 31.

```
[class,eq,'STOCK'],[symbol,eq,'YHOO'],[open,<,22] &
[class,eq,'STOCK'],[symbol,eq,'MSFT'],[open,>,31]
```

The detection of event patterns is carried out by the broker network in a distributed manner. In *topology-based* composite subscription routing [14], a composite subscription is routed as a unit towards potential publishers until it reaches a broker B at which the potential data sources are located in different directions in the overlay network. The composite subscription is split at broker B, called the *join point broker*, and each individual part is routed to potential publishers separately. Later, matching publications are routed back to the join point broker, which carries out the composite event detection. Notice that topology-based routing requires an acyclic overlay and does not consider dynamic network conditions.

4.1   Challenges

In a general broker overlay, multiple paths exist between subscribers and publishers, and the topology-based composite subscription routing does not necessarily result in the most efficient use of network resources. For example, composite event detection would be less costly if the detection is close to publishers with a higher publishing rate, and in a cyclic overlay, more alternative locations for composite event detection may be available. The overall savings are significant if the imbalance in detecting composite events at different locations is large.

In this paper, we develop a novel composite subscription routing algorithm that selects optimal join point brokers to minimize the network traffic and detection delay while correctly detecting composite events in a cyclic broker overlay. The approach benefits greatly from the flexibility made available by content-based routing in general overlays.

4.2 Dynamic Composite Subscription Routing

The *dynamic composite subscription routing* (DCSR) algorithm determines how a composite subscription should be split and routed. A composite subscription is represented as a tree where the internal nodes are operators, leaf nodes are atomic subscriptions, and the root node represents the composite subscription.

The DCSR algorithm traverses the subscription tree as follows: if the root of the tree is a leaf node, that is, an atomic subscription, the atomic subscription's next hop destination in the SRT is assigned to the root, and TID-based routing is applied to the atomic subscription. Otherwise, the algorithm recursively processes the left and right children separately. If the two children have the same destination, the root node is assigned this destination, and the composite subscription is routed to the next hop as a whole. If the children have different destinations, the algorithm has three choices: assigning the current broker or one of the children's destinations to the root node.

The composite subscription cost for each of these choices is estimated based on the cost model in Section 4.3. A destination broker with minimum cost will be assigned to the root node. If the root's destination is the current broker, the composite subscription is split. Otherwise, it is routed to one of the neighbors where further decisions are made. The recursive algorithm assigns destinations to the tree nodes bottom up.

4.3 Cost Model

A broker routing a composite subscription makes local optimal decisions based on the knowledge available at itself and its neighbors. The cost function can capture the use of resources such as memory, CPU, and communication. The *total routing cost* of a composite subscription CS at a broker is

$$TRC(CS) = RC(CS) + \sum_{i=1}^{n} RC_{N_i}(CS_{N_i}),$$

and includes the *routing cost* of CS at the broker and neighbor brokers (N_i, i = 1..n) where publications contributing to CS may come from. CS_{N_i} denotes the part of CS routed to broker N_i, and may be an atomic or composite subscription.

Routing cost at each broker: The cost of a composite subscription CS at a broker includes not only the time needed to match publications (from n neighbors) against CS, but also the time these publications spend in the input queue of the broker, and the time that matching results (to m neighbors) spend in the output queues. This cost is modeled as

$$RC(CS) = \sum_{i=1}^{n} T_{in}|P(CS_{N_i})| + \sum_{i=1}^{n} T_m|P(CS_{N_i})| + \sum_{i=1}^{m} T_{out_i}|P(CS)|,$$

where T_m is the average matching time at a broker, T_{in} and T_{out_i} are the average time messages spend in the input and output queues to the ith neighbor, respectively. $|P(S)|$, defined below, is the cardinality of (atomic or composite) subscription S. To compute the cost at a neighbor, brokers periodically exchange information such as T_{in} and T_m. This information is incorporated into an M/M/1 queueing model to estimate queueing times at neighbor brokers as a result of the additional traffic attracted by splitting a composite subscription there.

Subscription cardinality: The cardinality of a subscription S, denoted $|P(S)|$, is the number of matches of S per unit of time. First, we define the *selection factor* of subscription S. If S is atomic, its selection factor with respect to advertisement A is defined as $sf_A(S) = \prod_{i=1}^{k} sf_A(p_i)$, where p_i is the predicate of attribute a_i in S and $sf_A(p_i)$ is the selection factor of predicate p_i. The selection factors of individual predicates are computed based on the predicate's operator, and the distribution of attribute values d_{a_i} across publications, as shown in Table 1.

An advertisement's attribute distributions are disseminated as a histogram as part of the advertisement. We note two sources of inaccuracy in the selection factor estimation that arise from having to tradeoff accuracy with cost. First, the above equations do not consider the joint distribution among attributes, which would improve the estimation but require more information to be disseminated. Also, the accuracy of the attribute distributions themselves depends on the histogram bucket size and frequency of updates. We leave the exploration of these tradeoffs for future work.

We can now calculate the cardinality of an atomic subscription S that intersects advertisements $\{A_1, A_2, \ldots, A_q\}$, as $|P(S)| = \sum_{i=1}^{q} r_i * sf_{A_i}(S)$, where r_i is the publication rate associated with advertisement A_i. The cardinality of a composite subscription $CS = S_l \ op \ S_r$ is shown in Table 2.

4.4   Example

We now give an example of how the DCSR algorithm can route composite subscriptions based on the publication traffic and the status of the overlay. Fig. 4 shows a possible routing solution for composite subscription $CS = S_1 \& S_2$, where

Table 1. Selection Factor

Let $D = \int_{Min(a_i)}^{Max(a_i)} da_i$
$sf_A(a_i = val) = d_{a_i}(val)/D$
$sf_A(a_i > val) = \int_{val}^{Max(a_i)} da_i/D$
$sf_A(a_i < val) = \int_{Min(a_i)}^{val} da_i/D$

Table 2. Subscription Cardinality

$$|P(CS)| = \begin{cases} |P(S_l)| + |P(S_r)| & \text{if } op = \|; \\ min(|P(S_l)|, |P(S_r)|) & \text{if } op = \&. \end{cases}$$

the S_i are atomic. At Broker 6, CS is routed as a whole towards Broker 4, where the destinations of both S_1 and S_2 are different, and as a result, Broker 4 is the join point broker of CS in the topology-based routing algorithm. If the amount of data from S_1 is significantly larger than that from S_2, it may be more efficient to evaluate CS at Broker 3 rather than Broker 4. In the DCSR algorithm this dynamic evaluation occurs at each broker until a broker decides to split the composite subscription, say at Broker 1, in which case Broker 1 becomes the join point broker for CS.

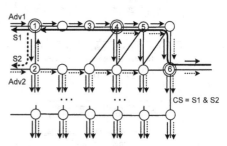

Since network conditions, such as delay and bandwidth, may change, the join point chosen by the DCSR algorithm may not remain optimal, and should be computed dynamically. If the join point broker finds a broker that is able to detect the composite event with a cost lower than itself, it initiates a join point movement [16].

Fig. 4. Dynamic CS routing

The DCSR algorithm determines the location that minimizes the network traffic and message delay costs of evaluating composite subscriptions. The DPR algorithm from Section 3.3 further reduces the cost of composite event detection.

5   Evaluation

In this section, we experimentally evaluate our routing protocols in general overlay topologies. For publications, we use stock quote traces obtained from Yahoo! Finance. Lacking real subscription traces, we generate subscriptions for the stock quote publication with predicates following a Zipf distribution in order to model locality among subscribers.[4] We explore the properties of the routing protocols by deploying a broker overlay in a controlled 20 machine local network consisting of machines with 4GB of memory and 1.86GHz CPUs. Unless otherwise stated, we evaluate the protocols in a 30 broker topology with an average connection degree (D) of 4. Each node is a complete content-based pub/sub broker that implements the protocols described in this paper. As well, 20 publishers and 30 subscribers join the system within the first 30 seconds of the experiment.

We compare the end to end notification delay of the fixed (Section 3.2) and dynamic (Section 3.3) algorithms and measure the CPU and memory usage per broker. For dynamic composite subscription routing, we observe the placement of the join point broker by measuring network traffic. To demonstrate robustness and scalability, we also evaluate broker networks deployed on PlanetLab.

End to End Notification Delay. The notification delay is computed as the average time between publishing at the publisher to the corresponding notification at the subscriber. This delay varies with the number of hops from the

---

[4] The datasets used in the experiments are available at [1].

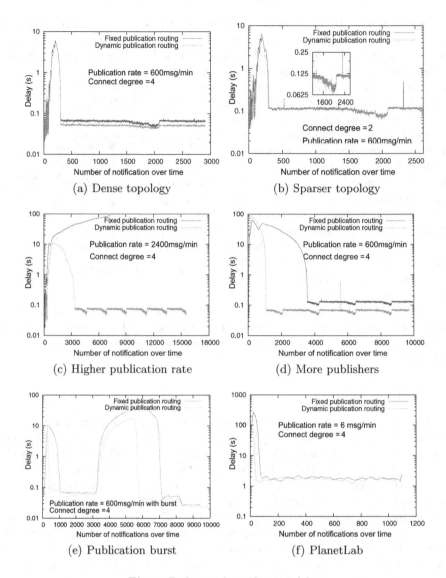

(a) Dense topology

(b) Sparser topology

(c) Higher publication rate

(d) More publishers

(e) Publication burst

(f) PlanetLab

Fig. 5. End to end notification delay

publisher to subscriber and the workload in the broker network, the latter of which depends on factors such as the overall publication rate and the number of subscriptions per broker. The delay metric includes the queueing delay, processing and matching time, and transmission delay at each hop.

When the publishers and subscribers join the system, advertisements are broadcast and subscriptions are matched with advertisements and forwarded towards potential publishers. This initial traffic contributes to network congestion and large notification delays, and is visible in Fig. 5(a) where the end to end delay is plotted (in log scale) for each notification. After initialization, the delays of both dynamic and fixed routing algorithms stabilize, with the dynamic algorithm producing a 20.3% shorter average delay than fixed routing. Our results show that brokers in the overlay have different traffic loads. In the fixed routing case, the output queueing delay of an overloaded broker constitutes 25% of the total end to end routing delay. The dynamic algorithm is able to detect such congestion and balance publication forwarding across the overlay.

In a less connected network, the benefit of dynamic routing is diminished due to a lack of alternate paths. In Fig. 5(b), with $D = 2$, the dynamic routing delay is only about 4.7% better than that of fixed routing. At some points in the experiment, the dynamic approach even performs worse than the fixed one because of the overhead of the path selection algorithm. While Fig. 5(a) and Fig. 5(b) demonstrate that the dynamic approach benefits from a well connected overlay, the benefit is not proportional to the connection degree. When the experiment is repeated with a fully connected topology, the delay with the dynamic approach is 4.1% worse than with the fixed approach. In this case, the overhead of maintaining link information does not offset gains in alternate path selection since all publishers and subscribers are already one hop from one another.

We observe that an increase in the publication rate causes the fixed routing approach to suffer worse notification delays. For instance, in Fig. 5(c) when the publication rate is increased to 2400 msg/min, the fixed algorithm becomes overloaded with messages queueing up at brokers along the routing path, whereas the dynamic routing algorithm continues to operate by offloading the high workload across alternate paths. The results suggest that dynamic routing is more stable and can handle heavier workloads, especially in a well connected network. Incidentally, the small but periodic decreases in delay are an artifact of the periodic publication workload. The publications near the end of the workload match fewer subscribers and are filtered by our routing algorithms before they propagate far into the network. This results in less congestion in the network and faster routing of the remaining publications. This phenomenon is apparent in all of the experiments that use this workload.

In the second scenario, we increase the number of publishers to 40, and their advertisements overlap each other. As described in Section 3.2, overlapping advertisements increase the number of potential alternate paths. Fig. 5(d) shows that the delay with the dynamic algorithm stabilizes 5 minutes sooner than with the fixed algorithm. Furthermore, the end to end delay with dynamic routing is 46.5% less than that with fixed routing. (We note again the log scale of the delay axis in Fig. 5). This compares with a relative benefit of 20.3% in Fig. 5(a) where there were fewer publishers and hence fewer alternate paths.

The third scenario evaluates a dynamic workload. A new publisher now joins the system five minutes after the other clients, whose publication rates range from 400~800msg/min, and publishes a burst of 1500 msg/min for two minutes. We further remove a publisher after the burst. As illustrated in Fig. 5(e), the dynamic approach stabilizes first as in previous experiments. While both algorithms suffer from increasing delays due to the burst, the dynamic algorithm maintains a smaller delay, is able to recover faster after the burst, and has a smaller steady state delay. Overall, the dynamic approach is more resilient to dynamic workloads.

In Table 3, we list the average end to end delay experienced by three subscribers that are 6, 10, and 12 hops away from the publisher. When the publisher and subscriber are close to one another, the dynamic algorithm has fewer opportunities to find suitable alternate paths. In Table 3, with a 6 hop path length, there is even a 0.8% performance degradation resulting from the overhead of the dynamic algorithm. When the distance increases to 12 hops, the improvement is up to 18.6%. We also observe, reading down the columns in Table 3, that the delay between the 6 and 12 hop subscribers with the fixed approach is 57.7%, while the corresponding difference with the dynamic algorithm is only 27.4%. This suggests that the dynamic approach is less sensitive not only to publication traffic but also to the path lengths between subscribers and publishers.

Table 3. Effect of subscriber distance on delay

Distance	Fixed (ms)	Dynamic (ms)	Improvement
6 hops	47.2	47.6	-0.8%
10 hops	64.5	52.9	18.0%
12 hops	74.4	60.6	18.6%
Max diff	57.7%	27.4%	

An important observation from the above results is that our pub/sub routing algorithms actually *benefit* from a cyclic overlay by reducing the notification delay and increasing the resilience to loads. To demonstrate the robustness and scalability of our approach, we repeat our experiments on PlanetLab with a 50 broker overlay network. The heterogeneous and shared PlanetLab nodes and network make it difficult to derive repeatable and reliable results, but our evaluations on PlanetLab support the conclusions made from the controlled environment experiments. Fig. 5(f) confirms that the dynamic algorithm stabilizes faster than the fixed one, and has a smaller notification delay.

Faster Matching. Both the fixed and dynamic routing algorithms have the potential to dramatically improve routing and matching performance. It takes our matching engine about 4.5 ms to match a publication against over 200,000 subscriptions per hop [14]. Once the TID attribute is bound (see Section 3.2), subsequent brokers only need to match the TID attribute instead of the full publication content. This can provide significant savings, especially with complex subscriptions, large workloads, or long path lengths. For the dynamic algorithm in the experiment associated with Fig. 5(a), 1926 publications issued by publishers resulted in 16997 publication messages, requiring 16997 matching operations by brokers. With TID routing, where only the first broker performs full matching, only $1926/16997 = 11.3\%$ of the matching operations are required.

Overhead of Dynamic Publication Routing. We measure the CPU and memory usage for all 30 brokers in the network over time for the experiment shown in Fig. 5(a). In the dynamic approach, we need to periodically (10 *ms* in this experiment) update a *link status table* at each broker. When a publication arrives, the broker selects a better path based on the link status table. The average CPU and memory usage per broker in the dynamic routing approach is 6.3% and 8.9% higher than those of the fixed routing approach, respectively. The busiest broker in the dynamic approach has the most neighbors and consumes up to 83.7% of the CPU processing capacity, while the other brokers only consume 16.6% of the CPU. The results show that fixed and dynamic publication routing consume similar CPU and memory usage. Therefore, the dynamic algorithm reduces the notification delay and the resilience to publication workloads without consuming much more system resources.

Dynamic Routing with Failures. In this experiment, we connect 20 publishers and 30 subscribers to a fully connected 30 broker network. We simulate broker failures by randomly killing some of the brokers, and measure the end to end delay of the dynamic routing approach with failures. The number of failures the system can tolerate depends on the connectivity of the network, and the position of the broker in the overlay. For example, a failure that partitions the network will render it impossible to deliver publications across the partitions.

In Fig. 6, immediately after the first broker failure, which occurs after about the 1000th notification, the notification delay increases by up to 89.1%. Routing around the failed broker temporarily introduces congestion at some other broker, but the dynamic routing algorithm detects the congestion and automatically balances the traffic among the remaining alternate paths. When the second broker failure occurs at around the 7000th notification, fewer alternate paths are available, and the notification delay now increases up to 217.5%. This

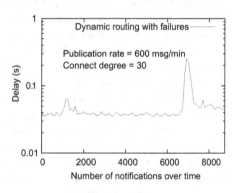

Fig. 6. Failures

time, however, the notification delay stabilizes at about 23.1% higher than before the failure, because the alternate paths the algorithm finds are longer. This experiment shows that the dynamic routing approach can route messages around failures and balance traffic among alternative paths.

Dynamic CS Routing. We evaluate the DCSR algorithm on PlanetLab using a topology similar to that in Fig. 4. Twenty publishers publish at rates ranging from 100 to 600 per minute, and 30 subscribers issue subscriptions, with one of them being a composite subscription. In Fig. 7 we measure the bandwidth of certain brokers located on the composite subscription routing path. The solid bars represent the number of outgoing messages at a broker, and the hatched bars are the number of incoming messages that are not forwarded. Note that the sum of the solid and hatched bars represents the total number of incoming messages at a broker. We also measure notification delays in Fig. 8, as measured

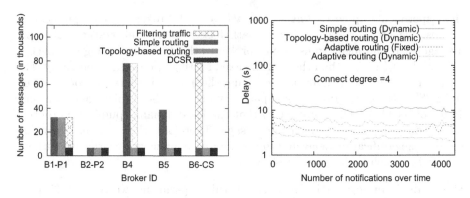

Fig. 7. CS traffic   **Fig. 8.** CS delay

from when the last publication contributing to the composite subscription is published to when the subscriber receives the notification.

The composite subscription is issued at Broker 6 in Fig. 4, and is routed to its potential publishers using simple routing, topology-based routing or DCSR. In simple routing, a composite subscription is split into atomic subscriptions at the broker that first receives the composite subscription from a subscriber. In this case, the split occurs at Broker 6, and all publications must be routed to this broker where the composite subscription is evaluated and unmatched publications are finally filtered out. This is illustrated in Fig. 7 where we see that with simple routing, only Broker 6 filters any messages, and therefore all preceding brokers incur higher than necessary message load. In topology-based routing, however, Broker 4 is the join point broker, and we observe the filtering that occurs here in Fig. 7, as well as the reduced message loads at Brokers 5 and 6. The DCSR algorithm determines the composite subscription detection location based on the potential publication traffic. In our topology, the publisher at Broker 1 has a higher publication rate, and hence this broker is an efficient point to detect the composite subscription. Fig. 7 shows that filtering indeed occurs at Broker 1 and that all subsequent brokers enjoy a reduced message load.

To summarize, the topology-based composite subscription routing algorithm imposes less traffic than simple routing by moving the join point into the network, and the DCSR algorithm further reduces traffic by moving the join point closer towards congested publishers as indicated by the cost model. In the scenario in Fig. 7, compared to simple routing, the DCSR algorithm reduces the traffic at Broker 1 by 79.5%, a reduction that is also enjoyed by all brokers downstream of the join point.

In Fig. 8 we see that with the DPR algorithm, the simple composite subscription routing performs the worst, and the DCSR the best. Even compared to the topology-based approach, the DCSR algorithm manages to reduce the notification delay by 55%, by filtering out messages early in the network and hence reducing queueing delays. In this scenario, we also evaluate fixed and dynamic publication routing with the DCSR algorithm. Fig. 8 shows that the dynamic approach improves the delay by 40.1% compared to fixed publication routing. We expect the benefits to be even more pronounced in larger networks since longer composite subscription paths in such topologies offer the potential for more savings in terms of traffic and delay.

6 Conclusions

Current pub/sub systems [5,8,19,23] assume an acyclic broker overlay network and do not provide special mechanisms to cope with cycles in the overlay. In this paper, we introduce a content-based routing protocol for general overlays supporting both atomic and composite subscription routing. Content-based routing in a general overlay improves the scalability and robustness of pub/sub systems by offering routing path alternatives. Our approach retains the original pub/sub interface and matching algorithms so it may be easily integrated into existing pub/sub systems. It also minimizes redundant traffic induced by cycles in the overlay and reduces message routing delay. Our protocols allow publications to select optimal paths to matching subscribers and composite subscriptions can be routed to the best event detection locations in order to satisfy potential quality of service constraints at the application level.

Experiments in both wide-area PlanetLab and controlled local environments confirm the benefits of the dynamic publication and composite event routing algorithms. Publication end to end routing is about 20% faster, stabilizes sooner after a burst, and is able to route around certain failures in the network. As well, dynamically determining the optimal composite subscription processing location saves about 80% of the network traffic and reduces end to end delay by more than half.

A worthwhile future research direction for this work is to investigate the feasibility of supporting some of the motivating applications from Section 1 with quality of service guarantees. As well, it would be useful to quantitatively compare content-based pub/sub algorithms designed for acyclic topologies to those in this paper.

Acknowledgments. The research was funded in part by CA, CFI, IBM, NSERC, OCE, OIT, and Sun. We would like to thank Serge Mankovski from CA and our colleagues including Bala Maniymaran for providing valuable feedback on earlier drafts of this paper. The completion of this research was also made possible thanks to Bell Canada's support through its Bell University Laboratories R&D program.

References

1. Experiment datasets, `http://research.msrg.utoronto.ca/Padres/DataSets`
2. Adler, M., Ge, Z., Kurose, J., Towsley, D., Zabele, S.: Channelization problem in large scale data dissemination. In: IEEE ICNP (2001)
3. Aekaterinidis, I., Triantafillou, P.: Pastrystrings: A comprehensive content-based publish/subscribe DHT network. In: IEEE ICDCS (2006)

4. Carzaniga, A., Rosenblum, D.S., Wolf, A.L.: Design and evaluation of a wide-area event notification service. In: ACM ToCS (2001)
5. Cugola, G., Nitto, E.D., Fuggetta, A.: The JEDI event-based infrastructure and its application to the development of the OPSS WFMS. In: IEEE TSE (2001)
6. Deering, S., Cheriton, D.R.: Multicast routing in datagram internetworks and extended LANs. In: ACM ToCS (1990)
7. Fawcett, T., Provost, F.: Activity monitoring: Noticing interesting changes in behavior. In: ACM SIGKDD (1999)
8. Fiege, L., Mezini, M., Mühl, G., Buchmann, A.P.: Engineering event-based systems with scopes. In: Magnusson, B. (ed.) ECOOP 2002. LNCS, vol. 2374, p. 309. Springer, Heidelberg (2002)
9. Gupta, A., Sahin, O.D., Agrawal, D., Abbadi, A.E.: Meghdoot: Content-based publish/subscribe over P2P networks. In: ACM Middleware (2004)
10. Koenig, I.: Event processing as a core capability of your content distribution fabric. In: Gartner Event Processing Summit, Orlando, Florida (2007)
11. Kumar, V., Cai, Z., et al.: Implementing diverse messaging models with self-managing properties using IFLOW. In: IEEE ICAC (2006)
12. Lee, S.-J., Su, W., Hsu, J., Gerla, M., Bagrodia, R.: A performance comparison study of ad hoc wireless multicast protocols. In: INFOCOM (2000)
13. Li, G., Hou, S., Jacobsen, H.-A.: A unified approach to routing, covering and merging in publish/subscribe systems based on modified binary decision diagrams. In: IEEE ICDCS (2005)
14. Li, G., Jacobsen, H.-A.: Composite subscriptions in content-based publish/subscribe systems. In: ACM Middleware (2005)
15. Li, G., Muthusamy, V., Jacobsen, H.-A.: Adaptive content-based routing in general overlay topologies. TR CSRG-584, University of Toronto (July 2008)
16. Li, G., Muthusamy, V., Jacobsen, H.-A.: Subscribing to the past in content-based publish/subscribe. TR CSRG-585, University of Toronto (January 2008)
17. Liu, H., Ramasubramanian, V., Sirer, E.G.: Client behavior and feed characteristics of RSS, a publish-subscribe system for Web micronews. In: IMC (2005)
18. Medhi, D., Ramasamy, K.: Network Routing: Algorithms, Protocols, and Architectures. Academic Press, London (2007)
19. Mühl, G.: Generic constraints for content-based publish/subscribe systems. In: Batini, C., Giunchiglia, F., Giorgini, P., Mecella, M. (eds.) CoopIS 2001. LNCS, vol. 2172, p. 211. Springer, Heidelberg (2001)
20. Mukherjee, B., Heberlein, L.T., Levitt, K.N.: Network intrusion detection. IEEE Network (1994)
21. Muthusamy, V., Jacobsen, H.-A.: Small-scale peer-to-peer publish/subscribe. In: MobiQuitous P2PKM (2005)
22. Nayate, A., Dahlin, M., Iyengar, A.: Transparent information dissemination. In: ACM Middleware (2004)
23. Opyrchal, L., Astley, M., et al.: Exploiting IP multicast in content-based publish-subscribe systems. In: ACM Middleware (2000)
24. Ostrowski, K., Birman, K.: Extensible Web services architecture for notification in large-scale systems. In: IEEE ICWS (2006)
25. Özsu, M.T., Valduriez, P.: Principles of Distributed Database Systems. Prentice Hall, Englewood Cliffs (1999)
26. Petrovic, M., Muthusamy, V., Jacobsen, H.-A.: Content-based routing in mobile ad hoc networks. In: MOBIQUITOUS (2005)
27. Picco, G.P., Cugola, G., Murphy, A.L.: Efficient content-based event dispatching in the presence of topological reconfiguration. In: IEEE ICDCS (2003)

28. Pietzuch, P., Bacon, J.: Hermes: A distributed event-based middleware architecture. In: IEEE ICDCS (2002)
29. Pietzuch, P., Shand, B., Bacon, J.: Composite event detection as a generic middleware extension. IEEE Network (2004)
30. Riabov, A., Liu, Z., Wolf, J.L., Yu, P.S., Zhang, L.: Clustering algorithms for content-based publication-subscription systems. In: IEEE ICDCS (2002)
31. Rose, I., Murty, R., et al.: Cobra: Content-based filtering and aggregation of blogs and RSS feeds. In: NSDI (2007)
32. Schuler, C., Schuldt, H., Schek, H.-J.: Supporting reliable transactional business processes by publish/subscribe techniques. In: Casati, F., Georgakopoulos, D., Shan, M.-C. (eds.) TES 2001. LNCS, vol. 2193, p. 118. Springer, Heidelberg (2001)
33. Tock, Y., Naaman, N., Harpaz, A., Gershinsky, G.: Hierarchical clustering of message flows in a multicast data dissemination system. In: IASTED PDCS (2005)
34. Triantafillou, P., Economides, A.: Subscription summarization: A new paradigm for efficient publish/subscribe systems. In: IEEE ICDCS (2004)

AlfredO: An Architecture for Flexible Interaction with Electronic Devices

Jan S. Rellermeyer, Oriana Riva, and Gustavo Alonso

Systems Group, Department of Computer Science, ETH Zurich
8092 Zürich, Switzerland
{rellermeyer,oriva,alonso}@inf.ethz.ch

Abstract. Mobile phones are rapidly becoming the universal access point for computing, communication, and digital infrastructures. In this paper we explore the software architectures necessary to make the mobile phone a truly universal access point to any electronic infrastructure. We propose AlfredO, a lightweight middleware architecture that allows developers to construct applications in a modular way, organizing the applications into detachable tiers that can be distributed at will to dynamically configure multi-tier architectures between mobile phones and service providers. Through AlfredO, a phone can lease on-the-fly the client side of an application and immediately become a fully tailored client. Our experimental results indicate that AlfredO has very little overhead, it is scalable, and yields very low latency. To demonstrate the feasibility and potential of the platform, in the paper we also describe AlfredOShop, a prototype application for spontaneously controlling information screens from a mobile phone.

Keywords: Mobile Phones, Software as a Service, Universal Interface, OSGi.

1 Introduction

The mobile phone is quickly transforming itself from a mobile telecommunication device into a multi-faceted information manager that can support not only communication among people, but also the processing and manipulation of an increasingly diverse set of interactions. The trend of a phone as a point of convergence for the user's activities, in some respects, has already begun. South Korea Telecom has introduced mobile payment technology and added RFID readers to phones to allow people to get information about shopping products [1]. Nokia has integrated GPS receivers to enable sports activity tracking, car navigation, and multimedia city guides [2,3]. Motorola is researching how to allow its nomadic devices to interact with a car's components: if the car airbags deploy, the phone makes an emergency call; if the driver is maneuvering on a busy road, an incoming phone call is postponed; and if an urgent calendar entry is approaching, it can pop up on the car's display [4].

V. Issarny and R. Schantz (Eds.): Middleware 2008, LNCS 5346, pp. 22–41, 2008.

Applications of this type are usually based on ad-hoc implementations and customized to specific scenarios. In this paper, we investigate the software architectures required to support rapid prototyping of such applications. Our objective is to allow a mobile phone to acquire on-the-fly the necessary elements to immediately turn into a fully tailored client for interaction with any encountered electronic device.

In the past, distributed systems have supported interactions among embedded devices by either statically preconfiguring the execution environment or by dynamically migrating code, data, and service state from one device to another. However, the lack of flexibility of the former approach and the increased security risks of the latter have hampered their actual deployability in mobile environments. To overcome these problems and make our approach feasible for resource-constrained mobile phones, we propose AlfredO, a lightweight middleware architecture that enables users to flexibly interact with other electronic devices while providing ease of maintenance and security for their personal devices.

AlfredO stems from two key insights. Our first insight is that most interactions with electronic devices such as appliances, touchscreens, vending machines, etc., are usually short-term and ad-hoc. Therefore, the classic approach of pre-installing device drivers for each target device is not practicable. Instead, we propose to adopt a software distribution model based on the concept of software as a service. Each target device represents its capabilities as modular service items that can be accessed on-the-fly by any mobile phone. Our second insight is that the evolution of client-server computing from mainframes hooked to dumb user terminals to two-tier architectures (i.e., the classical client-server architecture) and to three-tier architectures (e.g, Web applications) has shown how partitioning server functionality yields better overall performance, flexibility, and adaptability. Therefore, we model each service item as a decomposable multi-tier architecture consisting of a presentation-tier, a logic tier, and a data tier. These tiers can be distributed to the interacting mobile phone thus configuring multi-tier architectures between the mobile phone and the target device.

AlfredO provides several benefits:

- *Scalability* and *ease of administration*: with AlfredO a resource-constrained mobile device such as a mobile phone becomes capable of supporting an unbounded number of diverse interactions. Instead of downloading, installing, and constantly updating the software necessary to interact with every conceivable target device, a mobile phone can simply acquire a stateless interface to the service of interest.
- *Flexibility*: AlfredO permits configuring flexible client-server architectures. A mobile phone, for instance, can host a thin client that simply acquires the presentation tier of the target service for the time of the interaction and discards it upon completion. Alternatively, a phone may also decide to acquire parts of the service logic tier with the aim of providing faster performance and responsiveness even in high latency networking environments.
- *Device independence*: To cope with the diversity of the input/output capabilities of the appliances and electronic devices a phone may need to interact

with, AlfredO completely decouples the abstract design of a user interface from its implementation. Thereby, different renderings of the same abstract interface can be implemented on different devices. For example, a user interface can be rendered in one way on a notebook with mouse and large screen, in a different way on a phone with joystick and small screen, and in another way on a touchscreen.

- *Security*: AlfredO allows a phone to become a fully functional client by simply acquiring the presentation-tier of the target service. This can be achieved by simply shipping a "description" of the device's user interface to the mobile phone and letting the phone implement the actual user interface based on the abstract specifications. As this description file is not allowed to access the phone's local resources, this approach provides the security benefits of a sandbox model.
- *Efficiency*: AlfredO comes on a phone with a very low footprint of less than 300 kBytes. Yet, it permits interacting with a large variety of electronic devices while remaining latency-efficient. Our experiments show that a phone such as the Nokia 9300i can manage even 40 concurrent service interactions with an invocation latency of less than 150 msec over 802.11b WLAN. Furthermore, with AlfredO a phone is capable of turning in a fully operational client of a target service provider in a few seconds. This provides an end-user experience fully comparable to that of many other common applications available on phones, such as text editors, file managers, web browsers, etc.

We have implemented AlfredO using R-OSGi [5], a middleware platform that allows applications to be distributed using the modularity features of OSGi [6]. The OSGi framework implementation underneath is the very resource-efficient Concierge [7] platform. The next section gives an overview of the R-OSGi platform. Section 3 describes the design of AlfredO and gives insights into its implementation. Performance results are analyzed in Section 4. *MouseController* and *AlfredOShop*, two prototype applications built using AlfredO, are presented in Section 5. We discuss related work in Section 6 and conclude the paper in Section 7.

2   R-OSGi Overview

The R-OSGi [5] middleware extends the notion of OSGi [6] services to applications that run in a distributed manner. OSGi is an open standard which is maintained by the OSGi Alliance, a not-for-profit industry alliance with many major players of the software industry (like IBM, SAP, or Oracle) but also device vendors (like Nokia, Ericsson, or Motorola) involved. Traditionally, OSGi has been used to decompose and loosely couple Java applications into software modules. These modules encapsulate different parts of the whole functionality and their lifecycle can be individually controlled at runtime. For instance, each single functional module can be updated with a newer version without restarting the application, which makes OSGi popular for developing long-running applications such as the firmware of hardware devices, or extensible applications like the Eclipse IDE [8]. Modules typically communicate through services, which are ordinary Java classes published under a service interface in a central service registry. Through the service registry service consumers can retrieve a direct reference to the service object of interest. Hence, OSGi provides a very lightweight communication model that avoids performance-adverse indirections known from container systems such as EJB [9].

2.1   Key Principles

With R-OSGi, many of the benefits provided by the OSGi paradigm can be leveraged to distributed systems. OSGi modules are distributed across several devices and the R-OSGi middleware transparently manages interactions between services located on different devices by exploiting the loose coupling of services. Typically, a service consists of an implementation (i.e., an instance of a class), one or multiple service interfaces under which the service is published, and a set of service properties. Since the concrete implementation of a service is hidden behind the service interface registered with the local service registry, R-OSGi can dynamically build proxies for remote modules which exhibit the same service interface as the one registered with the local service registry. Thereby, remote modules invoke service functions as if they were locally implemented and thus remain transparent to the network communication involved.

The typical assumption of static and immutable composition of software does not apply to the OSGi model. Instead, OSGi provides a platform where modules are dynamic and applications are prepared to react upon service failures or other kinds of interruptions. Hence, the potentially harmful side effect of introducing a network link into an application does not break the application model. Furthermore, disconnections between services can be mapped to module unload events, which the software can handle gracefully.

Remote service invocations are essentially synchronous and blocking remote communications. R-OSGi additionally supports asynchronous non-blocking interactions through remote events. Likewise, this addition does not introduce any new concept to the application model. The OSGi specification already contains an event infrastructure that many applications use when running on a single Virtual Machine (VM). R-OSGi transparently forwards such events when it detects that a connected remote machine has a registered handler for a specific event type.

2.2   Service Proxies

In the simplest case, a machine publishes a service under a service interface and a client machine acquires access to this service by establishing a connection to its machine. As part of the handshake, the meta-information about registered services is exchanged. These service descriptions are synchronized between the devices so that changes of services or unregistration events are immediately visible to all connected machines. When a client wants to access a service, the service interface is shipped through the network and a *local proxy* for the service is created from this interface. This proxy is then registered with the local service registry as an implementation of the particular service. If it happens that the service interface references types provided by the original service module located on the remote machine, the corresponding classes will also be transmitted and injected into the proxy module (*type injection*).

However, the proxy itself can also provide more functionality than solely delegating service calls to the remote machine. *Smart proxies* implement the idea of moving parts of the service functionality to the client VM. The remote service can provide an abstract class as a smart proxy that is shipped to the client. All implemented methods run locally on the client machine whereas abstract methods are implemented as remote calls. Therefore, in this way, the service can explicitly push computation to the client side, if the client allows.

3   System Design and Implementation

Our approach aims to turn nearly-ubiquitous mobile phones into universal interfaces to the surrounding electronic world. Mobile phones nowadays have sufficient computation power to participate in sophisticated applications. However, they have by design inherent characteristics which distinguish them from typical general-purpose mobile computing devices, such as laptop computers. Phones have a different form factor, different display sizes and screen resolutions, and different input devices. Treating mobile phones like laptop computers overstrains their capabilities and provides unfeasible solutions. On the other hand, considering mobile phones as downsized versions of conventional computers neglects the benefits and unique capabilities they offer, such as built-in cameras and various sensor devices. Our goal is to look at the phone platform in its own right and leverage as much as possible its unique characteristics.

AlfredO incorporates three main mechanisms: (1) a *service-based software distribution model* for the support of an unbounded number of service interactions between phones and other electronic devices, (2) a *multi-tier service architecture* to flexibly configure the service interaction, and (3) a *device-independent presentation model* to achieve device independence and provide interface customizability.

3.1   Service-Based Software Distribution Model

When a phone needs to interact with an electronic device available in the surrounding environment, from where does it obtain the required software? A simple approach would be to preinstall the necessary software on the phone and require a third party to authenticate it. Yet, this approach would result in poor flexibility as mobile phones will more likely need to interact with devices casually encountered in the environment. Furthermore, each time the original software is updated, the update needs to be propagated to all phones where the software was previously installed. As the number and type of electronic devices increase, explicitly distributing, installing, updating software on each phone would become an unmanageable task.

Another possible approach is to dynamically transfer the software from the electronic device (or from the Internet) to the phone at the beginning of the transaction. Unfortunately, this approach would expose the phone to several security risks since in the common case the interaction occurs with unknown devices. Furthermore, downloading, installing, and configuring all necessary software is a time-consuming task that very often requires the user involvement and that consumes lots of communication and computational resources.

Our solution to software distribution is based on the concept of *Software as a Service (SaaS)*, which has been traditionally applied to Internet services. According to this logic, the new business model for most Internet's commodity software is not selling software, but building services enabled by that software. We believe SaaS can bring interesting benefits also to mobile phones, especially due to the impossibility for such resource-constrained devices to possess all software necessary for every possible interaction.

We adopt a service-based software distribution model where software available on electronic devices is made available to mobile phones in the form of flexible service items. Specifically, we package the functions provided by each electronic device as modular services that can be invoked, decomposed, and distributed using the service-oriented architectural approach of R-OSGi. In R-OSGi, services encapsulate whole functional units and dependencies between services are typically restricted to semantical dependencies at the application level. In the simplest case, a phone acquires on-the-fly the interface of a service of interest and discards it once the interaction is completed. In this way, phones are released from the duty of downloading, installing, and maintaining the software necessary to interact with all surrounding devices and the number of possible interactions can therefore grow unbounded. Furthermore, by letting phones acquire interfaces to arbitrary services high flexibility is provided and a phone's functonalities are not limited anymore to what their software platform and middleware layers are pre-configured for.

Another advantage that this service-based distribution model brings to mobile phones is its concept of software as a "process". Instead of software products that need to be engineered to exactly follow the given specifications, this model allows software to undergo frequent changes thus flexibly integrating a user's new requirements, technological advances, and emerging data models as soon as they become available. Hence, software on electronic devices can be changed and upgraded without compromising their interactions with the external world.

3.2   Multi-tier Service Architecture

We envision most interactions between mobile phones, called *clients*, and other electronic devices, called *target devices*, will occur in an ad-hoc manner. A mobile phone may contact a target service directly if its address is known (e.g., the contact address is provided at the bottom of the touchscreen) or upon service discovery. R-OSGi supports several service discovery protocols such as SLP [10,11]. Alternatively, the target device itself may periodically broadcast invitations to nearby devices. AlfredO makes the information about new devices available to

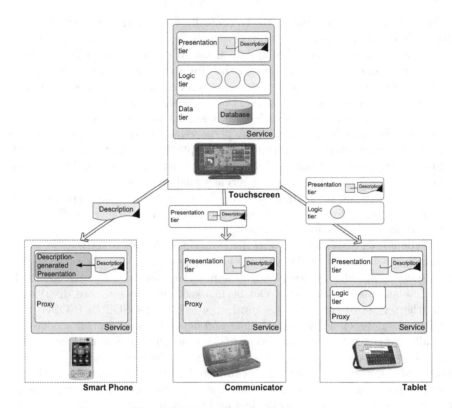

Fig. 1. Multi-tier service architecture

the user and the user can decide whether to connect to a discovered device. Once the connection is established, the two devices exchange symmetric leases that contain the name of the services that each device offers. Thereby, the user can choose which service to invoke.

As Figure 1 shows, in our approach, services are built using a multi-tier software architecture consisting of a presentation tier (i.e., the user interface), a logic tier (i.e., computational processes), and a data tier (i.e., data storage). Tiers can be distributed according to different distribution logics and the boundaries of distribution can be adjusted dynamically. Typically, at the beginning of an interaction, the phone and the target device agree on the distribution configuration. This decision may depend on the phone's capabilities as well as its current execution context. For example, if a phone has low free memory, only the presentation tier is shipped to the phone, whereas if the communication link is unstable also the logic tier is shipped, thus reducing the communication overhead.

In the current implementation, the data tier always resides on the target device, while the presentation tier always resides on the client. By default the service logic tier is not transferred to the mobile phone, but we support also the case in which parts of the service logic are transferred to the mobile phone .

Initially, the target device provides the mobile phone with two elements: the interface of the service of interest and a service descriptor. The *service interface* is used by the R-OSGi framework running on the mobile phone to build a corresponding service proxy (see Section 2.2 for the definition of service proxy). The *service descriptor* consists of three parts. First, it contains an abstract description of the user interface (UI) necessary to support the interaction with the target service. As explained in the next section, based on the UI description each phone platform can generate a UI customized to the phone capabilities. Second, it includes a list of services on which the service of interest depends. Third, for each service in the dependency list it includes an abstract description of its requirements (e.g., other service dependencies, memory and CPU lower boundaries, etc.).

The default behavior is to generate a local proxy for the service interface and host only the presentation tier on the mobile phone. The client device runs the UI locally and triggers computation on the remote target device by interacting with the local proxy. As all computation and data management occur on the target device, this configuration minimizes the load on the resource-constrained phone. The mobile phone either self-generates a suitable UI based on the abstract description of the UI (see the example with the smart phone in Figure 1) or directly receives the UI from the target device (see the example with the communicator in Figure 1). We envision this will be the case for most interactions as they are likely to occur in unknown and untrusted environments. Indeed, a main advantage of this configuration is security. On the server side, the target device has full control on the implementation of its functions thus limiting attacks from malicious clients. On the client side, the device can decide which capabilities to expose to the target device in order to support the interaction. Furthermore, if only a stateless description of the UI is shipped to the mobile phone the configuration provides the security benefits of a sandbox model.

AlfredO also permits configuring more complex two-tier architectures, where the client not only acquires the presentation tier but also parts of the service logic (see the example with the tablet in Figure 1). The client can request additional services that appear in the list of service dependencies provided by the descriptor and run them locally. For each requested service, the client receives the associated descriptor (listing the service dependencies of the new service) and its service interface. In trusted environments, this approach can be effective in reducing the communication overhead and improving the application's responsiveness.

The descriptor provides a declarative description of the system comparable to other declarative approaches like XForms [12], but it allows for more flexibility. Indeed, our approach is not restricted to typical interfaces with input validation and content submission. Instead, it supports all the interaction patterns of the R-OSGi middleware, such as asynchronous communication through events, high-volume data exchange through transparent stream proxies, and synchronous service invocations between services.

The example in Figure 2 shows how a mobile phone can configure a customized client application capable of interacting with the remote target device.

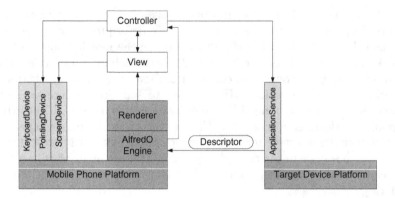

Fig. 2. An example of system configuration based on the service descriptor

In a typical interaction some services will run on the mobile phone's platform (e.g., KeyboardDevice, PointingDevice, etc.) and others on the target device's platform (e.g., ApplicationService). The client device receives a descriptor of the target service and generates the application's *View* and *Controller*.

Instead of defining layouts that typically break on different screen resolutions and ratios, the UI is specified using abstract controls and relationships. The *Renderer* running on the mobile phone decides how to turn this abstract UI into an implementation (the application's View) that is tailored to the phone's hardware capabilities.

The *AlfredOEngine* generates the application's Controller based on the service requirements specified in the descriptor. The Controller defines how events generated through the UI (View) can affect the state of the application consisting of application data as well as configuration parameters and proxy settings. For example, at some point of the interaction, in order to improve the application's responsiveness the client can decide to acquire additional services currently running on remote devices. Likewise, the Controller also defines how events generated by the target device can modify the application's state. The Controller, for instance, may periodically poll a certain service method provided by the remote device and react to its changes by invoking another service method or by changing the implementation of a control command of the UI.

3.3   Device-Independent Presentation Model

In our approach, we consider mobile phones as general-purpose platforms for interactions with various electronic devices and applications but without disregarding the specific characteristics of each device. Electronic devices provide a wide range of different input and output hardware capabilities. In many cases, these are customized to the functions each device is designed for. Clearly, a phone cannot offer every conceivable hardware capability, but capabilities of one device can be mapped to those of another one. For example, the mouse of a desktop computer is equivalent to the joystick of a phone or the knob of a coffee machine.

The service descriptor provides a device-independent specification of the UI. Ideally, an application developer should describe the input and output needs of his applications through this description, devices should provide specifications of their input and output capabilities, and users should specify their preferences [13]. The system can then self-implement a suitable interaction technique that takes all these requirements into account.

In AlfredO, the service logic remains agnostic to the specific hardware drivers available on each device. In other words, the logic tier builds on an abstract UI. Input and output capabilities that are used by a specific UI are modeled as OSGi services and accordingly their abstract definition is given by their corresponding service interfaces. All OSGi service interfaces are then organized in a hierarchy. For example, the *NotebookKeyboard* service implements the *KeyboardDevice* service interface which is used for entering characters as well as the *PointingDevice* service interface which is used for moving the mouse pointer through the cursor keys.

Depending on the capabilities offered by the interacting phone, the abstract description of the UI can be rendered differently, i.e, each phone generates the UI in a different manner. A device platform without a mouse or trackpoint can only build a GUI implementing the *KeyboardDevice* interface and without the *PointingDevice* service. Or a phone may have the choice to use a trackpoint or an accelerometer to implement the *PointingDevice* interface. Likewise, on a phone a *KeyboardDevice* interface may be implemented using the small keyboard of the phone or a handwriting detection that operates with a stylus. In principle, multiple devices can be federated to implement the abstract specifications of the given UI. Furthermore, the UI can be partly on the local phone, partly on the target device, and partly on other external devices. For example, in Figure 2, the phone may decide to use a notebook's screen with larger resolution; in this case, the *ScreenDevice* service would be implemented remotely by the notebook platform and invoked on the phone through a local proxy.

The implementation of the UI can use different rendering engines that are provided by the client platform. Currently, the default rendering engine produces a Java AWT [14] application where the abstract user interface is rendered with AWT panels. Another supported rendering engine is based on the SWT [15] toolkit. This is especially useful for devices for which an implementation of the Embedded Rich Client Platform (eRCP) [16] exists. As eRCP runs on top of OSGi, it requires only a small set of additional bundles to turn an eRCP device into an AlfredO client. For phone platforms that do not support any graphical toolkit, it is possible to use a web browser that is fed by a servlet [17] renderer. This produces HTML enriched with AJAX [18]. In this case, the web browser can serve as a graphical environment to interact with the headless AlfredO platform.

4   Experimental Evaluation

The goal of this experimental evaluation is threefold. First, it quantifies the footprint of AlfredO on resource-constrained mobile phones. Second, it assesses the latency to acquire the presentation tier from a target device. Third, it evaluates the scalability of AlfredO in terms of number of parallel service interactions that can be supported between a mobile phone and any target device.

4.1 Resource Consumption

As AlfredO is based on a layered and decomposable architecture, the actual size of the software stack on a phone depends on the actual deployment and the size of the renderers utilized for generating the user interface. The minimal core platform consists of an OSGi framework, the R-OSGi system, and the AlfredO core functionality. Using the very lightweight Concierge [7] OSGi implementation, in total this amounts to a footprint of about 290 kBytes. The renderers typically have a footprint of around 40 kBytes, except the servlet renderer that has additional dependencies from the OSGi HTTP service implementation and adds a total of 160 kBytes when running with the Concierge HTTP service prototype.

To assess the runtime costs, we use our two prototype applications (*MouseController* and *AlfredOShop*), which are discussed in detail in the following section. The proxy bundle generated for the *MouseController* consumes 6 kBytes on the file system and the *AlfredOShop* proxy bundle takes 7 kBytes.

Runtime memory consumption is hard to measure on embedded devices like phones because it depends on the state and the timing of the garbage collector. In a controlled environment on a desktop Java VM, however, the *MouseController* consumes about 200 kBytes of memory and the *AlfredOShop* 30 kBytes. The higher memory footprint of the *MouseController* application is due to application-generated data (i.e., the RGB bitmap image that the application periodically receives from the controlled device and that is stored in the local memory).

Summarizing, the resource consumption of AlfredO is minimal and therefore very well suits the resource requirements of mobile phones. The whole software stack has a footprint that can nowadays be easily compared with the footprint of an average single page of an internet website. For comparison, a hardcopy of the first page of the ETH Zurich web site (which is not especially fancy), creates a storage footprint of 200 kBytes. Proxy bundles for services that are no longer available are not cached but immediately uninstalled as soon as the interaction is terminated. Therefore, an AlfredO client does not store outdated data over time. Compared to device drivers or web clients, this is clearly an advantage and allows much more versatile interactions. The memory footprint is also not an issue for today's mobile phones. Even when more complex services and user interfaces are involved, the memory is not a limiting factor.

4.2 Latency Performance

In these experiments we measure the time a phone client needs to contact and establish an interaction with a target service. In these tests the phone acquires only the presentation tier of the service. This includes the interface of the service of interest, a description of the service requirements and a description of the abstract UI. We use a Nokia 9300i that runs a 150 MHz ARM9 processor and offers both 802.11b wireless LAN and Bluetooth (BT) connectivity, the latter, however, only with the CLDC VM but not with the CDC VM. As R-OSGi runs on the CDC VM, for the experiments in BT networks we employ a second phone, a Sony Ericsson M600i that runs a 208 MHz ARM9 processor. Both phones interact with a regular desktop machine (single core Pentium 4 class).

We measure the initial start time necessary to contact a service and acquire its interface, build the proxy bundle, install it on the local R-OSGi framework, and get the proxy running on the mobile phone (i.e., Start proxy bundle). The experiment is run with the two different applications, the *MouseController* and the *AlfredOShop* service. The amount of data transferred to the phone accounts for about 2 kBytes for each application.

Table 1 and Table 2 report the results. The network communication necessary to acquire the service interface is not the dominant factor in determining the total start time. Building, installing, and starting the proxy on the phone takes much longer. Therefore, the time is not primarily influenced by the size of the service interface. On the other hand, it strongly depends on the phone platform in use. On the SonyEricsson phone, which has a more powerful processor, the performance is in average 40% faster. However, from a user point of view, total start times of both applications are more than acceptable if compared to startup delays of typical phone applications. On the 9300i Nokia communicator, for instance, the startup time of the built-in *Document* text editor application is about 3 seconds, the startup time of the *FileManager* is around 6 seconds, and starting a web browser and displaying the default Nokia homepage takes about 17 seconds (assuming the phone is already connected to the Internet).

Table 1. Initial delay for service interaction on a Nokia 9300i over WLAN

	Nokia 9300i WLAN, in ms	
Operation	MouseController	AlfredOShop
Acquire service interface	94	110
Build proxy bundle	3125	3110
Install proxy bundle	703	703
Start proxy bundle	1000	359
Total start time	4922	4282

Table 2. Initial delay for service interaction on a SonyEricsson M600i over BT

	SE M600i BT, in ms	
Operation	MouseController	AlfredOShop
Acquire service interface	263	312
Build proxy bundle	1882	1881
Install proxy bundle	259	260
Start proxy bundle	892	246
Total start time	3296	2699

4.3 Scalability

An important goal of AlfredO is to ensure that phone clients and service providers can scale to a sufficient number of interactions. We first assess the scalability performance of the service provider and then of the phone client.

In the first set of experiments, the server runs on a typical desktop machine, i.e., a single core Pentium 4 class. To put the server under stress, multiple concurrent clients run on another machine of the same type. Client and server machines are connected through a 100 Mbit/s ethernet network link. Clients connect to the server and perform a service invocation of the same service method every 100 ms. In the tests, a new client instance is started every second. We measure the average invocation time of the last client instance, which is started when all other client instances are already running. The average is computed over a period of at least 90 seconds.

Figure 3 shows the results of this experiment. The server performs very fast and provides an average invocation time of only 1 ms. The invocation time slightly increases with an increasing number of clients but even with 128 clients the invocation time is below 2.5 ms.

However, with this configuration we could not run tests with a number of clients larger than 128. This is because the client machine reaches its upper bound when running 128 Java VMs concurrently. To investigate the scalability boundary of our system, we therefore ran a second set of tests, in which the clients run simultaneously on a cluster of six machines and perform the same experiment as before. The six client machines are two-processor dual-core AMD opteron 2.2 GHz machines and are connected through a switched 1000 Mb/s ethernet network. The service provider is an identical machine in the same network.

As depicted in Figure 4, also in these tests AlfredO performs very efficiently. The server can handle 384 client interactions while providing an average invocation time of 2.2 ms. Given the latency increase observed with 768 concurrent clients (not shown in the figure), it can be estimated that the scalability limit is between 400 and 800 clients. Specifically, with 540 clients the latency is 3.6 ms,

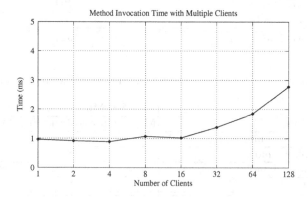

Fig. 3. Invocation time with multiple concurrent clients on a single machine

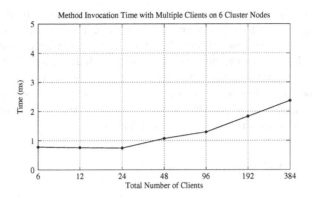

Fig. 4. Invocation time with multiple concurrent clients on six cluster nodes

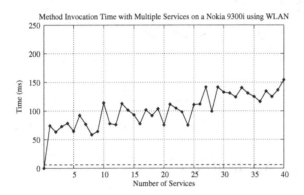

Fig. 5. Invocation time on a Nokia 9300i Phone over 802.11b WLAN

whereas 600 clients lead to a delay over 42 ms per invocation. Therefore, we can conclude that the upper boundary in this configuration is about 550 concurrent clients. This boundary on the server scalability enormously exceeds the require-ments of the applications that we currently envision. A service running on a coffee machine, on a touchscreen in a shop, or on a vending machine may need to support an average of 2-3 concurrent users and a maximum of 30 concurrent users, which still represents only a 5% of the available service capacity.

In the second part of the study, we investigate the scalability of the client side. The client runs on a Nokia 9300i phone. This time we install 1024 distinct services on the server. The mobile phone is configured to get a new service every 10 seconds and then continuously invoke a service method on all acquired services every second. The measured values represent the average invocation time of the first instance in each of these time windows over multiple runs of the experiment. Figure 5 shows the results. The dotted line represents the latency baseline, an ICMP ping over the network link. As observed on the server side, AlfredO provides high scalability on the client side as well. The average latency is around 100 ms.

We then ran the same experiment on the Sony Ericsson M600i phone (see Figure 6) using the built-in Bluetooth 2.0 interface. The results are comparable to the previous platform even though WLAN has in theory an almost four times higher bandwidth. However, since the messages exchanged are fairly small, the bandwidth is not a dominating factor unless a larger amount of data is shipped through the network. For instance, the type of network employed had a larger impact on the latency to acquire the service interfaces (roughly 2 kBytes of data) in the experiments reported in Table 1 and Table 2.

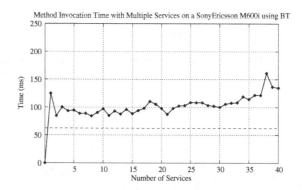

Fig. 6. Invocation time on a Sony Ericsson M600i phone over Bluetooth 2.0

5   Prototype Applications

Using AlfredO we have built two prototype applications: *MouseController* and *AlfredOShop*.

5.1   MouseController

To demonstrate how AlfredO allows a phone to quickly transforming itself in a universal remote controller we have built *MouseController*. This is a very simple but very powerful service that allows a mobile phone to control the movement of the mouse on a notebook's screen. Figure 7 shows how a browser application running on a notebook can be controlled using the communicator's cursor keys. In the figure, the user is minimizing the window opened on the notebook's screen.

The user interface of the same service (i.e., controlling the mouse pointer) is rendered in different ways on different phone clients depending on the capabilities of each particular device. For example, the description of the user interface retrieved by the phone specifies that input commands utilize the *PointingDevice* service interface. On a Nokia 9300i phone, this interface is implemented with the cursor keys of the keyboard. On an iPhone, the same interface is implemented using the integrated accelerometer, thus allowing the user to move the mouse pointer on the notebook's screen by moving the phone itself.

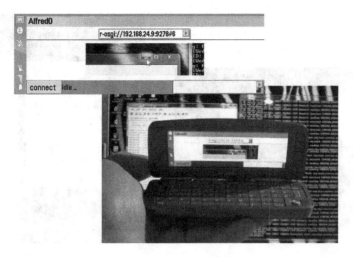

Fig. 7. MouseController running on a Nokia 9300i phone

On the phone's screen a small snapshot of the notebook's screen is displayed. Since the interactions causing the mouse to move are typically occurring at a high update rate, there is often not enough network bandwidth left to send the large updates of the snapshot back to the phone. Therefore, the application uses asynchronous events between the service and the phone and sends updates whenever there is enough bandwidth.

5.2   AlfredOShop

AfredOShop is a prototype application that allows users to interact with information screens using their mobile phones. For instance, by interacting with an information screen placed behind a shop window, a user can browse and compare shop's products even when the shop is closed (e.g., when passing by in the night). The mobile phone is used as a remote controller of the screen on which the product description is visualized.

Figure 8 shows *AlfredOShop* running on Nokia 9300i phone while the user is browsing the details of the beds available in the shop. In this example, the information screen is a notebook computer that displays the shop's interface.

Implementing this application using AlfredO brings several benefits both to the customer and to user. On the customer side, the application can contribute increasing the shop's revenue by making the shop accessible 24 hours a day. Furthermore, a shop's owner does not incur in any security risk because AlfredO provides him a full control on which information to display. On the user side, the interaction only requires a phone's keyboard and cursor. Security is guaranteed because only a passive description of the UI is retrieved from the information screen and no computation takes place on the actual phone.

Since the *AlfredOShop* application uses a rich user interface with multiple informational and control widgets, AlfredO plays an important role in adapting

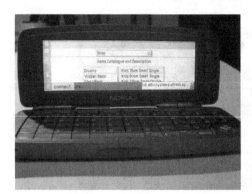

Fig. 8. AlfredOShop on a Nokia 9300i   **Fig. 9.** AlfredOShop on an Apple iPhone

the user interface to different phone capabilities as well as to different screen sizes and output devices. On the Sony Ericsson M600i, AlfredO uses an AWT rendering. On the Nokia 9300i an eRCP renderer efficiently creates the service presentation in SWT. Furthermore, as the Sony Ericsson phone has a portrait-oriented display and the Nokia a landscape-oriented display the output interface is adapted accordingly. The iPhone platform currently does not run any Java implementation that supports the graphical toolkit of the device. However, the AlfredO servlet renderer can be used to generate an AJAX-enhanced set of dynamic web pages that can be viewed and controlled through the built-in web browser (Figure 9). In terms of functionality, the AJAX version provides the same features as the other versions, such as explicitly connecting to a known service, getting informed of newly discovered devices, and switching between the user interfaces of different devices and their services.

6   Related Work

Research on distributed systems and ubiquitous computing has variously focused on the problem of how users can dynamically interact with devices embedded in the surrounding environment. Proposed solutions can be roughly grouped into two categories: those that assume an *a priori* configuration of the interacting devices and those that configure the devices on-the-fly by downloading the necessary software from the Internet or by migrating it from a nearby device.

For example, systems like Personal Server [19] provide the user with a virtual personal computer environment. Data and code necessary to interact with external input/output interfaces are pre-stored and pre-installed on the mobile devices. As these approaches require a pre-configured infrastructure they can suit only static environments.

The second class of systems allows for increased flexibility and can therefore suit dynamic environments. Technologies based on mobile code [20] have been considered in several domains, but they are usually disregarded because of their security and trust concerns. These security problems are alleviated by systems that rely on a third party (e.g., Internet) for authentication purposes. CoolTown [21] assume a web presence that connects all embedded devices. Each device advertises its presence and offered services through URLs. SDIPP [22] augments the Bluetooth service discovery protocol with web access. A user can download the required service interface directly from the nearby device using Bluetooth or from service directories implemented as web services.

Although these approaches can provide some flexibility, AlfredO achieves even higher flexibility by organizing the services into decomposable tiers that can be distributed to configure one-tier or two-tier architectures among the interacting devices. Security is also improved by transferring to the mobile phone only a description of presentation tier, thus allowing the device to self-implement its UI. Furthermore, AlfredO does not rely on Internet connectivity and targets the resource constraints of mobile phones: it is lightweight and highly efficient.

Web services have also been considered in this context. Microservers [23] embed web servers in Bluetooth devices and use WAP over Bluetooth for communication. Specifically tailored to mobile phones, Mobile Web Server [24], also known as Raccoon, provides a mobile phone with a global URL and with HTTP access thus enabling a mobile phone to host a universally accessible website. Even though web services are not employed in the current implementation, they could be utilized as well. We opted for R-OSGi because it provides a lightweight implementation optimized to minimize the resource consumption on phones.

We borrow the notion of abstract user interfaces that can be rendered in different ways on different devices from other research projects [25,26], especially in the field of human-computer interaction [27]. However, these projects mostly focus on how to generate the user interface and typically rely on centralized infrastructures. Instead, our focus is on the system and infrastructure issues.

7   Conclusions

AlfredO enables mobile phones to become universal clients for interaction with an unbounded number of heterogeneous electronic devices. Ultimately, this approach blurs the boundaries between mobile phones, appliances, and other electronic devices and let resource-constrained mobile phones acquire larger value from services that reside elsewhere. Compared to previous approaches, AlfredO makes service interactions fully decomposable processes, thus providing high flexibility and customizable security. In addition, a mobile phone benefits from such an approach also in terms of easier administration (no need to install software) and automatic maintenance. Experience has shown that our implementation is highly efficient and it comes on phones with a file footprint of only 290 kBytes. Future work on AlfredO includes an online optimization mechanism to customize service distribution at runtime and an automatic distribution mechanism of the data tiers to provide transparent synchronization.

Acknowledgments

The work presented in this paper was partly supported by the National Competence Center in Research on Mobile Information and Communication Systems (NCCR-MICS), a center supported by the Swiss National Science Foundation under the grant number 5005-67322, and partly by the ETH Fellowship Program.

References

1. South Korea Telecom: SK Telecom Releases Upgraded Mobile RFID-based "Touch Book" Service (2007), http://www.sktelecom.com/eng/jsp/tlounge/presscenter/PressCenterDetail.jsp?f_reportdata_seq=3883
2. Nokia: Nokia N95 (2007), http://nokia.com/n95
3. Nokia Research Centre: Sports Tracker (2006), http://research.nokia.com/research/projects/SportsTracker/index.html
4. Motorola: Nomadic Device Gateway (2006), http://www.motorola.com/content.jsp?globalObjectId=8253
5. Rellermeyer, J.S., Alonso, G., Roscoe, T.: R-OSGi: Distributed applications through software modularization. In: Cerqueira, R., Campbell, R.H. (eds.) Middleware 2007. LNCS, vol. 4834, pp. 1–20. Springer, Heidelberg (2007)
6. OSGi Alliance: OSGi Service Platform, Core Specification Release 4, Version 4.1, Draft (2007)
7. Rellermeyer, J.S., Alonso, G.: Concierge: A service platform for resource-constrained devices. In: Proceedings of the 2007 ACM EuroSys Conference (EuroSys 2007), pp. 245–258. ACM, New York (2007)
8. Eclipse Foundation: Eclipse (2001), http://www.eclipse.org
9. Sun Microsystems: JSR 220: Enterprise Java Beans, Version 3.0 (2006)
10. Guttman, E., Perkins, C., Veizades, J.: Service Location Protocol, Version 2. RFC 2608, Internet Engineering Task Force (IETF) (1999), http://www.ietf.org/rfc/rfc2608.txt
11. Rellermeyer, J.S.: JSLP project, Java Service Location Protocol (2008), http://jslp.sourceforge.net
12. W3C: XForms 1.0, 3rd edn. (2007)
13. Myers, B., Hudson, S.E., Pausch, R.: Past, present, and future of user interface software tools. ACM Trans. Hum-Comput. Interact. 7(1), 3–28 (2000)
14. Zukowski, J.: Java AWT Reference. O'Reilly, Sebastopol (1997)
15. Eclipse Foundation: SWT: Standard Widget Toolkit (2004), http://www.eclipse.org/swt/
16. Eclipse Foundation: embedded Rich Client Platform, eRCP (2006), http://www.eclipse.org/ercp/
17. Sun Microsystems: Java Servlet Technology (1994)
18. Garrett, J.J.: Ajax: A New Approach to Web Applications (2005)
19. Want, R., Pering, T., Danneels, G., Kumar, M., Sundar, M., Light, J.: The personal server: Changing the way we think about ubiquitous computing. In: Borriello, G., Holmquist, L.E. (eds.) UbiComp 2002. LNCS, vol. 2498, pp. 194–209. Springer, Heidelberg (2002)
20. Fuggetta, A., Picco, G.P., Vigna, G.: Understanding code mobility. IEEE Transactions on Software Engineering 24(5), 342–361 (1998)

21. Kindberg, T., Barton, J., Morgan, J., Becker, G., Caswell, D., Debaty, P., Gopal, G., Frid, M., Krishnan, V., Morris, H., Schettino, J., Serra, B., Spasojevic, M.: People, places, things: Web presence for the real world. In: Proceedings of the 3rd IEEE Workshop on Mobile Computing Systems and Applications (WMCSA 2000), p. 19. IEEE, Los Alamitos (2000)
22. Ravi, N., Stern, P., Desai, N., Iftode, L.: Accessing ubiquitous services using smart phones. In: Proceedings of the 3rd IEEE International Conference on Pervasive Computing and Communications (PerCom 2005), pp. 383–393 (2005)
23. Hartwig, S., Stromann, J.P., Resch, P.: Wireless microservers. IEEE Pervasive Computing 1(2), 58–66 (2002)
24. Nokia: Mobile Web Server (2008),
    http://wiki.opensource.nokia.com/projects/Mobile_Web_Server
25. Ponnekanti, S., Lee, B., Fox, A., Hanrahan, P., Winograd, T.: ICrafter: A service framework for ubiquitous computing environments. In: Abowd, G.D., Brumitt, B., Shafer, S. (eds.) UbiComp 2001. LNCS, vol. 2201, pp. 56–75. Springer, Heidelberg (2001)
26. LaPlant, B., Trewin, S., Zimmermann, G., Vanderheiden, G.: The universal remote console: A universal access bus for pervasive computing. IEEE Pervasive Computing 3(1), 76–80 (2004)
27. Nichols, J., Myers, B., Higgins, M., Hughes, J., Harris, T., Rosenfeld, R., Pignol, M.: Generating remote control interfaces for complex appliances. In: Proceedings of the 15th annual ACM Symposium on User Interface Software and Technology (UIST 2002), vol. 2201, pp. 161–170. ACM Press, New York (2002)

Exo-Leasing: Escrow Synchronization for Mobile Clients of Commodity Storage Servers[*]

Liuba Shrira[1], Hong Tian[2], and Doug Terry[3]

[1] Brandeis University
[2] Amazon.com
[3] Microsoft Research

Abstract. Escrow reservations is a well-known synchronization technique, useful for inventory control, that avoids conflicts by taking into account the semantics of *fragmentable* object types. Unfortunately, current escrow techniques cannot be used on generic "commodity" servers because they require the servers to run the type-specific synchronization code. This is a severe limitation for systems that require application-specific synchronization but need to rely on generic components.

Our *exo-leasing* method provides a new way to implement escrow synchronization without running any type-specific code in the servers. Instead, escrow synchronization code runs in the client providing the ability to use commodity servers. Running synchronization code in the client provides an additional benefit. Unlike any other system, our system allows a disconnected client to obtain escrow reservation from another disconnected client, reducing the need to coordinate with the servers. Measurements of a prototype indicate that our approach provides escrow-based conflict avoidance at moderate performance overhead.

1 Introduction

Mobile collaborators wish to continue their collaborative work wherever they go. In spite of improving network connectivity, wide-area connectivity cannot be taken for granted because of physical, economic and energy factors. Moreover, the increasing trend towards storing data in utility data centers is making it harder for mobile workers to share and access their data while out of the office. It is useful, therefore, to develop techniques that enable mobile users to continue collaborative work while disconnected and operate independently without compromising data consistency.

Disconnected access to shared data is by now commonly supported via a well understood process [11]. A mobile client pre-loads objects before disconnecting and optimistically manipulates locally-cached copies of objects, periodically reconnecting to validate the changes against a "master copy" of data stored reliably at the storage server. If a conflict is detected the client has to abort the changes or reconcile them, possibly using application-specific resolvers [11,21].

---

[*] This research was partially supported by NSF grant CNS-0427408 and Microsoft Research, Cambridge, UK. The work was done while Hong Tian was at Brandeis University.

V. Issarny and R. Schantz (Eds.): Middleware 2008, LNCS 5346, pp. 42–61, 2008.

The penalty for aborts and after-the-fact conflict resolution, however, may be too high in some applications. For example, a mobile salesman may accept customer orders based on cached, but out-of-date information only to discover, upon returning to the office, that the purchased items are out of stock, thereby resulting in cancelled orders or unhappy customers. To avoid costly conflicts, a mobile client, before disconnecting, can obtain reservations [20](locks) that guarantee (in-advance) the successful completion of specific transactions while disconnected. *Escrow* synchronization [17] is a well-known simple scheme, useful for inventory control, that provides such reservations. It exploits the properties of *fragmentable* [29] object types to avoid conflicts when clients make concurrent changes to shared objects [20]. For example, members of a mobile sales team can each obtain a reservation for a portion of the available sales items and independently validate sales transactions while disconnected.

Current escrow synchronization techniques suffer from a limitation that precludes the use of generic "commodity" servers because they require type-specific escrow synchronization code at the servers. Most data centers will not allow customers to run unproven custom code on shared storage system servers for performance and security reasons. This is a problem for systems that require application-specific synchronization but rely on generic components to exploit economies of scale (for example, "cloud computing" systems are likely to have this problem).

The contribution of our paper is to fix this limitation. We describe a new technique called *exo-leasing* that provides escrow without running type-specific code at the servers. Instead, this code runs in the client. New applications using escrow and other fragmentable object types can be developed without modifying the servers. The result is a modular system with the ability to use commodity servers. An additional benefit of exo-leasing is the ability to provide new functionality. Unlike any other system, we allow a disconnected mobile salesman on a sales trip to split and transfer part of a reservation to a partner. Exo-leasing makes this possible because the synchronization code running at the client encapsulates the complete synchronization logic. Disconnected reservation split and transfer reduces the need to communicate with the servers, providing a complementary benefit to disconnected cooperative caching [18,24] that transfers data but not reservations.

We prototyped MobileBuddy, an exo-leasing escrow synchronization system on top of a generic transaction system, and evaluated the performance overheads introduced by our techniques. Measurements indicate that if the client obtains reservations but does not benefit from them, our techniques impose a moderate performance penalty. If the client benefits from conflict avoidance, enabled by the reservation and reservation transfer, the cost is reasonable since conflict avoidance saves work.

To summarize, this paper attacks an important insufficiently studied problem in mobile computing space, namely, how a commodity storage server can support escrow synchronization so that client applications can control shared inventory data while avoiding conflicting updates that later need to be aborted or resolved.

The paper makes the following contributions: 1) It introduces exo-leasing, a new approach that combines escrow reservations with optimistic concurrency control. By offloading the type-specific escrow code from the servers to the clients, it provides the ability to use commodity servers, making escrow reservations practical in commodity storage systems. 2) It describes a novel reservation split and transfer facility enabled by exo-leasing, describing its semantics and new transactional mechanisms for implementing the semantics. 3) It provides measurements of a prototype system, supporting our performance claims.

2   Our Approach

Our goal is to provide effective support for disconnected client transactions using escrow synchronization in systems such as inventory control. Specifically, using the mobile sales example, we require:

1. Ability to acquire sales reservations so that a salesman can carry out sales transactions while disconnected and be sure the transactions will commit without conflicts.
2. A proper outcome in the absence of failures. For example, the salesman should be able to commit only the sales he ultimately manages to finalize.
3. A proper outcome in case of failure. For example if the salesman never finalizes the sale, the reservation should be released.

Our new approach, based on specialized escrow objects, supports these requirements, and, unlike prior work, requires no special processing on the storage server nodes. This is attractive because one can use generic commodity nodes. Prior work also made use of specialized escrow data types to avoid concurrency conflicts and developed a number of implementations [12,17,29]. However, these approaches involved the use of specialized code running at the server node. Using our approach, prior escrow schemes can be adapted to use unmodified generic servers.

In our scheme, the persistent storage for objects resides on storage servers while mobile clients cache and access local copies of these objects. A disconnected client runs top-level disconnected transactions that contain within them special smaller *revertible* (*open nested* [30]) transactions. The revertible transactions perform modifications to objects that are cached on a mobile client and are used to commit changes, e.g. reservations to items in stock, that may be cancelled later. They allow clients to coordinate their changes. Fig. 1 summarizes the steps taken by a mobile client both when connected and disconnected from the server (for now ignore the split and transfer steps that will be explained later).

Our requirement to not run any special code at the storage nodes implies that storage nodes do not know anything about the revertible changes. Instead, storage nodes process all commit requests, including revertible transactions, identically. Our approach, instead, has special processing performed at the client machines. These computations run on cached copies of data from the storage server nodes, and these copies will reflect the changes made by other committed

```
Begin top-level transaction
Obtain reservations
Loop {
        Refresh/load objects into local cache
        Disconnect from server
        Loop{
                Perform local tentative transactions
                Validate tentative transactions against reservations
                Record transaction results
                Connect to collaborator  // Start reservation split and transfer
                    Refresh/load objects if desired
                    Provide some reservations if desired
                    Obtain new reservations if desired
                }                                           // End reservation split and transfer
        Connect to the server
        Release some reservations if desired
        Renew or obtain new reservations if necessary
}
Commit top-level transaction i.e.
atomically validate/abort local transactions and
        release unused reservations.
```

Fig. 1. Mobile client steps

transactions, including both committed top-level transactions and committed revertible transactions. Thus the computations can observe the revertible changes
of other disconnected transactions and take these into account. Our approach
makes use of special *escrow objects*. Such an object provides the normal operations, including obtaining or releasing a reservation for a resource. Additionally,
these objects are prepared to handle the changes committed by revertible transactions. When the user calls a modification operation on such an object, the
operation performs the modification and records the execution of the operation
in a log along with a lease. The lease stores the time at which the revertible
operation will expire. The information about the revertible modifications and
their leases is part of the representation of the object, and thus is written to the
storage server when the mobile client reconnects and the application commits
the revertible transaction. Other clients, upon connecting to the shared storage
server, will observe the revertible modification on the special escrow object.

When the client reconnects and is ready to commit the top-level transaction,
it must first call a special *confirm* operation on all escrow objects on which it
wants the revertible change to become permanent. This operation updates the
status of that change so that it *no longer* appears revertible. Additionally, the
transaction can call a special *release* operation to undo the modifications that
are no longer of interest to it. Thus when the top-level transaction commits, all
of the escrow objects whose modifications have been confirmed will be stored
with those changes having really happened, and objects whose changes have
been released will have those modifications cancelled. Note that the application
need not explicitly cancel (release) the changes that are no longer needed, since

these modifications will be undone automatically when those objects are used by other transactions after the leases expire. However, cancelling is desirable since it can release the resource earlier, before their leases expire.

3   Exo-Leasing

Consider the value of the shared object tracking the balance of in-stock items for sale in the disconnected sales application, and consider the write/write conflicts that occur when concurrent transactions add or remove item reservations. These conflicts are superfluous in the sense that, as long as there remain available items for sale, no matter in what order the reservations are interleaved they produce the same in-stock balance. A type-specific synchronization scheme called *escrow* [17] avoids these unneeded conflicts by exploiting the semantics of the *escrow* type. An object of *escrow* type provides two commutative operations: *split(delta)* and *merge(delta)*. A transaction calls the split operation to make a reservation for specified (delta) escrow amount, and calls the merge operation to return the unused escrow amount. As long as the in-stock balance is positive, the escrow locking protocols allows concurrent transactions to interleave the split and merge operations without conflicts. The escrow type is a representative of a general class of *fragmentable* objects [29]. Objects of this class have commutative operations that can be exploited by type-specific synchronization schemes like escrow to avoid conflicts.

Escrow is a simple and effective synchronization method that has been well-known for a long time but has not been widely deployed in commercial systems. A principle barrier to the adoption in practice has been the need to modify the (legacy) concurrency engine since prior proposals run escrow synchronization code in the server. We show how to implement escrow at the clients yet allow the same concurrent operation inter-leavings allowed by other escrow proposals. Our disconnected client/server system runs transactions on cached state in the client, using a generic fine-grain read/write concurrency control scheme, and a cache coherence protocol that sends invalidation to the client if the object cached at the client becomes stale (because another client has modified it).

Server-side escrow. The server-side implementation of a sales account service using escrow synchronization consists of an object (service object) that exports a collection of methods. The methods include *acquire*, *release*, and *expire* operations that can be overridden by different fragmentable object implementations. The object implementation consists of the procedures implementing the operations and the representation of the shared state they manipulate. The representation includes a set of outstanding reservations and an internal in-stock balance object that implements the escrow operations. The *split(delta)* operation is called by the acquire request to obtain the reserved escrow amount, and the *merge(delta)* operation is called by the release request to return the unused escrow amount. The *merge(delta)* operation is also called by the expire method that is invoked internally by the service system when a reservation expires. The reservation requests run as atomic transactions. The acquire request atomically commits the modifications to the in-stock-balance object and inserts a record describing the reservation into the reservation set. The reservation record specifies the reservation expiration time, and the recovery actions that need to be performed if the reservation expires. These *reconciler* actions are type-specific, they perform the inverse of the operation invoked by the acquire request. The release and expire requests atomically commit the effects of the corresponding merge operation and remove the reservation.

The synchronization code described above resembles a concurrent object with a type-specific lock manager implemented using a monitor where monitor procedures implement the reservation requests, and monitor state encapsulates the internal in-stock-balance object and the outstanding reservation set. Within the monitor, the procedures use a simple mutex to serialize accesses to the shared monitor state.

Client-side escrow. A disconnected client/server system that runs transactions on cached state in the client, validates read/write conflicts at the server, using a cache coherence protocol that detects stale cache entries, can run the concurrent object on the client side. This is achieved by simply storing the persistent monitor state at the server, caching at the client the monitor code and state, running the monitor procedures on the cached state, and replacing the mutex synchronization with the cache coherence protocol that coordinates access to cached state by validating read/write conflicts at the server. When the client is connected and issues a reservation acquire request, the corresponding monitor procedure updates the client's cached state (the reservation set and the state of the in-stock-balance object) to reflect the reservation and sends the modified state to the server. If the state sent to the server is not stale, the server can commit the request making the updated state persistent. If the cached state is stale because another client has committed a reservation, the server aborts the request and informs the client. The client gets from the server the up-to-date monitor state, re-runs the request, and tries to commit with the new state. Eventually the request will succeed. If a client needs to return unused reservation the commit of the release request is similar to the acquire request in that it may need to be retried.

Lease expiration. In the server-side scheme, the monitor code notices an expired reservation and invokes the expire request to release the reservation. In the client-side scheme, the monitor code at a client notices the expired reservation. Such a client invokes the expire request to release the reservation. There is no problem with concurrent duplicate invocations of the expire request for the same expired reservation at multiple clients since after the first release commits other cached monitor copies become stale. A reservation expiration may not be noticed for a long time if no client runs a reservation request. On the other hand, the expiration is of no interest until then. We assume the server enforces object access controls so that only clients having suitable permissions are allowed to modify the monitor state. Since all escrow reservation requests require write permission the expired reservation can be reconciled by any client that makes a reservation request. Otherwise, the reservation reconciliation may need to wait until noticed by a client with appropriate permissions. Note, that a client with a fast clock could expire the lease too soon. To avoid this, we use the server time for lease expiration (assuming monotonic clocks). That is, a client must have received a message from the server with a timestamp greater than the lease expiration time.

We call the above client-side synchronization approach *exo-leasing* (externalized leasing), and refer to the object running the escrow synchronization code at the client simply as *escrow object*. We showed how exo-leasing works for escrow type. The same approach works for other fragmentable types [29]. A general transformation from a server-side type-specific synchronization scheme to a client-side scheme is described in [23].

Considerations. Moving code to the client can adversely impact the performance of the system if the monitor object is large and the contention is high. In general, however, we expect the synchronization objects to be small and contention levels to be moderate. Moving code to the client raises a security concern if servers are trusted and clients and servers belong to different administrative domains. A rogue client could corrupt the monitor code, e.g. expire a lease "too early", and commit changes that depend on the expiration request. Digital signatures could allow to detect a rogue client after-the-fact, but may introduce overhead. The security concern is mitigated if a client runs in a secure appliance. A possible general approach, considered future work, is to exploit recently introduced hardware TCB extensions.

4   2-Level Transactions with Exo-Leasing

We have designed a 2-level transaction system that supports escrow synchronization for disconnected client transactions accessing shared objects stored in generic storage servers. In the 2-level system, a generic *base* transaction system, assumed as given, provides disconnected client/server storage for persistent objects. The base transactions synchronize using *read/write* optimistic concurrency control. Higher-level transactions, called *application transactions*, correspond to activities meaningful to the application. For example, reserving items for sale, running a disconnected sale, and then committing the sales transaction upon reconnection, may constitute one application transaction. Application transactions synchronize using escrow objects. We describe how we use the base system to implement escrow objects, to provide application transaction atomicity in the presence of client crashes and failures to reconnect, and to support disconnected application transaction validation. A technical report [25] considers the ACID properties in our 2-level system.

Base transactions. MX disconnected object storage system [24] provides base transactions, though we could use other generic client-server storage system that supports cached transactions, e.g. SQL server replication. A disconnected mobile client runs *tentative transactions*, accessing the local copies of the cached objects stored persistently in storage servers. A tentative transaction records intention to commit and allows the client to start up a next transaction. Tentative commits lead to *dependent commits* [9]: transaction T_j *depends* on T_i if it uses objects modified by T_i because if T_i ultimately aborts so must T_j. A tentative commit that is not a dependent commit, defines an *independent action*: [5] a transaction T_j that does not use objects modified by T_i can commit even if T_i aborts. To commit a tentative transaction persistently, the client connects to the server. An optimistic concurrency control scheme (adaptation of OCC [2]), provides efficient validation of disconnected client transaction read and write sets using invalidations. The server accumulates the invalidations for objects cached at a disconnected client, allowing, upon reconnection, to validate client transactions efficiently, including transactions accessing objects acquired from other clients while disconnected (using disconnected cooperative caching [24]). A transaction that passes server validation is committed, and its results are stored persistently at the server (without re-executing it).

Application transactions and escrow objects. Application transactions invoke operations on regular cached objects and encapsulated escrow objects. An application transaction runs as a top-level transaction that contains nested base transactions (tentative or durable). Application transaction effects become durable when it commits a base transaction at the server.

The escrow object operations (e.g. acquire, release and expire) run as base transactions nested inside the top-level transaction. They manipulate an escrow object representation consisting of regular cached objects. For example, the operation to acquire an escrow reservation that reserves a number of sales items reads the cached copy of the escrow variable to check if a sufficient amount of sales items is available for the reservation, and updates the cached representation to reflect an acquired amount. The base transaction that commits the acquire operation updates the *durable copy* of the escrow object at the server.

The nested transaction that commits an update to an escrow object at the server, without committing the top-level transaction, exposes the effects of the top-level transaction to other clients. Such open nesting [16,30] allows to synchronize top-level transactions running in concurrent clients to avoid conflicts (e.g. another client can observe the existing reservations and reserve the remaining sales items). Note, that since base transactions are optimistic, the server will abort a client base transaction if the cached escrow object state is stale, i.e. has been modified by another client. In such a case, the first client re-fetches the new state of the escrow object, re-executes the nested transaction on the fresh state, and retries the commit of the base transaction. The nested transaction is retried without undoing the top-level transaction.

Recovery. We want to guarantee the atomicity (all-or-nothing) property for top-level transactions. A top-level transaction that exposes its effects by committing open nested transactions (running escrow operations) can subsequently crash or abort. The exposed effects need to be undone (recovered) by running escrow operations that revert the effects. The protocol that accomplishes this resembles logical recovery for highly-concurrent data structures, e.g. ARIES recovery for indexes [7]. Likewise, its mechanisms, *cleanup* and *reconcilers*, resemble, respectively, logical recovery procedure and logical undo records. Our protocol differs because it runs on the client side, and deals with leases rather than locks.

Cleanup runs when transactions commit or abort. The goal of the *abort cleanup* is to revert the exposed effects of an open nested transaction when the top-level transaction aborts. The goal of the *commit cleanup* is to ensure that the exposed effects are not reverted when the top-level transaction commits. The cleanup actions invoke operations called *reconcilers*, defined by the escrow objects. Reconcilers revert the effect of escrow operations. For example, the reconciler for an operation that acquires an escrow lease on an item, is an escrow merge operation that returns the item. The reconcilers are stored in the part of the escrow object representation, called the *reconciler log*. A reconciler is recorded in the log when the open nested transaction runs the associated escrow operation. A reconciler becomes durable when the open nested transaction commits at the server. The reconciler entry in the reconciler log can be *active, deactivated,* or *timed-out*. The open nested transaction commits an *active* reconciler that includes the lease expiration time.

An abort cleanup, running when a top-level transaction aborts, invokes and deactivates the *active* reconcilers recorded by its open nested transactions. An abort cleanup can also run on a different client that observes a *timed-out* reconciler in the reconciler log. Such abort cleanup runs when the top-level transaction at the observing client commits or aborts. A commit cleanup, running when a top-level transaction commits, deactivates the *active* reconcilers that have been recorded by its open nested transactions (without invoking them). The commit cleanup resembles the release of locks at transaction commit time in read/write locking schemes but there is an important difference. Where the release of read/write locks only affects performance, escrow leases must be removed (deactivated) atomically with the top-level commit to maintain correctness. This is because, if the top-level transaction commits and subsequently client crashes without removing the escrow leases, the time-out of the escrow lease will revert the effects of the lease, thus violating the all-or-nothing property of the top-level transaction whose commit depends on the acquire of the lease.

A top-level transaction assembles the cleanup actions by registering callbacks to escrow object handlers called *cleanup handlers* when open nested transactions invoke escrow operations. In addition, validation procedures check the leases in the reconciler logs, and register handlers for the timed-out reconcilers so that commit or abort cleanup at the observing client will invoke the timed-out reconciler and deactivate it. A cleanup action runs as a nested base transaction that commits (or aborts) atomically with the top-level transaction. To commit a nested transaction as part of the top-level transaction commit, the client simply includes the read/write sets of the nested transaction with the parent read/write sets. If the server can not commit the joint transaction because the escrow object was stale, the client receives an invalidation for the escrow object, re-fetches the new state of the object, and retries the joint commit without aborting the top-level transaction. Note, that if other data (not the escrow object) was stale, the application will need to resort to after-the-fact reconciliation for that particular data.

Example execution. Fig. 2 shows the state of the reconciler logs at the server and two concurrent clients C1 and C2 running top-level transactions using an escrow object. The initial escrow object state at the server contains 15 in-stock escrow items and an empty reconciler log. C1 runs a top-level transaction T1 acquiring a reservation for 5 items by committing (step 1) a connected open nested transaction that updates at the server the escrow variable e to 10 items to reflect the remaining in-stock amount, recording a leased reconciler [merge 5/C1] that will undo its effect if C1 does not reconnect in time (lease time omitted to avoid clutter). Note, unlike for regular cached objects, after invoking acquire, the cached escrow amount at the client and at the server are different. A concurrent client C2 runs a top-level transaction T2 that acquires a reservation for 3 items (step 2) updating the durable escrow variable e to 7 to reflect the remaining in-stock amount, and recording a reconciler [merge 3/C2]. C1 consumes 2 escrow items while disconnected (running a special validated DON-transaction explained below that records tentative update to the cached escrow variable) resetting cached e to 3. If T1 were to abort at this point, the entire acquired amount has to be reconciled. If T1 were to commit, only the remaining unconsumed amount, as indicated by the cleanup handlers onCommit and onAbort registered with T1 (depicted within unshaded box). C1 reconnects and commits (step 3) the parent transaction T1, releasing the unused escrow amount, and resetting the durable value of e to 10. The commit deactivates C1's reconciler

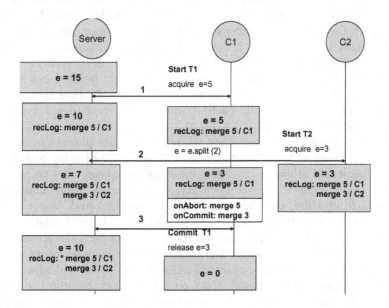

Fig. 2. Reconciler logs in escrow leasing

in the durable reconciler log (deactivated is entry marked *[merge 3/ C1]). The durable reconciler log at the server still contains the active reconciler for the open nested transaction committed by C2. If C2 crashes, or does not reconnect in time, the reconciler will be invoked and deactivated by another client that accesses this escrow object and observes the expired reconciler.

Disconnected validation. Our system supports *disconnected validation* [20] for top-level transactions. Disconnected validation guarantees, at the cost of extra checking at tentative commit time, that transactions will pass connected validation, provided the client reconnects in time. Validated transactions are a useful practical abstraction that reflects the reality of disconnected computation. For example, a "guaranteed mobile sales transaction" that performs a disconnected update to the escrow object, runs as a validated transaction. A new variant of disconnected tentative transaction we call *DON* (*disconnected open nested*) transaction supports disconnected validation. Unlike regular tentative transactions in the base transaction system, DON transactions run protected by the escrow lease and therefore can be validated by a disconnected client. Escrow operations runs as DON transactions. A specialized validation procedure provided by escrow objects checks lease expiration. Sec. 6 considers the performance overhead of disconnected validation.

5   Reservation Split and Transfer

A disconnected salesman may want to transfer a reservation to a partner. Our system allows a disconnected client (the requester) to acquire reservations from another client (the helper). Some disconnected client/server systems allow one disconnected client to obtain consistent objects from another client [3,18,24] but none support the split and transfer of reservations (locks or leases). Yet, such a feature might be useful since it reduces the need to communicate with the servers and permits a new pattern of collaboration within disconnected workgroups. Consider how reservation split and transfer might be used in a scenario where a team of three traveling salesman Joe, Sally and Mary share a sales service account. Mary and Sally each obtain a reservation to sell five items, disconnect and travel together to a sales destination where each completes a sales transaction selling one item each. Mary changes her plans, departing for a different destination. Mary would like to transfer her remaining reservations to Sally. This would allow Sally to guarantee the additional sales transactions she hopes to accomplish to cover for Mary. Sally acquires the remaining four reservations from Mary, completes five sales transactions and, before departing, transfers her remaining reservations to Joe who arrives to replace Mary. Sally reconnects to the server and successfully commits her sales transactions, recording the reservation transfers. The commit reflects the sales of six reserved items, removing the appropriate reservations for the sold items and adjusting the pending reservations to four items. Mary reconnects next, recording a reservation transfer to Sally, and commits her sales transaction. The commit reflects the sale of one reserved item, adjusting the pending reservations to three items. Joe gets distracted with other matters and lets the remaining reservations expire. The expire method is invoked canceling the expired reservations and making the three reserved items available again. At this point, to run a guaranteed sales transactions Joe would need to reconnect and acquire new reservations. Fig. 1 summarizes the steps taken by a mobile client using reservation transfer. Exo-leasing makes reservation split and transfer possible because the escrow object that runs at the client (rather than the server) encapsulates the complete logic of the escrow reservation manager. The reservation transfer is implemented by a special transfer procedure defined as part of the escrow object implementation.

Semantics. Escrow reservation split and transfer has to preserve the semantic invariants of the escrow type. Such transfer should have the same effect as if the helper never had the reservation, and the requester acquired the reservation by interacting with the server. That is, the transfer of a part of escrow reservation from the helper to the requester must simultaneously increase the amount of escrow in the requester and decrease by the same amount the reserved amount in the helper. The correctness condition for reservation split and transfer [25] requires that a transaction system that commits transactions using the transferred reservations is equivalent to a system that commits the same transactions without the transfer, where all reservations are obtained by interacting with the server. Of course, any one of the disconnected clients participating in the typed lease transfer can crash before reconnecting to the server. Moreover, the participating clients can reconnect in any order. For example, a requester that has acquired the reservation from a helper could reconnect first, and the helper that has supplied the reservation could crash while disconnected. The correctness condition for reservation needs to be maintained in the presence of disconnected client crashes and all possible participant reconnection orders.

Recovery. We implement the reservation split and transfer using a new kind of transaction. The new transaction, called a *2DON* transaction, involves two clients participating in the transfer, each client runs a nested tentative base transaction. 2DON transaction is tentative because one or both participants in the transfer could crash. It commits durably when one or both participants reconnect to commit the transaction at the server. To insure the atomicity of the transfer, the 2DON transaction has to record enough information in the participants to enable any reconnecting participant to recover independently, if the other participant does not reconnect in time. The reservation transfer procedure at the helper client calls the escrow object release operation to reflect the transfer. This updates the cached escrow variable and defines the appropriate commit and abort cleanup actions, recording the appropriate reconcilers in the reconciler log. These steps are identical to DON transaction. In addition, the reservation transfer procedure records the reconcilers of the other participant so that the reconciler logs at both participants contain identical sets of reconcilers reflecting the transfer. Using the reconciler logs the eventual cleanup actions insure that reconcilers for unused reservations are invoked (and deactivated), and the reconcilers for used reservations are deactivated.

In a client that reconnects first, the commit cleanup for the top-level transaction containing the transfer deactivates the durable original reconciler created when the reservation that got transferred was first acquired, and adds the two reconcilers, generated by the transfer. The reconciler for the amount held by the reconnecting committing client gets immediately deactivated when this reconnecting transaction commits. The reconciler for the amount held at the other participant will get deactivated when the second participant in the transfer reconnects (or by expiration). Our protocol guarantees that the appropriate cleanup actions for every reconciler will be invoked *exactly once*, in all three cases that constitute the possible outcomes of the transfer: when the second participant reconnects and commits in time, second participant fails to reconnect, or none of the participants reconnect in time. An example illustrates the protocol steps.

Example execution. Fig. 3 depicts the reconciler logs reflecting escrow reservation transfer. The execution steps are identical to the example in Figure 2, except for step 2 when helper client C1 connects to requester client C2 and splits and transfers a reservation for 3 items. The split and transfer runs as the 2DON transaction, resetting the escrow amount to 0 in the helper, and to 3 in the requester. The 2DON transaction records in the reconciler logs of the participants the leased reconcilers reflecting the transfer (same expiration time as the original helper lease). The requester transfer reconciler [merge 3/C2] accounts for the case when the requester does not reconnect in time. Such lost transferred amount needs to be recovered by merging it back into the total available amount. The reconnecting helper C1 will durably commit this reconciler at the server. The expiration of this reconciler will trigger the intended cleanup. This

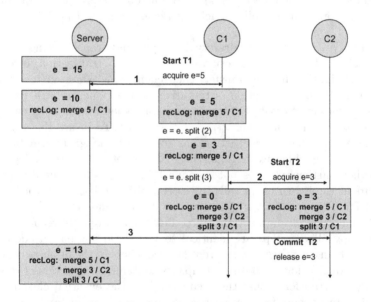

Fig. 3. Reconciler logs in escrow split and transfer

reconciler will be deactivated by the requester C2 if it reconnects in time as part of the commit of the top-level transaction T2 that run the 2DON transaction. The helper transfer reconciler [split 3/C1] accounts for the situation where the helper does not reconnect in time and therefore does not deactivate the durable reconciler [merge 5/C1] generated by C1's open nested transaction that obtained the original reservation. The timeout of the original acquire reconciler could (incorrectly) merge back the entire amount not accounting for the transferred amount. This is not a problem because the reconnecting C2 has the reconciler [split 3/C1] generated by the 2DON transaction, and will durably commit it at the server. The expiration of this reconciler, together with the original acquire reconciler will trigger the execution of both reconcilers during cleanup, correctly adding back 2 escrow units. Both reconcilers (corresponding to acquire and transfer) would be deactivated if C1 reconnects on time as part of the top-level transaction T1 commit. In the example, C2 reconnects to the server first (step 3), releases all the reservations (no reservations were used up), updates the server escrow amount to 13 to reflect the returned escrow, deactivates the requester's transfer reconciler, and updates the server reconciler log to include the helper's reconciler. All of the above actions commit atomically in a base transaction. After the commit, the cached requester state contains no reservations (not shown). Consider the possible ways the execution could proceed. If C1 reconnects and commits on-time, this would not change the durable escrow value but would deactivate the helper's reservations and corresponding reconcilers, as explained above. Alternatively, if C1 does not reconnect, the reconciler log at the server containing the helper's reconcilers [merge 5/C1] and [split 3/C1] would eventually be observed and invoked at some other client adding back 2 units. If both the requester and helper fail to reconnect in time, some client eventually accessing the escrow object would invoke the timed out reconciler [merge 5/C1] stored originally in the reconciler log.

6 Experimental Evaluation

We have implemented MobileBuddy, a prototype 2-level transaction system with exo-leasing and evaluated its performance. MobileBuddy provides disconnected application transactions and supports escrow reservations and disconnected reservation split and transfer, implementing the protocols described in Sec. 4 and Sec. 5 on top of the base MX disconnected object storage system [24]. To support expressive applications, following Mobisnap [20], in addition to escrow objects, MobileBuddy provides a set of additional generic leases corresponding to the locking modes supported by SQL systems. For brevity, we omit the details of the MobileBuddy system implementation in MX that are straightforward and can be found in a technical report [25,28]. Here we describe our performance experiments.

Methodology and findings. Exo-leasing provides two types of benefits for disconnected collaborators. First, the ability to obtain reservations and to validate disconnected transactions avoids loss of work due to conflicts and eliminates in the normal case some of the potentially high (but not entirely avoidable) costs of external compensation actions. This benefit, determined by the transaction workload and application-specific costs, reduces to the general benefit of type-specific and generic locking, and has been studied before (e.g. the results in [20] apply). Second, obtaining a reservation from a nearby collaborator, instead of the server is advantageous when the cost of communicating with the server is high. This benefit reduces to the benefit of disconnected cooperative caching and has been studied before (e.g. the results in MX system [24], and others [3,18] apply). We do not repeat the evaluation of the known *benefits* of exo-leasing. Instead, we evaluate the *overhead* introduced by the validated DON transactions, the new feature supported by exo-leasing that has not been studied before.

We evaluate this overhead using the example mobile salesman scenario described in Sec. 5, considering two possible situations. In one case, transactions run with sufficient leases for all the objects they access and therefore validated transactions can provide a practical benefit to the client. In the other case, transactions run with insufficient leases and therefore the validations fails. Our experiments highlight the performance differences between the two cases. The findings, using transactions running a standard benchmark indicate that in a mobile transactional object system (many small objects), the extra overhead imposed by enabling validated DON transactions can be high for application transactions that do not benefit from the leases (i.e. fail validation, or do not need to be validated). For transactions that benefit, the overhead is reasonable. As expected, the overhead for lease transfer is offset by the cost of accessing the server when network latency is non-negligible. Note, that MobileBuddy system incurs no additional overhead if the client holds no leases.

Experimental Configuration. We run MobileBuddy in a system configuration where a server and the clients ran each on a 850MHz Intel Pentium III processor based PC, 256MB of memory, and Linux Red Hat 9.0, an obsolete version compatible with the aging MX system implementation. The experiments ran in an isolated system in the Utah experimental testbed emulab.net [1] that enables access to older operating systems versions, on a dedicated system. The cost of the leases is independent of the size of the collaborative group, given the small group sizes expected in MobileBuddy, and given we do not expect high lease contention. A system configuration containing a server and two clients is sufficient therefore for our experiment. All reported experimental measurements are averages of three trial runs showing minimal variance with hot caches.

The OO7 Benchmark. Our workloads are based on the multi-user OO7 benchmark [4]; this benchmark is intended to capture the characteristics of complex data in many different CAD/CAM/CASE applications, but does not model any specific application. We use OO7 because it allows us to control the sharing of complex data and because it is a standard benchmark for measuring object storage system performance. To study the cost of leases, we extended the OO7 database to support escrow objects. Now each atomic part has two additional escrow objects, so the application can acquire leases on the escrow objects. Otherwise, the database is the same as a normal OO7 database. The cost of checking the leases is workload-dependent, proportional to the number of objects accessed by a transaction. In the extended OO7 benchmark, each transaction accesses 72,182 objects.

Overheads. Validated transactions incur overhead at three points:

1. Tentative commit: each one of the objects accessed in the tentative transaction (the read set) is checked whether it is protected by a lease, to determine whether the tentative transaction (and its updates) can pass disconnected validation.
2. Transfer: all tentative transactions that have accessed objects without leases before lease transfer are re-validated using the acquired leases.
3. Durable commit at reconnect: the client runs cleanup handlers registered by transactions using escrow objects.

We distinguish between the validated transaction overhead in the situation where client holds insufficient leases, and the overhead in the situation where client holds sufficient leases, referring to the former as *Penalty* and later as *Cost*. *Penalty* is our main concern since in this case there is no benefit to the client. For *Cost*, our concern is whether the overhead is reasonable.

Penalty. Consider the mobile sales scenario discussed in Section 5. Suppose a salesperson Mary disconnects with leases, but her tentative transactions use objects unprotected by the leases. Assuming Mary enables the disconnected validation, each time Mary commits a tentative transaction, the transaction is validated introducing penalty *Tentative*, defined as the time of the check relative to the total tentative commit time. This cost is 9% in our experiment, but is workload dependent and is higher when the violation is detected later in the check since the check stops when violation is detected. In terms of absolute time, in the worst case if all 72,182 objects are checked, this penalty adds 62ms per tentative commit.

In our scenario, when Mary meets with John, she further obtains some leases from John. Since her tentatively committed transactions have not used objects protected by leases, the transfer causes the validation of all her tentative transactions against the transferred leases resulting in penalty *Transfer* (*Tentative* per transaction). This cost would be offset by the cost of fetching leases from the server when the network latency is non-negligible.

When Mary reconnects to the server, the transaction commit protocol checks invalidations and runs cleanup handlers that update the persistent copies of escrow objects, removing leases and returning the unused amounts. We conservatively consider the worst case when Mary has obtains leases on all escrow objects, and all her escrow objects have pending invalidations due to John's reservations. In this case, the client-side commit penalty *DurableCommit* is 32%. This includes *InvalidationChecks*, adding 7% extra relative the total reconnection validation time, and *CleanupHandlers*, adding 25% extra to total validation time. In absolute time, *DurableCommit* adds 305ms to the total reconnection validation. A realistic workload is unlikely to have that many escrow leases so the overhead will be lower.

Cost. In this situation, Mary disconnect with leases that are now used by her tentative transactions. Mary's disconnected validation succeeds each time, but to detect this, she performs the validation at each commit checking all the objects that the transaction has accessed. This introduces the overhead *Tentative*, defined the same way as in *Penalty* above. This overhead is high, 47% in our experiment. Recall, the difference between this overhead and the corresponding one in *Penalty* situation is that when Mary does not use leases, the checking procedure stops when it finds the first unprotected access in Mary's tentative transaction read set. In contrast, when she has enough leases, the procedure checks the entire read set.

Table 1 summarizes the client-side overheads *Penalty* and *Cost* for validated DON transactions.

Table 1. Overheads of validated DON transactions

	Cost	*Penalty*
TentativeCommit	47 %	9%
Transfer	-	*TentativeCommit* * number of transactions
DurableCommit	32%	32%

Two things to note. First, recall the *Penalty* for lease transfer is incurred for each tentative transaction accessing objects without holding leases. There is no corresponding validation *Cost* associated with lease transfer since in this case transactions committed before the transfer have accessed objects while holding leases. Second, the *Penalty* and *Cost* overheads for *DurableCommit* are equal. Whether client uses a lease, or not, the connected durable commit cleanup actions check the invalidations and remove the lease, returning unused escrow amount. In addition, note that client-side *DurableCommit* overhead is also incured to obtain the leases before disconnection. The server-side overhead of obtaining and removing a lease is simply the cost of an update transaction.

Summary. Our experiment indicates that if the client obtains escrow leases but does use them, the penalty of validated DON transactions is non-negligible. If the client relies on the reservations, using them to achieve disconnected validated transactions, then the client pays for the benefit brought by the reservations. We consider the cost reasonable.

7   Related Work

Our work blends a number of prior ideas, optimistic disconnected client/server systems, cooperative caching, escrow synchronization and multi-level transactions. To our best knowledge, none of the prior work has considered moving the synchronization out of the server, or disconnected client-to-client synchronization.

Most disconnected client/server systems are optimistic and handle conflicts after-the-fact. Coda servers [11] handle conflicting directory updates in a type-specific way. Coda clients handle conflicting updates to files using application-specific resolvers (ASR) [13], as do Ficus clients [21]. Exo-leasing differs from ASR because it avoids conflicts (in the normal case) by coordinating *in advance*, enabling disconnected validation.

MX [24] introduced disconnected cooperative caching, a feature allowing a mobile client to transfer consistent objects to another client without contacting a server. Ensemblue [18] mobile appliance system, PRACTI [3] replication framework, and Sailhan et al [22] also provide this feature. MobileBuddy is implemented on top of MX. Most peer-to-peer systems that transfer mutable objects support weak consistency. Lazy Replication [14] and Bayou [27] provide strong consistency for objects and allow to handle conflicts in a type-specific way. The mobile epidemic quorum system [10] provides multi-object transactions with standard locking.

Multi-level transactions and escrow have attracted significant research interest (most relevant approaches identified below), but no commercial systems that we know about have deployed these techniques. The need to modify the concurrency engine in the server has been the principal barrier. Weikum [30] proposed multi-level transactions with open nesting in a locking system, Lomet [15] described multi-level recovery. Unlike these systems, our base transactions are optimistic, similar to Manon et al [16], and our recovery approach handles leases [6] rather than locks. The middleware implementation [19] of the J2EE Activity Service increases concurrency for long-running connected transactions using semantic locks [7], as does the promises system [8]. A position paper [23] shows how to achieve a similar benefit for both long-running transactions and snapshot queries using exo-leasing with general type-specific synchronization [26]. Escrow synchronization was introduced by O'Neil [17] and extended to replicated systems by Kumar and Stonebraker [12]. Walborn et al [29] generalizes escrow to fragmentable and reorderable data types. The approach in Mobisnap [20] mobile client/server storage system is closest to ours and has inspired our work. Like exo-leasing, Mobisnap combines optimistic concurrency with lease-based conflict avoidance and supports disconnected validation. However, like all other proposals, Mobisnap implements the type-specific synchronization at the server.

8   Conclusion

This paper attacks a pracrical problem in the mobile computing space, namely, how to support escrow synchronization in a client/server storage systems so that disconnected clients can operate independently on shared data and validate transactions to avoid conflicting updates that later need to be aborted or reconciled. To that effect, this paper makes the following contributions: 1) It describes exo-leasing, a new modular approach to escrow synchronization that avoids type-specific code at the server providing the ability to use commodity servers. 2) It describes a reservation split and transfer mechanism that can aid collaboration in disconnected groups and is enabled by exo-leasing. 3) It presents performance measurements of MobileBuddy, a prototype escrow synchronization and reservation transfer system based on exo-leasing, evaluatinf the client-side overhead of running disconnected validated transactions.

Acknowledgments. We thank the anonymous referees for helpful suggestions and Butler Lampson, Barbara Liskov, and Mike Stonebraker for useful comments.

References

1. 'emulab.net', the Utah Network Emulation Facility. supported by NSF grant ANI-00-82493
2. Adya, A., Gruber, R., Liskov, B., Maheshwari, U.: Efficient Optimistic Concurrency Control Using Loosely Synchronized Clocks. In: Proc. of the ACM SIGMOD (May 1995)
3. Belaramani, N., Dahlin, M., Gao, L., Nayate, A., Venkataramani, A., Yalagandula, P., Zheng, J.: Practi replication. In: Proc. of the NSDI (April 2006)
4. Carey, M., et al.: A Status Report on the OO7 OODBMS Benchmarking Effort (October 1994)
5. Gifford, D., Donahue, J.: Coordinating Independent Atomic Actions. In: Proc. of IEEE COMPCON Digest of Papers (February 1985)
6. Gray, C., Cheriton, D.: Leases: An Efficient Fault-tolerant Mechanism for Distributed File Cache Consistency. In: Proc. the 12th SOSP (October 1989)
7. Gray, J., Reuter, A.: Transaction Processing: Concepts and Techniques (1993)
8. Greenfield, P., Fekete, A., Jang, J., Kuo, D., Nepal, S.: Isolation support for service-based applications: A position paper. In: Proc. of CIDR (January 2007)
9. Gruber, R., Kaashoek, F., Liskov, B., Shrira, L.: Disconnected Operation in the Thor Object-Oriented Database System. In: Proc. of the IEEE Workshop on Mobile Computing Systems and Applications (December 1994)
10. Holliday, J., Steinke, R., Agrawal, D., Abbadi, A.E.: Epidemic quorums for managing replicated data. In: Proc. of the IEEE ICPCC (February 2000)
11. Kistler, J., Satyanarayanan, M.: Disconnected operation in the Coda file system. In: ACM TOCS (February 1992)
12. Kumar, A., Stonebraker, M.: Semantics based transaction management techniques for replicated data. ACM SIGMOD Record 17(3), 117–125 (1988)
13. Kumar, P., Satyanarayanan, M.: Supporting application-specific resolution in an optimistically replicated file system. In: Workshop on Workstation Operating Systems, pp. 66–70 (1993)
14. Ladin, R., Liskov, B., Shrira, L., Ghemawat, S.: Providing High Availability Using Lazy Replication. ACM TOCS 22(3) (November 1992)
15. Lomet, D.B.: Mlr: A recovery method for multi-level systems. In: Proc. of ACM SIGMOD (June 1992)
16. Ni, Y., Menon, V., Adl-Tabatabai, A., Hosking, A., Hudson, R., Moss, E., Saha, B., Shpeisman, T.: Open nesting in software transactional memory. In: Proc. of the PPOP (November 2007)
17. O'Neil, P.: The escrow transaction method. ACM Transactions Database Systems 11(4), 406–430 (1986)
18. Peek, D., Flinn, J.: Ensemblue: Integrating distributed storage and consumer electronics. In: Proc. of OSDI (November 2006)

19. Perez-Sorrosal, F., Patino-Martinez, M., Jimenez-Peris, R., Vuckovic, J.: Highly available long running transactions and activities for j2ee applications. In: Proc. of the IEEE ICDCS (2006)
20. Preguica, N., Martins, J.L., Cunha, M., Domingos, H.: Reservations for Conflict Avoidance in a Mobile Database System. In: Proc. of the 1st MobiSys (May 2003)
21. Reiher, P.L., Heidemann, J.S., Ratner, D., Skinner, G., Popek, G.J.: Resolving file conflicts in the ficus file system. In: Proc. of the Usenix Technical Conference (1994)
22. Sailhan, F., Issarny, V.: Cooperative caching in ad hoc networks. In: Proc. of the 4th Mobile Data Management Conference (January 2003)
23. Shrira, L., Dong, S.: Exosnap: a modular approach to semantic synchronization and snapshots. In: Proc. of the 2nd Workshop WDDDM, EuroSys 2008, Glasgow, UK (March 2008)
24. Shrira, L., Tian, H.: MX: Mobile Object Exchange for Collaborative Applications. In: Proc. of ECOOP (July 2003)
25. Shrira, L., Tian, H., Terry, D.: Exo-leasing: Escrow synchronization for mobile clients of commodity storage servers. Technical Report MSR-TR-2008-112, Microsoft Research Silicon Valley (August 2008)
26. Shrira, L., Xu, H.: Snap: a non-disruptive snapshot system. In: Proc. of the ICDE, Tokyo, Japan (April 2005)
27. Terry, D.B., Theimer, M.M., Petersen, K., Demers, A.J., Spreitzer, M.J., Hauser, C.H.: Managing update conflicts in Bayou, a weakly connected replicated storage system. In: Proc. of the ACM SOSP (1995)
28. Tian, H.: MX: Mobile Object Exchange for Collaborative Applications. Ph.D thesis, Brandeis University (2005)
29. Walborn, G.D., Chrysanthis, P.K.: Supporting semantics-based transaction processing in mobile database applications. In: Proc. of the SRDS (1995)
30. Weikum, J.: A theoretical foundation of multi-level concurrency control. In: Proc. of the ACM PODS (1986)

Subscription Subsumption Evaluation for Content-Based Publish/Subscribe Systems

Hojjat Jafarpour, Bijit Hore, Sharad Mehrotra,
and Nalini Venkatasubramanian

Department of Computer Science, University of California at Irvine
{hjafarpo,bhore,sharad,nalini}@ics.uci.edu

Abstract. In this paper we address the problem of subsumption checking for subscriptions in pub/sub systems. We develop a novel approach based on negative space representation for subsumption checking and provide efficient algorithms for subscription forwarding in a dynamic pub/sub environment. We then provide heuristics for approximate subsumption checking that greatly enhance the performance without compromising the correct execution of the system and only adding incremental cost in terms of extra computation in brokers. We illustrate the advantages of this novel approach by carrying out extensive experimentation.

Keywords: Publish/Subscribe, Subscription Subsumption, Message-oriented middleware.

1 Introduction

Content-based Publish/Subscribe (pub/sub) is a customized many-to-many communication model that can satisfy requirements of many modern distributed applications [1]. In a pub/sub scheme, subscribers express their interest in content by issuing a subscription (query). Whenever some content is produced, it is delivered to the subscribers whose query parameters are satisfied by the content in the publication. By decoupling communication parties, a pub/sub system provides anonymous and asynchronous communication making it an attractive communication infrastructure for many applications. Such applications include selective information dissemination, location-based services, and workload management [1].

In order to distribute the load of publications and subscriptions a distributed content-based pub/sub system uses a set of network brokers (nodes). Different architectures have been proposed for connecting brokers in a pub/sub network [2, 12, 11]. Routing protocols for publications and subscriptions in brokers aim to reduce network traffic that results from transferring publications and subscriptions between nodes. One way in which publication traffic can be reduced is by enabling filtering of publications close to their sources. This can be achieved by flooding each subscription to all brokers in the network. However, such a naive approach significantly increases subscription dissemination traffic. Broadcasting all subscriptions over the network also increases subscription

V. Issarny and R. Schantz (Eds.): Middleware 2008, LNCS 5346, pp. 62–81, 2008.

table size at nodes which makes content matching more expensive during publication dissemination. An optimization for reducing subscription dissemination traffic is to exploit "covering" relationship between a pair of subscriptions. In this case, if a new subscription is covered by an existing subscription, it is not forwarded. Applying subscription covering in every broker in a pub/sub overlay network can greatly reduce the subscription dissemination traffic. Most of the existing pub/sub systems like SIENA [2], REBECA [6] and PADRES [4] implement *pair-wise* subscription cover checking to reduce redundancy in subscription forwarding. Efficient techniques for checking pair-wise subscription covering have also been proposed in the other works [5, 7].

A more efficient approach for reducing subscription dissemination traffic and subscription table size is to exploit subscription subsumption relationship between a new subscription and a set of existing active subscriptions. In this case, if a new subscription is completely covered (subsumed) by the set of existing subscriptions, then it is not forwarded. Clearly, since subscription covering is a special case of subscription subsumption checking for the latter results in greater efficiencies both in terms of reducing traffic between nodes and reducing size of the subscription table at nodes. Efficient subscription subsumption checking is not a trivial task. The subsumption checking problem where subscriptions can be represented as convex polyhedra has been shown to be co-NP complete [10][1]. To the best of our knowledge the only work that considers subscription subsumption in pub/sub systems is a 'Monte Carlo type' algorithm for probabilistic subsumption checking proposed by Ouksel *et al.* [3]. However, this technique may falsely determine a subscription to be subsumed by a set of existing subscriptions when in fact it isn't. This may result in false negatives in publication dissemination meaning that a publication may not be delivered to subscribers with matching subscription. In fact not forwarding some of subscriptions changes behavior of pub/sub system from deterministic into probabilistic. While it may be acceptable in some systems, having false negatives in publication dissemination may not be tolerable in pub/sub systems that are used for dissemination of vital information such as financial information and stock market data.

Main idea: In this paper we propose a novel approach for exact subscription subsumption evaluation in d-dimensional content space. Our proposed approach is based on the following observation: *Verifying whether a set of existing subscriptions (covered region) subsumes a new subscription is exactly the same as verifying whether the new subscription intersects with the uncovered region (i.e., portion of the domain which is not covered by any existing subscription)*. We refer to the uncovered portion of the domain as the *negative space*. Then, one only needs to forward the subscriptions that overlap with the negative space to other nodes in the network. In a *d*-dimensional content space where subscriptions are *d*-dimensional rectangles, we can always represent the negative space using a set of *non-overlapping d*-dimensional rectangles. The main drawback of

---

[1] Note that while subsumption problem in general case is co-NP complete, if the subscriptions are d-dimensional rectangles as we show in this paper the problem can be solved in $O(n^d)$ where n is the number of existing subscriptions.

considering an exact representation of the negative space is that it might require maintaining a large number of rectangles. One can show that in the worst case this may lead to $O(n^d)$ rectangles where n is the number of active subscriptions. Besides the storage complexity, this can lead to poor performance during subsumption checking and creation of new negative rectangles as we will show later in the paper. To alleviate this problem, we propose an approximate subsumption evaluation technique that enhances performance significantly while adding a small overhead in terms of not determining some of subsumed subscription. This leads to a minor increment in subscription forwarding traffic without compromising the correctness of the pub/sub functionality, as illustrated by our experiments. The approximate approach provides knobs to control the accuracy of subsumption checking by adjusting the required space and time.

The remainder of the paper is organized as follows. In the next section we formalize the subscription subsumption problem. In Section 3 we present our approach for subsumption evaluation and subscription and unsubscription forwarding algorithms. Section 4 describes approximate subsumption evaluation along with the corresponding subscription and unsubscription algorithms. We evaluate the proposed approach in Section 5 followed by an overview of the related work in Section 6. Finally, we draw our conclusion in Section 7.

2   Problem Formulation

The architecture of pub/sub system consists of a set of broker nodes interconnected through transport-level links which form an *acyclic* overlay network. Each client is connected to one of these nodes that act as the proxies of the clients on this network. When a client issues a subscription to the node it is connected to, it in turn forwards the subscription (if need be) to its neighbors in the network. Forward propagation is carried out till every node in the network receives the subscription. When a client publishes an event, it sends the event to its designated node (broker) that forwards the content through the overlay network to the nodes that have a matching subscription. Finally, the node delivers the content to the actual client that subscribed to it. Figure 1 depicts a sample broker overlay network with 11 broker nodes and shows the clients connected to one of these nodes.

Subscription & publication routing: Subscriptions are broadcast to all nodes in the overlay network. Each node stores subscriptions in its subscription-table along with the information about which neighbor requested for which subscription. Upon receiving a publication from a neighbor or one of its clients, a broker matches it against the subscriptions in its table and forwards the publication to a neighbor if and only if it has received a matching subscription from that neighbor. Since the content matching operation is performed at every node along the path from publisher broker to subscribers, matching time has a significant effect on the speed of publication dissemination. Several efficient matching techniques have been proposed in the literature to reduce matching time [8, 9].

Redundancy minimization using pair-wise covering information: To prevent unnecessary dissemination of subscriptions and reduce the size of

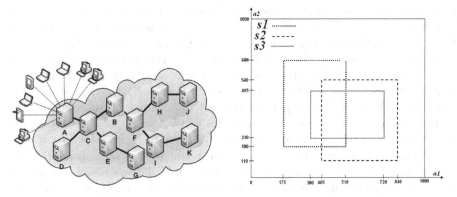

Fig. 1. A sample broker overlay network   **Fig. 2.** s_3 is subsumed by s_1 and s_2

subscription tables, pub/sub systems use subscription covering and subsumption techniques. A subscription s_1 covers subscription s_2 if and only if all publications matching s_2 also match s_1. When a node N receives a new subscription from one of its neighbors, say subscription s_2 from N', such that it is covered by some previous subscription s_1 also forwarded by N' to N, then node N can simply drop s_2 without forwarding it to its other neighbors[2]. Since the covered subscriptions are not disseminated to all brokers, it results in lower network traffic and compact subscription tables. Note that N stores s_2 in its *passive subscription list* since it may need to forward s_2 should its covering subscriptions s_1 (and potentially others) be cancelled by an unsubscription request. If s_1 were to be unsubscribed, it is removed from N's (active) subscription table and the subscription(s) that were covered by s_1, such as s_2 in the passive subscription list are moved to its subscription table and forwarded to the neighbors along with the unsubscription request for s_1.

Optimal redundancy minimization using subsumption information: While the above discussion illustrates a simplistic approach to reducing subscription traffic, we address this problem in its most general form. In the general case, as long as the union of an existing set of subscriptions covers a new subscription entirely, the new subscription need not be forwarded. It is easy to see that pair-wise covering is a special case of the more general subsumption checking problem. Our goal in this paper is to develop an efficient approximation scheme for the subsumption checking problem. We define the problem formally below after describing the notations used in the rest of the paper.

2.1 Notation

C_d denotes the d-dimensional content space where each dimension represents an attribute. The set of independent (orthogonal) attributes along which

---

[2] Note that if s_2 was forwarded by some other neighbor N'' then, N would have to forward s_2 to N'.

subscriptions and publications are specified is denoted by the set $A=\{a_1, a_2, ..., a_d\}$. The domain of each attribute is also pre-specified and is assumed to be ordered[3]. One may visualize the content space as a d-dimensional rectangular region of space. We represent the lowest and highest values taken by an attribute a_i by l_i and u_i respectively. Each publication represents a point in the content space that is represented by a d-dimensional point $p = (v_1, v_2, ..., v_d)$ where v_i is the value of attribute a_i in the publication and $v_i \in [l_i, u_i]$. A subscription s is represented as a *conjunction* of d predicates where the ith predicate represents an interval on the ith attribute's domain. Each predicate in subscription s_j is represented as $[low_i^j, up_i^j]$ that indicates the boundaries of the subscription for i^{th} attribute[4]. Thus, a subscription corresponds to a d-*dimensional rectangle* in the content space. Subscription rectangles partition the content space into two parts, *positive space* and *negative space*.

Definition 1. For a given set of subscriptions, $S = \{s_1, s_2, .., s_n\}$, we define the *positive* space as the parts of the content space that are covered by at least one subscription rectangle. We represent the positive space as C_S^+ where $C_S^+ = \bigcup_{s_i \in S} s_i$. We also define the *negative* space as the portions of the content space that are not covered by any subscription rectangle. We represent the negative space as C_S^-. Of course, $C_S^+ \cup C_S^- = C_S$ and $C_S^+ \cap C_S^- = \varnothing$.

We say that publication p matches(satisfies) subscription s_j if and only if for each v_i in p, $v_i \in [low_i^j, up_i^j]$. Subscription s is subsumed by set of subscriptions $S = \{s_1, s_2, .., s_n\}$ if and only if for every publication p matching s, there is a $s_i \in S$ that matches p. We denote subsumption as $s \sqsubseteq S$.

2.2   Subscription Subsumption Problem

We define the subscription subsumption problem for pub/sub system as follows:

Definition 2. Given $S = \{s_1, s_2, .., s_n\}$ is the set of existing subscriptions, is a new subscription s subsumed by S?

The solution to the above problem is a "true" if and only if for every publication p matching s, there is a $s_i \in S$ that matches p. More succinctly, we denote this fact by "$s \sqsubseteq S$ iff $s \subset C_S^+$". A solution to the subscription subsumption problem returns a "true" or "false" when posed with an instance of the problem.

Figure 2 depicts the subscription subsumption concept in a 2-dimensional content space. There are three subscriptions in this example where $s_1 = \{[175, 510],$ $[180, 680]\}$, $s_2 = \{[405, 840], [110, 540]\}$ and $s_3 = \{[380, 720], [230, 495]\}$. Neither subscription s_1 nor subscription s_2 completely cover subscription s_3. However, s_3 is fully covered by the union of s_1 and s_2.

---

[3] In case of nominal attributes, we assume some random order is assigned to the domain values. Alternatively, a partial order in the form of a taxonomy might also be utilized to assign the nominal values some numeric identifiers from an ordered domain.

[4] If no interval is specified along a dimension, the selectivity of the corresponding predicate is assumed to be equal to the whole domain of the attribute.

3   Exact Subscription Subsumption Checking

In this section we present the exact subsumption checking approach and describe the subscription and unsubscription routing algorithms. We also present a discussion on the complexity of the proposed algorithms.

As mentioned earlier, if $s \subset C_S^+$ then $s \sqsubseteq S$. However, since the positive space consists of the set of subscription rectangles which may be overlapping with each other subsumption evaluation can be more complicated. On the other hand, we can easily represent the negative space using a set of non-overlapping rectangles and more importantly this set can be maintained easily under updates (addition and deletion of subscriptions). Using negative rectangles we simply need to determine if a new subscription intersects with at least one of the negative rectangles. If this is the case, we can right away conclude that the new subscription is not subsumed by previous subscriptions.

Proposition 1. Subscription s is not subsumed by the set of existing subscriptions $S = \{s_1, s_2, .., s_n\}$ if and only if $s \cap C_S^- \neq \varnothing$.

Initially, when there is no subscription in the system the whole d-dimensional domain denotes the negative space, $C_S^- = C_d$ and the positive space $C_S^+ = \varnothing$. When the first subscription, s_1 is received we will have $C_S^- = C_S - \{s_1\}$ and $C_S^+ = \{s_1\}$ which means that the subscription is added to the positive space (and forwarded to the neighboring nodes) and at the same time, is subtracted from the negative space. The remainder of the negative space is not necessarily a complete rectangle, therefore, it needs to be partitioned into a set of smaller non-overlapping rectangles. Figure 3 depicts one of the several possible ways of

FUNCTION Subtract:
Input ← subscription s
Input ← A negative rectangle r
Input ← i: Subtraction dimension.
Output ← R_{new} set of new non-overlapping negative rectangles

1) $R_{new} = \varnothing$.
2) If $i \geq d$ then RETURN R_{new}
3) $NonCoverRange(i) = r(i) - s(i)$.
   (0, 1 or 2 ranges in i^{th} dimension)
4) For each range $\delta \in NonCoverRange(i)$ {
5)   Create new rectangle r_ρ where i^{th} dimension range is δ
6)   and the rest of ranges are the same as r.
7) $R_{new} = R_{new} \cup \{r_\rho\}$.
8) }
9) $r_{Remaining}$: Remainig negative space where i^{th} dimension
10) range is $s(i)$ and the rest of ranges are the same as r.
11) $R_{new} = R_{new} \cup Subtract(s, r_{Remaining}, i + 1)$.
12) RETURN R_{new}

Fig. 3. Negative space partitioning

Fig. 4. Rectangle subtraction function for d-dimensional space

partitioning the negative space after adding the first subscription. We will refer to this as a *rectangle splitting* operation.

Figure 4 depicts the rectangle splitting function which returns the set of non-overlapping negative rectangles after subtraction of a subscription from a negative rectangle. The function receives the subscription and the intersecting negative rectangle along with the dimension number, (i), that the splitting should be done along with. The initial call of the function must pass dimension number zero $(i = 0)$. For the given splitting dimension number i, the function subtracts the subscription range from the given negative rectangle range in the ith dimension and returns the remaining ranges as a set of non-overlapping ranges in i^{th} dimension (Line 3). Depending on the intersection form, the subtraction of the subscription range from the negative rectangle's range can split the rectangle's range into one, two or three sub ranges where only one of them intersect with the subscription's range in the ith dimension. The sub ranges that are not intersecting with the subscription's range generate new non-overlapping negative rectangles with the other ranges of the negative rectagle in the other dimensions (Lines 4-8). The intersecting section of the rectangle range along with the ranges in other dimensions represent the remaing part of the negative rectangle. The function then recursively splits the remaining negative rectangle along with the other dimensions (Line 11).

In the example in figure 3, the split leads to 4 smaller rectangles, that is 3 more rectangles than before the split. Figure 5 also depicts the partitioned negative space after adding s_1, s_2 and s_3. The general case of d dimensions is captured in the proposition below.

Proposition 2. In a d-dimensional content space, a rectangle splitting operation can lead to at most $2d$ - 1 new negative rectangles.

Proof. After subtracting the intersecting region of a subscription from a negative rectangle, the remaining negative region can always be split into γ smaller rectangles, where γ is the number of surfaces of the subscription that completely or partially intersect with the negative rectangle. Since there are 2d faces of a d-dimensional rectangle, we have at most 2d-1 new rectangles generated in this process (counting one of them as the old rectangle).   □

Observation. After n subscriptions have been added, let the negative space be represented as an union of some m non-overlapping rectangles, then after the $(n + 1)^{th}$ subscription, the new (reduced) negative space can still be represented as an union of non-overlapping rectangles by carrying out at most $O(m)$ rectangle splitting operations.

On an average, the number of splitting operations is much smaller than $O(m)$. We represent the set of non-overlapping negative rectangles as $R(C_S^-) = \{r_1^-, r_2^-, .., r_m^-\}$. As stated in the proposition 2 above, this set can be constructed and maintained incrementally. We illustrate the subsumption checking procedure using a sequence of 3 subscriptions in Figure 5.

As it can be seen, the negative space is partitioned into four new non-overlapping rectangles. Assume we use the partitioning method depicted in figure 3 and we add subscription s_2 which is depicted in figure 2. In this case since subscription s_2 intersects with negative rectangles r_3 and r_4 the subscription is not subsumed and we need to add it into the active subscription list. We also need to subtract the subscription from the intersecting rectangles and represent the remaining parts of each negative rectangle after subtraction as non-overlapping rectangles. The new partitioning of the negative space after adding subscription s_2 is depicted in figure 5. The negative space now consists of seven non-overlapping rectangles. Finally, when we add subscription s_3, since it does not intersect between the subscription and any of the negative rectangles, we conclude that the subscription s_3 is subsumed.

Next, we formally describe the subscription and unsubscription forwarding algorithms.

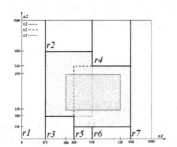

```
Input ← subscription s
Input ← set of negative rectangles R = {r_1, r_2, .., r_n}
Input ← set of active subscriptions, S_A
Input ← set of passive subscriptions, S_P

1) Find R_intersect: the set of intersecting rectangles in R.
2) If R_intersect = ∅ then { //s is subsumed and is not forwarded.
3)     S_P = S_P ∪ {s}.
4)     RETURN.
5) }
6) Otherwise { // s is NOT subsumed and is forwarded.
7)     S_A = S_A ∪ {s}.
8)     For every r_i ∈ R_intersect do {
9)         R = R − {r_i}.
10)        R_i^Remaining = r_i − s.
11)        Partition R_i^Remaining into non-overlapping rectangles.
12)        and add them to (R_{r_i}) set.
13)        R = R ∪ R_{r_i}.
14)    }
15)    Forward s.
16) }
```

Fig. 5. Negative space partitioning after adding subscriptions s_1, s_2 and s_3

Fig. 6. Subscription forwarding Algorithm with exact subsumption cheching

3.1   Subscription Forwarding Algorithm

When a new subscription is issued, we need to quickly determine if it intersects with any negative rectangle and if so, we need to identify all the rectangles that may potentially undergo splitting. Any popular multidimensional indexing structure such as R-Tree or KD-Tree [13, 14] can be used to speed up access to the rectangles. The data structure used by the algorithm maintains the following information: (i) The set of negative rectangles; (ii) The list of active subscriptions consisting of the subscriptions that have been forwarded; (iii) The list of passive subscriptions that contains the subscriptions that are subsumed and therefore, have not been forwarded. Figure 6 represents the subscription forwarding algorithm with exact subsumption checking.

The algorithm starts with finding all the negative rectangles that intersect with the subscription. If the set of intersecting negative rectangles is empty, the subscription is subsumed and there is no need to forward it. In this case the subscription is added to the list of passive subscriptions (Lines 2-5). On the other hand, if the set of intersecting negative rectangles is not empty, this implies that the subscription is not subsumed and it must be forwarded. In this case, the algorithm first adds the subscription into the list of active subscriptions. For each of the negative rectangles in the intersecting set, it removes the negative rectangle from the data structure (Line 9) and carries out the rectangle splitting operation after determining the intersection area (Line 10-12). Then, the newly created rectangles are added to the set representing the cover of the negative space. Finally, the new subscription is forwarded to neighbor brokers except the one that it was received from.

The space and time complexity of the subscription forwarding with exact subsumption checking depends on the number of the non-overlapping negative rectangles. Assuming the number of such rectangles is $m(i)$ after i subscriptions have been forwarded, we require $O(m(i))$ space to represent these rectangles. In the worst-case, the time complexity of the $(i+1)^{th}$ subscription forwarding step is $O(d.m(i))$ where d is the dimension of the content space. This is so, because the $(i+1)^{th}$ subscription may intersect with $O(m(i))$ negative rectangles resulting in $O(d(m(i))$ splitting related operations. To represent the complexity of the algorithm based on the number of subscriptions we present an upper bound for m. We start our analysis with the following proposition about the number of partitions in one dimensional space.

Proposition 3. In a one dimensional domain n ranges result in at most $2n+1$ non-overlapping ranges.

Proof. Proof is based on induction. Each range has two bounding points, start and end. Initially there is only one range which covers all the domain. After adding the first range, the domain will contain at most three ranges (2*1+1). Assuming the maximum number of partitions resulting from n ranges is $2n+1$, we add the $(n+1)^{th}$ range. The boundaries of the new range will intersect with at most two of the existing non-overlapping ranges which results in partitioning each of these two ranges into two smaller ranges. Therefore, two new ranges is added to the number of partitions and the number of non-overlapping ranges that the domain is partitioned into will be $2n+1+2 = 2(n+1)+1$.   □

Using the above proposition, we can provide an upper bound for the number of rectangles (positive and negative) that can be generated by n rectangles.

Theorem 1. Given a set of n rectangles in d-dimensional space, an upper bound to the number of non-overlapping rectangles that can partition the space based on these rectangles is $O(n^d)$.

Proof. Each of the rectangles has a range in each dimension. Therefore, the domain of each dimension is partitioned with n ranges. The maximum possible number of non-overlapping ranges resulting from this partitioning is $2n+1$ in each dimension (according to the Proposition 3). Using the partitioning ranges in each dimension, the d-dimensional space can be partitioned at most into $(2n+1)^d$

non-overlapping rectangles. Therefore, the maximum number of non-overlapping rectangles partitioning the space is $O(n^d)$.   □

Based on the above theorem, the following theorem provides an upper bound for the number of negative rectangles when there are n subscriptions.

Theorem 2. Given a set of n rectangles in d-dimensional space, an upper bound for the number of non-overlapping rectangles that partition the negative space is $O(n^d)$.

Proof. According to the Theorem 1 we know that the upper bound for total number of rectangles partitioning all the space resulted from n rectangles is $O(n^d)$. Each of the given positive rectangles at least include one of the partitioning rectangles. Therefore, the number of remaining rectangles for the negative space is at least $O(n^d - n)$ which is $O(n^d)$.   □

Since, the number of negative rectangles can grow really fast ($O(n^d)$ for n subscriptions), the time and space complexity of the algorithm can become prohibitive. This motivates our approximation algorithm which checks this growth and which will be discussed in Section 4.

3.2   Subscription Cancellation Algorithm

If a subscriber wants to cancel a subscription, it makes a "unsubscription" request that is forwarded along the path that the corresponding subscription was forwarded earlier. When such a request arrives at a broker, it needs to check which subscriptions in the passive list might now get uncovered due to removal of this subscription and ensure that these queries are forwarded. Figure 7 shows the algorithm.

To cancel a subscription s the unsubscription algorithm first checks if s is in the passive set of subscriptions. If it is, then the subscription is subsumed by previously forwarded queries (active subscriptions) and he only needs to remove it from the list of passive subscriptions (Lines 1-4). Otherwise, it first removes the subscription from the list of active subscriptions (Line 5). Then, it finds $S_A^{intersect}$ which is the set of all active subscriptions that intersect with s. Unsubscribing s can result in some uncovered space that needs to be added to the negative cover. Obviously, the regions within s that are covered by other active subscriptions should not be added to the negative space. To compute these regions, the algorithm iterates over the set of intersecting active rectangles in $S_A^{intersect}$ and subtracts these regions from the s (Lines 8-19). Finally, the new negative space (if there is one) is added to the set of negative rectangles in line 20. Now, the algorithm needs to take care of the set of affected passive subscriptions which is done in lines 21-26. Here, all the passive subscriptions that intersect with s are detected and removed from the passive subscription list. Then, each of these subscriptions are evaluated for subsumption against the new set of negative rectangles. The subscriptions that are not subsumed anymore are then forwarded to neighbors along with the unsubscription request.

Input ← subscription s that must be cancelled
Input ← set of negative non-overlapping hyper rectangles $R = \{r_1, r_2, .., r_n\}$
Input ← set of active subscriptions, S_A
Input ← set of passive subscriptions, S_P

1) If $s \in S_P$ {
2) $S_P = S_P - \{s\}$.
3)   RETURN.
4) }
5) $S_A = S_A - \{s\}$
6) Find $S_A^{intersect}$: the set of active subscriptions in S_A that intersect with s.
7) Set $R_{newNegative} = \{s\}$ as the set of new negative rectangles.
8) For every $s_i \in S_A^{intersect}$ do {
9) $S_A^{intersect} = S_A^{intersect} - \{s_i\}$.
10) $R_{newNegative}^{s_i} = \varnothing$.
11) For every $r_j \in R_{newNegative}$ do {
12)   If $r_j \cap s_i \neq \varnothing$ {
13) $R_{newNegative} = R_{newNegative} - \{r_j\}$.
14) $R_{r_j} = r_j - s_i$ where R_{r_j} is in the form of non-overlapping rectangles.
15) $R_{newNegative}^{s_i} = R_{newNegative}^{s_i} \cup R_{r_j}$.
16)   }
17) }
18) $R_{newNegative} = R_{newNegative} \cup R_{newNegative}^{s_i}$.
19) }
20) $R = R \cup R_{newNegative}$.
21) Find $S_P^{intersect}$: the set of passive subscriptions in S_P that intersect with s.
22) $S_{newActive} = \varnothing$.
23) For each $s_i \in S_P^{intersect}$ do {
24) $S_P = S_P - \{s_i\}$
25) Subscribe(s_i, R, S_A, S_P).
36) }

Fig. 7. Unsubscription algorithm for the exact case

The unsubscription algorithm searches the negative rectangles, the active subscription and the passive subscription lists. Therefore, the time complexity of the unsubscription algorithm is $O(d.(m + |S_A| + |S_P|))$.

As we mentioned above, the number of negative rectangles can grow very quickly and make the subscription forwarding as well as unsubscription procedures very expensive. We now develop an approximation algorithms that remarkably enhances the efficiency at the cost of slightly increased traffic.

4 Approximate Subscription Subsumption Checking

In this section we introduce a heuristic that help maintain an acceptable upper bound on the number of negative rectangles. The proposed heuristic pays a small penalty in terms of falsely concluding some subscriptions as being "not subsumed" when in reality they are subsumed by the set of active subscriptions. However, such false decisions do not have any effect on the correct execution of the pub/sub system.

Subsumption checking heuristic: We restrict the number of new negative rectangles that are created after adding a new subscription to at most k, a user specified constant. Assume $R_{intersect} = \{r_1, r_2, .., r_\alpha\}$ is the set of α negative rectangles that intersect with a new subscription s. If $\alpha > k$, we choose a $R_{intersect}^{Selected} \subseteq R_{intersect}$ such that the number of new negative rectangles created from subtracting s from rectangles in $R_{intersect}^{Selected}$ is at most k. The remaining rectangles in $R_{intersect}$ are not modified. This relaxation increases the chance of wrongly concluding that a latter query is not subsumed when it is in fact subsumed. Restricting the number of newly generated rectangles to k results in at most $O(k.n)$ negative rectangles after n active subscriptions, which is a significant improvement over the $O(n^d)$ worst-case bound.

Tuning the accuracy of the approximate approach: We can control the accuracy of subsumption detection by adjusting the value of k. By varying k one can explore the tradeoff space between the probability of false-positives in subscription dissemination and the number of negative rectangles generated.

The approximate subsumption checking can either assume a fixed value for k or a dynamic threshold which changes for each subscription based on the number of existing negative rectangles. The dynamic approach allows more fine tuning to balance the two competing factors. For instance, let the threshold be a function of the order of the subscription, say $\zeta(i) = k.i - m_{i-1}$ where $k.i$ is the maximum possible number of negative rectangles after i queries and m_{i-1} is the actual number after $i - 1$ queries. This implies, if the number of negative rectangles in the system is less than the maximum expected number, for the new subscription s_i, we can add a larger number of rectangles to the system and therefore increase the accuracy of subsequent subsumption checks.

Top-k selection: Given the maximum number of new rectangles allowed (k or $\zeta(i)$), we need to select the best candidates for splitting. We propose a model based on *benefit/cost* for selecting these rectangles. We define the *benefit* of partitioning a negative rectangle with respect to a subscription as the "volume" of the intersecting region. We define the corresponding *cost* to be "the number of new negative rectangles that are created". The benefit is proportional to the increase in chance of determining subsumption while the cost is proportional to the space required for the new rectangles as well as the increase in computational cost to determine intersections for new subscriptions. Therefore, we choose the top-k negative rectangles with highest benefit to cost ratio are chosen for splitting. Figure 8 shows the approximate subsumption checking algorithm.

The approximate subsumption checking algorithm in addition to the standard inputs, also requires the set $CoveredBy_s$ to be specified. This is the set of rectangles in the content space that are covered only by subscription s. We also specify k which is the maximum number of new rectangles allowed per subscription (we only provide the algorithm for the constant k case. The version for variable ζ is similar). Similar to the exact algorithm, if the subscription does not intersect with the negative space it is subsumed (Lines 1-5). Otherwise it is added to the active subscription set. Then for each of the intersecting negative rectangles,

Input ← subscription s
Input ← $CoveredBy_s = \varnothing$: list of content space sections covered only by s
Input ← k: maximum number of new negative rectangle for s
Input ← set of negative non-overlapping hyper rectangles $R = \{r_1, r_2, .., r_n\}$
Input ← set of active subscriptions, S_A
Input ← set of passive subscriptions, S_P
1) Find $R_{intersect}$: the set of rectangles in R that intersect with s.
2) If $R_{intersect} = \varnothing$ then { // s is subsumed.
3) $S_P = S_P \cup \{s\}$.
4)   RETURN .
5) }
6) Otherwise { // s is **NOT** subsumed.
7) $S_A = S_A \cup \{s\}$.
8)   For every $r_i \in R_{intersect}$ do {
9) $r_i^{Remaining} = r_i - s$.
9)   If $r_i^{Remaining}$ is a complete rectangle {
10) $CoveredBy_s = CoveredBy_s \cup (r_i \cap s)$.
11) $R = R - \{r_i\}$.
12) $R = R \cup \{r_i^{Remaining}\}$.
13)   }
14)   Otherwise {
15)   Compute the selection metric ($\frac{Benefit}{Cost}$) for r_i.
16)   Add r_i to the $IntersectingSelectionList$.
17)   }
18)   }
19)   newNegativeCount = 0
20)   While (newNegativeCount $\leq$ k) {
21) r_i = the negative rectangle in $IntersectingSelectionList$ with the maximum selection
metric value ($\frac{Benefit}{Cost}$).
22) $R = R - \{r_i\}$.
23) $r_i^{Remaining} = r_i - s$.
24)   Partition $r_i^{Remaining}$ into non-overlapping rectangles.
25)   and add them to (R_{r_i}) set.
26)   newNegativeCount = newNegativeCount + $|R_{r_i}|$
27) $R = R \cup R_{r_i}$
28) $CoveredBy_s = CoveredBy_s \cup (r_i \cap s)$.
29)   }
30)   Forward s.
31) }

Fig. 8. subscription forwarding algorithm with approximate subsumption checking

the algorithm checks if the remaining rectangle after subtracting the subscription from it is a complete rectangle. If the remaining is a complete rectangle subtracting the subscription does not create a new negative rectangle and the algorithm updates the negative rectangle (Lines 9-13). Otherwise, the selection metric value is computed for the intersecting negative rectangle and the rectangle is added to the $IntersectingSelectionList$ (Lines 14-17). The $IntersectingSelectionList$ contains the set of negative rectangles that intersect with subscription s (i.e., those that create extra negative rectangles after subtracting s from them). The algorithm then picks the negative rectangle with the highest benefit/cost ratio and removes it from the set of negative rectangles. Then, the algorithm subtracts the subscription from it and updates the set of negative rectangles. It also adds the intersecting section to the $CoveredBy_s$ list since this section is only covered by this subscription. The algorithm iterates till the number of extra negative rectangle reaches k (Line 19-29).

The unsubscription algorithm can be quite complicated depending on the level of accuracy. We propose an approximate unsubscription algorithm that may result in larger negative space. However, as mentioned before the larger negative space only results in not detecting some of subsumption and does not affect the correctness of the pub/sub system. Also, assuming the rate of unsubscriptions is much lower that the rate of subscriptions such expansion of the negative space may be tolerated in many cases. Figure 8 shows the approximate unsubscription algorithm.

Input ← subscription s
Input ← $CoveredBy_s$: list of content space sections covered only by s
Input ← set of negative non-overlapping hyper rectangles $R = \{r_1, r_2, , r_n\}$
Input ← set of active subscriptions, S_A
Input ← set of passive subscriptions, S_P

1) If $s \in S_P$ {
2) $S_P = S_P - \{s\}$.
3)   RETURN.
4) }
5) $S_A = S_A - \{s\}$
6) $R = R \cup CoveredBy_s$
7) Find $S_P^{intersect}$: the set of passive subscriptions in S_P that intersect with $CoveredBy_s$.
8) $S_{newActive} = \emptyset$.
9) For each $s_i \in S_P^{intersect}$ {
10) $S_P = S_P - \{s_i\}$
11)   Boolean isActive = Subscribe(s_i, R, S_A, S_P).
12)   If isActive=TRUE {
13) $S_{newActive} = S_{newActive} \cup \{s_i\}$.
14)   }
15) $S_A = S_A \cup S_{newActive}$.
16)   Forward all subscriptions in $S_{newActive}$ along with unsubscription message.
17) }

Fig. 9. Approximate unsubsumption agorithm

Similar to the exact case the subsumed subscription is only removed from the passive subscription list (Lines 1-4). When a request for cancellation of an active subscription is received, the algorithm first removes the subscription from the active subscription list (Line 5). Then, the rectangles in $CoveredBy_s$ are added to the list of negative non-overlapping rectangles (line 6). The algorithm then detects all the passive subscriptions that intersect with the new negative rectangles in $CoveredBy_s$ (Line 7). For each passive subscription that is not subsumed anymore the algorithm forwards it along with the unsubscription request to its neighbors (Lines 9-17).

The approximate unsubscription may increase the negative space volume incrementally that may affect the subsumption evaluation accuracy for later subscriptions. In order to achieve more accurate subsumption checking, we can reconstruct the whole negative space using the set of subscriptions in the system.

This can be done periodically in an offline manner, where one can recompute the negative space by making one pass over complete set of existing subscriptions. If the number of subscriptions is very large, then some pre-processing can be done to speed up this computation. We will not go into the details of such a step in this paper. We simply note that such a re-computation process results in new S_A, S_P, R and $CoveredBy_s$ sets.

5   Experimental Evaluation

In this section we evaluate the effectiveness of our proposed subscription subsumption checking approach using extensive simulations. As described in previous sections, the efficiency of our approach directly depends on the number of negative rectangles stored. We now describe the setup and the various experiments that we carried out.

Simulation setup: We perform our simulations using 10,000 subscriptions in 2, 3, 4 and 5 dimensional content space. The domain of each dimension is set as the range [0,1000] and the subscriptions are d-dimensional rectangles in this domain. We generate the subscriptions by fixing the lower end-point of the range along each dimension, say x and then selecting the size of the range randomly from the interval $[0, 1000 - x]$ which determines the upper end-point along that dimension. We sample the Zipfian distribution to pick the lower end-point of a range along each dimension.

For the approximate subsumption checking experiments, we fix the value of k to be 50. This implies that we limit the number of new negative rectangles that are added to the index for each new subscription to at most 50. Recall that, when the actual number of rectangles is more than k, we compute the best set of rectangles to split by computing the ratio of benefit to cost and choosing the ones that yield the highest values. For a negative rectangle and a subscription the benefit is measured as the volume of the intersecting region and the cost is the number of newly created negative rectangles as a result of the intersection.

Measuring advantage of subsumption checking: To compare the relative merit of subsumption checking against the pair-wise covering approach, we measure how many messages were prevented from being forwarded by employing each of these approaches. Figure 10 plots the number of redundant subscriptions detected by the subsumption checking algorithm and the pair-wise subscription covering approach. The results shown are for 2, 3 and 4 dimensional content space. As expected, the number of redundant subscriptions detected using the subsumption checking algorithm is always greater that the covering one. The graph shows another interesting fact, that the number of subsumed subscriptions is an inversely proportional to the dimension of the content space. This can be justified by observing that the probability of overlap reduces with increasing dimensionality, therefore reducing the probability of subsumption. The same trend is seen in the covering relation between subscriptions and increasing dimensionality of the space. However, even at higher dimensions, the number

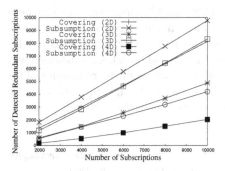
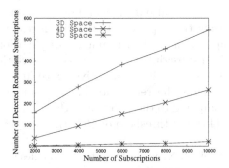

Fig. 10. Subscription Subsumption vs. Covering

Fig. 11. Extra traffic reduction by approximate subsumption algorithm

of queries subsumed by the union of 2 or more queries is substantially greater than number of pair-wise coverings. This result reveals the significance of exploiting subscription subsumption compared to using only pair-wise subscription covering. Figure 11 depicts the same results for the approximate subsumption checking.

Negative rectangle creation rate: The number of negative rectangles directly affects the efficiency of our subsumption checking algorithm. Therefore, we measure how the number of negative rectangles vary with increasing number of subscriptions and as well as content space dimensionality. Table 1 shows the number of negative rectangles generated against number of subscriptions and number of dimensions for the exact subsumption checking algorithm. Generally, by adding more subscriptions, the number of negative rectangle grows. However, in 2-dimensional space the observed behavior is counter-intuitive, wherein the number of negative rectangles sharply grow for the first 100 subscriptions and then remains steady between 140 and 200. This behavior can be explained considering the number of covered and subsumed subscriptions for 2-dimensional scenario in our simulations. As depicted in figure 10 more than 95% of subscriptions are subsumed in this scenario and since these subscriptions do not generate new negative rectangles, the total number of negative rectangles in the 2-dimensional scenario remains significantly small. On the other hand, the number of negative rectangles significantly increases for 3 and 4 dimensional case. If we store the negative rectangles in broker's memory the algorithm may consume all of the available memory as it is shown in the table for 4-dimensional case with more than 4000 subscription and a machine with 1GB memory. The significant number of negative rectangles is a clear justification for using our approximate subsumption checking algorithm.

Table 2 represents the number of negative rectangles resulting from usage of the approximate algorithm with value of k set to 50. As we expected, the number of negative rectangles significantly drops for 4-dimensional space which results in less space requirement and faster subsumption evaluation. However, this comes at the cost of not detecting all the subsumed subscriptions.

Table 2 also depicts an unexpected trend for 2 and 3 dimensional space where using the approximate algorithm results in more negative rectangles. Since the approximate algorithm may not partition all the intersecting negative rectangles for a subscription, subsequent subscriptions that would have been subsumed will intersect with the negative space and generate more negative rectangles. This explains the reason for having more negative rectangles in approximate case compared to the exact case. However, the number of negative rectangles remains below the threshold of $O(k.n)$.

Table 1. Number of negative rectangles for exact subsumption

	2000	4000	6000	8000	10000
2D	181	118	81	73	66
3D	15983	20154	19667	20756	22230
4D	364740	665000	–	–	–

Table 2. Number of negative rectangles for approximate subsumption

	2000	4000	6000	8000	10000
2D	367	405	430	438	443
3D	27928	30221	31755	33071	34079
4D	13455	23414	32148	39969	47064

Approximate algorithm: As mentioned earlier, the approximate algorithm substantially improves the space and time complexities of subsumption checking by restricting the number of new negative rectangles. We evaluate the advantage of using the approximate algorithm for two main decision factors. First, we investigate the effect of threshold k on the number of detected subsumptions and the number of new negative rectangles created. Then we evaluate the approximate algorithm based on the function that is used to select the negative rectangles for partitioning. The subsumed subscriptions detected in the following experiments are in addition to the covered subscriptions and can not be detected using traditional pair-wise covering techniques.

Effect of k: Figure 12 depicts the advantage of using the approximate algorithm for three different k values, 10, 50 and 100 in a 3-dimensional content space. As we expected, by increasing the value of k the number of detected subscription subsumptions also increases. Increasing the value of k from 10 to 50 results in

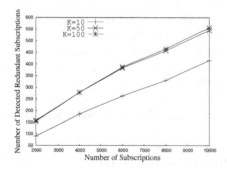

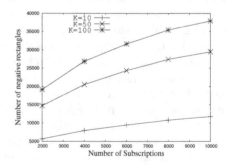

Fig. 12. Effect of k on subsumtion detection

Fig. 13. Negative rectangles for different k values

considerable improvement in subsumption detection, however, as it can be seen in the graph there is no considerable improvement in increasing the value of k from 50 to 100. On the other hand, as shown in figure 13 the number of negative rectangles considerably increases when we vary k from 50 to 100. Based on the results in figures 12 and 13 we can conclude that increasing k may not always result in significant improvement in subsumption detection, however, it results in increasing number of negative rectangles. Therefore, selecting proper value for k can improve the performance of the approximate algorithm significantly.

Other Selection Metric Value Function: Figures 14 and 15 show the results for three different negative rectangle selection functions. Recall, the default selection function is the ratio of the intersecting areas volume (benefit) to the number of new generated negative rectangles (cost). We consider two other functions where in the first one we only consider the benefit as the selection function and in the other one we consider the inverse of cost as the selection function. As it can be seen, using the ratio of benefit to cost results in better detection of subsumed subscriptions and fewer negative rectangles. The graphs also show that considering benefit alone performs slightly better than considering the cost. The reason is that despite considering only cost reduces the number of new negative rectangles for a new subscription but it may result in more intersections and therefore more negative rectangles for the future subscriptions. On the other hand, if we select negative rectangles based on the intersecting volume, we increase the probability of detecting subsumption for future subscriptions and therefore resulting in fewer negative rectangles.

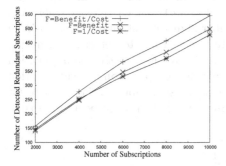 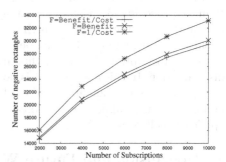

Fig. 14. Effect of negative rectangle selection function

Fig. 15. Number of negative rectangles for different selection functions

6 Related Work

Subscription covering concept in pub/sub systems was introduced in Siena event dissemination system [2]. Siena organizes subscriptions in a partially ordered set (poset) where the order is defined by covering relation. Siena only considers pair-wise covering relation between subscriptions and does not exploit subsumption. REBECA is another pub/sub system that not only uses covering, but also considers subscription merging [6]. Subscription covering and merging algorithms in REBECA have linear execution time regarding to the number of subscriptions.

Li *et al.* propose a representation of subscriptions using modified binary decision diagrams (MBD) in PADRES pub/sub system [4]. They propose subscription covering, merging and content matching algorithms based on this representation. However, the MBD-based approach does not consider subscription subsumption relation among subscriptions.

Shen *et al.* propose a novel approach for approximate subscription covering detection using Space Filling Curves(SFC) [15]. In this approach a subscription $s = \{[low_1, up_1],...,[low_d, up_d]\}$ in d-dimensional space which is a d-dimensional rectangle is transformed into a point $p(s) = \{-low_1, up_1,...,-low_d, up_d\}$ in 2d-dimensional space. Considering each subscription as a point, the covering problem in d-dimensional space is converted into point dominance problem in 2d-dimensional space. The point dominance problem then is answered using space filling curve where the rectangle corresponding to a subscription is represented as set of one dimensional ranges using SFC and if the point of another subscription falls into these ranges it is covered by the subscription. However, the proposed approach can only detect covering and it is not clear how to extend it for subsumption.

To effectively detect covering subscriptions Triantafillou *et al.* propose an approach based on subscription summaries [7]. Attributes of each incoming subscription are independently merged into their corresponding summary structures. The summaries will ensure reduction in the network bandwidth required to propagate subscriptions and the storage overhead to maintain them.

Ouksel *et al.* present a Monte Carlo type probabilistic algorithm for the subsumption checking [3]. The algorithm has $O(k.m.d)$ time complexity where k is the number of subscriptions, m is the number of distinct attributes (dimensions) in subscriptions, and d is the number of tests performed to detect subsumption of a new subscription. This algorithm may result in false negatives in publication dissemination. In this algorithm it is possible that propagation of a subscription is stopped while it is not subsumed by the existing subscriptions. This may result in not delivering publications to some subscribers that may not be acceptable in applications like stock ticker.

7   Conclusion and Future Work

In this paper, we studied the problem of subsumption checking for queries in publish/subscribe (pub/sub) systems. Efficient query subsumption checking can greatly improve the performance of pub/sub systems by reducing subscription routing traffic between brokers. We developed a novel approach based on negative (uncovered) space representation which allows for fast subsumption checking. Specifically, we provided algorithms to maintain a cover of the negative space using a set of disjoint rectangles, in a dynamic environment where both subscription and unsubscriptions requests are made by clients. Further, since certain query workloads can lead to large number of covering (negative) rectangles that can adversely effect performance and storage, we developed a heuristic that checks the growth of the cover-size. Our approximate subsumption checking algorithm reduces subscription forwarding traffic without affecting the correctness of execution. Finally, we carried out extensive simulated experiments to illustrate the advantage of our proposed approach.

As our ongoing and future work, we will be investigating some of other heuristics for efficiency of subsumption checking as well as carry out tests in a real system. We will look at the other strategies like rectangle merging to reduce the number of negative rectangles. An interesting direction is to extend this approach to other more complex query classes and different query workloads, with higher proportions of unsubscription request.

References

1. Eugster, P.T., Felber, P.A., Guerraoui, R., Kermarrec, A.-M.: The many faces of publish/subscribe. ACM Computing Surveys 35(2) (2003)
2. Carzaniga, A., Rosenblum, D.S., Wolf, A.L.: Design and Evaluation of a Wide-Area Event Notification Service. ACM Transactions on Computer Systems 19(3), 332–383 (2001)
3. Ouksel, A.M., Jurca, O., Podnar, I., Aberer, K.: Efficient Probabilistic Subsumption Checking for Content-Based Publish/Subscribe Systems. In: Proceedings of Middleware 2006, pp. 121–140 (2006)
4. Li, G., Hou, S., Jacobsen, H.-A.: A Unified Approach to Routing, Covering and Merging in Publish/Subscribe Systems Based on Modified Binary Decision Diagrams. In: Proceedings of IEEE ICDCS 2005, pp. 447–457 (2005)
5. Shen, Z., Tirthapura, S.: Approximate Covering Detection among Content-Based Subscriptions Using Space Filling Curves. In: Proceedings of IEEE ICDCS (2007)
6. Mühl, G.: Large-scale content-based publish/subscribe systems. Ph.D Dissertation, University of Darmstadt (September 2002)
7. Triantafillou, P., Economides, A.: Subscription Summarization: A New Paradigm for Efficient Publish/Subscribe Systems. In: Proceedings of ICDCS 2004, pp. 562–571 (2004)
8. Fabret, F., Jacobsen, H.A., Llirbat, F., Pereira, J., Ross, K.A., Shasha, D.: Filtering algorithms and implementation for very fast publish/subscribe systems. In: Proceedings of ACM SIGMOD 2001, pp. 115–126 (2001)
9. Carzaniga, A., Wolf, A.L.: Forwarding in a Content-Based Network. In: Proceedings of ACM SIGCOMM 2003, pp. 163–174 (2003)
10. Srivastava, D.: Subsumption and indexing in constraint query languages with linear arithmetic constraints. Annals of Mathematics and Artificial Intelligence 8, 315–343 (1992)
11. Costa, P., Picco, G.P.: Semi-Probabilistic Content-Based Publish-Subscribe. In: Proceedings of ICDCS 2005, pp. 575–585 (2005)
12. Castelli, S., Costa, P., Picco, G.P.: HyperCBR: Large-Scale Content-Based Routing in a Multidimensional Space. In: IEEE INFOCOM (2008)
13. Guttman, A.: R-trees: a dynamic index structure for spatial searching. In: Proceedings of ACM SIGMOD 1984, pp. 47–57 (1984)
14. Preparata, F.P., Shamos, M.I.: Computational Geometry: An Introduction. Springer, Heidelberg (1985)
15. Moon, B., Jagadish, H.V., Faloutsos, C., Saltz, J.H.: Analysis of the Clustering Properties of the Hilbert Space-Filling Curve. IEEE Trans. Knowl. Data Eng. 13(1), 124–141 (2001)

Diagnosing Distributed Systems with Self-propelled Instrumentation

Alexander V. Mirgorodskiy[1] and Barton P. Miller[2]

[1] VMware, Inc.
mirg@vmware.com
[2] Computer Sciences Dept, University of Wisconsin
bart@cs.wisc.edu

Abstract. We present a three-part approach for diagnosing bugs and performance problems in production distributed environments. First, we introduce a novel execution monitoring technique that dynamically injects a fragment of code, the *agent*, into an application process on demand. The agent inserts instrumentation ahead of the control flow within the process and propagates into other processes, following communication events, crossing host boundaries, and collecting a distributed function-level trace of the execution. Second, we present an algorithm that separates the trace into user-meaningful activities called *flows*. This step simplifies manual examination and enables automated analysis of the trace. Finally, we describe our automated *root cause analysis* technique that compares the flows to help the analyst locate an anomalous flow and identify a function in that flow that is a likely cause of the anomaly. We demonstrate the effectiveness of our techniques by diagnosing two complex problems in the Condor distributed scheduling system.

Keywords: distributed debugging, performance analysis, dynamic instrumentation, trace analysis, anomaly detection.

1 Introduction

Quickly finding the cause of software bugs and performance problems in production environments is a crucial capability. Despite its importance, the task of problem diagnosis is still poorly automated, requiring substantial time and effort of highly-skilled analysts. We believe that such diagnosis can be substantially simplified with *automated* techniques that work on *unmodified systems* and use *limited application-specific knowledge*. In this paper, we present our diagnostic framework, demonstrate that it is able to work on complex distributed systems, and describe real-world problems that it enabled us to diagnose in the Condor distributed cluster management software [28, 41].

The ability to collect and analyze traces from unmodified and unfamiliar systems is crucial in production environments, where the following three challenges significantly complicate problem investigation. First, many problems in production environments are difficult to reproduce on another system. Such problems require analysis in the field and demand collaboration between the customer

V. Issarny and R. Schantz (Eds.): Middleware 2008, LNCS 5346, pp. 82–103, 2008.

and the developers. Second, modern systems are built of interacting black box components that often come from different vendors and provide limited support for execution monitoring. Finally, if a system does support detailed execution monitoring, the volume of collected data can be exceptionally high and often impossible to analyze by hand.

Our diagnostic approach uses a previous observation that problems often correspond to infrequent execution paths or paths that have properties deviating from common behavior [5,10,17,20,27]. By finding where the execution diverged from the norm, we may be able to determine the problem location. Our approach monitors system execution at a fine granularity, discovering and instrumenting communicating processes on-the-fly, and collecting function-level traces in distributed environments. Our trace analysis algorithm automatically compares traces to each other to identify unusual activities and point the analyst to a possible root cause of the problem. While there are several projects that collect event traces or profiles and analyze them automatically to simplify problem diagnosis [5,10,11,15,16,20,27,30,44], the following features of our approach make it suitable for on-demand diagnosis in production environments:

Dynamic binary instrumentation across processes and hosts. We use *self-propelled instrumentation* to collect detailed function-level control flow traces from unmodified and unfamiliar systems [34]. The corner stone of self-propelled instrumentation is an autonomous fragment of code called *the agent* that is injected into the system on a user-provided external event. After injection, the agent starts monitoring system execution by inserting trace statements into the system's code ahead of the flow of control. With this technology, tracing can be rapidly enabled on demand so that the users experience no overhead if the system operates normally and no tracing is necessary.

This paper extends self-propelled instrumentation to propagate from one process to another on inter-process communication. It allows us to discover communicating components and obtain distributed control flows. For example, we can start tracing a Web browser and propagate into the Web server and other components of an e-commerce system to obtain the complete control flow trace from the request to the reply.

Identification of concurrent flows with limited system knowledge. In a system that processes more than one request at a time, the collected trace may contain events of concurrent requests arbitrarily interleaved. The presence of unlabeled events from multiple unrelated activities may be confusing for manual trace examination. Furthermore, events that belong to unrelated requests may occur in a different order in different runs. This behavior complicates automated analysis: a normal trace being examined may appear substantially different from previous ones and thus marked as an anomaly. To overcome these limitations, we decompose the trace into a collection of per-request traces that we call *flows*. Each flow is user-meaningful and more deterministic than the original trace.

Our flow-construction approach uses application-independent rules where possible but can incorporate application-specific knowledge into analysis. As a result, our framework is likely to be easier to apply to a new system than previous application-specific techniques [5, 10, 24, 26]. Yet, unlike the application-independent techniques of DPM [32] and Whodunit [9], the user can improve the accuracy of flow construction by providing additional knowledge into analysis. Unlike the technique of Aguilera et al. [3], our approach is not probabilistic and can construct accurate flows even for infrequent requests.

Root cause analysis with limited user effort. Similar to dynamic program dicing [11,30], Triage [43], and Pinpoint [10], we focus our analysis on differences in coverage between successful and failed flows. We look for functions that have been executed only in the successful or only in the failed flows. Such functions are correlated with the occurrence of the problem and often point to its root cause. In our experiments however, the number of differences in call path coverage perfectly correlated with failures proved to be large and most such differences corresponded to normal variations between flows. The key feature of our analysis is its ability to further reduce the number of differences to be examined manually yet attempt to retain the cause of the problem. The following sections discuss our approach in detail and show its effectiveness, finding the causes of two non-trivial bugs in the Condor distributed batch scheduling system [28, 41].

2   Propagation and Tracing

We locate bugs and performance problems by comparing control-flow traces for normal and anomalous activities in a system, e.g., comparing per-request traces in an e-commerce environment. Here, we describe our trace collection approach that we call *self-propelled instrumentation*. The corner stone of self-propelled instrumentation is an autonomous agent that is injected in the system upon a user-provided external event (e.g., a keypress) and propagates through the code carried by the flow of execution. Propagation is the process of inserting monitoring statements ahead of the flow of execution within a process and across boundaries between communicating processes. The key feature of this approach is its ability to work on unmodified distributed systems and start collecting traces on demand without a system restart. When the user decides to stop tracing, the agent can be deactivated.

Within a process, we use the *spTracer* framework [34, 35] to intercept the execution of an application at function call instructions, though finer-grained branch-level instrumentation also can be implemented. The agent takes control at a call site in the application's code, generates a trace record, instruments the next point of interest, and returns control to the application.

This paper extends the self-propelled instrumentation technology to propagate across process and host boundaries on inter-process communication events. We follow the flow of control within a process where the start event happened, and carry the tracing over into another process when the two processes communicate. Each process generates an in-memory control-flow trace. When the user-specified deactivation event happens, we stop trace collection, assemble all per-host traces at a central location, and arrange observed events in a system-wide Parallel

Dynamic Program Dependence Graph (PDG) [13]. The PDG is a DAG where nodes represent observed events and edges represent happened-before dependences between the events [25].

To construct the PDG, we need to observe events in different processes and establish the correspondence between matching *send* events in one process and *recv* events in another. Our framework collects the necessary data dynamically, using five steps to propagate from one component to another: intercept a *send* event, identify the name of the destination process, inject the agent into the destination process (possibly, on a remote host), detect the receipt at the destination process, and follow the execution of the destination process. We begin by describing these steps for the foundational case of communication via TCP sockets and generalize it to other types of communication later.

2.1 Propagation over a TCP Socket

To enable the agent to propagate across host boundaries, we run daemon processes, called *spDaemons*, on all hosts in the system. These daemons can be started at system boot time, or they can be started by the agent on-demand, if nodes in the system support remote operations such as *SSH* (Secure Shell). Figure 1 shows how the agent in process P propagates into process Q. First, the agent library, *agent.so*, instruments the *send* and *write* routines in P. When reached, this instrumentation determines whether the accessed file descriptor corresponds to a TCP socket, and in that case, intercepts control of the process before it sends the message.

Second, the instrumentation determines the name of the peer process, a tuple $\langle hostid, pid \rangle$, where *hostid* is the IP address of the host and *pid* is the process identifier on that host. The remote *hostid* for a given socket can be found with the standard *getpeername* function. Since there is no standard mechanism for finding the remote *pid*, we use a two-step process to determine it. We use *getpeername* to find the remote port *portid* and send it to our *spDaemon* on the remote host. That daemon uses a technique similar to that of the *netstat* utility to map *portid* to *pid*: map port number to the inode number identifying the socket and scan the */proc* tree to locate processes that opened a socket with that inode.

Third, *spDaemon* injects a copy of the agent into the identified process using the Hijack mechanism [45]. This mechanism causes the process to load our shared

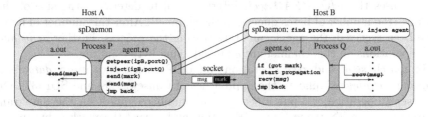

Fig. 1. Propagation of the agent from process P on host A to process Q on host B when P attempts to send a message to Q over a TCP socket

library at run time. Fourth, the sender's agent uses the TCP OOB (Out-of-band) mechanism to mark the first byte of the message and lets the application proceed with the *send* operation. At injection time, the receiver's agent also instruments the entry points for *recv* and *read* library calls to identify the moment when the message arrives. When this instrumentation is executed, it checks whether the file descriptor corresponds to the original socket and whether the OOB mark has arrived. If so, the current *recv* event corresponds to the *send* event that triggered cross-process propagation. Our agent instruments all functions on the stack, from *main* to the *recv* and starts the propagation procedure on the receiver side.

Subsequent *send* and *recv* operations on this socket are matched using *byte-counting*: counting the number of bytes sent and received by each endpoint. A socket can be shared by multiple processes on a host, e.g., multiple HTTP daemons often share the same listening socket to accept multiple concurrent connections. To address this scenario, we keep byte counts in shared memory and each agent updates them atomically.

Note that our technique does not send the code of the agent across the boundaries: each host uses a locally-installed copy of the agent and does not need to run untrusted downloaded code. This property can enable secure deployment of self-propelled instrumentation across administrative domains. To support such deployments, *spDaemons* could implement security policies specifying remote users who can request propagation through processes on this host and users who can download the resulting trace. This paper does not study this aspect further.

2.2   Other Communication Mechanisms

Similar to TCP sockets, our prototype propagates across UNIX pipes and UDP sockets. The primary difference between our support for these communication mechanisms lies in techniques for matching *send* and *recv* events. This task is non-trivial in presence of in-flight messages or for mechanisms that do not preserve the order of messages. In both cases, the first *recv* event observed after the injection may not correspond to the *send* event that triggered the injection.

As mentioned above, we address this problem for TCP sockets by using the OOB mechanism and subsequent byte-counting. The OOB mechanism is supported only for TCP sockets. For local order-preserving communication mechanisms such as pipes and UNIX-domain sockets we can use a different technique for dealing with in-flight messages. After injection, the agent in the receiving process uses the *FIONREAD ioctl* interface [40] to determine the size of the backlog (the number of bytes queued in the channel). After this number of bytes have been received, the agent can start tracing the process. Further *send* and *recv* operations on this channel are matched using byte-counting.

To match *send* and *recv* operations on UDP sockets, we use a *datagram-marking technique* similar to the approaches of Causeway [8] and SDI [37]. On each *send* operation, we put a sequentially-numbered mark on the datagram encoding it as a TS (timestamp) IP option and record the mark value in the local trace. On each *recv* operation, we extract the mark from the datagram and append it to the local trace. At the analysis time, *send* and *recv* operations with equal mark values can be matched together. The limitation of this technique is that routers and firewalls in some environments may remove IP options from forwarded packets, drop packets with options, or process them slower than normal packets. Determining how common such environments are and developing alternative solutions remain subjects for future work.

Shared memory communication creates other challenges, and for these situations, we plan to use the technique from Whodunit [9].

3   Reconstruction of Distributed Control Flows

Bugs and performance problems in complex systems are often manifested by deviations of control flow from the common path. To identify such deviations and determine the root cause of a problem, we collect control-flow traces and analyze them manually or automatically. In distributed environments however, collected traces may contain events that correspond to different concurrent activities such as HTTP requests, possibly of multiple users. Events that correspond to one request are not explicitly labeled in the trace and can appear interleaved with events from other requests. Such interleaving of unrelated activities complicates manual trace analysis. It also increases trace variability and thus presents challenges for automated analysis. Events from different activities may appear in a different order in different runs. As a result, a normal trace may appear substantially different from previous ones and can be marked as an anomaly.

To overcome these problems, we decompose the execution of an application into units that correspond to different semantic activities, referred to as *flows*. Flows are easier to analyze manually and automatically than the original trace. They contain logically-related events and there is little trace variability within a flow. For example, a Web server process can execute requests from two users in an interleaved order, as shown in Figure 2. Flows are shown as disjoint shaded areas in that figure. Unlike previous techniques for flow construction [3,5,9,10, 24,26,32], our approach uses general rules to construct flows but can incorporate application-specific knowledge into analysis when the rules are insufficient.

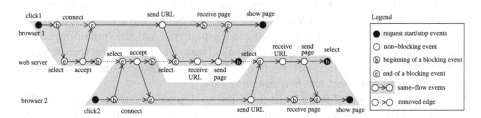

Fig. 2. Flows in a Web server executing requests from two Web browsers

3.1   Flow-Construction Algorithm

Our prototype traces function calls, returns, and communication events. This section describes our flow-construction algorithm in its general form since it also applies to a wider class of events. We define an *event* as an execution instance of an instruction in a process. Such an event can be represented by a tuple ⟨*location, seq_id*⟩, where *location* identifies the process and the instruction address within that process, while *seq_id* is a sequence number, i.e., the number of executions of this instruction in the history preceding this event. This definition includes message-passing *send* and *recv* events since they typically correspond to execution of system call trap instructions.

In our representation, flows are sets of events, where $x \in \Phi$ denotes that event x belongs to flow Φ. We formulate the task of constructing flows as a graph problem. First, we represent a system-wide control-flow trace as a PDG. This PDG is constructed from a set of start events S provided by the user (e.g., request-arrival events). Then, we apply several graph transformations to the PDG, removing and adding edges to the graph to partition it into disjoint subgraphs. Each subgraph represents one flow.

To transform the graph, we apply two application-independent rules to each pair of connected events u and v in the PDG. Both rules determine whether the pair of events must belong to the same flow. If these events do not satisfy either rule, we remove the edge $u \rightarrow v$ from the PDG. In the second step, we traverse the transformed PDG to find events reachable from events in the start set S. Events reachable from an event $s_i \in S$ compose flow Φ_i.

The first rule is the *communication-pair* rule that dictates that the pair of matching communication events belongs to the same flow: if s and r are matching *send* and *recv* events, then $\Phi(s) = \Phi(r)$. This rule implies that inter-process edges in the PDG must not be removed. The second rule is the *message-switch* rule that dictates that a process can switch from one flow to another only on receiving a message. A pair of adjacent events x_{i-1} and x_i in a process belong to the same flow unless the second event is a *recv* (a node with more than one immediate predecessor): if $deg^+(x_i) = 1$ then $\Phi(x_i) = \Phi(x_{i-1})$. Here, $deg^+(x)$ is the in-degree of x, the number of immediate predecessors of x in the PDG.

To illustrate our algorithm, consider Figure 2. Both requests are serviced by the same server process in the interleaved order. By locating all nodes in the PDG with the in-degree of two and removing intra-process edges incidental to such nodes, we obtain a transformed PDG where all edges satisfy our rules. Inter-process edges satisfy the communication-pair rule and the remaining intra-process edges satisfy the message-switch rule. Next, we traverse the transformed PDG beginning from the start events and construct two disjoint components that accurately represent the two user requests.

Our representation of flows is most similar to dependence trees of Magpie [5]. However, Magpie does not use such trees to separate events from different requests. Instead, it relies on application-specific rules provided by the user and builds a tree later to represent each already-separated request. In contrast, the graph representation is central to our algorithm: we construct requests by separating the PDG into disjoint subgraphs.

3.2   Custom Directives

Our application-independent algorithm may attribute some events to the wrong flow. Consider a single-process server that receives requests from clients, enqueues them, services them later, and replies to the clients. In Figure 3, the process receives a request from *client2*, enqueues it, dequeues an earlier request from *client1*, and handles it. While Figure 3 shows the correct assignment of events to requests, this assignment could not be generated without knowing the relationship between *enQ* and *deQ* operations. The enQ_2 and following deQ_1 events belong to different requests, but our message-switch rule would attribute them to the same flow since they are not separated by a *recv* node.

To provide application-specific knowledge to the analysis, we introduce the concept of a *mapping directive*. Each directive identifies a pair of events that should belong to the same flow. The added relation between two events allows us to insert a new edge into the PDG. An important simplification is our observation that each directive needs to connect two events within the same process (inter-process dependences are correctly constructed by the communication-pair rule already). To give directives preference over the message-switching rule, we insert the edges first, treat them as inter-process edges, and then apply the local edge-removing algorithm described in the previous section.

Since directives require knowledge of system internals, they can be provided by system developers, rather than end users. To specify directives, we apply the event-join formalism of Magpie [5] to control-flow traces: our directives have the form $\langle bb, jattr \rangle$, where *bb* is the address of a basic block in the code, *jattr* is a so-called *join attribute*, e.g., a program variable. The result of this directive is labelling an event corresponding to execution of *bb* with the join attribute of *jattr*. Control-flow events *u* and *v* with the same value of the join attribute are assigned to the same flow: if $v.jattr = u.jattr$, then $\Phi(v) = \Phi(u)$. We translate each directive into a code fragment that is inserted into the basic block *bb*. When executed, the fragment saves the value of *jattr* along with *bb* in the trace. At analysis time, events with the same value of *jattr* are assigned to the same flow.

To match the enqueue and dequeue events in Figure 3, we can provide a simple directive: $\langle enQ:entry, arg \rangle \rightarrow \langle deQ:exit, ret\_val \rangle$. This directive assumes that the argument to the *enQ* routine is the address of the request structure to enqueue; the *deQ* routine returns that address on exit. At analysis time, we identify trace

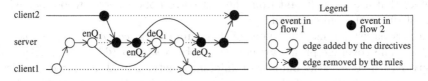

Fig. 3. Flows constructed with the help of directives

records where the argument to enQ was equal to the return value of deQ and introduce an artificial PDG edge between them. This operation increases the in-degree of the deQ node, causing us to remove the original intra-process edge incidental to deQ and allowing us to separate the two requests.

4   Identification of Anomalies and Their Causes

Specialized techniques aim at locating a single type of bugs, such as buffer over-runs, memory leaks, or race conditions. Our approach however, belongs to another class of techniques that can locate a wide variety of problems, provided that they are manifested by deviation of the execution from the norm.

Our approach looks for problems manifested by unusual control flow, such as functions that only executed in failed flows or took substantially more time in failed flows. To identify the causes of such problems, we use a two-step process. First, we perform *data categorization*: identify anomalous flows, i.e., one or several flows that are different from the rest and may correspond to failed requests. Second, we perform *root cause identification*: examine the differences between the anomalous flows and the normal ones to help the analyst identify the causes of the anomalies. To reduce the required manual effort, we eliminate some differences that are effects of earlier ones. We also rank the remaining differences to estimate their importance to the analyst.

4.1   Data Categorization

Our framework can be deployed in two different scenarios: on-demand diagnosis of a particular problem and always-on system monitoring. In the first scenario, the end user often is able to categorize collected flows manually. If the problem occurs for a particular HTTP request, the user can mark that request as an anomaly. For always-on system monitoring however, manual categorization may not be feasible. A flow may fail silently, without user-visible effects. A flow may also start misbehaving after a non-fail-stop failure.

To identify anomalous flows, we started with the algorithm of *spTracer* [35] and extended it to operate on distributed flows. *spTracer* summarizes each per-process control flow trace as a fixed-length vector (a *time profile*), defines a distance metric between pairs of profiles, and finds one or more profiles that are most distant from the rest. To extend this approach to the distributed scenario, we construct distributed per-flow profiles. Each profile now summarizes activities in a single flow, spanning multiple processes where these activities occurred. Profiles that are most distant from the rest correspond to flows whose behavior is most different from common.

In this paper, we use two types of flow summaries: *coverage* and *composite profiles*. The coverage profile for flow Φ is a bit vector $\boldsymbol{p}^v(\Phi) = \langle v_1, \ldots, v_F \rangle$ of length F, where F is the number of different functions in all executed binaries. Bit v_i is set if and only if the corresponding function f_i was executed in flow Φ. Therefore, the difference between two coverage profiles identifies functions present in one flow and absent from another. As a result, flows that execute similar code will result in similar coverage profiles and vice versa. Our profiles also include *call path profiles* if we treat different call paths from *main* to each function as a separate function. For simplicity, we refer to components of profile vectors as functions. The experiments in Section 5, use the path-based method due to its higher accuracy.

The composite profiles capture both the temporal behavior and the communication structure of a distributed application. A composite profile for flow Φ is a concatenation of two vectors: a *multi-process time profile* and a *communication profile*. The multi-process time profile $\boldsymbol{p}^t(\Phi) = \langle t_1, \ldots, t_F \rangle$ is a natural extension of single-process time profiles used by *spTracer*. Here, t_i is the fraction of time flow Φ spends on path i. The communication profile, is a vector $\boldsymbol{p}^s(\Phi) = \langle s_1, \ldots, s_F \rangle$. Here, s_i is the normalized number of bytes sent by path i on flow Φ. The addition of the communication structure allows us to detect anomalies that cause little change in the temporal behavior. For example, UDP message loss and retransmission will be visible in the communication profile while the time to handle this condition may not be noticeable in the time profile.

In Section 5, both composite and coverage profiles proved equally effective at identifying anomalous flows. In other scenarios, composite profiles may be more suitable for detecting problems that result in little change in function coverage: indefinite blocking in system calls, infinite loops, and performance problems. In contrast, coverage profiles may be more effective for locating anomalies in workloads with large normal variations in time or bytes sent on each flow. Furthermore, we use coverage profiles at the second stage of our diagnosis. They allow us to identify a problem even if it was in a short-running function that did not involve communication activities (e.g., a double *free* causing a later crash).

Once profiles are constructed, we compute a distance metric between each pair of profiles as the Manhattan norm of their per-component difference. Then, we use the pair-wise distance metric to compute the *suspect score* of a profile, that is the distance of the profile to common or known-normal behavior. Finally, we report the profile with the highest score to the analyst as the most unusual. An important feature of this algorithm is its ability to integrate prior examples of known-normal behavior into analysis and thus avoid reporting unusual but normal behaviors as anomalies.

4.2   Root Cause Identification

spTracer focused on finding the most visible symptom of a problem (the function where the most unusual amount of time was spent). This paper presents a root cause analysis approach that may identify more subtle problem causes occurring long before the failure. To locate such causes, we examine differences in coverage between normal and anomalous flows. Namely, we construct the set Δ_a containing call paths that are present in the anomalous profiles and absent from all normal ones, the set Δ_n containing call paths that are present in the normal profiles and absent from all anomalous ones, and their union $\Delta = \Delta_a \cup \Delta_n$. By inspecting each path in Δ and determining why it is present only in normal or only in anomalous flows, the analyst may be able to find the problem cause. For example, an intermittent double *free* bug would manifest itself by an extra call to *free* in anomalous flows, thus adding a path to Δ_a. Similarly, an attempt to reference unallocated memory would result in an extra call to *malloc* in Δ_n.

In our experience however, the number of call paths in Δ is often large. In addition to the call path corresponding to the root cause of the problem, Δ may contain subsequent symptoms of the same problem. We refer to such call paths as *problem-induced variations in coverage*. Δ may also contain unrelated paths that are caused by slight differences in system load or program input between flows. We refer to such call paths as *normal variations in coverage*.

While we cannot distinguish problem-induced variations from normal variations automatically, we can substantially reduce the number of variations of each type. In our experience, a single variation in the execution can generate multiple call paths in Δ. We attempt to retain one path for each cause by using two transformations of set Δ. We present these transformations on the example of Δ_a; the same techniques also apply to Δ_n.

First, assume that function *main* called functions A and D only in the anomalous run; function A also called functions B and C. As a result, set Δ_a will contain call paths $main \rightarrow A$, $main \rightarrow A \rightarrow B$, $main \rightarrow A \rightarrow C$, and $main \rightarrow D$. The corresponding call tree is shown in Figure 4a. To understand why the anomalous run was different from the normal run, we must explain why paths $main \rightarrow A$ and $main \rightarrow D$ are part of Δ_a. Longer paths, $main \rightarrow A \rightarrow B$ and $main \rightarrow A \rightarrow C$ would become part of Δ_a automatically: since $main \rightarrow A$ was never observed in a normal run, any longer path also could not be observed in a normal run. Our first transformation examines each path $\pi \in \Delta_a$ and discards all longer paths that contain π as a prefix. We denote the transformed set Δ_a as Δ_a' and show it in Figure 4b.

Second, we merge call paths in Δ_a' that differ only in the last call as such paths typically correspond to a single cause. The reason why functions A and D were invoked only in the anomalous flow is located in their parent, function *main*, thus making the parent, not the leaves, a potential problem location. We can therefore replace the two paths in Δ_a' with a single composite path $main \rightarrow [A, D]$, creating Δ_a'' shown in Figure 4c. If the application exhibited more than one problem in a single function, this optimization might hide one of the problems. However, we believe this case to be quite rare and the merging optimization to be widely beneficial.

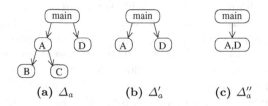

(a) Δ_a (b) Δ_a' (c) Δ_a''

Fig. 4. Call tree before and after the transformations

To further simplify examination of call paths in Δ_a'', we introduce two competing ranking techniques. The first technique arranges call paths in the order of their first occurrence in the trace. It assumes that the earlier differences between anomalous and normal flows are more likely to correspond to the root cause of a problem. This assumption holds for problem-induced variations in coverage (since all symptoms happen after the root cause). However, it may be violated for normal variations that can occur even before the root cause. Our second technique orders shorter call paths before longer ones. Shorter paths are easier to analyze. Furthermore, they often represent more substantial differences in the execution than longer paths.

5 Experience

Our earlier prototype proved useful for diagnosing bugs and performance problems in single-process scenarios and in a collection of identical processes [34, 35]. To evaluate our techniques in a distributed environment, we applied them to finding the causes of two bugs in the Condor distributed scheduling system. Condor provides batch scheduling, execution, and monitoring facilities for high-throughput computing tasks [28, 41]. It can schedule sequential and parallel jobs. Condor operates in a variety of environments from loosely-connected networks of desktop workstations to large-scale supercomputers and the Grid.

Condor is a complex system that has a multi-tier architecture where different services are performed by different daemons communicating over the network. A simple user job requires cooperation of six different daemons on multiple hosts and also several auxiliary programs. In complex Grid environments, it involves even more services. Internally, Condor uses several standard communication mechanisms including pipes, TCP sockets, and UDP sockets. It also implements custom primitives such as queues and timers for deferring actions.

5.1 File Transfer Problem

Condor allows the user to specify multiple jobs to be run as part of a single submission. Such a submission is referred to as a *cluster*. A recent bug caused the output files for some jobs in a cluster to be created in a wrong directory. The output for the first job is placed at the correct location, but the output for all subsequent jobs are created in the current working directory rather than the directory specified by the user. This problem has been fixed by Condor developers. Here, we describe how we found it with the help of our techniques.

To diagnose this problem, we submitted a cluster of five jobs to Condor (Version 6.7.17) and collected the traces starting from the *condor_submit* command. Our tracer propagated through all the daemons and auxiliary programs involved in handling the jobs. When the last job in the cluster terminated, we saved the traces to disk. Collected traces allowed us to construct the PDG for the execution. Figure 5 shows a summary diagram that we created automatically from the PDG and visualized the resulting graph with the *Graphviz* package [18]. It shows

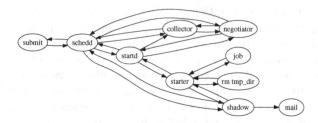

Fig. 5. Communication diagram for scheduling a Condor job. Manually annotated with process names.

the traces for a single-job submission since a five-job diagram and the full PDG are more complex. Each node in this diagram corresponds to a process that our agent traced. Each edge corresponds to one or several repeating communication events: sending a message, forking a child, or waiting for a child's completion.

This diagram allows us to understand the job scheduling process: *condor_submit* contacts the *schedd* daemon on the local host, and *schedd* adds the job to its scheduling queue. Next, the *schedd* contacts the *negotiator* daemon to find a matching execution host for the job. The *negotiator* uses information maintained by the *collector* daemon to find an idle execution host and contact its *startd* daemon. The *startd* spawns an auxiliary process called the *starter*, and the *schedd* on the submitting machine spawns a process called the *shadow*. The *starter* and the *shadow* communicate to transfer the job input to the execution machine, start and monitor the job, and transfer the output files to the submitting machine on job completion. Finally, Condor notifies the user via email.

Once all five jobs completed, we attributed collected events to separate flows, where each flow represented processing one user job. While following component interactions did not use Condor-specific knowledge, flow construction required directives. Without directives, communication diagrams for two consecutive identical jobs appeared substantially different from each other. By examining detailed flow graphs, we identified two instances where *schedd* switched from working on one job to another without a *recv* event. After introducing simple directives, the flows for identical jobs became visually similar.

To quantify the accuracy of flow construction, we reused the core of our anomaly detection algorithm. We computed the distance metric between coverage profiles for two known-different jobs and the distance between two known-similar jobs. The distance between different jobs was 4.7 times higher than that between similar jobs. That is, our algorithm constructed similar flows for similar activities and substantially different flows for different activities. Another approach for validating the results of flow construction is to use high-level knowledge about the system. Consider a system for example, where the event of sending a packet from the server to the client always belongs to the same flow as the earlier incoming request from the client. If the results of the automated algorithm satisfy this property, we obtain additional assurance that flows are constructed accurately. Such properties can be naturally expressed by our custom directives. The effectiveness of this technique remains to be seen.

Next, we obtained the profiles for each flow. In this study, profiles were already classified: the first job corresponded to the normal profile, subsequent ones corresponded to problem profiles. Therefore, we did not need to perform the anomaly detection step and directly applied our root cause identification technique. Namely, we compared the call path coverage profiles for the normal flow and the anomalous flow with the most similar coverage (corresponding to the second job). Each profile contained more than 80,000 distinct call paths.

We represented each call path as a string of function addresses, sorted them lexicographically, and found strings present in one flow but not the other. This technique identified more than 21,000 differences between the flows; examining them manually would be infeasible. However, the transformations described in Section 4.2 were able to reduce the number of differences to 107 paths, a factor of 200 reduction, thus enabling manual path investigation. This result shows that filtering is essential for analysis of detailed coverage data in distributed systems.

To locate the cause of the problem, we examined the remaining paths in the order of their first occurrence in the flow. Several early paths corresponded to normal variations in coverage: processing of the first job in the cluster requires additional initialization tasks. However, the 15th earliest difference pointed us to the root cause of the problem. The path $(main \rightarrow read\_condor\_file \rightarrow queue \rightarrow SetTransferFiles \rightarrow InsertJobExpr \rightarrow HashTable\langle MyString, int\rangle::lookup)$ in $condor\_submit$ was present in the anomalous flow but not in the normal one. By examining the source code for $SetTransferFiles$ and $InsertJobExpr$, we found that the name of the output file was incorrectly registered in a hash table as a per-cluster attribute. Per-cluster attributes are shared among all jobs in a cluster while the output file has to be unique for each job. Changing $SetTransferFiles$ to treat the output file name as a per-job attribute fixed the problem.

This study also uncovered a limitation of our current prototype. After fixing the problem, we discovered that the discussed path to $HashTable\langle MyString, int\rangle$ $::lookup$ was still part of the difference between the first and the second flow. Although this path was no longer taken when constructing the output file attribute, it was taken for several unrelated attributes that were correctly marked as per-cluster. Function $SetTransferFiles$ invoked $InsertJobExpr$ from several call sites, but our prototype did not distinguish these invocations as different paths. Unlike the path for the output file attribute however, these paths corresponded to normal variations between flows and must be ignored.

Such variations did not prevent us from finding the cause of this problem. However, finding the causes of other problems may require analysis of paths that are distinguished by the call site information. Since our agent already uses call site instrumentation, augmenting our approach to record the site address for each function call is straightforward. Our analyses would be able to handle call paths of the form $(main \rightarrow site_1 \rightarrow A \rightarrow site_2 \rightarrow B)$ without any modification.

5.2   Job-Run-Twice Problem

Techniques that allowed us to find the cause of the file-transfer problem also proved useful for finding another previously-diagnosed problem in the Condor environment. The *shadow* daemon contained an intermittent bug that could cause it to crash after reporting successful job completion. In such cases, the *schedd* daemon restarted the *shadow* and the job was run for the second time. Re-running the job after reporting its successful completion caused a higher-level work-flow management component built on top of Condor to abort; reporting job completion twice also was confusing for the end user.

To model this hard-to-reproduce problem in our test environment, we inserted a controlled intermittent fault in the Condor source code. If the fault occurs, it terminates the execution of the *shadow* daemon after it writes the job completion entry in the log; if the fault does not occur, the *shadow* completes successfully. Similar to the file-transfer problem, we then submitted a cluster of five identical jobs to Condor, obtained the system-wide trace that began at *condor_submit*, and separated the trace into flows. One of the flows contained an instance of the problem and our anomaly detection algorithm was able to identify such a flow as follows.

Figure 6a shows the suspect scores computed for *composite* profiles of all flows without prior reference traces. Flows 1 and 5 have higher scores than the rest of the flows. Detailed examination of their differences from the common behavior showed that these differences corresponded to normal variations in activities performed only for the first and the last job in the cluster. Therefore, this approach is unable to locate the true anomaly. Coverage profiles performed similarly to the composite profiles and also could not locate the anomaly.

Unlike the file-transfer scenario however, this problem was intermittent. As a result, we were able to obtain a set of known-correct traces, where the problem did not happen, and used them to improve the accuracy of anomaly detection. Figure 6b shows the suspect scores for all flows computed using such known-correct traces as a reference. Flows 1 and 5 receive low suspect scores because similar flows were present in the normal run. In contrast, Flow 3 exhibits an anomalous behavior; it has not been observed in previous normal executions. Analysis of coverage profiles showed similar results. By examining Condor job-completion log records, we confirmed that our automated approach identified the correct anomaly: Flow 3 corresponded to the job that was run twice.

To identify the root cause of this problem, we analyzed differences in call path coverage between Flow 3 in the anomalous run and Flow 3 in the known-normal previous run. The total number of paths present only in the anomalous flow or only in the normal flow was 964. After applying our filtering techniques, we reduced the number of paths to inspect to 37, a factor of 26. While substantial, the reduction factor was lower than that in the file-transfer problem since most differences corresponded to functions with smaller call path subtrees. Our techniques still enabled us to examine the remaining ones manually.

We ranked all the paths by time of first occurrence. Similar to the file-transfer problem, several early paths corresponded to normal variations in the workload

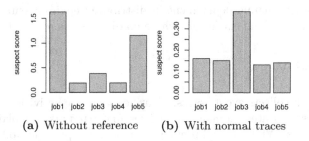

(a) Without reference   (b) With normal traces

Fig. 6. Suspect scores for five jobs with and without reference traces

rather than anomalies. However, the 14th path corresponded to an immediate effect of the fault: *schedd*'s function *Scheduler::child_exit* invoked *Daemon-Core::GetExceptionString* only in the anomalous flow. By examining the source code, we determined that *child_exit* calls *GetExceptionString* when the *shadow* crashes or aborts. Next, this function writes a warning record to the *schedd* log file and reschedules the job. Due to the large log file, and the large number of log files from other Condor components, finding this record via manual inspection of the logs would be difficult. In contrast, our approach presented a small number of reports to the analyst and significantly simplified locating the failed component. To find the location of the fault in the *shadow*, we examined the last functions the *shadow* called in the anomalous Flow 3. The call path at the crash time pointed to the location where we previously inserted the fault thus correctly identifying the cause of the problem.

To compare our ranking strategies, we also ordered call paths by their length. This strategy placed the call path to *DaemonCore::GetExceptionString* in the first position: this path was the shortest among the differences. Here, ranking by length was more effective than ranking by time of occurrence. In the file-transfer problem however, the true cause was ranked 31st by length and 15th by time. Determining which ranking technique works better in most environments and designing alternative ranking techniques remains future work.

5.3   Run-Time Overhead

In our previous experiments with real-life applications, the overhead of function-level instrumentation ranged from 35% for a call-intensive workload to less than 1% for an I/O-bound workload [33, 34, 35]. While some elusive problems may be masked by any amount of overhead, this limitation exists in all run-time diagnostic tools. Yet, they are still widely used and effective in many cases. Furthermore, the overhead of our tool might be lowered by using static structural analysis to reduce tracing of functions in inner loops. Another alternative is to combine our distributed propagation infrastructure with hardware branch-tracing capabilities available in recent Intel® processors [19]. Whether tracing every branch in hardware introduces less run-time overhead than tracing every function call with instrumentation is likely workload-specific. The efficacy of these optimizations is yet to be studied. Most importantly, the key feature of our approach is dynamic deployment in distributed environments, introducing zero overhead in normal execution, where no diagnosis is required.

6   Related Work

Our framework collects event traces, identifies semantic activities in the traces, such as requests, locates anomalous activities, and attempts to explain the causes of the anomalies. While several previous diagnostic approaches follow the same steps, we use substantially different techniques to target unmodified production environments. Below, we survey related work at each of these steps.

6.1   Techniques for Data Collection

Our approach can collect detailed traces from already-running unmodified distributed systems and it introduces zero overhead when disabled. AjaxScope diagnoses problems in a client's browser by instrumenting the JavaScript source passing through a proxy server [22]. This approach works on unmodified systems but applies only to scripting environments. Within a single host, our technique is most similar to dynamic binary translation [1,7,12,29,31,36,39]. Triage combines binary translation of PIN [29] with record-replay capabilities [43]. The novel feature of our approach however, is its ability to cross host boundaries, propagating from one process into another in a distributed system. This property enables system-wide on-demand analysis of individual requests in the field.

Unlike the single-host case, previous techniques for distributed tracing could not be applied to an already-running system and they typically collect coarse-grained traces that may be insufficient for accurate diagnosis. Magpie obtains traces of kernel events using probes already available in Windows and relies on binary rewriting for application-level tracing. Similarly, SysProf relies on static Linux kernel instrumentation [2]. Pinpoint and Stardust [42] collect traces of communication events by modifying middleware and applications.

Some mechanisms can obtain more detailed traces, but they still require system modification and restart. Traceback uses offline binary-rewriting to instrument application components [4]. King and Chen obtain system-wide dependence graphs from applications that communicate via standard UNIX mechanisms [23]. To intercept all communication operations, they run the entire system inside a virtual machine and modify the virtual machine monitor to capture all system calls made inside the guest operating system. Whodunit tracks communications through shared memory by running critical sections of the application in an instruction emulator [9]. To intercept message-passing communications, Whodunit uses *send* and *recv* wrappers in all components.

6.2   Techniques for Flow Reconstruction

A trace from a real-world distributed system may contain interleaved events from several concurrent user requests. To simplify trace analysis, several previous approaches attempted to separate events from different requests into flows [3,5,9, 10,24,26,32,42]. Our approach aims to support many systems with application-independent rules. These rules are similar to the algorithms of DPM [32] and Whodunit [9]. In scenarios where such rules are insufficient however, we allow the analyst to provide additional application-specific directives to analysis. These directives have the form similar to the event-join schema of Magpie [5]. The key feature of our flow-reconstruction approach is its ability to combine generic and application-specific knowledge in a uniform algorithm.

Aguilera et al. studied probabilistic techniques for building causal flows without application-specific knowledge [3]. This approach looks for frequent causal paths in the system and thus may be used for locating performance bottlenecks. However, results presented by the authors indicate that this probabilistic approach generates many false paths for rare requests. As a result, it may not be accurate for locating the causes of infrequent bugs and performance anomalies.

Another approach for flow construction is to assign a unique identifier to each request-arrival event and modify the source code of the system to pass this identifier to other components on inter-component communications. This technique has been used by Pinpoint [10], Stardust [42], the works of Li [26], and Krempel [24]. These projects can accurately track the paths of requests through components. However, they require extensive middleware modifications.

6.3   Techniques for Data Analysis

Our data analyses contain two steps. First, we use an anomaly detection algorithm to find an unusual request. In this step, we use the algorithm of *sp-Tracer* [35], extended to operate on distributed rather than per-process flows. Second, we perform root cause analysis to find why the identified request is unusual. Below, we focus on this step, surveying techniques for root cause analysis.

Several projects attempt to diagnose problems by correlating observed events with failures. Pinpoint looks for components (hosts or software modules) that are present only in failed requests. Jones et al. apply a similar idea at the program statement level, identifying statements that are frequently present in failed runs and absent in passing runs [20]. *Dynamic program dicing* [11,30] and Triage [43] compare the dynamic backward slice for a variable with an incorrect value (a set of program statements or basic blocks affecting the variable) to the slice for a variable with a correct value, e.g., the same variable in a successful run. Finally, Cooperative Bug Isolation CBI) samples various predicates during program runs (e.g., whether each conditional branch in the code was taken) and reports predicates correlated with failures to the analyst [27].

We apply a similar approach to function-level coverage data in a distributed system. Triage and dynamic program dicing have a finer level of detail, but they work in a single process. Another important feature of our approach is its ability to substantially reduce the number of differences to examine. In distributed environments, slicing-based approaches may also require similar filtering techniques though it remains to be seen. Similar to CBI and Jones et al., we also rank the differences so that more likely problem causes are ranked higher. However, our scheme can order even functions that are perfectly correlated with the failure rather than assigning the same highest rank to them.

Magpie attempts to locate the cause of the problem from raw traces rather than trace summaries [6]. It automatically builds a probabilistic state machine that accepts the collection of traces, processes each anomalous trace with the machine, and marks events that correspond to state transitions with low probabilities as the causes of anomalies. Pip also operates on raw traces of events and checks them against a manually-constructed model [38]. These techniques could also be applied to our function-level traces. In our experience however, function-level traces in distributed systems are highly variable and the first difference is often caused by minor variations in workload for different runs. We eliminate most of such variations by summarizing traces as call path profiles.

Yuan et al. propose a supervised technique for identifying known problems in failure reports coming from the field [44]. They summarize the system call trace for a failed run and find an already-diagnosed problem with the most similar summary. Cohen et al. construct signatures of application performance metrics and search the collection of signatures for previously-diagnosed performance problems [15]. Unlike both approaches, we operate on detailed function-level traces and thus can perform diagnosis with higher precision. Furthermore, these techniques target known problems and would be unable to diagnose new failures.

Finally, there are several approaches that attempt to localize the root cause of a problem via repetitive modification of system parameters. Delta Debugging [46] and the first stage of Triage look for the minimum change in program input that cause the incorrect run to complete successfully. Delta Debugging also attempts to isolate the problem to a minimum set of program variables. Choi and Zeller diagnose race conditions by finding the minimum change in thread schedules that would make the problem disappear [14]. Whether these techniques can be generalized to handle production distributed systems remains to be seen.

Acknowledgments

We wish to thank Naoya Maruyama, Ben Liblit, Somesh Jha, and Miron Livny for helpful comments and suggestions throughout this work. Discussions with Jaime Frey and Jim Kupsch helped us in our Condor experiments. This work is supported in part by Department of Energy Grants DE-FG02-93ER25176 and DE-FG02-01ER25510, and the National Science Foundation. The U.S. Government is authorized to reproduce and distribute reprints for Governmental purposes notwithstanding any copyright notation thereon.

References

1. Adams, K., Agesen, O.: A comparison of software and hardware techniques for x86 virtualization. In: 12th International Conference on Architectural Support for Programming Languages, ASPLOS (October 2006)
2. Agarwala, S., Schwan, K.: SysProf: Online Distributed Behavior Diagnosis through Fine-grain System Monitoring. In: 26th International Conference on Distributed Computing Systems (ICDCS), Lisboa, Portugal (July 2006)

3. Aguilera, M.K., Mogul, J.C., Wiener, J.L., Reynolds, P., Muthitacharoen, A.: Performance Debugging for Distributed Systems of Black Boxes. In: ACM Symposium on Operating Systems Principles, Bolton Landing, New York (October 2003)
4. Ayers, A., Schooler, R., Agarwal, A., Metcalf, C., Rhee, J., Witchel, E.: TraceBack: First-Fault Diagnosis by Reconstruction of Distributed Control Flow. In: Conf. on Programming Language Design and Implementation, Chicago, IL (June 2005)
5. Barham, P., Donnelly, A., Isaacs, R., Mortier, R.: Using Magpie for Request Extraction and Workload Modelling. In: 6th Symposium on Operating Systems Design and Implementation, San Francisco, CA (December 2004)
6. Barham, P., Isaacs, R., Mortier, R., Narayanan, D.: Magpie: real-time modelling and performance-aware systems. In: 9th Workshop on Hot Topics in Operating Systems, Lihue, Hawaii (May 2003)
7. Bruening, D., Duesterwald, E., Amarasinghe, S.: Design and Implementation of a Dynamic Optimization Framework for Windows. In: 4th ACM Workshop on Feedback-Directed and Dynamic Optimization, Austin, TX (December 2001)
8. Chanda, A., Elmeleegy, K., Cox, A.L., Zwaenepoel, W.: Causeway: Support For Controlling And Analyzing The Execution Of Web-Accessible Applications. In: 6th International Middleware Conference, Grenoble, France (November 2005)
9. Chanda, A., Cox, A.L., Zwaenepoel, W.: Whodunit: Transactional Profiling for Multi-Tier Applications. In: EuroSys, Lisbon, Portugal (March 2007)
10. Chen, M., Accardi, A., Kiciman, E., Lloyd, J., Patterson, D., Fox, A., Brewer, E.: Path-based Failure and Evolution Management. In: 1st Symposium on Networked Systems Design and Implementation, San Francisco, CA (March 2004)
11. Chen, T.Y., Cheung, Y.Y.: Dynamic Program Dicing. In: International Conference on Software Maintenance, Montreal, Canada (September 1993)
12. Chernoff, A., Hookway, R.: DIGITAL FX!32 Running 32-Bit x86 Applications on Alpha NT. In: USENIX Windows NT Workshop, Seattle, WA (August 1997)
13. Choi, J.D., Miller, B.P., Netzer, R.H.B.: Techniques for Debugging Parallel Programs with Flowback Analysis. ACM Transactions on Programming Languages and Systems 13(4) (1991)
14. Choi, J.D., Zeller, A.: Isolating Failure-Inducing Thread Schedules. In: International Symposium on Software Testing and Analysis, Rome, Italy (July 2002)
15. Cohen, I., Zhang, S., Goldszmidt, M., Symons, J., Kelly, T., Fox, A.: Capturing, indexing, clustering, and retrieving system history. In: 20th ACM Symposium on Operating Systems Principles, Brighton, UK (October 2005)
16. Dickinson, W., Leon, D., Podgurski, A.: Finding failures by cluster analysis of execution profiles. In: 23rd International Conference on Software Engineering, Toronto, Ontario, Canada (May 2001)
17. Engler, D., Chen, D.Y., Hallem, S., Chou, A., Chelf, B.: Bugs as deviant behavior: a general approach to inferring errors in systems code. In: 18th ACM Symposium on Operating Systems Principles (SOSP), Banff, Alberta, Canada (October 2001)
18. Gansner, E., North, S.: An open graph visualization system and its applications to software engineering. Software: Practice & Experience 30(11) (September 2000)
19. Intel Corp., Intel® 64 and IA-32 Architectures Software Developer's Manual, Volume 3B: System Programming Guide, Part 2, Order Number: 253669-022US (November 2006)
20. Jones, J.A., Harrold, M.J., Stasko, J.: Visualization of test information to assist fault localization. In: Intl. Conf. on Software Engineering, Orlando, FL (May 2002)
21. Kiciman, E., Fox, A.: Detecting Application-Level Failures in Component-based Internet Services. In: IEEE Trans. on Neural Networks: Spec. Issue on Adaptive Learning Systems in Communication Networks (September 2005)

22. Kiciman, E., Livshits, B.: AjaxScope: A Platform for Remotely Monitoring the Client-Side Behavior of Web 2.0 Applications. In: 21st Symposium on Operating Systems Principles (SOSP), Stevenson, WA (October 2007)
23. King, S.T., Chen, P.M.: Backtracking Intrusions. In: 19th ACM Symposium on Operating System Principles, Bolton Landing, NY (October 2003)
24. Krempel, S.: Tracing Connections Between MPI Calls and Resulting PVFS2 Disk Operations, Bachelor's Thesis. Ruprecht-Karls-Universität, Heidelberg (2006)
25. Lamport, L.: Time, clocks and the ordering of events in a distributed system. Commun. of the ACM 21(7) (1978)
26. Li, J.: Monitoring and Characterization of Component-Based Systems with Global Causality Capture, HP Labs Tech. Report HPL-2003-54 (2003)
27. Liblit, B., Naik, M., Zheng, A.X., Aiken, A., Jordan, M.I.: Scalable Statistical Bug Isolation. In: ACM SIGPLAN Conference on Programming Language Design and Implementation, Chicago, IL (June 2005)
28. Litzkow, M., Livny, M., Mutka, M.: Condor–a hunter of idle workstations. In: 8th Intl. Conf. on Distributed Computing Systems, San Jose, CA (June 1988)
29. Luk, C.K., Cohn, R., Muth, R., Patil, H., Klauser, A., Lowney, G., Wallace, S., Reddi, V.J., Hazelwood, K.: Pin: Building Customized Program Analysis Tools with Dynamic Instrumentation. In: ACM SIGPLAN Conference on Programming Language Design and Implementation, Chicago, IL (June 2005)
30. Lyle, J.R., Weiser, M.: Automatic Program Bug Location by Program Slicing. In: 2nd Intl. Conf. on Computers and Applications, Beijing, China (June 1987)
31. Maebe, J., Ronsse, M., De Bosschere, K.: DIOTA: Dynamic Instrumentation, Optimization and Transformation of Applications. In: Workshop on Binary Translation, Charlottesville, VA (September 2002)
32. Miller, B.P.: DPM: A Measurement System for Distributed Programs. IEEE Trans. on Computers 37(2) (February 1988)
33. Mirgorodskiy, A.V.: Ph.D. Thesis, University of Wisconsin–Madison (2006)
34. Mirgorodskiy, A.V., Miller, B.P.: Autonomous Analysis of Interactive Systems with Self-Propelled Instrumentation. In: 12th Multimedia Computing and Networking, San Jose, CA (January 2005)
35. Mirgorodskiy, A.V., Maruyama, N., Miller, B.P.: Problem Diagnosis in Large-Scale Computing Environments. In: SC 2006, Tampa, FL (November 2006)
36. Nethercote, N., Seward, J.: Valgrind: A program supervision framework. In: 3rd Workshop on Runtime Verification, Boulder, CO (July 2003)
37. Reumann, J., Shin, K.G.: Stateful distributed interposition. ACM Transactions on Computer Systems 22(1), 1–48 (2004)
38. Reynolds, P., Killian, C., Wiener, J.L., Mogul, J.C., Shah, M.A., Vahdat, A.: Pip: Detecting the Unexpected in Distributed Systems. In: 3rd Symposium on Networked Systems Design and Implementation (NSDI), San Jose, CA (May 2006)
39. Scott, K., Davidson, J.: Strata: a software dynamic translation infrastructure. In: Workshop on Binary Translation, Barcelona (September 2001)
40. Stevens, W.R.: UNIX Network Programming, 2nd edn., vol. 1. Prentice Hall, Englewood Cliffs (1998)
41. Thain, D., Tannenbaum, T., Livny, M.: Distributed Computing in Practice: The Condor Experience. Concurrency and Computation: Practice and Experience 17(2–4) (February– March 2005)
42. Thereska, E., Salmon, B., Strunk, J., Wachs, M., Abd-El-Malek, M., Lopez, J., Ganger, G.R.: Stardust: Tracking Activity in a Distributed Storage System. In: International Conf. on Measurement and Modeling of Computer Systems, Saint-Malo, France (June 2006)

43. Tucek, J., Lu, S., Huang, C., Xanthos, S., Zhou, Y.: Triage: Diagnosing Production Run Failures at the User's Site. In: 21st Symposium on Operating Systems Principles (SOSP), Stevenson, WA (October 2007)
44. Yuan, C., Lao, N., Wen, J.-R., Li, J., Zhang, Z., Wang, Y.-M., Ma, W.-Y.: Automated Known Problem Diagnosis with Event Traces. In: EuroSys, Leuven, Belgium (April 2006)
45. Zandy, V.: Force a Process to Load a Library,
    http://www.cs.wisc.edu/~zandy/p/hijack.c
46. Zeller, A.: Isolating Cause-Effect Chains from Computer Programs. In: Intl. Symposium on the Foundations of Software Engineering, Charleston, SC (November 2002)

Multithreading Strategies for Replicated Objects[*]

Jörg Domaschka[1], Thomas Bestfleisch[1], Franz J. Hauck[1], Hans P. Reiser[2],
and Rüdiger Kapitza[3]

[1] Department of Distributed Systems, Ulm University, Germany
{joerg.domaschka,thomas.bestfleisch,franz.hauck}@uni-ulm.de
[2] LaSIGE, Faculdade de Ciências da Universidade de Lisboa, Portugal
hans@di.fc.ul.pt
[3] Dept. of Comp. Sciences 4, University of Erlangen-Nürnberg, Germany
rrkapitz@cs.fau.de

Abstract. Replicating objects usually requires deterministic behaviour
for maintaining a consistent state. Multithreading is a critical source of
non-determinism, completely unsupported in most fault-tolerant middleware systems. Recent publications have defined deterministic scheduling
algorithms that operate at the middleware level and allow multithreading
for replicated objects. This approach avoids deadlocks, improves performance, and makes the development better resemble that of non-replicated
objects. This paper surveys those algorithms and analyses their differences. It also defines extensions to two efficient multithreading algorithms
to support nested invocations and condition variables with time-bounded
wait operations similar to the Java synchronisation model. In addition,
we provide an experimental evaluation and performance comparison of
the algorithms, indicating the areas in which each algorithm performs
best. We conclude that replication middleware should implement recon-
figurable multithreading strategies, as there is no optimal one-size-fits-all
solution.

1 Motivation

Object replication is an important mechanism for implementing reliable distributed applications. Many current object middleware systems support replication. For example, FT-CORBA [1] and Jgroup [2] are architectures for replicating
CORBA and Java RMI objects, respectively.

In many application domains of replication, such as file systems and data
bases, the aim of replication is data-centric. In contrast, the replication of objects leads to different requirements, as it not only requires consideration of the
state of the objects, but also of their activity. For example, an object method
can actively interact with external services, and concurrently executing methods
might use mechanisms such as semaphores, monitors, and condition variables for

[*] This work has been supported by the EC through FP6 Integrated Project IST2006-
0033576 (XtreemOS) and project NoE IST-4-026764-NOE (ReSIST), and by the
FCT, through the Multiannual Funding Programme.

V. Issarny and R. Schantz (Eds.): Middleware 2008, LNCS 5346, pp. 104–123, 2008.

coordination. A replication infrastructure should impose as few constraints as possible on the object implementations. This way, existing non-replicated implementations can be re-used directly for replication, and the developer can make use of the programming model he is used to, without paying a lot of attention to replication-induced restrictions.

Object replication strategies are typically classified as *active* or *passive*. In active replication, all replicas individually execute all requests, and the assumption of deterministic replica behaviour guarantees state consistency. In passive replication, only a single primary executes method invocations, and then transfers state updates to secondary replicas. At first sight, this strategy eliminates the need for determinism. However, sending state updates synchronously after each state modification is expensive. Often, the primary state is only periodically transferred to secondary replicas, and a message log is used to store client requests that the primary has executed since the last checkpoint. A secondary replica has to have the same deterministic behaviour if it wants to obtain a state identical to that of a failed primary by re-executing requests from such a log.

Multithreaded execution is a source of non-determinism, as multiple threads might execute at unknown relative speeds and might modify the object state in an unpredictable order. Non-replicated objects usually use mechanisms such as locks to coordinate concurrent state modifications. Nevertheless, different replicas of an object can grant locks in a different order, thus causing inconsistencies between replicas. Most object replication infrastructures avoid this problem by executing methods strictly sequentially.

In the past few years several authors have proposed solutions that to some extent enable deterministic multithreading in replicated objects [3,4,5,6]. The main motivation for multithreading is either to improve the efficiency of replicated objects, thus reducing the performance difference between replicated and non-replicated applications, to avoid inherent deadlock problems of single-threaded executions [7], or to provide a programming model that is as close as possible to the non-replicated case. This paper builds upon these previous works by enhancing some known algorithms and by providing a comparative analysis. The specific contributions of this paper are as follows:

- It presents a survey of all existing multithreading strategies for replicated objects known to the authors, clearly stating their differences in objectives, assumptions, and achieved properties.
- It augments two previously known algorithms with extensions that permit the use of these algorithms in a broader application spectrum.
- It provides an experimental evaluation and performance comparison of all algorithms, indicating the areas in which each algorithm performs best, and demonstrating that a middleware should provide configurability of the multithreading strategy, as there is no best algorithm for all situations.

This paper is structured as follows. The next section discusses the necessity of multithreading in replicated objects. Section 3 discusses and compares the existing algorithms. Section 4 defines extended variants of two algorithms, PDS and LSA. Section 5 presents an experimental evaluation based on several use cases. Finally, Section 6 concludes.

2   Background and Related Work

Many distributed object replication systems, such as OGS [8] and GroupPac [9], do not support multithreading in replicated objects. Method invocation requests from clients are executed in a strictly sequential order; a request is processed only after the preceding request has been completed. This approach avoids any non-determinism that can arise from thread scheduling, and it provides implicit synchronization of state modifications, as multiple threads cannot attempt to modify the state concurrently.

There are, however, several reasons that argue for the use of multithreading in replicated objects [7]. First of all, multithreading can enhance performance. On one hand, the computational power of multi-CPU hardware can be utilized better. On the other hand, multithreading allows the system to process additional method invocations whenever the system becomes idle because the current thread has to wait, e.g., during external invocations.

Second, a single-threaded execution excludes coordination via condition variables. For example, a thread might want to interact with an external service by first issuing an asynchronous external request, and then wait on a condition variable for the notification by a call-back of the external service.

Third, nested invocations can cause deadlocks in a single-threaded model, if a thread synchronously calls an external service, which in turn invokes a method at the originator.

Using multithreading in replicated objects requires that appropriate steps be taken to remove non-determinism. This means that in spite of concurrent execution of threads, the order of conflicting state manipulations must be made deterministic. The implementation of the replicated object must use some means to coordinate state modifications that happen concurrently in multiple threads. The use of explicit locks or monitors is the most popular model, but other mechanisms, such as non-blocking or wait-free synchronization, can also be found [10]. In this paper, we assume that multithreaded objects use lock synchronization; if these objects are replicated, the replication infrastructure must make sure that locks are granted in a consistent order on all replicas.

Some existing research projects use a modified Java virtual machine to implement deterministic replication. For example, *Napper et al.* (based on a modified Sun JDK 1.2) [11] and *Friedman and Kama* (based on a modified JikesRVM) [12] use this approach. Other systems ensure determinism at an even lower system level. For example, MARS [13] is strictly time-driven and periodic at the hardware level, which makes all functional and timing behaviour deterministic. The features of such a platform can be used for deterministic replication [14]. All these systems can execute multiple threads concurrently. They all require specifically designed hardware, operating systems, or Java virtual machines to achieve determinism.

In this paper we focus on means to enforce determinism of multithreaded replicated services purely at the middleware level, without requiring special low-level support in operating system or virtual machine. Several algorithms have been proposed in this area. On the basis of work by *Jiménez-Peris et al.* [15], *Zhao et al.* [3] propose a strategy to execute a new request during the idle time caused by a nested invocation of the main thread. Our ADETS-SAT algorithm [6] extends this approach with support for reentrant locks, condition variables, and time bounds on wait operations. These strategies allow the execution of a new thread only if the previous thread suspends. ADETS-MAT [7] is an improved version of ADETS-SAT that enables the concurrent execution of multiple threads. Basile's *Loose Synchronization Algorithm* (LSA) [4] supports true multithreading on the basis of a leader-follower model. Basile's *Preemptive Deterministic Scheduling* algorithm (PDS) [5] allows the concurrent execution of a fixed set of threads in periodic rounds, without requiring communication for consistency. We compare these algorithms in Section 3.2.

We use our FT*flex* replication infrastructure on top of the Aspectix middleware [16,17] for evaluating the multithreading strategies. FT*flex* supports deterministic multithreading on the basis of a plug-in interface for configurable ADETS (Aspectix DEterministic Thread Scheduler) modules.

3 Comparison of Algorithms

In this section, we define a set of criteria that allow a characterization of the various algorithms. These criteria include the *coordination model*, the *external interaction model*, the *deployment*, and the *multithreading model*. On this basis, we subsequently provide a systematic comparison of algorithms.

3.1 Criteria

Coordination Model. There are numerous different mechanisms for coordinating multiple concurrent threads. We restrict the discussion to *locks, monitors,* and *Java synchronization*, as these are most prevalent in existing systems.

Locks are a basic coordination mechanism that allows protecting the access to resources, using two operations `lock` and `unlock`. *Reentrant locks* allow one thread to acquire the same lock multiple times.

Monitors are a synchronization mechanism defined by Hoare that provides implicit locking around monitor procedures. Condition variables within the monitor allow threads to suspend and temporarily release the lock while waiting for a condition. Any thread that causes the condition to be true can signal the waiting thread, which in turn atomically regains the lock and resumes. By mapping a monitor procedure to a pair of `lock`/`unlock` operations, any scheduling algorithm for reentrant locks can be used for applications that use monitors for coordination. However, monitors in addition require support for condition variables by the scheduling algorithm.

Native Java synchronization uses a concept similar to Hoare monitors. It restricts the model by defining a single implicit condition variable for each monitor (instead of an arbitrary number). On the other hand, it supports time-bound wait operations, which allow a waiting thread to resume after a specific timeout.

Locks and monitors provide sufficient support to protect state modifications that should be made atomically. Condition variables are useful in situations in which threads wait for callbacks from external services and for coordinating in producer/consumer scenarios.

External Interaction Model. In terms of external interaction, we can distinguish between scheduling strategies that support *none (NO)*, and strategies that support *nested invocations (NI)* and *callbacks (CB)*. A nested invocation is an invocation of a function of a service B, issued by a service A during the execution of a client request. A callback is an invocation of a function of service A triggered by the nested invocation from A to a service B.

If a scheduling algorithm is deadlock-free for arbitrary nested invocations, it will also be deadlock-free for callbacks, which are a special kind of nested invocation. On the other hand, a scheduling algorithm can use thread IDs to detect that an incoming nested invocation belongs to an existing local (blocked) thread and thus identify it as a callback. Algorithms on this basis can supports deadlock-free callbacks, but are not necessarily deadlock-free for other nested invocations.

Deployment. Implementations of objects typically use either language-internal coordination mechanisms (such as in the case of Java) or invocations of synchronization methods of an external library (such as the pthread library for C++ objects). If such object implementations are deployed in a multithreading replication infrastructure, the synchronization methods have to be adjusted to interact with the replication infrastructure.

The simplest way is to provide *no support* at all, forcing developers to modify the implementation accordingly to interact with the replication infrastructure. A better alternative is an automated approach. Either, *code transformation* can be applied to alter the replica code automatically (as proposed for ADETS-SAT [6]). Or, *low-level interception* can redirect external library calls to the replication infrastructure (as used in Eternal [18]).

The deployment strategy could be considered as a concern orthogonal to deterministic scheduling. However, in ongoing work [19] we demonstrate that code analysis and transformation allows improving concurrency on the basis of prediction of future synchronization steps.

Multithreading Models. We classify the multithreading support of middleware infrastructures into four categories: *single thread (S)*, *single logical thread (SL)*, *single active thread (SA)*, and *multiple active threads (MA)*.

The S model is the simplest variant, in which the middleware starts executing a request R_{i+1} only after request R_i has fully completed its execution.

In the SL model, a single logical thread of execution exists. In a chain of nested invocations, the logical thread may call methods of the same object multiple times. For example, if a thread that executes m_{A1} at object A starts a chain of nested invocations that ultimately calls method m_{A2} at object A, the object A can detect that the invocation m_{A2} belongs to the same logical thread as m_{A1}. Thus, object A can execute m_{A2} using an additional physical thread. In a sequential execution model without the logical thread abstraction, nested invocations finally targeting the same object would cause a deadlock.

In the SA model, multiple independent physical threads can exist within a replica. Only one of them may be active at a time, while all other threads are blocked (e.g., waiting for a lock or for the return from a nested invocation). Consistency is obtained by a deterministic selection of the active thread. A running active thread is not preempted; if the active thread blocks or terminates, a deterministic strategy is required to resume one of the existing threads or to create a new active thread for handling the next request. If the strategy guarantees that the same choice is made in all replicas, consistency will be maintained.

The SA model does not require the identification of logical threads. However, such identification is mandatory if a system wants to support reentrant locks. For example, a method m_{A2}, called by m_{A1}, might want to acquire a lock already held by m_{A1}. We denote a SA model with appropriate logical thread identification as $SA+L$.

In MA, multiple threads may exist and run in parallel. Multiple threads may either be simultaneously active in a multi-CPU or multi-core CPU setting, or a low-level thread scheduler may execute them on a single CPU with preemption. To maintain consistency in true multithreading, all access to shared data structure needs to be made in a consistent order. The number of threads may be restricted by an algorithm.

3.2   Algorithms

This section discusses several different algorithms. Table 1 summarizes their different properties and models compared to a pure sequential execution.

SL in Eternal. The Eternal middleware was the first system to support the SL model [18] An infrastructure can support this model by tagging nested invocations with context information that identifies the originating logical thread.

SA and ADETS-SAT. Applying the approach of Jiménez-Peris et al. [15] to a CORBA middleware, Zhao et al. [3] implemented an algorithm for the SA

Table 1. Overview of multithreading algorithms and their properties

	Coordination	Deadl.-Free Interaction	Deployment	Multithreading
SEQ	implicit	NO	–	S
Eternal	implicit	CB	interception	SL
SAT	Locks	NI+CB	interception	SA
ADETS-SAT	Java	NI+CB	transformation	SA+L
ADETS-MAT	Java	NI+CB	transformation	MA
LSA	Locks/Monitor	NI+CB	manual	MA
PDS	Locks	NO	manual	MA (restr.)

model in Eternal. ADETS-SAT [6] is an extension of this algorithm that also offers support for reentrant locks and for Java condition variables. The algorithm ensures that threads calling wait() are enqueued in a deterministic manner and dequeued deterministically at a notify().

ADETS-MAT. The ADETS-MAT algorithm [7] works similar to ADETS-SAT, but instead of using only a single active thread, it allows additional concurrency. Beside a primary thread that works similar to the active thread in ADETS-SAT, multiple secondary threads are executed concurrently as long as they do not request additional mutex locks. ADETS-MAT requires no communication for granting locks, threads can be created at any time by client requests, and no restrictions are made on the number and frequency in which a thread requests locks. Concurrency is constrained by the fact that only the primary thread can acquire locks. It fully supports the native synchronization model of the Java programming language. One of the main objectives of the algorithm is to use the idle time during nested invocations.

LSA. In LSA [4], a single replica works as primary node. This node can execute an arbitrary number of threads without restrictions, and records the order in which locks are granted to threads as a sequence of *(lock, thread)* pairs. It broadcasts this data structure to all other replicas periodically. All follower nodes suspend threads that request a lock until the corresponding broadcast is received. While the basic operation of LSA is very simple, it requires a strategy to handle the failure of the primary node. *Basile et al.* define such a fail-over algorithm for crash failures as well as for Byzantine failures. Failure handling requires additional communication between replicas to maintain consistent scheduling. This is a significant difference to other algorithms that do not need any additional computation or communication to handle node failures.

PDS. *Basile et al.* have defined two variants of the PDS algorithm, PDS-1 and PDS-2 [5]. Both algorithms work in sequential rounds. In PDS-1, each thread can acquire at most one mutex per round. A thread is suspended when it requests a mutex; as soon as all threads are suspended, a new round is started. As the mutex requests of all threads are known at the beginning of the round, the mutexes can be assigned deterministically to all threads. If multiple threads request the same lock, they get the lock in increasing thread ID order. For example, if two threads T_1 and T_2 have both requested a mutex m, T_1 may execute and T_2 remains suspended. As soon as T_1 unlocks m, T_2 may execute concurrently with T_1. If T_1 suspends in the current round without unlocking m, T_2 remains suspended.

The PDS-2 variant improves concurrency by allowing threads to acquire up to two locks per round. A round is divided into two phases. Initially, a round starts execution in phase-1 in the same way as PDS-1, granting mutexes according to requests made before the start of the round. If a thread requests a new mutex during phase-1, it is not immediately suspended (as it would be in PDS-1). Instead, this second mutex is granted under the condition that it is available and all threads with lower thread IDs have already acquired such a phase-1 mutex. After the second mutex acquisition, the thread enters phase-2, in which a mutex request suspends a thread as in PDS-1. A new round is started as soon as all threads are suspended.

In both PDS algorithms, the number of threads is constant during the execution of a round. New threads may be created or removed only at the start of a new round. Even then, a deterministic rule for changing the set of threads is necessary. The state of the incoming message queue cannot be used for deciding an adjustment of the thread pool size, as the group communication system only ensures a consistent order of message reception, but no consistent time (i.e., some replica might already have received a message m, while other replicas have not). The PDS algorithms work best if all threads repeatedly execute lock requests followed by computations of approximately identical computation times. It requires no communication for deterministically assigning mutex locks to threads. The algorithm has two main disadvantages. First, as long as one single thread fails to request a mutex lock, no new round can be started. Second, the number of threads must be known deterministically at the start of each round. Incoming requests have to be mapped to a fixed-size thread pool. This means that in each round, new requests have to be assigned to threads that have finished executing their previous requests. If no new requests are available, the system cannot start a new round (as the idling thread will not acquire a lock). The only way to solve this problem is to deterministically create artificial requests in case that client requests do not arrive sufficiently frequently.

4   Extending LSA and PDS

In this section, we define extended versions of the LSA and PDS algorithms. Their primary goal is to support a system model that includes the following features: reentrant locks, nested invocations, condition variables, and time-bounded wait operations. The ADETS-SAT and ADETS-MAT algorithms already support all of these features. The semantics for condition variables is based upon the native Java programming language. In addition, we extend LSA to support an arbitrary number of mutexes without prior registration at the scheduler.

Reentrant locks can be implemented on the basis of any deterministic scheduling algorithm that supports just simple locks. A reentrant mutex is one that can be acquired multiple times by one thread. The transformation requires a data structure that, for each thread, stores the number of times a lock has been acquired. Only on the transitions from 0 to 1 (upon lock) and 1 to 0 (upon unlock), the lock/unlock functions of the base algorithms are called.

4.1   Extending LSA to ADETS-LSA

Nested invocations do not require any dedicated support in the implementation of the LSA algorithm. Nested invocations do not influence the order of mutex assignments. In LSA, a thread waiting for a nested invocation reply does not have any influence on the progress of other threads.

Condition variables without time bounds cause no problems in LSA. A wait() operation can be called locally at all replicas. Invocations of wait() and `notify()`/`notifyAll()` on the same condition variable have to be done in the same relative order. A deterministic order of such concurrent operations is easily obtained in all replicas by the LSA algorithm, as all operations on a condition variable are protected by the acquisition of the corresponding mutex. The basic LSA algorithm guarantees a deterministic order of these mutex acquisitions. Hence, the order of operations on the condition variable will be deterministic as well.

Time bounds on wait operations represent a more difficult source of nondeterminism. For example, two threads T_1 and T_2 might be waiting on a condition variable, with thread T_1 having specified a time bound. A third thread, T_3, might call a `notify()` operation. The timeout of T_1 and the notification of T_3 happen concurrently; thus, the order in which the two happen is non-deterministic. Two possible execution sequences are (a) that the timeout happens first, with the effect that T_1 is resumed by the timeout and, after that, T_2 is resumed by T_3's notify operation, and (b) that T_3's notification happens first, which cancels the timeout and resumes only T_1.

Handling such timeouts deterministically requires a non-trivial extension to LSA. In the solution that we provide in the ADETS-LSA algorithm, a local timeout of a wait operation does not resume the waiting thread directly. Instead, it creates a new thread, which is also subject to the ADETS-LSA scheduling. The thread tries to resume the waiting thread by locking the corresponding mutex and signalling the `wait()` operation to resume. Thus the basic scheduling algorithm guarantees that, due to the lock, the signalling is done in a consistent order on all replicas.

A sample execution of this extension is shown in Figure 1. Thread T_1 calls `wait()` with a timeout of $20ms$. This call causes the LSA scheduler to create a timeout thread (TO-Thread), which sleeps for $20ms$ and then tries to resume the wait. Concurrently, thread T_2 tries to call `notify()`. Both T_2 and TO-Thread

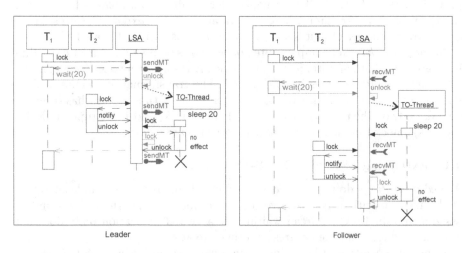

Fig. 1. Sample execution of timeout handling in ADETS-LSA

need to lock the same mutex. On the leader node, T_2 is faster, causing the notify() operation of T_2 to resume T_1, and the timeout thread has no effect. On the follower node, the timeout thread requests the lock first, but the LSA scheduler ensures that the lock is first assigned to T_2, resulting in a deterministic behaviour.

The original LSA algorithm assumes that globally known IDs for mutexes and for threads exist. *Basile et al.* describe a method for dynamically adding new mutexes and new threads by explicitly notifying the scheduler. Adding new threads is feasible in practice if the middleware infrastructure controls the creation of threads, as it can notify the scheduler. Mutexes, however, are not created explicitly. In Java, every object can be used as a mutex, and there are no globally consistent IDs for these objects. In ADETS-LSA, the leader replica assigns new mutex IDs automatically on the first lock operation on a not yet known mutex. Follower replicas instead suspend a thread upon a lock operation with an unknown ID. On all replicas, the lock operation can uniquely be identified by the thread ID, as the same thread will lock the corresponding mutex on all replicas. The leader sends its mutex ID with its periodic mutex table broadcast, which enables the follower replicas to learn the new mutex ID.

4.2   Extending PDS to ADETS-PDS

The PDS algorithm first raises the question of *assigning requests to threads*. The algorithm assumes that a thread pool of a fixed size is given. It does not allow the asynchronous creation of new threads for each incoming client request. The original publication simply assumes that sufficiently many requests arrive, so that all threads can continuously execute, without specifying a strategy for assigning requests to threads. In a practical middleware infrastructure, however, such a strategy needs to be implemented. The assignment of requests to threads must be made consistently in all replicas. We suggest two possible strategies:

- A *round-robin strategy* assigns incoming requests to all threads such that, given a thread-pool size of N, the i-th incoming request is assigned to thread $i \bmod N$. This strategy works fine if requests have identical computation times.
- In a *synchronized request assignment strategy*, a thread that has just finished processing of its last request locks the mutex of the incoming message queue. This mutex lock is granted consistently in all replicas, because this operation is also under the control of the PDS, and thus each request is assigned to the same thread in all replicas. Our current implementation uses this strategy.

Nested invocations have no impact on the order of lock assignments and thus are uncritical for consistency, but they can have a serious impact on performance. We propose two different strategies:

- First, nested invocations can be used simply without any support by the scheduling algorithm. In this case, however, a thread that waits for a nested invocation can block all other threads from starting a new round. This approach seems favourable if the duration of the nested invocation is short compared to the execution time between two mutex locks. This approach is used in the following experimental evaluation.

– Alternatively, the scheduler can consider a thread that has issued a nested invocation to be suspended. This enables all other threads to continue executing rounds, but requires a deterministic strategy to resume the thread. For example, if the reply message is processed within some round, the suspended thread can be scheduled for being resumed in the next round. This approach adds an additional delay to each nested invocation; thus, it is not useful with nested invocations that have short duration, like it is the case in our evaluation.

From a consistency point of view, *condition variables* can be supported in the PDS algorithm without much effort. All operations on condition variables are protected by mutex locks, and thus the relative order of these operations is deterministic on all replicas. The only requirement is that a `notify()` operation selects the thread to resume deterministically. This determinism is not guaranteed by the native Java notification mechanisms. By implementing a queue of waiting threads that is modified deterministically by each `wait()` operation, such determinism can easily be achieved though.

The integration into the round execution model is done in the following manner. Once a thread t calls `wait()` in some round, it is considered suspended. After a new round has been triggered, t is removed from the set of active threads. Consequently, the scheduling decisions in the subsequent rounds are done without t. When another thread calls `notify()` during some round, thread t is resumed immediately, but has first to aqcuire the corresponding lock. This lets thread t wait until the start of the next round.

Figure 2 shows a sample execution of two replicas A and B. On replica A the `wait()` operation of thread t_1 happens before the second mutex acquisition of

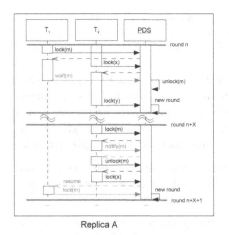
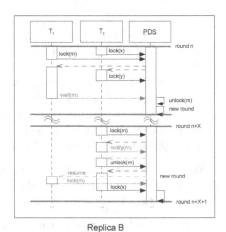

Replica A   Replica B

Fig. 2. Handling of condition variables in ADETS-PDS

t_2. Thus, the new round is triggered because of t_2. On replica B the opposite happens. The new round is triggered because of the wait() operation.

Having a thread pool of fixed size, however, the use of condition variables can cause deadlocks. If all available threads suspend in wait() operations, no more threads are available for handling requests that could resume a waiting thread. To avoid this problem, we implement a strategy for an automated adjustment of the thread-pool size. The original PDS algorithm supports changing the set of threads at the start of a new round. In a deadlock situation, the conditions for the start of a new round (i.e., all threads are blocked) are met. Thus, at the start of each round, the number of threads not blocked in a wait() operation is compared to a minimum threshold. If the number falls below the threshold, additional threads are added to the thread pool. On the other hand, if there are more non-waiting threads than the threshold and there are insufficient incoming requests (i.e., the request assignment strategy has to suspend a thread temporarily due to the lack of requests), the number of non-waiting threads is reduced to the minimum threshold.

Timeouts of *time-bounded wait operations* potentially occur concurrently with explicit notifications, and thus an extended algorithm has to make sure that any such non-determinism is avoided. We propose the same concept that is also used for ADETS-SAT and ADETS-MAT. After a timeout occurs, a timeout message is sent to all replicas via group communication. This message is handled by a normal request-handler thread, which notifies the waiting thread. As all notifications are synchronized by mutexes, a deterministic order is guaranteed.

5   Experimental Evaluation

This section presents an experimental evaluation of the scheduling strategies discussed in the previous sections. A set of benchmarks capture typical interaction patterns of distributed applications. Each of them is executed with purely sequential scheduling and with all four multithreaded ADETS variants.

5.1   Implementation Overview

All presented strategies have been implemented on the basis of our FT*flex* replication infrastructure [17], which extends the CORBA-based Aspectix middleware [16,17]. FT*flex* supports multithreading in object replicas using its configurable ADETS (Aspectix DEterministic Thread Scheduler) module. Each scheduling algorithm is implemented as a separate ADETS plug-in module.

Integrating the scheduling module in the middleware is relatively light-weight. We added it in between the group communication module, which delivers the requests, and the object adapter whose task is to enforce at-most-once semantics and to trigger dispatching and parameter unmarshalling. Thus, the scheduler instances are completely independent of the object implementation. We use code transformation to intercept calls of synchronisation-related operation in the object implementation [6].

At runtime, the group communication module receives a new request and passes it on to the scheduler instance. There, a thread that executes the request is created eventually; the creation happens according to the strategy implemented by the scheduler. As soon as the thread is running, the scheduler invokes the object adapter. If the execution of the requested method issues a lock/unlock operation or an operation on a condition variable, these calls are forwarded to the scheduler, which in turn handles these operations. The scheduler itself uses the group communication module to broadcast messages to the other replicas. Such broadcasts might be timeout messages after a time-bounded operation or update messages from the primary in case of the LSA scheduling strategy.

5.2 Benchmark Overview

The benchmarks cover three different scenarios: evaluation of local computations with lock-protected shared state, local computation together with nested invocations, and usage of condition variables. A final discussion analyses overall advantages and disadvantages.

All measurements presented in this section were made on a set of PCs with a AMD Athlon 2.0 GHz CPU and 1 GB RAM. The PCs were using Linux kernel 2.6.17 and were connected by a 100 MBit/s switched Ethernet. The current prototype of the Aspectix middleware was used on the basis of Sun's Java runtime environment version 1.5.0_03.

In each benchmark, active replicas of an object were placed on three nodes, and all clients on separate nodes are started simultaneously in each experiment. All measurements show the invocation times measured at the client side, averaged over at least 5,000 invocations; to minimize the effects of JIT compilation, the first 200 invocations of each client are not included in the average. In all benchmarks the size of the thread-pool in PDS was equal to the number of clients.

5.3 Local Computations

The first group of benchmarks assumes that the behaviour of object methods is limited to (a) performing local computations and (b) requesting and releasing mutex locks. In such a scenario, the only problem of a single-threaded execution is the lack of parallel execution, which primarily is a disadvantage on multi-CPU machines. In the benchmarks, a variable number of clients invoke object methods that have one of the behaviours shown in Figure 3. The measurements for the invocations were made on the client-side.

(a) compute
(b) compute − lock − state access − unlock
(c) lock − state access and compute − unlock
(d) lock − state access − unlock − compute

Fig. 3. Variants of the local computations benchmark

The pattern (a) does not access the shared object state and thus does not need any mutex access. The pattern (b) first computes and then locks a mutex, updates the object state, and unlocks the mutex again. This is a typical pattern for applications that first perform computations on the request arguments such as verifying digital signatures and preprocessing the client data, and then use this data to update the object state, using a mutex lock to synchronize the update. Pattern (c) is typical for applications that require simultaneous access to client arguments and object state for performing some calculations. The whole request execution is protected by a mutex lock. Pattern (d) can mainly be found in practice for methods that read the shared state and then perform computations (e.g., transformations of state data) to produce the return value for the client.

For the following measurements, it is assumed that the local computations take 100 ms. The availability of an unlimited number of CPUs on a single-CPU hardware is simulated by suspending the request-handler thread for the duration of the computation time instead of performing real computations, thus freeing the CPU for other threads. Furthermore, it is assumed that the methods of the replicated object use fine-grained locking. If all methods used the same mutex lock, this would result in a sequential execution. Instead, the benchmarks assume that 10 different mutexes are available, with each client invocation using a randomly selected mutex. The actual state access is assumed to take a negligible amount of time. Figure 4 shows the result of the benchmarks executed with three replicas and a variable number of clients.

With pattern (a), SAT executes all requests sequentially, while all other variants allow a fully concurrent execution. MAT and LSA perform best, as they can execute all requests immediately in the absence of any synchronization. PDS shows a slight overhead, because it requires internal synchronization (i.e., mutex locks for the incoming message queue) for assigning requests to threads.

Pattern (b) results in similar results. While SAT processes all requests sequentially, all other variants enable a concurrent execution of the computations. MAT is the superior variant, as LSA requires communication for the mutex locks, while PDS uses additional mutex locks for assigning requests to threads.

Pattern (c) produces different results. As all requests start with a lock operation and do not define internal scheduling points, the MAT algorithm delays all requests until they become primary and as a result serializes all requests, which leads to the same poor performance as the SAT algorithm. LSA and PDS both enable concurrency and show similar behaviour. With an increasing number of clients, the probability that two requests require the same mutex increases. Such a collision delays the start of a new round for the PDS algorithm; thus, with many clients, the LSA algorithm is superior.

Pattern (d) is similar to (c); the only difference is that mutex locks are released before the computation. The PDS algorithm benefits from this behaviour, as a collision between two request delays a new round only for the short duration of the state access, and not for the duration of the computation. As a result, PDS is the most efficient algorithm for this pattern, while LSA is slightly slower, and both SAT and MAT achieve no concurrent execution.

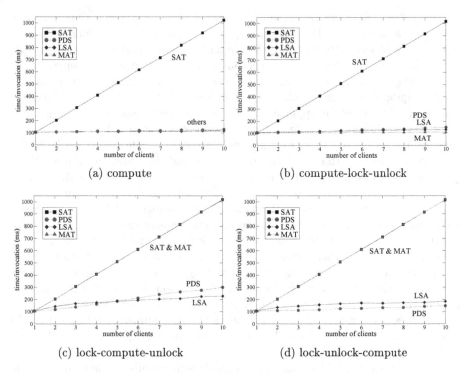

(a) compute

(b) compute-lock-unlock

(c) lock-compute-unlock

(d) lock-unlock-compute

Fig. 4. Measurements with local computations and mutex locks

The different benchmark patterns demonstrate that for each algorithm there are situations in which it performs well, and others in which it does not. Most important, the MAT algorithm is the most efficient one in the situations (a) and (b), while it fails to provide any advantage compared to SAT in the situations (c) and (d). The latter two situations represent worst-case scenarios for MAT. The poor performance of MAT can be alleviated by the introduction of *yield* operations, which enable a selection of a new primary thread without reaching an implicit scheduling point. Another approach for optimizing MAT is the use of source-code analysis to predict synchronization behaviour [19].

5.4   Nested Invocations

The second set of benchmarks adds nested invocations to the patterns. As explained in Section 2, nested invocations can result in deadlocks and reduce performance by causing idle time in a single-threaded execution model. Hence, application patterns with nested invocations are an important scenario even on a single-CPU machine.

In the first scenario, two replica groups A and B are created with each consisting of 3 replicas. A varying number of clients call a method at group A, which in turn calls a method at group B. Internally, both requests and the reply from group B to group A are delivered via group communication.

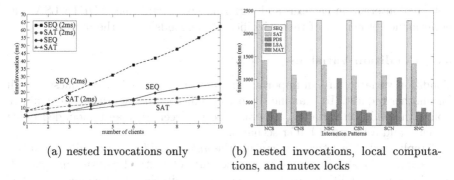

(a) nested invocations only

(b) nested invocations, local computations, and mutex locks

Fig. 5. Measurements with nested invocations

Figure 5(a) shows the average invocation time measured by the clients, using (i) a strictly sequential execution and (ii) the ADETS-SAT algorithm[1]. The solid lines (diamond and triangle symbols) refer to measurements in which the nested invocation returns immediately. Even in this situation, multithreading with ADETS-SAT is increasingly better with a rising number of clients. In a second measurement (dashed lines with circles and squares), the method called at B suspends for $2ms$ before it returns. In this case, the benefit from our multi-threaded approach (which allows to accept new requests at A while the invocation to B is in progress) is enormous compared to a single-threaded execution.

A comparison of all ADETS scheduling algorithms is provided on the basis of a set of more complex benchmarks. In each benchmark, the replicas execute the following operations: a nested invocation ($100\ldots150ms$, denoted as N), a local computation ($75\ldots125ms$, denoted as C), and a synchronized state update (lock und unlock operation, denoted as S).

The duration of nested invocations and local computations was simulated to have a uniform random distribution on the given interval. The three elements can be combined in six permutations (NCS, NSC, CNS, CSN, SNC, SCN). Figure 5(b) shows the result of the benchmarks with above parameters, run with ten clients.

The ADETS-SAT performs better than the single-threaded execution, because the idle time of a nested invocation is utilized. Local computations cannot be performed in parallel, however. Thus, the ADETS-SAT performs worse than the other algorithms. The performance of the ADETS-MAT algorithm heavily depends on the interaction patterns. In some situations (NCS, CSN), the algorithm performs best of all. In others (NSC, SCN) it offers no significant advantage compared to the ADETS-SAT algorithm. The problematic pattern is a state update (S) followed by a computation (C). The ADETS-PDS performs

---

[1] No other algorithms have been evaluated in this nested-invocation-only benchmark. As there are no lock operations, ADETS-MAT and ADETS-LSA would result in similar performance as ADETS-SAT. On the other hand, ADETS-PDS, which assumes that each thread acquires a lock in each round, would not work appropriately.

well in all interaction patterns and performs even better than ADETS-LSA. The performance of neither of them significantly depends on on the pattern.

5.5   Condition Variables

Condition variables are an important mechanism that enables a request to wait for another request. To examine the performance of the algorithms in combination with condition variables, we evaluated two scenarios, an unbounded buffer scenario and a bounded buffer scenario.

A replicated object that implements the *unbounded buffer* provides two methods, consume() and produce(). The consume() method returns an available data item on a condition variable if no item is available. The produce() method makes an item available, and notifies another request-handling thread that waits on the condition variable, if such a thread exists. Without support for condition variables, the consume method needs to be implemented differently; for the evaluation we use periodic polling for consume() with pure sequential scheduling.

Figure 6(a) shows the result of this experiment, using a single producer client and up to ten consumer clients. With an increasing number of consumers, the single-threaded execution shows an increasing disadvantage. This behaviour is to be expected due to the periodic polling: the number of unsuccessful iterations of consume() calls increases with a rising number of consumers competing for the producer. The other strategies, however, scale linearly because a thread is only notified if an item in the buffer exists. The ADETS-SAT performs minimally better than ADETS-MAT and ADETS-PDS. The ADETS-LSA, however, has a notable overhead due to the leader-follower communication.

The second benchmark for evaluating the scheduler behaviour in combination with condition variables implements a *bounded buffer*. In this experiment, both produce() and consume() block if the buffer is full or empty, respectively. Two condition variables are used: the first one is used to resume a blocked produce() call by a consume() call; the second one is used in the reverse direction. Figure 6(b) shows the result of the experiment, in which the same number of producers

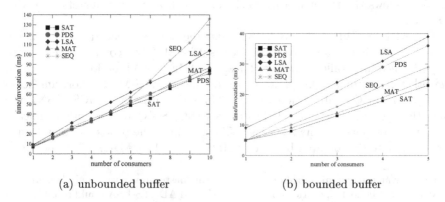

(a) unbounded buffer   (b) bounded buffer

Fig. 6. Measurements with condition variables

and consumers, each ranging from 1–5, have been used. The size of the buffer was set to 2. The graph shows the average time per consumer invocation; exactly the same average time was obtained for producer invocations.

Both experiments show that ADETS-SAT and ADETS-MAT are superior to all other execution strategies. ADETS-PDS and ADETS-LSA, on the other hand, show poor performance. In the experiment with the bounded buffer, they perform even worse than the sequential polling-based approach. With the ADETS-LSA algorithm, this is due to the additional communication caused by the scheduling algorithm. With ADETS-PDS, threads that resume from a wait operation need to be delayed until the next internal round starts; this delay increases the invocation times.

5.6   Overall Performance Comparison

Concluding, we state that the ADETS-SAT algorithm always performs better than the single-threaded execution. On the other hand, the main disadvantage is that it does not support true multithreading. As a result, when using multiple CPUs it yields significantly less performance than to the other strategies.

The ADETS-MAT algorithm in contrast supports true multithreading in typical usage patterns, such as preprocessing some data and then modifying the local state, but it does not perform well if calculations require a locked mutex, because different mutexes cannot be locked concurrently by different threads.

The ADETS-LSA strategy works well independent of a certain pattern. The leader-follower communication, however, is one disadvantage of the ADETS-LSA. Obviously, this issue is even more important when using the LSA in a WAN environment. Due to the communication, the ADETS-LSA also showed a noticeable overhead in scenarios with condition variables. A second disadvantage is the reconfiguration process that is necessary after the failure of the leader. This failure must first be detected, which leads to a delay until the reconfiguration process can be started. Furthermore, this reconfiguration defeats essential advantages of active replication, as it is typically used if minimal downtime after failures is required.

The ADETS-PDS has a good overall performance when all threads execute the same pattern concurrently. But it does not perform well in other scenarios when different patterns are executed, because the round execution model can cause high delays. Also, in conjunction with condition variables the PDS may perform worse than ADETS-SAT and ADETS-MAT.

6   Conclusions

In this paper, we have revisited the problem of multithreaded execution of methods at replicated objects. In active replication, multithreading is a potential source of non-determinism that has to be made deterministic by an adequate thread-scheduling strategy. Similar consistency problems can arise in passive replication if the re-execution of methods after a primary failure is inconsistent to the first execution of the primary before its failure. In our CORBA-based FT*flex* infrastructure for object replication, we have implemented four different strategies: ADETS-MAT, ADETS-SAT, ADETS-LSA, and ADETS-PDS.

The first contribution of this paper are the ADETS-LSA and ADETS-PDS algorithms, an extension of Basile's LSA and PDS algorithms. Our variants add support for the native Java synchronization model. Beside reentrant locks, the most important extensions are the support for condition variables and the deterministic handling of time bounds on wait operations. PDS was also extended to support nested invocations.

The second contribution is a comparison of the available thread-scheduling strategies. In a set of experiments, we have analysed the respective benefits of each algorithm. We show that the performance of an algorithm is highly dependent on the interaction patterns. No algorithm is clearly superior to all others. Our evaluation provides information about which algorithm works better in which application scenarios. We conclude that replication infrastructures should support variability of its thread-scheduling strategy. In all cases, however, a multithreaded strategy is superior to single-threaded request execution.

References

1. OMG: Common object request broker architecture: Core specification, version 3.0.3. Object Management Group (OMG) document formal/2004-03-12 (2004)
2. Montresor, A.: The Jgroup distributed object model. In: Proceedings of the IFIP WG 6.1 International Working Conference on Distributed Applications and Interoperable Systems II (1999)
3. Zhao, W., Moser, L.E., Melliar-Smith, P.M.: Deterministic scheduling for multithreaded replicas. In: WORDS 2005 (2005)
4. Basile, C., Whisnant, K., Kalbarczyk, Z., Iyer, R.: Loose synchronization of multithreaded replicas. In: SRDS 2002 (2002)
5. Basile, C., Kalbarczyk, Z., Iyer, R.: Preemptive deterministic scheduling algorithm for multithreaded replicas. In: DSN 2003 (2003)
6. Domaschka, J., Hauck, F.J., Reiser, H.P., Kapitza, R.: Deterministic multithreading for Java-based replicated objects. In: PDCS 2006 (2006)
7. Reiser, H.P., Hauck, F.J., Domaschka, J., Kapitza, R., Schröder-Preikschat, W.: Consistent replication of multithreaded distributed objects. In: SRDS 2006 (2006)
8. Felber, P., Guerraoui, R., Schiper, A.: The implementation of a CORBA object group service. Theory and Practice of Object Systems 4(2), 93–105 (1998)
9. Bessani, A.N., da Silva Fraga, J., Lung, L.C., Alchieri, E.A.P.: Active replication in CORBA: Standards, protocols, and implementation framework. In: DOA 2004 (2004)
10. Fich, F.E., Hendler, D., Shavit, N.: On the inherent weakness of conditional synchronization primitives. In: PODC 2004 (2004)
11. Napper, J., Alvisi, L., Vin, H.: A fault-tolerant Java virtual machine. In: DSN 2003 (2003)
12. Friedman, R., Kama, A.: Transparent fault tolerant Java virtual machine. In: SRDS 2003 (2003)
13. Kopetz, H., Damm, A., Koza, C., Mulazzani, M., Schwabl, W., Senft, C., Zainlinger, R.: Distributed fault-tolerant real-time systems — the Mars approach. IEEE Micro 9(1), 25–40 (1989)

14. Poledna, S., Burns, A., Wellings, A.J., Barrett, P.: Replica determinism and flexible scheduling in hard real-time dependable systems. IEEE Trans. Computers 49(2), 100–111 (2000)
15. Jiménez-Peris, R., Patiño-Martínez, M., Arévalo, S.: Deterministic scheduling for transactional multithreaded replicas. In: SRDS 2000 (2000)
16. Reiser, H.P., Hauck, F.J., Kapitza, R., Schmied, A.I.: Integrating fragmented objects into a CORBA environment. In: Proc. of the Net.ObjectDays, Erfurt, Germany (2003)
17. Reiser, H.P., Kapitza, R., Domaschka, J., Hauck, F.J.: Fault-tolerant replication based on fragmented objects. In: Eliassen, F., Montresor, A. (eds.) DAIS 2006. LNCS, vol. 4025, pp. 256–271. Springer, Heidelberg (2006)
18. Narasimhan, P., Moser, L.E., Melliar-Smith, P.M.: Enforcing determinism for the consistent replication of multithreaded CORBA applications. In: SRDS 1999 (1999)
19. Domaschka, J., Schmied, A.I., Reiser, H.P., Hauck, F.J.: Revisiting deterministic multithreading strategies. In: Int. Workshop on Java and Components for Parallelism, Distribution and Concurrency (2007)

A Component Framework for Java-Based Real-Time Embedded Systems*

Aleš Plšek, Frédéric Loiret, Philippe Merle, and Lionel Seinturier

INRIA Lille - Nord Europe, ADAM Project-team
USTL-LIFL CNRS UMR 8022
Haute Borne, 40, avenue Halley
59650 Villeneuve d'Ascq, France
{ales.plsek,frederic.loiret,philippe.merle,lionel.seinturier}@inria.fr

Abstract. The Real-Time Specification for Java (RTSJ) [13] is becoming a popular choice in the world of real-time and embedded programming. However, RTSJ introduces many non-intuitive rules and restrictions which prevent its wide adoption. Moreover, current state-of-the-art frameworks usually fail to alleviate the development process into higher layers of the software development life-cycle. In this paper we extend our philosophy that RTSJ concepts need to be considered at early stages of software development, postulated in our prior work [2], in a framework that provides continuum between the design and implementation process. A component model designed specially for RTSJ serves here as a cornerstone. As the first contribution of this work, we propose a development process where RTSJ concepts are manipulated independently of functional aspects. Second, we mitigate complexities of RTSJ-development by automatically generating execution infrastructure where real-time concerns are transparently managed. We thus allow developers to create systems for variously constrained real-time and embedded environments. Performed benchmarks show that the overhead of the framework is minimal in comparison to manually written object-oriented applications, while providing more extensive functionality. Finally, the framework is designed with the stress on dynamic adaptability of target systems, a property we envisage as a fundamental in an upcoming era of massively developed real-time systems.

Keywords: Real-time Java, RTSJ, component framework, middleware.

1 Introduction

1.1 Current Trends and Challenges

The future of distributed, real-time and embedded systems brings demand for large-scale, heterogeneous, dynamically highly adaptive systems with variously

---

* This work has been partially funded by the ANR/RNTL Flex-eWare project and by the Interuniversity Attraction Poles Programme Belgian State, Belgian Science Policy.

V. Issarny and R. Schantz (Eds.): Middleware 2008, LNCS 5346, pp. 124–143, 2008.

stringent QoS demands. Therefore, one of the challenges is the development of complex systems composed from hard-, soft-, and non-real-time units. The Java programming language and its Real-Time Java Specification [13] (RTSJ) represent an attractive choice because of their potential to meet this challenge. Moreover, they bring a higher-level view into the real-time and embedded world, which is desperately needed when avoiding accidental complexities and steep-learning curves. However, using RTSJ at the implementation level is an error-prone process where developers have to obey non-intuitive rules and restrictions (single parent rule [3], cross-scope communication [17], etc.).

One of the answers to these issues are component-oriented frameworks for RTSJ, such as [10,12,14], abstracting complexities of the RTSJ development from the developers. Nevertheless, the state-of-the-art solutions still need to fully address adaptability issues of real-time systems, separation of real-time and functional concerns, and suffer from the absence of a high-level process that would introduce real-time concerns during the design phase.

1.2   Goals of the Paper

A complete process for designing of real-time and embedded applications comprise many complexities, specially timing and schedulability analysis, which has to be included in a design procedure. The scope of our proposal is focused on non-distributed applications and is placed directly afterwards these stages, when real-time characteristics of the system are specified but the development process of such a system lies at its very beginning.

The goal of our work is to develop a component framework alleviating the RTSJ-related concerns during development of real-time and embedded systems. Our motivation is to consider real-time concerns as clearly identified software entities and clarify their manipulation through all the steps of software life cycle. The challenge is therefore to mitigate complexities of the real-time system development and offload the burden from users by providing a middleware layer for management of RTSJ concerns. We therefore summarize the main contributions that are addressed to achieve the goals:

- *Development Process.* To propose a methodology to develop RTSJ-based systems that mitigates possible complexities and allows full-scale introduction of code generation technics.
- *Transparently Implemented Systems.* To provide transparent implementation of systems with comprehensive separation of concerns and extensive support of non-functional properties.
- *Performance.* To achieve minimal overhead of the framework, its performance and memory overhead should be subtle enough to address real-time and embedded platforms. Different code-optimization levels should be introduced to address variously constrained environments.

1.3   Structure of the Paper

To reflect the goals, the paper is structured as follows. Section 2 provides an overview of RTSJ, introduces our example scenario, and presents the component-oriented principles we integrate in our solution. Section 3 proposes a new framework for developing real-time and embedded systems. In Section 4 we present selected design and implementation aspects of our framework. Section 5 evaluates our approach; we show benchmark results measuring the overhead of the framework and discuss further contributions of our work. We present related work in Section 6. Section 7 concludes and draws future directions of our research.

2   Background

2.1   Real-Time Java Specification

The Real-Time Java Specification [13] (RTSJ) is a comprehensive specification for development of predictable real-time Java-based applications. Between many constructs which mainly pose special requirements on underrunning JVM, two new programming concepts were introduced - real-time threads (`RealTimeThread`, `NoHeapRealTimeThread`) and special types of memory areas (`ScopedMemory`, `ImmortalMemory`).

`RealTimeThread` and `NoHeapRealTimeThread` (NHRT) are new types of threads that have precise scheduling semantics. Moreover, NHRT can not be preempted by the garbage collector, this is however compensated by a restriction forbidding to access the heap memory. RTSJ further distinguishes three memory regions: `ScopedMemory`, `ImmortalMemory`, and `HeapMemory`, where the first two are outside the scope of action of the garbage collector to ensure predictable memory access. Memory management is therefore bounded by a set of rules that govern access among scopes. Another important limitation is the *single parent rule* [3] defining that a memory region can have only one parenting scope.

2.2   Motivation Example

To better illustrate all the complexities of the RTSJ development, we introduce an example scenario that will be revisited several times through the course of this paper. The goal is to design an automation system controlling an output statistics from a production line in a factory and report all anomalies. The example represents a classical scenario, inspired by [8], where both real-time and non-real-time concerns coexist in the same system.

The system consists of a production line that periodically generates measurements, and of a monitoring system that evaluates them. Whenever abnormal values of measurements appear, a worker console is notified. The last part of the system is an auditing log where all the measurements are stored for auditing purposes. Since the production line operates in 10ms intervals, the system must be designed to operate under hard real-time conditions.

A class diagram of the system is depicted in Fig. 1. As we can see, real-time and non-realtime concerns are mixed together. Identification of those parts of the system that run under different real-time constrains is difficult, hence the design of communication between them is clumsy and error-prone. As a consequence,

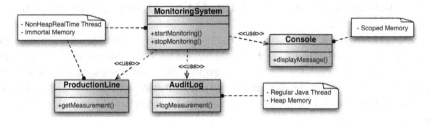

Fig. 1. Motivation Example

the developer has to face these issues at the implementation level which brings many accidental complexities.

To avoid this, a clear separation of real-time and memory management from the functional concerns is required. Moreover, the RTSJ concerns need to be considered at the design phase since they influence the architecture of the system. Therefore a proper semantics for manipulating RTSJ concerns during all the steps of system development has to be additionally proposed.

2.3   Component Frameworks

Component frameworks simplify development of software systems. A proper component model represents cornerstone for each component framework, its extensiveness substantially influences the capabilities of a component framework.

We have investigated several component models [7,9,11] to identify features suitable for our framework. Based on this we extract a fundamental characteristic of a state-of-the-art component model: A lightweight hierarchical component model that stresses on modularity and extensibility. It allows the definition, configuration, dynamic reconfiguration, and clear separation of functional and non-functional concerns. The central role is played by interfaces, which can be either *functional* or *control*. Whereas *functional interfaces* provide external access points to components, *control interfaces* are in charge of non-functional properties of the component (e.g. life-cycle or binding management). Components are sometimes divided into *passive* and *active*. Whereas passive components generally represent services, active components contain their own thread of control. Additionally, a feature so far provided only by the Fractal component model [11] is *sharing of components* which defines that a component could have several super-components.

Component models usually provide *container* (also referred as *membrane* or *membrane paradigm* in [18]) - a controlling environment encapsulating each component and supporting various non-functional properties specific to a given component. This brings better separation of functional and non-functional properties, which can be hidden in membranes, thus simplifying utilization of components by end users.

3   Component Framework for RTSJ-Based Applications

In our previous work [2], we claim that an effective development process of
RTSJ-compliant systems needs to consider RTSJ concerns at early stages of
the system design. Following this philosophy, our framework proposes a new
methodology that facilitate design and implementation of RTSJ-based systems.
We thus clarify manipulation of non-functional properties during all phases of
the system life cycle.

The cornerstone of our framework represents a component model, proposed by
our prior research, which allows us to fully separate functional and non-functional
concerns through all the steps of system development. We recapitulate the basic
model characteristics in Section 3.1. Then, a design methodology incorporated
into our framework is introduced in Section 3.2. As an outcome of this process
we obtain a real-time system architecture that can be used for implementation
of the system. Here, we benefit from separation of functional and non-functional
concerns and design an implementation process that addresses these concepts
separately - whereas functional concerns are developed manually by users, the
code managing non-functional concerns is generated automatically. We elaborate
on this implementation methodology in Section 3.3.

Our hierarchical component model with sharing [2] is depicted in Fig. 2. The
abstract entity *Component* defines that each component has sub components
expressing hierarchy, and super components, expressing component sharing. We
derive *Active* and *Passive* components, basic building units of our model, representing business concerns in the system. Each active component contains its
own thread of execution.

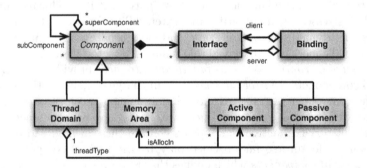

Fig. 2. A Real-Time Component Metamodel

3.1   A Real-Time Java Component Metamodel

ThreadDomain represents `RealTimeThread`, `NoHeapRealTimeThread`, and `Re-
gularThread` in a system. Each *ThreadDomain* component encapsulates all
the active components containing threads of control with the same properties

(such as thread-type or priority). *MemoryArea* representing `ImmortalMemory`, `ScopedMemory`, and `HeapMemory` encapsulates all subcomponents that are allocated in the same memory area. Therefore, we are able to explicitly model RT-concepts at the architectural level by using *ThreadDomain* and *MemoryArea* components. This brings us the advantage of creating the most fitting architecture according to real-time requirements of the system.

Composing and Binding RT-Components. The restrictions introduced by RTSJ impose several rules on the composition process. Since the component model includes RTSJ concerns, we are able to validate a conformance to RTSJ during the composition process. Additionally, our model allows sharing of components. Therefore, a set of super components of a given component directly defines its business and also its real-time role in the system. To give an example of such rules, the `ThreadDomain` and `MemoryArea` components are exclusively composite components, since they do not implement a functional behaviour. They specify non-functional properties which are commonly shared by their sub-components. Therefore, while `MemoryArea` components can be arbitrarily nested [1], it does not apply for `ThreadDomain`. Indeed, an *active component* should always be nested in a unique `ThreadDomain`. An another example of RTSJ constraints between thread and memory model concerns the `NoHeapRealTimeThread` which is not allowed to be executed in the context of the Java `heap` memory. Within our design space, this constraint is translated by a `NHRT ThreadDomain` which should not encapsulate a `Heap MemoryArea`, regardless of the hierarchical level specified by functional components.

Similarly, also the RTSJ conformance of bindings between components is evaluated at the design time. This allows developers to mitigate complexities of their implementation by choosing one of several communication patterns [1,5,17] already at the design time.

All these constraints are verified during the design process, which is presented in the following section.

3.2   Designing Real-Time Applications

This section further explains how we integrate the component model into the process of designing real-time applications. The *Design Views* and the *Design Methodology* are proposed with motivation to fully exploit the advantages of the component model at the design time.

Design Views. We define three basic views that allow designers to gradually integrate real-time concerns into the architecture: *Business View, Thread Management View*, and *Memory Management View*. Whereas the business view considers only functional aspects of the system, the two others stress on different aspects of real-time programming - realtime threads and memory areas

---

[1] RTSJ specification defines a hierarchical memory model for scoped memories, as introduces in Section 2.1.

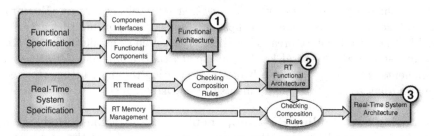

Fig. 3. RealTime Component Architecture Design Flow

management. These views therefore allow designers to architect real-time concerns independently of the business functionality. Additionally, the execution characteristics of systems can be smoothly changed by designing several different assemblies of components into *ThreadDomains* and *MemoryAreas*. This is beneficial when tailoring the same functional system for different real-time conditions.

Design Methodology. The methodology we propose progressively incorporates all the views into the design process. The new architecture design flow, depicted in Fig. 3, represents a procedure gradually introducing real-time concerns into the architecture. In three steps, we consequently employ the *Business, RealtimeThread* and *Memory Management views* to finally obtain RTSJ compliant architecture. The compliance with RTSJ is enforced during the design process. This provides an immediate feedback and the designer can appropriately modify an architecture whenever it violates RTSJ. Moreover, the verification process of the architecture identifies the points where a glue code handling RTSJ concerns needs to be deployed, which substantially alleviates the implementation phase.

Motivation Example Revisited. To fully demonstrate the design process proposed in this section, we revisit our example scenario. By using the business view, we construct the functional architecture. Then we deploy active components into appropriate `ThreadDomain` components, determining which parts of the application will be real-time oriented - the thread management view can be used here. After deploying all components into corresponding `ThreadDomain` components, the adherence to RTSJ is verified. As a result, the compositions violating RTSJ are identified and possible solutions proposed, for example using RTSJ-compliant patterns [1,5,17]. In the next step, the memory management of the system has to be designed - the memory management view can be used.

To finally create a complete RT System Architecture, the business view, the thread and memory management views are merged together. The final RT System Architecture can be seen in Fig. 4. The lower part of the figure presents the XML serialization of the resulting architecture. The structure of this language is consistent with the metamodel sketched out in Fig. 2. It provides the

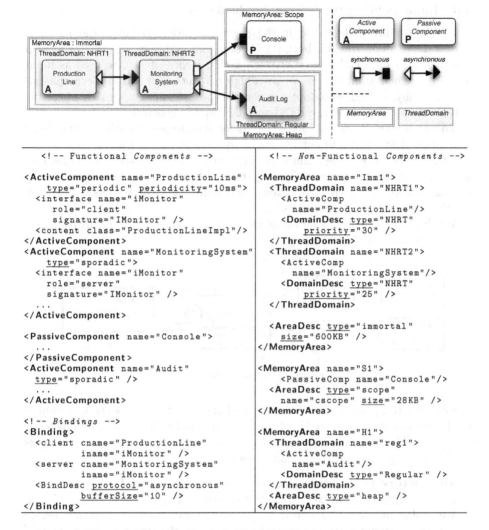

Fig. 4. Motivation Example: Real-time System Architecture

whole information needed to implement the execution infrastructure described in Section 3.3, for example:

- the functional component ProductionLine is defined as a *periodic active* component,
- the binding between MonitoringSystem and AuditLog active components specifies an asynchronous communication and its associated *message buffer size*,
- the non-functional components specify RTSJ-related attributes, such as a *memory type* and *size* of a MemoryArea, a *thread type* and a *priority* for a ThreadDomain.

3.3 Implementing Real-Time Applications

The design analysis described in the previous section yields in the *real-time system architecture* which is both RTSJ compliant and fully specifies the system together with its RTSJ related characteristics. Hence, it can be used as input for an implementation process where a high percentage of tasks is accomplished automatically. Indeed, we adopt a generative-programming approach where the non-functional code (e.g. the RTSJ-specific code) is generated.

This approach allows developers to fully focus on implementation of functional properties of systems and entrust the management of non-functional concepts into the competence of the framework. Thus we eliminate accidental complexities of the implementation process. The separation of concerns is also adopted at the implementation level where functional and non-functional aspects are kept in clearly identified software entities.

We therefore introduce a new implementation process incorporating code generation technics, depicted in Fig. 5.

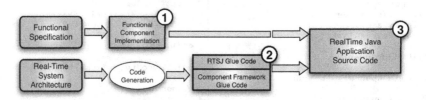

Fig. 5. Execution Infrastructure Generation Flow

Implementing Functional Concerns of Applications. As the first step of the implementation flow, see Fig. 5 step 1, functional logic of the system is being developed. The development process thus follows our approach where developers implement only component content classes.

Infrastructure Generation Process. As the second step of our development process, we generate an execution infrastructure of the system, in Fig. 5 step 2. We exploit an already designed RT System Architecture in order to generate a glue code managing non-functional properties of the system. The generation process implements several tasks, they are listed below, their implementation is described in further details in Section 4.

– **RTSJ-related Glue Code**
   • *Realtime Threads and MemoryArea management.* Real-time Thread and Memory Areas management is the primary task of the generated code. Automatical initialization and management of these aspects in conformance to RTSJ thus substantially alleviates the implementation process for the developers.
   • *Cross-Scope Communication.* Since the RT system architecture already specifies which cross-scope communication patterns will be used, their implementation can be moved under the responsibility of the code generation process.

- *Initialization Procedures.* The generated code has to be responsible also for bootstrapping procedures which will be triggered during the launch of the system. This is important since RTSJ itself introduces a high level of complexity into the bootstrapping process.
- **Framework Glue Code**
  - *Active Component Management.* For active components, the framework manages their lifecycle - generating code that activates their functionality.
  - *Communication Concepts.* Automatical support for synchronous/asynchronous communication mechanisms is important aspect offloading many burdens from developers.
  - *Additional Functionality.* Additionally, many other non-functional properties can be injected by the framework, e.g. a support for introspection and reconfiguration of the system.

Final Composition Process. Finally, by composing results of the functional component implementation and the infrastructure generation process we achieve a comprehensive and RTSJ-compliant source code of the system. Here, each functional component is wrapped by a layer managing its execution under real-time conditions. This approach respects our motivation for clear separation of functional and real-time concerns.

4   Framework Implementation Issues

The key design decision characterizing the framework is to employ component-oriented approach also during the implementation process of developed systems. Our motivation is therefore to preserve components at the implementation layer. Apart from well-know advantages of this concept, e.g. reusability of the code, this approach brings better transparency and separation of concerns. Specially separation of concerns is important here, since we need to implement functional and real-time concerns of the system but deploy them in separate entities.

Following these goals, we introduce *non-functional components* that are present at runtime. These components represent `ThreadDomain` and `MemoryArea` components, architected at the design time, and manage RTSJ-concerns of the system. This contributes to a full separation of functional and non-functional code. Moreover, this approach is further expanded by the membrane paradigm, introduced in Section 2.3, defining that each component is encapsulated by a membrane layer that manages its non-functional properties. RTSJ management is thus deployed at two places - in non-functional components, providing a coarse-grain approach, and in the membrane of each functional component, providing a fine-grain approach to management of RTSJ concerns for the specific functional logic.

Therefore, in Section 4.1 we first present the membranes and how they are employed in our solution to support RTSJ concerns of components. We also introduce non-functional components here. Consequently in Section 4.2, we explain detail implementation of membranes. Finally, Section 4.3 describes the infrastructure generation process generating membranes of components and introduces various levels of optimization heuristics which reduce overhead of the framework.

4.1 Component Framework Implementation

Component-Oriented Membrane. Membrane paradigm, originally introduced in [18], defines that each component is wrapped by a controlling environment called *membrane*. Its task is to support various non-functional properties of the component. The control membrane of a component is implemented as an assembly of so-called *control components*. Additionally, special control components called *interceptors* can be deployed on component interfaces to arbitrate communication between the component and its environment, they are also integrated in the membrane. Since membranes can be parameterized, the framework allows developers to deploy for each component its unequally designed membrane that directly fits its needs.

RTSJ-oriented Membrane. We employ the concept of membranes to develop our own set of controllers and interceptors which are specially designed to manage RTSJ-concerns in the system. We provide the following extensions of the control layer:

- **Active Interceptors** encapsulate *active components*. They implement a run-to-completion execution model[2] for each incoming invocation from their server interfaces and are configured by the properties defined by the enclosing *ThreadDomain* component.
- **Memory Interceptors** implement cross-scope communication and are deployed on each binding between different *MemoryAreas*. Their implementation depends on the design procedure choosing one of many RTSJ memory patterns [1,5,17].

Non-Functional Components. An additional construct for manipulation of RTSJ-concerns at the implementation layer represent *non-functional components*. These components correspond to `ThreadDomain` and `MemoryArea` components, created at the design time, and provide thus a coarse-grain approach to management of RTSJ-concerns in the system. More preciously, membranes of non-functional components contain real-time controllers and interceptors, which superimpose non-functional concerns over their subcomponents. Thus we manage RTSJ concepts of groups of functional components with identical RTSJ properties.

4.2 Membrane Architecture Analysis

The control components incorporated in membrane can be divided into two groups. First, the controllers which are specific to the non-functional needs of

---

[2] This execution model precludes preemption for *active components*.

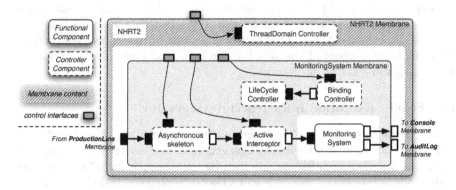

Fig. 6. Membrane Architecture, Illustration Example

the component - e.g. asynchronous communication controller, RTSJ-related controllers. These components have to be present in the membrane since they implement non-functional logic directly influencing components' execution. The second group of controllers represent units which are optional and are not directly required by the component's functional code, e.g. Binding or Lifecycle controllers. Access to membrane functionality is provided through *control-interfaces*, which are hidden at the functional level to avoid confusion with functional implementation.

Motivation Example Revisited. To illustrate the membrane architecture, we revisit our motivation example from Section 2.2, Fig. 6 shows a membrane of the MonitoringSystem component. In the picture we can see an active Monitoring-System component encapsulated by its membrane, this composition is then deployed in a non-functional component NHRT2, an instance of a ThreadDomain entity representing a NoHeapRealtimeThread. Inside the MonitoringSystem membrane, various controllers and interceptors are present. *ActiveInterceptor* implements execution model of an active component; *Asynchronous Skeleton* implements asynchronous communication. Both of them represent non-functional interceptors specific to the MonitoringSystem component. Contrarily, *Lifecycle* and *Binding Controllers* are present to implement introspection and reconfiguration of the system, and represent optional part of the membrane that is independent of functional architecture of the component. Finally, the NRHT2 component contains a ThreadDomain controller that implements logic for management of NoHeapRealtimeThread subcomponents.

Runtime Adaptability. Already the basic set of controllers - Binding Controller, Content Controller, and Lifecycle controller, supports introspection and dynamic adaptation of the system. Whereas regular-Java components in our framework can be flawlessly reconfigured, however, adaptation of real-time code brings additional challenges and complexities. Since every manipulation of RTSJ concepts is bounded by their specification rules, the reconfiguration process has to adhere to these restrictions as well. Investigation and research of these controlling mechanisms is however out of the scope of this paper. We therefore settle for basic support of the adaptability issue and plan to fully tackle this challenging topic in our future work.

4.3 Soleil - Execution Infrastructure Generator

For the infrastructure generation process we employ Soleil, an extension of *Juliac* - a Fractal [11][3] toolchain backend which generates Java source code corresponding to the real-time architecture specified by the designer, including membrane source code, a framework glue code and a bootstrapping code. Moreover, the tool offers different generation modes corresponding to various levels of functionality, optimization and code compactness:

1. `SOLEIL`. This default mode generates a full componentization of the execution infrastructure. The RTSJ interceptors and the reconfigurability management code are therefore implemented as non-functional components, within the *membranes*. The structure of the latter is also reified at runtime, as well as the `ThreadDomain` and `MemoryArea` composite components. This generation mode provides the complete introspection and reconfiguration capabilities of the component framework at functional and at membrane level.
2. `MERGE-ALL`. In this generation mode the implementation of functional component code and its associated membrane are merged into a single Java class. Therefore, it generates one class per each functional component defined by the developer. Since the number of Java objects in the resulting infrastructure is considerably decreased, this mode achieves also memory footprint reduction. In comparison with the `SOLEIL` mode, it corresponds to a first optimization level where several indirections introduced by the membrane architecture are replaced by direct method calls. As component membrane structures are not preserved at the runtime, the `MERGE-ALL` mode do not provides reconfiguration capabilities at membrane level. However, these capabilities are provided at the functional level.

   The source-to-source optimizations performed by the generation process are based on Spoon [16], a Java program processor, which allows fine-grained source code transformations.
3. `ULTRA-MERGE`. The most optimized mode achieves that the whole resulting source code fits into one unique class. Moreover, the generated code does not preserve the reconfiguration capabilities anymore. The resulting infrastructure is therefore purely static. It exclusively embeds the functional implementations merged to the code which takes into account the component activations, the asynchronous communications, and the RTSJ dedicated code.

---

[3] Available at http://fractal.ow2.org/

5   Evaluation

To show the quality of our framework, we evaluate it from several different perspectives. First, we conduct benchmark tests to measure performance of the framework. Then we evaluate the development process introduced by our solution from the code generation perspective. Finally, we summarize the contributions of the framework to the field of real-time and embedded systems development.

5.1   Overhead of the Framework

The main goal of this benchmark is to show that our framework does not introduce any non-determinism and to measure the performance/memory-consumption overhead of the framework. As one of the means of evaluation, we compare differently optimized applications developed in our framework against a manually written object-oriented application.

Benchmark Scenario. The benchmark is performed on the motivation case-study presented in Fig. 4. We measure the execution time of a complete iteration starting from the `ProductionLine` component. Its execution behavior consists of a production of a state message that is sent to the `MonitoringSystem` component using an asynchronous communication. The latter is a *sporadic active component* that is triggered by an arrival notification of the message from its incoming server interface. The scenario of this transaction finally ends after invocation of a synchronous method provided by the passive `Console` component and an asynchronous message transmission to the active `AuditLog` component.

Evaluation Platform. The testing environment consists of a Pentium 4 monoprocessor (512KB Cache) at 2.66 GHz with 1GB of SDRAM, with the Sun 2.1 Real-Time Java Virtual Machine (a J2SE 5.0 platform compliant with RTSJ), and running the Linux 2.6.24 kernel patched by RT-PREEMPT. The latter converts the kernel into a fully preemptible one with high resolution clock support, which brings hard realtime capabilities[4].

Benchmarking Method. The measurements are based on *steady state observations* - in order to eliminate the transitory effects of cold starts we collect measurements after the system has started and renders a steady execution. For each test, we perform 10 000 observations from which we compute performance results. Our first goal is to show that the framework does not introduce any non-determinism into the developed systems, we therefore evaluate a "worst-case" execution time and an average jitter. Afterwards, we evaluate the overhead of the framework by performance comparison between an application developed in the framework (impacting the generated code) and an implementation developed manually through object-oriented approach. Therefore, in the results presented bellow, we compare four different implementations of the evaluation

---

[4] The Linux RT-PREEMPT patch is available at
    `www.kernel.org/pub/linux/kernel/projects/rt/`

scenario. First, denoted as OO, is the manually developed object-oriented application. Then, denoted as SOLEIL, MERGE_ALL, and ULTRA_MERGE, are applications developed in our framework constructed with different levels of optimization heuristics. We refer the reader to Section 4.3 for detail description of the optimization levels.

Results Discussion. The results of the benchmarks are presented in Fig. 7, where the graph (a) presents the execution time distribution of the 10,000 observations processed. Fig. 7(b) sums up these results and gives their corresponding jitters. Fig. 7(c) presents the memory footprints observed at runtime.

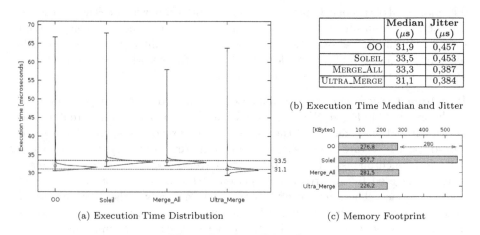

(b) Execution Time Median and Jitter

(a) Execution Time Distribution

(c) Memory Footprint

Fig. 7. Benchmark Results

Non-Determinism. As the first result, we can see that our approach does not introduce any non-determinism in comparison to the object-oriented one, as the execution time curves of OO and SOLEIL are similar. Moreover, the jitter is very subtle for all tests. This is caused by the execution platform which ensures that real-time threads are not preempted by GC, and provides a low latency support for full-preemption mechanisms within the kernel.

Performance Time. The median execution time for the SOLEIL test is 4.7% higher than for the OO one. This corresponds to the overhead induced by our approach based on component-oriented membranes. However, the performance of the ULTRA_MERGE is comparable to the manually implemented OO - it is even slightly better since ULTRA_MERGE' implementation is more compact.

Memory Footprint. Considering the memory footprint, SOLEIL consumes 280KB more memory than OO. The price paid for generated membranes providing RTSJ interception mechanisms, introspection and reconfigurability. MERGE_ALL, a test introducing the first level of optimizations, gives a more precise idea of the injected code which provides these non-functional capabilities at runtime: 4.7KB. The memory overhead purely corresponds to the algorithms and data structures used by our component framework. Finally, the ULTRA_MERGE is the most lightweight - even in comparison to OO.

Bottom Line. The bottom line is that our approach does not introduce any non-determinism. Moreover, the overhead of the framework is minimal when considering *MERGE_ALL*, but with the same functionality as our non-optimized code. Finally, we demonstrate a fitness for embedded platforms by achieving a memory footprint reduction (*ULTRA_MERGE*) that provides better results than the OO-approach.

5.2   RTSJ Code Generation Perspective

We further confront our generation process against the set of code generation requirements identified in [6]. The authors highlight importance of separation of concerns, stress on compactness of generated code, and demand clear distinction between generated and manually written code. All these requirements are met by our generation process since both generated and manually written code are deployed in clearly identified components. Moreover, an additional requirement demands a clear separation between functional and non-functional semantics. This is however supported directly in our component metamodel (`ThreadDomain` and `MemoryArea` components) and thus we inherently meet this requirement.

5.3   Summary of Our Contribution

We further summarize the main contributions of our work, they can be divided into two categories:

- **RTSJ-based Systems Development**
  - **Component Model.** The proposed component model allows designers to explicitly express an architecture combining real-time and business concerns.
  - **Designing Real-time Applications.** The component model further allows a separation of real-time concerns and to design them independently of the rest of the system. By combining different Thread and Memory Management compositions we can smoothly tailor a system for variously hard real-time conditions without necessity to modify the functional architecture. The verification process moreover ensures that compositions violating RTSJ will be refused.
  - **Implementing Real-time Applications.** Considering an implementation of each component, the designed architecture considerably simplifies this task. Functional and real-time concerns are strictly separated and a guidance for possible implementations of those interfaces that cross different concerns is proposed.
- **Framework Implementation**
  - **Separation of Concerns.** The separation of concerns is consistently respected through all the steps of development lifecycle. Membrane extensions and non-functional components are preserved also at the implementation layer to manage real-time concerns of the system.

- **Code Generation.** The code generation approach we integrate in our framework respects the set of requirements [6] that are key for the fitness of generated code from the RTSJ perspective.
- **Performance.** Our evaluations show that we deliver predictable applications and the overhead of the framework is considerably reduced by the optimizations heuristics we implement (MERGE_ALL optimization level). Moreover, we achieve an effective footprint reduction suitable for embedded systems (ULTRA_MERGE optimization level). Despite the wide functionality we provide through out the applications development and execution life-cycle, performance results are comparable with the object-oriented approach.
- **Dynamic Adaptation of Real-time Systems.** Although the dynamic adaptation of Java-based real-time systems is a novel and complex topic, we tackle this challenge by introducing a basic support for runtime adaptation of systems developed in our framework. We consider this feature as a potent starting point for our future research.

6   Related Work

Recently significant increase of interest in RT Java is reflected by an intensive research in the area. However, focus is laid on implementation layer issues, e.g. RTSJ compliant patterns [1,5,17], rather than on RTSJ frameworks where only a few projects are involved. Apart from these few frameworks, other projects are recently emerging with features similar to our work.

Compadres [14], one of the most recent projects, proposes a component framework for distributed real-time embedded systems. A hierarchical component model where each component is allocated either in a scoped or immortal memory is designed. However, the model supports only event-oriented interactions between components. On the contrary to our approach, components can be allocated only in scoped or immortal memories, therefore communication with regular non-real-time parts of applications can not be expressed. Since the co-existence of real-time and non-real-time elements of an application is often considered as one of the biggest advantages of RTSJ, we believe that it should be addressed also by its component model. Compadres also proposes a design process of real-time applications. However, a solution introducing systematically the real-time concerns into the functional architecture is not proposed, thus the complexities of designing real-time systems are not mitigated.

Work introduced in [12] also defines a hierarchical component model for Real-Time Java. Here, components can be either active or passive. Similarly to our work, active components with their own thread of control represent real-time threads. However, the real-time memory management concerns can not be expressed independently of the functional architecture, systems are thus developed already with real-time concerns which not only lay additional burdens on designers but also hinders later adaptability.

The project Golden Gate [10] introduces real-time components that encapsulate the functional code to support the RTSJ memory management. However, the work is focused only on the memory management aspects of RTSJ, the usage of real-time threads together with their limitations is not addressed.

The work published in [4] presents a new programming model for RTSJ based on aspect-oriented approach. Similarly to our approach, the real-time concerns are completely separated from applications base code. Although, as we have shown in [18], aspect- and component-oriented approaches are complementary, but the component-oriented approach offers more higher-level perspective of system development and brings a more transparent way of managing non-functional properties with only slightly bigger overhead.

The DiSCo project [15] addresses future space missions where key challenges are hard real-time constraints for applications running in embedded environment, partitioning between applications having different levels of criticality, and distributed computing. Therefore, similarly to our goals, the project addresses applications containing units that face variously hard real-time constraints. Here, an interesting convergence of both solutions can be revealed. The DiSCo Space-Oriented Middleware introduces a component model where each component provides a wide set of *component controllers* - a feature extensively supported by our solution.

The work introduced in [6] investigates fitness criteria of RTSJ in model-driven engineering process that includes automated code generation. The authors identify a basic set of requirements on code generation process. From this point of view, we can consider our generation tool as an implementation fully compatible to the ideas proposed in this work. We further confront our approach with these requirements in Section 5.2.

7   Conclusion and Future Work

This paper presents a component framework designed for development of real-time and embedded systems with the Real-Time Specification for Java (RTSJ). Our goal is to alleviate the development process by providing means to manipulate real-time concerns in a disciplined way during the development and execution life cycle of the system. Furthermore, we shield the developers from the complexities of the RTSJ-specific code implementation by separation of concerns and automatical generation of the execution infrastructure.

Therefore, we employ a component model comprising the RTSJ-related aspects that allows us to clearly define real-time concepts as software entities and to manipulate them through all the steps of the system development. Consequently, we define a methodology that gradually introduces real-time concerns into the system architecture, thus mitigating complexities of this process. Finally, we alleviate the implementation phase by providing a process generating automatically a middleware layer that manages real-time and non-functional properties of the system.

Our evaluation study shows that we deliver predictable systems and the overhead of the framework is considerably reduced by the optimization heuristics we implement. Moreover, we achieve an effective footprint reduction making the output systems suitable for the embedded domain.

As for the future work, our primary goal is to extend our framework to support design and infrastructure generation for additional non-functional properties, e.g. distribution support. Furthermore, we design our framework with stress on adaptability of real-time and embedded systems, thus the framework provides a basic support for dynamic adaptability of all system components. However, to comprehensively address this issue, adaptation of real-time components needs to be managed, we therefore plan to fully tackle this challenging topic in our future work.

References

1. Corsaro, A., Santoro, C.: The Analysis and Evaluation of Design Patterns for Distributed Real-Time Java Software. In: 16th IEEE International Conference on Emerging Technologies and Factory Automation (2005)
2. Plšek, A., Merle, P., Seinturier, L.: A Real-Time Java Component Model. In: Proceedings of the 11thInternational Symposium on Object/Component/Service-oriented Real-Time Distributed Computing (ISORC 2008), Orlando, Florida, USA, May 2008, pp. 281–288. IEEE Computer Society, Los Alamitos (2008)
3. Wellings, A.: Concurrent and Real-Time Programming in Java. John Wiley and Sons, Chichester (2004)
4. Andreae, C., Coady, Y., Gibbs, C., Noble, J., Vitek, J., Zhao, T.: Scoped Types and Aspects for Real-time Java Memory Management. Real-Time Syst. 37(1), 1–44 (2007)
5. Benowitz, E.G., Niessner, A.F.: A Patterns Catalog for RTSJ Software Designs. In: Meersman, R., Tari, Z. (eds.) OTM-WS 2003. LNCS, vol. 2889, pp. 497–507. Springer, Heidelberg (2003)
6. Bordin, M., Vardanega, T.: Real-time Java from an Automated Code Generation Perspective. In: JTRES 2007: Proceedings of the 5th international workshop on Java technologies for real-time and embedded systems, pp. 63–72. ACM, New York (2007)
7. Bures, T., Hnetynka, P., Plasil, F.: SOFA 2.0: Balancing Advanced Features in a Hierarchical Component Model. In: SERA 2006: Proc. of the 4th International Conference on Software Engineering Research, Management and Applications, USA, pp. 40–48. IEEE Computer Society, Los Alamitos (2006)
8. Gough, C., Hall, A., Masters, H., Stevens, A.: Real-Time Java: Writing and Deploying RT-Java Applications (2007),
http://www.ibm.com/developerworks/java/library/j-rtj5/
9. Clarke, M., Blair, G.S., Coulson, G., Parlavantzas, N.: An Efficient Component Model for the Construction of Adaptive Middleware. In: Guerraoui, R. (ed.) Middleware 2001. LNCS, vol. 2218, p. 160. Springer, Heidelberg (2001)
10. Dvorak, D., Bollella, G., Canham, T., Carson, V., Champlin, V., Giovannoni, B., Indictor, M., Meyer, K., Murray, A., Reinholtz, K.: Project Golden Gate: Towards Real-Time Java in Space Missions. In: ISORC, pp. 15–22 (2004)
11. Bruneton, E., Coupaye, T., Leclercq, M., Quéma, V., Stefani, J.B.: The Fractal Component Model and its Support in Java. Software: Practice and Experience 36, 1257–1284 (2006)

12. Etienne, J., Cordry, J., Bouzefrane, S.: Applying the CBSE Paradigm in the Real-Time Specification for Java. In: JTRES 2006: Proceedings of the 4th international workshop on Java technologies for real-time and embedded systems, USA, pp. 218–226. ACM, New York (2006)
13. Bollela, G., Gosling, J., Brosgol, B., Dibble, P., Furr, S., Turnbull, M.: The Real-Time Specification for Java. Addison-Wesley, Reading (2000)
14. Hu, J., Gorappa, S., Colmenares, J.A., Klefstad, R.: Compadres: A Lightweight Component Middleware Framework for Composing Distributed, Real-Time, Embedded Systems with Real-Time Java. In: Proc. ACM/IFIP/USENIX 8th Int'l Middleware Conference (Middleware 2007), vol. 4834, pp. 41–59 (2007)
15. Prochazka, M., Fowell, S., Planche, L.: DisCo Space-Oriented Middleware: Architecture of a Distributed Runtime Environment for Complex Spacecraft On-Board Applications. In: 4th European Congress on Embedded Real-Time Software (ERTS 2008), Toulouse, France (2008)
16. Pawlak, R., Noguera, C., Petitprez, N.: Spoon: Program Analysis and Transformation in Java. Technical report rr-5901, INRIA (2006)
17. Pizlo, F., Fox, J.M., Holmes, D., Vitek, J.: Real-Time Java Scoped Memory: Design Patterns and Semantics. In: Seventh IEEE International Symposium on Object-Oriented Real-Time Distributed Computing (ISORC 2004), pp. 101–110 (2004)
18. Seinturier, L., Pessemier, N., Duchien, L., Coupaye, T.: A Component Model Engineered with Components and Aspects. In: Gorton, I., Heineman, G.T., Crnković, I., Schmidt, H.W., Stafford, J.A., Szyperski, C., Wallnau, K. (eds.) CBSE 2006. LNCS, vol. 4063, pp. 139–153. Springer, Heidelberg (2006)

DeXteR – An Extensible Framework for Declarative Parameter Passing in Distributed Object Systems

Sriram Gopal, Wesley Tansey, Gokulnath C. Kannan, and Eli Tilevich

Department of Computer Science
Virginia Tech, Blacksburg, VA 24061, USA
{sriramg,tansey,gomaths,tilevich}@cs.vt.edu

Abstract. In modern distributed object systems, reference parameters are passed to a remote method based on their runtime type. We argue that such type-based parameter passing is limiting with respect to expressiveness, readability, and maintainability, and that parameter passing semantics should be decoupled from parameter types. We present *declarative parameter passing*, an approach that fully decouples parameter passing semantics from parameter types in distributed object systems. In addition, we describe DeXteR, an extensible framework for transforming a type-based remote parameter passing model to a declaration-based model transparently. Our framework leverages aspect-oriented and generative programming techniques to enable adding new remote parameter passing semantics, without requiring detailed understanding of the underlying middleware implementation. Our approach is applicable to both application and library code and incurs negligible performance overhead. We validate the expressive power of our framework by adding several non-trivial remote parameter passing semantics (i.e., copy-restore, lazy, streaming) to Java RMI.

Keywords: Extensible Middleware, Metadata, Parameter Passing, Aspect Oriented Programming, Declarative Programming.

1 Introduction

Organizations have hundreds of workstations connected into local area networks (LANs) that stay unused for hours at a time. Consider leveraging these idle computing resources for distributed scientific computation. Specifically, we would like to set up an ad-hoc grid that will use the idle workstations to solve bioinformatics problems. The ad-hoc grid will coordinate the constituent workstations to align, mutate, and cross DNA sequences, thereby solving a computationally intensive problem in parallel.

Each workstation has a standard Java Virtual Machine (JVM) installed, and the LAN environment makes Java RMI a viable distribution middleware choice. As a distributed object model for Java, RMI simplifies distributed programming by exposing remote method invocations through a convenient programming

V. Issarny and R. Schantz (Eds.): Middleware 2008, LNCS 5346, pp. 144–163, 2008.

model. In addition, the synchronous communication model of Java RMI aligns well with the reliable networking environment of a LAN.

The bioinformatics application follows a simple Master-Worker architecture, with classes `Sequence`, `SequenceDB`, and `Worker` representing a DNA sequence, a collection of sequences, and a worker process, respectively. Class `Worker` implements three computatinally-intensive methods: `align`, `cross`, and `mutate`.

```
interface WorkerInterface {
   void align(SequenceDB allSeqs, SequenceDB candidates, Sequence toMatch);
   Sequence cross(Sequence s1, Sequence s2);
   void mutate(SequenceDB seqs);
}
```

```
class Worker implements WorkerInterface { ... }
```

The `align` method iterates over a collection of candidate sequences (`candidates`), adding to the global collection (`allSeqs`) those sequences that satisfy a minimum alignment threshold. The `cross` method simulates the crossing over of two sequences (e.g., during mating) and returns the offspring sequence. Finally, the `mutate` method simulates the effect of a gene therapy treatment on a collection of sequences, thereby mutating the contents of every sequence in the collection.

Consider using Java RMI to distribute this application on an ad-hoc grid, so that multiple workers could solve the problem in parallel. To ensure good performance, we need to select the most appropriate semantics for passing parameters to remote methods. However, as we argue next, despite its Java-like programming model, RMI uses a different remote parameter passing model that is *type-based*. That is, the runtime type of a reference parameter determines the semantics by which RMI passes it to remote methods. We argue that this parameter passing model has serious shortcomings, with negative consequences for the development, understanding, and maintenance of distributed applications.

Method `align` takes two parameters of type `SequenceDB`: allseqs and candidates. allseqs is an extremely large global collection that is being updated by multiple workers. We, therefore, need to pass it by *remote-reference*. candidates, on the other hand, is a much smaller collection that is being used only by a single worker. We, therefore, need to pass it by *copy*, so that its contents can be examined and compared efficiently. To pass parameters by *remote-reference* and by *copy*, the RMI programmer has to create subclasses implementing marker interfaces `Remote` and `Serializable`, respectively. As a consequence, method `align`'s signature must be changed as well. Passing allSeqs by *remote-reference* requires the type of allSeqs to become a remote interface. Finally, examining the declaration of the remote method `align` would give no indication about how its parameters are passed, forcing the programmer to examine the declaration of each parameter's type. In addition, in the absence of detailed source code comments, the programmer has no choice but to examine the logic of the entire slice [3] of a distributed application that can affect the runtime type of a remote parameter.

Method **mutate** mutates the contents of every sequence in its **seqs** parameter. Since the client needs to use the mutated sequences, the changes have to be reflected in the client's JVM. The situation at hand renders passing by *remote-reference* ineffective, since the large number of remote callbacks is likely to incur a significant performance overhead. One approach is to pass **seqs** by *copy-restore*, a semantics which efficiently approximates *remote-reference* under certain assumptions [22].

Because Java RMI does not natively support *copy-restore*, one could use a custom implementation provided either by a third-party vendor or an in-house expert programmer. Mainstream middleware, however, does not provide programming facilities for such extensions. Thus, adding a new semantics would not only require a detailed understanding of the RMI implementation, but also sufficient privileges to modify the Java installation on each available idle workstation.

Finally, consider the task of maintaining the resulting ad-hoc grid distributed application. Assume that **SequenceDB** is a remote type in one version of the application, such that RMI will pass all instances **SequenceDB** by *remote-reference*. However, if a maintenance task necessitates passing some instance of **SequenceDB** using different semantics, the **SequenceDB** type would have to be changed. Nevertheless, if **SequenceDB** is part of a third-party library, it may not be subject to modification by the maintenance programmer.

To overcome the limitations of a type-based remote parameter passing model, we present an alternative, *declarative* model. We argue that remote parameter passing should resemble that of local parameter passing in mainstream programming languages. Following this paradigm, a passing mechanism for each parameter is specified at the declaration of each remote method. By decoupling parameter passing from parameter types, our approach increases expressiveness, improves readability, and eases maintainability.

Unsurprisingly, mainstream programming languages such as C, C++, and C# express the choice of parameter passing mechanisms through method declarations with special tokens instead of types. For example, by default objects in C++ are passed by *value*, but inserting the **&** token after the type of a parameter signals the by *reference* mechanism. We argue that distributed object systems should adhere to a similar declarative paradigm for remote method calls, but properly designed for distributed communication.

While Java always uses the by *value* semantics for local calls, we argue that distributed communication requires a richer set of semantics to ensure good performance and to increase flexibility. We also argue that IDL-based distributed object systems such as CORBA [11] and DCOM [1] with their **in**, **out**, and **inout** parameter modes stop short of a fully declarative parameter model and are not extensible.

Recognizing that many existing distributed applications are built upon a type-based model, we present a technique for transforming a type-based remote parameter passing model to use a declaration-based one. Our technique transforms parameter passing functionality transparently, without any changes to the underlying distributed object system implementation, ensuring cross-platform compatibility and ease of adoption. With Java RMI as our example domain, we combine aspect-oriented and generative techniques to retrofit its parameter passing functionality. Our approach is equally applicable to application classes, system classes, and third-party libraries.

In addition, we argue that a declarative model to remote parameter passing simplifies adding new semantics to an existing distributed object model. Specifically, we present an extensible plug-in-based framework, through which third-party vendors or in-house expert programmers can seamlessly extend a native set of remote parameter passing semantics with additional semantics. Our framework allows such extension in the application space, without modifying the JVM or its runtime classes. As a validation, we used our framework to extend the set of available parameter passing semantics of RMI with several non-trivial state-of-the-art semantics, introduced earlier in the literature both by us [22] and others [4,7,25].

One of the new semantics we implemented using our framework is an optimization of our own algorithm for *copy-restore* [22]. In the original implementation, the server sends back a complete copy of the parameter to the restore stage of the algorithm on the client, which is inefficient in high-latency, low-bandwidth networking environments. The implemented optimized version of the *copy-restore* algorithm, which we call *copy-restore with delta*, efficiently identifies and encodes the changes made by the server to the parameter, sending to the client only the resulting delta. Because the original *copy-restore* algorithm performs better in high-bandwidth networks, our extensible framework makes it possible to use different versions of the *copy-restore* algorithm for different remote calls in the same application.

We believe that the technical material presented in this paper makes the following novel contributions:

- A clear exposition of the shortcomings of type-based parameter passing models in modern distributed object systems such as CORBA, Java RMI, and .NET Remoting.
- An alternative declarative parameter passing approach that offers multiple design and implementation advantages.
- An extensible framework for retrofitting standard RMI applications to take advantage of our declaration based model and for extending the RMI native set of parameter passing semantics.
- An enhanced *copy-restore* mode of remote parameter passing, offering performance advantages for low bandwidth, high latency networks.

The rest of this paper is structured as follows. Section 2 presents DeXteR, our extensible framework. Section 3 describes how we used DeXteR to add several non-trivial parameter passing semantics to RMI. Section 4 discusses the advantages and constraints of our approach. Section 5 discusses related work. Finally, Section 6 outlines future work directions and conclusions.

2   The *DeXter* Framework

This section discusses the design and implementation of **DeXteR** (Declarative **Ext**ensible **R**emote Parameter Passing), a framework for declarative remote parameter passing.

2.1   Framework Overview

DeXteR implements declaration-based parameter passing semantics on top of standard Java RMI, without modifying its implementation. DeXteR uses a plug-in based architecture and treats remote parameter passing as a distributed cross-cutting concern. Each parameter passing style is an independent plugin component.

DeXteR uses the Interceptor Pattern [18] to expose the invocation context explicitly on the client and the server sites. While Interceptors have been used in several prior systems [8] to introduce orthogonal cross-cutting concerns such as logging and security, the novelty of our approach lies in employing Interceptors to transform and enhance the core functionality of a distributed object system, its remote parameter passing semantics.

Figure 1 depicts the overall translation strategy employed by DeXteR. The rank-and-file (i.e., application) programmer annotates an RMI application with the desired remote parameter passing semantics. The annotations processor takes the application source code as input, and extracts the programmer's intent. The extracted information parameterizes the source code generator, which encompasses the framework-specific code generator and the extension-specific code

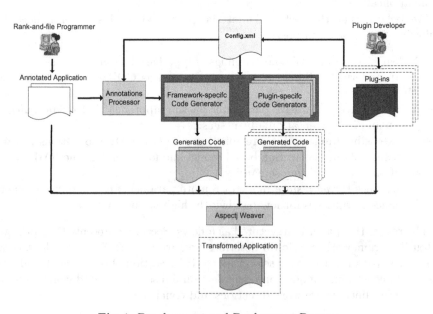

Fig. 1. Development and Deployment Process

generators. The framework-specific code generator synthesizes the code for the client and the server interceptors using aspects. The extension-specific code generators synthesize the code pertaining to the translation strategy for supporting a specific parameter passing semantics. DeXteR compiles the generated code into bytecode, and the resulting application uses standard Java RMI, only with a small AspectJ runtime library as an extra dependency. The generated aspects are weaved into the respective classes at load-time, thereby redirecting the invocation to the framework interceptors at both the local and the remote sites.

2.2 Framework API

DeXteR provides interception points for parameter passing plugins in the form of the `InterceptionPoint` interface. Developing a new plugin involves implementing this interface and identifying the interception points of interest, providing the functionality at these interception points, and registering the plugin with the framework.

```
interface InterceptionPoint {
    // Interception points on client-side
    Object [] argsBeforeClientCall(Object target, Object [] args);
    Object [] customArgsBeforeClientCall(Object target);
    Object retAfterClientCall(Object target, Object ret);
    void customRetAfterClientCall(Object target, Object [] customRets);

    // Interception points on server-side
    Object [] argsBeforeServerCall(Object target, Object [] args);
    void customArgsBeforeServerCall(Object target, Object [] customArgs);
    Object retAfterServerCall(Object target, Object ret);
    Object[] customRetAfterServerCall(Object target);

    // Plugin-specific code generator
    void generate(AnnotationInfo info);
}
```

The above interface exposes the invocation context of a remote call at different points of its control-flow on both the client and server sites. DeXteR exposes to a plugin only the invocation context pertaining to the corresponding parameter passing annotation. For example, plugin X obtains access only to those remote parameters annotated with annotation X. DeXteR enables plugins to modify the original invocation arguments as well as to send custom information between the client- and the server-side extensions. The custom information is simply piggy-backed to the original invocation context.

2.3 Implementation Details

The interception is implemented by combining aspect-oriented and generative programming techniques. Specifically, DeXteR uses AspectJ to add extra methods to RMI remote interface, stub, and server implementation classes for each remote method. These methods follow the Proxy pattern to interpose the logic required to support various remote parameter passing strategies. Specifically, the flow of a remote call is intercepted to invoke the plugins with the annotated parameters, and the modified set of parameters is obtained. The intercepted invocation on the client site is then redirected to the added extra method on the server. The added server method reverses the process, invoking the parameter passing style plugins with the modified set of parameters provided by their client-side peers. The resulting parameters are used to make the invocation on the actual server method. A similar process occurs when the call returns, in order to support different passing styles for return types.

For each remote method, DeXteR injects a wrapper method into the remote interface and the server implementation using *inter-type declarations*, and pointcuts on the execution of that method in the stub (i.e., implemented as a dynamic proxy) to provide a wrapper in the form of an *around* advice. All the AspectJ code that provides the interception functionality is automatically generated at compile time, based on the remote method's signature.

2.4   Bioinformatics Example Revisited

DeXteR enables the programmer to express remote parameter passing semantics exclusively by annotating remote method declarations with the intended passing semantics. A distributed version of the bioinformatics application from section 1 can be expressed using DeXteR as follows. The different parameter passing semantics are introduced without affecting the semantics of the centralized version of the application.

```
public interface WorkerInterface extends Remote
{
    void align(@RemoteRef SequenceDB matchingSeqs,
               @Copy SequenceDB candidates,
               @Copy Sequence toMatch) throws RemoteException;

    @Copy Sequence cross(@Copy Sequence s1, @Copy Sequence s2)
                        throws RemoteException;
    void mutate(@CopyRestore SequenceDB seqs)
                        throws RemoteException;
}
```

Since remote parameter passing annotations are part of a remote method's signature, they must appear in both the method declaration in the remote interface and the method definitions in all remote classes implementing the interface. This requirement ensures that the client is informed about how remote parameters will be passed, and it also allows for safe polymorphism (i.e., the same remote interface may have multiple remote classes implementing it). We argue, however, that this requirement should not impose any additional burden on the programmer. A modern IDE such as Eclipse, NetBeans, or Visual Studio should be able to reproduce the annotations when providing method stub implementations for remote interfaces.

3   Supporting Parameter Passing Semantics

This section describes the strategies for implementing several non-trivial parameter passing semantics previously proposed in the research literature [22,7,25,4] as DeXteR plugins. We restrict our description to parameters, as the strategies for handling return types are identical.

To demonstrate the power and expressiveness of our approach, we chose the semantics that have very different implementation requirements. While the lazy semantics requires flexible proxying on-demand, copy-restore requires passing extra information between the client and the server. Despite the contrasting nature of these semantics, we were able to encapsulate all their implementation logic inside their respective plugins and easily deploy them using DeXteR.

3.1   Lazy Semantics

Lazy parameter passing [7], also known as *lazy pass-by-value*, provides a useful semantics for asynchronous distributed environments, specifically in P2P applications. It works by passing the object initially by reference and then transferring it by value either upon first use (*implicitly lazy*) or at a point dictated by the application (*explicitly lazy*). More precisely, lazy parameter passing defines *if and when exactly an object is to be passed by value*.

The translation strategy for passing reference objects by *lazy* semantics involves using the plugin-specific code generator. As our aim is to decouple parameter types from the semantics by which they are passed, to pass a parameter of

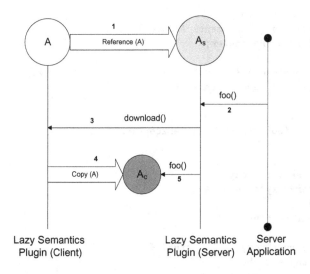

Fig. 2. Lazy Semantics Plugin Interaction Diagram (*A*: Serializable Object; A_s: Stub of A; A_c: Copy of A; (1) A is passed from client to server; (2) Server invokes foo() on stub A_s; (3) Server plugin calls download() on client plugin; (4) Client plugin sends a copy of A, A_c; (5) Server plugin calls foo() on A_c.)

type A by *lazy* semantics does not require defining any special interface nor A implementing one. Instead, the plugin-specific code generator generates a Remote interface, declaring all the accessible methods of A. To make our approach applicable for passing both application and system classes, we deliberately avoid making any changes to the bytecode of a parameter's class A. Instead, we use a delegating dynamic proxy (e.g., A_DynamicProxy) for the generated Remote interface (e.g., AIface) and generate a corresponding server-side proxy (e.g., A_ServerProxy) that is type-compatible with the parameter's class A. As is common with proxy replacements for remote communication [6], all the direct field accesses of the *remote-reference* parameter on the server are replaced with accessor and mutator methods.[1]

In order to enable obtaining a copy of the remote parameter (at some point in execution), the plugin inserts an additional method download() in the generated remote interface AIface, the client proxy A_DynamicProxy and the server proxy A_ServerProxy.

```
class A {
  public void foo() {...}
}

// Generated remote interface
interface AIface extends Remote {
    public void foo() throws RemoteException;
    public A download() throws RemoteException;
}

// Generated client proxy
class A_DynamicProxy implements AIface {
    private A remoteParameter;

    public A download() {
       // serialize remoteParameter
    }

    public void foo() throws RemoteException { ... }
}

// Generated server proxy
class A_ServerProxy extends A {
    private A a;
    private AIface stub;

    public A_ServerProxy(AIface stub) {
       this.stub = stub;
    }
```

---

[1] Replacing direct fields accesses with methods has become such a common transformation that AspectJ [13] provides special fields access pointcuts (i.e., set, get) to support it.

```
    synchronized void download() {
        // Obtain a copy of the remote parameter
        a = stub.download();
    }

    public void foo() {
        // Dereference the stub
        stub.download();
        // Invoke the method on the copy
        a.foo();
    }
}
```

Any invocation made on the parameter (i.e., server proxy) by the server results in a call to its `synchronized download()` method, if a local copy of the parameter is not yet available. The `download()` method of the server proxy relays the call to the `download()` method of the enclosed client proxy with the aim of obtaining a copy of the remote parameter.

The client proxy needs to serialize a copy of the parameter. However, passing a remote object (i.e., one that implements a `Remote` interface) by *copy* presents a unique challenge, as type-based parameter passing mechanisms are deeply entangled with Java RMI. The RMI runtime replaces the object with its stub, effectively forcing pass by *remote-reference*. The plugin-generated code overrides this default functionality of Java RMI by rendering a given remote object as a memory buffer using Serialization. This technique effectively "hides" the remote object, as the RMI runtime transfers memory buffers without inspecting or modifying their content. The "hidden" remote object can then be extracted from the buffer on the server-side and used as a parameter. Once the copy is obtained, all subsequent invocations made on the parameter (i.e., server proxy) are delegated to the local copy of the parameter.

Thus, passing an object of type A as a parameter to a remote method will result in the client-side plugin replacing it with its type-incompatible stub. The server-side plugin wraps this type-incompatible stub into the generated server-side proxy that is type-compatible with the original remote object.

We note that a subset of the strategies described above is used for supporting the native semantics *copy* and *remote-reference*.

3.2 Copy Restore Semantics

A semantics with a different set of implementation requirements than that of *lazy* parameter passing is the *copy-restore* semantics. It copies a parameter to the server and then restores the changes to the original object in place (i.e., preserving client-side aliases).

Implementing the *copy-restore* semantics involves tracing the invocation arguments and restoring the changes made by the server after the call. The task

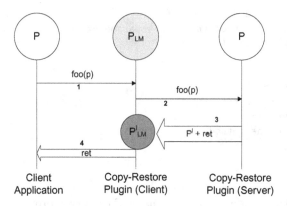

Fig. 3. Copy-Restore Semantics Plugin Interaction Diagram (P: Set of parameters passed to foo; P_{LM}: Linear map of parameters; P^l: Modified parameters (restorable data); *ret*: values returned by the invocation; $P^l{}_{LM}$: Modified linear map; (1) The client invokes method foo() passing parameter p; (2) The client-side plugin constructs a linear map P_{LM} and calls the original foo(p); (3) Server-side plugin invokes foo and returns modified parameters P^l and the return value *ret*; (4) Changes restored and the return value *ret* is passed to the client.)

is simplified by the well-defined hook points provided by the framework. Prior to the remote method invocation, the *copy-restore* plugin obtains a copy of the parameter A and does some pre-processing on both the client and the server sites. The invocation then resumes and the server mutates the parameter during the call. Once the call completes, the server-side plugin needs to send back the changes to the parameter made by the server to its client-side peer. This is accomplished using the custom information passing facility provided by the framework. The client-side plugin uses this information from its server-side peer to restore the changes to the parameter A in the client's JVM.

3.3   Copy Restore with Delta Semantics

For single-threaded clients and stateless servers, *copy-restore* makes remote calls indistinguishable from local calls as far as parameter passing is concerned [22]. However, in a low bandwidth high latency networking environment, such as in a typical wireless network, the reference *copy-restore* implementation may be inefficient. The potential inefficiency lies in the restore step of the algorithm, which always sends back to the client an entire object graph of the parameter, no matter how much of it has been modified by the server. To optimize the implementation of *copy-restore* for low bandwidth, high latency networks, the restore step can send back a "delta" structure by encoding the differences between the original and the modified objects. The necessity for such an optimized *copy-restore* implementation again presents a compelling case for extensibility and flexibility in remote parameter passing.

The following pseudo-code describes our optimized *copy-restore* algorithm, which we term *copy restore with delta*:

1. Create and keep a linear map of all the objects transitively reachable from the parameter.
2. On the server, again create a linear map, Lmap1, of all the objects transitively reachable from the parameter.
3. Deep copy Lmap1 to an isomorphic linear map Lmap2.
4. Execute the remote method, modifying the parameter and Lmap1, but not Lmap2.
5. Return Lmap1 back to the client; when serializing Lmap1, encode the changes to the parameter by comparing with Lmap2 as follows:
   (a) Write as is each changed existing object or a newly added object.
   (b) Write its numeric index in Lmap1 for each unchanged existing object.
6. On the client, replay the encoded changes, using the client-side linear map to retrieve the original old objects at the specified indexes.

Creating Linear Map. A linear map of objects transitively reachable from a reference argument is obtained by tapping into serialization, recording each encountered object during the traversal. In order not to interfere with garbage collection, all linear maps use weak references.

Calculating Delta. The algorithm encodes the delta information efficiently using a handle structure shown below.

```
class Handle{
    int id;
    ArrayList<Long> chId;
    ArrayList<Long> chScript;
    ArrayList<Object> chObject;
}
```

The identifier `id` refers to the position of an object in the client site linear map. The change indicator `chId` identifies the modified member fields using a bit level encoding. `chScript` contains the changes to be replayed on the old object. For a primitive field, its index simply contains the new value, whereas for an object field, its index points to `chObject`, which contains the modified references.

Restoring Changes. For each de-serialized handle on the client, the corresponding old object is obtained from the client's linear map using the handle identifier `id`. The handle is replaced with the old object, and the changes encoded in the handle are replayed on it. Following the change restoration, garbage collection reclaims the unused references.

As a concrete example of our algorithm, consider a simple binary tree, `t`, of integers. Every node in the tree has three fields: `data`, `left`, and `right`. A subset of the tree is aliased by non-tree pointers `alias1` and `alias2`. Consider a remote method such as the one show below, to which tree `t` is passed as a parameter.

```
void alterTree (Tree tree) {
    tree.left.data = 0;
    tree.right.data = 9;
    tree.right.right.data = 8;
    tree.left = null;
    Tree temp = new Tree (2, tree.right.right, null);
    tree.right.right = null;
    tree.right = temp;
}
```

Figure 4 shows the sequence of steps involved in passing tree t by *copy restore with delta* and restoring the changes made by the remote method alterTree to the original tree.

We measured the performance gains of our algorithm over the original copy-restore by conducting a series of micro-benchmarks, varying the size of a binary

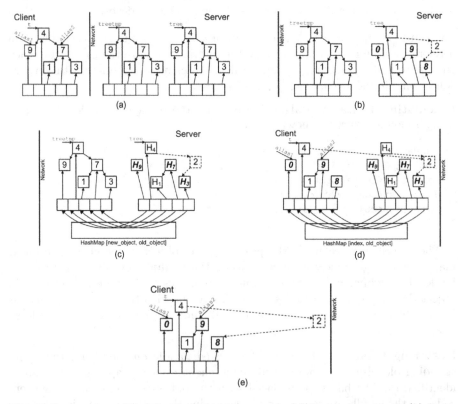

Fig. 4. *Copy-restore with delta* algorithm by example (a) State after step 3. (b) State after step 4. The remote procedure modified the parameter. (c) State during step 5. Copy the modified objects (even those no longer reachable through tree) back to the client; compute the delta script for modified objects using a hash map. (d) State during step 6. Replace the handles with the original old objects; replay the delta script to reflect changes. (e) State of the client side object after step 6.

tree and the amount of changes performed by the server. The benchmarks were run on Pentium 2.GHz (dual core) machines with 2 GB RAM, running Sun JVM version 1.6.0 on an 802.11b wireless LAN. Figure 5 shows the percentage of performance gain of copy-restore with delta over copy-restore. Overall, our experiments indicate that the performance gain is directly proportional to the size of the object graph and is inversely proportional to the amount of changes made to the object graph by the server.

By providing flexibility in parameter passing, DeXteR enables programmers to use different semantics or different variations of the same semantics as determined by the nature of the application. For instance, within the same application one can use regular *copy-restore* for passing small parameters and *copy-restore with delta* for passing large parameters.

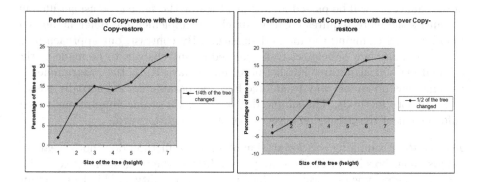

Fig. 5. Performance gain of copy-restore with delta over copy-restore

3.4   Other Semantics

Additional semantics we implemented using DeXteR include *streaming* [25], *parameter substitution a.k.a caching* [4], and some others. Due to space constraints, we do not explain them in detail.

DeXteR offers the advantages of supporting a wide variety of remote parameter passing semantics through a uniform API. Developments in hardware and software designs are likely to cause the creation of new parameter passing semantics. These semantics will leverage the new designs, but may be too experimental to be included in the implementation of a standard middleware system. DeXteR will allow the integration and use of these novel semantics at the application layer, without changing the underlying middleware. As a particular example, consider the introduction of massive parallelism into mainstream processors. Multiple cores will require the use of explicit parallelism to improve performance. Some facets of parameter passing are computation-intensive and can benefit from parallel processing. One can imagine, for instance, how marshaling could be performed in parallel, in which parts an object graph are serialized/deserialized by different cores.

4   Discussion

This section discusses the advantages of DeXteR as well as some of the constraints of our design.

4.1   Design Advantages

Expressing remote parameter passing choices as a part of the method declaration has several advantages over a type-based system. Specifically, a declarative approach increases expressiveness, improves readability, and eases maintainability. To further illustrate the advantages of our declarative framework, we compare and contrast our approach with that of Java RMI.

Expressiveness. Java RMI restricts expressiveness by assuming that all instances of the same type will be passed identically. Passing the same type using different semantics therefore requires creating subclasses implementing different marker interfaces and changing the method signature. By contrast, our approach does not require any new subclasses to be created or any changes to be made to the original method signature. Furthermore, under Java RMI, the programmer of the class has no simple way to enforce how the parameters are actually passed to its remote methods. The simple declarative style of our annotations makes enforcement of the parameter passing policies straightforward.

Readability. Examining the declaration of a remote method does not reveal any details about how its parameters are passed, forcing the programmer to examine each parameter type individually, which reduces readability and hinders program understanding. By contrast, our approach provides a single point of reference that explicitly informs the programmer about how remote parameters are passed.

Maintainability. An existing class may have to be modified to implement an interface before its instances can be passed as parameters to a remote method. This complicates maintainability as, in the case of third-party libraries, source code may be difficult or even impossible to modify. By contrast, our approach enables the maintenance programmer modify the semantics by simply specifying a different parameter passing annotation.

Extensibility. Even if the *copy-restore* semantics gets the attention of the Java community and is natively supported in the next version of Java, including new optimization mechanisms such as using *copy-restore with delta* would still mean modifying the underlying Java RMI implementation of both the client and the server. By contrast, our approach supports extending the native remote parameter passing semantics at the application-level, requiring absolutely no modifications to the underlying middleware.

Reusability. DeXteR also enables providing the parameter passing semantics as plugin libraries. Application programmers thus can obtain third-party plugins and automatically enhance their own RMI applications with the new parameter passing semantics.

Efficiency. Another advantage of our approach is its efficiency. That is, all the transformations described in Section 3 do not result in any additional overhead in using objects of type A until they are passed using a particular mode in an RMI call. This requires that one know exactly when an object of type A is used in this capacity. The insight that makes it possible to efficiently detect such cases is that the program execution flow must enter an RMI stub (dynamic proxy) for a remote call to occur.

To measure the overhead of DeXteR, we ran a series of microbenchmarks comparing the execution times of the DeXteR-based parameter passing semantics' implementations and their native counterparts, of which pass by *remote-reference* is of particular interest. In lieu of support for type-compatible dynamic proxies for classes in Java, our *remote-reference* DeXteR plugin emulates this functionality using a type-incompatible client-side dynamic proxy and a type-compatible server-side wrapper proxy. Thus, this emulated functionality introduces two new levels of indirection compared to the standard Java RMI implementation of this semantics. As any new level of indirection inherently introduces some performance overhead, it is important to verify that it is not prohibitively expensive.

To distill the pure overhead, we ran the benchmarks on a single machine. In the presence of network communication and added latency, the overhead incurred by the additional levels of local indirection would be dominated. Therefore, the results do not unfairly benefit our approach. The resulting overhead never exceeds a few percentage points of the total latency of a remote call executed on a single machine. Due to space constraints, we do not present the detailed results of this experiment here, but the interested reader can find them in reference [9]. In general, as the latency of a remote call is orders of magnitude greater than that of a local call, the overhead incurred by a DeXteR plugin adding a few simple local calls to a remote call should be negligible.

4.2   Design Constraints

Achieving the afore-mentioned advantages without changing the Java language required constraining our design in the following ways.

First, array objects are always passed by *copy* though the array elements could be passed using any desired semantics. While this is a limitation of our system, it is still nonetheless a strict improvement over standard RMI, which also passes array objects by *copy*, but passes array elements based on their runtime type.

Second, passing `final` classes (not extending `UnicastRemoteObject`) by *remote-reference* would entail either removing their `final` specifier or performing a sophisticated global replacement with an isomorphic type [23]. This requirement stems from our translation strategy's need to create a proxy subclass for *remote-reference* parameters, an impossibility for `final` classes. Since heavy transformations would clash with our design goal of simplicity, our approach issues a compile-time error to an attempt to pass an instance of a `final` class by *remote-reference*. Again, this limitation is also shared by standard RMI.

Finally, since our approach does not modify standard Java, it is not possible to support direct member field access for instances of system classes passed by

Table 1. Analysis of Java 6 JDK's public member fields (some overlap exists due to Exception classes spanning multiple packages)

Classes Analyzed	Total	Classes With Public Fields	Total Public Fields
All User-Accessible Classes	2732	57	123
GUI Classes	913	15	65
Exception Classes	364	33	34
RMI Classes	58	22	22
Java Bean Classes	56	3	3

remote-reference. While this is a conceptual problem, an analysis of the Java 6 library shown in Table 1 indicates that this is not a practical problem. For our purposes, we analyzed the java.* and javax.* classes, as they are typically the ones mostly used by application developers. As the table demonstrates, approximately 1% of classes contain non-final member fields. However, the vast majority of these classes are either GUI or sound components, SQL driver descriptors, RMI internal classes, or exception classes, and as such, are unlikely to be passed by *remote-reference.* Additionally, the classes in java.beans.* provide getter methods for their public fields, thereby not requiring direct access. The conclusion of our analysis is that only one (java.io.StreamTokenizer) of the more than 5,500 analyzed classes could potentially pose a problem, with two public member fields not accessible by getter methods.

5   Related Work

The body of research literature on distributed object systems and separation of concerns is extremely large and diverse. The following discusses only closely-related state of the art.

Separation of Concerns. Several language-based and middleware-based approaches address the challenges in modeling cross-cutting concerns.

Proxies and Wrappers [20] introduce late bound cross-cutting features, though in an application-specific manner.

Aspect Oriented Programming (AOP) [14] is a methodology for modularizing cross-cutting concerns. Several prior AOP approaches aim at improving various properties of middleware systems, with the primary focus on modularization [5,26].

Java Aspect Components (JAC) [17] and DJCutter [15] support distributed AOP. JAC framework enables the dynamic adding or removing of an advice. DJCutter extends AspectJ with *remote pointcuts*, a special language construct for developing distributed systems. DeXteR could use these approaches as an alternative to AspectJ.

A closely related work is the DADO [24] system for programming cross-cutting features in distributed heterogeneous systems. Similar to DeXteR, DADO uses hook-based extension patterns. It employs a pair of user-defined adaplets, explicitly modeled using IDL for expressing the cross-cutting behavior. To accommodate heterogeneity, DADO employs a custom DAIDL (an IDL extension) compiler, runtime software extensions, and tool support for dynamically retrofitting services into CORBA applications. DADO uses the Portable Interceptor approach for triggering the advice for cross-cutting concerns, which do not modify invocation arguments and return types. Thus, using DADO to change built-in remote parameter passing semantics would not eliminate the need for binary transformations and code generation.

Remote Parameter Passing. Multi-language distributed object systems such as CORBA [11], DCOM [1], etc., use an Interface Definition Language (IDL) to express how parameters are passed to remote methods. Each parameter in a remote method signature is associated with keywords `in`, `out`, and `inout` designating the different passing options. This approach however, does not completely decouple parameter passing from parameter types. When the IDL interface is mapped to a concrete language, the generated implementation still relies on a type-based parameter passing model of the target language. Specifically, in mapping IDL to Java [12], an IDL *valuetype* maps to a `Serializable` class, which is always passed by *copy*. Conversely, an IDL *interface* maps to a `Remote` class, which is always passed by *remote-reference*. Additionally, even if we constrain parameters to *valuetypes* only, the mapped implementation will generate different types based on the keyword modifiers present [10]. Thus, remote parameter passing in IDL-based distributed object systems is neither fully declarative, nor it is extensible.

.NET Remoting [16] for C# also follows a mixed approach to remote parameter passing. It supports the parameter-passing keywords *out* and *ref*. However, the *ref* keyword designates pass by *value-result* in remote calls rather than the standard pass by *reference* in local calls. This difference in passing semantics may lead to the introduction of subtle inconsistencies when adapting a centralized program for distributed execution. Furthermore, in the absence of any optional parameter passing keywords, a reference object is passed based on the parameter type. While this approach shares the limitations of Java RMI, *remote-reference* proxies are type-compatible stubs, which provide full access to the remote object's fields. Therefore, while the parameter passing model of .NET Remoting contains some declarative elements, it has shortcomings and is not extensible.

Doorastha [2] represents a closely related piece of work on increasing the expressiveness of distributed object systems. It aims at providing distribution transparency by enabling the programmer to annotate a centralized application with distribution tags such as *globalizable* and *by-refvalue*, and using a specialized compiler for processing the annotations to provide fine-grained control over the parameter passing functionality. While influenced by the design of Doorastha, our approach differs in the following ways. First, Doorastha does not completely decouple parameter passing from the parameter types, as it requires annotating classes of remote parameters with the desired passing style. Unannotated remote parameters are passed based on their type. Second, Doorastha does not support extending the default set of parameter passing modes. Finally, Doorastha requires a specialized compiler for processing the annotations. While Doorastha demonstrates the feasibility of many of our approach's features, we believe our work is the first to present a comprehensive argument and design for a purely declarative and extensible approach to remote parameter passing.

6   Future Work and Conclusions

A promising future work direction is to develop a declaration-based distributed object system for an emerging object-oriented language, such as *Ruby* [21], utilizing its advanced language features such as built-in aspects, closures, and co-routines. Despite its exploratory nature and the presence of advanced features, Ruby's distributed object system, *DRuby* [19], does not significantly differ from Java RMI.

We presented a framework for declarative parameter passing in distributed object systems as a better alternative to type-based parameter passing. We described how a declarative parameter passing model with multiple different semantics can be efficiently implemented on top of a type-based parameter passing model using our extensible framework, DeXteR. We believe that our framework is a powerful distributed programming platform and an experimentation facility for research in distributed object systems.

Availability. DeXteR can be downloaded from
http://research.cs.vt.edu/vtspaces/dexter.

Acknowledgments. The authors would like to thank Godmar Back, Doug Lea, Naren Ramakrishnan, and the anonymous reviewers, whose comments helped improve the paper. This research was supported by the Computer Science Department at Virginia Tech.

References

1. Brown, N., Kindel, C.: Distributed Component Object Model Protocol–DCOM/1.0 1998, Redmond, WA (1996)
2. Dahm, M.: Doorastha—a step towards distribution transparency. In: Proceedings of the Net. Object Days 2000 (2000)
3. De Lucia, A., Fasolino, A.R., Munro, M.: Understanding function behaviours through program slicing. In: 4th IEEE Workshop on Program Comprehension, pp. 9–18 (1996)
4. Eberhard, J., Tripathi, A.: Efficient Object Caching for Distributed Java RMI Applications. In: Guerraoui, R. (ed.) Middleware 2001. LNCS, vol. 2218, pp. 15–35. Springer, Heidelberg (2001)
5. Eichberg, M., Mezini, M.: Alice: Modularization of Middleware using Aspect-Oriented Programming. In: Gschwind, T., Mascolo, C. (eds.) SEM 2004. LNCS, vol. 3437. Springer, Heidelberg (2005)
6. Eugster, P.: Uniform proxies for Java. In: OOPSLA 2006: Proceedings of the 21st annual ACM SIGPLAN conference on Object-oriented programming systems, languages, and applications, pp. 139–152. ACM Press, New York (2006)

7. Eugster, P.T.: Lazy Parameter Passing. Technical report, Ecole Polytechnique Fédérale de Lausanne, EPFL (2003)
8. Fleury, M., Reverbel, F.: The JBoss Extensible Server. In: International Middleware Conference (2003)
9. Gopal, S.: An extensible framework for annotation-based parameter passing in distributed object systems. Master's thesis, Virginia Tech. (June 2008)
10. Object Management Group. Objects by value. document orbos/98-01-18, Framingham, MA (1998)
11. Object Management Group. The common object request broker: Architecture and specification, Framingham, MA (1998)
12. Object Management Group. IDL to Java language mapping specification, Framingham, MA (2003)
13. Kiczales, G., Hilsdale, E., Hugunin, J., Kersten, M., Palm, J., Griswold, W.G.: An overview of AspectJ. In: Knudsen, J.L. (ed.) ECOOP 2001. LNCS, vol. 2072, pp. 327–355, 110. Springer, Heidelberg (2001)
14. Kiczales, G., Lamping, J., Mendhekar, A., Maeda, C., Lopes, C., Loingtier, J.M., Irwin, J.: Aspect-Oriented Programming. In: Aksit, M., Matsuoka, S. (eds.) ECOOP 1997. LNCS, vol. 1241. Springer, Heidelberg (1997)
15. Nishizawa, M., Chiba, S., Tatsubori, M.: Remote pointcut: a language construct for distributed AOP. In: Proceedings of the 3rd international conference on Aspect-oriented software development, pp. 7–15 (2004)
16. Obermeyer, P., Hawkins, J.: Microsoft .NET Remoting: A Technical Overview. MSDN Library (July 2001)
17. Pawlak, R., Seinturier, L., Duchien, L., Florin, G., Legond-Aubry, F., Martelli, L.: JAC: an aspect-based distributed dynamic framework. Software Practice and Experience 34(12), 1119–1148 (2004)
18. Schmidt, D.C., Rohnert, H., Stal, M., Schultz, D.: Pattern-Oriented Software Architecture: Patterns for Concurrent and Networked Objects. John Wiley & Sons, Inc., New York (2000)
19. Seki, M.: DRuby–A Distributed Object System for Ruby (2007), http://www.ruby-doc.org/stdlib/libdoc/drb/
20. Souder, T.S., Mancoridis, S.: A Tool for Securely Integrating Legacy Systems into a Distributed Environment. In: Working Conference on Reverse Engineering, pp. 47–55 (1999)
21. Thomas, D., Hunt, A.: Programming Ruby. Addison-Wesley, Reading (2001)
22. Tilevich, E., Smaragdakis, Y.: NRMI: Natural and Efficient Middleware. IEEE Transactions on Parallel and Distributed Systems, 174–187 (February 2008)
23. Tilevich, E., Smaragdakis, Y.: J-Orchestra: Automatic Java Application Partitioning. In: Magnusson, B. (ed.) ECOOP 2002. LNCS, vol. 2374. Springer, Heidelberg (2002)
24. Wohlstadter, E., Jackson, S., Devanbu, P.: DADO: enhancing middleware to support crosscutting features in distributed, heterogeneous systems. In: Proceedings of the International Conference on Software Engineering, vol. 186 (2003)
25. Yang, C.C., Chen, C.K., Chang, Y.H., Chung, K.H., Lee, J.K.: Streaming support for Java RMI in distributed environments. In: Proceedings of the 4th international symposium on Principles and practice of programming in Java, pp. 53–61 (2006)
26. Zhang, C., Jacobsen, H.: Refactoring middleware with aspects. IEEE Transactions on Parallel and Distributed Systems 14(11), 1058–1073 (2003)

Performance Comparison of PHP and JSP as Server-Side Scripting Languages

Scott Trent, Michiaki Tatsubori, Toyotaro Suzumura, Akihiko Tozawa,
and Tamiya Onodera

IBM Tokyo Research Laboratory
16-23-14 Shimotsuruma Yamato-shi, Japan 242-8502
{trent,mich,toyo,atozawa,tonodera}@jp.ibm.com

Abstract. The dynamic scripting language PHP has become enormously popular for implementing lightweight web applications, and is widely used as a server-side scripting language for web servers. To contrast the performance of PHP and JSP for this purpose, we used the SPECweb2005 benchmark, which provides three application scenarios implemented in both PHP and JSP. This paper describes and contrasts the results of SPECweb2005 performance benchmark testing performed on different configurations of PHP and JSP using the popular web servers Apache and Lighttpd. Despite the execution overhead of interpretation in PHP engines observed in micro benchmarks, the experimental result of SPECweb2005 benchmark yields valuable performance data for web server implementers. The efficiency of scripting language runtimes still matters for the end-to-end performance. However, once carefully architected and tuned, the language runtime is less of a bottleneck than the web server performance itself.

Keywords: PHP, JSP, SPECweb, Benchmarking, Web Server.

1 Introduction

The dynamic scripting language PHP (PHP Hypertext Preprocessor) has become enormously popular for implementing lightweight web applications, and is widely used to access databases and other middleware. Apache module popularity surveys performed by Security Space in October 2007 indicate that 37% of Apache servers have PHP support enabled [11], making it the most popular Apache module by 10 percentage points. Businesses are quickly realizing the powerful combination of a service oriented architecture environment with dynamic scripting languages like PHP [5]. However, we believe that there are still critical performance issues involving PHP which remain to be investigated.

This paper focuses on the use of dynamic scripting languages to implement web server front-end interfaces. This corresponds with the way that the industry standard web server performance benchmark SPECweb2005 utilizes PHP and JSP (JavaServer Pages). In this case, scripts are used for the implementation of dynamic page generation, rather than the realization of complex business logic. This contrasts with

V. Issarny and R. Schantz (Eds.): Middleware 2008, LNCS 5346, pp. 164–182, 2008.

the traditional uses of complex JSP-based business logic implementation. While there are numerous studies on dynamic web content, this paper complements these studies with detailed analysis focusing on PHP. For example, following the performance study on CGI (Common Gateway Interface) based web servers for dynamic content by Yeager & McGrath back in 1995, researchers and practitioners have been examining the performance of more recent dynamic Web content generation technologies [3, 13, 15, 17]. These works, however, handle application scenarios where servlet front-ends implement relatively complex business logic.

Although Warner and Worley discuss the importance of also using PHP with SPECweb2005 [18], to the best of the author's knowledge, this paper is the first to publish a detailed analysis of SPECweb2005 experimental results using both PHP and JSP. The detailed analysis of PHP and JSP performance based on SPECweb2005 offered by this paper enables designers and implementers of web servers to understand the relative performance and throughput of different versions and configurations of PHP and JSP.

The rest of this paper is organized as follows. Section 2 discusses multi-tier web server architecture and the lightweight front-end approach using PHP and JSP. Section 3 reports on our findings regarding PHP and JSP language runtime micro benchmark performance. Section 4 details our SPECweb2005 benchmark methodology, environment, and test configurations. Section 5 analyzes SPECweb2005 benchmark throughput results, CPU usage profiling, and related performance metrics. Section 6 discusses the importance of these results. Section 7 covers related work, followed by our conclusions in Section 8.

2 Multi-tier Web Server Architecture: Lightweight Front-End Using PHP/JSP

Developers typically use PHP to implement a front-end interface to dynamic Web content generators, which are combined with web server software and back-end servers to provide dynamic content. The web server directly handles requests for static content and forwards requests for dynamic content to the dynamic content generator. The dynamic content generator, supported by back-end servers, executes code which realizes the business logic of a web site and stores dynamic state. Back-end servers may be implemented as a straight-forward database, or may be more complex servers handling the business logic of the web site. The front-end implementation may vary from heavy-weight business logic handlers to lightweight clients composing content received from back-end servers.

This paper focuses on multi-tier web site development scenarios utilizing such lightweight front-ends, supported by one or more layers of heavy-weight back-ends. This assumption is reasonable when considering Service-Oriented environments where PHP scripts are used to implement a "mash-up" of services provided elsewhere, in addition to the case of simple web sites such as bulletin boards where PHP scripts are just a wrapper to a database. Within the scenarios described in this paper, the dynamic content generator provides client implementation in addition to page composition. It connects to the back-end server through a network using either standard protocols such as HTTP or application/middleware-specific protocols.

JSP technology can be considered an alternative to PHP in implementing such front-ends. While it is part of the Java Servlet framework, developers typically use JSP to implement lightweight front-ends. Both PHP and JSP allow developers to write HTML embedded code. In fact, although there are language inherent differences between PHP and Java, the use of PHP scripts and JSP files can be very similar.

The objective of the experiments detailed in this paper is to measure the performance of lightweight front-end dynamic content generation written in PHP and JSP with popular web servers such as Apache and Lighttpd. This web server architecture scenario involves users who access a web server with pages written in plain static HTML, as well as JSP and PHP scripts which mix scripting language with HTML code. The configuration assumed within the paper is a typical one, where web server software, such as Apache, distinguishes between pure HTML, JSP, and PHP respectively with suffixes such as .html, .jsp, and .php. HTML code is directly returned to the requesting end-user's web browser, where JSP and PHP pages are respectively parsed by the Tomcat script engine and the PHP runtime engine which both provide pure HTML which is forwarded to the end-user on a remote system. (A sample comparison of similar trivial JSP and PHP scripts, along with resulting HTML code can be seen in Table 1) A common point between JSP and PHP is that implementations which perform well have a dynamically compiled and cached byte code. For example, the Java runtime used by the Tomcat script engine which we used performs much better when the Just-in-Time (JIT) compiler is enabled to create efficient cached native runtime code. Similarly, the Zend PHP runtime we used also performs significantly better when the Alternative PHP Cache (APC) is enabled, in which APC stores PHP byte codes compiled from the script source code in shared memory for future reuse.

Table 1. Sample PHP and JSP scripts with resulting HTML code

PHP Script	JSP Script	Resulting HTML Code

`<html> <body>`
`The date is`
`<?php`
`echo`
`date(DATE_RFC822);`
`?>`
`</body> </html>`
	`<html> <body>`
	`The date is`
	`<%=`
	`new`
	`java.util.Date();`
	`%>`
	`<body> </html>`
		`<html> <body>`
		`The date is`
		`Tue,  1   Jan   08`
		`12:00:00`
		`</body> </html>`

3   Language Runtime Performance Micro Benchmarking

To understand the difference in performance characteristics between PHP and Java at the language runtime level, we compared the following engines using a series of micro benchmark tests:

- PHP 4.4.7
- PHP 5.2.3
- Java 5 with Just-In-Time (JIT) compilation (IBM J9 VM 1.5.0 Build 2.3)
- Java 5 without Just-In-Time (JIT) compilation (same as above)

The PHP language framework allows developers to extend the language with library functions written in C. These functions, which are known as "extensions", are then available to be used within PHP scripts. The PHP runtime provides a variety of extensions for string manipulation, file handling, networking, and so forth. Since our first goal was to understand the performance of the PHP runtime itself, we conducted our experiments without the use of extensions. We developed the following micro benchmarks:

- A quick sort benchmark which sorts 100 integers,
- A Levenshtein benchmark which measures the similarity between two strings of 56 characters,
- A Fibonacci benchmark which calculates the 15th value in a Fibonacci series with two arbitrary starting values.

These PHP benchmarks were implemented entirely with PHP language primitives and avoided the use of PHP extensions. The Java versions also focused on using language primitives rather than standard classes. We compared the total run time of executing each test 10,000 times with each engine. We also executed each benchmark an additional 10,000 times as a warm-up, before the measured test. This prevents Java just-in-time compilation overhead from impacting the score in the Java tests. We ran the experiment on an Intel Pentium 4 CPU at 3.40 GHz with 3GB RAM Memory, with the Linux 2.6.17 kernel.

This test demonstrates large performance differences between each of the measured scripting languages and implementations. The experimental results in Figure 1 indicate that "Java 5 with JIT compilation" performs the best, followed by

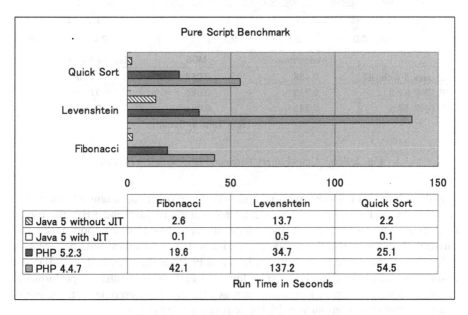

	Fibonacci	Levenshtein	Quick Sort
Java 5 without JIT	2.6	13.7	2.2
Java 5 with JIT	0.1	0.5	0.1
PHP 5.2.3	19.6	34.7	25.1
PHP 4.4.7	42.1	137.2	54.5

Run Time in Seconds

Fig. 1. Pure Script Benchmark Performance

"Java 5 without JIT compilation", "PHP 5.2.3", and "PHP 4.4.7" in all measured cases. Java 5 with JIT demonstrated nearly three orders of magnitude better performance due to the use of efficiently generated native code. It is also obvious that PHP 5.2.3 has a two to three times performance improvement over PHP 4.4.7 with the measured computations.

Secondly to determine the performance effect of PHP extensions compared with Java class methods, we developed and tested three additional micro benchmarks: regular expression matching, MD5 encoding, and Levenshtein comparison. For regular expression matching, the Perl Compatible Regular Expression extension (through the `preg_match()` function) was used in PHP, and the java.util.regex package was used in Java. For MD5 encoding, the MD5 extension was used in PHP and java.security.MessageDigest was used in Java. This experiment does not compare exactly the same logic, but rather demonstrates that the use of PHP extensions is competitive with Java using just-in-time compilation, as seen in Figure 2.

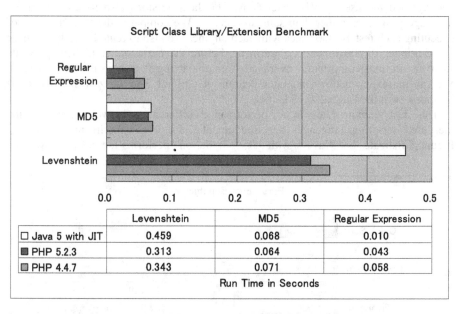

Fig. 2. Script Class Library/Extension Benchmark Performance

Although the pure script experiment showed three orders of magnitude difference between the performance of various implementations of Java and PHP, the use of PHP extensions (written in C) and compiled Java class libraries show much less variation. In the extreme, the regular expression test showed a maximum performance difference of about five times between Java and PHP, on the other end, the MD5 test results were nearly equivalent between Java and PHP. Thus a inherent performance risk of interpreted scripted languages such as PHP can be overcome with the use of efficient library functions such as PHP extensions written in C.

4   PHP/JSP SPECweb2005 Benchmark Methodology

Although micro benchmarks are simple to implement and analyze, and are thus often used in performance analysis, we next used the industry standard SPECweb2005 benchmark to understand the impact of different versions and configurations of PHP and JSP in more realistic situations. The SPECweb2005 benchmark, developed by the Standard Performance Evaluation Corporation (SPEC), is comprised of three test scenarios based on common website usage: a banking site scenario, an e-commerce site scenario, and a support site scenario. The banking site scenario allows for typical encrypted account transactions with Secure Sockets Layer (SSL) libraries where 60% of the data is generated through dynamic web pages. The e-commerce shopping site allows a user to browse catalogs and "purchase" products using both encrypted and unencrypted data. As shown in Table 2, experimentally about 5% of the data in the e-commerce scenario is transmitted using SSL encryption and 70% of the data transmitted is generated through dynamic web pages. Finally, the vendor support site provides downloading of large unencrypted support files such as manuals and software. As this scenario primarily allows for accessing large non-confidential static files, there is no encryption, and only 12% of the data transmitted is generated through dynamic web pages. Since SPECweb2005 is implemented in both PHP and JSP, it is particularly well suited for comparing performance between the two languages. Yet because every single officially published SPECweb2005 benchmark result as of Summer 2008 was performed using JSP rather than PHP [12], this paper provides a unique comparison of both implementations, which is valuable considering the popularity of real world web servers based on PHP.

Table 2. Experimentally measured percentage of encrypted and dynamic data transfered for each SPECweb2005 scenario

	Banking	Ecommerce	Support
Percentage of encrypted data	100%	4.4%	0%
Percentage of dynamic data e.g., script output	59.5%	71.6%	11.7%

A typical SPECweb2005 test bed has multiple client machines controlled by a Prime Client to provide a load on the System Under Test (SUT) to simulate hundreds to tens of thousands of users accessing the scenario web sites. Although multiple software components can run on the same physical system, a high level of distribution is desirable to provide a realistic environment. For example, an average of 22 physical clients were used in the officially published SPECweb2005 scores [12]. To reflect modern multi-tier web server architecture, SPECweb2005 uses one or more machines to serve as a Back End SIMulator (BESIM), emulating the function of a "Back End" database server.

4.1   SPECweb2005 Benchmark Environment

We used a single System Under Test machine running the web server, a BESIM server running the Back End SIMulation engine, a prime client machine, and three additional dedicated client machines. The computers were connected via a gigabit Ethernet network. The System Under Test was an IBM IntelliStation M Pro with a 3.4 GHz Xeon uniprocessor running Fedora Core 7 (kernel 2.6.23), Apache 2.2.6, and Lighttpd 1.4.18. Apache Tomcat was used as the JSP servlet container [1]. PHP 5.2.4, and Tomcat 5.5.25 were used in their respective tests. Tomcat was configured to use an IBM implemented Java Virtual Machine: J9 VM 1.5.0 Build 2.3. The standard distribution of SPECweb2005 was installed and configured as described in SPEC documentation [12].

4.2   Testing Methodology

In addition to following the guidelines laid down in the SPECweb2005 documentation [12] we developed a testing tool which could be configured to automatically run multiple tests, iterating such variables as the script engine language (PHP, JSP), the web server (Apache, Lighttpd), the number of simultaneous sessions, and the SPECweb2005 scenario (banking, ecommerce, and support), and other tuning factors. We varied the number of simultaneous sessions from 250 to 3000 by increments of 250. To ensure valid results, the SPECweb2005 test harness will abort individual tests when the web server response threshold is exceeded. We used 3000 simultaneous connections as our maximum because beyond this, with our configuration, it is rare for a test to run successfully to completion. To avoid genetic skewing of data, this paper only displays data for tests that ran successfully without repeated retries. Load levels that may not run to completion are extremely unlikely to result in a suitable Quality of Service (QoS) level to qualify as a valid SPECweb2005 test run.

   To assure a fair comparison, before each individual test is initiated, our testing tool restarted the SPECweb2005 client components, all middleware such as Tomcat, and web server, and otherwise ensured that the environment on each system in this distributed environment was in a consistent and receptive state. An officially published SPECweb2005 benchmark score is a single value which based on three 30-minute test runs from each of the three scenarios shows the performance improvement over SPEC's reference machine. This can be used to compare the relative perform-ance of web serving hardware platforms from different vendors. Since our goal was to analyze in detail how the use of different scripting languages and web servers affects performance, we used internal metrics such as the number of good/tolerable/failed requests served as reported from the SPECweb2005 test harness for each test. To improve test coverage in the time available, we used 10-minute test runs rather than the official 30-minute run, and only ran each test once rather than three times. Although our test runs are not suitable for reporting as an official score, they are very useful for identifying trends seen as over tens of tests, and variation seen with identical test runs was small as demonstrated in Figure 3. The vmstat command was also used to monitor such performance statistics as memory usage, swapping activity, and CPU utilization [6]. No swapping activity was observed during our reported tests. In separate test runs, we used the oprofile tool to identify process, module, and function CPU utilization.

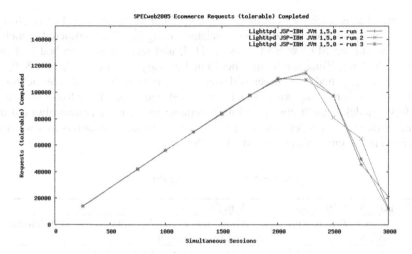

Fig. 3. Repeated test runs demonstrate similar results

We measured each of the SPECweb2005 scenarios with the following five configurations of scripting language and web server with the goal of contrasting JSP with PHP, and Apache with Lighttpd:

- JSP with Apache via mod_jk connector
- JSP with Lighttpd via mod_proxy module
- PHP with Apache via FCGI protocol
- PHP with Lighttpd via FCGI protocol
- PHP with Apache via in-process mod_php

While as the four potential combinations of two scripting languages and two web servers are obvious, the methods for connecting scripting languages and web servers are rather arcane. We chose connectors and connection methods based on availability and general practice. mod_jk is a commonly used connector between Apache and Tomcat using the Apache JServ Protocol (AJP). FCGI (Fast Common Gate Way Interface) is a protocol developed by Open Market to improve the performance and usability of the CGI model for web server to back-end (e.g., scripting language engine) communication which is commonly used with the Lighttpd web server. In our test, the Lighttpd mod_proxy module serves as a general purpose connector between Tomcat and the Lighttpd web server. mod_php is a dynamically loadable module for Apache which enables PHP script processing within the web server process via direct function calls rather than interprocess communication as used by the other methods. With Apache, mod_php is more common than FCGI for PHP script processing.

4.3 Tuning Considerations

Significant tuning effort was expended to ensure that performance was not limited by obvious configuration limitations or trivial system resource limitations. We removed unused daemons, services, and web server modules to reduce computational noise [8].

When initial tests suffered from thrashing under high loads, we added more physical memory, and paid attention to memory related tuning [6]. We considered guidelines used by published SPECweb2005 results [12], and techniques described in Linux, Apache, PHP, and Tomcat reference books and primary websites [2, 4, 6, 7, 8, 9, 14]. Although the Lighttpd web server is designed as a minimally threaded asynchronous event-handling program, with Apache we used the single-threaded/multi-process "prefork" model, since it considered more reliable and is more commonly used than the multi-threaded "worker" model. The significant tuning parameters that we found beneficial in our environment include the following.

Table 3. Significant Tuning Parameters

Tuning Modification	Benefit
/etc/security/limits.conf nofile 65536	Allow more files/sockets to be simultaneously opened by specific user.
sysctl fs.file-max=1000000	Allow more files/sockets to be open simultaneously.
Apache KeepAliveTimeout 2 on SUT	Reduce time an httpd process spends waiting for client response.
Apache KeepAliveTimeout 28800 on BESIM	Enable BESIM to use persistent http connections to reduce connection restart overhead.
Apache ServerLimit 1200	Specify enough httpd processes so that connection availability is not a bottleneck, yet not so many that httpd process memory usage causes thrashing.
Apache MaxRequestsPerChild 0	Avoid overhead of having httpd processes restarted after receiving a certain number of requests.
sysctl net.core.so.maxconn=10000	Increase the connection queue size to prevent denied connections.
vm.swappiness = 50	Improve caching throughput.
max*threads in tomcat5/server.xml = 15000	Improve the response time provided by JSP.
APC extension compiled into PHP	Improve PHP processing time. (Comparable to using JIT in Java.)
tmpfs filesystem used for /tmp	Improved performance for access to temporary files in /tmp.
Lighttpd max-procs=16, max-connections=8192, max-fds=16484, max-worker = 2	Ensure that lighttpd has sufficient sockets and FCGI processes to avoid bottlenecks.
Non-error logging minimalized	Avoid unnecessary overhead.
Debug modes disabled	Avoid unnecessary overhead.

5 PHP/JSP Performance Benchmark Results

5.1 Overall Performance

Figure 4 shows the maximum performance for each configuration and scenario, as determined by the maximum number of simultaneous sessions (e.g., users) which can be supported with acceptable Quality Of Service as defined by SPEC. The results were largely consistent between test scenarios, showing that JSP tended to perform better than PHP (yet PHP with Lighttpd performs nearly as well as the JSP test cases), and Lighttpd tends to perform better than Apache (yet, JSP with Apache performs nearly as well as Lighttpd). Although the Ecommerce test scenario stands as it handles as much as 50% more simultaneous sessions than the other scenarios, since the load per session is not normalized between test scenarios, one must conclude that a single user SPECweb2005 Ecommerce scenario session load is less than that of either a Banking or Ecommerce scenario user session load. However, the fact that the high performing JSP/Apache, JSP/Lighttpd, and FCGI PHP/Lighttpd configurations had a higher percentage performance increase in the Ecommerce scenario than Apache using either mod_php or FCGI PHP does emphasize the superiority of these configurations.

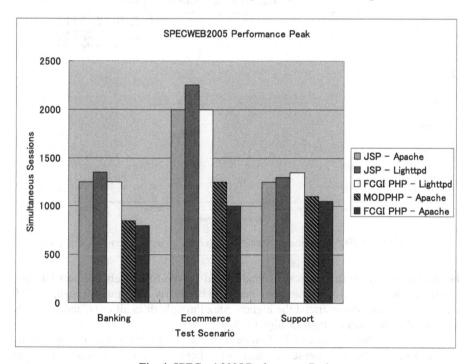

Fig. 4. SPECweb2005 Performance Peak

5.2 Throughput Results

Figures 5-7 show the number of tolerable (or better) requests fulfilled for each of the configurations. At low loads, throughput performance is not gated by SUT resources,

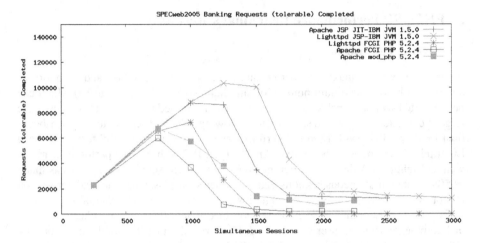

Fig. 5. SPECweb2005 Banking Scenario (Tolerable or better) Requests Completed

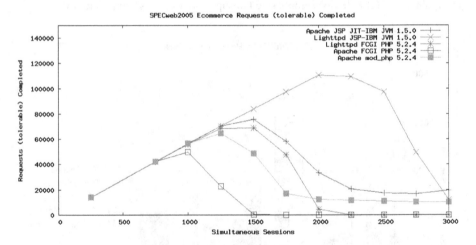

Fig. 6. SPECweb2005 Ecommerce Scenario (Tolerable or Better) Requests Completed

but rather simply by the amount of load placed by the SPECweb2005 test harness, hence at low loads all configurations demonstrate nearly the same throughput. JSP with both servers demonstrated the highest peak throughput in all tests, and generally performed better than PHP under high loads.

Although the performance of PHP in performing fine grain tasks such as executing trivial function calls and simple instructions has been shown to be hundreds of times slower than C, PHP does relatively better at coarse grain activities such as calling complex external libraries to perform actions such as DB access [10]. Ramana and Prabhakar [10] use micro benchmarks to demonstrate that file I/O on PHP is more efficient than, for instance, calculating Fibonacci numbers in PHP. (These results are also consistent with the micro benchmarks we used in Section 3 of this paper.) Thus

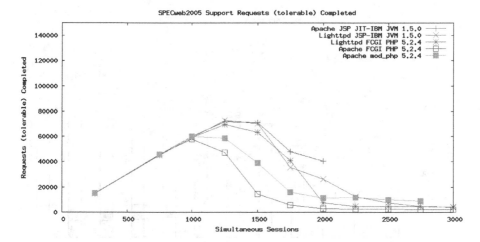

Fig. 7. SPECweb2005 Support Scenario (Tolerable or Better) Requests Completed

we theorize that although all scenarios in SPECweb2005 contain a significant number of fine grain tasks, the high level of file I/O performed in the SPECweb2005 Support scenario allowed PHP to narrow the performance gap with JSP under high loads in this case, as seen in Figure 7. This result implies that micro benchmarks of read performance for large static files would be comparable between PHP and JSP.

Figures 8-12 show detailed results of the Ecommerce scenario for each of our five configurations with test loads from 250 to 3000 simultaneous sessions. Similar results are observed with the Banking and Support scenarios, which are omitted to save space. Data on the number and quality of requests serviced at each point is gathered and shown in these graphs. A "Good Response" is one that is returned to the user within 2-3 seconds (depending on the scenario), a "Tolerable Response" is one that is returned within 4-5 seconds (depending on the scenario), a "Failed Response" is one that returns after that, and a "Validation Error" is a response which is incorrect irregardless of how fast or slow it is. As observed earlier, performance under low loads is the same with each configuration, since the limiting factor is simply the load provided by the SPECweb test suite. As load increases, the expected shifting of request categorization from Good to Tolerable to Failed is observable with all configurations. This shifting can be directly predicted by the increase in average response time reported by the SPECweb2005 test harness. The JSP Lighttpd configuration demonstrated the best performance, but the JSP/Apache and PHP (mod_php) Apache configurations continued to service 10-15% of their requests with good Quality of Service even under extremely high loads, where the other configurations did not. This indicates a wider standard deviation among request response time, implying a potentially "unfair" (e.g., not FIFO) scheduling algorithm with configurations that continue to return a percentage of "Good Responses" under very high load.

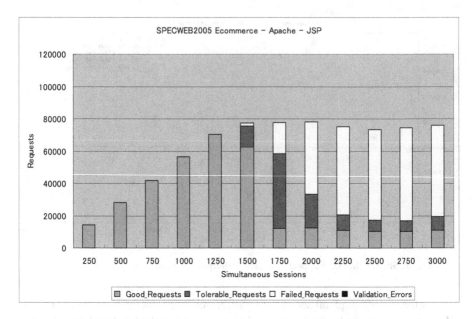

Fig. 8. SPECweb2005 Ecommerce Performance with JSP and Apache

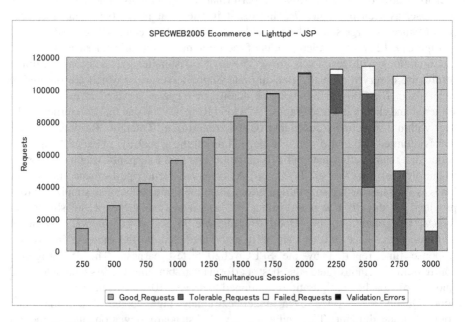

Fig. 9. SPECweb2005 Ecommerce Performance with JSP and Lighttpd

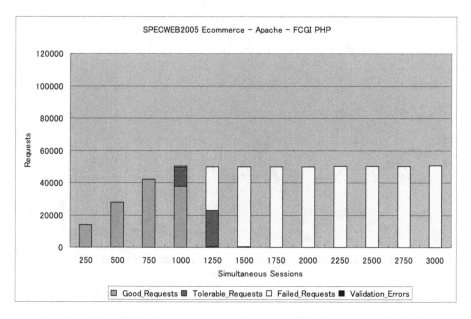

Fig. 10. SPECweb2005 Ecommerce Performance with PHP and Apache (via FCGI)

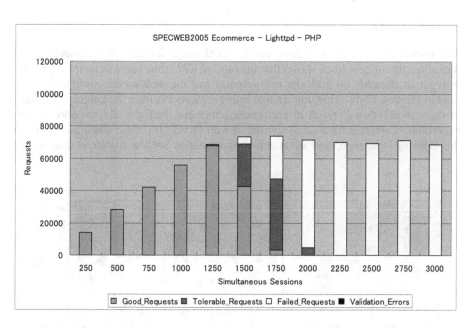

Fig. 11. SPECweb2005 Ecommerce Performance with PHP and Lighttpd (via FCGI)

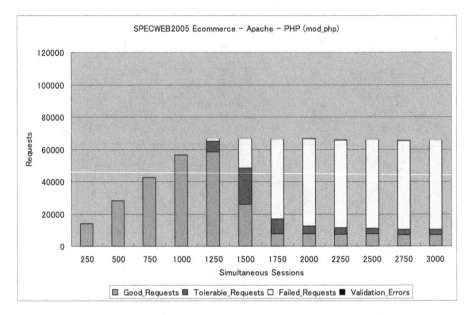

Fig. 12. SPECweb2005 Ecommerce Performance with mod_php and Apache

5.3   CPU Usage

Not surprisingly, using oprofile to profile CPU usage for each test scenario at the maximum throughput level shows that the ratio of CPU time spent in script engine vs. web server depends on both the test scenario and the web server configuration, as seen in Figures 13-15. This implies that improvements to either the language runtime, or the web server will result in performance increase. In Figure 14 we observe that encryption accounted for a large amount of web server CPU time when used (e.g., in the Banking scenario), and of course that scenarios with a higher percentage of

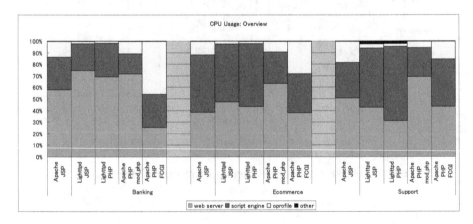

Fig. 13. High-Level View of CPU Usage for Each SPECweb Scenario

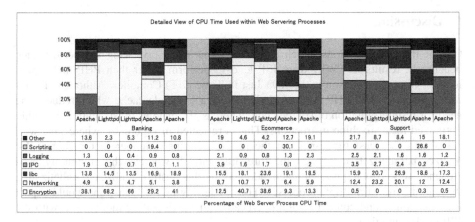

Detailed View of CPU Time Used within Web Servering Processes

	Apache	Lighttpd	Lighttpd	Apache	Apache	Apache	Lighttpd	Lighttpd	Apache	Apache	Apache	Lighttpd	Lighttpd	Apache	Apache
			Banking					Ecommerce					Support		
■ Other	13.6	2.3	5.3	11.2	10.8	19	4.6	4.2	12.7	19.1	21.7	8.7	8.4	15	18.1
□ Scripting	0	0	0	19.4	0	0	0	0	30.1	0	0	0	0	26.6	0
■ Logging	1.3	0.4	0.4	0.9	0.8	2.1	0.9	0.8	1.3	2.3	2.5	2.1	1.6	1.6	1.2
▣ IPC	1.9	0.7	0.7	0.1	1.1	3.9	1.6	1.7	0.1	2	3.5	2.7	2.4	0.2	2.3
■ libc	13.8	14.5	13.5	16.9	18.9	15.5	18.1	23.6	19.1	18.5	15.9	20.7	26.9	18.6	17.3
□ Networking	4.9	4.3	4.7	5.1	3.8	8.7	10.7	9.7	6.4	5.9	12.4	23.2	20.1	12	12.4
□ Encryption	38.1	68.2	66	29.2	41	12.5	40.7	38.6	9.3	13.3	0.5	0	0	0.3	0.5

Percentage of Web Server Process CPU Time

Fig. 14. Detailed View of CPU Time Used within Web Serving Processes

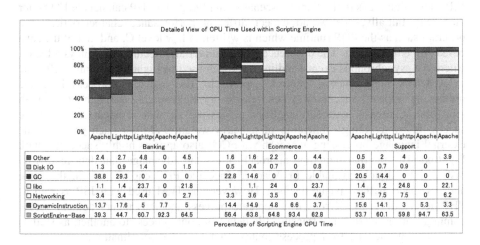

Detailed View of CPU Time Used within Scripting Engine

	Apache	Lighttpd	Lighttpd	Apache	Apache	Apache	Lighttpd	Lighttpd	Apache	Apache	Apache	Lighttpd	Lighttpd	Apache	Apache
			Banking					Ecommerce					Support		
■ Other	2.4	2.7	4.8	0	4.5	1.6	1.6	2.2	0	4.4	0.5	2	4	0	3.9
□ Disk IO	1.3	0.9	1.4	0	1.5	0.5	0.4	0.7	0	0.8	0.8	0.7	0.9	0	1
■ GC	38.8	29.3	0	0	0	22.8	14.6	0	0	0	20.5	14.4	0	0	0
□ libc	1.1	1.4	23.7	0	21.8	1	1.1	24	0	23.7	1.4	1.2	24.8	0	22.1
□ Networking	3.4	3.4	4.4	0	2.7	3.3	3.6	3.5	0	4.6	7.5	7.5	7.5	0	6.2
▩ DynamicInstruction	13.7	17.6	5	7.7	5	14.4	14.9	4.8	6.6	3.7	15.6	14.1	3	5.3	3.3
▩ ScriptEngine-Base	39.3	44.7	60.7	92.3	64.5	56.4	63.8	64.8	93.4	62.8	53.7	60.1	59.8	94.7	63.5

Percentage of Scripting Engine CPU Time

Fig. 15. Detailed View of CPU Time Used within Scripting Engine

dynamic data created by scripting engines tended to use more time in the script engine. The high percentage of SSL computation time spent in the Lighttpd as compared with Apache was puzzling until we identified that SSL connection negotiation data is not shared among multiple Lighttpd processes as it is with Apache. Data from vmstat show that the kernel accounted for 34-44% and user time accounted for 36-59% of CPU time. The seemingly high levels of system time are reasonable considering the disk and network I/O involved in running the SPECweb benchmark. At the function level, the memcpy() function call was observed as being a significant consumer of CPU in every configuration, implying that additional application of the zero-copy principal may be warranted [19].

6 Discussion

One of the first questions which comes to mind when reviewing the performance benchmark results is, "Why does JSP tend to perform better then PHP under high loads?" One major reason is the Java Just in Time (JIT) Compiler. Although JIT has been compared with PHP APC, APC is merely a bytecode cache which reduces the need for re-interpretation of source code, whereas JIT enables the execution of highly optimized local machine instructions. This is reflected in Figure 14, where Java with JIT shows the least time spent in the runtime engine. Another factor is that JSP realizes parallelization through the threading model, whereas the commonly used Apache worker/mod_php approach adopted in this testing realizes parallelization through the use of multiple processes. Thus under high CPU loads, one would expect less scheduling and context switch overhead with the threading model used with the JSP implementation.

Another seemingly anomalous point is that PHP used with Lighttpd outperformed JSP under high loads in the Support scenario, implying that PHP can handle I/O better than JSP. Initially, one would expect different performance characteristics of a program such as the PHP runtime which is written in low level C, and that of the Java based JSP environment. The difference in web server architectures also plays a factor, where the asynchronous event-handling approach used in Lighttpd appears preferable to Apache's multi-process "prefork" approach. The use of in-process language processing appears successful when reasonably lightweight, as is the case with mod_php. Likewise, external language processing as with Tomcat seems to be successful by avoiding replication of a heavy-weight JVM for each process. The external language processing approach via FCGI also appears highly successful with Lighttpd. The internal mod_php approach offers the advantage that data read from disk is immediately available to Apache, since the PHP engine runs in the same address space as the Apache daemon. However, the JVM used with JSP as well as PHP accessed via FCGI runs in a separate process and thus incurs domain socket communication overhead to transmit file data from one process to another, as well as potential inefficiencies from process context switching and coordination.

7 Related Work

Titchkosky and associates established that serving dynamic web content can reduce throughput by 8 times as compared with static web content [13], providing our team with encouragement to identify methods to reduce the negative performance impact of using scripted language dynamic web content. Ramana and Prabhakar analyzed the performance differences between PHP and compiled languages such as C, pointing out the relative performance downside of PHP [10], which corresponds with our tests on pure-script implemented benchmarks vs. scripts using standard class library or PHP extensions implemented in C language. The upside of our benchmarking is that we found the use of C-language PHP extensions for computationally intensive functions to enable PHP scripts to perform comparably with Java. Cecchet and colleagues analyze various middleware architectures based on technology such as Apache, PHP, Tomcat, MySQL, and JOnAS [3, 17], which helped guide our methodology. Warner and Worley describe the importance of using technology such as PHP rather than just JSP for real-world benchmarking with SPECweb2005 [18]. We have contributed to this line of reasoning as we were motivated to write this paper since we have not seen data from an industry standard web server benchmark that provides a detailed comparison of the performance PHP and JSP as a web server dynamic scripting language.

8 Conclusion

When implementing a web server system which will never experience high load, or in which performance, throughput, and reliability under high load is not an issue, then the use of any of the analyzed languages or web servers will achieve similar performance results. If outstanding performance and throughput is the primary goal, then the use of JSP over PHP is advisable. However, if a 5-10% difference in throughput and performance is acceptable, then the implementer of a web system can achieve similar results using either PHP or JSP. In which case, other requirements such as developer language familiarity and programming efficiency, maintainability, security, reliability, middleware compatibility, etc. would be the deciding factors. It is also reassuring to developers of both language runtimes and web servers, that enhancements to either can offer performance improvements to the community.

Acknowledgements

We are appreciative of the many useful discussions with Graeme Johnson and Andrew Low, from the IBM Ottawa Software Lab, which have provided valuable direction. Mathematical guidance from Mei Kobayashi, and perceptive feedback from the Systems Department, both at the IBM Tokyo Research Laboratory resulted in a more consistent and rigorous analysis. We are also deeply indebted to the feedback and comments regarding PHP and SPECweb2005 testing which we received from the PHP team at IBM Hursley.

References

1. Apache Software Foundation (2008), http://tomcat.apache.org
2. Bergsten, H.: Java Server Pages. O'Reilly, Sebastopol (2003)
3. Cecchet, E., Chanda, A., Elnikety, S., Marguerite, J., Zwaenepoel, W.: Performance Comparison of Middleware Architectures for Generating Dynamic Web Content. In: 4th ACM/IFIP/USENIX International Middleware Conference (2003)
4. Chopra, V., Galbraith, B., et al.: Professional Apache Tomcat (2003) ISBN 0-764-5372-5
5. IBM (2006),
   http://www-03.ibm.com/press/us/en/pressrelease/19822.wss
6. Johnson, S., Huizenga, G., Pulavarty, B.: Performance Tuning for Linux Servers. IBM Press (2005) ISBN 0-131-44753-X
7. Lecky-Thompson, E., Eide-Goodman, H., Nowicki, S., Cove, A.: Professional PHP5. Wrox Press (2005) ISBN 0-764-57282-2

8. Petrini, F., Kerbyson, D., Pakin, S.: The case of the Missing Supercomputer Performance: Achieving Optimal Performance on the 8,192 Processors of ASCI Q. In: Proceedings of IEEE/ACM SC (2004)
9. PHP Group (2008), http://www.php.net
10. Ramana, U., Prabhakar, T.: Some Experiments with the Performance of LAMP Architecture. In: Proceedings of the 2005 Fifth International Conference on Computer and Information Technology (2005)
11. Security Space (2007), http://securityspace.com
12. Standard Performance Evaluation Corporation (2008), http://www.spec.org
13. Titchkosky, L., Arlitt, M., Williamson, C.: A Performance Comparison of Dynamic Web Technologies. In: 11th IEEE/ACM International Symposium on Modeling, Analysis and Simulation of Computer Telecommunications Systems (2003)
14. Wainwright, P.: Professional Apache 2.0 (2002) ISBN 1-861-00822-1
15. Wu, A.W., Wang, H., Wilkins, D.: Performance Comparison of Alternative Solutions For Web-To-Database Applications. In: Proceedings of the Southern Conference on Computing (2000)
16. Garcia, D.F., Garcia, J.: TPC-W E-Commerce Benchmark Evaluation. IEEE Computer 36(2), 52–48 (2003)
17. Amza, C., et al.: Specification and implementation of dynamic Web site benchmarks. In: Proceedings of the 5th IEEE Workshop on Workload Characterization (2002)
18. Warner, S., Worley, J.: SPECweb2005 in the Real World: Using Internet Information Server (IIS) and PHP. In: 2008 SPEC Benchmark Workshop (2008)
19. Stancevic, D.: Zero Copy I: User-Mode Perspective. Linux Journal 3(105) (2003)

Debugging and Testing Middleware with Aspect-Based Control-Flow and Causal Patterns*

Luis Daniel Benavides Navarro, Rémi Douence, and Mario Südholt

OBASCO project; EMN-INRIA, LINA
Dépt. Informatique, École des Mines de Nantes
4 rue Alfred Kastler, 44307 Nantes cédex 3, France
{lbenavid,douence,sudholt}@emn.fr

Abstract. Many tasks that involve the dynamic manipulation of middleware and large-scale distributed applications, such as debugging and testing, require the monitoring of intricate relationships of execution events that trigger modifications to the executing system. Furthermore, events often are of interest only if they occur as part of specific execution traces and not all possible non-deterministic interleavings of events in these traces. Current techniques and tools for the definition of such manipulations provide only very limited support for such event relationships and do not allow to concisely define restrictions on the interleaving of events.

In this paper, we argue for the use of aspect-based high-level programming abstractions for the definition of relationships between execution events of distributed systems and the control of non-deterministic interleavings of events. Concretely, we provide the following contributions: we (i) motivate that such abstractions improve on current debugging and testing methods for middleware, (ii) introduce corresponding language support for pointcuts and advice defined in terms of causal event sequences by extending an existing aspect-oriented system for the dynamic manipulation of distributed systems, and (iii) evaluate our approach in the context of the debugging and testing of Java-based middlewares, in particular, JBoss Cache for replicated caching.

1 Introduction

Many tasks that involve the dynamic manipulation of middleware and large-scale distributed applications, such as debugging and testing, require the monitoring of intricate relationships of execution events that trigger modifications to the executing system. Such relationships, which often include events occuring on different hosts, have to be defined declaratively as well as monitored and modified efficiently. Consider, for instance, coherency of replicated data under transactional control in middleware cache infrastructures, such as JBoss Cache: in this

---

* Work partially supported by AOSD-Europe, the European Network of Excellence in AOSD (www.aosd-europe.net).

V. Issarny and R. Schantz (Eds.): Middleware 2008, LNCS 5346, pp. 183–202, 2008.

case, the correctness of sequences of events corresponding to executions of two-phase-commit protocols involving multiple machines has to be checked. Furthermore, execution events of a distributed system frequently are of interest only if they occur as part of specific execution traces but not in the presence of different interleavings of the events that are part of those traces and occur due to non-deterministic executions. The definition of reproducible test cases, for instance, frequently requires constraints to be imposed on non-deterministic executions.

Several approaches to define such relationships among and constraints on events in distributed systems have been proposed. Such approaches include, for example, causal event relationships based on logical clocks [1, 13, 17], data path expressions for concurrent programs [23], and control-flow based event relationships [18]. However, such declarative means for the definition of event relationships have not been integrated into mainstream middlewares and corresponding support in current tools for the debugging and testing of distributed infrastructures is very limited. Intricate relationships between distributed events and restrictions on the interleavings of concurrent events can be directly defined in current execution environments only in terms of conditions on the execution state of individual hosts. Hence, relationships involving multiple hosts have to be expressed using complex encodings that are difficult to understand, to maintain, and result in inefficient event monitoring and execution of modifications.

In this paper, we argue for the use of high-level abstractions for the definition of relationships between execution events of distributed systems, their modification and the control of non-deterministic interleavings of events. Concretely, we provide three contributions. First, we motivate that such mechanisms improve on current debugging and testing methods for distributed systems, in particular, real-world middleware infrastructures (Sec. 2). Second, we introduce corresponding aspect-based programming language support that provides declarative means to monitor and modify causal sequences of events in pointcuts and advice. We present suitable language support (Sec. 3) and a corresponding implementation (Sec. 4) in terms of an extension of the AWED language and system [2, 4] for the dynamic manipulation of distributed systems using distributed aspects. Third, we evaluate our approach in Sec. 5 in the context Java-based middlewares, in particular, for debugging and testing of JBoss Cache, a Java-based middleware for replicated caching, and ActiveMQ, the Apache message broker. We also show how current best practices for the debugging and testing of distributed systems can be improved using our approach in a practical and efficient manner. Related work is discussed in Sec. 6 and a conclusion given in Sec. 7.

A copy of the code, the benchmarks and evaluations in the context of JBoss-Cache and ActiveMQ can be found at [2].

2   Motivation

In this paper, we argue for the use of sophisticated relationships between events to be used to monitor and manipulate middleware and distributed infrastructures. We claim, in particular, that control-flow based relationships, sequence relationships and events that are causally-connected, *e.g.*, with respect to a notion of logical time, are crucial in this context. In this section, we motivate these claims for typical debugging and testing tasks of distributed infrastructures.

2.1 Expressive Breakpoints for Distributed Debugging

Current tools for distributed debugging, such as Eclipse and the Distributed Debugging Tool [12, 26], apply debugging techniques for sequential programs to distributed applications. Such tools almost always employ a centralized debugging component that coordinates execution of independent local debuggers that only support breakpoints in terms of local entities (*e.g.*, updates of local objects, local files, etc.). The distributed debugger can match local breakpoints in different machines and control the execution by, *e.g.*, stopping it and inspecting the local state of different machines. However, this kind of tools has not been widely adopted by developers, mainly because they do offer only small added value over the use of sequential debuggers on a per-machine basis.

We argue that there are two major reasons for this lack of added value:

- Lack of means for the expressive definitions of distributed breakpoints involving, in particular, control flow and sequence relationships between distributed execution events.
- Lack of means to handle non-determinism in distributed and concurrent applications.

In the following, we consider three basic debugging scenarios that frequently occur in middlewares to illustrate these issues involving control-flow relationships and non-deterministic relationships among events, especially ones involving causally-connected events (thus effectively extending discussions in recent work on distributed debugging [18, 20]).

Debugging control flow. As a first example, consider a distributed application that uses synchronous remote method invocation (*e.g.*, Java RMI) for communication between three different hosts. A developer may be interested in setting a line breakpoint in one host, H say, that is triggered only in the dynamic extent of a (previous) method call occuring on another host G. Note that such debugging scenarios are based on (typically implicit) specifications of correct program behavior. *e.g.*, that an erroneous execution path is characterized by the sequence of calls G;H on the mentioned hosts where H occurs before the call to G returns. Using current tools, the developer has three options:

- She can apply a breakpoint to the method called on host G and once this match is triggered she can, at runtime, add the line breakpoint at H. However, in this case all subsequent occurrences of the second breakpoint are matched: identifying a specific call of interest can be very difficult.
- The programmer could pollute the original code with state information to track the necessary control flow dependencies (*i.e.*, store state information that then has to be suitably forwarded to the other hosts) and match the specific breakpoint in H.

– The programmer could add a breakpoint directly on the execution of H, match the corresponding breakpoint there without taking into account the originating control flow and decide manually what to do at each match.

Using (formal or informal) reasoning mechanisms, all of these options could be proven to correctly identify the erroneous path with respect to the specifications above. However, clearly none of these situations is acceptable, because they are tedious to implement and are highly error prone. All three represent common practice with current debuggers for distributed middleware and applications, though.

Debugging non-deterministic event relations. Events that may occur concurrently and that should trigger debugging operations only if they are interleaved in specific ways further complicate matters. Debugging of replicated caching infrastructures, for example, may involve replication actions that originate from the same transaction but are triggered asynchronously (e.g. as part of a two phase-commit protocol). Errors often depend in this case on the order in which the replication actions are applied but the decision, as part of a debugging action, whether two actions occur in the relevant order is difficult to take if debugging processes (as is often the case) may introduce arbitrary delays in the observation of events.

Since current debugging tools do not provide abstractions to concisely express such cases, programmers once again have to resort to manually encode and interpret distributed state by applying one of the three options introduced above. This approach becomes, however, rapidly unmanageable if many events and many hosts are involved.

Often such debugging tasks can be much facilitated by ensuring that occurrences of events obey strict ordering requirements, possibly imposing deterministic sequences of events in a previously non-deterministic systems. This is useful, in particular, in order to systematically explore possible erroneous traces. Once again current debuggers do not support such facilities, but have to resort to encodings of distributed state. Extending previous work [14, 18, 20, 23] that has highlighted casual relationships as a means to remedy this problem, our approach seamlessly integrates notions of causality with expressive control-flow based event relationships.

2.2   Test-Driven Development

Current techniques for the test-driven development for distributed applications are also limited by a lack of support for the expression of distributed event relationships. Distributed unit test cases, in particular, are almost always implemented by means of sequential abstractions that test conditions of distributed concerns on the local state of individual machines. For example, test cases related to replication in JBoss Cache [15] frequently use a seemingly intuitive testing scenario: a test case is defined in terms of two cache instances, such that after an operation on a source cache, the state of the second cache can be tested to compare the new and old versions. This idiom seems obvious and simple; however, it does not allow to take into account, for example, the communication behavior, such as sequences of intermediate synchronous or asynchronous calls, which obviously may strongly interfere with the cache behavior. Consequently, the definition of reproducible test cases are subject to the same restrictions as discussed above, for example, if reproducibility depends on specific interleavings of a set of concurrent events being tested (that are part of a potentially much larger set of possible interleavings).

3 Language Support

In this section we propose a language to support manipulations and evolutions of distributed applications. It is based on the AWED system (Aspect With Explicit Distribution [4, 6]): that explicitly supports monitoring of sequences of distributed execution events that trigger dynamic modifications. This enables us to concisely express different debugging scenarios involving control-flow and sequence-like relationships between events. Furthermore, we introduce in this paper an extension of AWED in order to support causally-related events and causal communications (based on an event reordering mechanisms).

3.1 The AWED Language

Aspect Oriented Programming supports separation of concerns. An aspect modifies a base application: its pointcut specifies points of interest (i.e., events) in the base application execution and its advice specifies a piece of code to be executed before, after, or instead of such a point of interest. In this paper, a pointcut can denote a single event (e.g., a method call) or a sophisticated sequence of events. The base application and the aspect are woven into a single application where the aspect monitors the base program execution and triggers its advice.

AWED supports AOP in a distributed context. In particular, a pointcut can monitor events on several hosts. A sequence of events can involve different hosts. An advice can be executed remotely, synchronously or asynchronously to the base execution. Furthermore, an aspect can be deployed on a group of hosts.

The grammar shown in Fig. 1 shows the essentials of pointcut definitions in the AWED language (the full language definition can be found in [6]). The pointcut language allows matching of method calls (terminal `call`), nested calls (`cflow` means control-flow) and arbitrary (regular) sequences of method calls (non-terminal *Seq*). The constructors `host` and `on` specify (groups of) hosts where a pointcut is matched (or where an advice is executed). The constructors `target` and `args` bind values (such as the receiver or the arguments of a method call) to variables. This enables values to be passed from a matching execution event to the corresponding advice. Pointcuts can be composed using logical operators (union, intersection and complement). Sequences (*Seq*) are defined in terms of transitions of non-deterministic finite-state automata. An automaton is a set of transitions *Step*. Each transition has a label *id* and its pointcut *Pc*

// *Pointcuts*

$$
\begin{array}{lll}
Pc & ::= & \texttt{call}(\mathit{MSig}) \mid \texttt{cflow}(Pc) \mid \mathit{Seq} \\
   &   & \mid \texttt{host}(\mathit{Group}) \mid \texttt{on}(\{\ \mathit{Hosts}\ \}) \\
   &   & \mid \texttt{target}(\{\mathit{Type}\}) \mid \texttt{args}(\{\mathit{Arg}\}) \\
   &   & \mid Pc \parallel Pc \mid Pc\,\&\&\,Pc \mid !Pc \\
\mathit{Seq} & ::= & \mathit{Id}\colon \texttt{seq}(\{\mathit{Step}\}) \mid \texttt{step}(\mathit{Id},\mathit{Id}) \\
\mathit{Step} & ::= & \mathit{Id}\colon Pc \rightarrow \mathit{Target} \\
\mathit{Target} & ::= & \mathit{Id} \parallel \ ... \ \parallel \ \mathit{Id} \\
\mathit{Hosts} & ::= & \texttt{localhost} \mid \texttt{jphost} \mid "\mathit{Ip}\colon\!\mathit{Port}" \mid \mathit{GroupId}
\end{array}
$$

Fig. 1. The AWED language (excerpts)

non-deterministically leads to a set of *Id*. The constructor step identifies the transition in the automaton that should trigger advice.

3.2   Distributed Debugging with AWED

AWED can be applied to debug intricate relationships between execution events. It generalizes previous approaches to the debugging of control-flow based relationships between events. In this subsection we show how the original AWED model allows to handle debugging problems expressed in terms of control-flow-based and arbitrary sequence-based relationships between distributed events.

Distributed control flow. Sequences of calls that are nested within each other's control flow can be defined using the cflow pointcut constructor. Extending Nishizawa's *et al.* [22] work, AWED supports control-flow pointcuts over distributed executions taking into account Java's thread model as well: it enables matching of sequences of events that originate in local threads, span threads spawned at remote locations, and spawned child threads. The control-flow model is also transparent regarding synchronous and asynchronous communication contexts.

As an example consider testing and debugging of JBoss Cache as presented in the motivation section. A concrete problem of the two-phase commit protocol consists in ensuring that remote calls to **prepare** methods are always triggered by a corresponding call at a local cache site. A remote call that has not been appropriately triggered can be caught by the following pointcut:

!**cflow**(**call**(∗ Transaction.prepare(..)) && **host**("source"))
&& **call**(∗ Cache.remotePrepare(..)) && **host**("target")

This pointcut matches all the calls to the **remotePrepare** method on hosts belonging to the host (or host group) **target** that are not in the distributed control flow of calls occurring at source hosts. Hence, a simple pointcut definition can address the complexity of a distributed control flow breakpoint. Such control-flow relationships for debugging have already been studied, *e.g.*, as part of Li's work [18] for distributed (CORBA and COM) component-based systems and Chern and De Volder's work on sequential control-flow based breakpoints [9]: we extend such approaches by supporting the notion of control flow in the presence of asynchronous and synchronous method calls.

Distributed sequences of events. As introduced above, AWED supports pointcuts over sequences of execution events, *e.g.*, sequences of calls that do not have to be nested into other calls of the sequence. Hence, such sequences allow the definition of more general event-based contexts than the control-flow based event sequences considered above.

In the context of the debugging of JBoss Cache, for example, a very frequent requirement consists in the definition of contexts depending on the activation state of the cache. Concretely, one may want to identify remote **put** operations (which introduce data in the cache) that occur after the local cache has been initialized and before it has been stopped. A corresponding pointcut can be specified in AWED as follows:

```
a1 : seq(start > t1,
         t1: call(* Cache.start(..)) && host(localhost)> t2 || t3,
         t2: call(* Cache.put(..)) && !host(localhost) > t2 ||t3,
         t3: call(* Cache.stop(..)) && host(localhost) > t1)
      && step(a1,t2)
```

This pointcut defines an automaton named **a1** having three transitions **t1**, **t2** and **t3**: once started, **put** operations can occur or the cache can be stopped. Note that the **start** and **stop** operations of the cache are matched on the local host, while the **put** operations must not occur on the local host. The term **step(a1, t2)** allows an advice to be triggered relative to a specific transition **t2** of the automaton. At the first line **start > t1** defines that the initial transition is **t1**. The expression **t1 :**

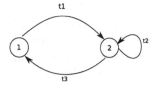

Fig. 2. Graphical representation of a start-action(s)-stop automaton

pointcutDef > t2 || t3 is interpreted as follows: if **pointcutDef** matches the current event, then the automaton is now ready to accept an execution event as defined by **t2** or **t3**. Figure 2 shows the graphical interpretation of the defined automaton.

The expressive power of our approach is mainly determined by the expressivity of our pointcut language. AWED basically provides regular pointcuts. An extension by guards on transitions of the corresponding finite-state machines, thus providing a turing-complete pointcut language, is however unproblematic (and is provided as part of the existing implementation). This feature would also allow to directly characterize concurrent and timed events. By explicitly providing regular pointcuts, existing analysis techniques of, *e.g.*, deadlocks using model checking of distributed and concurrent systems, should be applicable. This is, however, subject of future work.

A second element determining the power of our approach is the granularity of events that can be referred to by pointcuts. We have restricted the pointcut language deliberately to method calls: a more fine-grained event model that would allow, e.g., to refer to the evaluation of subexpressions of arithmetical expressions (that are supported by some aspect approaches) could incur considerable execution overhead and are less relevant for the debugging of middlewares.

The case for causality relationships. Sequence pointcuts in AWED do not guard against problems of the underlying communication network, in particular concerning message delivery such as inversion of sent messages due to random delays in message transmission. The previous sequence pointcut involving start, put and stop on JBoss Cache events is unproblematic in this respect since message inversions resulting in put operations outside the ordinary operating conditions of cache can be easily filtered out by additional pointcuts if necessary. In other cases, e.g., inversion of bank deposits and withdrawals, such problems would however wreak havoc.

Generally, AWED's automata-based pointcuts are therefore subject to two problems:

- They may not match valid sequences of events that happen to arrive in the wrong order at the host where the sequence is to be matched.
- They may match wrong sequences that stem from events that occur at different hosts in the wrong order but whose order has been inverted, e.g., because of message delays, at the host where the sequence is matched.

An AWED developer has to take care in order to avoid these problems: either by the careful definition of pointcuts and manual synchronization of distributed executions or by ensuring that additional constraints on the base application's semantics exclude them. The next subsection proposes new language constructs to enable pointcuts to directly support causality relationships and ordering constraints of messages.

3.3   AWED with Causal Pointcuts

Much research work has been done on orderings of distributed events starting with Lamport's landmark paper [17] on the use of *logical time*. In particular, vector clocks [19] can be used to enforce causal relations between events and implement causal communication by reordering events. We now show how we have integrated these notions into AWED.

Causal sequences without reordering. To extend AWED with causal information, without including reordering of messages, we have introduced a new sequence constructor seqCausal and two transition modifiers, causal and conc,

```
// Pointcuts
Seq      ::=  Id: SeqCons({Step})  |  step(Id,Id)
SeqCons  ::=  seq  |  seqCausal  |  seqCausalOrder
Step     ::=  [[!]causal  |  conc]Id: Pc → Target
```

Fig. 3. AWED with causal pointcuts

see Fig. 3. The two modifiers respectively ensure that the labelled transition is causally related to or concurrently executed with respect to the transitions leading to the start state of the labelled transition. The constructor seqCausal is syntactic sugar for sequence pointcuts whose transitions are by default labelled as causal unless they have been explicitly declared using conc to execute concurrently.

As an example let us consider the following pointcut definition:

a1 : seqCausal(causal s1: call(∗ Cache.prepare(..)) && host("source") > s2,
          conc s2: call(∗ Cache.commit(..)) && host("target") > s1)
    && step(a1, s2)

This sequence matches a prepare event in a JBoss Cache transaction, followed by a commit only if it is *not* causally related to the prepare event. Then the following prepare event is matched only if it is causally related to the previous matched commit event. This pointcut can therefore be used to test for unexpected calls to commit methods. As we show in the evaluation section, Sec. 5, this pointcut is useful to test for a real bug that affected the JBoss Cache infrastructure.

Causal pointcuts with reordering. Causal pointcuts without reordering only enforce that causally-related events are matched but they do not ensure all sequences will be matched.

To resolve this second problem, we harness the property — already demonstrated by Lamport's totally ordered broadcast operation [17] — that logical time values cannot only be used to test for causality relationships but that they also support the reordering of messages that arrive at a host in the wrong order. To allow reordering according to causal relationships, we have extended AWED with a third sequence pointcut constructor, seqCausalOrder that ensures that all causal relations are matched by, if necessary reordering, incoming events. Its semantics ensures that each event is delayed to wait for the event that precedes it causally.

As a concrete example, the following pointcut can be used to ensure that commit operations are correctly interleaved with prepare operations:

a1 : seqCausalOrder(
        t1: call(∗ Cache.prepare(..)) && host("source") > t2 || t3,
        t2: call(∗ Cache.commit(..)) && host("target") > t1,
        t3: call(∗ Cache.prepare(..)) && host("source"))
    && step(a1, t3)

Indeed, a cache web repeats sequences of prepare commit. So, two prepare should never occur in a row (transition t3): an error should be reported in this case. In order to prevent reporting of spurious errors (*e.g.*, when a commit occurs before prepare but is monitored after it) the messages must be ordered as specified by seqCausalOrder.

Note that this construct requires a larger overhead than the one without reordering. In particular with the previous construct the events are consumed as soon as they arrive, and causality is only an additional test defined by the causal and conc labels. In the case of causally ordered sequences, messages are delayed and processed only once all the causally preceding messages are received. The causal and conc labels are automatically supported in the totally ordered construct (they do not pose an additional overhead).

4   Implementation

In this section, we present how distributed aspects with support for causal events and message reordering have been implemented by extending the non-causal implementation of the AWED system [4, 5]. Note that while we present a Java-based implementation (and an evaluation of Java-based middlewares in the following section), conceptually our approach is not tied to Java. The Arachne aspect system, for instance, features (non causal) regular sequence pointcuts for C applications and has been applied to the modification of network protocols used for the communication in distributed systems [11].

In the following, we first present the overall architecture of the resulting system. Second, we discuss how AWED can be used to test causality on distributed infrastructures that have not been prepared for the provision or use of causality information. Third, we discuss the implementation of the framework that supports causal finite state machines to support causal sequences without message reordering. Finally, we will present the mechanisms for message reordering that were included to support the pointcut construct seqCausalOrder.

4.1   AWED Architecture

AWED is a dynamic aspect language that weaves aspects with classes at load time and allows aspect deployment and undeployment at execution time. Its implementation presents an optimized partially evaluated interpreter for distributed aspects. Figure 4 shows the overall architecture, i.e., its compilation chain and the main structures of its runtime framework. In the top left part of the figure we can see how the application and aspect code is compiled into Java bytecode. The bytecode is then read by AWED's instrumentation and transformation framework at load time, producing a version of the application that is instrumented at the necessary joinpoints (here a subset of the method calls). When executing the instrumented application, and once it reaches an instrumented joinpoint, the application dispatches joinpoint notifications to the Registry framework that takes care of the recognition of distributed sequence pointcuts. This framework passes the joinpoint notification to each aspect instance, that, in turn, evaluates each joinpoint to match pointcuts and to apply advice. An AWED runtime framework, including a registry, is running at runtime on each logical host, i.e., JVM. In order to support remote pointcuts each registry, i.e., each JVM, communicates joinpoint notifications to the other JVMs using an extension of the JGroups framework [16], one of the most popular Java-based middleware for group communication. This part of the infrastructure contains all necessary support for non-causal event relationships, in particular remote regular sequence pointcuts.

In figure 4, we have also detailed the two main extensions incorporated to the runtime framework in order to support the causal constructs. First, the communication framework (see the box labelled "JGroups extension" in the figure) has been extended to support causality-supporting protocols. The extended JGroups component uses the original JGroups framework augmented with specific protocols for causality. In the figure we show a traditional protocol stack that supports different protocols, including the User Datagram Protocol (UDP). The protocol stack shows, at the top, the `Causal AWED` protocol. This protocol can be any of two new protocols that we have implemented. Second, the pointcut class hierarchy (see the class diagram for causal pointcuts highlighted in magnifying glass in the figure) has been augmented by support for causal sequence-based aspects, concretely by support for causal pointcuts with or without reordering and a notion of transition guards. In the following we present both extensions in some more detail.

Causality-supporting protocols. The two new protocols that support causality do not modify actual communication, but just handle causality and delegate actual communication to the other protocols in the protocol stack. The first protocol that we have implemented is the `Causal tags + clock increase` protocol. This protocol tags the distributed messages with a vector clock time, and will calculate the value of the new vector clock times at a host upon arrival of new messages. This protocol can be used to detect causal relations, but it can not

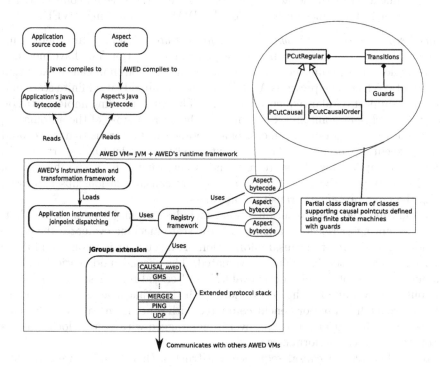

Fig. 4. AWED architecture

be used to impose causal ordering of messages. The second protocol that we have implemented is `Causal tags`. This is a more lightweight protocol that tags messages with vector clock times but does not update the vector clock. This protocol can be used with specialized adapters to add causality information to distributed infrastructures and applications that have not been aware of causality information in the first place.

4.2   Adding Causality to Non-causal Distributed Applications

Most distributed infrastructures and applications do not implement causality natively. Adapting such applications to support causality typically is very cumbersome and error prone. To avoid this problem, we propose specialized adapters that can be used to instrument causality transparently in legacy applications. To prove that this is a feasible solution we have implemented an adapter for RMI based applications, thus covering a wide spectrum of distributed Java applications. This adapter is realized using Java's notion of customized sockets.

The adapter basically implements a mechanism similar to that provided by the `Causal tags + clock increase` protocol. Thus, each message in the legacy application is now tagged with a vector clock and a local vector clock is updated upon arrival of each RMI message. This connector can be combined with the AWED framework that is running the `Causal tags` protocol to detect causal relations in the legacy application. This deployment do not need any particular modification of the legacy application. To use the specific connector, the programmer just specifies an option for the JVM when invoking AWED.

Causal sequence constructs with guarded finite state machines. In order to implement the causal sequence construct as presented in section 3 we have modified the compiler and the runtime infrastructure of the previous non-causal execution system of AWED. The previous AWED system has already used finite state machines to support regular sequence pointcuts. The corresponding implementation evaluates each join point and, depending on the current state of the automaton, accepts or rejects a joinpoint. In case of acceptance, a state transition is executed before executing the advice. We have extended this model to support guards. Thus, at compile time the state machine is constructed with specific guards, mainly to support the causal tests required by causal relationships expressed using the `conc` or `causal` transition modifiers.

At runtime, the new execution system includes two major extensions. First, before accepting or rejecting a joinpoint, the state machine evaluates the corresponding guard, *e.g.*, the causal information of the current joinpoint, and if the guard is satisfied the joinpoint is evaluated. The second modification address the management of vector clocks: evaluation of causal regular sequences has to compute a new value for the vector clock each time that it accepts a joinpoint. This approach has a major benefit compared with other frameworks implementing causality: finer grained control over events tagged with vector clocks and, as a consequence, less performance overhead.

To implement the causal sequence construct with reordering we have further extended the automata-based pointcut recognition component. Each such component now has its own vector clock that is advanced each time a message is processed (including messages not in the alphabet of the state machine). To address reordering, the state machine uses a delay queue where it stores the messages that do not arrive in the right (causal) order. The messages in this queue are causally ordered but not necessarily consecutive. Upon arrival of a new message it gets evaluated: if it is accepted and if the message causally is the next message with respect to the vector clock of the state machine, it is processed and the first message in the delay queue is evaluated again.

Finally, a note on the scalability of our approach: Concerning scalability of the pointcut matching, the principal property is that the AWED architecture (cf. Fig. 4) does not impose any centralized control, in particular, for the monitoring of pointcuts that involve causal relationships. The other components of the AWED architecture (principally matching of other pointcut types and execution of remote advice) do not require central control either as discussed as part of our previous work [4].

5   Evaluation

In this section we present a qualitative and quantitative evaluation of our approach using JBoss Cache [15], a Java-based middleware infrastructure for replicated caching (part of JBoss middleware tools). First, we analyze a non-trivial test case for replicated caching and show that aspects based on control-flow and causal patterns significantly improve the corresponding debugging and unit testing tasks. Second, we evaluate the performance of our prototype implementation in a two-fold manner. A series of micro-benchmarks provides evidence that our implementation supports regular causal sequences with no to reasonable small performance overhead. Finally, in order to provide concrete evidence that we meet the objectives set out in the motivation, we compare AWED's use of sophisticated regular causal sequences to the use of the Eclipse debugger as a popular tool for the debugging of distributed Java applications by means of loose coordination of per-host debugging sessions.

5.1   Qualitative Evaluation

In the following we present a qualitative evaluation of our approach involving debugging and testing scenarios in two Java-based middlewares, JBoss Cache [15] and Apache's ActiveMQ [27].

Deadlock testing in JBoss Cache. In JBoss Cache (Ver. 2.0.0GA) the method `performTest` of class `ReplicatedTransactionDeadlockTest` (see Fig. 5) implements a test case to detect a deadlock bug. The test case uses two caches, actions on the first cache are replicated onto the second cache by means of the replication framework. The method triggers multiple workers in multiple threads. Each worker starts a transaction, puts a value in the cache (all workers use the same memory position in the cache) and commits the transaction. The test has to be

```
1   private void performTest() throws Exception {
2       // repeat the test several times since it's not always reproducible
3       for (int i = 0; i < NUM_RUNS; i++) {
4           if (exception != null) { // terminate the test on the first failed worker
5               fail("Due to an exception: " + exception); }
6           // start several worker threads to work with the same FQN
7           Worker[] t = new Worker[NUM_WORKERS];
8           for (int j = 0; j < t.length; j++) {
9               t[j] = new Worker("worker " + i + ":" + j); t[j].start(); }
10          // wait for all workers to complete before repeating the test
11          for (Worker aT : t) aT.join(); } }
```

Fig. 5. Deadlock detection test case method

repeated a number of times (first **for** block in the figure) since it can't be reproduced easily. The original bug occurred when a worker, after a successful prepare phase of the two phase commit protocol, commits a transaction and releases the lock over the source cache after the local commit but before completing the final commit phase with the remote caches. In this case, other workers may interleave their transaction operations, in particular, acquire the lock at the same cache position and thus preclude the first transaction to terminate its remote commit phase, thus entering a deadlock situation, because no worker can acquire all necessary local and remote locks anymore.

A programmer dealing with that bug faces tree problems: (i) how two reproduce the problem, (ii) how to debug it and (iii) how to write a suitable test case to identify it in the future. To deal with the first problem the code shown in Fig. 5 triggers several threads that execute transactions concurrently, hoping for the bug to be reproduced. This approach is subject to several problems, in particular, that a unit test session could pass over the bug without noticing it. Regarding the second problem, as part of a corresponding debugging session a programmer would have to apply a breakpoint either to the line for remote prepare or in the line that throws the corresponding exception. In the first case the debugger will stop on each prepare (buggy or not). In the second case it will, eventually, stop only on an error of one of the threads. Then, depending of how threads are scheduled, it could stop the application(s) in a buggy state or in a correct state, because the other action could have or have not enough time to complete the transaction. Additionally, the programmer could perform many runs without reproducing the bug. A test case for this bug is, of course, subject to all the problems detailed above.

Using our approach we can improve on the three development scenarios: debugging, unit testing and bug reproduction. Fig. 6 shows a pointcut that can be used to define a breakpoint that will occur only if the bug appears. The pointcut implements a sequence (*i.e.*, finite state machine) with three states and three transitions. The first state accepts a call to the method **runPreparePhase**, from the **ReplicationInterceptor** class in the cache that belongs to the **source** group (**source** and **target** are dynamic groups that can be handled using AWED). Once such a method is received, the state machine changes its state to a state that accepts **tCommit** transitions and **tSecondPrepare**, the latter representing a prepare operation issued by another worker. If the target cache receives

```
1   pointcut deadlock():
2     s1:seqCausalOrder(
3       tPrep:
4         call(* ReplicationInterceptor.runPreparePhase(..)) && host(src) > tCommit || t2ndPrep,
5       tCommit: call(* PessimisticLockInterceptor.commit(..)) && host(targ) > tPrep,       .
6       tSecondPrepare: call(* ReplicationInterceptor.runPreparePhase(..)) && host(src)) &&
7     step(s1, tSecondPrepare);
```

Fig. 6. Pointcut for deadlock detection in a synchronous transactional cache

```
1    pointcut prepare(): call(* ReplicationInterceptor.runPreparePhase(..)) && host(src);
2    pointcut commit(): ... && call(* BaseRpcInterceptor.replicateCall(..)) && ...
3
4    pointcut generateDeadlock():
5      s1:seqOrderedCausal(
6        tPrep : prepare() > tCommit || t2ndPrep,
7        tCommit : commit() > tCommit || t2ndPrep,
8        t2ndPrep: prepare() );
9
10   before(): generateDeadlock() && step(s1, tCommit) { while(block){ Thread.yield(); } }
11   after(): generateDeadlock() && step(s1, t2ndPrep) { block=false; }
```

Fig. 7. Aspect ensuring the generation of the buggy behavior for deadlock detection

a `tCommit` message, the normal behavior, it returns to the first state. Finally, if the sequence detects, after the first `tPrepare` message, a `tSecondPrepare` message on the `source` cache, the state machine recognizes a deadlock state. Note that the sequence definition must be ordered causally in order to ensure that the events will be detected in the correct order in any distributed setting.

AWED's regular causal pointcut definitions can also be helpful for bug reproduction and unit testing. The main problem with current test case definitions, such as that introduced above, is that it is of haphazard nature, *i.e.*, it does not always allow to reproduce the bug situation. Figure 7 shows an excerpt of code from an aspect that will interact with the original test case of Fig. 5 to impose the desired order of events in the presence of only two workers. The aspect excerpt includes the definition of a state machine that matches a call to the method `runPreparePhase`, which means that the corresponding transaction has acquired the lock and is going to broadcast a prepare message to the target cache. Then, if it detects a call to the `replicateCall` method having as parameter a commit method call, a before advice will suspend the current thread until another `runPreparePhase` is detected. A buggy implementation will allow this reordering of events, a correct implementation will produce a lock-timeout exception because the cache node will be locked by the second transaction.

Debugging ActiveMQ. We have also performed experiments over the Apache project's ActiveMQ message broker [27] that is used, *e.g.*, for the integration of enterprise information systems. From an analysis of the list of the 359 open issues in ActiveMQ's bug tracking system as of Aug. 2008, we have found six issues classified as *blockers*: at least four of these are caused by the wrong ordering of events or messages. Similarly, out of the 13 messages classified as *critical* at least five are related to message or event ordering. We have successfully woven causal aspects on ActiveMQ. To test the applicability of our approach we have debugged a use case regarding a deadlock situation in a configuration setting with four brokers and a use case involving the wrong ordering of repeatedly delivered messages in the context of transactions session with roll back. In both cases we have successfully defined simple pointcut definitions that exactly test for the corresponding error situations. These tests provide evidence that our approach, in particular the AWED system, is applicable generally to Java-based middleware. Finally, as for JBoss Cache, these debugging experiments have incurred only minimal overhead in both the Java client and the ActiveMQ broker.

5.2   Micro-benchmarks

We have run performance tests of our implementation using the performance framework of JBoss Cache. This framework allows to run multiple performance test over cache configurations. The tests were performed in a cluster of 4 nodes. Each node was equipped with a double core AMD Opteron 250 (2400 MHz) processor in 32 bit mode, 4 GB of memory and a 1 GB network interface. The *test case scenario* we have used is the default Web-Session simulator of the JBoss Cache framework that basically simulates the interaction of a replicated http session in a cluster of application servers. This test can be parametrized on the number of requests and the ratio of reads to writes requests.

We have evaluated the performance of the extended protocols developed to support causality in AWED. To this end, we have compared four different protocol configurations: (i) the performance of JBoss Cache with a standard, non-causal, configuration of its communication protocol stack (denoted `Normal` below), (ii) the causality protocol `Causal` natively provided by JGroups and (iii) our new protocols `Causal tags` and `Causal tags + clock increment`.

Table 1 shows the results of several test sessions in our cluster. The first set of sessions was performed with a ratio of 80% reads and 20% writes over 100.000 operations (left part of the table) and the second set of tests considers a ratio of 20% reads and 80% writes (right part of the table). Each node in the test executes 100.000 requests and only the writes are replicated to the other members. The data shows that in both cases the `Normal` protocol and the `Causal tags` protocol presents the best performance average For the test with 20% writes, the `Causal` protocol (full causality, *i.e.*, vector clocks, clock

Table 1. Test results of 100.000 requests with respectively 20% and 80% writes

Protocol	Requests per second			
	20% writes		80% writes	
	Average	Standard dev.	Average	Standard dev.
Normal	63,350.23	7,004.93	58,033.77	9,792.51
Causal	60,961.14	11,867.69	53,814.05	7,085.89
Causal tags + clock inc.	52,107.34	27,790.92	53,463.53	7,310.65
Causal tags	60,396.03	7,420.05	59,487.43	7,405.64

increment and reordering) presents lower performance overhead than the `Causal tags + clock increment` protocol. Overall our new protocols do not impose a significant performance overhead (especially in the case of a large number of writes to the cache) compared to the standard JBoss Cache protocols.

5.3   Remote Debugging vs. Distributed Debugging

In order to provide evidence that we have achieved the main objective set out in the motivation part, that is, that regular causal sequences improve on a per-host approach to debugging, we compare the performance of a remote debugging session with Eclipse and a distributed debugging session with AWED. To this end, we have again used the JBoss Cache benchmark framework. We first compare two debugging sessions, one with Eclipse and one with AWED, without breakpoints in order to measure the overhead of the frameworks. We then compare both debugging sessions in the presence of a high-frequency breakpoint (*i.e.*, reached and fired many times).

AWED runtime overhead vs. Eclipse remote debugging overhead. Table 2 (left part) compares the overhead of the debugging infrastructure posed by eclipse in a debugging session and the overhead posed by our AWED prototype. This test doesn't include any breakpoint, thus it only compares the overhead of the execution frameworks. The table shows small and comparable overhead for both frameworks. This is not surprising due to the fact that both frameworks are based on the Java agent technology and no breakpoints are evaluated.

As a last experiment we have compared the overhead of Eclipse and AWED in the presence of a high-frequency breakpoint: a breakpoint in the method `invoke` of the interceptor class ReplicationInterceptor. Table 2 (right part) shows the behavior of the Eclipse debugger attached to four nodes running the JBoss Cache framework and the behavior of AWED breakpoints under such conditions. In table 2 the protocol configuration labeled as *invasive causality* implies that the application being debugged has been invasively modified with an adapter for causality, thus AWED system can predicate over application's own messages. Using the Eclipse debugger we have executed the benchmarks first in JBoss Cache normal configuration and then with JBoss Cache using JGroups default `CAUSAL` protocol. The performance in these configurations is very bad and after several problems with memory overflow and unacceptable delays for the test we have reduced the number of request to 100. On the other hand, the test of

Table 2. Debugging session without breakpoints (left half) and with a high-frequency breakpoint (right half)

	Protocol	Requests per second Average	Std. dev.	No. of requests	Requests per second Average	Std. dev.	No. of requests
Eclipse	Normal	55,111.79	7,792.45	10^5	2.80	0.21	100
Debugger	Causal	55,172.60	5,764,97	10^5	3.39	0.30	100
AWED	Causal tags + clock inc.	56,079.85	5,983.75	10^5	234.77	5.07	10^5
	Invasive causality	53,045.19	10,223.90	10^5	237.61	7.58	10^5

performance using the AWED framework are at least seventy times faster and do not impose any restrictions in the conditions of the test. This is due to the fact that, even tough the Eclipse debugger and AWED's dynamic framework use similar execution technology, AWED implements several optimization techniques and was designed with distribution in mind [6]. Our approach thus scales much better than the discussed debugging methods using Eclipse.

6   Related Work

Our approach for causality is based on the idea of causality based on vector clocks introduced by Mattern [19] (that itself extended Lamport's approach on logical time introduced in the landmark pape [17]). These results were later integrated into actual middleware for reliable distributed systems based on group communication,*e.g.*, see the Horus framework [28]. The benefits and limitations of using causal communications, in particular, the resulting overhead that is added to all communication, has been actively discussed [7, 8, 24]. Our approach extends similar current approaches, *e.g.*, the support for causality in JGroups [3] We have provided concrete evidence that expression of causal communication at the language level is useful in the presence of real-world debugging scenarios in current middleware.

Debugging of control-flow based relationships between execution events has been one of the main domains of application of causality and logical clocks, see *e.g.*, [10, 13, 14, 23, 25]. Hseush et al. [14] and Ponamgi et al. [23] have presented *Data Path Expressions* (DPE), a control-flow based debugging language for concurrent applications. Our sequence construct combined with the pointcut language provide similar flexibility as their theoretical language, additionally we provide a fully distributed solution with no central monitoring component.

More recently Sen et al. [25] proposed an algorithm for decentralized monitoring used to check violations of safety properties in distributed systems. Monitoring expressions in their approach are written in past time linear logic. Their proposal presents *knowledge vectors* (inspired by vector clocks) and propose the Diana tool and actors as an implementation support. Our approach provides richer expressivity because of our general notion of transition guards and allows group relationships to be expressed.

Other approaches have addressed the implementation and formalization of distributed models for debugging (*e.g.*, see [10, 21]). However, either they do not consider the causality concept and ordering of events (*e.g.*, De Rosa *et al.* [10]) or, they restrict the concept of causality to the concept of distributed control flow (*e.g.*, Mega and Kon [21] as well as Li's work on monitoring of component-based systems [18]) These approaches can only express a small subset of the relationships we consider. Finally, control flow relationships for the debugging using aspects have been considered only for the sequential case, notably by Chern and De Volder [9].

7   Conclusion

In this paper, we have argued for the use of programming abstractions as expressive support for the debugging and testing of distributed middleware, in particular for the definition of sophisticated relationships between distributed events and the recognition of event sequences in the presence of non-deterministic executions. We have presented a corresponding aspect-based language and implementation support that introduces causal event sequences into AWED, an aspect system for the dynamic manipulation of distributed systems. We have validated our approach in the context of Java-based middleware, in particular for the debugging and unit testing of a JBoss Cache and Apache's ActiveMQ. This evaluation has shown that our implementation has reasonable overhead and that our approach significantly improves on the use of debuggers, such as Eclipse, that are based on the manual coordination of per-host debugging sessions.

This work paves the way for several leads of future work. On a conceptual level, more flexible abstractions to define relationships that mix events that partially are causally ordered and partially are not are of foremost interest. Furthermore, exploring the use of our abstractions in other application domains, such as grid infrastructures, should be explored.

References

1. Anderson, J.H.: Lamport on mutual exclusion: 27 years of planting seeds. In: PODC 2001: Proceedings of the twentieth annual ACM symposium on Principles of distributed computing, pp. 3–12. ACM Press, New York (2001)
2. Awed home page (2008), http://www.emn.fr/x-info/awed
3. Ban, B.: JGroups, reliable multicast comm. (2002), http://www.jgroups.org/
4. Benavides Navarro, L.D., Südholt, M., et al.: Explicitly distributed AOP using AWED. In: Proceedings of the 5th ACM Int. Conf. on Aspect-Oriented Software Development (AOSD 2006). ACM Press, New York (2006)
5. Benavides Navarro, L.D., Südholt, M., Vanderperren, W., De Fraine, B., Suvée, D.: Explicitly distributed AOP using AWED. Research Report 5882, INRIA (March 2006)
6. Benavides Navarro, L.D., Südholt, M., Vanderperren, W., Verheecke, B.: Modularization of Distributed Web Services Using Aspects with Explicit Distribution (AWED). In: Meersman, R., Tari, Z. (eds.) OTM 2006. LNCS, vol. 4276, pp. 1449–1466. Springer, Heidelberg (2006)
7. Birman, K.: A response to cheriton and skeen's criticism of causal and totally ordered communication. SIGOPS Oper. Syst. Rev. 28(1), 11–21 (1994)
8. Cheriton, D.R., Skeen, D.: Understanding the limitations of causally and totally ordered communication. In: SOSP, pp. 44–57 (1993)
9. Chern, R., De Volder, K.: Debugging with control-flow breakpoints. In: AOSD 2007: Proceedings of the 6th international conference on Aspect-oriented software development, pp. 96–106. ACM, New York (2007)
10. De Rosa, M., Goldstein, S.C., Lee, P., Campbell, J.D., Pillai, P., Mowry, T.C.: Distributed watchpoints: Debugging large multi-robot systems. International Journal of Robotics Research (2007)

11. Douence, R., Fritz, T., Loriant, N., Menaud, J.-M., Ségura-Devillechaise, M., Südholt, M.: An expressive aspect language for system applications with arachne. In: Proc. of AOSD 2005. ACM Press, New York (2005)
12. Eclipse Foundation. Remote debugging in Eclipse (2008), http://www.eclipse.org
13. Fowler, J., Zwaenepoel, W.: Causal distributed breakpoints. In: Proceedings of the 10th International Conference on Distributed Computing Systems (ICDCS), Washington, DC, pp. 134–141. IEEE, Los Alamitos (1990)
14. Hseush, W., Kaiser, G.E.: Modeling concurrency in parallel debugging. In: PPOPP, pp. 11–20 (1990)
15. JBoss Cache home page (2008), http://labs.jboss.com/jbosscache
16. JGroups home page (2008), http://www.jgroups.org
17. Lamport, L.: Time, clocks, and the ordering of events in a distributed system. Commun. ACM 21(7), 558–565 (1978)
18. Li, J.: Monitoring and characterization of component-based systems with global causality capture. In: 23th Int. Conf. on Distributed Computing Systems, Providence, RI. IEEE, Los Alamitos (2003)
19. Mattern, F.: Virtual time and global states of distributed systems. In: Proceedings of the international Workshop on Parallel and distributed Algorithms, Chateau de Bonas, France (October 1988)
20. Mega, G., Kon, F.: Debugging distributed object applications with the Eclipse platform. In: Eclipse 2004: Proceedings of the 2004 OOPSLA workshop on eclipse technology exchange, pp. 42–46. ACM, New York (2004)
21. Mega, G., Kon, F.: An Eclipse-Based Tool for Symbolic Debugging of Distributed Object Systems. In: Meersman, R., Tari, Z. (eds.) OTM 2007, Part I. LNCS, vol. 4803, pp. 648–666. Springer, Heidelberg (2007)
22. Nishizawa, M., Shiba, S., Tatsubori, M.: Remote pointcut - a language construct for distributed AOP. In: Proc. of AOSD 2004. ACM Press, New York (2004)
23. Ponamgi, M.K., Hseush, W., Kaiser, G.E.: Debugging multithreaded programs with MPD. IEEE Software 6(3), 37–43 (1991)
24. Schwarz, R., Mattern, F.: Detecting causal relationships in distributed computations: in search of the holy grail. Distrib. Comput. 7(3), 149–174 (1994)
25. Sen, K., Vardhan, A., Agha, G., Rosu, G.: Efficient decentralized monitoring of safety in distributed systems. In: ICSE, pp. 418–427. IEEE, Los Alamitos (2004)
26. Allinea Software. Distributed debugging tool (2008), http://www.allinea.com/
27. The Apache software foundation. Apache ActiveMQ is an open source message broker (2008), http://activemq.apache.org/
28. van Renesse, R., Birman, K.P., Maffeis, S.: Horus: a flexible group communication system. Commun. ACM 39(4), 76–83 (1996)

Enabling Resource Sharing between Transactional and Batch Workloads Using Dynamic Application Placement

David Carrera[1], Malgorzata Steinder[2], Ian Whalley[2], Jordi Torres[1],
and Eduard Ayguadé[1]

[1] Technical University of Catalonia (UPC) - Barcelona Supercomputing Center (BSC)
Barcelona, Spain
{david.carrera,jordi.torres,eduard.ayguade}@bsc.es
[2] IBM T.J. Watson Research Center
Hawthorne, NY 10532
{steinder,inw}@us.ibm.com

Abstract. We present a technique that enables existing middleware to fairly manage mixed workloads: batch jobs and transactional applications. The technique leverages a generic application placement controller, which dynamically allocates compute resources to application instances. The controller works towards a fairness goal while also trying to maximize individual workload performance. We use relative performance functions to drive the application placement controller. Such functions are derived from workload-specific performance models—in the case of transactional workloads, we use queuing theory to build the performance model. For batch workloads, we evaluate a candidate placement by calculating long-term estimates of the completion times that are achievable with that placement according to a scheduling policy. In this paper, we propose a lowest relative performance first scheduling policy as a way to also achieve fair resource allocation among batch jobs. Our technique permits collocation of the workload types on the same physical hardware, and leverages control mechanisms such as suspension and migration to perform online system reconfiguration. In our experiments we demonstrate that our technique maximizes mixed workload performance while providing service differentiation based on high-level performance goals.

1 Introduction

Transactional applications and batch jobs are widely used by many organizations to deliver critical services to their customers and partners. For example, in financial institutions, transactional web workloads are used to trade stocks and query indices, while computationally intensive non-interactive workloads are used to analyse portfolios or model stock performance. Due to intrinsic differences among these workloads, they are typically run today on separate dedicated hardware, which contributes to resource under-utilization and management complexity. Therefore, organizations demand management solutions that permit such workloads to run together on the same hardware, improving resource utilization while continuing to offer performance guarantees.

Integrated performance management of mixed workloads is a challenging problem. First, performance goals for different workloads tend to be of different types. For

V. Issarny and R. Schantz (Eds.): Middleware 2008, LNCS 5346, pp. 203–222, 2008.
© IFIP International Federation for Information Processing 2008

interactive workloads, goals are typically defined in terms of average or percentile response time or throughput over a short time interval, while goals for non-interactive workloads concern the performance (e.g., completion time) of individual jobs. Second, due to the nature of their goals and short duration of individual requests, interactive workloads lend themselves to automation at short control cycles, whereas non-interactive workloads typically require calculation of a schedule for an extended period of time.

In addition, different types of workload require different control mechanisms for management. Transactional workloads are managed using flow control, load balancing, and application placement. Non-interactive workloads need scheduling and resource control. Traditionally, these have been addressed separately.

To illustrate the problems inherent in managing these two types of workload together, let us consider a simple example. Consider a system consisting of 4 identical machines. At some point in time, in the system there is one transactional application, TA, which requires the capacity of 2 machines to meet its average response time goal. The system also includes 4 identical batch jobs, each requiring one physical machine for a period of time t and having completion time goal of $T = 3t$. The jobs are placed in a queue and are labeled J1, J2, J3, and J4, according to their order in the queue. The system must decide how many jobs should be running—that is, how many machines should be allocated to the transactional application and to batch jobs respectively. Let us consider two of the possible configurations. In the first configuration, one machine is allocated to batch workload and three machines are used by TA. Thus, jobs execute in sequence and complete after time t, $2t$, $3t$, and $4t$. As a result, J4 violates its SLA goal, while TA overachieves its SLA target. In the second configuration, two machines are allocated to batch workload, which permits the four jobs to complete at times t, t, $2t$ and $2t$, respectively. Thus all jobs exceed their SLA goal, while TA also meets its SLA target. Clearly, the second configuration is a better choice.

Let us now assume that that the second configuration is put into effect, but then, at time $t/2$, the workload intensity for TA increases such that it now requires all 4 machines to meet its SLA goal. In the current configuration, all jobs will exceed their SLA goals, but TA will violates its goal. If, for the sake of easy calculation, we assume that the response time of TA is proportional to the inverse of its allocated capacity, then TA will violate its response time goal by 100%. Therefore, it makes sense to consider suspending one of the running jobs, J2, and allocating its capacity to TA. If this change occurs at time $t/2$, then J1, J2, J3, and J4, complete at times t, $1.5t$, $2.5t$, and $3.5t$ respectively—all jobs run in series on a single machine, and J2 resumes halfway through its execution. Thus, J1, J2, and J3 exceed their SLA goals, J4 violates its goal by about 16%, and TA violates its goal by about 33%. This results in an allocation that, when the goals of all workloads cannot be met, spreads goal violations among workloads so as to achieve the smallest possible violation for each application.

These examples show that in order to manage resource allocation to a mix of transactional and batch workloads, the system must be able to make placement decisions at short time intervals, so as to respond to changes in transactional workload intensity. While making decisions, the system must be able to look ahead in the queue of jobs and predict the future performance (relative to goals) of all jobs—both those started now, and those that will be started in the future. It must be able to make trade-offs between the various jobs and the transactional workload, taking into account their goals.

Enabling resource sharing between transactional and batch workloads also introduces a number of challenges in the area of application deployment, update, configuration, and performance and availability management. Many of these challenges are addressed by virtualization technologies, which provide a layer of separation between a hardware infrastructure and workload, and provide a uniform set of control mechanisms for managing these workloads embedded inside virtual containers. Our technique relies on common virtualization control mechanisms to manage workloads.

In addition, our system uses Relative Performance Functions (RPF from here on) to permit trade-offs between different workloads. The RPFs define application performance relative to that application's goal. It can therefore be seen that equalizing the achieved relative performance between two applications results in "fairness"—the applications will be equally satisfied in terms of relative distance from their goals. The original contribution of this paper is a scheme for modeling the performance of, and managing, non-interactive long-running workloads.

This paper is organized as follows. In Section 2, we explain the contributions of this paper in the context of related work. In Section 3, we present our approach to managing heterogeneous workloads using resource allocation driven by application relative performance. In Section 4, we describe the calculation of the relative performance function for non-interactive applications. In Section 5 we evaluate our approach via simulation.

2   Related Work

The explicit management of heterogeneous workloads was previously studied in [1], in which CPU shares are manually allocated to run mixed workloads on a large multiprocessor system. This is a static approach, and does not run workloads within virtual machines. Virtuoso [2] describes an OS scheduling technique, VSched, for heterogeneous workload VMs. VSched enforces compute rate and interactivity goals for both non-interactive and interactive workloads (including web workloads), and provides soft real-time guarantees for VMs hosted on a single physical machine. VSched could be used as a component of our system for providing resource-control automation mechanisms within a machine, but our approach addresses resource allocation for heterogeneous workloads across a cluster of machines.

The relative performance functions we use in our system are similar in concept to the utility functions that have been used in real-time work schedulers to represent the fact that the value produced by such a system when a unit of work is completed can be represented in more detail than a simple binary value indicating whether the work met its or missed its goal. In [3], the completion time of a work unit is assigned a value to the system that can be represented as a function of time. Other work in the field of utility-driven management are summarized in [4] with special focus on real-time embedded systems. In [5], the authors present a utility-driven scheduling mechanism that aims to maximize the aggregated system utility. Our technique does not focus on real-time systems, but on any general system for which performance goals can be expressed as relative performance functions. In addition, we introduce the notion of fairness into our application-centric management technique—our objective is not to maximize the system relative performance, but to at least maximize the performance of the least performing application.

Outside of the realm of the real-time systems, the authors of [6] focus on a utility-guided scheduling mechanism driven by data management criteria, since this is the main concern for many data-intensive HPC scientific applications. In our work we focus on CPU-bound heterogeneous environments, but our technique could be extended to observe data management criteria by expanding the semantics of our RPFs.

Despite the similarity between an RPF and a utility function, one difference should be pointed out. While utility functions are typically used to model user satisfaction or business value resulting from a particular level of performance, an RPF is merely a measure of relative performance distance from the goal. Hence, unlike in [7,8] we do not study the correctness of RPFs with respect to modeling user satisfaction. If such a satisfaction model exists, it may be used to transform an RPF into a utility function.

There is also previous work in the area of managing workloads in virtual machines. Management of clusters of virtual machines is addressed in [9] and [10]. The authors of [9] address the problem of deploying a cluster of virtual machines with given resource configurations across a set of physical machines. The authors of [10] define a Java VM API that permits a developer to set resource allocation policies. In [11] and [12], a two-level control loop is proposed to make resource allocation decisions within a physical machine, but these do not address integrated management of multiple physical machines. The authors of [13] study the overhead of a dynamic allocation scheme that relies on virtualization as opposed to static resource allocation. Their evaluation covers both CPU-intensive jobs and transactional workloads, but does not consider mixed environments. Neither of these techniques provides a technology to dynamically adjust allocation based on SLA objectives in the face of resource contention.

Placement problems in general have also been studied in the literature, frequently using techniques including bin packing, multiple knapsack problems, and multi-dimensional knapsack problems [14]. The optimization problem that we consider presents a non-linear optimization objective while previous approaches [15,16] to similar problems address only linear optimization objectives. In [17], the authors evaluate a similar problem to that addressed in our work (restricted to transactional applications), and use a simulated annealing optimization algorithm. Their strategy aims to maximize the overall system utility while we focus on first maximizing the performance of the least performing application in the system, which increases fairness and prevents starvation, as was shown in [18]. In [19], a fuzzy logic controller is implemented to make dynamic resource management decisions. This approach is not application-centric—it focuses on global throughput—and considers only transactional applications. The algorithm proposed in [20] allows applications to share physical machines, but does not change the number of instances of an application, does not minimize placement changes, and considers a single bottleneck resource.

3   Integrated Management of Heterogeneous Workloads

3.1   System Architecture

We consider a system that includes a set of heterogeneous physical machines, referred to henceforth as *nodes*. Transactional web applications, which are served by application servers, are replicated across nodes to form *application server clusters*. Requests to these applications arrive at an entry router which may be an L4 or L7 gateway that distributes requests to clustered applications according to a load balancing mechanism. Long-running jobs are submitted to the *job scheduler*, placed in its queue, and dispatched based on the resource allocation decisions of the management system.

The request router monitors incoming and outgoing requests and measures their service times and arrival rates per application. It may also employ an overload protection mechanism [21,22] by queuing requests that cannot be immediately accommodated by server nodes. A separate component, called the *work profiler* [23], monitors resource utilization of nodes and (based on a regression model that combines the utilization values with throughput data) estimates an average CPU requirement of a single request to any application. Based on these findings, our system builds performance models that allow it to predict the performance of any transactional application for any given allocation of CPU power. The size and placement of application clusters is determined by the *application placement controller* (APC).

Batch jobs are submitted to the system via the *job scheduler*. Each job has an associated performance goal. Currently we support completion time goals, and we plan to extend the system to handle other performance objectives. The job scheduler uses APC as an advisor as to where and when a job should be executed. When APC makes a decision, actions pertaining to batch jobs are given to the scheduler to be put into effect. The job scheduler also monitors job status and notifies APC, which uses the information in subsequent control cycles. A *job workload profiler* estimates job resource usage profiles, which are fed into APC. Job usage profiles are used to derive an RPF of a given resource allocation to jobs, which is used by APC to make allocation decisions.

APC operates in a control loop with period T, which is of the order of minutes. A short control cycle is necessary to allow the system to react quickly to transactional workload intensity changes which may happen frequently and unexpectedly. In each cycle, APC examines the placement of applications on nodes and their resource allocations, evaluates the relative performance of this allocation and makes changes to the allocation by starting, stopping, suspending, resuming, relocating or changing CPU share configuration of some applications. In the following sections we will concentrate on the problem solved by APC in a single control cycle.

3.2   Problem Statement

We are given a set of nodes, $\mathcal{N} = \{1, \ldots, N\}$ and a set of applications $\mathcal{M} = \{1, \ldots, M\}$. We use n and m to index into the sets of nodes and applications respectively. With each node n we associate its memory and CPU capacities. With each application, we associate its load independent demand, that represents the amount of memory consumed by this application whenever it is started on a node. We use symbol P to denote a placement matrix of applications on nodes. Cell $P_{m,n}$ represents the number of instances of application m on node n. We use symbol L to represent a load placement matrix. Cell $L_{m,n}$ denotes the amount of CPU speed consumed by all instances of application m on node n. A RPF for each application may be expressed as a function of L.

Use of Relative Performance Functions. A relative performance function for a given application is a measure of the relative distance of the application's performance from its goal. It has a value of 0 when the application exactly meets its performance goal. Values greater than 0 and less than 0 represent the degree with which the goal is exceeded or violated, respectively. In our system we associate an RPF to each existing application.

RPFs are used to model the relation between delivered service level and application satisfaction. For resource allocation purposes, such functions can be transformed to model application satisfaction given particular resource allocation. Notice that application satisfaction can be understood as a measurement of relative performance. Section 3.3 and Section 4 describe how RPFs are calculated for both transactional applications and long-running jobs in our system. Our system aims to make fair placement decisions in terms of relative performance – application performance relative to its goal. The use of RPFs in our system is justified by the fact that they provide uniform workload-specific performance models that allow fair placement decisions across different workloads.

Although in our system we use linear functions, other models could be decided as it is discussed in section 2. Deciding the best shape for application performance models is out of the scope of this particular work, but the technique here presented will continue to work for any existing monotonic growing model.

Optimization Objective. Given an application placement matrix P and a load distribution matrix L, a relative performance value can be calculated for each application. The performance of the system can then be measured as an ordered vector of application relative performance. The objective of APC is to find the best possible new placement of applications as well as a corresponding load distribution such that maximizes the performance of the system.

The optimization objective is an extension of a max min criterion, and differs from it by explicitly stating that after the max min objective can no longer be improved (because the lowest performing application cannot be allocated any more resources), the system should continue improving the relative performance of other applications. The APC finds a placement that meets the above objective while ensuring that neither the memory nor CPU capacity of any node is overloaded. In addition, APC employs heuristics that aim to minimize the number of changes to the current placement. While finding the optimal placement, APC also observes a number of constraints, such as resource constraints, collocation constraints and application pinning, amongst others.

Algorithm Outline. The application placement problem is known to be NP-hard and heuristics must be used to solve it. In this paper, we leverage an algorithm proposed in [18].

The core of the algorithm is a set of three nested loops. An outer loop iterates over nodes. For each visited node, an intermediate loop iterates over application instances placed on this node and attempts to remove them one by one, thus generating a set of configurations whose cardinality is linear in the number of instances placed on the node. For each such configuration, an inner loop iterates over all applications, attempting to place new instances on the node as permitted by the constraints.

The order in which nodes, instances, and applications are visited is driven by relative performance functions. In the process, the algorithm examines application relative performance asking the following questions:

- What is the relative performance of an application in the specified placement?
- Given application placement, how much additional CPU power must be allocated to an application such that it achieves the specified relative performance value?

In Section 3.3, we briefly explain how these questions are answered for web workloads. Section 4 introduces the relative performance function for long-running workloads, which is an original contribution of this paper.

3.3 Performance Model for Transactional Workloads

In our system, a user can associate a response time goal, τ_m with each transactional application. Based on the observed response time for an application t_m, we evaluate the system performance with respect to the goal using an objective function u_m, which is defined as follows:

$$u_m(t_m) = \frac{\tau_m - t_m}{\tau_m} \tag{1}$$

We leverage the request router's performance model and the application resource usage profile to estimate t_m as a function of the CPU speed allocated to the application, $t_m(\omega_m)$. This allows us to express u_m as a function of ω_m, $u_m(\omega_m) = u_m(t_m(\omega_m))$.

Given a placement P and the corresponding load distribution L, we obtain $u_m(L)$ by taking $u_m(\omega_m)$, where $\omega_m = \sum_n L_{m,n}$. Likewise, we can calculate the amount of CPU power needed to achieve a relative performance u by taking the inverse function of u_m, $\omega_m(u)$.

The performance model for transactional workloads is not an original contribution of this work, but is in the core of the middleware upon which our work relies. Thus, the reader is referred to [21] for a detailed description of the model.

4 Performance Model for Non-interactive Workloads

In this section, we focus on applying our placement technique to manage long-running jobs. We start by observing that a performance management system cannot treat batch jobs as individual management entities, as their completion times are not independent. For example, if jobs that are currently running complete sooner, this permits jobs currently in the queue (not yet running) to complete sooner as well. Thus, performance predictions for long-running jobs must be done in relation to other long-running jobs.

Another challenge is to provide performance predictions with respect to job completion time on a control cycle which may be much lower than job execution time. Typically, such a prediction would require the calculation of an optimal schedule for the jobs. To trade-off resources among transactional and long-running workloads, we would have to evaluate a number of such schedules calculated over a number of possible divisions of resources among the two kinds of workloads. The number of combinations would be exponential in the number of nodes in the cluster. We therefore propose an approximate technique, which is presented in this section.

4.1 Job Characteristics

We are given a set of jobs. With each job m we associate the following information:

Resource Usage Profile. A resource usage profile describes the resource requirements of a job and is given at job submission time—in the real system, this profile comes from the job workload profiler. The profile is estimated based on historical data analysis. Each job m consists of a sequence of N_m stages, $s_1, \ldots, s_{N_m}$, where each stage s_k is described by the following parameters:

- The amount of CPU cycles consumed in this stage, $\alpha_{k,m}$.
- The maximum speed with which the stage may run, $\omega_{k,m}^{max}$.
- The minimum speed with which the stage must run, whenever it runs, $\omega_{k,m}^{min}$.
- The memory requirement $\gamma_{k,m}$.

Performance Objectives. The SLA objective for a job is expressed in terms of its desired completion time, τ_m, which is the time by which the job must complete. Clearly, τ_m should be greater than the job's desired start time, τ_m^{start}, which itself is greater than or equal to the time when the job was submitted. The difference between the completion time goal and the desired start time, $\tau_m - \tau_m^{start}$, is called the relative goal.

We are also given an RPF that maps actual job completion time t_m to a measure of satisfaction from achieving it, $u_m(t_m)$. If job m completes at time t_m, then the relative distance of its completion time from the goal is expressed by the RPF of the following form.

$$u_m(t_m) = \frac{\tau_m - t_m}{\tau_m - \tau_m^{start}} \tag{2}$$

Runtime State. At runtime, we monitor and estimate the following properties for each job: Current status, which may be either running, not-started, suspended, or paused; and CPU time consumed thus far, α_m^*.

4.2 Hypothetical Relative Performance

To calculate job placement, we need to define an RPF which APC can use to evaluate its placement decisions. While the actual relative performance achieved by a job can only be calculated at completion time, the algorithm needs a mechanism to predict (at each control cycle) the relative performance that each job in the system will achieve given a particular allocation. This is also the case for jobs that are not yet started, for which the expected completion time is still undefined. To help answer questions that APC is asking of the RPF for each application, we introduce the concept of *hypothetical relative performance*.

Estimating Application Relative Performance Given Aggregate CPU Allocation.
Suppose that we deal with a system in which all jobs can be placed simultaneously, and
in which the available CPU power may be arbitrarily finely allocated among the jobs.
We require a function that maps the system's CPU power to the relative performance
achievable by jobs when placed on it.

Let us consider job m. Based on its properties, we can estimate the completion time
needed to achieve relative performance u, $t_m(u) = \tau_m - u(\tau_m - \tau_m^{\text{start}})$. Then we can
calculate the average speed with which the job must proceed over its remaining lifetime
to achieve u, as follows:

$$\omega_m(u) = \frac{\alpha_{N_m,m}^{cr}}{t_m(u) - t_{\text{now}}} \tag{3}$$

where we define $\alpha_{N_m,m}^{cr}$ as the remaining work to complete all stages up to stage
N_m, m.

To achieve the relative performance of u for all jobs, the aggregate allocation to all
jobs must be $\omega_g = \sum_m \omega_m(u)$. To create the RPF, we sample $\omega_m(u)$ for various values
of u and interpolate values between the sampling points.

Let $u_1 = -\infty, u_2, \ldots, u_R = 1$, where R is a small constant, be a set of sampling
points (target relative performance values from now on). We define matrices W and V
as follows:

$$W_{i,m} = \begin{cases} \omega_m(u_i) & \text{if } u_i < u_m^{\text{max}} \\ \omega_m(u_m^{\text{max}}) & \text{otherwise} \end{cases} \tag{4}$$

$$V_{i,m} = \begin{cases} u_i & \text{if } u_i < u_m^{\text{max}} \\ u_m^{\text{max}} & \text{otherwise} \end{cases} \tag{5}$$

Cell $W_{i,m}$ contains the average speed with which application m should execute starting from t_{now} to achieve relative performance u_i, and cell and $V_{i,m}$ contains the relative
performance value u_i if it is possible for application m to achieve this performance level
u_i. If relative performance u_i is not achievable by application m, these cells instead contain the average speed with which the application should execute starting from t_{now} to
achieve its maximum achievable relative performance, and the value of the maximum
relative performance, respectively.

For a given ω_g, there exist two values k and $k + 1$ such that:

$$\sum_m W_{k,m} \leq \omega_g \leq \sum_m W_{k+1,m} \tag{6}$$

Allocating a CPU power of ω_g to all jobs will result in a relative performance u_m
for each job m in the range $V_{k,m} \leq u_m \leq V_{k+1,m}$. That corresponds to a hypothetical
CPU allocation ω_m in the range $W_{k,m} \leq \omega_m \leq W_{k+1,m}$.

At some point the algorithm needs to know the relative performance that each application will achieve (u_m) if it decides to allocate a CPU power of ω_g to all applications
combined. We must find values ω_m and u_m for each application m such that equation 6
is satisfied and that fall within the ranges described above. It must also be satisfied that
$\sum_m \omega_m = \omega_g$. As finding a solution for this final requirement implies solving a system
of linear equations, which is too costly to perform in an on-line placement algorithm, we
use an approximation based on the interpolation of ω_m from cells $W_{k,m}$ and $W_{k+1,m}$,

where k and $k + 1$ follow equation 6, and deriving u_m from ω_m. This technique is not included here because of space constraints, but is described in detail in [24].

Evaluating Placement Decisions. Let P be a given placement. Let ω_m be the amount of CPU power allocated to application m in placement P. For applications that are not placed, $\omega_m = 0$.

To calculate the relative performance of application m given a placement P calculated at time t_{now} for a control cycle of length T, we calculate a hypothetical relative performance function at time $t_{now} + T$. For each job, we increase its α^* by the amount of work that will be done over T with allocation ω_m. We use thus obtained hypothetical relative performance to extrapolate u_m from matrices W and V for $\omega_g = \sum_m \omega_m$.

Thus, we use the knowledge of placement in the next cycle to predict the job's progress over the cycle's duration, and we use the hypothetical function to predict job performance in the following cycles. We also assume that the total allocation to long-running workload in the following cycles will be the same as in the next cycle. This assumption helps us balance batch work execution over time.

4.3   Hypothetical Relative Performance: An Illustrative Example

In this example (created using the simulator discussed in more detail in Section 5) we illustrate how the hypothetical relative performance guides our algorithm to make placement decisions.

We use three jobs, J1, J2, and J3, with properties shown in Table 1, and a single node with 2000MB of RAM and one 1000MHz processor. The memory characteristics of the jobs and the node mean that the node can host only two jobs at a time. J1 can completely consume the node's CPU capacity, whereas J2 and J3, at maximum speed, can each consume only half of the node's CPU capacity.

We execute two scenarios, S1 and S2, which differ in the setting of the completion time factor for J2, which in turn affects the completion time goal for J2, as illustrated in Table 1. Note that J3 has a completion time factor of 1, which means that in order to meet its goal it must be started immediately after submission and that it must execute with the maximum speed throughout its life. To improve the clarity of mathematical calculations, we also use unrealistic execution times (in the order of seconds) and a control cycle $T = 1s$.

Figure 1 shows cycle-by-cycle executions of the algorithm for S1 and S2, respectively, illustrating relevant placement alternatives that are considered in successive

Table 1. Hypothetical Relative Performance Example: System Properties

Job property	J1	J2	J3	Job property	Scenario 1 J1 J2 J3	Scenario 2 J1 J2 J3
Start time [s]	0	1	2	Relative goal factor	5 4 1	5 3 1
Max speed [MHz]	1,000	500	500	Relative goal [s]	20 16 8	20 12 8
Mem requirement [MB]	750	750	750	Completion time goal [s]	20 17 10	20 13 10
Work [Mcycles]	4,000	2,000	4,000			
Min execution time [s]	4	4	8			

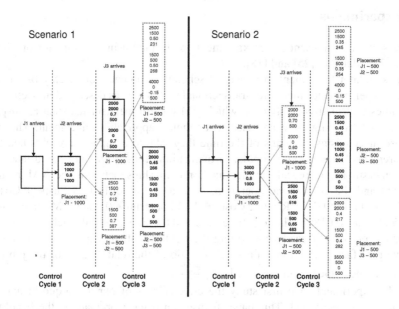

Fig. 1. Hypothetical Relative Performance Example: Cycle-by-cycle execution. Rectangular boxes show the outstanding work, $\alpha_m - \alpha_m^*$, work done, α_m^*, value of hypothetical relative performance and corresponding CPU allocation for each job currently in the system.

control cycles. The boxes with solid outlines show the choices that the algorithm makes, and those with dotted outlines indicate viable alternatives that are not chosen. The reasoning for the choices made is described below.

In cycle 1 of S1 and S2, only one job, J1, is in the system, hence the only reasonable placement is the one that allocates the maximum speed to J1. After the arrival of J2, in cycle 2, two placements are considered: P1, in which both J1 and J2 are running with an allocated speed of 500 MHz (for J1 this amounts to 50% reduction of the capacity allocated in cycle 1), and P2, in which J2 is not placed and J2 continues to run at maximum speed. In S1, P1 and P2 have the same relative performance value of 0.7 to both applications. Therefore, P2 is selected, since it does not require any placement changes. In S2, due to the tightened goal of J2, the utilities of P1 and P2 are $(0.65, 0.65)$ and $(0.6, 0.7)$, respectively, where (x, y) is an increasingly ordered vector of utilities for J1 and J2. Therefore, in S2, P1 is better choice as it equalizes the relative distance of the performance of J1 and J2 from their respective goals.

The difference in the value of hypothetical utilities between S1 and S2, can be illustrated using J2 as an example. If J2 is not started in cycle 2, and hence is started in cycle 3 or later, its earliest possible completion time is 19. In S1, this results in a maximum achievable relative performance of 0.65 ($\approx (16 - 5)/16$), whereas in S2, it is only 0.6 ($\approx (12 - 5)/12$).

Since in cycle 2 of S1 and S2 the algorithm has made different decisions, from this point the scenarios diverge. However, a similar rationale may be used to explain the decisions made by the algorithm in cycle 3, also shown in Figure 1.

5 Experiments

In this section we present three experiments performed using a simulator previously used and validated in [25] and [18].

The simulator implements a variety of scheduling policies for batch jobs and also includes a performance model for transactional workloads, as described in Section 3.3. It assumes a virtualized system, in which VM control mechanisms such as suspend, resume, and live migration are used to configure application placement. The costs of these mechanisms, in terms of the time they take to complete, are obtained from measurements taken using a popular virtualization product for Intel-based machines. These measurements reveal simple linear relationships between the VM memory footprint and the cost of the operation, and can be described as Suspend Cost = VM Footprint $*$ $0.0353s$, Resume Cost = VM Footprint $*$ $0.0333s$, Migrate Cost = VM Footprint $*$ $0.0132s$. The boot time observed for all our virtual machines was $3.6s$.

For the purpose of easily controlling the tightness of SLA goals, we introduce a relative goal factor which is defined as the ratio of the relative goal of the job to its execution time at the maximum speed, $\frac{\tau_m - \tau_m^{start}}{t_m^{best}}$.

In the experiments, we first study the effectiveness of our technique in handling a homogeneous workload. This paper focuses on batch workload, as the benefits of our approach in managing transactional workload have been shown previously [18]. This permits us to study the algorithm's behavior with a reduced number of variables, while also providing an opportunity to compare our techniques to existing approaches. In the final experiment, we evaluate the effectiveness of our technique in managing a heterogeneous mix of transactional and long-running workloads.

5.1 Experiment One: Relative Performance Prediction Accuracy

In this experiment, we examine the basic correctness of our algorithm by stressing it with a sequence of identical jobs—jobs with the same profiles and SLA goals. We use this scenario to examine the accuracy with which hypothetical relative performance predicts the actual job performance.

When jobs are identical, the best scheduling strategy is to make no placement changes (suspend, resume, migrate). This is because there is no benefit to job completion times (when considered as a vector) to be gained by interrupting the execution of a currently placed job in order to place another job.

We consider a system of 25 nodes, each of which has four 3.9GHz processors and 16GB of RAM. We submit to this system 800 identical jobs with properties shown in Table 2. Jobs are submitted to the system using an exponential inter-arrival time

Table 2. Properties of Experiment One

Property	Value	Property	Value
Maximum speed [MHz]	3,900 (1 CPU)	Minimum execution time [s]	17,600
Memory requirement [MB]	4,320	Relative goal factor	2.7
Work [Mcycles]	68,640,000	Relative goal [s]	**47,520**

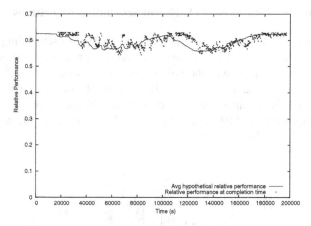

Fig. 2. Experiment One: Average hypothetical relative performance over time and actual relative performance achieved at completion time

distribution with an average inter-arrival time of 260s. This arrival rate is sufficient to cause queuing at some points during the experiment. The control cycle length is 600s.

Observe that each job's maximum speed permits it to use a single processor, and so four jobs could run at full speed on a single node. However, the memory characteristics restrict the number of jobs per node to three. Consequently, no more than 75 jobs can run concurrently in the system. Each job, running at maximum speed, takes 17,600s to complete. The relative goal factor for each job is 2.7, resulting in a completion time goal of 47,520s ($2.7 * 17,600$), as measured from the submission time.

The maximum achievable relative performance for a job described in Table 2 is 0.63. This relative performance will be achieved for a job that is started immediately upon submission and runs at full speed for 17,600s. In that case, the job will complete 29,920s before its completion time goal, and thus will have taken 37% of the time between the submission time and the completion time goal to complete. This relative performance is an upper bound for the job, and will be decreased if queuing occurs.

In Figure 2, we show the average hypothetical relative performance over time as well as the actual relative performance achieved by jobs at completion time. When no jobs are queued, the hypothetical relative performance is 0.63 and it decreases as more jobs are delayed in the queue. Notice that the relative performance achieved by jobs at their completion time has a shape similar to that of the hypothetical relative performance, but is shifted in time by about 18000 sec. This is expected, as the hypothetical relative performance is predicting the actual relative performance that jobs will obtain at the time they complete, as thus is affected by job submissions, while the actual relative performance is only observed at job completion. The algorithm does not elect to suspend or migrate any jobs during this experiment, hence we do not include a figure showing the number of placement changes performed. Finally, we evaluated the execution time for the algorithm at each control cycle when running on a 3.2GHz Intel Xeon node. In normal conditions, the algorithm produces a placement for this system in about 1.5s. We also observed that when all submitted jobs can be placed concurrently, the algorithm is able to take internal shortcuts, resulting in a significant reduction in execution time.

5.2   Experiment Two: Comparing Different Scheduling Algorithms

In this experiment, we compare our algorithm with alternative scheduling algorithms. We do so in a system presented with jobs with varying profiles and SLA goals. The relative goal factors for jobs are randomly varied among values 1.3, 2.5, and 4 with probabilities 10%, 30%, and 60%, respectively. The job minimum execution times and maximum speeds are also randomly chosen from three possibilities—9,000s at 3,900MHz, 17,600s at 1,560MHz, and 600s at 2,340MHz which are selected with probabilities 10%, 40%, and 50%, respectively.

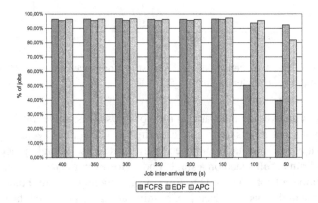

Fig. 3. Experiment Two: Percentage of jobs that met the deadline

We compare our algorithm (referred to as APC) with simple, effective, and well-known scheduling algorithms: Earliest Deadline First (EDF) and First-Come, First-Served (FCFS). Note that while EDF is a preemptive scheduling algorithm, FCFS does not preempt jobs. In both cases, a first-fit strategy was followed to place the jobs.

We use eight different inter-arrival times, ranging from 50s to 400s, and continue to submit jobs until 800 have completed. The experiment is repeated for the three algorithms: APC, EDF, and FCFS. In the paper we concentrate on the results for inter-arrival times of 200s and 50s due to space limitations (see [24] for more results).

Figure 3 shows the percentage of jobs that met their completion time goal. There is no significant difference between the algorithms when inter-arrival times are greater than 100s—this is expected, as the system is underloaded in this configuration. However, with an inter-arrival period of 100s or less, FCFS starts struggling to make even 50% of the jobs meet their goals. EDF and APC have a significantly higher, and comparable, ratio of jobs that met their goals. At a 50s inter-arrival time, the goal satisfaction rate for FCFS has dropped to 40%, and the goal satisfaction rate is actually higher for EDF than for APC. However, Figures 4 and 5 show the penalties for EDF's slightly (10%) higher satisfaction rate.

Figure 4 shows that one of these penalities is that EDF makes considerably more placement changes than does the APC once the inter-arrival time is 150s or less. Recall that FCFS is non-preemptive, and so makes no changes. Note that in this experiment,

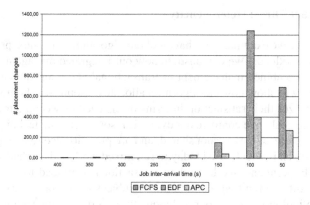

Fig. 4. Experiment Two: Number of jobs migrated, suspended, and moved_and_resumed

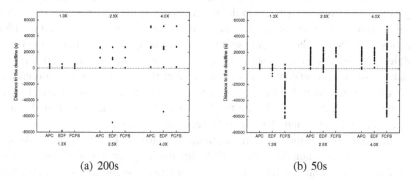

(a) 200s   (b) 50s

Fig. 5. Experiment Two: distribution of distance to the goal at job completion time, for two different mean inter-arrival times (50s and 200s)

we did not consider the cost of the various types of placement changes—this does not change the conclusions, as our technique is making many fewer changes that EDF under heavy load. This figure, coupled with Figure 3, shows our algorithm's ability to making few changes to the system whilst still achieving a high on-time rate.

Figure 5 shows the distribution of distance to the deadline at job completion time for the three different relative goal factors (1.3, 2.5 and 4.0). We show these results for inter-arrival times of 200 and 50 seconds, in Figure 5 (a) and (b), respectively. Points with distance to the goal greater than zero indicate jobs that completed before their goal. Observe that for inter-arrival times of 200s, all three algorithms are capable of making the majority of jobs meet their goal, and the points for each algorithm are concentrated—for each algorithm and each relative goal factor, the distance points form three clusters, one for each minimum execution time. However, at an inter-arrival time of 50s, the algorithms produce different distributions of distances to the goal. In particular, observe that for APC the data points are closer together than for EDF (this is most easily observed for the relative goal factor of 1.3). This illustrates that APC outperforms EDF in equalizing the satisfaction of all jobs in the system.

5.3 Experiment Three: Heterogeneity

In this experiment, we examine the behavior of our algorithm in a system presented with heterogeneous workloads. We demonstrate how our integrated management technique is applicable to combined management of transactional and long-running workloads. The experiment will show how our algorithm allocates resources to both workloads in a way that equalizes their satisfaction in terms of distance between their performance and performance goals. We compare our dynamic resource sharing technique to a static approach in which resources are not shared, and are pre-allocated to one type of work. This static approach is widely used today to run mixed workloads in datacenters.

We extend Experiment One by adding transactional workload to the system, and compare three different system configurations subject to the same mixed workload. In the first configuration we use our technique to perform dynamic application placement with resource sharing between transactional and long-running workloads. In the second and third configurations we consider a system that has been partitioned into two groups of machines, each group dedicated to either the transactional or the long-running workload. In both configurations, we use a First-Come First-Served (FCFS) to place jobs—FCFS was chosen because it is a widely adopted policy in commercial job schedulers. Notice that creating static system partitions is a common practice in many datacenters. In the second configuration, we dedicate 9 nodes to the transactional workload (9 nodes offer enough CPU power to fully satisfy this workload), and 16 nodes to the long-running workload. In the third configuration, we dedicate 6 nodes to the transactional application and 19 to the long-running workload.

To simplify the experiment, the transactional workload is handled by a single application, and is kept constant throughout. Note that the long-running workload is exactly the same as that presented in Section 5.1. The memory demand of a single instance of the transactional application was set to a sufficiently low value that one instance could be placed on each node alongside the three long-running instances that fit on each node in Experiment One. This was done to ensure that the two different types of workload compete only for CPU resources (notice from Experiment One that a maximum of 3 long-running instances can be placed in the same node because of memory constraints).

The relative performance of transactional workloads is calculated as described in Section 3.3. A relative performance of zero means that the actual response time exactly meets the response time goal: lower relative performance values indicate that the response time is greater than the goal (the requests are being serviced too slowly), and higher relative performance values indicate that the response time is less than the goal (the requests are being serviced quickly). In this experiment, the maximum achievable relative performance for the transactional workload is around 0.66, at an approximate allocation of 130,000MHz. Allocating CPU power in excess of 130,000MHz to this application will not further increase its satisfaction: that is, it will not decrease the response time. This is normal behavior for transactional applications—the response time cannot be reduced to zero by continually increasing the CPU power assigned. Notice that 130,000MHz is less than to the CPU capacity of 9 nodes, and so the transactional workload can be completely satisfied by 9 nodes.

The experiment starts with a system subject to the constant transactional workload used throughout, in addition to a small (insignificant) number of long-running jobs

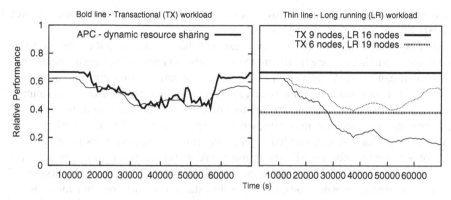

Fig. 6. Experiment Three: actual relative performance for the transactional workload and average calculated hypothetical relative performance for the long-running workload

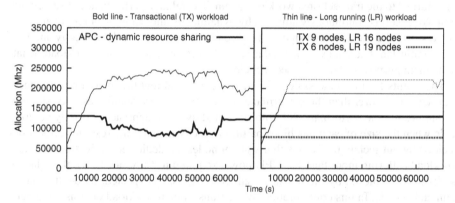

Fig. 7. Experiment Three: CPU power allocated to each workload for the three system configurations

already placed. Then, we start submitting a number of long-running jobs using an inter-arrival time short enough to produce some job queueing. As more long-running jobs are submitted, following the workload properties described in Section 5.1, more CPU demand is observed for the long-running workload. In the end of the experiment, the long-running job inter-arrival time is increased to a value high enough to expect that the job queue length will start decreasing.

Figures 6 and 7 show the results obtained for the three system configurations described above. Figure 6 shows the relative performance achieved by both the transactional and long-running workload for each of the configurations. For the transactional workload we show actual relative performance, and for the long-running workload we show hypothetical relative performance, described in Section 4.2. Although hypothetical relative performance is a predicted value, previous experiments have already shown that this approximation is accurate enough for performance prediction purposes. In addition, we verified for this particular experiment that the utilities achieved by jobs at completion time, long after they were submitted and placements calculated, met their predicted performance. Figure 7 shows the CPU power allocated to each workload over the experiment.

Looking at the results for our dynamic resource sharing technique it can be observed that at the beginning of the experiment the transactional application gets as much CPU power as it can consume, as there is little or no contention with long-running jobs—obtaining its maximum achievable relative performance of 0.66. As more long-running jobs are submitted, the hypothetical relative performance for those long-running jobs starts to decrease as the system becomes increasingly crowded. As soon as the hypothetical relative performance calculated for the long-running jobs becomes lower that the relative performance observed for the transactional workload (that is to say, no more resources can be allocated to the long-running workload without taking CPU power away from the transactional workload), our algorithm starts to reduce the allocation for the transactional workload and give that CPU power instead to the long-running workload, until the relative performance each achieves is equalized. At the end of the experiment, the job submission rate is slightly decreased, which results in more CPU power being returned to the transactional workload again. The relative performance observed for both workloads is continuously adjusted by dynamically allocating resources over time. The result is that the resource sharing between both workloads is dynamically and unevenly adjusted, but achieving a similar relative performance for each workload, what is the main purpose of our proposed technique.

The results for the static system configurations reveal that the overall performance they deliver is lower than the performance observed for our dynamic resource sharing technique, and the performance of both static and dynamic approaches is only comparable when the size of each machines partition exactly matches the resource allocation decided by our technique. Notice that when 9 nodes are dedicated to the transactional workload (offering more than the CPU power required to fully satisfy it), the relative performance achieved by the transactional workload is, as expected, 0.66—the maximum achievable. In this configuration, while transactional workload obtains good performance, long-running jobs struggle to meet their completion time goals, as shown by the low achieved relative performance values. When only 6 nodes are dedicated to the transactional workload, the relative performance that it achieves is consistently lower than that achieved with our dynamic resource sharing technique, while the performance benefits observed for the long-running jobs are not obvious when compared to the results obtained with our technique. Recall also that relative performance represents the relative distance to the goal achieved by each particular workload—distance to the response time goal for the transactional application and distance to the completion time goal for long-running jobs. Thus, relative performance is a direct measurement of the performance obtained by each workload.

6   Conclusions and Future Work

In this paper we present a technique that allows integrated management of heterogeneous workloads composed of transactional applications and long-running jobs, dynamically placing the workloads in such a way as to equalize their satisfaction. We use relative performance functions to make the satisfaction and performance of both workloads comparable. We formally describe the technique, and then demonstrate that it not only performs well in presence of heterogeneous workloads but it also shows consistent performance in presence only of long-running jobs compared to other well-known scheduling algorithms. We perform our experiments with a simulator already used and validated against a system prototype in [25,18]. While here we mainly focus on the description and evaluation of the management of long-running jobs, transactional workloads were extensively covered in [18]. We expect to extend this technique in the future to offer explicit support for parallel jobs, and we also need to work on the on-the-fly generation of job profiles. The optimization technique could also be extended to focus on resources other than CPU.

Acknowledgments

This work is partially supported by the Ministry of Science and Technology of Spain and the European Union (FEDER funds) under contract TIN2007-60625 and by the BSC-IBM collaboration agreement SoW Adaptive Systems.

References

1. Sun Microsystems: Behavior of mixed workloads consolidated using Solaris Resource Manager software. Technical report (May 2005)
2. Lin, B., Dinda, P.: VSched: Mixing batch and interactive virtual machines using periodic real-time scheduling. In: Proc. ACM/IEEE Supercomputing, Seattle, WA (November 2005)
3. Jensen, E.D., Locke, C.D., Tokuda, H.: A time-driven scheduling model for real-time operating systems. In: IEEE Real-Time Systems Symposium, pp. 112–122 (1985)
4. Ravindran, B., Jensen, E.D., Li, P.: On recent advances in time/utility function real-time scheduling and resource management. In: ISORC 2005: Proceedings of the Eighth IEEE International Symposium on Object-Oriented Real-Time Distributed Computing (ISORC 2005), Washington, DC, USA, pp. 55–60. IEEE Computer Society, Los Alamitos (2005)
5. Balli, U., Anderson, J.S.: Utility accrual real-time scheduling under variable cost functions. IEEE Trans. Comput. 56(3), 385–401 (2007); Member-Haisang Wu and Senior Member-Binoy Ravindran and Member-E. Douglas Jensen
6. Vengerov, D., Mastroleon, L., Murphy, D., Bambos, N.: Adaptive data-aware utility-based scheduling in resource-constrained systems. Sun Technical Report TR-2007-164, Sun Microsystems (April 2007)
7. Lee, C.B., Snavely, A.E.: Precise and realistic utility functions for user-centric performance analysis of schedulers. In: HPDC 2007: Proceedings of the 16th international symposium on High performance distributed computing, pp. 107–116. ACM, New York (2007)
8. Chun, B.N., Culler, D.E.: User-centric performance analysis of market-based cluster batch schedulers. In: CCGRID 2002: Proceedings of the 2nd IEEE/ACM International Symposium on Cluster Computing and the Grid, Washington, DC, USA, p. 30. IEEE Comp. Society, Los Alamitos (2002)
9. Foster, I., Freeman, T., Keahey, K., Scheftner, D., Sotomayor, B., Zhang, X.: Virtual clusters for grid communities, Singapore (May 2006)
10. Czajkowski, G., Wegiel, M., Daynes, L., Palacz, K., Jordan, M., Skinner, G., Bryce, C.: Resource management for clusters of virtual machines, Cardiff, UK, pp. 382–389 (May 2005)

11. Zhu, X., Wang, Z., Singhal, S.: Utility-driven workload management using nested control design. In: American Control Conference, June 14-16, 2006, p. 6 (2006)

12. Padala, P., Shin, K.G., Zhu, X., Uysal, M., Wang, Z., Singhal, S., Merchant, A., Salem, K.: Adaptive control of virtualized resources in utility computing environments. In: EuroSys 2007: Proceedings of the ACM SIGOPS/EuroSys European Conference on Computer Systems 2007, pp. 289–302. ACM, New York (2007)

13. Wang, Z., Zhu, X., Padala, P., Singhal, S.: Capacity and performance overhead in dynamic resource allocation to virtual containers. In: 10th IFIP/IEEE International Symposium on Integrated Network Management, 2007. IM 2007, May 21–25, 2007, pp. 149–158 (2007)

14. Kellerer, H., Pferschy, U., Pisinger, D.: Knapsack Problems (2004)

15. Karve, A., Kimbrel, T., Pacifici, G., Spreitzer, M., Steinder, M., Sviridenko, M., Tantawi, A.: Dynamic placement for clustered web applications. In: WWW Conference, Edinburgh, Scotland (May 2006)

16. Kimbrel, T., Steinder, M., Sviridenko, M., Tantawi, A.: Dynamic application placement under service and memory constraints. In: International Workshop on Efficient and Experimental Algorithms, Santorini Island, Greece (May 2005)

17. Wang, X., Lan, D., Wang, G., Fang, X., Ye, M., Chen, Y., Wang, Q.: Appliance-based autonomic provisioning framework for virtualized outsourcing data center. In: ICAC 2007: Proceedings of the Fourth International Conference on Autonomic Computing, Washington, DC, USA, p. 29. IEEE Computer Society, Los Alamitos (2007)

18. Carrera, D., Steinder, M., Whalley, I., Torres, J., Ayguadé, E.: Utility-based placement of dynamic web applications with fairness goals. In: 11th IEEE/IFIP Network Operations and Management Symposium (NOMS 2008), Salvador Bahia, Brazil (2008)

19. Xu, J., Zhao, M., Fortes, J., Carpenter, R., Yousif, M.: On the use of fuzzy modeling in virtualized data center management. In: Xu, J., Zhao, M., Fortes, J., Carpenter, R., Yousif, M. (eds.) ICAC 2007. Fourth International Conference on Autonomic Computing, June 11-15, 2007, p. 25 (2007)

20. Urgaonkar, B., Shenoy, P., Roscoe, T.: Resource overbooking and application profiling in shared hosting platforms. In: Proc. Fifth Symposium on Operating Systems Design and Implementation, Boston, MA (December 2002)

21. Pacifici, G., Spreitzer, M., Tantawi, A., Youssef, A.: Performance management for cluster-based web services. IEEE Journal on Selected Areas in Communications 23(12) (December 2005)

22. Pacifici, G., Segmuller, W., Spreitzer, M., Steinder, M., Tantawi, A., Youssef, A.: Managing the response time for multi-tiered web applications. Technical Report Tech. Rep. RC 23651, IBM (2005)

23. Pacifici, G., Segmuller, W., Spreitzer, M., Tantawi, A.: Dynamic estimation of cpu demand of web traffic. In: VALUETOOLS, Pisa, Italy (October 2006)

24. Carrera, D., Steinder, M., Whalley, I., Torres, J., Ayguadé, E.: Managing SLAs of heterogeneous workloads using dynamic application placement. Technical Report RC 24469, IBM Research (January 2008)

25. Steinder, M., Whalley, I., Carrera, D., Gaweda, I., Chess, D.: Server virtualization in autonomic management of heterogeneous workloads. In: 10th IEEE/IFIP Symposium on Integrated Management (IM 2007), Munich, Germany (2007)

Biologically-Inspired Distributed Middleware Management for Stream Processing Systems

Geetika T. Lakshmanan and Robert E. Strom

IBM T. J. Watson Research Center, Hawthorne, NY 10532, USA
{gtlakshm,robstrom}@us.ibm.com

Abstract. We present a decentralized and dynamic biologically-inspired algorithm for placing dataflow graphs composed of stream processing tasks onto a distributed network of machines, while minimizing the end-to-end latency. Our algorithm responds on-the-fly to placement requests of new flow graphs or to modifications of an already running stream processing flow graph, and dynamically adapts to changes in performance characteristics such as message rates or service times as well as to changes in processor availability or link performance during runtime. Our algorithm is derived by analogy to pheromone-based cooperation between ants to fulfill goals such as food discovery. We have conducted extensive simulation experiments to show the scalability and adaptability of our algorithm.

Keywords: Distributed Stream Processing, Task Placement, On-The-Fly Management, Biologically-Inspired, Self-Managing Middleware.

1 Introduction

The complexity of current computer systems has motivated computer scientists to turn towards nature for inspiration. The fault tolerance properties and decentralized control achieved in natural systems combined with the intuitive simplicity of their design make them particularly appealing for solving problems in computer systems. Immune system architectures for computer security methods [1], firefly-inspired synchronicity for wireless sensor networks [2], bee colony behavior-based middleware platforms [3] and ant-based ad hoc network multicasting [4] are but a few examples of the ways in which biology has influenced the design of computer systems. Investigation of the collective foraging behavior of ants has sparked the field of *ant colony optimization* (ACO) algorithms [5]. These are probabilistic techniques for solving computational problems which can be reduced to finding optimal paths in graphs. Ant-based algorithms have been applied to solve combinatorial optimization problems such as the travelling salesman problem, quadratic assignment problem, graph coloring, job-shop scheduling, sequential ordering and vehicle routing [5]. In addition to these static problems, where characteristics do not change over time, ant-based algorithms have also been applied to stochastic time varying problems such as routing in telecommunications networks [6]. Given the adaptive capabilities built into

V. Issarny and R. Schantz (Eds.): Middleware 2008, LNCS 5346, pp. 223–242, 2008.

ant-based algorithms, they are particularly well suited to such problems where solutions must be adapted online to changing conditions.

Adaptive online task placement is currently an important problem in distributed stream processing systems [7,8,9,10,11,12,13]. A distributed stream processing system (DSPS) streams data from multiple data sources or *producers* to multiple clients or *consumers* interested in the results derived from processing conducted on the data. Between the producer and consumer the data is processed through a number of computational tasks that are linked via a dataflow graph. Each task receives one or more streams of input data messages, either from a producer or from an upstream task, each message in a stream arriving asynchronously. In response to a message, a task performs a computation, which may access the message, read and modify internal state representing past history, and may or may not generate one or more messages which are sent either to consumers or to downstream tasks. Examples of tasks include operators, such as an incremental join, an aggregation, or a facial recognition operator. Flow graphs may be designed by an application designer, or may be separately specified by consumers who write queries. Each query defines the particular messages a particular consumer requires and the operators or computational tasks needed to derive these messages from producer streams.

There are a number of well known distributed stream processing systems in both academic and commercial settings [7,8,9,10,11,12,13]. These systems support applications such as processing financial market data, managing sensor network data collected from geographically dispersed sources and detecting network intrusion and other kinds of security violations in computer systems. Stream data sources typically produce large volumes of data at high and variable rates. Providing low latency, high throughput execution in the midst of dynamically changing data and network conditions as well as new, diverse processing requests is a challenge. One way to reduce traffic and improve performance of the DSPS is by dynamically placing stream processing tasks on the machines available in the stream processing network in order to maximally satisfy some objective function.

In this paper we present a biologically-inspired algorithm for dynamically placing tasks on a network of machines in a distributed stream processing system. Obtaining an optimal solution to the static task assignment problem, where the problem characteristics do not change, is computationally intractable [14]. The problem we address in this paper is even more difficult, due to the following additional requirements:

- **Dynamic and incremental:** We cannot assume that the entire flow graph and network description is known once and for all prior to deployment. The placement may need to react to changes, which may be (a) changes to the flow graph, such as a new query, or new consumer, (b) changes to the performance characteristics of the streams or operators, (c) changes to the availability or capacity of the machines or links. The system must react incrementally: that is, small changes to part of the system may induce small changes to the placement, rather than re-doing a single placement algorithm from scratch.

- **Decentralized:** We cannot assume a centralized server with global knowledge; instead we require that the placement execute in a distributed fashion on the same network of machines on which the stream processing system is executing.

Our biologically-inspired solution is grounded on techniques from ACO. ACO-based algorithms have several salient features that make them appealing for placement in distributed systems. ACO algorithms translate problems into finding optimal paths in graphs. Finding optimal paths is achieved through *stigmergy* [5], a method of indirect communication in a self-organizing emergent system. Stigmergy is achieved in ants through pheromone deposits. The concentration of pheromone guides ants towards appropriate routes. Simulating stigmergy in the context of ants in a computer system can be done in a completely decentralized manner using routing tables stored at every node. Successful global behavior is achieved by purely local decisions made at each node. The routing tables are updated by ant-like agents that carry very little state, and perform simple computations at nodes in order to update routes. Ant-like agents can be implemented online, in parallel with the functionality of the data processing system. As a result, the solution is naturally decentralized and dynamic.

Simulating stigmergy alone is not sufficient to achieve distributed task placement in stream processing systems using ants. Establishing an optimal path between the producers and consumers of a query requires ensuring that the path qualifies in terms of some quality of service metric (for instance the end-to-end latency between the producers and consumers of the query), as well as ensuring that the nodes in this path have sufficient capacity to process operators of the query without adversely affecting the performance of queries whose operators are already deployed on these nodes. The algorithm we present in this paper accomplishes both of these goals by introducing different "species" of ants and relying on a queueing model to estimate service time of tasks on a server. Placement in our algorithm is orchestrated by three different species of ants. *Routing ants* establish paths between the producers and consumers of a query by depositing pheromone in pheromone tables maintained at every node. *Scouting ants* estimate the cost of placing query operators on a set of machines in a path between a producer and a consumer of that query. *Enforcement ants* execute the placement of a query on a path. To the best of our knowledge, this work represents the first biologically-inspired algorithm for dynamic task placement in distributed stream processing systems.

The rest of this paper is organized as follows. After describing related work in Section 2, we provide complete details of our algorithm in Section 3. In section 4 we investigate our algorithm in simulation and end with conclusions.

2   Related Work

Operator placement has received significant attention in the distributed stream processing systems community. Existing literature consists of a wide variety of heuristic algorithms that range from static global optimization solutions to complete or partial decentralized solutions that perform local adjustments to placement dynamically during runtime.

Query Operator Placement in Distributed Stream Processing Systems. In Flux, a dynamic load balanced strategy is developed in the context of continuous queries [15]. A centralized controller is responsible for collecting workload information and making load balancing decisions. Another approach computes placement by minimizing the average time, estimated by a queueing model, required for an event originating at the producer to reach its destined consumer, also using a centralized controller[16]. Operator placement has also been examined in the context of in-network stream query processing for sensor network environments with progressively increasing computational power network bandwidth up a hierarchy of nodes[14]. This approach provides theoretical analysis of a centralized placement algorithm that minimizes the total cost of computation as well as communication, but does not consider how the algorithm will respond to dynamic changes during runtime. A global optimization scheme for maximizing the weighted throughput of all queries in the system is proposed in [17]. Weights are provided as input and represent the importance or priority of a query operator. With the exception of[17], these placement schemes require a centralized controller to recompute the placement of the entire operator graph in order to respond to dynamic changes in the environment such as the introduction of new operators, changes in the network data rates, and changes in the availability of machines and network links. In [17], rather than recomputing an optimal placement in response to bursty data rates, a centralized controller jointly optimizes the input and output rates of operators, as well as their instantaneous processing rates. The global optimization scheme does need to be re-run however, when new operators need to be deployed, and when existing operators expire. Most recently a centralized placement algorithm has been proposed for a scheduler for *System S*, a distributed stream processing middleware, which balances the load on nodes and network traffic, and minimizes the inter-node traffic while respecting a host of constraints [18].

Decentralized algorithms have been proposed to minimize *network usage* and dynamically adjust placement in response to network changes during runtime [19,20]. These algorithms focus on minimizing communication cost, and do not explicitly have a load-balancing strategy. One of these algorithms also considers reusing computation between overlapping queries [19]. It does not, however, compute the performance impact of reusing queries on existing queries. Reusing existing computation is important in certain stream processing applications where a majority of query processing requests are redundant, such as in the financial services industry. An approach has been developed to address this that focuses exclusively on reusing component streams to satisfy new placement requests using a queueing-based quality-of-service impact projection algorithm [21]. This scheme does not outline how to compute an optimal placement when no existing computation can be reused.

Several decentralized algorithms only consider load management for computing an optimal placement [10,22]. A data flow aware load selection strategy has been proposed in [23]. This approach aims to achieve lower communication cost by restricting the scattering of data flows, but does not assign placement by explicitly minimizing the end-to-end latency between the producers and consumers of queries. Furthermore, the load balancing scheme in this algorithm is based on partner selection which assigns a fixed number of load balancing candidate partners for each node, and load is moved individually for each machine between its partners. Another approach uses runtime monitoring information to adapt a decentralized placement algorithm that maximizes business utility which is defined as a function of the required bandwidth, available bandwidth and delay on a given edge of the network [24]. This approach proposes stream management middleware in which nodes self-organize into utility-aware clusters and requires cluster coordinators to maintain state for all nodes in a cluster. A component composition algorithm has also been proposed that dynamically composes quality-aware and resource-efficient stream processing applications from a system's currently available components while balancing the load [25]. Although this approach utilizes distributed composition probing, it requires global state.

Biologically-Inspired Task Placement. ACO algorithms have been applied to static task placement problems in which task and machine characteristics are fixed. In [26] the authors address the Quadratic Assignment Problem where each ant visits nodes and assigns a task to each node such that the product of the flows between activities is minimized by the distance between their locations. Tasks are assumed to be static and data rates are constant. Another variant is the Job-Shop Scheduling problem [27] where a job consists of an ordered sequence of operations. The problem is to assign the operations to time intervals in such a way that the maximum of the completion times of all operations is minimized and no two jobs are processed at the same time on the same machine. The static nature of the problems is a critical assumption that bolsters the success of these algorithms, and therefore they cannot simply be extended to solve dynamic task placement problems. In [6], an ant-colony optimization scheme is applied to dynamic traffic monitoring and routing. They outline how latency minimizing paths can be established between sources and destinations using ant colonies.

On the evolutionary front, considerable work has concentrated on applying genetic algorithms to static and dynamic task placement. None of these algorithms, however, are applicable to data stream processing systems where placement is concerned with tasks that are part of data flow graphs and execute on continuous streams of data.

3   Design and Algorithm

In this section we define our model, introduce necessary terminology, and present details of our ant-inspired task placement algorithm for distributed stream processing systems.

3.1   Stream Processing Model

We assume that every data source has knowledge of the flow graphs which specify the tasks executed on the data streams it produces. We also assume that stream processing tasks are asynchronous software components with multiple inputs, multiple outputs, and possible internal state. Tasks may execute asynchronously; messages sent between tasks are asynchronous. Task topology may change in response to dynamic requests to change the graph, but such changes are assumed to happen at rates much less frequent than the input streaming message rates. Servers can be actual machines, or processes or threads within a machine. At any point during execution, a server has some number of tasks assigned to it, representing a partition of the total dataflow graph. There is a single queue of messages waiting to be processed by the server. When the server is idle and the queue is non-empty, a message is dequeued, delivered to the appropriate task, and processed by that task, which may in turn generate internal messages for other downstream tasks in the same server. Processing of the message finishes when all such downstream tasks have finished executing. There may be one or more messages queued up for delivery to consumers or to downstream tasks in other servers; these messages are queued to links which are assumed to asynchronously transport these messages to consumers or to the queues in the appropriate servers. In this paper we do not address how to resolve problems such as lost messages that result from link or server failure. There are several well known techniques that address this [28].

Total latency depends upon the sum of server queueing delay, task processing time in each server, link queueing delay and link latency in each link, across the paths between producers and consumers.

In our approach, the streaming data messages and the tasks are augmented with ants (following our biological metaphor) and *cells*. Ants are implemented as special control messages distinct from data messages; cells are implemented as special tasks distinct from the tasks being placed. Each server contains one cell containing information about that server and its neighbors. Cells hold data, called *pheromones*, again following our metaphor; ants travel back and forth between cells carrying various information depending upon the kind of ant.

3.2   Approach Overview

Inspired by the success of Di Caro and Dorigo [6] in using ants to establish routes in telephone networks, we extend their work to accomplish task placement in a stream processing system. In particular we enhance their work to incorporate a queueing model as well as different species of ants. In addition to *routing ants*, we introduce *scouting ants*, and *enforcement ants*. These ants are responsible for placing each query. Placement is conducted through three stages. First, routing ants are dispatched by *leaders*, located at producers. Routing ants continuously travel between producers and destinations, depositing pheromones on their return trip in routing tables at every server that reflect different preference weights given to alternative next hops. Their destinations represent consumers of a query. Pheromone concentrations guide ants along best paths to their destinations. Once routing ants have established paths to the destination of a query, the leader dispatches scouting ants towards the same destination. Each scouting ant travels a particular path guided by pheromone concentrations towards its destination and computes the cost of a proposed hypothetical placement of the query along the path. Upon reaching its destination, it returns to the leader with its hypothetical placement report. In the third stage, after the leader has received enough reports from the scouts it had previously dispatched, it picks the best report, and dispatches an enforcement ant to execute the placement of the query outlined by the report. Once a query has been placed, the leader periodically dispatches routing and scouting ants for the query in order to ensure that its placement adapts to changes in the query tasks, as well as to changes in network conditions, data characteristics, and other queries being placed. If a more optimal placement of the query is found, then the leader picks the new placement, and dispatches enforcement ants to execute the new placement and discontinue the previous one. The concept of the pheromone vector and the role of routing ants are exactly as defined in the model by Di Caro and Dorigo [6]. The additional role of scouting ants and enforcement ants as well as the incorporation of the queueing model represent our novel contribution.

3.3 Pheromone Vector

There exists one cell per server which contains state relevant to an ant traversing this server. Each cell is aware of the set of destinations. Each cell C has a set of neighbors $N(C)$. For each destination D, a cell C maintains a pheromone vector [6] that maps each neighbor n into a probability $\Phi_{D,n}^C$ of choosing neighbor n as the next hop to travel from cell Cs server to destination D. Because these are probabilities, $\sum_{n \in N(C)} \Phi_{D,n}^C = 1$, for each destination D. Initially, when no information is known about one route versus another, the values of $\Phi_{D,n}^C$ may be set to be equiprobable (uniformly distributed). For each destination D, a cell C also maintains $\Gamma_C = \{\mu_{C \to D}, \sigma_{C \to D}^2\}$, where $\mu_{C \to D}$ is the mean and $\sigma_{C \to D}^2$ is the variance of the time to traverse both links and service queues on the best path from C to D.

Each query has one or more producers. Each producer site (or, if the producer is an external site, then at the server site which is the point of attachment of the producer, and which will act as a proxy for the producer for the purpose of this algorithm) contains a *leader*. Whenever a query is added, deleted, or changed, or whenever an unchanged query is requested to redo its placement, a leader at one producer is selected. If there is a single producer, the selected leader is the leader at that single producer. If there are multiple producers, the producer along the longest path to the consumer is selected. Thus the flow graph is clipped to a single linear chain of tasks, which we refer to as a *subquery*. Figure 1(b) shows the path selected by the ants for placement of the query in Figure 1(a) which has fan-in. Once the subquery is placed, the same algorithm is re-executed, one producer at a time, to place the tasks on paths from other producers that join in to a task on this path. Figure 1(d) shows the path selected by the ants for the placement of the query in Figure 1(c) which has fan-out. Once the subquery is placed, the same algorithm is re-executed, one consumer at a time, to place the tasks on paths that span out of the fan-out point.

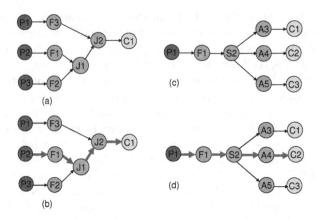

Fig. 1. (b) shows the path selected by ants for placement for the query in (a) which has fan-in. (d) shows the path selected by ants for the placement of the query in (c) which has fan-out. P and C stand for producers and consumers. F stands for the FILTER operator, J for JOIN, S for SPLIT, A for AGGREGATION.

3.4   Routing Ants: Forward Direction Seeking Paths

Intermittently, a leader residing at a producer of a query, releases a routing ant with destination D, the server ID of a consumer of the query, and source cell C_S. The number of ants and how frequently they are released are set as user defined parameters in our implementation. The ant carries on its back (i.e. the payload of a control message contains) the following information: its destination D, the path it has taken so far (the ID of each server hosting each cell it has passed through), and the delay it has experienced so far at each hop, passing through processing queues and link queues. Initially, only the source cell C_S is in the path. At each step, at a cell C that is not the destination D, the routing ant does the following:

1. It records on its back how long it has waited in the server queue at cell C.
2. It chooses a next hop towards D, by making a probabilistic choice of next hop neighbor, i, based upon the pheromone vector $\Phi_{D,i}^C$ at C, choosing among the neighbors it did not already visit, or over all the neighbors in case all of them had been previously visited.
   If a cycle is detected, that is, if an ant is forced to return to an already visited node, the cycle's nodes are removed from the ant's memory, and all information relating to them is destroyed. If the cycle lasted longer than the lifetime of the ant before entering the cycle, (that is if the cycle is greater than half the ant's age) the ant is destroyed.
3. It enqueues itself on the link towards the next hop neighbor, i, waiting to crawl through the link.
4. When it arrives at the next hop neighbor, i, it records on its back how long it has waited in queueing and propagation time passing through the link.

5. If it is not now at the destination D, it queues itself at the tail of the server queue of the next hop neighbor, i. Once it is dequeued, it repeats steps 1-5.
6. If it is now at the destination D, it turns around and begins its reverse journey back towards C_S.

3.5   Routing Ants: Reverse Direction Reinforcing Paths

Once a routing ant has reached destination D, it reverses direction and crawls backward towards the server C_S hosting its source cell. It knows how to reach its source, because it has stored on its back the path it had actually taken. On the reverse path, at each hop, it bypasses the server queues and goes directly to each cell C, to update its pheromone vector $\Phi_{D,n}^C$ and the estimates, Γ_C. After arriving at cell C from a cell $C-1$, the ant will update $\Phi_{D,C-1}^C$, which represents the probability of choosing cell $C-1$ as the next hop when attempting to reach D from C. The pheromone vector at cell C is updated by incrementing the probability $\Phi_{D,C-1}^C$ associated with neighbor cell $C-1$ and the destination D, and decreasing (by normalization) the probabilities $\Phi_{D,n}^C$ associated with other neighbor nodes $n, n \neq C-1$. The update procedure modifies the probabilities of the various paths, based on the *experience* the ant had recorded on its back when it chose the particular next hop neighbor on its forward path from C_S to D. While this experience can incorporate a variety of factors, in our implementation, we restrict it to $\frac{1}{T_{C_S \to D}}$, the inverse of the trip time, which can be computed using the information the ant loads on its back in the forward path to D, outlined in Section 3.4. Inverse trip time alone cannot be treated as an exact error measure, given its dependence on the load on the network. Therefore, the values stored in the model Γ_C are used to guide the adjustment of the trip times. Di Caro and Dorigo experiment [6] with a number of linear, quadratic and hyperbolic combinations of the trip time values and the estimates, Γ_C in order to create a reinforcement signal, $r \equiv r(\frac{1}{T_{C \to D}}, \Gamma_C), r \in [0,1]$. In our implementation, we define r as $\frac{1}{T_{C_S \to D}}$ and use Γ_C to decide when to update the pheromone vector. If the elapsed trip time of a sub-path is statistically *good* (i.e. it is less than $\mu + I(\mu, \sigma)$, where I is an estimate of the confidence interval for μ), then the time value is used to update the pheromone vector $\Phi_{D,n}^C$ and the estimates, Γ_C. On the other hand, trip times of sub-paths not deemed good, in the same statistical sense, are not used. The pheromone vector value $\Phi_{D,C-1}^C(t)$ at time t is increased by the reinforcement value at time $t+1$ as follows:

$$\Phi_{D,C-1}^C(t+1) = \Phi_{D,C-1}^C(t) + r.(1 - \Phi_{D,C-1}^C(t)) = \Phi_{D,C-1}^C(t).(1-r) + r. \quad (1)$$

Thus the probability is increased by a value proportional to the reinforcement received, and to the previous value of the node probability. Given the same reinforcement, small probability values are increased proportionally more than big probability values.

The probability $\Phi_{D,n}^C$ for all neighbor nodes $n \in N(C)$ where $n \neq C-1$ is decayed. This is essential to eliminate poor quality paths to D. These $n-1$ nodes receive a negative reinforcement by normalization. Normalization is necessary to ensure that the sum of probabilities for a given pheromone vector is 1.

$$\Phi_{D,n}^{C}(t+1) = \Phi_{D,n}^{C}(t).(1-r), n \neq C - 1 . \tag{2}$$

After the routing ant has performed the reinforcement step on the cell at each hop back to the source, it dies. If a cell's pheromone vector for a destination is not updated beyond a given amount of time, the vector is destroyed. This ensures that a cell only maintains information that is relevant to the current set of queries deployed in the stream processing system, and furthermore prevents cell size from exploding arbitrarily.

3.6   Queueing Model

In this section we summarize the queueing-based flow performance model, presented in [16], which is utilized by ants in our algorithm to estimate the queueing delay experienced by a data packet in a server.

We define a *flow* as a path in a flow graph from a producer to a consumer that consists of an ordered sequence of tasks. Each server hosts a subset of the queries deployed in the stream processing network. This subset can consist of a number of logically unrelated segments of various flows, denoted as F. The service time of a flow is the sum of the service times of the tasks in the flow. Since some tasks are executed more than once if their ancestors in the execution sequence produce more than one event, batch sizes are incorporated in this calculation. For a given flow f, let θ_i be the set of tasks in the path from task t_i to the root task t_1, the entry task for events in this flow, with $\theta_1 = \{\}$. Let B_j represent the batch size of task t_j, task i's ancestor, such that $j < i$ and $j > 0$. The service time S_f of a flow $f \in F$ is the total amount of time a server is occupied due to an incoming event arriving at f, and this can be calculated as:

$$S_f = \sum_i S_i \prod_{j|t_j \in \theta_i} B_j . \tag{3}$$

The key insight driving the method in [16] is to first aggregate the input streams to a server into a single stream and simulate the behavior of all task flows through the server as one flow. Marginal metrics for individual flows can then be computed from the combined result. The aggregation/disaggregation approach proposed by Whitt [31] for servers with multiple incoming streams and multiple flows is appropriate for computing this. We begin by presenting the aggregation formulas applicable to our model.

The aggregate flow service rate, $\hat{\mu}$, the sum of the expected values of individual flow service rates, can be computed as:

$$\hat{\mu} = \frac{\hat{\lambda}}{\sum_f \frac{\lambda_f}{\mu_f}} . \tag{4}$$

where $\mu_f = \frac{1}{S_f}$ is the service rate of flow f and λ_f is its input rate, and the aggregate $\hat{\lambda}$ is the sum of the expected values of the individual flow input rates. The squared coefficient of variance for all the flow service times can be computed as:

$$c_s^2 = \frac{\hat{\mu}^2}{\hat{\lambda}} \left(\sum_f \frac{\lambda_f}{\mu_f^2} (c_{s_f}^2 + 1) \right) - 1 . \tag{5}$$

where $c_{s_f}^2 \equiv \frac{\sigma^2[S_f]}{E[S_f]^2}$ is the squared coefficient of the variance of flow f in which $E[S_f]$ is the flow's mean service time, and $\sigma^2[S_f]$ is the variance of the flow's service time. Assuming a general distribution for arrivals, Whitt's formula [31] can be used:

$$\hat{c_a^2} = (1 - w) + w \left(\sum_f c_{a_f}^2 \frac{\lambda_f}{\lambda} \right) . \tag{6}$$

where

$$w = [1 + 4(1 - \rho)^2 (v - 1)]^{-1} . \tag{7}$$

where

$$v = [\Sigma_f (\frac{\lambda_f}{\lambda})^2]^{-1} . \tag{8}$$

where $c_{a_f}^2$ is the coefficient of variance for the flow f, and $\rho = \frac{\hat{\lambda}}{\hat{\mu}}$, is the load.

We can now use these to compute the expected queueing delay, Q_f, for a given flow in a server via a $G/G/1$ approximation due to Marchal[32]:

$$Q_f = \left(\frac{\rho}{1 - \rho} \right) \left(\frac{\hat{c_a^2} + \hat{c_s^2}}{2} \right) \left(\frac{1}{\hat{\mu}} \right) . \tag{9}$$

We can now compute the expected latency L_f of a flow f through a server as the sum of its expected service time and the queueing delay:

$$L_f = Q_f + S_f . \tag{10}$$

We can model the delay experienced by a packet across a network link in the standard way employed in queueing theory. The link is modeled as a server, and a packet on the link experiences a queueing delay and a transmission delay. The queueing delay is a function of the link bandwidth and size of the messages crossing the link.

3.7   Scouting Ants: Hypothetical Placement

Once a threshold number of routing ants return, the selected leader dispatches multiple scouting ants. Each scouting ant carries information about the tasks in the subquery to be placed, as well as the ID of the server hosting C_S, the cell releasing the scout, and D, the ant's destination which is the consumer connected to the subquery. Each scouting ant will explore, in parallel with its team members, one hypothetical alternative for placing these tasks along a path from the given producer to the consumer. Exploration proceeds along cells selected on a hop-by-hop basis using the weighted probabilities in the pheromone vector in each cell. At each cell residing at a server, the scouting ant computes a hypothetical placement of tasks in the subquery. It uses a queueing model to estimate: (1) The given servers contribution to the latency of the hypothetically placed tasks, denoted as L_{new}; (2) the computational time of other tasks currently deployed on this server, denoted as L_{prev}, given the hypothetically placed tasks. Hypothetical placement calculations do not affect actual placement. The computational time of tasks currently deployed on the server has to be taken into account because it is affected and augmented by the additional stream volume introduced by a hypothetically placed task. In particular, when a new data stream is directed through a server, it affects the queueing delay experienced by data packets in all other data streams flowing through the server, and consequently affects the time it takes to service tasks on these other data streams. The ant greedily places tasks on a server provided that the sum of L_{new} and L_{prev} does not exceed a user-specified delay threshold, L_T:

$$L_{new} + L_{old} < L_T . \tag{11}$$

The queueing model summarized in the previous section is used to perform this estimate. If the delay threshold, L_T, is not specified by the user, then the ant ensures that the load on a server resulting from the combined existing and hypothetical flows does not become unacceptable. Specifically, the ant ensures that the load on a server, defined as $\rho = \frac{\hat{\lambda}}{\hat{\mu}}$ in section 3.6, where $\hat{\lambda}$ is the sum of the expected values of the individual stream input rates and $\hat{\mu}$, the sum of the expected values of individual stream service rates, is strictly less than a constant α, $\alpha \in [0, 1]$.

A parameter g, such that $g > 0$ and $g \in \mathbb{Z}$, represents the level of greediness of the scout, and controls the number of tasks the scout is willing to hypothetically place on the server, which is not necessarily the maximum number of tasks that can be placed on the server without violating the delay threshold, before moving on to the next server. The leader initializes scouts with randomly generated values for the parameters α and g.

At each cell, the scout records in its placement report (a) the ID of the server at which the cell resides, (b) which tasks it is placing on the server, and the sum of (c) the component of the latency of the hypothetically placed subquery at that server, and the impact on the latency of tasks in other subqueries deployed at that server. It then crawls to the next cell, using the pheromone vector exactly as the routing ants do. If it reaches the destination D without having been able to place all of its tasks, it declares failure and remains at the cell, C_D, in the destination server. If a number of failed scouts that traversed the same path with different levels of greediness, g, accumulate at C_D, one of them re-traces its steps to C_S and applies a negative reinforcement to the path in order to discourage future ants from pursuing the same path. If the scout succeeds in placing the tasks, it retraces its steps, and presents its scouting report to the producer. On its reverse path, the scout may conduct local load balancing of hypothetically placed tasks by estimating and comparing the service times of the same task on adjacent servers, and moving the task to the server on which placement is more efficient.

3.8   Enforcement Ants

If a scout succeeds in hypothetically placing all the tasks of the subquery, it returns to its dispatch leader, carrying a scouting report, consisting of the complete hypothetical placement, together with the latency statistics it recorded at each step. The leader waits a designated period of time for scouts to return. When a threshold number of scouts return the leader selects the best scouting report and dispatches enforcement ants to perform the placement outlined in this report. If a timeout occurs with too few scouts returning successfully, the leader may send out more scouts. Although, generally, the leader will wait for a threshold number of reports to return before making a decision about which placement to execute, if one of the scouts returns with an outstanding report, i.e. one with that has insignificant computational impact on the servers, the leader will proceed to execute this report without completing its wait for a threshold number of scouts to return. Before executing placement at each node, the enforcement ant will recalculate the placement cost of tasks that need to be placed at each server, and compare this against the statistics in the scout report. If the current cost of placement exceeds the cost stated in the scout's report by more than a threshold, the enforcement ant will return without executing placement, and the as a result the leader will dispatch more routing and scouting ants to discover other potential placements of the subquery. Thus, our placement strategy is most effective when local network conditions do not change significantly during the placement of a subquery.

Once the subquery has been placed, placement is recursively executed for other linear task chains in the flow graph. If a query has more than one producer, join points in the query are selected and the placement algorithm is recursively executed from each of these producers to this join point. Specifically, the ID of a server hosting a join point for a query is initialized as the destination in the routing, scouting and enforcement ants. These ants are released in parallel from each of the other producers of the query, and they are responsible for completing the placement of the subqueries that connect to the join point. For instance in Figure 1(b), the first subquery comprising of the chain of operators F1, J1 and J2 is placed. Then placement is re-executed from P1 to place F3 with J2 as the destination and from P3 to place F2 with J1 as the destination. If a query has fan-out, then multiple scouting and routing ants are dispatched from the producer to the point of fan-out. From this point the ants are dispatched in parallel to each consumer, in order to establish paths and place the remaining parts of the query between the point of fan-out and the other consumers. For instance in Figure 1(d), the first subquery comprising of the chain of operators F1, S2, and A4 is placed. Then placement is re-executed from S2 to place A3 with C1 as the destination, and from S2 to place A5 with C3 as the destination.

3.9   Updating Placement

Once a leader completes the placement of a query through enforcement ants, it periodically dispatches routing and scouting ants to seek more appropriate placements of the query in response to changing network conditions, such as changes in message rates, or changes in the network topology. The number of routing and scouting ants and the frequency with which they are periodically dispatched by a leader are initialized as user assigned parameters. The routing ants update routes to the consumers of the query. The scouting ants traverse the updated routes to determine new potential placements for the query. The leader periodically retrieves the current end-to-end service time for a query by sending an ant along the path on which the query is placed, and compares this with the service time of hypothetical placement reports of the query gathered by scouts. If the end-to-end latency of a hypothetical placement of a query is less than its most recently retrieved end-to-end latency (resulting from an existing deployment) by a factor β, such that $\beta > 0$ and $\beta \in \mathbb{R}_{\geq 0}$, then the leader dispatches enforcement ants to execute the new placement of the query, and discontinue the previous placement of the query. In the case where the query has one or more stateful tasks that must be moved as a result of the change in placement, there is a problem of conveying the state from the old location to the new location, or reconstructing the state at the new location. There are several well known techniques that address this [15,29,30], and we intend to examine this in future work.

Placement can also be explicitly updated by a user-initiated request in response to changes in performance or resource or flow graph characteristics. Users can initiate an updated query placement request accompanied with a request to terminate the deployment of the previous version of the query or request relevant producers to incrementally redo placement of one or more queries.

3.10   Task Reuse

Operator reuse is incorporated into our model. When a scouting ant conducts hypothetical placement of a task on a server, it retrieves the currently hosted tasks on that server. If the scout finds a reusable task that produces the same result as the task to be placed, it reuses this task instead of hypothetically instantiating a new instance. When executing a placement order by the leader, enforcement ants first check for reusable tasks on each node instead of instantiating a new instance.

4   Experimental Evaluation

To evaluate the performance of our algorithm we implemented a discrete event simulator in Java. We randomly generated queries with both fan-in and fan-out. Each edge in a query graph is labelled with: (1) the *message input rate* in units of messages/millisecond, and (2) the *message size* in units of bytes/message. For each task, we define its *mean service time* in terms of a virtual work unit (VWU), which corresponds to a time unit (say, 1 second) on some standard machine such as an IBM ThinkPad T40. The VWU concept is mainly introduced to accommodate different processing capacities of the machines. Tasks in our queries include query operators such as SELECT, JOIN, PROJECT, AGGREGATION and SPLIT. Producers and consumers are assumed to be pinned to machines in the network. Although we randomly generated queries, we used meaningful values for the data on query edges and tasks that emulate workloads of data streams in the financial services industry. The network topology fed to the simulator was a transit-stub topology, generated by the GT-ITM internetwork topology generator. Nodes and links are assigned processing and communication capacities from discrete classes to simulate a heterogeneous system. The machine processing capacities are defined in units of VWU/millisecond such that if a T40 ThinkPad has processing capacity of 1, then a twice as fast machine would have a capacity of 2.

For comparison, we also implement three other common approaches: *optimal, random and centralized*. The optimal algorithm chooses the best possible placement with the lowest end-to-end latency based on an exhaustive search over all possible placements. The random algorithm selects a server for hosting each task at random and serves as a worst case comparison. We also compare against a centralized placement algorithm [16] whose goal is to produce an assignment of unpinned tasks to servers such that the expected average latency from producers to consumers over all paths is minimized. The centralized algorithm also utilizes a queueing model of the flow graph to determine how to compute the expected latencies due to the combination of delays for a given assignment. It employs a steepest descent search to find an approximate solution to the problem of minimizing the latencies. The algorithm accepts one flow graph as input which represents the concatenation of all queries that need to be placed. Placement of the entire flow graph has to be recomputed each time a new query needs to be placed, or there is a change in the data or network characteristics.

We evaluate our ant-inspired algorithm in terms of (1) the quality of its solution, (2) its adaptability and self-management capabilities, and (3) its scalability. Figure 2(a) compares the end-to-end latency of a flow graph placed by the optimal algorithm with our ant-inspired decentralized algorithm for an increasing number of query tasks. We observe that although the ant-inspired decentralized algorithm does not guarantee optimal results, the end-to-end latency of the query

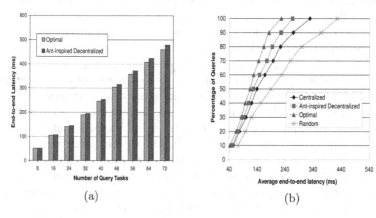

(a)   (b)

Fig. 2. Evaluation of the quality of our algorithm's placement solution. (a) Comparison of end-to-end latency achieved for increasing number of query tasks. (b) Comparison of end-to-end latency achieved for increasing number of queries.

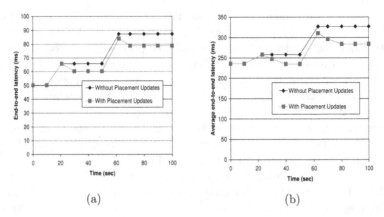

Fig. 3. Evaluation of our algorithm's adaptability and self-optimization capabilities. (a) End-to-end latency variation for a query with and without self-optimization when data rates are increased at time 20 and at time 60. (b) Average end-to-end latency variation of 200 concurrently executing queries with and without self-optimization when 50 additional queries are added at time 20 and at time 60.

graph placed by it is not much worse than the end-to-end latency of the query graph placed by the optimal algorithm. Figure 2(b) compares the average end-to-end latency of all queries deployed on the network by the centralized, random and optimal algorithms with our ant-inspired decentralized algorithm. The total number of queries placed is 100. In this experiment 100 ants are released from each producer every 5 seconds. We observe that our ant-inspired decentralized algorithm consistently achieves better performance than other heuristic algorithms and similar performance as the optimal algorithm. While conducting this experiment, we also recorded the predicted running time of our distributed algorithm as output by our simulator and compared it against the running time of the centralized algorithm. We find that for queries compiled into flow graphs with more than 150 nodes, the centralized algorithm takes on the order of hours to run, where as the predicted running time of our algorithm is on the order of seconds.

Second, we evaluate the effectiveness of dynamically updating placement during runtime by our algorithm in response to changes in data characteristics. Figure 3(a) shows the variation in end-to-end latency for a 10-node query graph with and without self-optimization while network conditions are changing. During the 100 second simulation, the data rates at all producers of the query are increased by 10 ms at time 20 and then again by the same amount at time 60. We sample the end-to-end latency of the query every 10 seconds. The performance with self-optimization involving dynamic placement updates is clearly better than without self-optimization. Figure 3(b) shows the variation in average end-to-end latency for 200 concurrently executing queries with and without self-optimization in response to new queries being placed. 50 additional queries are placed at time 20 and at time 60. We observe that our decentralized and incremental algorithm generates a globally improved solution, as the average

Table 1. Loss and number of placement updates for different values of β

β	Number of Placement Updates	Latency-Loss (ms)
1.1	15	0
1.25	10	25.87
1.5	7	59.23
1.75	2	78.67
2.0	1	101.23

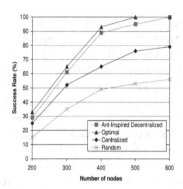

Fig. 4. Scalability of our algorithm: success rate of deploying 300 queries on distributed systems with different number of nodes

end-to-end latency over all queries, with self-optimization, decreases. We also observe that the change in average end-to-end latency consistently decreases and reaches a point where it stops decreasing, indicating that our algorithm does not continue to update placement indefinitely.

Recall from section 3.9 that a decision to discontinue a query's placement and move it to a new placement is made when the end-to-end latency of a hypothetical placement of the query is less than its most recently retrieved end-to-end latency (resulting from an existing deployment) by a factor β, such that $\beta > 0$ and $\beta \in \mathbb{R}_{\geq 0}$. We calculate the loss in end-to-end latency incurred due to sub-optimal deployments of a 10-node query using different values of β in the presence of network perturbations (cross-traffic). The results are shown in Table 1. The loss is calculated as the integral over time of the difference between the maximum achievable end-to-end latency and the current end-to-end latency of the deployed flow-graph. The loss incurred is sufficiently low for a large number of values of β, and thus an appropriate value for β can be used to trade-off latency for a lower number of placement updates.

Finally, we evaluate the scalability of the our algorithm illustrated by Figure 4. We use different distributed stream processing systems with 200 to 600 nodes. As we add more nodes into the distributed stream processing system, the number of candidate servers for hosting tasks increases proportionally, so as to increase the capacity of the distributed stream processing system. We impose the same workload of 300 queries on those different distributed stream processing systems. Figure 4 shows the performance comparison results. We observe that our algorithm achieves similar scaling property as the optimal algorithm. For this experiment, we also recorded the message overhead added by our algorithm to the traffic in the network. We find that, on average, ant messages occupy 0.01% of the traffic on a link in the network of 200 nodes, and 0.022% of the traffic on a link in the network of 600 nodes.

5 Conclusion and Future Work

In this paper we have presented a biologically-inspired, distributed placement algorithm that reacts on-the-fly to placement requests of new flow graphs or to modifications of an already running stream processing flow graph, and dynamically adapts to changes in performance characteristics such as message rates or service times as well as to changes in processor availability or link performance during runtime. Our incremental algorithm is inspired by pheromone-based cooperation in ants and possesses many good properties that emerge as a result of this analogy such as completely decentralized control and no requirements for global state. Our simulation results show that our algorithm maintains scalable and effective self-management, while achieving high quality placement in terms of end-to-end latency. Although we choose to optimize placement for end-to-end latency, our model is generic enough to incorporate other metrics such as bandwidth or the product of bandwidth and latency. Instead of recording time at every hop along their forward routes, routing ants can record other metric related information from links and servers and use it to create and update pheromone entries on their return routes. Although we discussed and evaluated our algorithm in the context of tasks which are database query operators, it is applicable to the placement of any sequence of tasks on streams of data.

As future work we plan to develop a theoretical model of our algorithm and prove its correctness given concurrent placement of tasks by ants. We also intend to define some load placement primitives for each ant in order to prevent situations where placement continuously oscillates between two or more configurations. This can occur when data rates are particularly bursty. In addition to a queueing model, we would like to explore other methods to estimate the cost of hypothetical placement that are more suitable for real stream processing systems. We also intend to implement our algorithm on a real stream processing system.

References

1. Harmer, P.K., Williams, P.D., Gunsch, G.H., Lamont, G.B.: An artificial immune system architecture for computer security applications. J. Evolutionary Computation 23(6), 252–280 (2002)
2. Werner-Allen, G., Tewari, G., Patel, A., Welsh, M., Nagpal, R.: Firefly-Inspired Sensor Network Synchronicity with Realistic Radio Effects. In: ACM Conference on Embedded Networked Sensor Systems (2005)

3. Suzuki, J., Suda, T.: A Middleware Platform for a Biologically Inspired Network Architecture Supporting Autonomous and Adaptive Applications. IEEE Journal On Selected Areas In Communications 23(2), 249–260 (2005)
4. Lee, S.-Y., Chang, H.S.: An ant system based multicasting in mobile ad hoc network. IEEE Congress on Evolutionary Computation 2, 1583–1588 (2005)
5. Bonabeau, E., Dorigo, M., Theraulaz, G.: Swarm Intelligence. Oxford University Press, Oxford (1999)
6. Di Caro, G., Dorigo, M.: AntNet: Distributed Stigmergetic Control for Communications Networks. Journal of Artificial Intelligence Research 9, 317–365 (1998)
7. Exploratory Stream Processing Systems, http://domino.research.ibm.com/comm/research_projects.nsf/pages/esps.index.html
8. Financial Services: Real Time Data Processing with a Stream Processing Engine. White paper, http://www.streambase.com/knowledgecenter.htm
9. Abadi, D., et al.: The design of the borealis stream processing engine. In: Proceedings of CIDR, Asilomar, CA (2005)
10. Cherniack, M., et al.: Scalable Distributed Stream Processing. In: Conference on Innovative Data Systems Research (2003)
11. Motwani, R., et al.: Query Processing, Resource Management, and Approximation in a Data Stream Management System. In: Conference on Innovative Data Systems Research (2003)
12. Chandrasekaran, S., et al.: TelegraphCQ: Continuous Dataflow Processing for an Uncertain World. In: Conference on Innovative Data Systems Research (2003)
13. Damani, O., Strom, R.: Smart Middleware and Light Ends for Simplifying Data Integration. In: Conference on Information Reuse and Integration (2006)
14. Srivastava, U., Mungala, K., Widom, J.: Operator Placement for In-Network Stream Query Processing. In: Proc. Principles of Distributed Systems, pp. 250–258 (2005)
15. Shah, M., Hellerstein, J., Chandrasekaran, S., Franklin, M.: Flux: An adaptive partitioning operator for continuous query systems. In: International Conference on Data Engineering (2003)
16. Pandit, V., Strom, R., Buttner, G., Ginis, R.: Performance Modeling and Placement of Transforms for Stateful Mediations, IBM Technical Report No. RI08002 (2004), http://www.domino.research.ibm.com/library/cyberdig.nsf/index.html
17. Amini, L., Jain, N., Sehgal, A., Silber, J., Verscheure, O.: Adaptive control of extreme-scale stream processing systems. In: International Conference on Data Engineering (2006)
18. Wolf, J., et al.: SODA: An Optimizing Scheduler for Large-Scale Stream-Based Distributed Computer Systems. In: ACM Middleware (2008)
19. Pietzuch, P., Ledlie, J., Shneidman, J., Roussopoulos, M., Welsh, M., Seltzer, M.: Network-aware operator placement for stream-processing systems. In: Proc. of 22nd ICDE (2006)
20. Ahmad, Y., Cetintemel, U.: Network-aware query processing for stream-based applications. In: Proceedings of Very Large Data Bases, VLDB (2004)
21. Repantis, T., Gu, X., Kalogeraki, V.: Synergy: Sharing-aware component composition for distributed stream processing systems. In: ACM Middleware, pp. 322–341 (2006)
22. Balazinska, M., Balakrishnan, H., Stonebraker, M.: Contract-based load management in federated distributed systems. In: Symposium on Networked Systems Design and Implementation (2004)

23. Zhou, Y., Ooi, B., Tan, K., Wu, J.: Efficient dynamic operator placement in a locally distributed continuous query system. In: International Conference on Cooperative Information Systems (2006)
24. Kumar, V., Cooper, B., Schwan, K.: Distributed stream management using utility-driven self-adaptive middleware. In: International Conference on Autonomic Computing (2005)
25. Gu, X., Yu, P., Nahrstedt, K.: Optimal component composition for scalable stream processing. In: 25th IEEE ICDCS, Columbus, OH (2005)
26. Maniezzo, V., Colorni, A.: The Ant System Applied to the Quadratic Assignment Problem. IEEE Transactions on Knowledge and Data Engineering 11(5), 769 (1998)
27. Colorni, A., Dorigo, M., Maniezzo, V., Trubian, M.: Ant System for Job-Shop Scheduling. JORBEL – Belgian Journal of Operations Research, Statistics and Computer Science 34, 39–53 (1994)
28. Balazinska, M., Hwang, J.-H., Shah, M.: Fault-tolerance and high availability in data stream management systems. In: Encyclopedia of Database Systems (to appear)
29. Liu, B., Zhu, Y., Jbantova, M., Momberger, B., Rundensteiner, E.: A dynamically adaptive distributed system for processing complex continuous queries. In: Proceedings of Very Large Data Bases, VLDB (2005)
30. Yang, Y., Kramer, J., Papadias, D., Seeger, B.: HybMig: A Hybrid Approach to Dynamic Plan Migration for Continuous Queries. IEEE Transactions on Knowledge and Data Engineering 19(3), 398–411 (2007)
31. Whitt, W.: The queueing network analyzer. Bell Systems Technical Journal 66, 2779–2813 (1983)
32. Marchal, W.: Some simpler bounds on the mean queueing time. Operations Research 22, 1083–1088 (1978)

pMapper: Power and Migration Cost Aware Application Placement in Virtualized Systems

Akshat Verma[1], Puneet Ahuja[2], and Anindya Neogi[1]

[1] IBM India Research Lab
[2] IIT Delhi

Abstract. Workload placement on servers has been traditionally driven by mainly performance objectives. In this work, we investigate the design, implementation, and evaluation of a power-aware application placement controller in the context of an environment with heterogeneous virtualized server clusters. The placement component of the application management middleware takes into account the power and migration costs in addition to the performance benefit while placing the application containers on the physical servers. The contribution of this work is two-fold: first, we present multiple ways to capture the cost-aware application placement problem that may be applied to various settings. For each formulation, we provide details on the kind of information required to solve the problems, the model assumptions, and the practicality of the assumptions on real servers. In the second part of our study, we present the pMapper architecture and placement algorithms to solve one practical formulation of the problem: minimizing power subject to a fixed performance requirement. We present comprehensive theoretical and experimental evidence to establish the efficacy of pMapper.

1 Introduction

Resource provisioning or placement of applications on a set of physical servers to optimize the application Service Level Agreements (SLA) is a well studied problem [6,24]. Typically, concerns about application performance, infrequent but inevitable workload peaks, and security requirements persuade the provisioning decision logic to opt for a conservative approach, such as hardware isolation among applications with minimum sharing of resources. This leads to sub-optimal resource utilization. Bohrer et al. have studied real webserver workloads from sports, e-commerce, financial, and internet proxy clusters to find that average server utilization varies between 11% and 50% [3]. Such inefficient provisioning leads to relatively large hardware and operations costs when compared to the actual workload handled by the data center. However, recently two important trends, *viz.* server virtualization and the heightened awareness around energy management technologies, have renewed interest in the problem of application placement. The placement logic in the middleware now need to look beyond just application SLAs into increasing energy-related operations costs. In this paper, we investigate the *Power-aware Application Placement* problem and

V. Issarny and R. Schantz (Eds.): Middleware 2008, LNCS 5346, pp. 243–264, 2008.

present *pMapper*, an application placement controller that dynamically places applications to minimize power while meeting performance guarantees.

System management costs have escalated rapidly with the growing number of densely packed under-utilized machines in the data center. Virtualization is seen as a solution that can provide the required isolation layer to consolidate applications running on a large number of low utilization servers to a smaller number of highly utilized servers. The virtualization layer typically provides flexible runtime mechanisms for fine grain resource allocation. In fact, high speed live migration of virtual machines is also possible between the physical servers in a cluster. This enables applications in virtual machine containers to be moved at runtime in response to changing workload to dynamically optimize the application placement on physical servers. Thus mechanisms to allow dynamic resizing and migration of virtual machine containers among physical servers enables research in dynamic application placement middleware beyond static provisioning.

A second trend that is important for dynamic application placement is the growing awareness about energy consumption in data centers and the significant adverse impact on the environment in terms of CO_2 emissions from the cooling systems. The current power density of data centers is typically around 100 Watt per sq.ft. and growing at the rate of $15 - 20\%$ per year [17]. Thus, it is increasingly being realized that inefficient use of servers in a data center leads to high energy costs, expensive cooling hardware, floor space, and also adverse impact on the environment. There is a large initiative in the industry as well as academia to develop technologies that will help to create "green" or environment-friendly data centers that will optimize energy consumption and consolidate hardware resources, besides being sensitive to application performance and availability SLAs. To this extent, a dynamic application placement controller can use virtualization to resize VM containers of applications or migrate VMs at runtime to consolidate the workload on an optimal set of physical servers. Servers unused over a period of time can be switched to low power states to save energy. Further, we observed a fairly large dynamic power range (e.g., the static power of an IBM HS-21 blade was 140Watt and the dynamic potentially non-linear power range was almost 80Watt for the **daxpy** benchmark). Hence, even in scenarios where servers can not be switched off by consolidation, power savings can be obtained by packing the servers at optimal target utilization.

The use of power management techniques during application placement has its own implications. A dynamic application placement controller uses live migration and we found from our testbed experimentation that the cost of live migration is significant, and needs to be factored by the dynamic placement controller. For example, a 512MB VM running HPC benchmarks require almost a minute to migrate and causes a 20-25% drop in application throughput during the live migration. We also observed that a large number of live migrations are required for dynamic placement, thus emphasizing the importance of taking migration cost into account.

Contributions: In this paper, we make the following contributions to advance the state of the art. We describe the architecture and implementation of a *power-aware application placement framework*, called *pMapper*, which can incorporate various scenarios involving power and performance management using virtualization mechanisms. *pMapper* provides the solution to the most practical possibility, i.e. power minimization under performance constraints. We have implemented the framework, some algorithms, and the interfaces with an existing commercial IBM performance-oriented workload manager. We have benchmarked applications on virtualized server platforms to create utilization-based *power models* of application and server combinations and quantify the virtualization related costs. The characterization study provides us with insights into the structure of the power-aware placement problem that can be used to design tractable application placement solutions. We used the power models, migration cost models, and power-aware placement algorithms to design a dynamic placement controller that, under various assumptions, performs better than a static or load balancing placement controller with increasing heterogeneity of the server platforms, i.e. their power models. All input models and assumptions in *pMapper* have been validated on a testbed using a set of benchmark applications. The various algorithms implemented in *pMapper* have been compared through simulation on real utilization trace data obtained from a large production environment.

The rest of the paper is organized as follows. Section 2 describes the various flavors of the problem and the tool architecture. Section 3 discusses the assumptions made in the formulation and validates the assumptions through testbed experiments. Section 4 provides the details of the algorithms. Section 5 describes our implementation and a trace-driven evaluation study of our algorithms. Section 6 presents a comparative discussion with the related work.

2   pMapper: Power and Migration Cost-Aware Application Placement Framework

In this section, we present the *pMapper* application placement framework for power management and the various optimization formulations for power-aware application placement. We first present the *pMapper* architecture framework that leverages power management techniques enabled by virtualization.

2.1   Architecture

We have designed the *pMapper* framework to utilize all the power management capabilities available in virtualized platforms. As per the terminology used in [15], power management actions can be categorized as (i) soft actions like CPU idling in the hypervisor, (ii) hard actions like DVFS or throttling and (iii) consolidation actions. Commercial hypervisors drop all the power management actions that are taken by the OS. Further, for multi-tiered applications, a single VM instance may not be able to determine the application end-to-end QoS thus necessitating the need for a power management channel from the the management

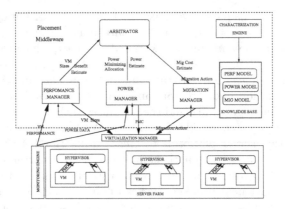

Fig. 1. *pMapper* Application Placement Architecture

middleware. In *pMapper*, all the power management actions are communicated by three different managers, with an arbitrator ensuring consistency between the three actions. The soft-actions like VM re-sizing and idling are communicated by the *Performance Manager*, that has a global view of the application in terms of QoS met and performance SLA. *Power Manager* triggers power management at a hardware layer whereas a Migration Manager interfaces with the Virtualization Manager to trigger consolidation through VM live migration.

The resource management flow of *pMapper* starts with the *Monitoring engine*, which collects the current performance and power characteristics of all the VMs and physical servers in the farm. *Performance Manager* looks at the current performance and recommends a set of target VM sizes based on the SLA goals. In case, the target VM sizes are different from the current VM sizes, it also presents an estimate of the benefit due to resizing. Similarly, *Power Manager* looks at the current power consumption and may suggest throttling (by DVFS or explicit CPU throttling). The central intelligence of *pMapper* lies in *Arbitrator*, which explores the configuration space for eligible VM sizes and placements and implements an algorithm to compute the best placement and VM sizes, based on the estimates received from *Performance*, *Power* and *Migration* managers.

Performance Manager supports interfaces using which the *Arbitrator* can query for the estimated benefit of a given VM sizing and placement (for all the VMs). In order to cater for heterogeneous platforms, the *Performance Manager* consults a *Knowledge Base* to determine the performance of an application, if one of its VM is migrated from one platform to another. Similarly, *Power Manager* supports interfaces using which *Arbitrator* can get the best power-minimizing placement for a given set of VM sizes. Also, *Power Manager* uses a power model in the *Knowledge Base* to determine the placement, as well as estimate the power for a given placement. *Migration Manager* estimates the cost of moving from a given placement to a new placement and uses the *Migration Model* for making the estimate. Once the *Arbitrator* decides on a new configuration, *Performance Manager*, *Power Manager*, and *Migration Manager* execute the VM sizing, server throttling and live migration operations, respectively.

We note that for standalone applications running on power-aware virtualized platforms such as [15], our framework can make use of the OS hints by passing them on to the *Arbitrator*. Hence, our framework and proposed algorithms (Section. 4) can also be used in other power management frameworks [15,23].

2.2   Optimization Formulations

We now formulate the problem of placing N application on M virtualized servers that have power management capabilities. The power-aware application placement problem divides the time horizon in time windows. In each window, we compute the application placement that optimizes the performance-cost trade-off, i.e., maximizes performance and minimizes cost. The cost metric may consist of management cost, power cost or the application cost incurred due to the migrations that are required to move to the desired placement. We next present various formulations of the application placement problem.

Cost Performance Tradeoff. The generic formulation of the problem solves two sub-problems: (i) application sizing and (ii) application placement. Given a predicted workload for each application, we resize the virtual machine hosting the application and place the virtual machines on physical hosts in a manner such that the cost-performance tradeoff is optimized. In this paper, we focus on the power and migration costs only. Formally, given an old allocation A_o, a performance benefit function $B(A)$, a power cost function $P(A)$, and a migration cost function Mig for any allocation A, we need to find an allocation A_I defined by the variables $x_{i,j}$, where $x_{i,j}$ denotes the resource allocated to application V_i on server S_j, such that the net benefit (defined as the difference between performance benefit and costs) is maximized.

$$maximize \sum_{i=1}^{N} \sum_{j=1}^{M} B(x_{i,j}) - \sum_{j=1}^{M} P(A_I) - Mig(A_o, A_I) \qquad (1)$$

Cost Minimization with Performance Constraint. Data centers today are moving towards an SLA-based environment with fixed performance guarantees (e.g., response time of 100 ms with throughput of 100 transactions per second). Hence, in such a scenario, performance is not a metric to be maximized and can be replaced by constraints in the optimization framework. In practice, it amounts to taking away the VM sizing problem away from the *Arbitrator*. The VM sizes are now fixed by the *Performance Manager* based on the SLA and the *Arbitrator* only strives to minimize the overall cost of the allocation. Hence, the optimization problem can now be formulated as

$$minimize \sum_{j=1}^{M} P(A_I) + Mig(A_o, A_I) \qquad (2)$$

Performance Benefit Maximization with Power Constraints. A third formulation for the application allocation problem is to maximize the net performance benefit given a fixed power budget for each server, where the net benefit is computed as the difference between the performance benefit and migration cost.

$$maximize \sum_{i=1}^{N} \sum_{j=1}^{M} B(x_{i,j}) - Mig(A_o, A_I) \tag{3}$$

We next present the various model assumptions that $pMapper$ needs to make to solve the application placement problem.

3   Model Assumptions and Experimental Reality

In this section, we study the various underlying model assumptions and the feasibility of constructing estimation models required by the three formulations of the application placement problem.

Our testbed to experimentally validate the model assumptions consists of two different experimental setups. The first setup is an IBM HS-21 Bladecenter with mutiple blades. Each blade has 2 Xeon5148 dual-core Processors and runs two compute-intensive applications from an HPC suite, namely $daxpy$ and fma and a Linpack benchmark HPL [16] on VMWare ESX Hypervisor . Each blade server has an L2 cache of 4MB, FSB of 1.33 GHz, with each processor running at 2.33 GHz. The second setup consists of 9 IBM x3650 rack servers running VMWare ESX with L2 cache of 4MB. Each server has a quad-core Xeon5160 processor running at 2.99 GHz. This setup runs the Trade6 application as well as the two HPC applications $daxpy$ and fma. The overall system power is measured through IBM Active Energy Manager APIs [13]. We now list the key model assumptions and our experimental findings on the veracity (or the lack of it) of the assumptions. We use these findings to investigate the practicality of the optimization formulations discussed earlier.

3.1   Performance Isolation in Virtualized Systems

Virtualization allows applications to share the same physical server by creating multiple virtual machines in a manner such that each application can assume ownership of the virtual machine. However, such sharing is possible only if one virtual machine is isolated from other virtual machines hosted on the same physical server. Hence, we first studied this fundamental underlying assumption by running a background load using fma and a foreground load using $daxpy$. The applications run on two different VMs with fixed reservations. We varied the intensity of the background load and measured the performance (throughput) of the foreground daxpy application (Fig. 2(a)).

One can observe that the $daxpy$ application is isolated from the load variation in the background application. However, we conjectured that applications may only be isolated in terms of CPU and memory, while still competing for the shared cache. To validate this conjecture, we increased the memory footprint of

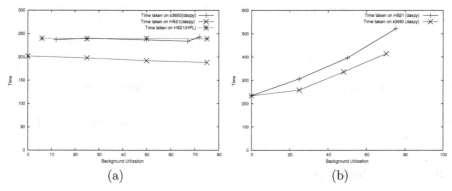

Fig. 2. Running Time of 30 Billion daxpy operations with change in background load on HS-21 and x3650 systems at (a) low memory footprint and (b) high memory footprint

both the foreground *daxpy* and background *fma*. We observed that as the size of the arrays being operated exceeded the L2 cache size ($4MB$), the applications were no longer isolated (Fig. 2(b)). The throughput of the foreground application decreases with increase in background traffic as a result of the large number of cache misses, which are due to increased cache usage by the background application. However, as one increases the memory footprint of each application beyond the cache size, the applications are no longer able to use the cache even in isolation. Hence, we concluded that for a large range of application use (small and large working set sizes), virtualization is able to successfully isolate two VMs from each other.

3.2   Migration Cost Modeling

We have proposed the application placement problem as a continual optimization problem, where we dynamically migrate the live virtual machines from one physical server to another in order to optimize the allocation. The migration of virtual machines requires creation of a checkpoint on secondary storage and retrieval of the VM image on the target server. Applications can continue to run during the course of migration. However, the performance of applications is impacted in the transition because of cache misses (hardware caches are not migrated) and possible application quiesces. Thus, each migration is characterized by a migration duration and a migration cost. The *Migration Manager* in *pMapper* needs to estimate this migration cost for use by the *Arbitrator*. Hence, we next studied the feasibility of characterizing migration cost for an application and study the parameters that affect this cost.

We observed (Fig. 3) that the impact of migration was independent of the background load and depends only on the VM characteristics. Hence, the cost of each live migration can be computed *a priori*. This cost is estimated by quantifying the decrease in throughput because of live migration and estimating the revenue loss because of the decreased performance (as given by SLA). Hence,

Background Load (CPU)	Migration Duration	Time (w/o Mig)	Time (With Mig)
0	60	210s	259s
12	70	214s	255s
30	63	209s	261s

Fig. 3. Impact of Migration on application throughput with different background traffic

we conclude that it is possible to estimate the cost of live migration of each application for use by *pMapper*.

3.3   Power Modeling

The power-aware application placement controller explores various candidate placements and needs to estimate the overall power drawn for each candidate placement while selecting a good placement. This estimation is especially required to solve the power-constraints and power-performance tradeoff formulations. We next study the feasibility of modeling the power for a server given a mix of applications running on it.

Give a set of N applications and M servers, we can potentially mix a large variety of applications on each server. Further, any optimization algorithm may seek to change the ratio of various applications on a server. Hence, creating a model for all mixes of all applications on all the servers is practically infeasible. Thus, we may be able to estimate the power drawn by a server only if it is independent of the applications running on it. We next conducted experiments to validate this assumption by creating power models for various applications on the two testbeds.

We found (Fig. 4(a)) that the power drawn by a server varies with the applications running on it. Hence, an algorithm that requires an exact power model

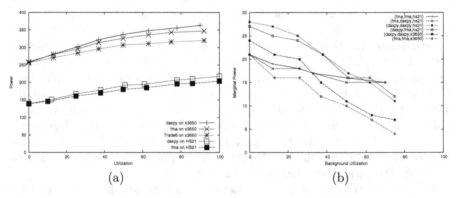

(a)   (b)

Fig. 4. (a) Power drawn by various applications with change in server utilization. (b) Marginal Power consumed by HPC applications on various platforms with change in background load and background mix. (A, B, C) denotes incremental power drawn by A with background traffic of B on platform C.

for each allocation may be infeasible in practice. Further, since migration takes a significant amount of time, any measurement-based strategy that tries to learn the power models for all used application mixes is also practically infeasible in a dynamic consolidation setting.

We concluded that the power-capping and power-performance tradeoff frameworks, though interesting in theory, are not feasible in practice as they need one to compute the exact power consumed by an application. However, we note that an algorithm to solve the power minimization problem does not need actual power numbers. The problem that the power minimization framework solves is to minimize power, without really knowing what the exact power would be. Hence, an algorithm that can be listed out as a sequence of steps, where each step is a decision problem for some application to determine which of the candidate servers the application should be placed on, does not need estimates of power values. Instead, if the algorithm can figure out which server minimizes the incremental increase in total power due to the new application being placed, then it can place the application appropriately.

One may, however, note that this approach restricts the algorithm choices to only those algorithms that take a local view of the problem, and hence can be locally optimal in the best case. Further, one still needs to solve the ordering problem, where for any given placement of $N - 1$ applications on M servers, we should be able to estimate the best server (in terms of power minimization) to place the Nth application. We next investigate two properties such that even if any one of them holds, one can make this decision.

Definition 1. Ordering Property: *For any two applications VM_i and $VM_{i'}$ and servers S_j and $S_{j'}$ at loads ρ_j and $\rho_{j'}$ respectively, if the server S_j is more power efficient than $S_{j'}$ for VM_i, then S_j is more power-efficient than $S_{j'}$ for all $VM_{i'}$ as well. Hence, the slopes for any two servers satisfy a uniform ordering across all applications.*

Definition 2. Background Independence Property: *An application and a server are said to satisfy that Background Independence Property if the incremental power drawn due to the application on the server depends only on the background load intensity and is independent of the traffic mix in the background.*

We next investigate if these properties can be made to hold in certain situations where we know about the class of applications we are placing. For example, if we restrict ourselves to consider only HPC applications or only J2EE applications in a cluster we can demonstrate that these properties hold. We ran two applications on the two testbeds for various mixes of background traffic picked from the HPC benchmarks. We observed the *Ordering Property* to hold for the two applications on the two testbeds. We noted (Fig. 4(b)) that the x3650 platform is more power-efficient (incrementally) for both the applications. This is true even when we changed the background traffic from *daxpy* to *fma* on the HS21 Blades. We also observe that the incremental power drawn by *daxpy* for both the background traffic at any given background load value is almost same. Hence, one can assume the *Background Independence Property* to hold at a coarse granularity in most scenarios. We next propose algorithms that use these properties to solve the power-minimization optimization problem.

4   Application Placement Algorithms

In this section, we describe the various placement algorithms designed for minimizing the overall cost, while meeting a fixed performance SLA. The algorithms assume that a performance manager provides them with a VM size for each application, that can meet its performance goals. We start with a brief description of the key ideas behind the algorithms.

4.1   Algorithm Idea

Our application placement algorithms that minimize the power and migration costs are based on three key observations

1. Estimating the power cost of a given configuration may not be possible because power drawn by a server depends on the exact application mix on a server.
2. Background Independence Property and Ordering Property allows one to pick a server for an application that will minimize the incremental power due to the new application. Hence, local searches are feasible.
3. The above properties may not hold always if servers are equally loaded. However, the properties will definitely hold if we compare an idle server with a loaded server.

The first two observations dictate the design of algorithms to be based on local searches. One can view the application placement problem as a bin-packing problem with differently sized bins. The servers represent the bins and the virtual machines represent the balls. The power drawn by a server is represented as the cost of the bin and the power-minimizing allocation is a packing that minimizes the cost of the packed bins. Since power drawn by a server depends on the actual mix of applications, the cost of packing a bin varies depending on the balls being packed in the bin. Bin packing has many local search algorithms like First-Fit Decreasing(FFD) [25], Best-Fit and Worst-fit.

We took a close look at FFD, where balls are ordered by size (largest first). The balls are then packed in the first bin that can accommodate them. We observed that if servers are ordered based on power efficiency (static power per unit capacity), then the FFD algorithm can employ the Ordering property to minimize power. This is because FFD unbalances load, and as per our third observation, the Ordering property always holds if we are comparing an idle server with a loaded server. Further, by placing servers based on their power efficiency, we ensure that more power efficient servers are the ones that are utilized first. Finally, FFD has good theoretical bounds and is also known to perform well in practice [25]. Hence, we focus on adapting First Fit to work for different sized bins with ball-dependent cost functions.

4.2 Algorithm Details

We first present an algorithm *min Power Parity* (*mPP*) in Fig. 5 to place the
VMs on the given set of servers in a manner such that the overall power consumed
by all the servers is minimized. The algorithm takes as input the VM sizes for
the current time window that can meet the performance constraints, a previous
placement and the power model for all the available servers. It then tries to place
the VMs on the servers in a manner that minimizes the total power consumed.

$algorithm\ mPP$
$Input : \forall i V M_i, Alloc_{old}\quad Output = Alloc_{new}$
$\forall Server_j$
$\quad Alloc_j = \phi, Used_j = 0$
$Sort\ VMs\ by\ size\ in\ decreasing\ order$
$for\ i = 1\ to\ N$
$\quad \forall Server_j\ compute\ Slope(Used_j)$
$\quad Pick\ the\ Server_{min}\ with\ the\ least\ Slope$
$\quad Add\ VM_i\ to\ Alloc_{min}, Used_{min}+ = Size(VM_i)$
$End\ For$
$Alloc_{new} = FFD(\mathbf{Used})$
$return Alloc_{new}$
$end\ mPP$

Fig. 5. Power-minimizing Placement Algorithm

mPP works in two phases: In the first phase, we determine a target utilization
for each server based on the power model for the server. The target utilization
is computed in a greedy manner, where we start with a utilization of 0 for each
server. We then pick the server with the least power increase per unit increase
in capacity. We continue the process till we have allocated capacity to fit all the
VMs. Since we may not be able to estimate the server with the least slope for all
possible background traffic mixes, we pick an arbitrary traffic mix to model the
power for each application and use this model in the selection process. We will
later show that modeling based on an arbitrary background traffic mix also leads
to a good solution. In the second phase, we call the bin-packing algorithm *FFD*
based on *First Fit Decreasing* to place the VMs on the servers, while trying to
meet the target utilization on each server. The bins in our version have unequal
capacity, where the capacity and order of each bin is defined in the first phase
whereas standard FFD that works with randomly ordered equal-sized bins.

Theorem 1. *If the* Ordering Property *or the* Background Independence Property *hold for a given set of servers and applications, then the allocation values
obtained by mPP in its first phase are locally optimal.*

Proof. Let there be any two servers S_j and S_k such that we can shift some load
between the two. For simplicity, assume that the load shift requires us to move

```
algorithm iFFD
Input : Alloc_o, Used    Output = Alloc_n
  Donors = φ, Receivers = φ
  For all servers S_j
    Prev_j =sum of VMs in S_j by Alloc_o
    If(Prev_j > Used_j)
      Add S_j to Donors
      Mig_j = Prev_j - Used_j
    Else
      Add S_j to Receivers
  End - For
  For all S_j in Donors
    Pick the smallest VMs that add upto
    Mig_j and add them to MigList
  End - For
  Sort MigList based on size
  For all VM_i in MigList
    Place VM_i on the first Donor_j that
    can pack it within Used_j
  End - For
  Return Alloc_n
```
(a)

```
algorithm pMaP
Input : Alloc_o, VM_i    Output : Migs
  Alloc_n = mPPH(Alloc_o, VM_i)
  MList = getMigList(Alloc_o, Alloc_n)
  ∀Server_j with no VMs placed in Alloc_n
    VG_j =VMs placed on Server_j in Alloc_o
    Add VG_j to MList
  ∀mig_i ∈ MList
    Cost_i = getMigrationCost(mig_i),
    Benefit_i = getBenefit(mig_i)
  Sort MList by Benefit_i/cost_i (decreasing)
  mig_best = most profitable entry in MList
  while(profit_best > cost_best)AND(MList≠ Φ)
    Migs = Migs ∪ mig_best
    Delete mig_best from MList
    Recompute Cost and Benefit for MList
  End While
  return Migs
end pMaP Algorithm
```
(b)

Fig. 6. (a)History Aware Packing Algorithm, (b) Migration Cost-aware Locally Optimal Placement Algorithm

the VM VM_i from S_j (at load ρ_j) to S_k (at load ρ_k). Also, since we had selected S_j over S_k for the additional load, there exists some VM $VM_{i'}$ for which the slope of S_j at load ρ_j is less than the slope for the server S_k at load ρ_k. However, by the *Ordering* assumption, such a VM $VM_{i'}$ can not exist. This leads to a contradiction and proves the required result.

The proof for the *Background Independence Property* is straightforward. If this property holds, then the incremental load due to application VM_i is independent of the workload mix, and as a result, we can always compute the exact increase in power on all candidate servers for VM_i and pick the best server. Hence, the shares allocated to the servers are locally optimal. This completes the proof.

One may also observe that if all the power models are concave, then the utilization allocation obtained is globally optimal as well. However, we did not observe this property to hold in our experiments and concluded that mPP can provably lead to locally optimal allocations only.

The mPP algorithm is designed to minimize power. However, it is oblivious of the last configuration and hence may entail large-scale migrations. This may lead to a high overall (power + migration) cost. Hence, we next propose a variant of FFD called *incremental FFD* ($iFFD$) for packing the applications on physical servers, given a fixed target utilization for each server in Fig. 6(a).

$iFFD$ first computes the list of servers that require higher utilization in the new allocation, and labels them as receivers. For each donor (servers with a target utilization lower than the current utilization), it selects the smallest sized applications to migrate and adds them to a VM migration list. It then runs FFD

with the spare capacity (target capacity - current capacity) on the receivers as
the bin size and the VM migration list as the balls. $iFFD$ has the nice property
that it starts with an initial allocation, and then incrementally finds a set of
migrations that will help it reach the target utilization for each server. Hence,
the packing algorithm migrates VMs only to the extent required to reach the
target utilization for each server.

We use $iFFD$ to design a power-minimizing placement algorithm that includes history, and is aptly named as *min Power Placement algorithm with History mPPH*. It works identically as mPP in the first phase. For the second
phase, it invokes $iFFD$ instead of FFD, thus selecting a placement that takes
the earlier placement as a starting point. $mPPH$ algorithm tries to minimize migrations by migrating as few VMs as possible, while moving to the new optimal
target utilization for the servers. However, even though it is migration aware, it
does not compromise on the power minimization aspect of the algorithm. Hence,
if the target utilization for servers change significantly in a time-window, $mPPH$
still resorts to large scale migrations to minimize power cost.

We next propose an algorithm $PMaP$ that takes a balanced view of both
power and migration cost, and aims to find an allocation that minimizes the sum
of the total (power + migration) cost. $pMaP$ (Fig. 6(b)) continually finds a new
placement for VMs in a fashion that minimizes power, while taking the migration
cost into account. The algorithm is based on the fundamental observation that
all the migrations that take us from an old power-minimizing placement to a
new power-minimizing placement may not be optimizing the power-migration
cost tradeoff. Hence, the algorithm first invokes any power-minimizing placement
algorithm ($mPPH$ is our choice) and gets a new power-minimizing placement. It
then computes the difference between the two placements (the set of migrations
that will change the old placement to the new placement) and determines a
subset to select. The selection process is based on sorting all the migrations
based on their incremental decrease in power per unit migration cost. We note
that a set of multiple migrations may be atomic and have to be separately
considered en masse as well, while estimating their incremental decrease in power
per unit migration cost. We then select the most profitable migration if the
power savings due to migration is higher than the migration cost. We repeat the
above procedure till no migrations exist that optimize the power-migration cost
tradeoff. We prove the following *Local Optimality* property for $PMaP$ along the
same lines as Theorem 1.

Lemma 1. *If pMaP at any given time has a placement P, then the next migration selected by P achieves the highest power-migration cost tradeoff. Hence,
every iteration that selects the next migration in pMaP is locally optimal.*

5   pMapper Implementation and Experimental Validation

We now present our implementation of $pMapper$ and an experimental study to
demonstrate its effectiveness.

5.1 Implementation

We have implemented *pMapper* to solve the cost minimization problem described in Eqn. 2. In this formulation, the *Arbitrator* is driven by performance goals and only arbitrates between the *Power Manager* and *Migration Manager* to find a placement that optimizes the power-migration cost tradeoff. The *Power Manager* implements the power-minimization algorithms *mPPH* and *mPP*, whereas the *Arbitrator* implements the *pMaP* algorithm to optimize the power migration tradeoff.

We use IBM Active Energy Manager [13] for monitoring power usage and EWLM [14] as the performance manager. In order to use the Active Energy Manager for monitoring, we have writen a monitoring agent that is co-located with the IBM Director Server and uses network sockets to communicate with the *pMapper* framework. EWLM uses a metric called Performance Index (PI) to indicate if an application is meeting its required SLA. A PI value of 1 is achieved when the response time of the application equals the target response time as specified in its SLA. Whenever, an application fails to meet its PI or outperforms its SLA, EWLM automatically resizes the VM so that the PI value for the application reaches 1. We have implemented our *Arbitrator* to work with a workload manager independent datastructure that captures a configuration in terms of VM sizes and their placements. Hence, the *Arbitrator* uses an adapter that allow it to understand the performance characteristics and partition sizes as reported by EWLM. We have implemented *pMapper* for VMWare ESX-based platforms and hence we use VMWare Virtual Center as the *Virtualization Manager*. We use the VI API provided by VMWare ESX 3.0 to communicate with the Virtualization Manager and execute migration actions. In order to execute throttling actions, we use the IBM Active Energy Manager interface that directly communicates with the BMC via IPMI commands.

We next describe our experimental setup for the performance study.

5.2 Experimental Setup

Our experimental testbed is driven by server utilization traces obtained from the server farm of a large data center. We initially wanted to conduct our experiments on the complete implementation of *pMapper*. However, we soon realized that this would take an inordinately long time (running the experiments for Fig. 7(b) only would take 4 months as it required 60 different runs). Initially, we looked at ways to speed up the experiments but we could not do so because the data refresh rate of Active Energy Manager was 5 minutes. We realized that our implementation was not focussing on performance (which was out-sourced to EWLM) and we only needed to study the power and migration cost minimization ability of *pMapper*.

Hence, we simulated the performance infrastructure by replacing the *Performance Manager* with the application trace data. Further, once the *Arbitrator* came up with a final placement, we fed the output to a *Simulator* that estimated the overall cost of the placement. Since we had characterized the applications on the platform earlier, we could design a table-driven simulator that was accurate with 99% confidence. The *Simulator* simulates the placement of these servers on a HS-21 Bladecenter according to the configuration given by the *Arbitrator*. For comparison, we used the following algorithms

- *Load Balanced*: This placement strategy places the VM in a manner such that the load is balanced across all the blades in the Bladecenter.
- *Static*: This algorithm takes long term history into account to find the placement that minimizes the power. The algorithm first estimates the minimum number of servers required to serve all the requests without violating blade server capacities. It then places the VMs (only once) on the servers to minimize power
- *mPP*: The minPowerPlacement Algorithm dynamically determines the placement that minimizes the power for that time window and is based on FFD.
- *mPPH*: The minPowerPlacement with History Algorithm determines the power-minimizing placement that takes into account the previous placement.
- *PMaP*: The PMaP Algorithm optimizes the tradeoff between power cost and migration cost, while computing the new placement for the window.

In our experiments, the *Performance Simulator* maps each server utilization trace to a Virtual Machine (VM) on the HS-21 with the VM size being set to the CPU utilization on the server. The trace is divided into time windows, and in each time window, the *Arbitrator* determined a new placement for each of the placement strategies based on the utilization specified by the *Performance Manager* in the time window. We feed the placements to the *Simulator*, which estimates the cost of each placement and logs it.

We studied the various methodologies with respect to the power consumed, the migration cost incurred, and the sum of power cost and migration cost. We then conducted a comparative study of the algorithms with change in server utilization. We also increased the number of blades in the Bladecenter to investigate the ability of the algorithms to scale and deal with fragmentation. We used a metric to quantify the relative impact of migration cost with power cost and termed it *MP Ratio*. The migration cost is determined by estimating the impact of migration on application throughput and consequent revenue loss, computed as per the SLA. This cost is compared with the power cost using the power drawn and the price/watt paid by the enterprise. We pick a reasonable value for this ratio in our baseline setting based on typical SLAs and then vary this ratio to study its impact on the performance of various algorithms. We also plugged in some other power models to investigate if the algorithms are dependant on specific power models. Further, by mixing different kinds of physical servers (with different power models), we investigate the ability of the algorithms to handle heterogeneity. We finally studied the practicality of the assumptions made.

5.3   Results

We first study the behaviour of various algorithms as the traces are played with time (Fig. 7(a)). The aggregate utilization of the VMs varies during the run and the dynamic algorithms continually try to adapt to the changed workload. We

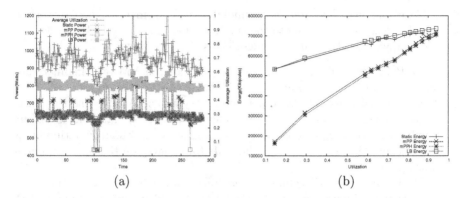

Fig. 7. Power consumed by various placements strategies with (a) time and (b) increasing overall utilization

observe that the dynamic algorithms mPP and $mPPH$ are able to save about 200W of power (25%) from the Load Balanced and Static Placements. However, as the utilization exceeds 0.75, the savings drop significantly. This is because, at high utilization, there is not much scope for consolidation. However, even at high loads, our algorithms are able to save some power by taking the decreasing slope of the power curves into account. We observed that our algorithms try to run most servers at close to their full capacity because the power-curve saturates at high capacity. Hence, instead of balancing the load across all servers, it makes sense to unbalance load even when all the servers are switched on. We also observe that the proposed algorithms show very strong correlation with the average utilization. This establishes their ability to continually adapt to workload variations and save power accordingly.

We next investigate the impact on power at different average utilization values. Towards this purpose, we compressed (or decompressed) all the traces so that the average utilization of the servers could be varied. The trace was compressed to achieve a higher utilization than the baseline, and decompressed to achieve lower utilizations. We observed that the power savings obtained by the proposed power-minimizing algorithms is significant at low utilization values. This is because our algorithms are able to consolidate the VMs on a few servers only, and save a significant amount of power due to the high static power cost. Our study (Fig. 7(a)) reaffirms that most savings come from consolidation and not by unbalancing load. This is evident because the savings of proposed algorithms increase significantly when the average utilization goes below 0.75 and 0.5. These are the utilization values at which one can switch off an additional server. Note that the discontinuities are not so noticeable in Fig. 7(b). However, since at an average utilization of 0.75, there are many time instances where the utilization goes beyond 0.75 and no server can be switched off, the difference between overall energy consumption between average utilization of 0.7 and 0.75 is not as large as one would expect from Fig. 7(a).

We have only investigated the performance of algorithms w.r.t power consumed by their corresponding placements. We now take into account the

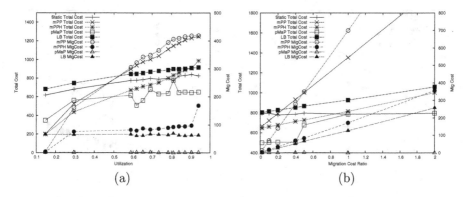

Fig. 8. Migration Cost and Overall Cost with (a) increasing overall utilization (b) change in MP (Migration to Power Cost) Ratio

migration cost and compare the power-minimizing algorithms with the migration cost aware $pMaP$ algorithm as well (Fig. 8(a)). We observe that even though the power drawn by $pMaP$ (difference of total cost and migration cost) is higher than mPP or $mPPH$, the total cost of $pMaP$ is the least amongst all competing algorithms. This establishes the importance of taking both the migration and power cost into account, while coming up with a new placement. We also observe that mPP pays a very high migration cost at higher utilization, and underperforms even the $LB(Load-balanced)$ and $Static$ placements at very high loads. On the other hand, $mPPH$ incurs very low migration cost (of the same order as load-balanced) and as a result, has a total cost very close to the best performing algorithm $pMaP$. This is a direct result of the fact that $mPPH$ takes the previous placement into account while computing a new placement, and tries to minimize the difference between the two placements. Hence, even though $mPPH$ does not compromise on saving power as opposed to $pMaP$, which can prefer a placement with high power and low migration cost, the migration costs incurred by $mPPH$ are not significant. This establishes $mPPH$ as a good alternative to $pMaP$, because of its relative simplicity.

The MP ratio (migration to power cost ratio) varies from one enterprise to another and depends on factors such as energy cost and SLA revenue models. We next investigate the various algorithms at different MP ratio. We observed (Fig. 8(b))that MP ratio directly affects the overall performance of mPP. Hence, mPP is the best performing algorithm (approaching $mPPH$ and $pMaP$) at low migration costs and underperforms even the power-unaware algorithms at very high migration cost. This underscores the importance of taking migration cost into account, along with the power cost for dynamic placement. On the other hand, $pMaP$ takes the increased migration cost factor into account by cutting down migrations. Hence, a high MP ratio does not affect its performance.

In our next set of experiments, we investigated the scalability of the algorithms along with their ability to deal with fragmentation (large VM sizes). Hence, we increased the number of servers from 4 to 16. We observed that $pMaP$ and

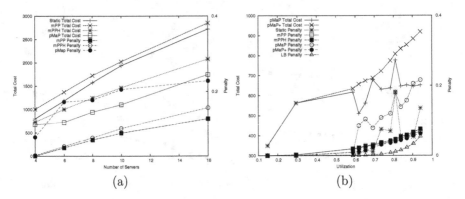

Fig. 9. (a) Overall Cost and Penalty with increase in servers (b) Power and Penalty with increase in fragmentation for penalty aware and unaware algorithms

$mPPH$ are the top two performing algorithms even with increased number of servers. However, we observed (Fig. 9(a)) that while aiming to unbalance load for minimizing power, $pMaP$ was leading to a large number of requests being dropped (or delayed). We call the drop in requests as *Penalty* of a placement. A reason for this penalty is the huge variance in workload. Hence, at an average load of 0.7 approximately, there are many instances when the transient load goes beyond 1.0 and, as a result, many requests need to be dropped (irrespective of the placement methodology). However, since $pMaP$ is unaware of penalties, it drops more requests than others, while striving to minimize cost. This makes $pMaP$ undesirable for use at high load intensities.

We next engineered $pMaP$ to take penalty into account, while exploring the search space between the old placement and the new placement. The modified algorithm $pMaP+$, during its exploration, picks only those intermediates whose penalty are below a bound. We fixed the bound to be 0.1 in our experiments. We observe (Fig. 9(b)) that the penalty aware algorithm $pMaP+$ now incurs the least penalty amongst mPP, $mPPH$, $pMaP$ and static. The penalty seen by the Load Balanced algorithm is the baseline penalty incurred solely because of traffic variations and $pMaP+$ now has a penalty approaching that of Load Balanced. This engineering allows $pMaP+$ to again be the algorithm of choice under all scenarios. We also observe that the penalties of the *Static* placement also varies a lot, approaching 20% in certain cases. This is again, a result of the load-shifts that happen with time, re-affirming the importance of a dynamic placement strategy.

In this set of experiments, we simulate heterogeneity with various power models. We simulate another server with a power model where the static power or the dynamic power or both may be reduced to half. We increase the number of such servers from 0 to 2 to increase the complexity in Static Power or Dynamic Power (Fig. 10(a)). We observed that increased complexity (due to heterogeneity) leads to higher power savings relative to the Static Placement, which is the best power-unaware placement method. Further, the power savings are almost

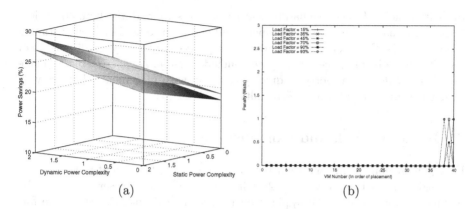

Fig. 10. (a) Power Savings of mPP and $mPPH$ in comparison to Static Placement with increasing heterogeneity. (b) Penalty incurred because of the Ordering Assumption.

additive with increase in static or dynamic complexity. Hence, the proposed algorithms are capable of working even better in heterogeneous clusters, thus establishing their efficacy in a wide variety of settings.

Our algorithms are based on the assumption that for each application being placed, we can characterize the incremental power drawn by it at various workloads on all the server platforms. We can then use this incremental power table to decide which server to place the application on, during dynamic application placement. We now investigate the practicality of this assumption. In order to study this, we looked at a a random sample of 100 points from this selection trace log and measured the incremental power drawn due to our selection and the incremental power drawn by selecting any other server. Fig. 10(b) shows the accuracy of our estimate in terms of the penalty accrued due to wrong selection for each placed application. If we made the right selection, we get a penalty of 0 whereas if there was another server with less incremental power, we incur a penalty equal to the difference. We observe that the *Ordering* property holds for most of the applications with a few errors resulting in an error of 1 watts or less. As compared to the total power consumption of about $750W$, this error is insignificant. Further, we observe that the property does not hold only for the last few applications being placed. Hence, any errors made do not get cascaded to other applications, as most of them were already placed. This is a direct result of the fact that we chose to adapt FFD, which leads to unbalanced load. Hence, for most of the comparisons that used the *Ordering* property, we compared an idle server with a loaded server, and very clearly the loaded server was selected because of the huge static power cost. Hence, our local search based on the *Ordering* property worked close to optimal. Further, a closer look at the plots reveal that we pay the penalty only when the overall load approaches 50% or 75%. This is because in these cases all the servers that were loaded were close to their capacity. Hence, we had to select between servers that where all loaded. In such a scenario, the *Ordering* property did not seem to hold in a few instances (about 1 in 5). However, this scenario encompasses only a very small portion of the overall problem space. Hence, we conclude that *pMapper* is able to make use of the *Ordering* property to quickly come up with placements that are very close to optimal (less than 0.2% penalty).

6   Related Work and Conclusion

Energy management in server clusters has been a popular area of research since the beginning of this decade [1,12]. Chen et al. [6] combine server level CPU scaling techniques with the application provisioning problem in the same formulation. However, in contrast to *pMapper*, they do not work in a virtualized setting with migration costs and only deal with homogeneous clusters for placement. Muse pose a resource allocation problem in [4], where services are allocated to enough number of resource containers on physical servers based on an economic model. Since energy cost is part of the model and the load is dynamic, resources are allocated dynamically in a manner that is aware of the energy costs. However, the model does not explicitly consider migration costs of containers or deal with the complexity of application specific power models in a heterogeneous server cluster. Bobroff et al. [2] describe a runtime application placement and migration algorithm in a virtualized environment. The focus is mainly on dynamic consolidation utilizing the variability in workload but they do not perform power-aware placements on heterogeneous servers.

Most of the cluster energy management literature addresses the problem of distributing requests in a web server cluster in such a way that the performance goals are met and the energy consumption is minimized [4,5,10,19,21]. There are a number of papers that describe server or cluster level energy management using independent [8,18] or cooperative DVS techniques [7,11]. There are other efforts in reducing peak power requirements at server and rack level by doing dynamic budget allocation among sub-systems [9] or blades [20].

In this work, we have presented an application placement controller *pMapper* that minimizes power and migration costs, while meeting the performance guarantees. *pMapper* differs from all existing literature because it addresses the problem of power and migration cost aware application placement in heterogeneous server clusters that support virtualization with live VM migration. It investigates the viability of using CPU utilization based application specific power models to develop placement algorithms and validates the assumptions through testbed experimentation. Through a carefully designed experimental methodology on two server platforms, we concluded that only a power minimization framework is feasible practically. We use insights from our study to pin down the conditions under which this problem can be solved. We proposed three dynamic placement algorithms to minimize power and migration cost and experimentally demonstrated the various scenarios in which each algorithm is effective. We established the superiority of our most refined algorithm $pMaP+$ under most settings over other power unaware algorithms as well as power aware algorithms both theoretically and experimentally.

References

1. Bianchini, R., Rajamoni, R.: Power and energy management for server systems. IEEE Computer, 68–76 (November 2004)
2. Bobroff, N., Kochut, A., Beaty, K.: Dynamic placement of virtual machines for managing sla violations. In: IEEE IM (2007)
3. Bohrer, P., et al.: The case for power management in web servers. In: Power Aware Computing (2002)
4. Chase, J., Anderson, D., Thakar, P., Vahdat, A., Doyle, R.: Managing energy and server resources in hosting centers. In: Proc. ACM SOSP (2001)
5. Chase, J., Doyle, R.: Balance of power: Energy management for server clusters. In: HotOS (2002)
6. Chen, Y., Das, A., Qin, W., Sivasubramaniam, A., Wang, Q., Gautam, N.: Managing server energy and operational costs in hosting centers. In: Sigmetrics (2005)
7. Elnozahy, E., Kistler, M., Rajamony, R.: Energy- efficient server clusters. In: Proceedings of the Workshop on Power-Aware Computing Systems (2002)
8. Elnozahy, M., Kistler, M., Rajamony, R.: Energy conservation policies for web servers. In: Proc. of USITS (2003)
9. Felter, W., Rajamani, K., Keller, T., Rusu, C.: A performance-conserving approach for reducing peak power consumption in server systems. In: ICS (2005)
10. Heath, T., Diniz, B., Carrera, E., Meira Jr., W., Bianchini, R.: Energy conservation in heterogeneous server clusters. In: Proc. of ACM PPoPP (2005)
11. Horvath, T.: Dynamic voltage scaling in multitier web servers with end-to-end delay control. IEEE Trans. Comput. 56(4) (2007)
12. Lefurgy, C., Rajamani, K., Rawson, F., Felter, W., Kistler, M., Keller, T.W.: Energy management for commercial servers. IEEE Computer 36(12), 39–48 (2003)
13. IBM Active Energy Manager,
    http://www-03.ibm.com/systems/management/director/extensions/actengmrg.html
14. IBM Enterprise WorkLoad Manager,
    http://www.ibm.com/developerworks/autonomic/ewlm/
15. Nathuji, R., Schwan, K.: Virtualpower: coordinated power management in virtualized enterprise systems. In: ACM SOSP (2007)
16. HPL-A Portable Implementation of the High Performance Linpack Benchmark for Distributed Memory Computers, http://www.netlib.org/benchmark/hpl/
17. Control power and cooling for data center efficiency HP thermal logic technology. An hp bladesystem innovation primer (June 2006)
18. Rajamani, K., Hanson, H., Rubio, J., Ghiasi, S., Rawson, F.: Application-aware power management. In: IISWC, pp. 39–48 (2006)
19. Rajamani, K., Lefurgy, C.: On evaluating request-distribution schemes for saving energy in server clusters. In: ISPASS (2003)
20. Ranganathan, P., Leech, P., Irwin, D., Chase, J.: Ensemble-level power management for dense blade servers. In: ISCA (2006)

21. Rusu, C., Ferreira, A., Scordino, C., Watson, A.: Energy-efficient real-time hetero-geneous server clusters. In: Proc. of RTAS (2006)
22. VMWare Distributed Resource Scheduler,
    http://www.vmware.com/products/vi/vc/drs.html
23. Stoess, J., Lang, C., Bellosa, F.: Energy management for hypervisor-based virtual machines. In: Proc. Usenix Annual Technical Conference (2007)
24. Urgaonkar, B., Pacifici, G., Shenoy, P., Spreitzer, M., Tantawi, A.: An analytical model for multi-tier internet services and its applications. In: Sigmetrics (2005)
25. Yue, M.: A simple proof of the inequality $ffd(l) \leq (11/9)opt(l) + 1$, for all l, for the ffd bin-packing algorithm. Acta Mathematicae Applicatae Sinica (1991)

Burstiness in Multi-tier Applications:
Symptoms, Causes, and New Models*

Ningfang Mi[1], Giuliano Casale[1], Ludmila Cherkasova[2], and Evgenia Smirni[1]

[1] College of William and Mary, Williamsburg, VA 23187, USA
{ningfang,casale,esmirni}@cs.wm.edu
[2] Hewlett-Packard Laboratories, Palo Alto, CA 94304, USA
lucy.cherkasova@hp.com

Abstract. Workload flows in enterprise systems that use the multi-tier paradigm
are often characterized as bursty, i.e., exhibit a form of temporal dependence.
Burstiness often results in dramatic degradation of the perceived user performance, which is extremely difficult to capture with existing capacity planning
models. The main reason behind this deficiency of traditional capacity planning
models is that the user perceived performance is the result of the complex interaction of a very complex workload with a very complex system. In this paper, we
propose a simple and effective methodology for detecting burstiness symptoms in
multi-tier systems rather than identifying the low-level *exact* cause of burstiness
as traditional models would require. We provide an effective way to incorporate
this information into a surprisingly simple and effective modeling methodology.
This new modeling methodology is based on the index of dispersion of the service
process at a server, which is inferred by observing the number of completions
within the concatenated busy periods of that server. The index of dispersion together with other measurements that reflect the "estimated" mean and the 95th
percentile of service times are used to derive a Markov-modulated process that
captures well burstiness and variability of the true service process, despite inevitable inaccuracies that result from inexact and limited measurements. Detailed
experimentation on a TPC-W testbed where all measurements are obtained by HP
(Mercury) Diagnostics, a commercially available tool, shows that the proposed
technique offers a simple yet powerful solution to the difficult problem of inferring accurate descriptors of the service time process from coarse measurements
of a given system. Experimental and model prediction results are in excellent
agreement and argue strongly for the effectiveness of the proposed methodology
under both bursty and non-bursty workloads.

Keywords: Capacity planning, multi-tier systems, transactions, sessions, bursty
workload, bottleneck switch, index of dispersion.

1 Introduction

The performance of a multi-tier system is determined by the interactions between the
incoming requests and the different hardware architectures and software systems that

---

* This work is partially supported by NSF grants CNS-0720699 and CCF-0811417, and a gift
from HPLabs. A short version of this paper titled "How to Parameterize Models with Bursty
Workloads" appeared in the HotMetrics 2008 Workshop (non-copyrighted) [5].

V. Issarny and R. Schantz (Eds.): Middleware 2008, LNCS 5346, pp. 265–286, 2008.
© IFIP International Federation for Information Processing 2008

serve them. In order to model these interactions for capacity planning, a detailed characterization of the workloads and of the application is needed, but such a "customized" analysis and modeling may be very time consuming, error-prone, and inefficient in practice. An alternative approach is to rely on live system measurements and to assume that the performance of each software or hardware resource is completely characterized by its *mean* service time, a quantity that is easy to obtain with simple measurement procedures. The mean service times of different classes of transaction requests together with the transaction mix can be used as inputs to the widely-used Mean Value Analysis (MVA) models [13,26,30] to predict the overall system performance under various load conditions. The popularity of MVA-based models is due to their simplicity and their ability to capture complex systems and workloads in a straightforward manner. In this paper, we present strong evidence that MVA models of multi-tier architectures can be unacceptably inaccurate if the processed workloads exhibit *burstiness*, i.e., short uneven spikes of peak congestion during the lifetime of the system. Motivated by this problem, we define here a new methodology for effective capacity planning under bursty workload conditions.

Internet flash-crowds are familiar examples of bursty traffic and are characterized by periods of continuous peak arrival rate that significantly deviate from the average traffic intensity. Similarly, a footprint of burstiness in system workloads is the presence of short uneven peaks in utilization measurements, which indicate that the server periodically faces congestion. In multi-tier systems, congestion may arise from the super-position of several events including database locks, variability in service time of software operations, memory contention, and/or characteristics of the scheduling algorithms. The above events interact in a complex way with the underlying hardware/software systems and with the incoming requests, often resulting in short congestion periods where the entire system is significantly slowed down. For example, even for multi-tier systems where the database server is highly-efficient, a locking condition on a database table may slow down the service of multiple requests that try to access the same data and make the database the bottleneck server for a time period. During that period of time, the database performance dominates the performance of the overall system, while most of the time another resource, e.g., the application server, may be the primary cause of delays in the system. Thus, the performance of the multi-tier system can vary in time depending on which is the current bottleneck resource and can be significantly conditioned by *dependencies* between servers that cannot by captured by MVA models. However, to the best of our knowledge, no simple methodology exists that captures in a simple way this time-varying *bottleneck switch* in multi-tier systems and its performance implications.

In this paper, we present a new approach to integrate workload burstiness in performance models, which relies on server busy periods (they are immediately obtained from server utilization measurements across time) and measurements of request completions within the busy periods. All measurements are collected with coarse granularity. After giving quantitative examples of the importance of integrating burstiness in performance models, we analyze a real three-tier architecture subject to TPC-W workloads with different burstiness profiles. We show that burstiness in the service process can be inferred effectively from traces using the *index of dispersion* for counts of completed requests, a measure of burstiness frequently used in the analysis of time series and network traffic [8,11]. The index of dispersion jointly captures service *variability* and *burstiness* in a single number and can also be related to the well-known Hurst parameter used in the analysis of long-range dependence [4]. Furthermore, the index of dispersion can be inferred reliably also if the length of the trace is short. Using the index of dispersion, we show that the accuracy of the model prediction can be increased by up to 30% compared to standard queueing models parameterized only with mean service demands [21].

Exploiting basic properties of bursty processes, we are also able to include in the analysis the 95th percentile of service times, which is widely used in computer performance engineering to quantify the peak-to-mean ratio of service demands. Therefore, our performance models are specified by three parameters only for each server: the mean, the index of dispersion, and the 95th percentile of service demands, making a strong case of being practical, easy, yet surprisingly accurate. To the best of our knowledge, this paper makes a first strong case in the use of a new practical modeling paradigm for capacity planning that encompasses workload burstiness. We stress that the prediction models we propose do not require explicit identification of the cause(s) of the observed burstiness. Instead, they use a powerful but simple abstraction that captures the effects of burstiness in complex multi-tiered environments.

The rest of the paper is organized as follows. In Section 2, we introduce service burstiness using illustrative examples and present the methodology for the measurement of the index of dispersion to parameterize the proposed model. In Section 3, we discuss the multi-tier architecture and the TPC-W workloads used in experiments and show that existing queueing models can not work if bottleneck switch exists in the system. The proposed modeling paradigm that integrates burstiness in performance models is presented in Section 4. Section 4 also shows the experimental results that validate the accuracy of the new methodology in comparison with standard mean-value based capacity planning. Finally, Section 6 draws conclusions.

2   Burstiness in Performance Models: Do We Really Need It?

In this section, we show some examples of the importance of burstiness in performance models. In order to show that burstiness can consistently affect the performance of a system and gain intuition about its fundamental features, we use a simple example. Let us consider the four workloads shown in Figure 1.

Each plot represents a sample of $20,000$ service times generated from the same hyperexponential distribution with mean $\mu^{-1} = 1$ and squared coefficient-of-variation $SCV = 3$. The only difference is that we impose to each trace a unique burstiness profile. In Figure 1(b)–(d), the large service times progressively aggregate in bursts, while in Figure 1(a) they appear in random points of the trace. In particular, Figure 1(d) shows the extreme case where all large requests are compressed into a single large burst. Thus, we use the term "burstiness" to indicate traces that are not just "variable" as the sample in Figure 1(a), but that also aggregate in "bursty periods" as in Figure 1(b)–(d).

What is the performance implication on systems of the different burstiness profiles in Figure 1(a)-(d)? Assuming that the request arrival times to the server follow an exponential distribution with mean $\lambda^{-1} = 2$ and 1.25, a simulation analysis of the

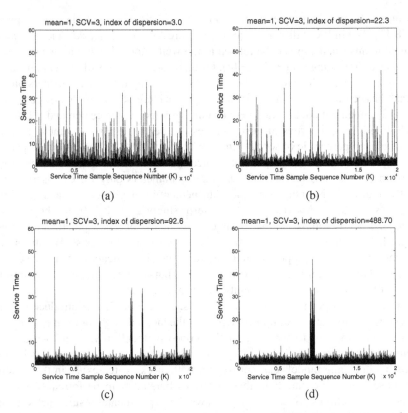

Fig. 1. Four workload traces with identical hyper-exponential distribution (mean $\mu^{-1} = 1$, $SCV = 3$), but different burstiness profiles. Given the identical variability, trace (d) represents the case of maximum burstiness where all large service times appear consecutively in a large burst. The index of dispersion I, introduced in this paper for the characterization of workloads in multi-tier architectures and reported on top of each figure, is able to capture the significantly different burstiness of the four workloads. As the name suggest, the dispersion of the bursty periods increases up to the limit case in Figure (d) as I grows.

$M/Trace/1$ queue[1] at 50% and 80% utilization, respectively, provides the response times, i.e., the service time plus waiting/queueing times in a server, shown in Table 1.

Irrespectively of the identical properties of the service time distribution, burstiness clearly has paramount importance for queueing prediction, both in terms of response time mean and tail. For instance, at 50% utilization the mean response time for the trace in Figure 1(d) is approximately 40 times slower than the service times in Figure 1(a) and the 95th percentile of the response times is nearly 80 times longer. In general, the performance degradation is monotonically increasing with burstiness; therefore it is important to distinguish the behaviors in Figure 1(a)–(d) via a quantitative index.

---

[1] We remark that workload burstiness rules out independence of service time samples, thus the classic Pollaczek-Khinchin formula for the $M/G/1$ queue does not apply if the service time distribution is bursty.

Table 1. Response time of the $M/Trace/1$ queue relatively to the service times traces shown in Figure 1. The server is evaluated for utilizations $\rho = 0.5$ and $\rho = 0.8$.

	Response Time (util=0.5)		Response Time (util=0.8)		Index of Dispersion
Workload	mean	95th percentile	mean	95th percentile	I
Fig. 1(a)	3.02	14.42	8.70	33.26	3.0
Fig. 1(b)	11.00	83.35	43.35	211.76	22.3
Fig. 1(c)	26.69	252.18	72.31	485.42	92.6
Fig. 1(d)	120.49	1132.40	150.32	1346.53	488.7

Overall the results in Table 1 give intuition that we really need burstiness in performance models. The index of dispersion introduced in the next section is instrumental to capture the difference in the burstiness profiles and provides a simple way to generalize queueing models to effectively capture the performance of bursty workloads and the effects of bottleneck switch.

2.1   Characterization of Burstiness: The Index of Dispersion

We use the *index of dispersion I* for counts to characterize the burstiness of service times [8,11]. This is a standard burstiness index used in networking [11], which we apply here to the characterization of workload burstiness in multi-tier applications.

The index of dispersion has a broad applicability and wide popularity in stochastic analysis and engineering [8]. From a mathematical perspective, the index of dispersion of a service process is a measure defined on the squared coefficient-of-variation SCV and on the lag-k autocorrelations[2] ρ_k, $k \geq 1$, of the service times as follows:

$$I = SCV \left(1 + 2 \sum_{k=1}^{\infty} \rho_k \right). \tag{1}$$

The joint presence of SCV and autocorrelations in I is sufficient to discriminate traces like those in Figure 1(a)–(d), e.g., for the trace in Figure 1(a) the correlations are statically negligible, since the probability of a service time being small or large is statistically unrelated to its position in the trace. However, for the trace in Figure 1(d), consecutive samples tend to assume similar values, therefore the sum of autocorrelation in Eq. (1) is maximal in Figure 1(d). The last column of Table 1 reports the values of I for the four example traces. The values strongly indicate that I is able to reflect the different burstiness levels in Figure 1(a)–(d) which directly affect the performance results.

Note that $I = 1$ if service times are exponential, then the index of dispersion may be interpreted qualitatively as the ratio of the observed service burstiness with respect to a Poisson process; therefore, values of I of the order of hundreds or more indicate a clear

---

[2] Autocorrelation is used as a statistical measure of the relationship between a random variable and itself [4]. In a time series of random variables $\{X_n\}$, where $n = 0, \ldots, \infty$, ρ_k expresses the value of the autocorrelation coefficient as follows: $\rho_k = \frac{E[(X_t - \mu^{-1})(X_{t+k} - \mu^{-1})]}{\sigma^2}$, where μ^{-1} is the mean, σ^2 is the common variance of $\{X_n\}$, and k denotes the time separation between the occurrences X_t and X_{t+k}.

departure from the exponentiality assumptions and, unless the real SCV is anomalously high, I can be used as a good indicator of burstiness. Although the mathematical definition of I in Eq. (1) is simple, this formulation is not practical for estimation because of the infinite summation involved and its sensitivity to noise. In the next subsection, we describe a simple alternative way of estimating I.

2.2   Measuring the Index of Dispersion

Instead of Eq. (1), we provide an alternative definition of the index of dispersion for a service process as follows. Let N_t be the number of requests completed in a time window of t seconds, where the t seconds are counted *ignoring* the server's idle time (that is, by conditioning on the period where the system is busy, N_t is a property of the service process which is independent of queueing or arrival characteristics). If we regard N_t as a random variable, that is, if we perform several experiments by varying the time window placement in the trace and obtain different values of N_t, then the index of dispersion I is the limit [8]:

$$I = \lim_{t \to +\infty} \frac{Var(N_t)}{E[N_t]},\qquad(2)$$

where $Var(N_t)$ is the variance of the number of completed requests and $E[N_t]$ is the mean service rate during busy periods. Since the value of I depends on the number of completed requests in an asymptotically large observation period, an approximation of this index can be also computed if the measurements are obtained with coarse granularity. For example, suppose that the sampling resolution is $T = 60s$, and assume to approximate $t \to +\infty$ as $t \approx 2$ hours, then N_t is computed by summing the number of

---

Input
T, the sampling resolution (e.g., $60s$)
K, total number of samples, assume $K > 100$
U_k, utilization in the kth period, $1 \le k \le K$
n_k, number of completed requests in the kth period, $1 \le k \le K$
tol, convergence tolerance (e.g., 0.20)
Estimation of the Index of Dispersion I
1.   get the busy time in the kth period $B_k := U_k \cdot T, 1 \le k \le K$;
2.   initialize $t = T$ and $Y(0) = 0$;
3.   do
    a.   for each $A_k = (B_k, B_{k+1}, \dots, B_{k+j}), \sum_{i=0}^{j} B_{k+i} \approx t$,
    aa.   compute $N_t^k = \sum_{i=0}^{j} n_{k+i}$;
    b.   if the set of values N_t^k has less than 100 elements,
      bb.   stop and collect new measures because the trace is too short;
    c. $Y(t) = Var(N_t^k)/E[N_t^k]$;
    d.   increase t by T;
    until $|1 - (Y(t)/Y(t - T))| \le tol$, i.e., the values of $Y(t)$ converge.
5.   return the last computed value of $Y(t)$ as estimate of I.

Fig. 2. Estimation of I from utilization samples

completed requests in 120 consecutive samples. Repeating the evaluation for different positions of the time window of length t, we compute $Var(N_t)$ and $E[N_t]$. Here, we use the pseudo-code in Figure 2 to estimate I directly from Eq. (2). The pseudo-code is a straight-forward evaluation of $Var(N_t)/E[N_t]$ for different values of t. Intuitively, the algorithm in Figure 2 calculates I of the service process by observing the completions of jobs in concatenated busy period samples. Because of this concatenation, queueing is masked out and the index of dispersion of job completions serves as a good approximation of the index of dispersion of the service process.

3   Burstiness in Multi-tier Applications: Symptoms and Causes

Today, a multi-tier architecture has become the industry standard for implementing scalable client-server enterprise applications. In our experiments, we use a testbed of a multi-tier e-commerce site that is built according to the TPC-W specifications. This allows to conduct experiments under different settings in a controlled environment, which then allows to evaluate the proposed modeling methodology that is based on the index of dispersion.

3.1   Experimental Environment

TPC-W is a widely used e-commerce benchmark that simulates the operation of an online bookstore [10]. Typically, this multi-tier application uses a three-tier architecture paradigm, which consists of a web server, an application server, and a back-end database. A client communicates with this web service via a web interface, where the unit of activity at the client-side corresponds to a webpage download. In general, a web page is composed by an HTML file and several embedded objects such as images. In a production environment, it is common that the web and the application servers reside on the same hardware, and shared resources are used by the application and web servers to generate main HTML files as well as to retrieve page embedded objects. We opt to put both the web server and the application server on the same machine called the front server[3]. A high-level overview of the experimental set-up is illustrated in Figure 3 and specifics of the software/hardware used are given in Table 2.

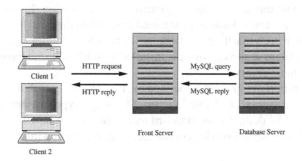

Fig. 3. E-commerce experimental environment

---

[3] We use terms "front server" and "application server" interchangeably in this paper.

Table 2. Hardware/software components of the TPC-W testbed

	Processor	RAM	OS
Clients (Emulated-Browsers)	Pentium D, 2-way x 3.2 GHz	4 GB	Linux Redhat 9.0
Front Server - Apache/Tomcat 5.5	Pentium D, 1-way x 3.2 GHz	4 GB	Linux Redhat 9.0
Database Server - MySQL5.0	Pentium D, 2-way x 3.2 GHz	4 GB	Linux Redhat 9.0

Table 3. The 14 transactions defined in TPC-W

Browsing Type	**Ordering** Type
Home	Shopping Cart
New Products	Customer Registration
Best Sellers	Buy Request
Product detail	Buy Confirm
Search Request	Order Inquiry
Execute Search	Order Display
	Admin Request
	Admin Confirm

Since the HTTP protocol does not provide any means to delimit the beginning or the end of a web page, it is very difficult to accurately measure the aggregate resources consumed due to web page processing at the server side. Accurate CPU consumption estimates are required for building an effective application provisioning model but there is no practical way to effectively measure the service times for *all* page objects. To address this problem, we define a *client transaction* as a combination of *all* processing activities that deliver an entire web page requested by a client, i.e., generate the main HTML file as well as retrieve embedded objects and perform related database queries.

Typically, a continuous period of time during which a client accesses a Web service is referred to as a *User Session* which consists of a sequence of consecutive individual transaction requests. According to the TPC-W specification, the number of concurrent sessions (i.e., customers) or emulated browsers (EBs) is kept constant throughout the experiment. For each EB, the TPC-W benchmark defines the user session length, the user think time, and the queries that are generated by the session. In our experimental environment, two Pentium D machines are used to simulate the EBs. If there are m EBs in the system, then each machine emulates $m/2$ EBs. One Pentium D machine is used as the back-end database server, which is installed with MySQL 5.0 having a database of 10,000 items in inventory.

There are 14 different transactions defined by TPC-W. In general, these transactions can be roughly classified of "Browsing" or "Ordering" type, as shown in Table 3. Furthermore, TPC-W defines three standard transaction mixes based on the weight of each type (i.e., browsing or ordering) in the particular transaction mix:

- the *browsing mix* with 95% browsing and 5% ordering;
- the *shopping mix* with 80% browsing and 20% ordering;
- the *ordering mix* with 50% browsing and 50% ordering.

One way to capture the navigation pattern within a session is through the *Customer Behavior Model Graph (CBMG)* [16], which describes patterns of user behavior, i.e., how users navigate through the site, and where arcs connecting states (transactions) reflect the probability of the next transaction type. TPC-W is parameterized by the set of probabilities that drive user behavior from one state to another at the user session level. During a session, each EB cycles through a process of sending a transaction request, receiving the response web page, and selecting the next transaction request. Typically, a user session starts with a Home transaction request.

The TPC-W implementation is based on the J2EE standard – a Java platform which is used for web application development and designed to meet the computing needs of large enterprises. For transaction monitoring, we use the HP (Mercury) Diagnostics [29] tool which offers a monitoring solution for J2EE applications. The Diagnostics tool collects performance and diagnostic data from applications without the need for application source code modification or recompilation. It uses bytecode instrumentation, which enables a tool to record processed transactions and their database calls over time as well as to measure their execution time (both transactions and their database calls). We use the Diagnostics tool to measure the number of completed requests n_k in the kth period having a granularity of 5 seconds. We also use the `sar` command to obtain the utilizations of two servers across time with one second granularity.

3.2 Bottleneck Switch in TPC-W

For each transaction mix, we run a set of experiments with different numbers of EBs ranging from 25 to 150. Each experiment runs for 3 hours, where the first 5 minutes and the last 5 minutes are considered as warm-up and cool-down periods and thus omitted in the analysis. User think times are exponentially distributed with mean $Z = 0.5s$. Figure 4 presents the overall system throughput, the mean system utilization at the front server and the mean system utilization at the database server as a function of EBs. Figure 4(a) shows that the system becomes overloaded when the number of EBs reaches 75, 100, and 150 under the browsing mix, the shopping mix, and the ordering mix, respectively. Beyond these EB values, the system throughput remains asymptotically flat. This is due to the "closed loop" aspect of the system, i.e., the fixed number of EBs

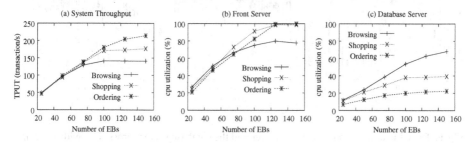

Fig. 4. Illustrating a) system overall throughput, b) average CPU utilization of the front server, and c) average CPU utilization of the database server for three TPC-W transaction mixes. The mean think time Z is set to 0.5 seconds.

(customers), that is effectively an upper bound on the number of jobs that circulate in the system at all times.

The results from Figures 4(b) and 4(c) show that under the shopping and the ordering mixes, the front server is a bottleneck, where the CPU utilizations are almost 100% at the front tier but only 20–40% at the database tier. For the browsing mix, we see that the CPU utilization of the front server increases very slowly as the number of EBs increases beyond 75, which is consistent with the very slow growth of throughput. For example, when the front server is already 100% utilized under the shopping and the ordering mixes, the front server for the browsing mix is just around 80%. Meanwhile, for the browsing mix, the CPU utilization of the database server increases quickly as the number of EBs increases. When the number of EBs is beyond 100, it is not obvious which server is responsible for the bottleneck: the average CPU utilizations of two servers are about the same, differing by a statistically insignificant margin. In presence of burstiness in the service times, this may suggest that the phenomenon of *bottleneck switch* occurs between the front and the database servers *across time*. This phenomenon is not specific to the testbed described in the current work. In an earlier paper [31], a similar situation was observed for a different TPC-W testbed. That is, a server may become the bottleneck while processing consecutively large requests, but be lightly loaded during other periods. In general, additional investigation to determine the existence of bottleneck switch is required when the average utilizations are relatively close or when the workloads are known to be highly variable.

To confirm our conjecture about the existence of bottleneck switch in the browsing mix experiment, we present CPU utilizations of the front and the database servers across time for the browsing mix, as well as for the shopping and the ordering mixes with 100 EBs, see Figure 5. A bottleneck switch occurs when the database server utilization becomes significantly higher than the front server utilization, as clearly visible in Figure 5(a) under the browsing mix workload. As shown in Figures 5(b) and 5(c), there is no bottleneck switch for the shopping and the ordering mixes, although these two workloads are also highly variable.

The bottleneck switch is a characteristic effect of burstiness in the service times. This unstable behavior is extremely hard to model. Later, in Section 4.3, we show that the

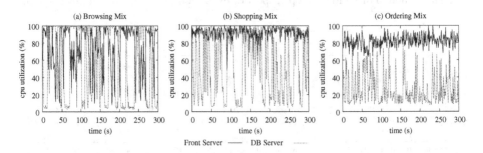

Fig. 5. The CPU utilization of the front server and the database server across time with 1 second granularity for (a) the browsing mix, (b) the shopping mix, and (c) the ordering mix under 100 EBs. The monitoring window is 300 seconds.

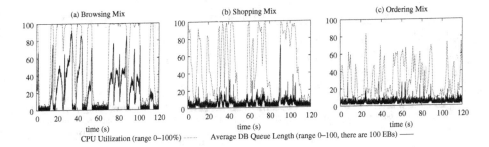

Fig. 6. The CPU utilization of the database server (dashed lines) and average queue length at the database server (solid lines) across time for (a) the browsing mix, (b) the shopping mix, and (c) the ordering mix. In this figure, the y-axis range of both performance metrics is the same because there are 100 EBs (clients) in the system. The monitoring window is 120 seconds.

browsing mix exhibits a significantly higher index of dispersion for both the front and database server compared to the shopping and ordering mixes.

3.3   The Analysis of Bottleneck Switch

Now, we focus on the burstiness in a multi-tier application to further analyze the symptoms and possible causes of the bottleneck switch. Indeed, for a typical request-reply transaction, the application server may issue multiple database calls while preparing the reply of a web page. This cascading effect of various tasks breaks down the overall transaction service time into several parts, including the transaction processing time at the application server as well as all related query processing times at the database server. Therefore, the application characteristics and the high variability in database server may cause burstiness in the overall transaction service times.

To verify the above congecture, we record the queue length at the database server at each instance that the database request is issued by the application server and a prepared reply is returned back to the application server. Figure 6 presents the queue length across time at the database server (see solid lines in the figure) as well as the CPU utilizations of the database server (see dashed lines in the figure) for all three transaction mixes.

Here, in order to make the figure easy to read, we show the case with 100 EBs such that the y-axis range for both performance metrics (i.e., queue length and utilization) is the same. First of all, the results for the browsing mix in Figure 6(a) verify that burstiness does exist in the queue length at the database server, where the queue holds less than 10 jobs for some periods, while sharply increases to as high as 90 jobs during other periods. More importantly, the burstiness in the database queue length exactly matches the burstiness in the CPU utilizations of the database server. Thus, at some periods almost all the transaction processing happens either at the application server (with the application server being a bottleneck) or at the database server (with the database server being a respective bottleneck). This leads to the alternated bottleneck between the application vs the database servers.

In contrast, no burstiness can be observed in the queue length for the shopping and the ordering mixes, although these two workloads have also high variability in their

Fig. 7. The overall queue length at the database server (dashed lines) and the number of current requests in system for the *Best Seller* transaction (solid lines) across time for (a) the browsing mix, (b) the shopping mix, and (c) the ordering mix, with 100 EBs and mean think time equal to 0.5*s*. The monitoring window is 120 seconds.

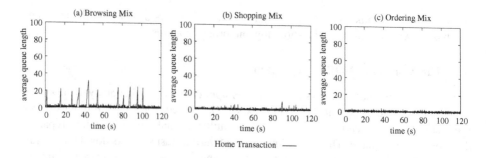

Fig. 8. The number of current requests in system for the *Home* transaction across time for (a) the browsing mix, (b) the shopping mix, and (c) the ordering mix, with 100 EBs and mean think time equal to 0.5*s*. The monitoring window is 120 seconds.

utilizations, see Figures 6(b) and 6(c). These results are consistent with those shown in Figures 5(b) and 5(c), where the application server is the main system bottleneck.

According to the TPC-W specification, different transaction types may have different number of outbound database queries. For example, the *Home* transaction has two database queries in maximum and one in minimum for each transaction request while the *Best Seller* transaction always has two outbound database queries per transaction request. To analyze whether burstiness in the database queue length originates from some particular transaction types, we measure the number of current requests for each transaction type over time. After revisiting all 14 transaction types, we find that the sources of this burstiness are indeed due to specific transaction types. Figures 7 and 8 show the results for two representative transaction types, the *Best Seller* transaction and the *Home* transaction, under three transaction mixes.

In Figure 7, the overall database queue length across time is also plotted as a base line. As shown in Figure 7(a), although in the browsing mix only 11% of requests belongs to the *Best Seller* transaction type, the number of these requests dominates the overall database queue length: the spikes in the overall queue length in the database clearly originate from this particular transaction type. Furthermore, there is burstiness in the number of requests for this transaction type and this burstiness "matches" well the overall queue length in the database server. In addition, for some extremely high spikes, e.g., at timestamp 40 in Figure 7(a), the requests of another popular transaction type, the *Home* transaction, also contribute to burstiness (see Figure 8(a)). These figures indicate that *Best Seller* and *Home* transactions share some resources required for their processing at the database server, and it leads to extreme burstiness during such time periods.

For the shopping and the ordering mixes, there is no visible burstiness in either the queue length at the database server or the number of current requests for each transaction type, as shown in Figure 7(b)-(c) and Figure 8(b)-(c), respectively.

In summary, we showed that

- burstiness in the service times can be a result of a certain workload combination (mix) in the multi-tier applications (e.g., burstiness in the service times may exist under the browsing mix in the TPC-W testbed);
- burstiness in the service times can be caused by a bottleneck switch between the tiers, and can be a result of "hidden" resource contention between the transactions of different types and across different tiers.

Systems with burstiness result in unstable behavior that is extremely hard to express and model. The super-position of several events, such as database locking conditions, variability in service time of software operations, memory contention, and/or characteristics of the scheduling algorithms, may interact in a complex way, resulting in burstiness in the system. The question is whether instead of identifying the low-level *exact* causes of burstiness as traditional models would require, one can provide an effective way to infer this information using live system measurements in order to capture burstiness into new capacity planning models.

3.4   Traditional MVA Performance Models Do Not Work

In this section, we use standard performance evaluation methodologies to define an analytical model of the multi-tier architecture presented in Section 3.1. Our goal is to show that existing queueing models can be largely inaccurate in performance prediction if the system is subject to bottleneck switches. We show in Section 4 how performance models can be generalized to correctly account for burstiness and bottleneck switches based on the index of dispersion.

We model the multi-tier architecture studied in our experiments by a closed queueing network composed of two queues and a delay center as shown in Figure 9. Closed queueing networks (see [13] for an introduction) are established as the standard capacity planning models for predicting the performance of distributed architectures using inexpensive algorithms, e.g., Mean Value Analysis (MVA) [22]; we refer to these models in the rest of the paper as *MVA models*.

In the MVA model shown in Figure 9, the two queues are used to abstract performance of the front server and of the database server, respectively. The delay center is instead representative of the average user think time Z between receiving a Web page

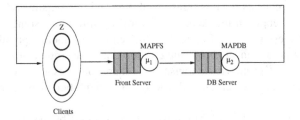

Fig. 9. The closed queueing network for modeling the multi-tier system

and submitting a new page download request[4]. The two queues serve jobs according to a processor-sharing scheduling discipline. In the real application, the servlet code is a mix of instructions at the front server and the database server: without an expensive analysis of the source code, it is truly difficult to characterize the switch of the execution from the front server to the database server and back, we thus make a simplification by assuming that requests first execute at the front server without any interruption and then the residual service time is processed at the database server[5]. Consequently, with this simplification, the two queues in Figure 9 are connected in series.

The proposed MVA model can be immediately parameterized by the following values:

- the mean service time S_{FS} of the front server;
- the mean service time S_{DB} of the database server;
- the average user think time Z;
- the number of emulated browsers (EBs).

Note that the arrival process at the multi-tier system, which is in the real system the arrival of new TPC-W sessions, is fully reproduced by the Z parameter. In fact, a new TPC-W session is generated in Z seconds after completion of a previously-running user session: thus, the feedback-loop aspect of TPC-W is fully captured by the closed nature of the queueing network and the user think time Z completes the model of the TPC-W arrival process.

The values of S_{FS} and S_{DB} can be determined with linear regression methods from the CPU utilization samples measured across time at the two servers [30]. Instead, Z and the number of EBs are imposed to set a specific scenario. For example, in Figure 10, we evaluate an increase of the number of EBs under the fixed think time $Z = 0.5s$; other choices of the delay are possible, see Section 4.2 for a discussion. Indeed, increasing the

---

[4] The main difference between a queue and a delay server is that the mean response time at the latter is *independent* of the number of requests present.

[5] In the following sections, we consider the burstiness associated to the execution of these requests at the front server and at the database server. Our abstraction ignores the order of execution of portions of the servlet code and has no impact on the burstiness estimates because the requests complete *faster* than the monitoring window of the measurement tool. Thus, for an external observer, it would be impossible to distinguish between samples collected from the real system and those of the abstracted system where the code first executes only at the front server and then completes at the database server.

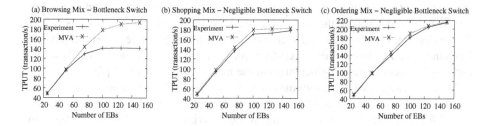

Fig. 10. MVA model predictions versus measured throughput

EB number is a typical way in capacity planning to explore the impact of increasingly larger traffic intensities on system performance. Figure 10 shows the results of the MVA model predictions versus the actual measured throughputs (TPUTs) of the system as a function of the number of EBs.

The three plots in the figure illustrate the accuracy of the MVA model under the browsing, shopping, and ordering mixes. The results show that the MVA model prediction is quite accurate for the shopping and ordering mixes, while there exists a large error up to 36% between the predicted and the measured throughputs for the browsing mix, see Figure 10(a). This indicates that MVA models can deal very well with systems *without* burstiness (e.g., the ordering mix in Figure 10(c)) and with systems where burstiness does *not* result in a bottleneck switch (e.g., the shopping mix in Figure 10(b)). However, the fundamental and most challenging case of burstiness that causes bottleneck switches reveals the limitation of the MVA modeling technique, see Figure 10(a). This is consistent with established theoretical results for MVA models, which rule out the possibility of capturing the bottleneck switching phenomenon [2].

4   Integrating Burstiness in Performance Models

Here, we use a measure of burstiness for the parameterization of the performance model presented in Figure 9. In Section 4.1, we first present the methodology for integrating the burstiness in queueing models and then discuss the impact of measurement granularity in Section 4.2. The experimental results that validate the proposed model are given in Section 4.3.

4.1   Integrating I in Performance Models

In order to integrate the index of dispersion in queueing models, we model service times as a two-phase Markovian Arrival Process (MAP(2)) [6,19,23]. An MAP(2) is a Markov chain that jumps between two states and the active state determines the current rate of service. For example, one state may be associated with slow service times, the other may represent fast service times. While processing the sequence of jobs, the MAP(2) jumps between these two states according to predefined frequencies. Simultaneously, the service rate offered to the jobs changes according to the current state. The variation of service rates of the MAP(2) is sufficient to reproduce the burstiness observed in the measured trace. The challenge is to assign the service rates of the two states and the jumping frequencies such that the service times received by the jobs served by the MAP(2) in the queueing model have the same burstiness properties of the service times in the measured trace. Fortunately, MAP(2) service rates and jumping frequencies can be fitted with closed-form formulas given the mean, SCV, skewness, and lag-1 autocorrelation coefficient ρ_1 of the measured service times [7,9].

We use these closed-form formulas to define the MAP(2) as follows. After estimating the mean service time and the index of dispersion I of the trace, we also estimate the 95th percentile of the service times as we describe at the end of this subsection. Given the mean, the index of dispersion I, and the 95th percentile of service times, we generate a set of MAP(2)s that have ±20% maximal error on I, see [1,12] for computational formulas of I in MAP(2)s. Among this set of MAP(2)s, we choose the one with its 95th percentile closest to the trace. Overall, the computational cost of fitting the MAP(2)s is negligible both in time and space requirements. For instance, the fitting of the MAP(2)s has been performed in MATLAB in less than five minutes[6] for the experiments in this paper.

We conclude by explaining how to estimate the 95th percentile of the service times from the measured trace. We compute the 95th percentile of the measured busy times B_k in Figure 2 and scale it by the median number of requests processed in the busy periods. If the trace has high dispersion (e.g., $I >> 100$), this estimate is very accurate because the n_k jobs that are served in the kth busy period receive a similar service time S_k and the busy time is therefore $B_k \approx n_k S_k$. This approximation consists in assuming that n_k is always constant and equal to its median value $med(n_k)$. Under this hypothesis the 95th percentile of B_k is simply $med(n_k)$ times the 95th percentile of S_k. Conversely, if the trace has low dispersion (e.g., $I < 100$), the estimation is inaccurate. Nevertheless, we observe that we can still use this simplification, because under low-burstiness conditions the queueing performance is dominated by the mean and the SCV of the distribution, and therefore a biased estimate of the 95th percentile does not have any appreciable effect on accuracy. In practice, we have found this estimation approach to be highly satisfactory for system modeling as shown by the experimental results reported in the next sections.

4.2   Impact of Measurement Granularity and Monitoring Windows

Starting from the MAP-based model defined in the previous section, we validate the accuracy of the new analytic model using the same experimental setup as in Section 3.4. We denote by Z_{qn} the think time used in the capacity planning queueing network model that represents the system presented in Section 3.4. For validation, we always compare the predictions of this model with a real experiment where the TPC-W has think time Z_{qn}. The notation Z_{estim} denotes the TPC-W think time used in experiments to generate the traces from which we estimate I and the MAP(2)s. In general, Z_{estim} can differ from Z_{qn}, e.g., if we want to explore the sensitivity of the system to

---

[6] Occasionally, and only for certain combinations of I and 95th percentile, there may exist more than one MAP(2) with identical mean, I, and 95th percentile. We have not found this case during the experiments in this paper, but in general we recommend to choose the MAP(2) with largest lag-1 autocorrelation since this results in a slightly more aggressive burstiness profile that provides conservative capacity planning estimates.

different think times we may consider models with different Z_{qn}, but the MAP(2)s are parameterized from the same experimental trace obtained for a certain $Z_{estim} \neq Z_{qn}$. A robust modeling methodology could predict well the performance of the system also for $Z_{qn} \neq Z_{estim}$ and we are seeking for a robust characterization of the service processes which is insensitive to the value Z_{estim} that describes a characteristic of the arrival process to the multi-tier system, rather than a property of the servers.

In all validations, we set $Z_{qn} = 0.5s$ and evaluate throughput and an increase of the number of EBs. The default think time value for the TPC-W benchmark is $7s$, but setting $Z_{qn} = 7s$ we would need to set the number of EBs as high as 1200 to reach heavy-load. Unfortunately, no existing numerical approach can solve the model for exact solutions when the system has such a large number of EBs. Since in this work we are interested in validating models with respect to their exact accuracy, we have explored exact solutions in Section 3.4 by reducing the user think time to $Z_{qn} = 0.5s$, such that the system becomes overloaded when the number of EBs is around $100 - 150$. Models with larger number of EBs should be evaluated with approximations, e.g., with the class of performance bounds presented in [6]. In the rest of paper, we only consider queueing network models with $Z_{qn} = 0.5s$. By building the underlying Markov chain and solving the system of linear equations, we solve the new analytic model and get the analytic results, see [6] for a description of the Markov chain underlying a MAP queueing network.

Here, we first present validation results on the browsing mix for different values of the measurement granularity Z_{estim}. Since measurements should not interfere with normal server operations, we have set the monitoring window resolution of the Diagnostics tool to a standard $W = 5s$, which means that hundreds of requests may be served between the collection of two consecutive utilization samples. For instance, when the user think time in TPC-W is set to $Z_{estim} = 0.5s$ and the number of EBs is 50, there are on average 465 requests completed in a monitoring window of $W = 5s$. A reduction of the frequency of sampling makes it difficult to collect a large number of samples (e.g., tens of thousands), and this significantly reduces the statistical robustness of the index of dispersion estimates[7]. Conversely, we have found that decreasing the mean throughput of the system by an increase of Z_{estim} can have beneficial effects on the quality of the index of dispersion estimation without having to modify the monitoring window resolution.

Figure 11 compares the analytic results with the experimental measurements of the real system for the browsing mix. A summary of the think time values used in the two models is given in Table 4. In all models, we set the mean user think time to $Z_{qn} = 0.5s$ and vary the system loads with different EBs. To evaluate the effect of the measurement granularity on the analytic model, we have estimated two sets of MAP(2)s by using the measured traces from the experiments with 50 EBs and two different levels of measurement granularity, i.e., the user think time $Z_{estim} = 0.5s$, and $Z_{estim} = 7s$, respectively. As Z_{estim} increases, we are getting monitoring data of finer granularity,

---

[7] Robustness depends on the relative frequency of service time peaks, e.g., if congestion events due to bursty arrivals as in Figure 1(d) are not frequent, then a large volume of experimental data may be needed to distinguish such events from outliers and correctly identify the bursty behavior.

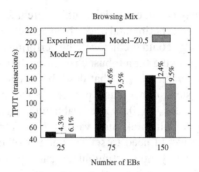

Fig. 11. Comparing the results for the model which fits MAPs with different $Z_{estim} = 0.5s$ and $Z_{estim} = 7s$. On each bar, the relative error with respect to the experimental data is also reported.

Table 4. Think time values considered in the accuracy validation experiments

	Queueing Network	MAP(2) Estimation
Model-Z0.5	$Z_{qn} = 0.5s$	$Z_{estim} = 0.5s$
Model-Z7	$Z_{qn} = 0.5s$	$Z_{estim} = 7s$

because in the same monitoring window W a smaller number of requests is completed. This makes the estimation of the variance of N_t in the algorithm in Figure 2 more accurate as the finer granularity reveals better the nature of the service times. This is intuitive, e.g., in the extreme case where Z_{estim} is so large that only a single request is completed during a single monitoring window W, then our measurement corresponds to a direct measure of the request service time and the estimation becomes optimal[8].

In Figure 11, the corresponding relative prediction error, which is the ratio of the absolute difference between the analytic result over the measured result, is shown on each bar. The figure shows that precision increases non-negligibly when a finer granularity of monitoring data is used. As the system becomes heavily loaded, the model with finer granularity (i.e., Z_{estim} as high as $7s$) dramatically reduces the relative prediction error to 2.4%.

4.3 Validation of Prediction Accuracy on Different Transaction Mixes

Figure 12 compares the analytical results with the experimental measurements of the real system for the three transaction mixes. The values of the index of dispersion for the front and the database service processes are also shown in the figure. Throughout all experiments, the mean user think time Z_{qn} is set to $Z_{qn} = 0.5s$; the MAP(2)s are obtained from experimental data collected with $Z_{estim} = 7s$.

---

[8] Indeed, a large increase of Z_{estim} to this level would be unrealistic because it would hide possible slowdowns in service times that become evident only when several requests are served simultaneously, e.g., increased memory access times in algorithms due to an increase in size of shared data structures. For this reason, it is always advisable to increase Z_{estim} such that there are some tens of requests completed in a time window W during the experiment.

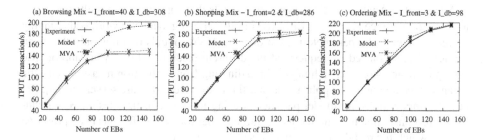

Fig. 12. Modeling results for three transaction mixes as a function of the number of EBs

Figure 12 gives evidence that the new analytic model based on the index of dispersion achieves gains in the prediction accuracy with respect to the MVA model on *all* workload mixes, showing that it is reliable also when the workloads are not bursty. In the browsing mix, the index of dispersion enables the queueing model to effectively capture *both* burstiness and bottleneck switch. The results of the proposed analytic model match closely the experimental results for the browsing mix, while remaining robust in all other cases.

The shopping mix presents an interesting case: as already observed in Section 3.4, the MVA model performs well on the shopping mix despite the existing burstiness because, regardless of the variation of the workload at the database server, the front server remains the major source of congestion for the system and the model behaves similarly to a MVA model (i.e., there is no bottleneck switch).

In the ordering mix, the feature of workload burstiness is almost negligible and the phenomenon of bottleneck switch between the front and the database servers cannot be easily observed, see Section 3.2. For this case, MVA yields prediction errors up to 5%. Yet, as shown in Figure 12(b) and 12(c), our analytic model further improves MVA's prediction accuracy. This happens because the index of dispersion I is able to capture detailed properties of the service time process, which can not be captured by the MVA model.

All results shown in Figure 12 validate the analytic model based on the index of dispersion: its performance results are in excellent agreement with the experimental values in the system, and it remains robust in systems *with* and *without* the feature of workload burstiness and bottleneck switch.

5 Related Work

Capacity planning of multi-tier systems is a critical part of the architecture design process and requires reliable quantitative methods, see [17] for an introduction. Queueing models are popular for predicting system performance and answering what-if capacity planning questions [17,26,27,28]. Single-tier queueing models focus on capturing the performance of the most-congested resource only (i.e., bottleneck tier): [28] describes the application tier of an e-commerce system as a M/GI/1/PS queue; [20] abstracts the application tier of a N-node cluster as a multi-server G/G/N queue.

Mean Value Analysis (MVA) queueing models that capture all the multi-tier architecture performance have been validated in [26,27] using synthetic workloads running on real systems. The parameterization of these MVA models requires only the mean service demand placed by requests at the different resources. In [24] the authors use multiple linear regression techniques for estimating from utilization measurements the mean service demands of applications in a single-threaded software server. In [15], Liu et al. calibrate queueing model parameters using inference techniques based on end-to-end response time measurements. A traffic model for Web traffic has been proposed in [14], which fits real data using mixtures of distributions.

However, the observations in [18] show that autocorrelation in multi-tier systems flows, which is ignored by standard capacity planning models, must be accounted for accurate performance prediction of multi-tiered systems. Indeed, [3] presents that burstiness in the World Wide Web and its related applications peaks the load of the Web server beyond its capacity, which results in significant degradation of the actual server performance. In this paper we have proposed for the first time robust solutions for capacity planning under workload burstiness. The class of MAP queueing networks considered here has been first introduced in [6] together with a bounding technique for approximate model solution. In this paper, we have proposed a parameterization of MAP queueing networks using for the service process of each server its mean service time, the index of dispersion, and the 95-th percentile of service times. The index of dispersion has been frequently adopted in the networking literature for describing traffic burstiness [11,25]; in particular, it is known that the performance of the G/M/1/FCFS queue in heavy-traffic is completely determined by its mean service time and the index of dispersion [25]. Further results concerning the characterization of index of dispersion in MAPs can be found in [1].

6 Conclusions

Today's IT and Services departments are faced with the difficult task of ensuring that enterprise business-critical applications are always available and provide adequate performance. Predicting and controlling the issues surrounding system performance is a difficult and overwhelming task for IT administrators. With complexity of enterprise systems increasing over time and customer requirements for QoS growing, effective models for quick and automatic evaluation of required system resources in production systems become a priority item on the service provider's "wish list".

In this work, we have presented a solution to the difficult problem of model parameterization by inferring essential process information from coarse measurements in a real system. After giving quantitative examples of the importance of integrating burstiness in performance models pointing out its role relatively to the bottleneck switching phenomenon, we show that coarse measurements can still be used to parameterize queueing models that effectively capture burstiness and variability of the true process. The parameterized queueing model can thus be used to closely predict performance in systems even in the very difficult case where there is persistent bottleneck switch among the various servers. Detailed experimentation on a multi-tiered system using the TPC-W benchmark validates that the proposed technique offers a robust solution to predict performance of systems subject to burstiness and bottleneck switching conditions.

The proposed approach is based on measurements that can be routinely obtained from existing commercial monitoring tools. The resulting parameterized models are practical and robust for a variety of capacity planning and performance modeling tasks in production environments.

References

1. Andersen, A.T., Nielsen, B.F.: On the statistical implications of certain random permutations in markovian arrival processes (MAPs) and second-order self-similar processes. Perf. Eval. 41(2-3), 67–82 (2000)
2. Balbo, G., Serazzi, G.: Asymptotic analysis of multiclass closed queueing networks: Common bottlenecks. Perf. Eval. 26(1), 51–72 (1996)
3. Banga, G., Druschel, P.: Measuring the capacity of a web server under realistic loads. World Wide Web 2(1-2), 69–83 (1999)
4. Beran, J.: Statistics for Long-Memory Processes. Chapman & Hall, New York (1994)
5. Casale, G., Mi, N., Cherkasova, L., Smirni, E.: How to parameterize models with bursty workloads. In: Proceedings of First Workshop on Hot Topics in Measurement & Modeling of Computer Systems, HotMetrics 2008 (2008)
6. Casale, G., Mi, N., Smirni, E.: Bound analysis of closed queueing networks with workload burstiness. In: Proceedings of ACM SIGMETRICS, pp. 13–24 (2008)
7. Casale, G., Zhang, E., Smirni, E.: Interarrival times characterization and fitting for markovian traffic analysis. Number WM-CS-2008-02 (2008), http://www.wm.edu/computerscience/techreport/2008/WM-CS-2008-02.pdf
8. Cox, D., Lewis, P.: The Statistical Analysis of Series of Events. John Wiley and Sons, New York (1966)
9. Ferng, H., Chang, J.: Connection-wise end-to-end performance analysis of queueing networks with MMPP inputs. Perf. Eval. 43(1), 39–62 (2001)
10. Garcia, D., Garcia, J.: TPC-W E-commerce benchmark evaluation. In: IEEE Computer, pp. 42–48 (February 2003)
11. Gusella, R.: Characterizing the variability of arrival processes with indexes of dispersion. IEEE JSAC 19(2), 203–211 (1991)
12. Heindl, A.: Traffic-Based Decomposition of General Queueing Networks with Correlated Input Processes. Ph.D. Thesis. Shaker Verlag, Aachen (2001)
13. Lazowska, E.D., Zahorjan, J., Graham, G.S., Sevcik, K.C.: Quantitative System Performance. Prentice-Hall, Englewood Cliffs (1984)
14. Liu, Z., Niclausse, N., Jalpa-Villanueva, C.: Traffic model and performance evaluation of web servers. Perform. Eval. 46(2-3) (2001)
15. Liu, Z., Wynter, L., Xia, C.H., Zhang, F.: Parameter inference of queueing models for it systems using end-to-end measurements. Perf. Eval. 63(1), 36–60 (2006)
16. Menascé, D.A., Almeida, V.A.F.: Scaling for E-Business: Technologies, Models, Performance, and Capacity Planning. Prentice-Hall, Inc., Englewood Cliffs (2000)
17. Menascé, D.A., Almeida, V.A.F., Dowdy, L.W.: Capacity planning and performance modeling: from mainframes to client-server systems. Prentice-Hall, Inc., Englewood Cliffs (1994)
18. Mi, N., Zhang, Q., Riska, A., Smirni, E., Riedel, E.: Performance impacts of autocorrelated flows in multi-tiered systems. Perf. Eval. 64(9-12), 1082–1101 (2007)
19. Neuts, M.F.: Structured Stochastic Matrices of M/G/1 Type and Their Applications. Marcel Dekker, New York (1989)
20. Ranjan, S., Rolia, J., Fu, H., Knightly, E.: Qos-driven server migration for internet data centers. In: The 10th International Workshop on Quality of Service (IWQoS 2002) (2002)

21. Reiser, M.: Mean-value analysis and convolution method for queue-dependent servers in closed queueing networks. Perf. Eval. 1, 7–18 (1981)
22. Reiser, M., Lavenberg, S.S.: Mean-value analysis of closed multichain queueing networks. JACM 27(2), 312–322 (1980)
23. Robertazzi, T.G.: Computer Networks and Systems. Springer, Heidelberg (2000)
24. Rolia, J., Vetland, V.: Correlating resource demand information with arm data for application services. In: Proceedings of WOSP 1998, pp. 219–230. ACM, New York (1998)
25. Sriram, K., Whitt, W.: Characterizing superposition arrival processes in packet multiplexers for voice and data. IEEE JSAC 4(6), 833–846 (1986)
26. Urgaonkar, B., Pacifici, G., Shenoy, P., Spreitzer, M., Tantawi, A.: An analytical model for multi-tier internet services and its applications. In: Proceedings of the ACM SIGMETRICS Conference, Banff, Canada, pp. 291–302 (June 2005)
27. Urgaonkar, B., Shenoy, P., Chandra, A., Goyal, P.: Dynamic provisioning of multi-tier internet applications. In: ICAC 2005: Proceedings of the Second International Conference on Automatic Computing, pp. 217–228 (2005)
28. Villela, D., Pradhan, P., Rubenstein, D.: Provisioning servers in the application tier for e-commerce systems. ACM Trans. Interet Technol. 7(1), 7 (2007)
29. Mercury Diagnostics, www.mercury.com/us/products/diagnostics
30. Zhang, Q., Cherkasova, L., Mathews, G., Greene, W., Smirni, E.: R-capriccio: A capacity planning and anomaly detection tool for enterprise services with live workloads. In: Proceedings of Middleware, Newport Beach, CA, pp. 244–265 (2007)
31. Zhang, Q., Cherkasova, L., Smirni, E.: A regression-based analytic model for dynamic resource provisioning of multi-tier applications. In: Proceedings of ICAC 2007, p. 27 (2007)

Towards End-to-End Quality of Service: Controlling I/O Interference in Shared Storage Servers

Gokul Soundararajan and Cristiana Amza

Department of Electrical and Computer Engineering
University of Toronto

Abstract. Due to the imperative need to reduce the costs of management, power and cooling in large data centers, operators multiplex several concurrent applications on each physical server of a server farm connected to a shared network attached storage. Determining and enforcing per-application resource quotas on the fly in this context poses a complex resource allocation and control problem spanning many levels including the CPU, memory and storage resources within each physical server and/or across the server farm. This problem is further complicated by the need to provide end-to-end Quality of Service (QoS) guarantees to hosted applications.

In this paper, we introduce a novel approach towards controlling application interference for resources in shared server farms. Specifically, we design and implement a minimally intrusive method for passing application-level QoS requirements through the software stack. We leverage high-level per-application requirements for controlling I/O interference between multiple database applications, by QoS-aware dynamic resource partitioning at the storage server. Our experimental evaluation, using the MySQL database engine and OLTP benchmarks, shows the effectiveness of our technique in enforcing high-level application Service Level Objectives (SLOs) in shared server farms.

1 Introduction

As the costs of management, power and cooling in large data centers become prohibitive, automated *server consolidation* techniques for better resource usage while providing differentiated Quality of Service (QoS) to applications become increasingly important. With *server consolidation*, several concurrent applications are multiplexed on each physical server of a server farm connected to consolidated network attached storage (see Figure 1). Such architectures are common in large data centers and consist of multiple levels of software, including web and application servers, database servers, operating systems and the storage server at the lowest level. The challenge for providing QoS to applications in these environments lies in the complexity of the dynamic resource partitioning problem for avoiding application interference at multiple levels, i.e., for CPU, memory and storage.

V. Issarny and R. Schantz (Eds.): Middleware 2008, LNCS 5346, pp. 287–305, 2008.
© IFIP International Federation for Information Processing 2008

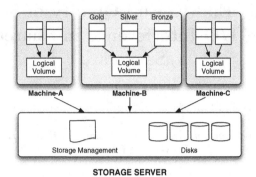

Fig. 1. Modern enterprise architecture: Server farm with resource consolidation

Previous work on dynamic resource partitioning in shared server environments focuses on partitioning a single resource within a single software tier at a time. Specifically, resource virtualization through virtual machine monitors (VMMs) has been used in both generic server systems [3] and database systems [14,15] to enforce per-application CPU quotas. Similarly, memory quota enforcement has been studied within the buffer pool of a database system running several applications [4,5]. Finally, several techniques have been studied for partitioning the I/O bandwidth between applications within the storage server [11,12,19]. However, the above approaches fall short of providing effective resource partitioning due to the following two reasons.

The first reason is that application QoS is usually expressed as a high-level Service Level Objective (SLO), e.g., desired latency or throughput, not as per-resource priorities or quotas. There is currently no automatic mechanism to assign the relative priority levels or resource quotas for applications corresponding to a high-level application metric. A dynamic approach to resource allocation is clearly more desirable than extensive off-line profiling in modern data center environments, where the set of co-scheduled applications, and/or the type and availability of hardware resources may change frequently and unpredictably.

The second reason that prevents current approaches from providing effective resource partitioning is the absence of coordination between different resource controllers. This absence of coordination might lead to situations where local goals may conflict with each other, or with the high-level per-application goals. For instance, the operating system may optimize fairness in thread scheduling across applications, while the storage server may optimize I/O latency. Each resource controller optimizes local goals, oblivious to the goals of other resource controllers, and to the per-application SLO's. There is little or no previous work on correlating priority or quota enforcement across several resources or software components.

To address the dynamic resource allocation problem in consolidated server environments, we introduce a novel technique for controlling application interference.

Our technique determines per-application resource quotas on the fly, with minimal application instrumentation. To achieve this, we monitor application-level metrics relative to SLOs periodically and pass these as application utility values down through all levels of the software stack i.e., from the DBMS to the OS running on each physical server in a server farm, and then to the shared storage server.

The monitored application-level metrics are utilized by a coordinated distributed learning technique, with one adaptive controller per software component. Each resource controller uses a reinforcement learning algorithm, called *learning automata* (LA) [13], for resource allocation. Specifically, each LA controller employs a feedback loop to dynamically converge towards a resource partitioning setting that minimizes the perceived penalties for all applications.

Though our technique is general enough to be applied for partitioning all shared resources, at all tiers, in this paper, we focus on dynamically partitioning the storage bandwidth. Towards this goal, we implement our technique in a prototype that enforces coordinated resource quotas per application at two levels: i) at the operating system I/O scheduler within each physical server of the server farm and ii) at the shared storage level. Our prototype implementation shows that our approach can be integrated in existing environments and applications with minimal changes to interfaces between components.

Specifically, we modify the Linux kernel and the Network Block Device (NBD) protocol, a network block protocol that is bundled with the Linux kernel, to allow passing the application-level utility on I/O calls, and to implement our learning and I/O scheduling algorithms. Our technique is sufficiently flexible to enforce resource quotas and to change them dynamically, for different applications, but also per application thread within the same application e.g., to enforce differentiated QoS for performance-critical transactions or queries.

We perform experiments on a cluster of dual processor servers connected to a storage server with external direct attached storage. We use the MySQL database engine and two applications: DBT-2 and the ORION (Oracle IO Numbers) storage utility. DBT-2 is a classic OLTP workload similar to TPC-C. Orion emulates part of the common I/O workload of the Oracle database server. We run experiments in several configurations where instances of the two applications share physical servers as well as the storage server. We show convergence to the per-application quotas that meet the high-level application SLO's for each application when using our coordinated dynamic learning technique.

The remainder of this paper is structured as follows. Section 2 describes the role of each software component in servicing I/O requests and the motivation to use end-to-end resource partitioning. Section 3 describes the architecture of our system and introduces our coordinated learning and our I/O bandwidth partitioning technique. Section 4 describes our prototype implementation. Section 5 presents our benchmarks and experimental platform, while Section 6 presents the results of our experiments on this platform. Section 7 discusses related work and Section 8 concludes the paper.

2   Background and Motivation

Enterprise storage servers (Figure 1) provide an abstraction of a single large logical storage device carved into several logical volumes. An application, like a database system or file system, mounts the logical volumes and uses the underlying storage. Within this storage hierarchy, we focus on the following two levels of control: (1) the OS I/O scheduler, which schedules I/O requests from a storage client to the underlying storage device, and (2) the storage server I/O scheduler, which manages bandwidth allocations to different logical volumes.

The interactions between the storage client and server travel through the operating system's *block layer*. The *block layer* maps logical to physical accesses on block devices e.g., in a RAID. It provides a wide range of functionality from request sorting and merging, prefetching, to I/O scheduling i.e., reordering requests to optimize the disk seek time. Due to this commonly used optimization objective, physically sequential I/O will be preferentially scheduled, typically regardless of its high-level application SLO. To counter starvation, implementations of I/O scheduling either attach a deadline for every request or provide fairness among several streams. However, these approaches are typically unaware of application SLOs. Similar to the operating system I/O scheduler, the storage server schedules I/O requests from different logical volumes. While the operating system I/O scheduler attempts to minimize seek times, the storage server I/O scheduler controls when each workload's request is sent to the disk firmware e.g., in order to meet a pre-specified I/O *latency* [12], but oblivious to the high-level application SLO.

As we can see from our description of the storage hierarchy described above, storage bandwidth allocations are influenced by both the operating system and the storage server, in an uncoordinated, SLO unaware, and possibly conflicting manner. In the following, we show through a motivating experiment that unpredictably large performance degradation can occur for co-scheduled applications due to I/O interference, whether or not CPU priorities are enforced at the OS level.

2.1   Motivating Example

Using current I/O schedulers in existing operating systems, we show that the performance of an application can be severely affected when paired with another I/O intensive process, whether or not we enforce per-application CPU priorities at the operating system level.

We run DBT-2, a TPC-C like workload, on MySQL, concurrently with OLTP-A, an online transaction processing (OLTP) workload, generated using the ORION (Oracle IO Numbers) tool. We configure DBT-2 to use 200 warehouses, resulting in a database size of 64GB. We provide additional details of our workloads in Section 6. In our experiments, we run MySQL/InnoDB on direct-attached storage and show the effects of I/O interference between applications. In our experimental setup, we use either the cfq scheduler, recently added to the Linux kernel, which attempts to provide fair queuing among several processes, or

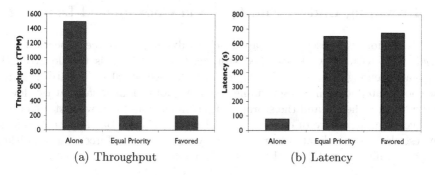

(a) Throughput   (b) Latency

Fig. 2. Co-scheduling DBT-2/OLTP-A on Direct-Attached Storage with CFQ scheduling

the more traditional `deadline` scheduler in Linux, which primarily targets minimizing I/O seek time. Neither the `cfq` scheduler, nor the `deadline` scheduler support enforcement of application SLOs.

Figure 2 shows the I/O interference between DBT-2 and OLTP-A when using the `cfq` scheduler at the operating system. We see that, when DBT-2 runs alone, it achieves 1498 TPM (transactions per minute) and its 90th percentile latency is 78 seconds. However, when DBT-2 is co-scheduled with OLTP-A, there is a significant slowdown. DBT-2's throughput is only 13% of its throughput running in isolation and the latency is 8.3x the original latency. In an attempt to achieve better performance for DBT-2, we set the CPU nice levels for DBT-2 to -10 (high priority) and OLTP-A to +10 (low priority) and re-run the experiment. We see a very small gain in DBT-2's performance. The throughput increases slightly from 196 TPM to 198 TPM.

The interference effect is even more pronounced when using the traditional `deadline` scheduler in Linux. In this case, DBT-2's throughput when co-scheduled with OLTP-A is only 2.3% of its throughput when running in isolation i.e., 80 TPM compared to 3391 TPM. As before, setting the DBT-2 process to a higher priority, by using the UNIX nice utility, does not significantly alleviate the problem.

These results show that there is currently no method of enforcing I/O requirements of applications at the operating system level. Furthermore, there is no method of communicating application SLO requirements and enforcing them at the storage server. Since both the OS and the storage server perform I/O scheduling in a per-application QoS oblivious manner, current architectures are unable to enforce end-to-end quality of service. As we have shown, this results in potentially high performance degradation for the high priority application.

In this paper, we address these issues by providing a method of transmitting application SLO requirements throughout the storage hierarchy. This allows the individual I/O controllers at each level to determine the bandwidth allocations dynamically.

3   Providing End-to-End QoS Via Coordinated Learning

In this section, we describe our approach to dynamic resource allocation in a server farm with network attached storage. Our objective is to allocate each application enough resources (i.e., bandwidth) to meet its SLO. Towards this, we use coordinated learning to determine resource quotas dynamically, at two levels in the system: the OS and the storage server. In the following, we first introduce the overall architecture of our system and an overview of our approach. Then, we describe our coordinated learning and dynamic quota enforcement algorithm in detail. Finally, we discuss the trade-offs made in our design.

3.1   Architecture and Problem Statement

The architecture of our system is presented in Figure 1. We show the storage server hosting a number of virtual devices connected to several physical servers i.e., machines A, B, and C. Each physical server hosts a number of application classes, e.g., *gold*, *silver*, and *bronze* hosted on Machine-B in the Figure.

In this environment, the problem of resource allocation can be described as follows. For k servers hosting n application classes connected to s virtual volumes hosted on the storage server, we need to find the following proportions in order to meet the specified SLOs: i) We need to find proportions $P_{S_1}, P_{S_2}, \ldots, P_{S_s}$ for enforcing disk bandwidth partitioning among the workload for the virtual volumes at the storage server. and ii) At each machine $m \in \{1, 2, \ldots, k\}$, we need to determine the proportions $P_{m_1}, P_{m_2}, \ldots, P_{m_n}$ for scheduling the respective requests to the virtual device at the level of the OS I/O scheduler (e.g., $P_{B_{gold}}$, $P_{B_{silver}}$, and $P_{B_{bronze}}$ for the OS on Machine-B in Figure 1.

Finding an optimal solution to this problem is challenging since there is no clear mapping from the specified SLOs to disk bandwidth. As such, we use adaptive machine learning techniques as described next.

3.2   Overview of Approach

Towards achieving the specified SLOs, we embed resource controllers at the OS and at the storage server. All resource controllers use a learning algorithm for dynamic resource partitioning at its level. Specifically, each resource controller changes its own per-workload proportions dynamically, converging to a local solution based on application-level feedback values.

We coordinate learning between the OS and the storage server through a token-passing scheme. The learners at the two levels take turns in making actions and observing the application feedback. In this way, each level can observe the application feedback based only on its actions, thus converging to a solution. We ensure convergence to a stable global resource partitioning solution for the different learners by using the same feedback metric for learners at both the OS and the storage server levels. This application-level feedback metric, called *Deviance from Target* (dft), is periodically monitored for each application. The most recent dft is then passed from the application level through all levels of the software stack, including the OS, to the storage server on each I/O call of the corresponding application. Finally, each resource controller enforces the learned resource partitioning through quanta based scheduling for its workloads. Modifications to existing interfaces between components are minimal; all information exchanged between the two levels is piggybacked on regular communication.

In the following, we introduce the high-level application metric we use for coordinated learning (the dft metric). Next, we introduce the learning algorithm employed at each resource controller and the coordination between resource controllers. Finally, we explain the quanta-based scheduling algorithm used by each resource controller for enforcing the resource partitioning.

3.3 Deviance From Target (DFT) Metric

We use a single high-level application-level metric, called *Deviance from Target* (dft), for guided learning at all resource controllers. The dft represents the utility to the service provider from meeting the service level objective (SLO) of the corresponding application. This utility is typically mapped directly to an expected monetary reward (or penalty) for hosting a particular application and it may combine two factors: i) a performance indicator i.e., the relative distance of a pre-specified application metric, such as transaction throughput, or latency from a contracted SLO value over time and ii) the contracted client priority or class for the corresponding application e.g., gold/silver/bronze or best-effort.

Without loss of generality, for the purposes of this paper, we use as performance indicator a number that indicates the deviation from expected application performance, where a 0.0 value corresponds to *target achieved*, a positive value means we have exceeded the objective and a negative value means a violation of the contracted performance, hence a penalty for the service provider. For example, in order to compute the dft for a particular high priority OLTP application, we periodically sample the transactions completed. Then we compute the normalized distance between the average transaction throughput value over the last sampling interval and the contracted/expected throughput value (the SLO). To produce the dft, this value would be typically weighted to include the priority class. For simplicity, for the purposes of this paper, we use only two classes: priority and best effort. For a best effort application we always provide a dft feedback value of 0.0 regardless of the performance indicator. For a priority application, we provide its performance indicator as the dft feedback.

Finally, we also support assigning different dft values for different threads, transactions or queries inside an application. Specifically, we support selectively tagging fine-grained application contexts with the overall dft value of an application, while all other I/O from that application should be classified as best effort. For example, a database application may signal that a DBMS application thread carries its overall utility rather than a DBMS statistics logger thread; alternatively, the application may assign all its utility to a key transaction type e.g., a payment transaction.

In the following, we describe our learning algorithm at each resource controller. We then introduce a lightweight and minimally intrusive technique to coordinate the multiple controllers implemented at different levels in order to provide end-to-end QoS.

3.4   Learning at Each Resource Controller

We determine the workload proportions dynamically using a reinforcement learning algorithm [18]. In reinforcement learning, the learning agent learns how to use various *actions* to maximize a numerical *reward*. We use a simple reinforcement learning algorithm named *learning automata* (LA) [13].

Learning automata are adaptive decision-making devices that operate in unknown environments. A learning automaton has a finite set of actions and each action has a certain probability (unknown to the automaton) of getting rewarded by the environment of the automaton. The aim is to learn to choose the optimal action (i.e. the action with the highest probability of being rewarded) through repeated interactions with the system. If the environment is sufficiently stationary during the learning period, the iterative process of interacting with the environment in the LA algorithm is guaranteed to converge to the optimal solution [13]. We use a linear reward-penalty learning automata, where an automaton can probabilistically choose one of r actions $\{a_1, a_2, \ldots, a_r\}$ with associated probabilities $\{p_1, p_2, \ldots, p_r\}$ respectively. Let $p(k)$ denote the probability of an action to be taken at iteration k and suppose action a_i is taken at iteration k.

The result of an action a_i is mapped to a range between 0.0 and 1.0, where 0.0 represents the maximum positive feedback and 1.0 represents the maximum negative feedback. The feedback for the kth action is represented using the variable $f(k)$. The probabilities for taking each action are updated as follows. The probability p_i corresponding to action a_i is updated to:

$$p_i(k+1) = p_i(k) - \beta f(k)p_i(k) + \alpha(1 - f(k))(1 - p_i(k)) \qquad (1)$$

All other actions, a_j where $i \neq j$ are updated to:

$$p_j(k+1) = p_j(k) + f(k)(\frac{\beta}{r-1} - \beta p_j(k)) - \alpha(1 - f(k))p_j(k) \qquad (2)$$

The parameters α and β scale the reward and penalty. Typically, $\alpha > \beta$ for faster convergence.

We describe how we adapt the LA learning algorithm to enable dynamic allocations in our controller. The goal at each controller is to minimize the sum of the squared deviations from 0.0 (*error*) for the dft of all applications. For example, if the storage server was hosting s virtual volumes with each virtual volume hosting n applications, then the *error* (e) would be computed as

$$e = \sum_{i=1}^{s} \sum_{j=1}^{n} [dft_{i,j}]^2 \qquad (3)$$

Each controller dynamically determines proportions between its workloads, i.e., between applications in the operating system and between virtual devices in the storage server scheduler, with the objective of minimizing the error (e). For instance, consider a controller which schedules two workloads at the storage server. Such a controller will simply have to determine the proportion $0 \leq P \leq 1.0$, such that one workload receives a fraction P and the other workload receives $1 - P$ of the resource. For that particular controller, in order to determine P, we define a number of actions for the LA learning algorithm representing bandwidth allocations. The controller's action sets the proportions by picking from a collection of discrete choices. In our example here, a possible collection of choices might be $\{10/90, 30/70, 50/50, 70/30, 90/10\}$.

At each learning iteration, the controller first measures the current error, e_{cur}, in the system. Then, it probabilistically selects an action to take. For example, the controller may select the action corresponding to enforcing a proportion of 50/50. After selecting an action, the controller waits until the effects of its action are visible, for either a fixed time interval or a fixed number of requests. It then evaluates the application-level feedback, computes the new *error* value, e_{new}, and updates the variable $f(k)$ with a new value between 0.0 and 1.0, depending on the perceived benefit of its action. Finally, the controller updates the probabilities corresponding to taking each action using the new value of $f(k)$ in the formulas above.

3.5   Coordinated Learning

While all controllers in our system have the same goal, i.e., to optimize the dft error for all applications, each learns iteratively through trial and error. Thus, if all learners actuate their proportions in parallel, the feedback received by each learner is the result of actions taken by all controllers, not just by itself. To enable accurate feedback, hence convergence towards an end-to-end solution, we coordinate the multiple learners in the hierarchy using a simple token passing scheme. We thus let either the OS-level controllers or the storage server controller learn at a given time, while keeping the proportions fixed at the other level. Token requests and replies are passed on regular requests and replies between the two levels. Whenever holding the token, a learner takes a number of actions actuating its per-workload proportions and observes the application feedback on incoming requests.

3.6   Enforcing Proportions through Quanta-Based Scheduling

We enforce proportions by using quanta-based scheduling [19] at both the OS and storage resource controllers. Specifically, we partition a scheduling period into time intervals and assign intervals to workloads to meet their respective proportions. For example, let the scheduling period be 100 milliseconds with 100 slices. If two applications, A and B require equal proportions, then, each would be given exclusive access to storage for 50 milliseconds in every 100 milliseconds scheduling period. Scheduling based on time quanta allows for a good combination of enforcing proportions between workloads as well as taking advantage of the usual storage optimizations for per-workload locality. This is because when only one workload is allowed to run during a time interval, during that time, both the OS/storage I/O schedulers can optimize disk seeks with the usual techniques e.g., using elevator scheduling and also exploit the disk cache for that workload.

3.7 Discussion

In this section we discuss the trade-offs in our scheduling technique. We then present a theoretical argument for convergence to a global optimal solution for our end-to-end approach.

Trade-offs in Scheduling Technique. While quanta-based scheduling ensures that each workload receives a share of the disk bandwidth, there is an inherent tradeoff between using coarse-grained versus fine-grained scheduling intervals, hence quanta. At the limit, the scheduler can simply not use time quanta at all, and issue requests proportionally from each workload. Using large quanta may waste disk bandwidth if insufficient requests from the respective workload are available to the scheduler during a particular quantum. On the other hand, as mentioned before, using coarse-grained quanta has the advantage of reducing the potential disk seeks and cache conflicts caused by switching between multiple workloads.

We note that in many practical cases, the adaptivity inherent in our approach will naturally alleviate penalties, by self-regulating the quanta granularity. For example, assume that a sequential workload suffers due to increased disk seeks when interleaved with a random-access workload at the storage. If these penalties are significant, they will be reflected in the application's high-level metrics. Hence, the sequential workload will automatically receive a larger proportion of I/O bandwidth. The larger bandwidth allocation will implicitly translate into a *larger quanta*.

Global Convergence to an Optimal Solution. Our coordinated learning technique will converge towards a state with the minimum penalties achievable for the applications, hence for the service provider, if the application behavior and environment does not substantially change *during learning*.

When using multiple learners with a common feedback signal, as in our case, each environment state is determined by a combination of actions from all learners. In this case, the environment states form a composite environment which is referred to as Markovian Switching Environment. In such an environment, it can be theoretically shown [13] that a variable-structure automata with ergodic techniques, such as the linear reward-penalty learning automata we use, converges to the optimal set of actions by the multiple learners within a margin of error due to the continuous learning and exploratory nature of LA controllers.

The ideal solution, where all application dft's are 0.0 may be, however, unattainable, e.g., because of insufficient overall I/O bandwidth, and dynamic provisioning of additional resources may become necessary.

4   Prototype Implementation

In this section, we describe our prototype implementation for passing high-level application metrics through the software stack to the storage controller, and our virtual storage controller implementation.

4.1   Overview of Prototype Implementation

We embed our LA controller into Linux and our virtual storage prototype. We leverage the Network Block Device (NBD) code available with Linux for this purpose. NBD is a standard storage access protocol, similar to iSCSI, supported by Linux. NBD provides a method for a storage client (in our case MySQL) to communicate with a storage server over the network; specifically, NBD provides a pair of client/server modules, which run on the same physical machines as the storage client/server, respectively.

We implement a Linux-based virtual storage prototype, which we deploy on top of our commodity storage (RAID) firmware. We modify the existing *client* and *server* NBD protocol processing modules in order to pass high-level application metrics to our LA storage bandwidth controller. Specifically, we piggyback the application's performance (dft), the application identifier, and a learning token on the I/O call path. Our storage controller enforces bandwidth quota allocations, maps virtual to physical block accesses and issues the appropriate I/O requests to disk.

4.2   Code Changes

We instrument MySQL to capture the application-level metrics of interest, periodically, and to compute the *dft* metric relative to a predefined SLO for each application context. For example, for DBT-2, we monitor transaction throughput as application level metric and for Orion we use latency, which are the standard QoS metrics for these applications.

For every I/O call made from MySQL on behalf of the application, we add arguments to the corresponding system call and pass the application context identifier and the periodically updated *dft* metric for that application context. Context identifiers are assigned in such a way to be unique cluster-wide. In order to support differentiated QoS for fine-grained and/or dynamic application-level contexts, e.g., per application thread, or per-transaction, we also add a new system call, ioprio_context(), to the Linux kernel. ioprio_context() signals the beginning and end of an application context. We add corresponding system calls in MySQL, reusing pre-existing begin and end markers in the application structure e.g., for transaction begin and commit or thread creation and destruction. We modify the Linux kernel and the NBD packet format to tag each I/O call with the application-level information and pass this information through the respective software layers. In addition, for the coordinated learning algorithm, we piggyback the learning token on request and reply NBD packets.

4.3   I/O Scheduling Implementation

When a workload is given a quantum, we first determine the number of requests we can issue to disk such that they complete within the workload's quantum. To compute this value, we maintain an exponentially weighted average of the disk service time and the application's concurrency level. Using these two values, we compute the number of requests that can be issued per workload such that all requests finish within the quantum. First, we issue requests that were enqueued while waiting for the quantum to begin. Then, we issue requests that arrive during the scheduling quantum. We stop issuing requests if we determine that by issuing a request, we will exceed the workload's quantum. In this case, new requests will be enqueued as we wait for the requests to return from disk before the next quantum begins.

5   Experimental Methodology

We create a multi-tier system with shared storage using NBD, as shown in Figure 3. We use three machines: a storage server (S) and two application servers (A and B). In this system, we can run 4 applications, A_0, A_1, B_0, and B_1. The storage server (S) serves two virtual block devices which are mounted by machines A and B, respectively. The applications A_0 and A_1 share one virtual block device and B_0 and B_1 share the other. In addition, each machine runs a LA based controller that determines the bandwidth allocation for the two incoming streams. Machine A determines P_A, the fraction of the bandwidth allocated to A_0. Conversely, A_1 receives $(1-P_A)$ bandwidth. Similarly, Machine B determines P_B and the storage server S determines P_S.

The application servers are Dell PowerEdge SC1425 with dual Intel Xeon processors running Ubuntu Linux 6.06 with our modifications, and connected by Gigabit Ethernet. The storage server is a Dell PowerEdge PE1950 with 4 Intel Xeon processors running at 3Ghz and 3GB of memory. The storage server is connected to an external direct attached storage with 15 10K RPM SAS hard

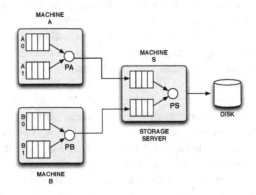

Fig. 3. Experimental Multi-tier System with Shared Storage

drives. The attached storage is configured using RAID-0. We benchmark the direct attached storage using ORION and found it provides 800 IOPS for our microbenchmark OLTP-A. Our NBD based storage server increases the latency by at most 10%.

We use MySQL/InnoDB and configure it to use a raw device and a buffer pool of 512 MB. We use ORION (Oracle IO Numbers) as a I/O load generator. ORION is a calibration tool released by Oracle to benchmark different storage architectures for database workloads. It allows the user to set different parameters like block size, read/write ratio, and number of outstanding I/Os. By changing the parameters, one can generate different types of database workloads. We set these parameters to generate an OLTP-like workload classified with equal amount of reads and writes, many random I/O accesses (16KB block size) and some large I/O (1MB blocks).

5.1 Benchmarks

OLTP-A: OLTP-A is an OLTP-*like* workloads we generate using the ORION tool. It is characterized by many random I/O accesses of 16KB and some large I/O of 1MB. The read/write ratio is 50%. We configure ORION to have 100 outstanding small I/O and 10 outstanding large I/O. OLTP-A issues I/O to a 64GB raw partition.

DBT-2: DBT-2 is an OLTP workload derived from TPC-C benchmark [16]. It simulates a wholesale parts supplier that operates using a number of warehouse and sales districts. Each warehouse has 10 sales districts and each district serves 3000 customers. The workload involves transactions from a number of terminal operators centered around an order entry environment. There are 5 main transactions for: (1) entering orders, (2) delivering orders, (3) recording payments, (4) checking the status of the orders, and (5) monitoring the level of stock at the warehouses. We scale DBT-2 by using 256 warehouses and the footprint of the database is 60GB. In our experiments, we simulate 1000 users connected to the system.

6 Experimental Results

We present an experimental evaluation of our end-to-end I/O bandwidth allocation technique. All results are obtained on our experimental configuration described in the previous section. We first evaluate our learning technique for enforcing end-to-end resource allocations. We then show the benefits of coordinated versus uncoordinated learning in two sharing scenarios, using the ORION and DBT-2 benchmarks.

6.1 Benefits of Coordinated Learning

We show the benefits of coordinated versus uncoordinated learning with two sharing scenarios. First, we run four instances of OLTP-A. Next, we co-schedule

DBT-2 with three instances of OLTP-A. For both scenarios, we compare both coordinated and uncoordinated learning with two ideal scenarios, where proportions are set manually for either i) one resource controller or ii) both resource controllers. In more detail, we evaluate four schemes:

1. **Optimal Settings:** We set all proportions manually to the optimal configuration.
2. **Single Storage Learner:** We set the proportions manually in the OS schedulers (P_A and P_B) but we determine P_S at the storage through learning.
3. **Uncoordinated Learning:** We let all controllers find the optimal values in parallel.
4. **Coordinated Learning:** We enable our token passing algorithm to coordinate the controllers. For uncoordinated and coordinated learning, we initialize the probabilities in each controller to $\frac{1}{5} = 0.2$ such that each action is equally likely.

In all experiments, we plot the *dft* (deviation from target) versus time. If $dft < 0$ this signifies that the application did not meet its SLO and a $dft > 0$ indicates that the application performed better than its SLO. Ideally, the $dft = 0$ throughout the duration of the experiment.

OLTP-A: In the first experiment, we run 4 instances of OLTP-A, two on each of our physical servers in our experimental setup. Since all workloads are identical, the optimal configuration is 0.5 at P_A, 0.5 at P_B and 0.5 at P_S. Figure 4 shows the performance of OLTP-A when allocations were optimally chosen. We show the results of all four OLTP-A instances. Since there is no learning stage, the allocations are met from the beginning of the experiment. In the second experiment, we fixed $P_A = 0.5$ and $P_B = 0.5$ and we used our controller to determine P_S. Figure 5 shows that the storage controller initially explores the solution space. At about the 300 second mark, the controller converges to the optimal action. After convergence, each application is on target with slight variations due to the adaptive and exploratory nature of the controller.

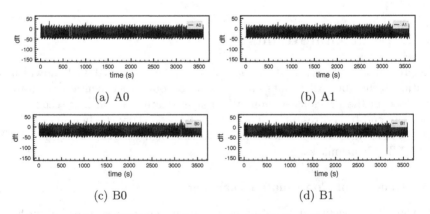

(a) A0   (b) A1

(c) B0   (d) B1

Fig. 4. OLTP-A performance using Optimal Settings

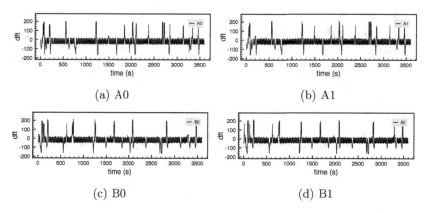

(a) A0   (b) A1

(c) B0   (d) B1

Fig. 5. OLTP-A performance using Single Learner

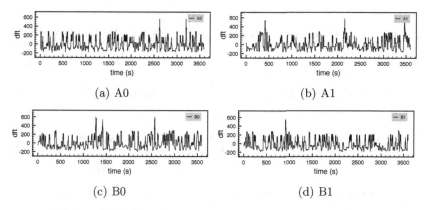

(a) A0   (b) A1

(c) B0   (d) B1

Fig. 6. OLTP-A performance using Uncoordinated Learning

As shown in Figure 6, the uncoordinated controllers are not able to converge within the duration of the experiment. Given the duration of the experiment of almost one hour, each SLO violation shown in the figure is of substantial amplitude, on the order of minutes in duration, and occurs roughly every 5-10 minutes. Hence, the QoS provided is unacceptable, and performance of all applications is poor. In contrast, as Figure 7 shows, the token passing algorithm allows the controllers to converge to an optimal allocation. At about the 2000 second mark, the three controllers arrive at the optimal solution and the performance of each application reaches its target. We observe that the token passing algorithm slows the learning process since each controller can run only while holding the token.

DBT-2/OLTP-A: We run DBT-2 with one OLTP-A workload on one physical server and 2 OLTP-A workloads on the second server. For DBT-2, we set the SLO at 80% percent its throughput running alone in the system (as measured in transactions/minute, TPM) and we classify it as a high priority application. We classify all OLTP-A workloads as best effort. With these requirements, our

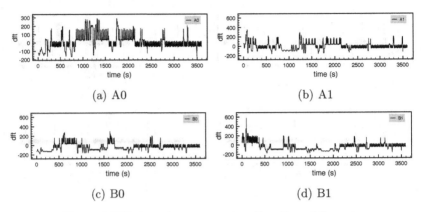

(a) A0   (b) A1

(c) B0   (d) B1

Fig. 7. OLTP-A performance, using Coordinated Learning

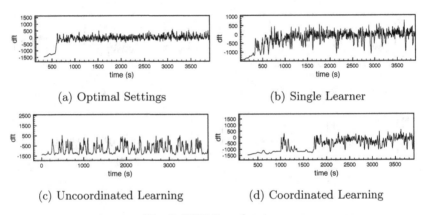

(a) Optimal Settings   (b) Single Learner

(c) Uncoordinated Learning   (d) Coordinated Learning

Fig. 8. DBT-2 performance

goal is to satisfy the performance demands of DBT-2 and divide the remaining bandwidth to the OLTP-A workloads.

We run the same four experiments as before. In the first experiment, we set the values of $P_A = 0.9$, $P_B = 0.5$ and $P_S = 0.9$ such that DBT-2 receives $P_A * P_S = 0.9 * 0.9 = 0.81 = 81\%$ of the available storage bandwidth. Figure 8(a) shows that, after an initial warmup stage, DBT-2 quickly reaches the target performance and stays on target for the duration of the experiment.

In the second experiment, we fixed $P_A = 0.9$ and $P_B = 0.5$ but we allow the controller to determine the optimal value of P_S. As shown in Figure 8(b), the storage controller arrives at the optimal configuration after the initial learning stage. This experiment also highlights the resilience of our controller. DBT-2 has an initial warmup stage before it begins to run the measurement stage. In the warmup stage, the workload uses fewer clients thus placing a smaller demand on the system. Therefore, the controller chooses a proportion that is optimal for the warmup stage. When DBT-2 begins the measurement stage, the controller adapts by selecting a different proportion that is optimal for the measurement stage of DBT-2. The results show that, even with the dynamic nature of DBT-2, the controller is able to adapt and arrive at the optimal configuration by the 1000 second mark of the experiment.

As before, the uncoordinated learners are not able to converge to the optimal configuration during our experiment (as shown in Figure 8(c). This results in poor performance for DBT-2, which does not converge to its target performance. In contrast, Figure 8(d) shows that with coordinated learning, the controllers are able to converge to the ideal solution at about the 2000 second mark of the experiment and are able to meet the DBT-2 performance target. The highest probability actions at each level of control after convergence, are close to the ideal proportion settings: 90/10 for DBT-2/OLTP-A, and 50/50 for OLTP-A/OLTP-A for the proportions at the two OS controllers, respectively and 90/10 for the proportions at the storage controller. Thus, while the DBT-2 performance target is achieved, requests from the best effort OLTP-A applications are also serviced.

7 Related Work

Resource allocation is a well known technique for improving system performance. Traditionally, resource scheduling has been achieved using either a *priority-based* mechanism or a *quanta-based* mechanism. Under priority-based mechanisms, applications with low priority are prone to starvation. This makes such mechanisms inappropriate when the objective is to provide per application QoS guarantees. In contrast to priority-based mechanisms, quanta-based scheduling mechanisms guarantee that each transaction acquires a fair portion of the shared resource e.g., as in *lottery scheduling* where processes are assigned *tickets* proportional to their share [21]. However, in this work, administrators need to manually specify the proportions for each application. *Real-rate scheduling*, is another policy with similarities to our own, in which the applications provide the OS scheduler a notion of *progress* through timestamps [9]. Using this information, the real-rate scheduler employs a feedback loop to determine resource requirements and specifies them to a proportion-period scheduler.

Dynamic allocation of the disk bandwidth has been studied to provide QoS at the storage server. Just like in our prototype, SLEDS [8], Façade [12], SFQ [10], and Argon [19] place a scheduling tier above the existing disk scheduler which controls the I/Os issued to the underlying disk. Argon [19] uses a quanta-based scheduler, while SLEDS [8] uses a *leaky-bucket* filter to throttle I/Os from clients exceeding their given fraction. Similarly, SFQ dynamically adjusts the deadline of I/Os to provide fair sharing of bandwidth. Furthermore, Cello [17] and YFQ [6] build QoS-aware disk schedulers, which make low-level scheduling decisions that strive to minimize seek times, as well maintain quality of service. All previous work in this area has studied methods on disk bandwidth allocation at a single level, either at the operating system level or at the storage level. We have shown that layering of several controllers leads to oscillation, hence suboptimal behavior. Through our context aware approach, we coordinate the controllers at both the operating system and at the storage server to provide QoS guarantees. Moreover, our technique is general and can easily be extended to coordinated resource partitioning of different resources e.g., CPU and disk, and/or resource controllers for the same resource located within different tiers.

Resource allocation has also been studied in database systems. Current implementations of DBMS rely on simple policies like Round-Robin for scheduling transaction access to CPU [1,7]. More sophisticated adaptive algorithms providing per-class response time goals for queries of multiple classes have been studied for dynamic buffer pool partitioning [4,5]. On the other hand, I/O scheduling as well as resource allocation to improve application defined metrics have not been studied in detail in database systems.

Finally, *resource containers* and *Virtual Machine Monitors (VMM)* provide mechanisms to enforce resource allocation [2]. For example, the VMWare ESX server employs memory allocation algorithms to facilitate the execution of multiple virtual machines on a system and offers a performance guarantee to each [20]. However, I/O performance isolation at the storage level, which is the main bottleneck in modern enterprise environments, is currently not guaranteed with these mechanisms.

8   Conclusion

We study techniques for enforcing end-to-end Quality of Service for applications in shared server farms. We introduce a unifying approach for controlling application interference for resources at all levels of the storage stack. Our approach uses coordinated learning based on the degree of achievement of high-level per-application service level objectives.

We implement our approach with minimal changes to existing interfaces in a state-of-the-art shared infrastructure using commodity software and hardware components. We focus on dynamically partitioning I/O bandwidth at two levels: the operating system I/O scheduler and the shared storage scheduler.

We evaluate coordinated versus uncoordinated learning as well as coordinated learning versus the optimal manually set configuration for enforcing I/O bandwidth allocations. We show experimentally, using industry standard benchmarks, that our technique converges towards the optimal configuration and is effective in enforcing high-level application SLOs at the storage server.

References

1. Abbott, R.K., Garcia-Molina, H.: Scheduling real-time transactions with disk resident data. In: VLDB, pp. 385–396 (1989)
2. Banga, G., Druschel, P., Mogul, J.C.: Resource containers: A new facility for resource management in server systems. In: OSDI, pp. 45–58 (1999)
3. Barham, P.T., Dragovic, B., Fraser, K., Hand, S., Harris, T.L., Ho, A., Neugebauer, R., Pratt, I., Warfield, A.: Xen and the art of virtualization. In: SOSP, pp. 164–177 (2003)

4. Brown, K.P., Carey, M.J., Livny, M.: Managing memory to meet multiclass workload response time goals. In: VLDB, pp. 328–341 (1993)
5. Brown, K.P., Carey, M.J., Livny, M.: Goal-oriented buffer management revisited. In: Jagadish, H.V., Mumick, I.S. (eds.) SIGMOD Conference, pp. 353–364. ACM Press, New York (1996)
6. Bruno, J.L., Brustoloni, J.C., Gabber, E., Özden, B., Silberschatz, A.: Disk scheduling with quality of service guarantees. In: ICMCS, pp. 400–405 (1999)
7. Carey, M.J., Jauhari, R., Livny, M.: Priority in DBMS Resource Scheduling. In: VLDB, pp. 397–410 (1989)
8. Chambliss, D.D., Alvarez, G.A., Pandey, P., Jadav, D., Xu, J., Menon, R., Lee, T.P.: Performance virtualization for large-scale storage systems. In: SRDS, pp. 109–118. IEEE Computer Society, Los Alamitos (2003)
9. Goel, A., Walpole, J., Shor, M.: Real-rate scheduling. In: IEEE Real-Time and Embedded Technology and Applications Symposium, pp. 434–441. IEEE Computer Society, Los Alamitos (2004)
10. Goyal, P., Vin, H.M., Cheng, H.: Start-time fair queueing: a scheduling algorithm for integrated services packet switching networks. IEEE/ACM Trans. Netw. 5(5), 690–704 (1997)
11. Gulati, A., Merchant, A., Varman, P.J.: pclock: an arrival curve based approach for qos guarantees in shared storage systems. In: Golubchik, L., Ammar, M.H., Harchol-Balter, M. (eds.) SIGMETRICS, pp. 13–24. ACM, New York (2007)
12. Lumb, C.R., Merchant, A., Alvarez, G.A.: Façade: Virtual storage devices with performance guarantees. In: FAST (2003)
13. Narendra, K.S., Thathachar, M.A.L.: Learning Automata: An Introduction. Prentice Hall, Englewood Cliffs (1989)
14. Ozmen, O., Salem, K., Uysal, M., Attar, M.H.S.: Storage workload estimation for database management systems. In: Chan, C.Y., Ooi, B.C., Zhou, A. (eds.) SIGMOD Conference, pp. 377–388. ACM, New York (2007)
15. Padala, P., Shin, K.G., Zhu, X., Uysal, M., Wang, Z., Singhal, S., Merchant, A., Salem, K.: Adaptive control of virtualized resources in utility computing environments. In: EuroSys, pp. 289–302. ACM, New York (2007)
16. Raab, F.: TPC-C - The Standard Benchmark for Online transaction Processing (OLTP). In: Gray, J. (ed.) The Benchmark Handbook. Morgan Kaufmann, San Francisco (1993)
17. Shenoy, P.J., Vin, H.M.: Cello: a disk scheduling framework for next generation operating systems. SIGMETRICS Perform. Eval. Rev. 26(1), 44–55 (1998)
18. Sutton, R.S., Barto, A.G.: Reinforcement Learning: An Introduction. MIT Press, Cambridge (1998),
    http://www.cs.ualberta.ca/~sutton/book/ebook/the-book.html
19. Wachs, M., Abd-El-Malek, M., Thereska, E., Ganger, G.R.: Argon: performance insulation for shared storage servers. In: FAST, Berkeley, CA, USA, pp. 61–76. USENIX Association (2007)
20. Waldspurger, C.A.: Memory Resource Management in VMware ESX Server. In: OSDI (2002)
21. Waldspurger, C.A., Weihl, W.E.: Lottery Scheduling: Flexible Proportional-Share Resource Management. In: OSDI, pp. 1–11 (1994)

SODA: An Optimizing Scheduler for Large-Scale Stream-Based Distributed Computer Systems

Joel Wolf[1], Nikhil Bansal[1], Kirsten Hildrum[1], Sujay Parekh[1], Deepak Rajan[1],
Rohit Wagle[1], Kun-Lung Wu[1], and Lisa Fleischer[2]

[1] IBM T.J. Watson Research Center, Hawthorne, NY 10532, USA
[2] Dartmouth College, Hanover, NH 03755, USA
{jlwolf,nikhil,hildrum,sujay,drajan,rwagle,klwu}@us.ibm.com,
lkf@dartmouth.edu
http://www.ibm.com

Abstract. This paper describes the *SODA* scheduler for *System S*, a
highly scalable distributed stream processing system. Unlike traditional
batch applications, streaming applications are open-ended. The system
cannot typically delay the processing of the data. The scheduler must
be able to shift resource allocation dynamically in response to changes
to resource availability, job arrivals and departures, incoming data rates
and so on. The design assumptions of *System S*, in particular, pose additional scheduling challenges. *SODA* must deal with a highly complex
optimization problem, which must be solved in real-time while maintaining scalability. *SODA* relies on a careful problem decomposition, and
intelligent use of both heuristic and exact algorithms. We describe the design and functionality of *SODA*, outline the mathematical components,
and describe experiments to show the performance of the scheduler.

Keywords: stream processing, scheduling, admission control, flow balancing.

1 Introduction

The authors of this paper are involved in an ambitious project, started in 2003,
known as *System S* [1,2,3,4,5,6]. *System S* is highly scalable distributed computer system middleware designed to handle complex jobs involving enormous
quantities of streaming data. A prototype of this system has been built and
continues to evolve.

Early examples of distributed stream processing systems have mostly involved
relational databases augmented with streaming operations [7,8,9,10]. In contrast, *System S* supports arbitrarily complex processing, both in terms of the
design of the basic units of computational software, known as *processing elements* (PEs), and the way in which these PEs are interconnected via streams.
Additionally, when designing *System S* a key assumption was that the offered
load would far exceed system capacity much of the time. Therefore it is expected
that the processing nodes in *System S* will need to be utilized as close to fully

V. Issarny and R. Schantz (Eds.): Middleware 2008, LNCS 5346, pp. 306–325, 2008.

as possible. Scheduling in such a complex, overloaded streaming environment is challenging problem and requires novel solution techniques.

This overview paper describes the *System S* scheduler, known as *SODA*. (*SODA* stands for *Scheduling Optimizer for Distributed Applications*.) We motivate the design of the scheduler, emphasizing its objectives and functionality. We describe the four major mathematical components of *SODA* at a relatively high level: Space considerations prevent us from giving complete details, but we refer the interested reader to [11]. We sketch three infrastructure components which provide critical *SODA* input. Finally, we describe a number of experiments which illustrate *SODA* performance.

1.1 *SODA* Objectives and Functionality

In contrast with more traditional jobs, stream processing jobs are typically openended. A stream job could in theory continue to execute as long as input data are available. As a result, standard scheduling metrics involving completion times and/or makespan are no longer relevant. Figure 1(a) shows the *data flow graph* of a typical *System S* stream processing job. The PEs of the job are the nodes in the digraph, and streams, in turn, correspond to the directed arcs. Such digraphs are typically acyclic, as is the case in this figure. Thus, given a topological ordering, processing of data by the job will proceed from left to right. One can make a reasonable analogy to a factory assembly line. Raw packets enter in *primal* streams at the left. (Primal streams originate externally to systems.) Processing proceeds through the various PEs along the way, with streams carrying the progressively more "finished" packets. The final product or products is produced at the right of the data flow graph, where *sink PEs* consume the final products and possibly interface with the external (non-*System S*) world to deliver these results. The final streams flowing into the sink PEs are called *terminal streams*, and denoted with a star in Figure 1(a). This motivates our choice of objective function: *SODA* schedules to maximize a utility-theoretic function based on the "importance" measured at the terminal streams of the data flow graphs. We will give a formal definition of importance in Section 3, but it is typically based on a quantity or quality measure of the stream.

Each PE can only be expected to run satisfactorily if the processing power allocated to it is within some acceptable range. Thus the overloaded nature of

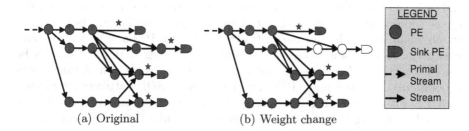

(a) Original   (b) Weight change

Fig. 1. Job Data Flow Graph

System S motivates an important scheduler function: *SODA* must be prepared to reject some jobs. Otherwise some PEs may not be given their minimum acceptable allocations. Some distributed stream processing systems employ load shedding to deal with momentary processing node overload conditions [12], but we know of no other actual systems which consider job admission. When the system is frequently rather than rarely overloaded, shedding load is not enough. Job admission is essential.

Technically, *System S* may provide *SODA* with more than one data flow graph per job. Each such alternative data flow graph is known as a *template*. There might, for example, be a higher and a lower quality template. The natural trade-off is that the higher quality template would require more processing resources than the lower quality one. The templates themselves could be very similar or very different. So an additional and novel function of *SODA* is the decision of which template to choose for each admitted job.

Optimizing the allocation of processing resources to the PEs in the chosen templates of the accepted jobs is extremely difficult for two reasons. The first reason is the highly interconnected (producer/consumer) nature of the PEs, potentially even across jobs. These PEs are *not* independent. The resources allocated to a PE which produces a stream affects the resources required for the PE(s) that consume that stream. Flow imbalances can lead on one hand to buffer overflows (and loss of data), and on the other to under-utilization of processing nodes. The second reason is again the overloaded nature of *System S*. In an underloaded system, flow imbalances simply matter less. A PE can use more of its allotted resources if needed because the resources are likely to be available. But in an overloaded system, there is no margin for error. Thus the scheduler must be parsimonious and carefully balance the allocated resources. We know of no other schedulers for distributed stream processing systems which perform this flow balanced resource allocation optimization.

Finally, *SODA* assigns the PEs in the chosen templates of the accepted jobs to processing nodes. Here there is a tradeoff between the load on the processing nodes and stream traffic on the network. Assigning two PEs connected by a stream to the same processing node eliminates the contribution of that stream to network traffic, but may contribute instead to overloading the processing node. So *SODA* attempts to achieve a balanced placement that does not overload either network links or node capacities. In fact, it attempts to minimize a weighted average of six separate metrics associated with processing loads on the nodes and traffic on the network links. The assignment problem is made more complex by the addition of many special constraints imposed by *System S*. These include, among many others, hardware constraints for certain PEs and nodes (*resource matching*), security and license constraints, constraints that pairs of PEs be placed together (*colocation*), or that pairs of PEs be placed on distinct nodes (*exlocation*). Of course, many PEs may share a node. *SODA* attempts to provide each PE with a fraction of the processing power of any node to which it is assigned, matching as closely as possible the overall PE flow balancing goals already computed.

To summarize, the functionality of the *SODA* scheduler for *System S* includes:

- **Job admission.** *SODA* determines which jobs should be accepted and which jobs should be rejected.
- **Choice of templates.** For those jobs which are accepted *SODA* chooses the template alternative which is most appropriate for the amount of resources available.
- **PE resource allocation.** *SODA* determines how many resources to allocate to each PE in the chosen template of an accepted job.
- **PE fractional assignment.** *SODA* assigns each PE in the chosen template of an accepted job to fractions of one or more processing nodes.

Additionally, *SODA* optimizes two key metrics as it makes its scheduling decisions:

- **Importance.** *SODA* attempts to maximize a utility-theoretic measure of the "goodness" of the work in the system.
- **Resource utilization.** *SODA* attempts to balance the load across all resources (node processing capacity, network bandwidth) in the system by minimizing a weighted average of metrics that model resource utilization.

1.2 *SODA* Design Overview

Another original design requirement for *System S* was the ability to react quickly in a highly dynamic environment. Data rates may change suddenly and dramatically; new jobs may be submitted; jobs may be canceled. The available resources may also change: Processing nodes may go offline; new nodes may go online. Even the notion of what is important may change. The scheduler must be able to incrementally adjust the set of admitted jobs, the PE resource allocations and the fractional assignments to accommodate these changes.

For this reason *SODA* is an *epoch*-based scheduler. At the beginning of each epoch, *SODA* obtains as input a snapshot of the current system state, including the jobs running on the system and the jobs waiting to be admitted. It then computes for most of an epoch, finally outputting its scheduling decisions at the end of the epoch. That is, it produces a list of accepted and rejected jobs. For the accepted jobs it produces a choice of templates and a set of fractional allocations of the PEs to processing nodes. Those decisions are enforced by *System S* during the following epoch, and the entire process repeats indefinitely. Epoch lengths are a *SODA* settable parameter, but epochs on the order of a minute are typical. This is a reasonable compromise between the staleness of the input data and the time required for the mathematical components of *SODA* to make high quality decisions.

To make the scheduling problem tractable, each *SODA* epoch is divided into four mathematical phases. For reasonably sized *System S* installations they are solved sequentially. Each of the four phases corresponds to a mathematical optimization module. The first two phases are known collectively as the *macro* model, while the second two are known as the *micro* model.

- The *macro model* chooses the jobs that will be admitted, the templates for those jobs, and the so-called *candidate* nodes to which the PEs in those jobs and templates can be assigned. These candidate nodes are a subset of the resource matched nodes, chosen to balance system load and simultaneously respect various constraints (security, licensing, colocation, exlocation and so on). The point is that candidate node choices made in the macro model are respected by the subsequent micro model, and this makes the decisions of the micro model easier and more effective.
- The *micro model* chooses the fractional allocations of the PEs in the jobs and templates that have been chosen by the macro model. Fractional allocations of PEs are 0 for a particular node *unless* that node has been chosen as a candidate node by the macro model. For this reason the *micro* model does not have to consider the difficult constraints handled in the macro model: They are satisfied automatically.

Within both the *macro* and *micro* model, the first (*quantity*) phase computes the resource allocation goals, and the second (*where*) phase computes the actual assignments. For this reason the four mathematical phases in *SODA* are known as *macroQ*, *macroW*, *microQ*, and *microW*, respectively. These decouplings make solving the individual optimization problems more efficient.

The remainder of this paper is organized as follows. In Section 2 we give an overview of *System S*. Section 3 contains a glossary of key new terms used by *SODA*. Understanding these terms is critical to following the overviews of the four mathematical components in Section 4. In Section 5 we describe experiments showing the performance benefits of the *SODA* scheduler. Section 6 contains a brief review of related work. Conclusions and future work are given in Section 7.

2   Overview of *System S*

We briefly describe some key components of *System S*. Readers are referred to [4,6] for more details. *System S* is distributed stream processing middleware, and its components provide efficient services to enable the simultaneous execution of multiple stream processing jobs on a large cluster of machines. A functional prototype of *System S* exists on a Linux cluster consisting of about 125 nodes interconnected by a Gigabit switched Ethernet network.

Aside from *SODA*, key run-time components of *System S* include the *Job Manager (JMN)* and the *Stream Processing Core (SPC)*. The JMN is a framework upon which job management, dispatching and node control are built. The JMN consists of a central orchestrator, a *Master Node Controller (MNC)*, and a *Resource Manager (RMN)*. Providing the execution and communication substrate for System S, the SPC consists of four major components: the *Dataflow Graph Manager (DGM)*, the *Data Fabric (DF)*, the *Node Controller (NC)*, and the *PE Execution Container (PEC)*. The DGM determines stream connections among PEs and matches descriptions of output ports with the flow specifications of input ports. The DF is the distributed data transport component, consisting of a set of daemons, one on each node. The NC manages PEC agents, and each

PEC manages one or more PEs. The PEC provides a run-time context and acts as a security barrier, preventing the user-written applications from corrupting the *System S* middleware as well as each other.

Each job can be described by one or more data flow graphs, as shown in Figure 1(a). The nodes in the directed graph correspond to the PEs, and the arcs to the streams. (One stream may show up as several arcs with the same source.) The PEs consume and produce data streams through their input and output ports, respectively. These data flow graphs are defined in a *job configuration* file, and specify how different PEs are to be connected via *flow specifications*. Stream connections are created between input and output ports based on a publish-subscribe model. *System S* dynamically determines the PE connections at run-time by matching stream data types with flow specifications. This allows PEs to discover new streams that match their flow specifications whenever such streams become available, allowing an application designer to avoid hard-wiring PE connections.

3 Glossary of Key New *SODA* Terms

SODA employs a number of terms that have very specific meanings to the scheduler. We list these below, with explicit definitions. The first two items, the *value function* and *weight*, are the key components of the third item, *importance*. Importance, in turn, is the metric that *SODA* tries to maximize. The fourth item, the *resource function (RF)*, is the atomic unit by which we iteratively compute this notion of importance. Finally, *rank*, the fifth item, is an orthogonal notion to importance: It is a priority metric assigned to each job; the lower the better. Jobs which produce little importance but have a low rank may get done *instead* of jobs which have more importance but have a higher rank.

Each derived stream produced by a potential *System S* job has a *value function* associated with it. This is an arbitrary non-negative real-valued function. The domain of this function might typically be the projected rate of the stream. Or it might instead be a stream quality measure, such as projected goodput. In theory it could be a cross product of a variety of quantity, quality and even other "goodness" measures. The definition is intentionally general, though early *SODA* instances have employed rate-based value functions. Also note that value functions which are 0 everywhere will typically predominate: Although the notion is also intentionally general we expect to see non-trivial value functions mostly on terminal streams of various jobs. These are, of course, the "end products" of *System S* work, and one would thus naturally want to measure goodness there.

Each derived stream produced by a potential *System S* job also has a *weight* associated with it. This is a non-negative real number. Non-trivial weights will also typically be quite sparse, as the weight may as well be 0 unless the stream also has a non-zero value function. Weights are automatically assigned based on job topology unless explicitly set by the user.

Each derived stream produced by a potential *System S* job has an *importance* which is the product of the weight and the value function. Importance is therefore a function of the rate or quality of the stream, which in turn depends on the resources allocated to all the upstream PEs – those PEs which helped to produce the stream. The summation of this importance over all derived streams is the *overall importance* being produced by *System S*, and this is what *SODA* attempts to maximize. (Again, a large majority of streams will typically not contribute to this importance metric.) Consider Figure 1 again. In Figure 1(a), all starred streams have positive weights. But in Figure 1(b) the second weight has been changed to 0. It follows that the 2 PEs immediately upstream of that weight cannot do work which contributes to overall importance. *SODA* will therefore not allocate resources to them. (Other PEs, further upstream, do useful work in support of streams with positive weights. They may get fewer resources than they would in the previous figure, but not necessarily none.) Weights are thus an easy "knob" to turn on and off portions of a job and also a way to adjust relative importance.

If importance is the metric to be maximized, the natural question is how to compute it. The first part of the answer is as follows: Each derived stream s in *System S* (and by approximate terminology the PE that produces that stream) has an *RF* associated with it. The *RF* is multidimensional. If there are n input streams to the producer PE, then the *RF* has $n + 1$ input parameters. There is one parameter for each of the input streams, each with the same domain as the value function. These measure the goodness of the respective input streams. The final input dimension is the (computational) resources which may be allocated to the PE, in *millions of instructions per second* (mips). The output of this function is again in terms of the same domain, and measures the goodness of stream s. See, for example, Figure 2. Assuming the domain to be rate-based, the *RF* for stream s_4 takes 4 parameters as input. The first three are the rates of streams s_1 through s_3, and the fourth is the *mips* allocated to PE 4. The output is the rate of stream s_4. The *RF* needs to be learned over time by a *SODA* infrastructure component known as the *Resource Function Learner (RFL)*. The *RFL* component provides crucial input data for *SODA* and is the subject of continuing research.

The second part of computing importance involves iteratively traversing the data flow graphs from "left" to "right", ending in a final value function calculation. Consider Figure 3. By topologically sorting [13] a directed acyclic graph, we can apply ready list scheduling [14] to compute the importance for stream s_5. In the figure three *RF*s are initially ready because they are fed by primal

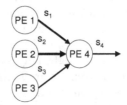

Fig. 2. The resource function for s_4 takes the *mips* of PE 4 and rates of s_1, s_2, and s_3 as input

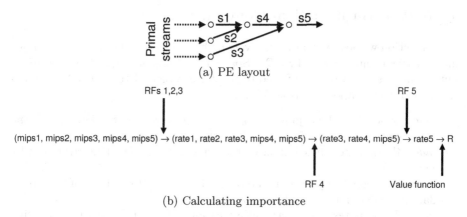

(a) PE layout

(b) Calculating importance

Fig. 3. Calculation of Importance

streams. So we obtain the rates at streams s_1 through s_3. Then an additional *RF* becomes ready (because its inputs have been computed), and we obtain the rate at stream s_4. Next we compute the rate at stream s_5. Finally we apply the weighted value function at s_5 to obtain importance. (*SODA* can also handle data flow graphs with cycles, but we omit details.)

Each job in *System S* has a *rank*, a positive integer which is used to determine whether the job should be run at all. The importance, on the other hand, determines the amount of resources to be allocated to each job that will be run. A lower job rank is better than a higher one. *SODA* admits jobs such that there is a specific job rank for which the following holds: All jobs with lower ranks are admitted, and all jobs with higher ranks are not admitted. Jobs with that rank may or may not be admitted, depending on the available resources and the importance associated with the (streams of the) jobs themselves. We call this property *rank-legality*. (This statement is a slight simplification, since one needs to account for inter-job dependencies.) Figure 4 shows job admission in two different load conditions. Each of the alternatives is rank-legal.

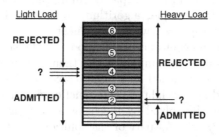

Fig. 4. Rank-Legal Job Admission

4   *SODA* Mathematical Components

In this section we describe, at a relatively high (qualitative) level, the four major mathematical components of *SODA*. Space limitations prevent a full exposition, but the interested reader is referred to [11] for complete details. The basic functionality of the components is as follows.

- *macroQ* decides which jobs to admit, which templates to choose, and the processing power goals for each PE in those jobs and templates.
- *macroW* computes the candidate processing nodes for the PEs given to it by *macroQ*.
- *microQ*, revises the processing power goals for the PEs in light of the candidate node decisions made by *macroW*.
- *microW* computes the fractional allocations of the PEs to the processing nodes based on the output of *macroW* and *microQ*.

Each *SODA* component has an internal *deadline*. Remember that *SODA* has slightly less than one epoch to solve the *macroQ*, *macroW*, *microQ* and *microW* problems. So the *SODA* scheduler itself has a scheduler.

4.1   *macroQ*

The *macro quantity* model, *macroQ*, finds a set of jobs to admit during the next epoch. For each admitted job it chooses a template from among the alternatives given to it. The jobs have ranks, and the jobs that are chosen by *macroQ* must respect the rank-legality constraint. Required jobs must be admitted. Minimum and maximum PE *mips* constraints must also be respected. The goal of the *macroQ* model is to maximize the projected importance of the streams produced by the admitted jobs and chosen templates. There is a total amount of processing power in the system, namely the sum of the power of all the processing nodes.

Thus *macroQ* becomes a resource allocation problem (RAP) [15]. We solve a discrete version of the RAP. So we divide the total processing power of the system into units of equal sized resolution. Also assume a specific rank-legal set of jobs and templates. The data flow graphs of these jobs and templates may be interconnected, and we form a digraph by gluing them together appropriately. *macroQ* is a divide and conquer algorithm, and the division is based on the partitioning of this digraph into weak components.

So consider for the moment one such component. The corresponding discrete RAP within the PEs of that component can then be solved. Note that the objective function can be regarded as a "black box", calculated by iterative *RF* compositions followed by a weighted value function calculation, as noted in Section 3. This RAP can be solved by a scheme known as *Non-Serial Dynamic Programming (NSDP)* [15]. As part of the solution we obtain the optimal importance for each level of resolution up to the total resources in the system.

Having performed this NSDP on *each* component we now consider the problem of optimizing over *all* components. The good news here is that the problem is a *separable* RAP. Separability here means that each summand is a function of a single decision variable, and such resource allocation problems are inherently easier to solve. In fact, if the component importance functions happen to be *concave* the problem can be solved by fast algorithms due to Fox or Galil and Megiddo. If the component importance functions, on the other hand, are not concave, the problem may still be solved by dynamic programming. See [15] for details on all of these algorithms. It turns out that concavity is not an uncommon condition for our component importance functions. So *macroQ* tests each component for concavity and employs the fastest combinations of these algorithms depending on the results.

At the end of this step we have computed the optimal *mips* allocations for each PE. But this can be regarded as just the inner loop of a three step nested process. In the central loop we evaluate all rank-legal templates. In the outer loop we evaluate successively finer resolution granularities.

The evaluation of all rank-legal templates is obviously exponential [13] in nature, though most jobs, in fact, only have a single template. The rank-legality constraints adds another exponential term, but these calculations can be streamlined, depending on the *macroQ* deadline.

The resolution granularity loop is simple in nature: *macroQ* starts with a coarse resolution to obtain a quick solution. Then it uses the time already spent to estimate the finest resolution it believes it can solve in the time remaining, subject to a reasonable minimum *mips* value. It outputs the best importance found, typically the finer resolution.

4.2   *macroW*

The *macro where* model, *macroW*, inputs from *macroQ* the set of resource allocation goals for PEs in chosen templates of admitted jobs, as well as the estimates of stream traffic between pairs of those PEs. The goal of *macroW* is to find a balanced allocation of these PEs to candidate nodes. Recall that these candidate nodes are a subset of the resource matched nodes, and that these choices will be respected by the *micro* model. These candidate nodes need to respect a large number of constraints, including several types of security and licensing constraints, memory, colocation and exlocation, limits on the maximum PEs per node, maximum degrees of parallelism for each PE, fixed PEs, and incremental constraints.

To balance between the processing node and the bandwidth usage, *macroW* minimizes a weighted average of six separate metrics: These consist of the average and maximum estimated utilizations of the processing nodes, the average and maximum projected bandwidth of any network link, and the average and maximum projected utilization of any processing node's network interface.

macroW uses a two-pronged approach. First, the problem is modeled as a mixed-integer optimization program [16], and solved using a state-of-the-art commercial software CPLEX [17]. But the structure of the problem lends itself to a local search heuristic. So we have also developed a submodule of *macroW*, known as *miniW*, to do local search on the space of PE candidate node assignments. This serves as a back-up to the *macroW* solution, and as a post-processing heuristic to the "exact" solution provided by CPLEX.

In fact this heuristic has several advantages:

- Fault-tolerance: In case the CPLEX-based solution fails, the heuristic provides a backup solution.
- Robustness: For large problem instances, integer programming may be slow and not converge by the *macroW* deadline. Thus, an alternative that always produces a (possibly sub-optimal) solution quickly is crucial.
- Accuracy: Traffic components of the linear programming (LP) formulation are inherently quadratic in nature, and this results in weak LP relaxations being used by our CPLEX-based *macroW*. For large problem instances some of these non-linearities are ignored for smaller streams. A good solution to a more accurate model may be better than an exact solution to a less accurate one.

We describe the phases of *miniW* briefly.

First, a *preprocessing* phase shrinks the problem size. In particular, PEs with fixed candidate node assignments are removed, and appropriate bookkeeping is performed to reduce the remaining processing power of the relevant nodes. Likewise, streams whose PEs are fixed are removed, and the bandwidth on the relevant network links are reduced. Processing nodes which are down or fully utilized are removed from the problem as well. The reduced problem is often of much smaller size than the original, yielding significant time savings.

Next, the *initialization* phase provides a first feasible solution. There are several algorithms implemented here. In one example, streams are sorted based on traffic, and processing nodes sorted in terms of available load. Then, the PEs in these streams are mapped to the nodes, while ensuring feasibility. Another example is a round-robin approach: First, PEs from previous epochs are assigned to their previous candidate nodes. (This avoids incremental movement constraints as much as possible.) The remaining PEs are assigned to candidate nodes in round-robin fashion, again ensuring feasibility. A round-robin approach attempts to ensures that no processing node is overly loaded in terms of number of allocated PEs. All these solutions are compared with the solution obtained via CPLEX, and the best solution is used as a starting point for the next phase.

In the *local improvement* phase, *miniW* attempts to iteratively improve the solution by a variety of techniques. It may move a single PE from one candidate node to another, provided that move is feasible and the objective function decreases. (In the neighborhood search literature this is traditionally called a *1-opt* move.) The algorithm may try swapping the candidate nodes of two PEs. (This is a 2-opt move.) It may assign two PEs connected by a stream to the same candidate node. (This is also a 2-opt move.) This reduces traffic, but increases node utilization. Finally, it may swap all the PEs on a pair of candidate nodes. Each of these techniques can be helped by judicious orderings of the PEs, streams and processing nodes. The idea is to calculate how important each is to the overall solution, and sort by those metrics. For instance, PEs are ordered by decreasing *mips* requirements, decreasing traffic requirements, or exclusivity. Processing nodes are ordered by decreasing load. Streams are ordered by decreasing traffic requirements, or by decreasing allocation goals of the corresponding PEs.

Finally, there may be a *perturbation* phase. *miniW* is designed to run until it reaches its deadline or cannot improve the solution. So if the local improvement phase reaches a locally optimal solution, *miniW* will perturb that solution, insisting on feasibility but ignoring the fact that the solution does not improve. The same techniques as the local improvement phase are employed, with the hope of escaping the local minimum. The process then continues until the *macroW* deadline is reached.

4.3   *microQ*

The role of *microQ*, the *micro quantity* model, is to adjust the PE processing allocation goals from *macroQ* based on the PE candidate nodes determined in *macroW*. Recall that *macroQ* knows only the total resources available in *System S*, not information on the individual processing nodes. Only *macroW* considers the processing node information. So *microQ* effectively corrects problems that may arise from the decoupling of the *macro* model into two sequential problems.

The PEs are grouped into (weak) components, as per *macroQ*. The desired resource allocation for a particular PE depends on the overall allocation of *mips* to the component that contains it. This connection is described via *pacing constraints* that specify, for each level of allocation of *mips* to the component, the proportion of these *mips* that should be allocated to each PE. For each component, we use *macroQ* to determine a piecewise-linear, concave function which approximately maps the resources allocated to the component to *importance*. The goal is to allocate resources to components to maximize total importance, satisfying the component-PE pacing constraints.

Since this problem is nonlinear, we do not solve it directly. Instead, we take an iterative approach, as follows: We estimate the resource allocation for each component. This determines a set of *linear* pacing constraints to enforce. Now, the problem can be solved as an LP that is actually a network flow problem [16] with these additional pacing constraints. If any component in the solution falls into a linear segments other than the one assumed, we impose the "revised" pacing constraints, and re-solve. The final solution is obtained when the process converges, or when the time allotted to *microQ* runs out.

4.4   *microW*

The goal of *microW*, the *micro where* model, is to make actual fractional assignments of PEs to processing nodes. The idea is to match as closely as possible the overall processing power goals computed for each PE by the *microQ* model, while meeting various constraints on incremental movement and node changes, fixed PEs, legal fractional allocations and so on. One constraint, for example, limits the cumulative amount change in fractional assignment values from the previous epoch. Another does so on a per PE basis, and a third on the number of processing nodes that can be modified during the current epoch.

The *microW* problem is solved via suitably modified techniques borrowed from the network flow literature [16]. We build and maintain a directed graph with three types of nodes:

- On the left side the nodes are the under-allocated PEs, ordered from most under-allocated to least under-allocated.
- In the middle the nodes are the processing nodes themselves.
- On the right side the nodes are the over-allocated PEs, ordered from least over-allocated to most over-allocated.

Directed arcs in this digraph exist if it is possible to push flow for a particular PE from one node of the digraph to another. The *microW* algorithm can be described as a doubly nested loop. The outer loop is performed on the under-allocated PEs, from most under-allocated to least under-allocated. The inner loop is performed on the over-allocated PEs, from most over-allocated to least over-allocated. A shortest path is chosen between the under-allocated PE and the over-allocated PE, and the maximal feasible flow is pushed along this path. After each successful flow push we perform the relevant bookkeeping and maintenance, adjusting the constraints, recomputing the under- and over-allocated PEs and incrementally reconstructing the directed graph. If there are no under- or over-allocated PEs *microW* ends with a perfect solution. The *microW* scheme also ends if flow push failures occur through an iteration of the entire doubly nested loops or if *microW* reaches its deadline.

5   Experimental Evaluation

5.1   Methodology

We evaluate *SODA* in the context of two qualitatively different *System S* applications: LSD [1], and DAC [6]. The LSD application is a large application intended to process high incoming data rates. It is composed of 104 jobs and 737 PEs. The LSD PEs are generally lightweight, but because the final job graph is large and highly connected, producing a flow-balanced schedule is difficult. The DAC application is smaller but provides scheduling challenges because its PEs have a wide range of processing requirements. It consists of six jobs and 51 PEs. For the experiments, the jobs corresponding to each application are submitted to the *System S* cluster, where they are run for ten minutes to collect relevant data. For both these applications, SODA takes less than a minute to compute a solution.

We compare the *SODA* PE placement decisions to three other approaches:

- **Random (RAND):** PEs are assigned to nodes uniformly at random. In expectation, each processing node hosts the same number of PEs, but in fact, the number of PEs hosted by a node may vary quite a bit.
- **Round-robin (RR):** PEs are processed sequentially and each PE is assigned to a node with the minimum PEs assigned so far. This is a very naive load balancing of PEs across the nodes.

- **Expert (EXP):** The application developers for LSD and DAC decide on the number of nodes and an allocation of PEs to nodes based on both their knowledge of the application as well as several trial-and-error runs where all PEs are resource matched to specific nodes. These placements are often tested in underloaded test environments, and cannot be expected to scale to overloaded environments. But they offer a reasonable measure of performance, one that must at least be matched, even in overloaded settings, by the scheduler.

These three schemes only perform PE placement–they do not address admission control, template choice or PE fractional allocations.

We evaluate each scheduler using the following metrics:

- *Ingest rate:* This is a measure of how much data (in Mbps) could be processed by the system. It is intended as a measure of the system's "effective capacity", and should be correlated to importance.
- *Importance:* The importance of a job is measured at the sink PEs as a quantity-based metric that depends on the data rates at the sink PEs. In our experiments, the streams into the sinks have unit weights and identity value functions, while all other streams have zero weights and value functions. As a result, the importance of a job is measured by the data rate flowing into its sink PEs.
- *Stream affinity:* One way to measure the quality of the placement is in terms of the traffic load on the system. We compute the amount of traffic that is sent between PEs on the same node divided by the total traffic. The higher this quantity, the better, since PEs which share a stream should be put on the same node (or nearby) to minimize network utilization.

These metrics are computed from the raw system metrics such as CPU usage per PE and traffic consumed and produced by each PE.

In the experiments below, we test the scheduler performance under different resource conditions ranging from under-provisioned to over-provisioned, which is achieved by varying the number of nodes made available to the scheduler. This allows us to see how the performance will change as the *raw* system capacity changes, and also which scheduler is better at achieving higher system utilizations and better *effective* system capacity. We perform three runs for each combination of scheduler and node pool size, and analyze the average across these runs.

5.2   Results

The carefully constructed EXP placements use 82 nodes for LSD and 30 nodes for DAC. *SODA* uses far fewer nodes yet achieves a higher quality placement than EXP. In particular, *SODA* performs favorably with as few as 30 nodes for LSD and 9 nodes for DAC, 36% and 30% of the number of nodes used in the expert placement, respectively. To compare with these, we also present the results for RAND and RR for two scenarios: 30 and 70 nodes for LSD, and 9 and

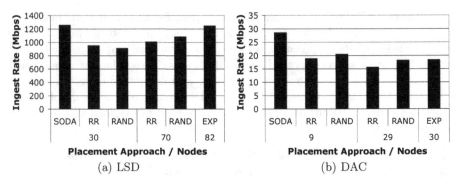

Fig. 5. Ingest rate: LSD and DAC

29 nodes for DAC. These allow us to compare their performance with *SODA*'s placement at one end of the spectrum (less nodes), and with EXP at the other end (more nodes).

Figure 5 compares the ingestion rates of *SODA*, EXP, RR, and RAND. From the figure, we see that *SODA* is able to ingest as much traffic as EXP with far fewer nodes (30) for LSD. For DAC, *SODA* outperforms EXP by over 50% with just 9 nodes. This is largely because EXP seeks to ensure that all PEs receive sufficient MIPS. As a result, the PEs are spread across many more nodes than they need to be, while SODA recognizes that nine nodes is enough and so saves on traffic. For a given node pool size, the *SODA*-computed placement also consistently ingests more traffic than RAND or RR. The performance of both RR and RAND is, not surprisingly, poorer than EXP. For instance, with 70 nodes for LSD, RR is able to ingest 25% less traffic than EXP, and with 29 nodes for DAC, RR is able to ingest 15% less traffic than EXP.

One of the metrics that SODA tries to maximize is the importance. Figure 6 presents the importance of DAC, as optimized by SODA in *macroQ*; recall from Section 3 that in our case this corresponds to the net traffic flowing into the sink PEs. Here, we see that *SODA* matches the performance of EXP in spite of using a third of the nodes. On the other hand, RR and RAND perform more than 10% worse than EXP, even when using 29 nodes. In particular, RR achieves only 84% of the traffic rates at the sinks attained by EXP and SODA.

Another goal of SODA is to ensure the network and nodes are not overloaded. The effect of the schedulers in terms of two system metrics is shown in Figure 7, which plots the stream affinity and maximum load for LSD and DAC. Stream affinity is the fraction of traffic that is sent on streams that have both source and destination PEs on the same node; higher is better. The load is indicated by the maximum CPU utilization across the nodes in the cluster; lower is better. From the figure, we see that *SODA* increases the intra-node traffic fraction without significantly increasing the maximum node load.

Considering traffic, with 30 nodes, the *SODA* placement for LSD sends less than 30% of the traffic over the network (over 70% on the same node); compared to 66% for EXP with 82 nodes. In addition to helping reduce network congestion,

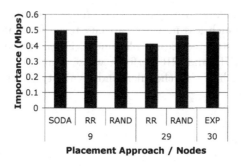

Fig. 6. Importance: DAC

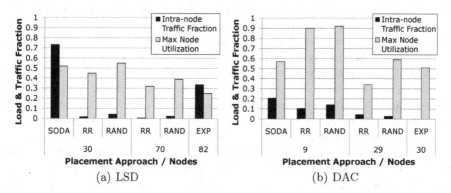

Fig. 7. Placement tradeoffs: LSD and DAC

this also contributes to the stronger throughput results obtained by *SODA*, since the overhead of sending data to a PE on the same node is lower. Naturally, RAND and RR fare poorly on this metric since they do not use stream information in their placement algorithm, and in fact are susceptible to exceeding the network capacity. In particular, for the case of LSD with 30 nodes, *SODA* is able to achieve much higher stream affinity (70%) than RAND and RR (less than 10%) with the comparable maximum loads (around 50%). For DAC, with 9 nodes, *SODA* places 20% more of the traffic on the same node, even though the maximum load is comparable to EXP, resulting in a significantly larger ingest rate.

Now considering load, we see that with DAC, RR and RAND do rather poorly with 9 nodes, by causing some nodes to be highly loaded. This is because the DAC PEs have dramatically different CPU requirements. In contrast, *SODA* balances the PEs across the nodes, thereby resulting in a much lower load, only slightly higher than the EXP with larger number of nodes. For LSD, the PEs are much more uniform, so RR and RAND perform satisfactorily in this metric. SODA results in a slightly higher load, but due to the higher intra-node traffic and more balanced placement, it is nevertheless able to achieve a higher ingest rate. Further, this maximum utilization of 52% is not in the problematic range.

In all our experiments, we observe that *SODA* requires significantly fewer nodes, and utilizes much less network capacity to perform as well, if not better than, a carefully constructed expert placement. Furthermore, we see that naive approaches like RAND and RR perform worse than *SODA* in general. This illustrates the strength of the scheduler, and its ability to schedule effectively in overloaded systems.

6   Related Work

Stream processing systems have been an active area of research in recent years. Example systems include Borealis [7], TelegraphCQ [8], STREAM [9], Aurora and Medusa [10]. These systems process voluminous quantities of incoming stream data, typically performing relational operations such as joins and selections on them. In contrast, *System S* is much more general, allowing arbitrarily complex operators, including relational ones.

Most of these stream processing systems are designed to be run on more than one node, and thus there has also been work on scheduling and load-balancing the operators. While these scheduling approaches have some of the flavor of the work we present here, none targets our problem exactly. We describe some of these related approaches here.

The FIT algorithm [12] is a load-shedding algorithm which intelligently drops load. Determining where best to drop load can be quite a complex problem, since dropping at a particular operator has an effect on the downstream operators, sometimes an unintended one. In some cases, shedding load on a particular operator increases the resources for other operators on that node, and so could *increase* load at nodes downstream. FIT cleverly addresses this problem in a distributed way, but without a global notion of importance. The *SODA* scheduler provides this same functionality as part of its resource allocation and scheduling, and does so in a way that takes into account the processing graph for a job and the total system objectives.

Xing et al. [18, 19] addresses the problem of variance in stream rates. Both papers describe a way to distribute the load so that changes in input rate have a smaller chance of overloading the system. However, they do not address the case when the system is overloaded, and make no decisions about job admission.

Pietzuch et al. [20] provides a scheduling algorithm for a wide-area network that places operators so as to minimize network latency. In the local area network that we address, bandwidth, not network latency, is the main concern. In addition, their work does not address the problem of job admission. Lakshmanan et al. [21] also addresses scheduling to minimize latency.

The STREAM project [22] has goals somewhat similar to those presented in this paper. Their system handles queries in an SQL-like language. When resources are tight, they revise queries by dropping packets and/or changing internal parameters.

Xia et al. [23] address the admission control problem in a hypothetical stream processing system. Their model assumes a linear processing graph. In other words, the input stream is processed, successively, by a series of operators. Thus, no operator takes input from more than one source stream.

7 Conclusions and Future Work

In this paper we have introduced *SODA*, a scheduler for very large-scale distributed stream processing applications. This scheduler is implemented and running as a component in the *System S* project. We have shown that *SODA* is practical, novel, and effective, scheduling as well as or better than expert placement but using well under half the nodes. While schedulers of other stream processing systems have some features of *SODA*, *SODA* is unique in that in addition to allocating processing to nodes, it also controls job admission and weights the resources given to the admitted jobs. This overview paper provides an introduction to the problem, high level descriptions of the solution, and an experimental analysis which demonstrates *SODA*'s performance.

One of the more novel features of *SODA* scheduler is that it can schedule itself as a separate PE. The value function for *SODA* would measure the effect of additional processing resources on solution quality. Giving more resources to *SODA* would make the solution quality better at the possible expense of giving other work in the system more resources. We plan to create a *SODA* PE which can be scheduled in the near future.

Note that the notion of *SODA* scheduling itself is very different from the notion in Section 4 that *SODA* has a scheduler. We plan to improve this *SODA* scheduler as well.

Though *System S* is oriented towards streaming applications, traditional work will invariably be performed as well. So we have created (but not yet integrated) a scheduler for the more traditional sorts of jobs that invariably are needed in any system.

For very large problem instances we expect to design a variant of *SODA* in which epochs are arranged in a two level temporal hierarchy. In this case, the *macro* model will run in a *macro epoch*, and the *micro* model will run in a *micro epoch*. There will be a number of micro epochs in each macro epoch, allowing the computationally expensive *macro* models more time for their optimization. (We have not yet seen problem instances in which this approach would be necessary.) For truly large problems we have a design, not yet fully coded, to partition the work in *SODA*, allowing for vast scaling, though potentially at some loss of accuracy.

System S was built for a traditional packet-based network. But there is actually great affinity between *System S* and circuit switching architectures: Communication between PEs is long-lived, on the order of multiple minutes or more. *Optical Circuit Switches (OCS)* provide all of the benefits of circuit switching and make the bandwidth of the system more flexible. We have developed (and are continuing to refine) an extension to *SODA* that allows it to make *link assignments* (defining the network topology) at the same time it performs its traditional role of making PE candidate assignments. A lab prototype has been built.

References

1. Amini, L., Andrade, H., Bhagwan, R., Eskesen, F., King, R., Selo, P., Park, Y., Venkatramani, C.: SPC: A distributed, scalable platform for data mining. In: International Workshop on Data Mining Standards, Services and Platforms (2006)
2. Douglis, F., Palmer, J., Richards, E., Tao, D., Tetzlaff, W., Tracey, J., Yin, J.: Position: Short object lifetimes require a delete-optimized storage system. In: ACM SIGOPS European Workshop (2004)
3. Hildrum, K., Douglis, F., Wolf, J., Yu, P.S., Fleischer, L., Katta, A.: Storage optimization for large-scale stream processing systems. In: ACM Transactions on Storage (2008)
4. Jain, N., Amini, L., Andrade, H., King, R., Park, Y., Selo, P., Venkatramani, C.: Design, implementation and evaluation of the linear road benchmark on the stream processing core. In: ACM SIGMOD International Conference on Management of Data (2006)
5. Jacques-Silva, G., Challenger, J., Degenaro, L., Giles, J., Wagle, R.: Towards autonomic fault recovery in System-S. In: International Conference on Autonomic Computing (2007)
6. Wu, K.-L., Yu, P.S., Gedik, B., Hildrum, K.W., Aggarwal, C.C., Bouillet, E., Fan, W., George, D.A., Gu, X., Luo, G., Wang, H.: Challenges and experience in prototyping a multi-modal stream analytic and monitoring application on System S. In: International Conference on Very Large Data Bases (2007)
7. Abadi, D.J., Ahmad, Y., Balazinska, M., Cetintemel, U., Cherniack, M., Hwang, J.H., Lindner, W., Maskey, A.S., Rasin, A., Ryvkina, E., Tatbul, N., Xing, Y., Zdonik, S.: The design of the Borealis stream processing engine. In: Conference on Innovative Data Systems Research (2005)
8. Chandrasekaran, S., Cooper, O., Deshpande, A., Franklin, M.J., Hellerstein, J.M., Hong, W., Krishnamurthy, S., Madden, S.R., Raman, V., Reiss, F., Shah, M.A.: TelegraphCQ: Continuous dataflow processing for an uncertain world. In: Conference on Innovative Data Systems Research (2003)
9. Arasu, A., Babcock, B., Babu, S., Datar, M., Ito, K., Motwani, R., Nishizawa, I., Srivastava, U., Thomas, D., Varma, R., Widom, J.: STREAM: The Stanford stream data manager. IEEE Data Engineering Bulletin 26 (2003)
10. Zdonik, S., Stonebraker, M., Cherniack, M., Cetintemel, U., Balazinska, M., Balakrishnan, H.: The Aurora and Medusa projects. IEEE Data Engineering Bulletin 26(1) (2003)
11. Wolf, J., Bansal, N., Hildrum, K., Parekh, S., Rajan, D., Wagle, R., Wu, K.L., Fleischer, L.: Scheduling optimizer for distributed applications: A reference paper. Technical Report 24453, IBM Research Report (2007)
12. Tatbul, N., Çetintemel, U., Zdonik, S.: Staying fit: Efficient load shedding techniques for distributed stream processing. In: International Conference on Very Large Data Bases, pp. 159–170 (2007)
13. Cormen, T., Leiserson, C., Rivest, R.: Introduction to Algorithms. McGraw-Hill, New York (1985)
14. Blazewicz, J., Ecker, K., Schmidt, G., Weglarz, J.: Scheduling in Computer and Manufacturing Systems. Springer, Heidelberg (1993)
15. Ibaraki, T., Katoh, N.: Resource Allocation Problems. MIT Press, Cambridge (1988)
16. Nemhauser, G.L., Wolsey, L.A.: Integer and Combinatorial Optimization. John Wiley and Sons, New York (1988)

17. ILOG: CPLEX, http://www.ilog.com/products/cplex
18. Xing, Y., Hwang, J.H., Çetintemel, U., Zdonik, S.: Providing resiliency to load variations in distributed stream processing. In: International Conference on Very Large Data Bases, VLDB Endowment, pp. 775–786 (2006)
19. Xing, Y., Zdonik, S., Hwang, J.H.: Dynamic load distribution in the Borealis stream processor. In: IEEE International Conference on Data Engineering, Washington, DC, USA, pp. 791–802. IEEE Computer Society, Los Alamitos (2005)
20. Pietzuch, P., Ledlie, J., Shneidman, J., Roussopoulos, M., Welsh, M., Seltzer, M.: Network-aware operator placement for stream-processing systems. In: IEEE International Conference on Data Engineering, Washington, DC, USA. IEEE Computer Society, Los Alamitos (2006)
21. Lakshmanan, G.T., Strom, R.E.: Biologically-Inspired Distributed Middleware Management for Stream Processing Systems. In: Issarny, V., Schantz, R. (eds.) Middleware 2008. LNCS, vol. 5346, pp. 223–242. Springer, Heidelberg (2008)
22. Motwani, R., Widom, J., Arasu, A., Babcokc, B., Babu, S., Datar, M., Manku, G., Olston, C., Rosenstein, J., Varma, R.: Query processing, approximation, and resource management in a data stream management system. In: Conference on Innovative Data Systems Research (2003)
23. Xia, C.H., Towsley, D., Zhang, C.: Distributed resource management and admission control of stream processing systems with max utility. In: ICDCS 2007: Proceedings of the 27th International Conference on Distributed Computing Systems (2007)

Toward Massive Query Optimization in Large-Scale Distributed Stream Systems

Yongluan Zhou[1], Karl Aberer[2], and Kian-Lee Tan[3],[*]

[1] University of Southern Denmark
[2] EPFL, Switzerland
[3] National University of Singapore

Abstract. Existing distributed stream systems adopt a tightly-coupled communication paradigm and focus on fine-tuning of operator placements to achieve communication efficiency. This kind of approach is hard to scale (both to the nodes in the network and the users). In this paper, we propose a fundamentally different approach and present the design of a middleware for optimizing massive queries. Our approach takes the advantages of existing Publish/Subscribe systems (Pub/Sub) to achieve loosely-coupled communication and to "intelligently" exploit the sharing of communication among different queries. To fully exploit the capability of a Pub/Sub, we present a new query distribution algorithm, which can adaptively and rapidly (re)distribute the streaming queries at runtime to achieve both load balancing and low communication cost. Both the simulation studies and the prototype experiments executed on Planet-Lab show the effectiveness of our techniques.

Keywords: Distributed Stream Systems, Publish/Subscribe Systems, Query Optimization, Load Balance, Overlay Network.

1 Introduction

There is a recently emerging demand for large-scale and widely distributed stream processing systems. Below is an example scenario, which is also the application context of this paper.

With the rapid development of sensor network technologies, more and more sensor networks are being deployed by many different organizations, such as research institutes and governments etc., to monitor and study our surrounding environment. The SensorScope project at EPFL (http://sensorscope.epfl.ch) is one such example. One can imagine that a stream processing system would be installed locally at each deployment to perform real-time data collection and analysis. It is desirable to pose queries involving multiple deployments across the border of countries and even continents. This demands a large-scale and loosely-coupled architecture to exploit the autonomous and distributed stream systems to provide a global stream processing service.

---

[*] Kian-Lee Tan is partially supported by research grant R-252-000-237-112 from the National University of Singapore.

V. Issarny and R. Schantz (Eds.): Middleware 2008, LNCS 5346, pp. 326–345, 2008.

While such a system is desirable, two problems should be carefully considered. First, the communication cost could be very high as it may involve inter-country and even inter-continental communication. Moreover, streams are typically of a very high rate and have to be transferred continuously. In comparing to the abundant processing power provided by the large number of servers, network bandwidth is the bottleneck in such a context. Hence, it is critical to perform query optimization to achieve high communication efficiency.

Second, for such an autonomous system, it is desirable to adopt a loosely-coupled communication architecture, where data sources can just push their data to the network without keeping track of the destinations, and a data consumer can retrieve data of its interest without knowing the location of the sources.

1.1   Existing Distributed Stream Systems

In existing distributed stream systems [1,3,13,17,18], the communication between data sources and consumers adopts the tightly-coupled client-server paradigm. A node directly connects to the sources to get the streams it wants. As mentioned, this is not desirable in our context.

Furthermore, operator placement algorithms [1,3,13,17] are often employed to optimize communication efficiency. Such schemes typically adopt a two-phase optimization algorithm, which resembles the earlier work on query optimization for distributed database systems, such as [22]. In the first phase, all the user queries are collected to a central place and then a global operator graph is generated. In the second phase, optimization algorithms are run to distribute the operators to minimize the communication cost [3,17]. Let us look at an illustrating example. Figure 1(a) is an example network composed by seven nodes. Nodes n_7 and n_6 issue two queries Q_1 and Q_2 (written in CQL [23]) respectively. The first phase optimization generates a global operator graph for these two queries as shown in Figure 1(b). Then the second phase may place the operators as depicted in Figure 1(c).

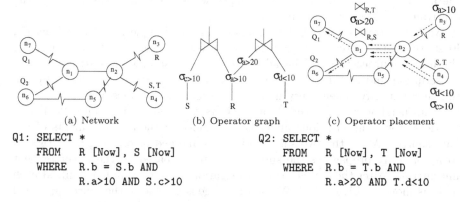

(a) Network   (b) Operator graph   (c) Operator placement

```
Q1: SELECT *
    FROM   R [Now], S [Now]
    WHERE  R.b = S.b AND
           R.a>10 AND S.c>10
```

```
Q2: SELECT *
    FROM   R [Now], T [Now]
    WHERE  R.b = T.b AND
           R.a>20 AND T.d<10
```

Fig. 1. Operator placement

While this approach is effective, it assumes that an optimized global operator graph is available. So far, it lacks scalable algorithm to generate a good global operator graph. It is even harder to maintain the global operator graph if new queries were admitted and old queries were terminated frequently. In addition, the operator placement algorithm assumes the knowledge of the underlying overlay network. This tightens the coupling between the network layer and the application layer which may not be desirable for a large-scale system.

1.2 Pub/Sub Systems

Looking from a different angle, we observe that the above optimization can be divided into three sub-tasks. (1) Avoid duplicate data transfer. In the above example, both Q_1 and Q_2 are interested in stream R. It is desirable to send the data of R only once over each link along the path to the destinations. This can be done by sharing the data access of stream R of the two queries. (2) Perform early data filtering. In the example, this is done by allocating the selection operators close to the source nodes of the streams. (3) Place the query operators in proper places. The placement should consider the data rate of the operators' input and output as well as the common data interest among the different operators. For example, in Figure 1(c), the two join operators are allocated to the same place. Hence they can share the bandwidth consumption of transferring data from stream R. Otherwise, if, for example, we place one of the join operators to node n_5 instead, then extra bandwidth will be consumed. Furthermore, if their output rates are much higher than their input rates, then it might be more beneficial to place them at their respective destinations (i.e. n_6 and n_7).

It is interesting to note that the first two sub-tasks have been solved nicely in the literatures of Distributed Publish/Subscribe systems [2,7,16] or Content-Based Networking (CBN) [10]. In these systems, messages are routed based on their contents as well as the interest profiles of nodes rather than the IP addresses of the destinations. Each message is represented as a set of attribute/value pairs. The interest profile (or subscription) of a node is specified as constraints on the attribute values. Only those messages whose attribute values satisfy the constraints will be sent to that node.

We illustrate more details by a scenario in an example Pub/Sub: Siena [7]. First, the data source n_3 in Figure 2(a) advertises the data that it provides through a multicast tree. The advertisement has similar data structure as a subscription and specifies the constraints that the messages produced by the source will satisfy. Then every node knows what kind of messages will be sent from its neighbors. Now, the data receivers (n_6 and n_7 in Figure 2(b)) can multicast their subscriptions under the guidance of the advertisements of the data sources. At n_1 the two subscriptions are merged before being propagated to n_2. n_2 only propagates the subscription to n_3 based on the advertisement information. After the subscription propagation, a routing table is built at each node as shown in Figure 2(c). When a message is produced, the source just send it to the neighbor who is interested in the message. Figure 2(d)shows how two example messages are routed in the network.

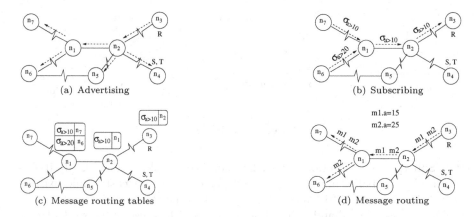

Fig. 2. Distributed Pub/Sub Systems

It can be seen that a Pub/Sub inherits the advantage of the multicast communication paradigm where a message is sent over each link at most once. Furthermore, the messages are filtered as soon as possible on the way to the interested parties. More importantly, this is done without global planning. Finally, data sources and destinations in a Pub/Sub are loosely-coupled as they need not keep track of each other. As mentioned, this is desirable in our context.

1.3   COSMOS

Based on the above observation, we intend to build our distributed stream processing system by using a Pub/Sub as the communication substrate to achieve loosely-coupled communication. We design a middleware, called COSMOS (CO-operated and Self-tuning Management Of Streaming data), which perform query optimization by leveraging the underlying Pub/Sub to accomplish the searching of common data interest of the queries and the global tuning of the placement of filters along the overlay paths (from the sources to the destinations).

Now what is left behind is the third sub-task of the optimization: placing the query operators in the proper locations. To do so, a new query distribution scheme is proposed.

In this paper, we distribute the query loads in the unit of queries (instead of operators) to reduce the complexity of the problem and make the adaptation algorithms run faster at runtime. Furthermore, allocating operators of a query to multiple nodes would require synchronizations among the nodes, including the synchronizations during query processing as well as those during query insertions and removals. This not only impairs the scalability of the system but also hard to be implemented in a loosely-coupled and autonomous system.

Our query distribution scheme distinguishes itself in several aspects: (1) It is more scalable. It does not require global planning to generate a global operator graph. Moreover, new hierarchical techniques are also employed to enhance the algorithm's scalability. (2) It takes the communication characteristics of a

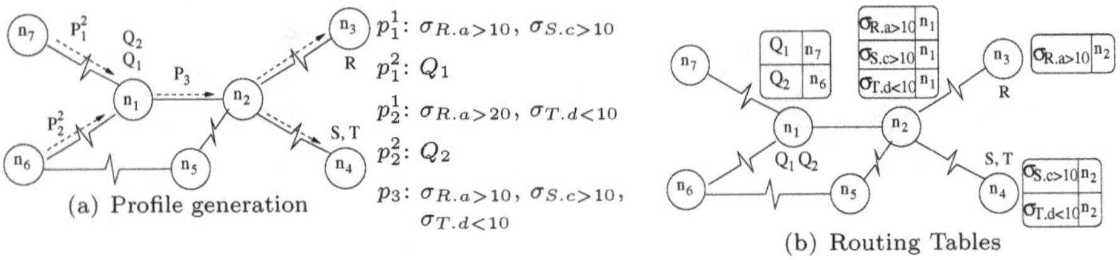

Fig. 3. COSMOS

Pub/Sub into consideration, which has not been explored before. (3) It targets both load-balancing and minimizing communication cost, while existing approaches [3,15,17,20,21,24] only focus on either one of them. (4) It stresses the problem of fast arrival and removal of queries, which is also often overlooked in most existing work.

Figure 3(a) shows an example distribution with both Q_1 and Q_2 distributed to n_1. Then, n_1 will generate two subscriptions for each query. For example, for Q_1, one subscription p_1^1 is generated to retrieve the source data to feed Q_1. Furthermore, another subscription p_1^2 is generated and sent to the query originator n_7. p_1^2 is inserted into the Pub/Sub by n_7 to receive the result stream of Q_1. Similarly p_2^1 and p_2^2 are generated for Q_2. At n_1, the two subscriptions p_1^1 and p_2^1 will be merged into a subscription p_3, which will then be inserted into the Pub/Sub. Figure 3(b) shows the routing tables at each node after all the subscriptions are inserted. Finally, queries are evaluated at n_1 when the data are received from the underlying Pub/Sub. The results will then be transfered by the Pub/Sub to n_6 and n_7 respectively.

In short, we propose a fundamentally different query optimization approach to achieve communication efficiency, which does not require the maintenance of a global operator graph. It leverages Pub/Sub to eliminate duplicate data transfer, to perform early data filtering and to achieve loose-coupling of data sources from data consumers.

1.4   Paper Layout

The rest of the paper is organized as follows. We first present an overview of the system in Section 2. The load distribution scheme is presented in Sections 3. Section 4 presents the results of a performance study of the load distribution scheme. Section 5 concludes the paper.

2   System Overview

The whole system consists of a number of, say N, distributed processors interconnected with a widely distributed overlay network. In addition, a number of data sources continuously publish their data to the network through the processors. A user first connects to a processor, which works as the proxy for him. In this case, the user and the proxy are said to be local to each other. User queries,

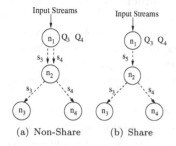

Input Streams   Input Streams

(a) Non-Share   (b) Share

Fig. 4. Result stream delivery

Table 1. Example queries

Q_3:	SELECT	S2.*
	FROM	Station1 [Range 30 Minutes] S1, Station2 [Now] S2
	WHERE	S1.snowHeight > S2.snowHeight S1.snowHeight $\geq$ 10
Q_4:	SELECT	S1.snowHeight, S1.timetamp, S2.snowHeight, S2.timestamp
	FROM	Station1 [Range 1 Hour] S1, Station2 [Now] S2
	WHERE	S1.snowHeight > S2.snowHeight
Q_5:	SELECT	S2.*, S1.snowHeight, S1.timestamp
	FROM	Station1 [Range 1 Hour] S1, Station2 [Now] S2
	WHERE	S1.snowHeight > S2.snowHeight

specified in an SQL-like language similar to CQL [23], are submitted through their proxies. The proxy is also responsible for retrieving the result stream and sending it back to the user. For simplicity, only continuous queries are considered and no stored tables are involved. The query is first passed to the COSMOS middleware, which places the query at an appropriate processor to optimize the system performance. This paper focuses on solving this optimization problem.

The delivery of data streams are handled by the Pub/Sub middleware, which is assumed to support subscriptions similar to those in Siena [7]. Below, we use an example to illustrate how COSMOS leverage the Pub/Sub component.

2.1 An Illustrating Example

Table 1 lists a few queries specified using CQL [23]. These queries are extracted and simplified from the typical snow drift monitoring tasks performed by the environmental scientists.

Let us first look at Q_3. Assume it is distributed to a processor, say n_1, by COSMOS. Then the COSMOS component at n_1 generates two subscriptions. The first one, p_1^3, will be used by n_1 to fetch the source data requested by Q_3 via the Pub/Sub component. The content of p_1^3 contains the following:

- A list of streams that are requested by Q_3: $\mathcal{S} = \{S1, S2\}$. This is used by the Pub/Sub to select the data based on their source stream.
- A list of requested data attributes: $\mathcal{P} = \{S2.*\}$. The Pub/Sub can perform projection of the unnecessary attributes as soon as possible to reduce the network traffic.
- A list of filters: $\mathcal{F} = \{S1.snowHeight > 10\}$. This will be used to perform early data filtering in the Pub/Sub.

The second subscription, p_2^3, is generated for the user to fetch the query result stream. To do so, a unique stream name is created for the result stream (by using the unique identifier of the processor n_1, such as the IP address). Then p_2^3 contains this stream name.

Assume another user submits another query Q_4 to the system (the second query in Table 2), which is also allocated to processor n_1. We can generate the first subscription, p_1^4, in a similar way. Pub/Sub can automatically perform data communication sharing.

The tricky part is the second subscription, p_2^4. A naive way is to generate separate result stream for Q_4. Hence we can use the unique name of Q_4's result stream to compose p_2^4. This situation is shown in Figure 4(a). The result streams of Q_3 and Q_4, i.e. s_3 and s_4 are transfered separately to the two users' proxies, n_3 and n_4, respectively.

However, it can be easily seen that the result streams of Q_3 and Q_4 could have significant overlapping contents. Therefore these common contents have been transferred twice over the link between n_1 and n_2 in the above scheme. To further reduce the cost, we should exploit the sharing of result stream delivery.

At each site, if there are multiple queries with overlapping results, the COS-MOS component will compose a new query Q whose result is the superset of the overlapping queries and only inserts this Q into the processing engine. In our example, Q_5 (the third query in Table 1) would be created and inserted into the processing engine at node n_1 instead of the two individual queries Q_3 and Q_4. As shown in Figure 4(b), Q_5 is run in n_1 and its result stream $s5$ is sent to n_2, where it is "split" into two streams. The "splitting" is fulfilled by composing appropriate subscriptions for the users to retrieve their results. In our example they can be composed as follows:

- p_2^3: $\mathcal{S}=\{s_5\}, \mathcal{P}=\{S2.*\}, \mathcal{F} = \{-30(minute) \leq S1.timestamp - S2.timestamp \leq 0$ AND $S1.snowHeight \geq 10\}$.
- p_2^4: $\mathcal{S} = \{s_5\}, \mathcal{P} = \{S1.snowHeight, S1.timetamp, S2.snowHeight, S2.timestamp\}, \mathcal{F} = \{-1(hour) \leq S1.timestamp - S2.timestamp \leq 0\}$

To implement this approach, we extend traditional query containment and equivalence theorems to continuous window-based queries. Readers can refer to [25] for more details of this approach.

3   Query Distribution

In this section, the details of the query distribution algorithms in the COSMOS middleware is presented. For ease of exposition, it is assumed that a data source is also a processor in this paper. Hence, we refer to all the nodes in the network as processors. The word "data source" refers to those processors which are the origins of one or more source streams.

In the following subsections, we first present the theoretical model of the problem and then present the proposed solution.

3.1   Problem Modeling

In the problem model, we assume we do not have the knowledge of the overlay network topology of the Pub/Sub component. This is to achieve loose coupling between the components.

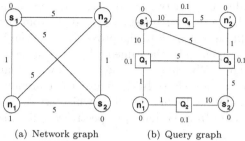

(a) Network graph   (b) Query graph

Table 2. Mapping Schemes

	Scheme	Load	WEC
Scheme 1	$Q_1, Q_2 \to n_1$	n_1: 0.2	165
	$Q_3, Q_4 \to n_2$	n_2: 0.2	
	$s_i \to s'_i,\ n_i \to n'_i$		
Scheme 2	$Q_1, Q_4 \to n_1$	n_1: 0.2	115
	$Q_2, Q_3 \to n_2$	n_2: 0.2	
	$s_i \to s'_i,\ n_i \to n'_i$		
Scheme 3	$Q_1, Q_3 \to n_1$	n_1: 0.2	110
	$Q_2, Q_4 \to n_2$	n_2: 0.2	
	$s_i \to s'_i,\ n_i \to n'_i$		

Fig. 5. Graphs

3.1.1 Objectives

Two objectives are considered in our algorithms:

– Balance the load among the processors. We assume the relative computational capability (the CPU speed) of a processor n_i is known and we quantify it as c_i. Furthermore, the load of a query is estimated as the CPU time that it will consume for every unit time in a processor with $c_i = 1$. Hence if the total query load is L and the total capability of the processors is C, the maximum load that can be allocated to a processor n_i is $(1 + \alpha) \cdot c_i \cdot \frac{L}{C}$. Parameter α is added to allow slight load imbalance to trade for better communication efficiency. It is set to 0.1 in our experiments.

– Minimize the total communication cost. The communication cost can be divided into two parts: (1) transferring source streams from the sources to the processors; (2) transferring query results from the processors to the users. Similar to existing work [3,17,15], to measure the communication efficiency, we use the weighted unit-time communication cost $\sum_{\forall i,j} r(n_i, n_j) \cdot d(n_i, n_j)$, where $r(n_i, n_j)$ is the per-unit time traffic (bit/s) on the link between n_i and n_j, and $d(n_i, n_j)$ is the transfer latency of the link.

To achieve both of the above two goals, the queries should be allocated onto the N processors such that the communication cost is minimized without violating the load constraints. To develop the algorithm, we model the problem as a graph mapping problem in the following subsection.

3.1.2 Graph Mapping Model

We first construct a network graph $NG = \{V_n, E_n, W_n\}$, where each vertex $v_i \in V_n$ represents a processor in the network and there is one edge $e_{ij} \in E_n$ between each pair of vertices v_i and v_j. The weight of each vertex v_i is given by $W_n(v_i)$. $W_n(v_i)$ is equal to c_i, the processor's capability value. Furthermore, the weight of an edge e_{ij} is also given by $W_n(e_{ij})$ and is equal to the communication latency between v_i and v_j. Figure 5(a) shows an example network graph. Here, there are two data sources, s_1 and s_2, which have no computational capability (in terms of complex query processing) and two processors, n_1 and n_2, have the same c_i.

Second, a *query graph*, $QG = \{V_q, E_q, W_q\}$, is constructed. There are two types of vertices in V_q: query vertex (q-vertex) representing a query and network vertex (n-vertex) representing a node in the network. An edge between a q-vertex and a n-vertex represents either a query requests source data from the data source or a query's result should be sent back to the proxy. In addition, if a query's data source and its proxy happen to be the same node, only one edge connects the query and that node. Figure 5(b) shows the query graph when four queries are submitted to the network of Figure 5(a). In the figure, there are four q-vertices, which are drawn in rectangles, and four n-vertices, which are drawn in circles. Q_1 and Q_2 request source data from s_1 and s_2 respectively and their results should be sent back to n_1.

In a query graph, each q-vertex is weighted with the estimated query load, while n-vertices are assigned with zero weights. In addition, each edge is weighted with the estimated data rate (bit/s) of the corresponding streams. For example, in Figure 5(b), Q_1's load is of value 0.1. In addition, it requests 10 bit/s data from source s_1 and generates 1 bit/s result streams to n_1.

However, the above model is still not enough for our problem. It ignores the sharing of data communication among queries in a Pub/Sub. To accurately model the communication cost, we add one edge between each pair of queries that have overlap in their data interest. The edge weight is equal to the rate of the data that are of interest to both of its end vertices (queries). The intuition is to penalize allocation schemes that distribute the two queries to two nodes that are very far away from each other. In Figure 5(b), the data requested by Q_1 from s_1 happens to contain those of Q_3. So the weight of the edge between Q_1 and Q_3 is equal to the one between s_1 and Q_3.

Now, we can model the query distribution problem as a graph mapping problem which maps the vertex set of one graph to the vertex set of another graph. A mapping from a vertex set V_1 to another vertex set V_2 is defined as a boolean function $M(v_i, v_j)$, where $v_i \in V_1$ and $v_j \in V_2$, under the constraint that for each $v_i \in V_1$ there is exactly one $v_j \in V_2$ such that $M(v_i, v_j) = true$. The formal problem statement is as follows:

Given a query graph $QG = (V_q, E_q, W_q)$ and a network graph $NG = (V_n, E_n, W_n)$, find a mapping M from V_q to V_n, such that the mapping

*1. **obeys network constraint:** an n-vertex v_i in V_q is mapped to a vertex v_j in V_n which represents the same network node as v_i;*

*2. **and obeys load-balancing constraint:***

$$\forall v_j \in V_n, \sum_{\substack{v_i \in V_q \\ M(v_i, v_j)}} W_q(v_i) \leq (1 + \alpha) \cdot W_n(v_j) \cdot \frac{W_q^v}{W_n^v}, \qquad (3.1)$$

where $W_q^v = \sum_{v_i \in V_q} W_q(v_i)$ and $W_n^v = \sum_{v_j \in V_n} W_n(v_j)$;

*3. **and minimizes the Weighted Edge Cut (WEC):** which is given by*

$$WEC = \sum_{\substack{v_k \in V_n \\ v_l \in V_n}} \sum_{\substack{v_i \in V_q \\ v_j \in V_q \\ M(v_i, v_k) \\ M(v_j, v_l)}} W_q(e_{ij}) \cdot W_n(e_{kl}). \qquad (3.2)$$

In Table 2, we present three mapping schemes from the query graphs to the network graphs in Figure 5, which obey both the network constraint and the load-balancing constraint. In scheme 1, we map all the queries to their own local processors, while scheme 2 is the optimal mapping if we ignore the potential sharing of communication of Q_1 and Q_3. We can see that scheme 3 is a better mapping, which has a smaller WEC value.

3.2   Challenges and Approach Overview

There are a few practical difficulties to solve this problem. First, it is hard to construct the global network graph and query graph when the size of the network and the number of queries scales up. A scalable algorithm is required. Second, even if we have the global graphs, finding the optimal mapping is an NP-Hard problem [19]. Hence, an efficient heuristic-based approach is needed. Third, the queries and stream statistics could change over runtime. A runtime algorithm is required to redistribute the queries.

To address the problems, distributed coordinators are employed to perform the heuristic graph mapping and remapping algorithms. They are organized into a hierarchical tree. Each leaf coordinator constructs a network (sub)graph which consists of an exclusive set of processors while a parent coordinator constructs a network (sub)graph composed by its child coordinators. This provides a hierarchical view of the network graph. On the other hand, each coordinator also holds a query (sub)graph which is a coarsened overview of its descendants' and this constructs a query graph hierarchy. Each coordinator only performs the mapping and runtime remapping of its query (sub)graph to its network (sub)graph. The rest of this section presents the detail of our scheme.

Finally, it is required to frequently estimate the overlaps between a pair of queries in the following algorithms, which could be very expensive if it is done by semantical reasoning. Therefore, we partition each stream into a number of substreams, and represent each query's data interest as a bit vector indicating whether a substream overlaps with its interest. In this way, efficient bit operations could be used to quickly perform the estimation.

3.3   Network Graph Hierarchy

The coordinators are a subset of processors chosen from all the processors in the system. Each such processor performs two separate logical roles: the stream processor and the coordinator. We assume that separate resources of these processors are reserved for these two roles. For non-coordinators, they perform only the stream processor role. Hereafter, the words "processor" and "coordinator" refer to the logical roles.

The coordinators are organized into a hierarchical tree. At the bottom level, each processor forms a separate cluster and the processor is also called the parent of this cluster. At the second level, the processors are clustered into multiple close-by (in terms of transfer latency) clusters. Within each cluster, the median is selected as the coordinator of the cluster which is also called the cluster's

---

Algorithm 1. Query graph coarsening algorithm

---

1 **while** $|V| > v_{max}$ **do**
2   Set all the vertices as unmatched;
3   **while** $\exists$ *unmatched vertices* $\wedge$ $|V| > v_{max}$ **do**
4   Randomly select an unmatched vertex u;
5          $A \leftarrow adj(u) - mat(adj(u))$;
6   **if** $is\_n(u)$ **then**
            $A \leftarrow A - \{v | v \in adj(u) \wedge is\_n(v) \wedge (u.clu \neq v.clu \vee v.clu = unknown)\}$;
7   Select a vertex v from A such that the edge $e(u, v)$ is of the maximum weight;
8   Collapse u and v into a new vertex w;
9   Set w as matched;
10         $w.weight \leftarrow u.weight + v.weight$;
11   Re-estimate the weights of the edges connected to w;
12   **if** $is\_n(u)$ OR $is\_n(v)$ **then**
13            $is\_n(w) \leftarrow true$;
14            $w.clu = is\_n(u)?u.clu : v.clu$;

---

parent. The median of a set of processors $\{n_1, n_2, \ldots, n_l\}$ is defined as the processor n_i with minimum total transfer latency to all processors in the cluster, i.e. $\sum_{1 \leq j \leq l} d(n_i, n_j) \leq \sum_{1 \leq j \leq l} d(n_k, n_j)$ for any n_k. These coordinators are also clustered level by level in a similar way. We say a processor belongs to a cluster of an internal coordinator (at any level) if it is the descendant of this coordinator.

Each coordinator constructs a network subgraph containing only its child coordinators (or child processors for the leaf coordinators). Here, the weight of a vertex is equal to the total capability values of all its descendant processors.

We adapt schemes proposed by the networking community to construct a hierarchical tree of coordinators, such as [5]. The mechanism in [5] tries to maintain a tree with the following properties: (1) the size of the cluster in each level is between k and $3k - 1$ (except the cluster of the root whose size could be less than k); (2) the parent is the median of its cluster. The tree is constructed incrementally and dynamically. Interested readers can refer to [5].

3.4 Query Graph Hierarchy Construction

In this subsection, we look at how to construct the query graph hierarchy. To begin, each leaf coordinator collects the query specifications from its child nodes and generates a query graph over them. If the number of vertices of the query graph is larger than v_{max}, then it runs Algorithm 1 to coarsen the query graph. The graph mapping algorithm at each coordinator, which will be presented in the following sections, is performed on this coarsened query graph. The coarsening algorithm repeatedly collapses two selected vertices until the number of vertices is smaller than or equal to v_{max}. In the algorithm, a vertex u tends to collapse with a neighbor v which has an edge $e_{u,v}$ with a larger weight, because these two vertices are more likely to be mapped to the same vertex in the network graph. For ease of exposition, we define the following functions: (1) $adj(u)$ returns the set of adjacent vertices of u; (2) $is\_n(u)$ returns true if u is an n-vertex; (3) $matched(A)$ is all the matched vertices in a vertex set A. In addition, for each n-vertex u, a field clu indicates which child cluster of the current coordinator covers u. Two n-vertices belong to two different child clusters shall not be merged together because they have to be mapped to different child clusters in the graph mapping algorithm. Note that if u is not covered by any child cluster of this coordinator, then their clu field is set as unknown.

The q-vertices in the (coarsened) graph are tagged with the current coordinator's name and then submitted to the parent coordinator who will perform the same procedure after receiving all the (coarsened) graphs from its children. Note that the procedure is run in parallel in different subtrees to accelerate the whole procedure. The procedure stops when the root gets the (coarsened) query graph. Now every coordinator holds its query graph. Finally,each coordinator periodically propagates the update of its query graph to its parents at runtime.

3.5   Initial Query Distribution

Once the initial query graph hierarchy is constructed, the root coordinator starts mapping its (coarsened) query graph to its network (sub)graph. The query subgraph mapped to each child is uncoarsened one level back and sent to the child. This procedure repeats at each level until all the queries are assigned to the processors. Note that, to uncoarsen a vertex, information of the finer-grained vertices, if necessary, is retrieved from the corresponding coordinator based on the tags of the vertex.

The algorithm is illustrated in Algorithm 2. It starts by using a greedy algorithm to get an initial mapping:

(a) Map each n-vertex to a child that manages the node that n-vertex represents.
(b) Map the q-vertices one by one in descending order of their weights. For each q-vertex, among the children that can accommodate it (i.e. their load-balancing constraints will not be violated after mapping the q-vertex to anyone of them), map it to the one that minimizes the current WEC. If no children can accommodate it, then map it to the one with the minimum violation of the load-balancing constraint.

Note that finding a mapping that satisfies the load-balancing constraint is an NP-Complete problem. Our algorithm does not guarantee finding such a mapping.

Lines 2-2 iteratively improve the mapping by trying to remap the q-vertices to other vertices in NG. Here, we use the value of $gain(v_i, v_k)$ to heuristically guide our remapping, which is equal to the reduction of the WEC value by remapping $v_i \in V_q$ to $v_k \in V_n$. To achieve some capability of climbing out of local minima, a q-vertex v_i with a negative $gain(v_i, v_k)$ value would be considered for remapping as long as its gain value is the highest and its remapping will not violate the load-balancing constraint of v_k. The mapping with minimum WEC value will be restored at the beginning of each outer iteration.

Algorithm 2. Graph mapping algorithm

Input: $NG = (V_n, E_n, W_n), QG = (V_q, V_q, W_q)$

1 use a greedy algorithm to get the initial mapping;
2 compute the gain $gain(v_i, v_j)$ for each q-vertex $v_i \in V_q$ and each $v_j \in V_n$;
3 $minWEC \leftarrow$ current WEC; $minMapping \leftarrow$ current mapping;
4 **repeat**
5   current mapping $\leftarrow minMapping$;
6   **repeat**
7       $maxGain \leftarrow -\infty$; $vertexToRemap \leftarrow \emptyset$; $vertexToRemapTo \leftarrow \emptyset$;
8   **for** *each $v_j \in V_n$* **do**
9   Find an unmatched q-vertex $v_i \in V_q$ currently mapped to v_j and a vertex $v_k \in V_n$, $gain(v_i, v_k)$ is maximized and remapping v_i to v_k does not violate load-balancing or improves a violation (if any);
10   **if** $gain(v_i, v_k) > maxGain$ **then**
11             $maxGain \leftarrow gain(v_i, v_k)$; $vertexToRemap \leftarrow v_i$; $vertexToRemapTo \leftarrow v_k$;

12   **if** $vertexToRemap \neq \emptyset$ **then**
13   set $vertexToRemap$ as matched;
14   remap $vertexToRemap$ to $vertexToRemapTo$;
15   update $gain(v_i, v_k)$ for any v_i directly connected to $vertexToRemap$;
16   **if** *current $WEC < minWEC$* **then**
17             $minWEC \leftarrow$ current WEC;
18             $minMapping \leftarrow$ current mapping

19   **until** $vertexToRemap = \emptyset$;
20 **until** $minWEC$ *is the same as the last iteration*;

3.6 Online New Query Insertion

Unlike prior work which assumes queries are relatively stable, our system stresses the problem of fast query streaming. The new queries have to be quickly distributed to the desirable processors. A good distribution can avoid runtime query migration at a later time (see the next subsection).

While there are many possible new query distribution schemes, in this paper, we only study the use of the hierarchical coordinator tree and show the significance of new query insertion for the system performance. In this scheme, a new query is first routed to the root coordinator which then routes it to one of its children. The routing is done level by level until the query is assigned to a processor. At each coordinator, the query is added to the query graph and the weights of the new edges are estimated. Then the new vertex is mapped to a vertex in the network graph such that the resulting WEC is minimized.

Although all queries have to be routed through the root coordinator, this scheme is scalable to very fast query streams. This is because it only needs to route the queries to a few children based on some coarse-grained information. As shown in Section 4, it can handle more than 800,000 queries per second in our experimental PC. For higher query stream rates, we can perform online

---

Algorithm 3. Adaptive load re-balance

---

1 **begin**
2   Compute the diffusion solution m_{ij} for every i, j pair;
3   **while** *there exists an* $m_{ij} > 0$ **do**
4   Randomly select a pair i, j such that $m_{ij} > 0$;
5        $V \leftarrow$ query vertices in n_i whose benefits differ up to $x\%$ from the largest benefit;
6        $V_d \leftarrow$ the dirty query vertices in V;
7   **if** $V_d = \emptyset$ **then** $V_d \leftarrow V$;
8   Remapping the vertex $v \in V_d$ from n_i to n_j such that it is of the largest load density and m_{ij} is larger than 90% of its weight;
9 **end**

---

routing only on some queries while simply keeping the other queries at their proxies. Further trade-offs between routing quality and routing efficiency is an interesting piece of future work.

3.7 Adaptive Query Redistribution

During runtime, the queries, the workload of processors and the characteristics of data streams may change. Hence the initial allocation of queries may become suboptimal. Thus adaptive adjustment of the query distribution has to be performed. Again we employ a hierarchical scheme. The adaptation works in rounds and each round is initiated by the root coordinator periodically. After making the redistribution decisions, the root coordinator would transfer the change of the distribution to each of its children. Each child coordinator retrieves the finer-grained information of the vertices newly allocated to it from their original coordinators. Then the child coordinators would perform the same procedure to make redistribution decisions. This process continues until the leaf coordinators are done with the redistribution. Note that the actual migration of queries happens after all decisions are made and is done among the processors.

The adaptive redistribution algorithm in each coordinator is composed of two phases: load re-balancing followed by distribution refinement. In the load re-balancing phase, the coordinator tries to re-balance the load among its children. Besides that, there are a few other goals to be achieved:

1. Minimize the WEC of the mapping.
2. Minimize the query migration time. Since migrating queries may incur the migration of stateful operators (e.g. join), we should minimize the size of the states to be moved.

In the load balancing phase, to avoid re-mapping from scratch, which may incur too many query migrations, we adopt a load diffusion approach [14]. A diffusion solution specifies the load m_{ij} that should be migrated from a coordinator n_i to another coordinator n_j for each (i, j) pair. Authors in [14] proposed a method to derive a diffusion solution such that the Euclidean norm of the transferred load is minimized which results in a small number of query migrations. Our redistribution algorithm is presented in Algorithm 3. As n-vertices are not considered for redistribution, the vertices in the algorithm only refer to the q-vertices. The benefit of remapping a vertex from n_i to n_j is defined as the reduction of the WEC given by Eqn (3.2). To achieve good mapping quality, our algorithm tends to remap those vertices with large benefits.

Furthermore, a vertex is called *dirty* if it had been picked for remapping in the earlier iterations in the same adaptation round. We give these vertices higher remapping priority because moving them again would not increase the amount of query migration (Note that queries are actually moved after all the decisions are made in one round.). In addition, the *load density* of a vertex is equal to the weight divided by the size of its state. We favor remapping the denser ones because it may result in less state movement. The value of x in line 3 can be used to trade mapping quality for lower migration cost. With a larger x value, we can consider more vertices with lower migration benefit. In our experiments, we set $x = 10$.

The distribution refinement phase attempts to reduce the WEC while maintaining the load balancing condition. Again the query vertices are visited randomly and checked to see whether they belong to one of the following categories:

(1) Mapping the vertex back to its original location can maintain load balance and the current WEC.
(2) Mapping the vertex to another node can decrease the current WEC without violating load balance.

The checks are performed in the order given above. Whenever such a vertex is found, the remapping is performed.

3.8   Statistics Collection

Stream statistics are periodically multicast to the coordinators from the sources. As stated before, we partition the data streams into multiple substreams and the data interest of a user query is represented as a bit vector. Hence the stream statistics we need is the data rate of each substream. In addition, each processor periodically collects the average CPU time that each of its running queries consumes per unit time. If any value is changed, then it will be (re)submitted to the parent coordinator to (re)estimate the workload that the query may incur.

4   Experiments

This section presents a performance study of the proposed techniques. Two sets of experiments are conducted. In the first one, simulations of a large scale distributed system and a huge query set are conducted to test the various performance aspects of COSMOS. In the second one, we deploy our system prototype over PlanetLab with a real data set to compare the performance of COSMOS with the state-of-the-art operator placement algorithms. All software are implemented in C/C++.

4.1   Simulation Study

A network topology with 4096 nodes is generated using the Transit-Stub model in the GT-ITM topology generator. Among these nodes, 100 nodes are chosen as the data stream sources, and 256 nodes are selected as the stream processors, and the remaining nodes act as the routers.

The default cluster size parameter k used in the coordinator tree construction is set to 4, which will be varied in the experiments. All the streams are partitioned into 20, 000 substreams and they are randomly distributed to the sources. The arrival rate of each substream is randomly chosen from 1 to 10 (bytes/seconds). To simulate clustering effect of user behaviors, $g = 20$ groups of user queries are generated and each group has different data hot spots. The group that a query belongs to is chosen randomly and the number of substreams that a query requests is uniformly chosen from 100 to 200. For the queries within every group, the probability that a substream is selected conforms to a zipfian distribution with $\theta = 0.8$. To model different groups having different hot spots, we generate g number of random permutations of the substreams. The number of queries are varied from 5, 000 to 60, 000 and we set their workload to be proportional to their input stream rates. The adaptive interval of the adaptive query redistribution algorithm is set to 200 seconds. Because the cost of transmitting the result streams from the processors to their local users are identical for any query distribution scheme, we subtract such cost from the reported figures to ease the comparison.

4.1.1   Initial Query Distribution

In the first experiment, we study the performance of the initial query distribution scheme with different number of queries. It is compared with three approaches: (a) Naive: allocate the queries to their local processors. (b) Greedy: only run the greedy algorithm in Algorithm 2. (c) Centralized: a centralized node constructs a global query graph and a global network graph, and runs Algorithm 2 to perform a global mapping. While this approach is limited in its scalability, it serves as a benchmark to examine the optimality of other approaches. Figure 6(a) presents the results of all the four approaches. Naive performs the worst because it cannot identify the data interest of the queries and optimize their locations. Greedy works a lot better. The two graph mapping algorithms perform the best and their performances are similar. This also verifies that the graph coarsening procedure in our hierarchical mapping algorithm does not incur much errors.

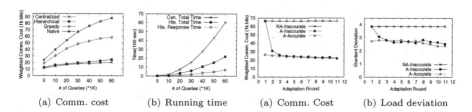

(a) Comm. cost   (b) Running time   (a) Comm. Cost   (b) Load deviation

Fig. 6. Varied #queries   **Fig. 7.** Adapting to inaccurate statistics

We also report the response time (i.e. the time interval from the begin to the end of the mapping) and the total time (i.e. the total CPU time consumed in all the coordinators) of the centralized and hierarchical graph mapping algorithms in Figure 6(b). Note that the response time and total time are equivalent for the centralized approach. It is shown that both the response time and total time of the hierarchical approach are much lower than the centralized one.

4.1.2   Adaptive Query Distribution

In the second set of experiments, we study the performance of the adaptation scheme. In the above experiments, the graph mapping algorithms perform well if accurate apriori statistics exist. However, apriori statistics are hard to collect in a large scale system. Hence, in the first experiment, we study the situation that the apriori statistics are inaccurate. We model this situation by using a random initial query allocation scheme. Three algorithms are compared: (1) NA-Inaccurate: non-adaptive algorithm with inaccurate statistics; (2) A-Inaccurate: adaptive algorithm with inaccurate statistics; (3) A-Accurate: Adaptive algorithm with accurate statistics. Figures 7(a) and 7(b) present the communication cost and the standard deviation of the system load over the observation period. It can be seen that the adaptive algorithm can gradually refine the initial query distribution scheme to minimize the communication cost and balance the system load.

In another experiment, we study the situation that new queries arrive in the system. Initially, there are 30,000 queries and new queries are added into the system incrementally at a 200 seconds interval. At the start of each interval, there are 1,500 new queries coming in. We reported the average communication cost during each interval and the standard deviation of the processor loads. Three schemes are compared: (1) Random: randomly allocate the new queries without considering their interest; (2) Online: use our online new query insertion algorithm; (3) Online-Adaptive: use both the online new query insertion and the adaptive query redistribution. The results are shown in Figure 8(a) and 8(b). The performance of Random gets worse with more queries added, while Online can maintain low communication cost but with increasing load imbalance. Online-Adaptive performs the best in both metrics because of its ability to re-balance the load distribution and to refine the query distribution.

In the fourth experiment, we examine the scalability of our system to fast query streams. The settings are similar to that of the above experiment. We collect the time for the root coordinator to distribute a query and then compute

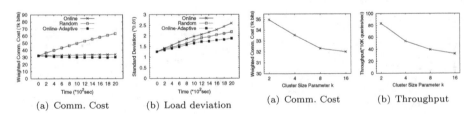

| (a) Comm. Cost | (b) Load deviation | (a) Comm. Cost | (b) Throughput |

Fig. 8. New query arrival   **Fig. 9.** Varied Cluster Size

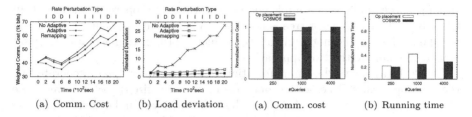

Fig. 10. Perturbation of stream rates   Fig. 11. Prototype study

the maximum query rate that it can accommodate. We study the root coordinator because it is the potential bottleneck of the system. We vary the cluster size parameter k. The results are shown in Figure 9. We can see that, with a smaller value of k, the query distribution quality is worse. That is because there are more levels in the coordinator tree and more graph coarsening is performed. On the other hand, the throughput of query streams gets better with a smaller value of k. The reason is the root coordinator needs to route queries to fewer number of children. Hence, adaptively setting the parameter k is an interesting piece of future work.

Finally, we examine the situation when the rates of streams change. At runtime, we increase (denoted by "I") or decrease (denoted by "D") the rates of 800 random streams several times so that load imbalance exists within the system. Here, we compare the adaptive scheme with two schemes: (1) Re-mapping: use the centralized mapping algorithm to remap the global query graph to the global network graph; (2) Non-Adaptive: no adaptation is done. Figures 10(a) and 10(b) depict the communication cost as well as the standard deviation of the load in the system after each change. It is clear that adaptive query redistribution performs close to centralized remapping and can re-balance the system load to adapt to the new data characteristics without increasing the communication cost. While the remapping algorithm can achieve better results, it incurred about 7 times more query migrations than the adaptive algorithm did.

4.2 Prototype Study

In this experiment, our prototype system is deployed on 30 nodes over PlanetLab from different countries and continents. We use our stream processing system, GSN (http://gsn.sourceforge.net), which is tailored for processing data from heterogeneous sensor networks. Real readings from 100 sensors deployed in our SensorScope project (http://sensorscope.epfl.ch) are used as the dataset. 5 nodes act as the data sources, each with equal number of sensors. A number (250 ~ 4000) of random queries are generated. Each query contains one to three random selection predicates on the sensor readings and sensor types together with one to three join predicates on the timestamp. A random node is chosen as the proxy for each query.

In the operator placement approach, an algorithm similar to [12] is implemented to generate an optimized global operator graph. In addition, the algorithm proposed in [3] is also implemented to optimize the operator placement. In COSMOS, the coordinator tree is constructed such that each cluster has $2 \sim 3$ members. Since [3] did not study adaptive query optimization, a static query set is used to compare the two approaches.

Figure 11(a) shows the communication cost of the query plans generated by the two approaches. To ease the comparison, we normalize the values over those of COSMOS. One can see that COSMOS can achieve similar communication efficiency as the existing operator placement algorithms with varied number of queries. The slight difference can be partially attributed to the fact that the operator placement algorithms in [3] do not consider load balancing and hence it can obtain a plan with lower communication cost. In Figure 11(b), we depict the response time of the two algorithms. In this figure, we normalize the values over the largest one (i.e. the response time of the operator placement algorithm with 4,000 queries) to see the trend with increasing number of queries. The result suggests that COSMOS is much more scalable than the existing operator placement algorithms with larger number of queries. This confirms the efficiency of the new system architecture and the hierarchical query placement algorithm.

5   Conclusion

This paper proposes a massive query optimization approach for distributed stream systems. A Pub/Sub is adopted as the communication substrate. Techniques are proposed to leverage the Pub/Sub to "intelligently" eliminate duplicate data transmission and perform early data filtering in a scalable way. Furthermore, a scalable load distribution scheme further improves the system's performance. The load distribution problem is modelled as a graph mapping problem, which considers both load balancing and communication cost minimization and also takes account of the communication characteristics of a Pub/Sub. Both static and adaptive query distribution algorithms are proposed. A new hierarchical scheme is utilized to enhance the algorithms' scalability. An extensive simulation study verifies the efficacy and efficiency of all the proposed techniques.

References

1. Abadi, D.J., et al.: The design of the borealis stream processing engine. In: CIDR (2005)
2. Aguilera, M.K., et al.: Matching events in a content-based subscription system. In: PODC (1999)
3. Ahmad, Y., et al.: Networked query processing for distributed stream-based applications. In: VLDB (2004)
4. Amini, L., et al.: Adaptive control of extreme-scale stream processing systems. In: ICDCS (2006)
5. Banerjee, S., et al.: Scalable application layer multicast. In: SIGCOMM (2002)
6. Carney, D., et al.: Monitoring streams: A new class of data management applications. In: VLDB (2002)

7. Carzaniga, A., et al.: Design and evaluation of a wide-area event notification service. ACM Transactions on Computer Systems 19(3), 332–383 (2001)
8. Carzaniga, A., et al.: A routing scheme for content-based networking. In: INFO-COM (2004)
9. Carzaniga, A., Wolf, A.L.: Forwarding in a content-based network. In: SIGCOMM (2003)
10. Carzaniga, A., Wolf, A.L.: Content-based networking: A new communication infrastructure. In: Infrastructure for Mobile and Wireless Systems (2001)
11. Chandrasekaran, S., et al.: TelegraphCQ: Continuous dataflow processing for an uncertain world. In: CIDR (2003)
12. Chen, J., et al.: NiagaraCQ: A Scalable Continuous Query System for Internet Databases. In: SIGMOD (2000)
13. Cherniack, M., et al.: Scalable distributed stream processing. In: CIDR (2003)
14. Hu, Y.F., Blake, R.J.: An optimal dynamic load balancing algorithm. Technical report, Daresbury laboratory (1995)
15. Kumar, V., et al.: Resource-aware distributed stream management using dynamic overlays. In: ICDCS (2005)
16. Papaemmanouil, O., et al.: Semcast: Semantic multicast for content-based data dissemination. In: ICDE (2005)
17. Pietzuch, P., et al.: Network-aware operator placement for stream-processing systems. In: ICDE (2006)
18. Repantis, T., et al.: Synergy: sharing-aware component composition for distributed stream processing systems. In: Middleware (2006)
19. Schloegel, K., et al.: Graph partitioning for high-performance scientific simulations, pp. 491–541 (2003)
20. Shah, M.A., et al.: Flux: An adaptive partitioning operator for continuous query systems. In: ICDE (2003)
21. Srivastava, U., et al.: Operator placement for in-Network stream query processing. In: PODS (2005)
22. Stonebraker, M., et al.: Mariposa: A New Architecture for Distributed Data. In: ICDE (1994)
23. The STREAM Group. STREAM: The stanford stream data manager. IEEE Data Engineering Bulletin (2003)
24. Xing, Y., et al.: Dynamic load distribution in the borealis stream processor. In: ICDE (2005)
25. Zhou, Y., et al.: Rethinking the design of distributed stream processing systems. In: NetDB (2008)

QoS Allocation Algorithms for Publish-Subscribe Information Space Middleware*

Joseph Loyall, Matthew Gillen, and Praveen Sharma

BBN Technologies
Cambridge, MA

Abstract. Information spaces have emerged as a powerful concept for providing managed exchange of information between members of communities of interest (COIs), including information brokering and dissemination by publish-subscribe-query middleware. To support COIs with real-time or critical information exchange requirements, information spaces require quality of service (QoS) management algorithms that consider the complex system dynamics within information spaces, that allocate multiple resources, and that scale to information spaces of reasonable size. This paper presents two algorithms for multi-resource QoS allocation within information spaces. The first algorithm always provides an optimal allocation and includes optimizations that enable it to scale to information spaces of moderate size. The second algorithm is an approximation algorithm that provides near optimal solutions in most situations and scales to much larger information spaces. The paper also presents analyses and experimental results of the effectiveness and efficiency of the algorithms.

Keywords: Quality of service, multi-resource allocation, publish-subscribe-query information spaces.

1 Introduction

The concept of *information spaces* has emerged to support information exchange within communities of interest (COIs), collections of users that are related by shared interests or participation in a common mission [23]. Information spaces consist of the following:

- Middleware services for brokering and managing information exchange
- A collection of information producing and consuming clients
- The clients' shared vocabulary
- The set of managed information objects (MIOs) that clients exchange [2].

In the information space model [12], *clients* are information publishers and consumers, communicating anonymously with other clients via an *information management*

---

* This work was supported by the USAF Air Force Research Laboratory under contract FA-8750-05-C-0267.

V. Issarny and R. Schantz (Eds.): Middleware 2008, LNCS 5346, pp. 346–365, 2008.

system (IMS) [2] with managers that monitor and control the information space. Information published into the information space is in the form of typed managed information objects (MIOs) consisting of payload and metadata. Consumers make requests for future (*subscriptions*) or past (*query*) information using predicates over MIO types and metadata values. Information spaces provide topic-based information exchange, brokering, discovery, and shared understanding [12]. Clients do not need to be aware of one another, the source of information they consume, or the consumers of information they publish.

The IMS that we utilize in this work, *Apollo* [24], builds upon work in distributed object, component, and service oriented middleware. It provides a set of services that allow the registration of subscription predicates (specified using XQuery [26]), matching of metadata for published MIOs (specified using XML [27]), and delivering matched MIOs to clients using the Java Message Service [20]. Client-side distribution middleware exposes publication, subscription, and query interfaces conforming to the *Joint Battlespace Infosphere Common API (CAPI)* [10] using SOAP messages over HTTP or HTTPS.

We have developed quality of service (QoS) management middleware for information spaces with dynamic interoperability and real-time requirements. Our QoS management capability extends existing IMS middleware to manage the production, delivery, and consumption of information that meets client needs within available resources, to mediate competing demands for resources, and to adjust to dynamic conditions. Our *QoS Management System (QMS)* middleware, illustrated in Figure 1, builds upon our previous work in QoS management for distributed object and component systems [7, 15, 16, 17, 18, 19, 28]. The QMS is multi-layered middleware, described in more detail in [14], with an information space QoS manager (ISQM)[1] that provides aggregate QoS allocations and policy for clients and operations throughout an information space. The ISQM is collocated with the information brokering service and provides policy to local QoS managers (LQM), each of which enforce the policy at a local control point, making local decisions as necessary to achieve and maintain

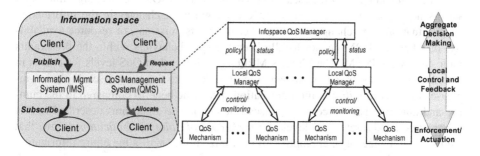

Fig. 1. The QMS layered architecture provides QoS management for an information space IMS

---

[1] The ISQM is called a *System Resource Manager (SRM)* in [14], a historical term that is not as accurate with regard to its function. Likewise, the LQM element is referred to as a local resource manager (LRM) in that document.

the desired QoS. The QMS also includes QoS mechanisms that control and monitor resource usage and shape information elements under control of an LQM. The QMS manages QoS in dynamic information spaces with clients that come and go, and goals, roles, and priorities that change with time and circumstances.

One of the challenges of providing QMS middleware is the development of algorithms for allocating QoS levels and their associated resources among the varying numbers of clients, operations, and applications using an information space. These *Multi-Resource QoS (MRQ) allocation algorithms* must consider the complex system dynamics of information spaces, be efficient enough to be used in real-time QoS management, and scale to the sizes of envisioned information spaces. Multi-resource QoS allocation is NP-hard[2], partially because of the following characteristics:

- There are complex system dynamics among the QoS needs within an information space. That is, how one resource is allocated can impact the demand positively or negatively for other resources. For example, a client who is interested in compressing information to lower bandwidth usage may require a higher amount of CPU.
- There is frequently no direct correlation between how important an application is and the amount of resources it needs.
- The relative ordering of QoS levels does not necessarily reflect the relative amount of resources that each level uses. That is, a higher QoS level (e.g., with higher precision, rate, or accuracy of information exchange) does not imply more resource usage than a lower QoS level and, in fact, might use more of some resources and fewer of others.
- Resource bottlenecks can change dynamically. That is, addressing a bottleneck caused by a highly constrained resource can result in a bottleneck in another resource.

This paper describes a set of multi-resource QoS allocation algorithms that we have developed for use within our prototype QMS. The MRQ algorithms are used by the information space QoS manager to select aggregate QoS allocations that are then enforced and maintained by the local QoS managers. The ISQM runs the algorithms and selects new QoS allocations when there are significant changes in the information space situation (e.g., change in the number of clients, missions, or resource availability) or when the LQM cannot locally keep the QoS behaviors within the constraints indicated by the ISQM. The ISQM's MRQ algorithms select QoS levels for clients in information spaces based on a benefit/cost ratio, i.e., the amount each choice increases the overall *utility* of the information space (the benefit) compared to the number and amount of resources that it uses (the cost). The algorithms described in this paper consider discrete QoS levels for each *control point* or *application* (terms that we use interchangeably), attempting to maximize utility across the entire information space within the available resources.

Because multi-resource QoS allocation is NP-hard, there is a tension between optimality and timeliness in the algorithms. Optimality refers to the ability of an algorithm

---

[2] Lee et al have reduced the problem to the 0-1 knapsack problem [11].

to produce the highest utility QoS allocation possible within the available resources. Timeliness refers to the amount of time needed to determine a QoS allocation. For the class of MRQ problems, one can arrive at an optimal solution by examining a search space of all combinations of the applications and all the QoS levels in which they can operate, but examining this search space can take exponential time.

In this paper, we describe two algorithms for multi-resource QoS allocation in information spaces that manage the tradeoff between optimality and timeliness in different ways:

- *Optimizing Brute-Force* always provides an optimal solution but potentially runs in exponential time. The algorithm includes two optimizations that can prune the search space and reduce the runtime significantly in some situations.
- *Greedy Approximation* is an approximation algorithm based on 0-1 integer programming. The algorithm produces a near optimal allocation in many scenarios and runs in polynomial time.

We evaluate each algorithm's efficacy (how close to optimal the allocations computed by the algorithms are) and efficiency (how quickly the algorithms can produce an allocation).

The rest of this paper is organized as follows. First, we describe the MRQ algorithms, including an analysis of their efficiency. We then present our efficacy and efficiency experiments, including the experimental setup and metrics. Following this, we present some related work. Finally, we summarize our results.

2 Information Space QoS Allocation Algorithms

The MRQ algorithms that we present in this section select an allocation of QoS levels for all control points in the information space. Each *control point* represents a logical set of related points at which QoS can be affected, such as the information consumption, processing, and production for a single application[3]. The algorithms consider the resources needed by each QoS level at each control point[4], and attempt to maximize a measure of overall benefit (i.e., a *utility function*) defined for an information space within the available resources. One can determine an optimal solution by examining a search space of all possible allocations, but this is an exponential search in general and infeasible for all but modestly sized information spaces. Therefore, we took two

---

[3] Although each of these (consumption, processing, and production) can be controlled separately, choices made at each will affect the others. Thus they require a consistent logical QoS level, e.g., the rate and format of data inputs (consumption) must take into account the speed of information processing and production.

[4] The algorithms need the list of applications, their QoS levels, and their resource usage as input. The QoS levels should be defined to represent the QoS characteristics of most importance to the end user, from the most desirable level of QoS to the least acceptable level of QoS. The resource usage can be determined by off- or on-line profiling, or by analysis in some cases (e.g., bandwidth used by a periodic publisher can be calculated by multiplying the number of information objects per second that are published times the size of each object).

simultaneous approaches: (1) developing optimizations that can reduce the search space, and (2) developing an approximation algorithm that runs in less than exponential time in the worst case. This results in an *Optimizing Brute-Force* algorithm that produces optimal solutions and a *Greedy Approximation* algorithm that produces approximate solutions but runs in polynomial time.

The goal of each MRQ algorithm is to select an *allocation* of QoS levels for applications that simultaneously:

- Is *feasible*, i.e., fits within the resources available in the information space. An infeasible allocation cannot be deployed and hence is not an acceptable solution.
- Maximizes information space *utility*, i.e., allocates the applications of most importance to the overall COI goals and provides higher QoS where it is most useful to the COI.

The utility for any given client corresponds to a higher perceived user perception, which generally increases as throughput and information quality (e.g., resolution, precision) increase and as latency and jitter decrease. However, when tradeoffs must be made, particular QoS attributes will be more desirable than others and these tradeoffs are captured in the sets of QoS levels for each client. For example, a user that is watching video is willing to sacrifice some initial latency (for buffering) for a significant decrease in jitter. The QoS levels for that user would attach a much higher utility value to a level that introduced some delay but maintained a steady rate than to one with lower delay but greater variance in the rate. For the overall information space, the utility function must combine the utilities for the levels of each of the information space, but also attach a greater weight to the more important users. That is, just as the least important attributes for a given user should be degraded when necessary, the ISQM should degrade QoS for the least important users when necessary. While the best utility function to use can vary for given situations, goals, or domains, a reasonable utility function to use for information spaces is one that calculates utility based on the criticality of the applications that are run and the QoS level at which they are run. That is, the utility is increased by any of the following factors: (1) running more applications (i.e., servicing more clients), (2) running higher priority applications, and (3) running any application at a higher QoS level. For an information space with A applications, we define utility as follows:

$$Utility = \sum_{i=1}^{A} (w_c C_i)(w_q Q_i) \qquad (1)$$

where:

- C_i (>= 0) is the relative criticality of application i compared to other applications.
- Q_i (>= 0) is the relative quality of QoS level i compared to other QoS levels for the same application or control point.
- w_c and w_q are weighting factors (to control the tradeoff of running more applications or applications at higher QoS levels).

The feasible allocation with the highest utility is considered the *optimal* allocation. Notice that there could be multiple allocations with equal utilities, so there could be multiple optimal solutions. For the experiments described in Section 0, we use a scenario generator that generates utility measures for each combination of application and QoS level, simulating in one value the criticality, QoS level value, and relative weights of these terms.

The above utility function and our experiments do not explicitly consider resource efficiency, so that two allocations could have equal utilities even if one uses fewer resources than the other[5]. However, keeping resources in reserve could lead to more effective QoS management in dynamic information spaces because wholesale reconfigurations will be reduced if there are resources available to handle overload situations or the addition of new applications. We accomplish this by adding a *reserve factor* to the utility function, i.e., a numerical measure of the benefit for having resources available, as follows:

$$Utility = \left(\sum_{i=1}^{A} (w_c C_i)(w_q Q_i) \right) + w_r R \tag{2}$$

where R is a measure of the resources available, and w_r is a (non-negative) weighting factor to control the tradeoff of using available resources now to run more applications (or higher QoS levels) or keeping the resources in reserve.

2.1 The Optimizing Brute-Force Algorithm

The Optimizing Brute-Force algorithm searches a combinatorial decision tree built from the control points and their QoS levels. As depicted in Figure 2, each level of the decision tree represents a control point (e.g., CP-a, CP-b, CP-c, etc.) and each branch represents a QoS level choice at its parent's control point (e.g., CP-a has QoS level choices 1 and 2, CP-b has QoS level choices 3 and 4, and so forth). Each non-leaf node represents an allocation of control points and QoS levels for the nodes above it in the graph (e.g., CP-b0 represents an allocation of QoS level 1 to CP-a, while CP-c2 represents an allocation of QoS level 2 to CP-a and QoS level 3 to CP-b). The leaf nodes represent combinations of an entire set of control points and QoS levels (i.e., the complete set of potential allocations) in an information space.

Without optimizations, a brute-force search would traverse the tree recursively and examine each leaf node for feasibility and utility. If a node is feasible, its utility is compared with the highest utility of previously evaluated feasible solutions. If the utility of the node is higher, then it becomes the new best solution. The best solution after evaluating all the leaf nodes is the optimal allocation, i.e., the feasible solution with the highest utility.

The brute-force search with no optimizations runs in $\Theta(q^a)$ where q is the number of QoS levels for each control point[6], and a is the number of control points[7]. For the

---

[5] However, resource efficiency is considered by the Greedy Approximation algorithm's *effective gradient* computation, described in Section 2.2.
[6] Assuming the same number of discrete QoS levels for each application.

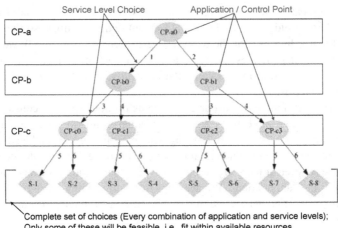

Fig. 2. Decision tree that the Brute-Force algorithm creates and traverses to allocate resources

Optimizing Brute-Force algorithm, we use the following optimizations to prune the search space, significantly in some cases.

Pruning Using an Infeasibility Check. This optimization utilizes the fact that as the algorithm traverses down from the root node to leaf nodes, the number of applications and QoS levels represented in the nodes increases. Consequently if the partial allocation represented by any non-leaf node is not feasible (i.e., it requests more resources than are available), then all the nodes in the subtree under the non-leaf node are also infeasible (because each will add applications to the already infeasible partial allocation). The entire subtree can be bypassed. This optimization works well (i.e., it leads to significant pruning) when many of the leaf nodes represent infeasible allocations.

Pruning Using a Utility Check. This optimization utilizes the fact that as the algorithm traverses down from the root node to leaf nodes (increase in depth of a tree), the utility associated with each node will be more than that of its parent node. At each point in the traversal of the tree, the algorithm walks the path of highest utility first (essentially following the branches of highest QoS levels whether they are feasible or not). If the leaf node reached is lower utility than the best solution reached so far, the entire subtree can be pruned, since all other paths would lead to even lower utility. This optimization works well when the algorithm finds a high utility feasible solution early, enabling pruning of many subtrees with lesser utility.

The Optimizing Brute-Force algorithm uses both of the above optimizations together, along with ordering the tree to maximize the pruning possible. However, in the worst case, the algorithm finds many feasible nodes and relatively low utility solutions, resulting in little or no pruning. In these cases, the algorithm may still end

---

[7] Θ notation is a tight upper and lower bound on the algorithm execution, i.e., the algorithm will check every node of the tree, i.e., exactly q^a *nodes*.

up examining nearly the entire tree. Therefore, the Optimizing Brute-Force algorithm is $O(q^a)$.

2.2 The Greedy Approximation QoS Management Algorithm

Our Greedy Approximation algorithm is based on a 0-1 integer programming algorithm in [21]. 0-1 integer programming tries to maximize the *objective function*:

$$\sum_{i=1}^{m} p_i x_i \tag{3}$$

subject to

$$\sum_{i=1}^{m} H_{ij} x_i \leq L_j \tag{4}$$

for j = 1, 2, ..., n, where:

- Each x_i is an application at a particular QoS level
- p_i is the priority of the application
- H_{ij} is the resource usage of x_i
- L_j is the vector of the capacity of the resources
- m is the number of applications and n is the number of resources.

Our Greedy Approximation algorithm greedily allocates QoS levels to applications contending for resources using an *effective gradient* measure, a ratio of the benefit that each application provides and the cost that it incurs. The algorithm measures the benefit of an application as the value it contributes to the objective function above. It measures the cost of an application at a particular QoS level as the amount of resources requested. The algorithm aggregates the resources into a single dimension and assigns a *penalty* to increase the cost associated with requesting a highly contended resource (i.e., a resource for which a significant amount has already been allocated to other applications).

Our algorithm extends the algorithm in [21] in the following ways:

1. We have two variable dimensions that need to be considered. Each application can have multiple QoS levels from which to choose. In the algorithm in [21], each application has one service level. Our algorithm treats each combination of application and QoS level as a separate viable choice, while ensuring that only one QoS level can be chosen for each application.
2. We compute an initial penalty vector for resource usage. The algorithm in [21] only computes penalties as the algorithm progresses, which can lead to significantly suboptimal allocation. That is, it treats all resources equally and completely available at the beginning. In reality, some resources are more likely to become bottlenecks (e.g., because more applications request them or applications request higher amounts of them) than others. Our algorithm performs an initial pass and

assigns an initial penalty to resources, making it cost more to request highly contended resources.

3. We guarantee a solution by including a *starvation* choice at each level, i.e., a QoS level that uses no resources and provides no benefit and represents starving a particular application if there are not enough resources to run it at any level.

After computing the initial penalty, the greedy approximation algorithm computes the total number of application-QoS level combinations as described in 1 above. It iterates over the following steps until either all the applications have been assigned a QoS level or there are no more resources left to allocate to any remaining choices:

1. It computes the effective gradient for each application-QoS level combination as the ratio of benefit divided by cost. The benefit is the utility that a given application at a given QoS level provides. The cost is the resources requested adjusted by the penalty.
2. It selects the application and QoS level combination with the highest effective gradient and eliminates further consideration of the other QoS levels for this application.
3. It allocates the resources needed by the application and QoS level combination selected in step 2, removing those resources from the available resources.
4. It prunes the list of application-QoS level combinations of any infeasible choices.

2.2.1 Analysis of the Runtime of Greedy Approximation
Pseudocode for the Greedy Approximation algorithm follows:

```
1:  initializeList(CP-QoSLevelList)
2:  while (CP-QoSLevelList not empty) {
3:    next = find_max_gradient(CP-QoSLevelList);
4:    addToUsedResources(next.resourceUsage)
5:    removeChosenCP's Other Service Levels
6:    removeInfeasible(CP-QoSLevelList)
7:  }
```

Step 1 is the creation of the initial penalty vector. It makes a single pass through the list of every control point and QoS level choice, *CP-QoSLevelList*, i.e., $a*q$ elements where a is the number of control points and q is the number of QoS levels. The loop bounded by steps 2 and 7 is executed at most a times, since step 5 removes at least $q-1$ elements from the list each time. Step 6 could remove more, so the actual number of times through the loop could be fewer than a times. Steps 3 and 4 are linear time operations on the current list of control points × QoS levels and resources, respectively.

Therefore, the worst case runtime is equal to *(aq) + a(arq)*, or $O(a^2qr + aq)$, where:

- a is the number of applications,
- q is the number of QoS levels, and
- r is the number of resources

Furthermore, notice that the operation in step 6 affects the runtime of future iterations. If step 6 prunes a significant number of infeasible allocations from the *CP-QoSLevelList*, then the number of times through the loop is significantly reduced. In scenarios where 100% of solutions are feasible, step 6 will never remove anything and the algorithm will run in worst case time. In scenarios where step 6 removes most of the elements because many allocations are infeasible, the algorithm will run much faster. Regardless, in worst case its runtime is polynomial or, more precisely, *quadratic* in the number of applications.

2.3 Applying the QoS Management Algorithms to Dynamic Information Spaces

As illustrated in Fig. 1, the algorithms described above are used by the ISQM layer of a multi-layered QoS management architecture. The ISQM uses the allocation algorithms to select a set of QoS levels to apply at the control points throughout an information space. The QoS levels are enforced at local control points by LQMs, which control the rate, size, processing, and other controllable attributes of information through the system.

The multi-layered approach also allows for QoS enforcement at different granularities of time. At the lowest layers, QoS mechanisms and LQMs maintain QoS levels by adjusting parameters like rate, compression level, and scaling factor as frequently as they need to, with feedback control to avoid thrashing. The execution of the QoS allocation algorithms and subsequent distribution of new QoS levels is expected to be much less frequent in general and associated with discrete events affecting the entire information space, such as changes in information space makeup (new clients or clients leaving), resource availability, or goals and priorities. In cases where the effects of changes can be limited, running the allocation algorithms and distributing new policies might be avoided altogether. For example, a new client that is relatively lower importance than other existing clients need not lead to recalculation of QoS levels for other clients. Likewise, if a client leaves, the resources that it is using can be kept in reserve rather than reallocating the information space, unless there is a critical need for higher QoS somewhere.

This motivates an important area for future research, namely that of limiting the effects of changes in allocations. That is, if a change to state occurs requiring the ISQM to run the QoS allocation algorithms to choose an allocation of QoS levels across the information space, it is desirable for the selected allocation to require as few changes at individual control points as possible. This means the ISQM needs to evaluate possible allocations not only in terms of their feasibility and utility values, but also in terms of their differences from the last deployed allocation. This is an area that we have not investigated fully yet.

3   Experimental Evaluation of the QoS Allocation Algorithms

We conducted a set of experiments to evaluate the relative performance of the algorithms, in terms of quality of the solution produced and the speed of execution to reach a solution. This section describes these experiments and their results.

3.1 Experimental Setup

We executed the experiments on a personal computer with a 2.80 GHz Intel® Pentium®-4 CPU with 512 MB RAM, running the Linux (Fedora Core Release 6) operating system.

We developed a *scenario generator* that randomly generates scenarios used as input to a *simulator* that we developed to execute the algorithms on the scenarios. Each scenario consists of a set of applications, a set of QoS levels for each application, a utility value for each QoS level, and a set of resources and amount used by each QoS level. The generator accepts the following arguments: the number of applications (control points) in the scenario, the number of QoS levels for each application, the total number of resources in an information space, and the number of resources (to be chosen from the total number of resources) for each QoS level. The generator produces a random value for utility for each combination of application and QoS level, randomly chooses the resources to use for each QoS level from among those available, and selects a random amount of each resource that is requested for each QoS level, generating a discrete uniform distribution of scenarios.

The simulator takes as input a set of scenarios, runs the MRQ algorithms on each scenario, and produces the solution allocation, the utility of the solution, the runtime of the algorithm, and values for the metrics described in Section 3.2.

In general, for each of the experiments described in this report, we use the scenario generator to generate a sizable set of scenarios with the following parameters: 3 QoS levels, 6 resources per QoS level, and 110 total resources. We varied the number of applications. For each application set, we generated 100 scenarios. For other experiments, we will describe the specific experiment design as we describe the experimental results.

3.2 Experimental Metrics

Algorithm Metrics. We collected the following metrics to compute the efficacy and the efficiency of the QMS algorithms:

- *Percent of Optimality:* The optimal solution is the feasible solution with the highest utility. For the solution returned by any algorithm, we compute its percent of optimality by dividing its utility by the utility of the optimal solution. For any given scenario, we use the utility reported by the Optimizing Brute-Force algorithm as the baseline against which the optimality of all the algorithms are compared.
- *Runtime:* We use the simulator to measure how fast each algorithm executes in our experiments. Although the absolute runtime depends on the hardware on which the algorithm is executed, the relative runtimes of various algorithms are comparable because we ran all our experiments on the same machine.

Contention Metrics. As part of our experiments, we evaluated the effect of *contention* on our algorithms, i.e., how resource rich or resource scarce the scenario is, and collected contention metrics to support this. We use the following contention metric in the experiments described in this paper:

- *Percent of infeasible solutions* measures the total number of infeasible solutions out of the total number of possible solutions (leaf nodes in the search tree created by the Optimizing Brute-Force algorithm). For example, the total number of possible solutions (i.e., possible allocations) for 10 applications and 3 QoS levels is 59,049 solutions. If only 200 solutions are feasible, we compute the percent of infeasibility as (59049-200)/59049. The percent of infeasibility is directly proportional to the level of contention, i.e., the higher the percentage of infeasible solutions, the higher the contention for resources in the scenario.

3.3   Percent of Optimality and Runtime of the Optimizing Brute-Force Algorithm

The Optimizing Brute-Force algorithm always produces an optimal solution (i.e., 100% optimality). Hence, we use this as the baseline algorithm for measuring the effectiveness of the other algorithms.

However, in the worst case Optimizing Brute-Force runs in exponential time. Furthermore, the runtime grows exponentially as either the number of applications or the number of QoS levels increase. Figure 3 shows *boxplots* of the results for an experiment in which we generated scenarios with the number of applications varying from 10 to 110 by steps of 10, with 100 scenarios at each step. Each application had 3 QoS levels, and each QoS level used 6 resources selected randomly from a total of 110 resources.

Boxplots [22] are a visual means of examining and comparing sets of data, regardless of their distributions, that readily indicates their medians, variance, and skew. As shown in Figure 3, the box of each dataset displays the interquartile range (IQR), i.e., the range from the first to the third quartile in which the middle 50% of data values lie. The thick black line in the middle of the box represents the median. Vertical lines extending out from the box and ending in horizontal bars, called whiskers, represent the extent of the (non-outlier) observed values. Circles beyond the whiskers represent outliers, i.e., values above 1.5 × IQR + the upper quartile value or less than -1.5 × IQR below the lower quartile value.

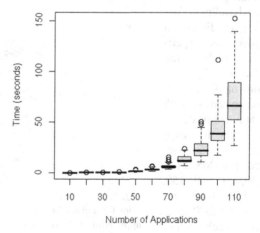

Fig. 3. Impact of varying the number of applications on the runtime of the Optimizing Brute-Force algorithm

As Figure 3 indicates, the runtime is good (near one second) until about 40-50 applications, after which the median runtime and the variance in runtime increase dramatically. The median runtime increases to about 70 seconds at 110 applications, with a worst case runtime of 150 seconds and best case of about 30 seconds. The increased variance is due to the difference in pruning possible from scenario to scenario. The scenarios with the highest runtime allow little pruning, causing the Optimizing Brute-Force algorithm to search nearly the entire space. In contrast, the best measured runtime (about 25 seconds for 110 applications, 6× faster than the worst case time) are for scenarios that allow significant pruning (i.e., many infeasible solutions and/or quickly found high-utility solutions).

Figure 4 depicts the runtime of Optimizing Brute-Force when either the number of QoS levels or the number of applications increases. For this experiment, we generated scenarios that varied the number of QoS levels from 1 to 20 for each number of applications and that varied the number of applications from 1 to 20 for each number of QoS levels. The runtime is acceptable up to about 10 of either, then increases dramatically.

3.4 Percent of Optimality and Runtime of the Greedy Approximation Algorithm

Our experiments indicate that the Greedy Approximation algorithm produces solutions that are close to optimal, with a significant improvement in runtime over the Optimizing Brute-Force baseline. The boxplot in Figure 5 represents an experiment in which we ran the Greedy Approximation algorithm on 50,000 scenarios, with 10 applications[8], 3 QoS levels for each application, 3 resources per QoS level, and 30, 70, 110, 150, and 190 total resources (10,000 scenarios for each level of

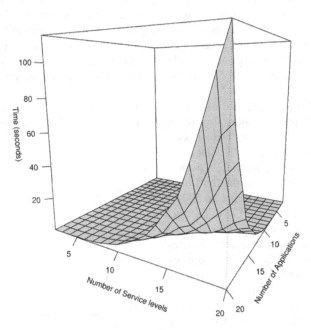

Fig. 4. The impact of simultaneously varying number of applications for a given QoS level and number of QoS levels for a given application when running the Optimizing Brute-Force

---

[8] We had to generate scenarios with a modest number of applications in order to have an optimality baseline against which to compare, since we have to run the Optimizing Brute-Force algorithm on each of the 50,000 scenarios to get the optimal solution.

total resources). The median solution is 96% of optimal (the thick black line near the top of the boxplot), and 75% of the solutions are over 90% of optimal or better (the grey box and above), with all but the outliers producing solutions 80% optimal or better. The worst solution is 40% of optimal.

In experiments designed to identify the source of the low optimality outliers, we determined that contention adversely impacts the effectiveness of Greedy Approximation. Specifically, we observed the median optimality decline to 75% as the level of contention increases significantly. Figure 6 illustrates experiments run with the number of applications varying from 10 to 110, 3 QoS levels, 6 resources per QoS level, and 20 total resources. In these experiments, the median percent of optimality varied between only 75-85%, although the worst case percent optimality is approximately the same as the experiment in Figure 5.

The difference in the number of resources being used by each application and the number of resources available causes the experiments depicted in Figures 5 and 6 to exhibit different contention characteristics. The experiments depicted in Figure 5 (selecting 3 resources from 30, 70, 110, 150, or 190 resources)

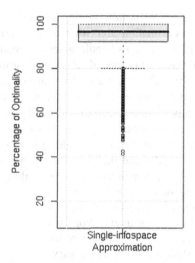

Fig. 5. Optimality of the Greedy Approximation algorithm on 50,000 scenarios with 10 applications, 3 QoS levels per appli-cation, 3 resources per QoS level, and 30, 70, 110, 150, and 190 total resources (10,000 scenarios each)

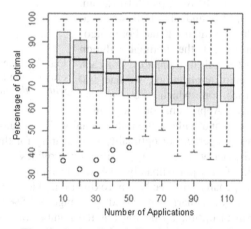

Fig. 6. Optimality of Greedy Approximation on 50,000 scenarios with a varying number of applications, 3 QoS levels per application, 6 resources per QoS level, and 20 total resources

had scenarios with the percentage of feasible solutions ranging from under 10% to 100%, whereas in the experiments depicted in Figure 6 (selecting 6 resources from 20 available), all of the scenarios had fewer than 0.5% feasible allocations. This provides evidence that the level of contention affects the optimality of the Greedy Approximation algorithm.

Effectiveness of the initial penalty optimizing factor. As described in Section 2.2, our Greedy Approximation algorithm uses an initial penalty vector. We introduced the initial penalty vector to handle a set of scenarios (that we dubbed *Greedy Achilles' Heel* scenarios) that produced sub-optimal solutions in the base algorithm (without the initial penalty). These scenarios have one or more high utility applications that request a significant amount of a highly contended resource. Since the algorithm without an initial penalty treated all resources equally and completely available at the beginning, these applications would be greedily assigned resources and potentially starve a large number of other applications resulting in a significantly suboptimal solution. To prevent this, we enhanced the algorithm to perform an initial pass and assign an initial penalty to highly contended resources, making it cost more to request these resources.

We conducted experiments to evaluate the effectiveness of the initial penalty enhancement. For this experiment, we generated Greedy Achilles' Heel scenarios with a varying number of applications, 3 QoS levels for each application, and 6 resources selected randomly from 110 resources for each QoS level. We varied the number of applications from 10 to 40 in steps of 10 (again, the upper bound of 40 allows us to run the Optimizing Brute-Force algorithm to get the optimal solution against which to compare). For each number of applications, we had 100 scenarios on which we ran the Greedy Approximation algorithm

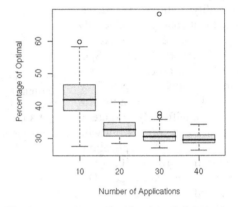

Fig. 7. Percentage of optimality of Greedy Approximation for Greedy Achilles' Heel scenarios *without the initial penalty optimization*

both with and without the initial penalty. The results show that the initial penalty improves the percent of optimality significantly for this class of scenarios. Without the initial penalty, Greedy Approximation provides a low median percent of optimality ranging from approximately 30% to approximately 42% (Figure 7). When we add the initial penalty to Greedy Approximation, the median percent of optimality on the same set of scenarios improved to a range of 75% to 85% (Figure 8). Notice that the percent of optimality declines as the number of applications increase in both cases, due to an increase in contention (more applications competing for the same number of resources).

The effect of the number of applications and the number of resources on the runtime of Greedy Approximation. We also ran experiments that varied the number of applications and the number of resources, the two scenario attributes that we believed might scale to large numbers in realistic scenarios. From the analysis in Section 2.2.1, we expected varying the number of applications to affect the runtime quadratically and varying the number of resources to affect the runtime approximately linearly.

For the experiment varying the number of applications, we increased the applications from 10 to 300 in steps of 10, with 100 scenarios for each discrete number of applications. Each application had 3 QoS levels, and each QoS level used 6 resources selected randomly from a total of 110 resources.

As expected from the analysis above, we observed that the runtime of Greedy Approximation increases polynomially with the increase in the number of applications (Figure 9). As comparison, executing the Greedy Approximation algorithm on a randomly generated scenario with 110 apps took less than 0.10 seconds versus 60 seconds for the Optimizing Brute-Force algorithm. We observed subsecond runtimes for up to hundreds of applications (0.6 seconds for 300 applications).

Figure 10 illustrates the results of an experiment to evaluate the effects of varying the number of resources. In this experiment, we randomly generated scenarios with 100 applications, 3 QoS levels per application, 3 resources per QoS level, and total resources varying from 30 to 180, in steps of 10. We generated 100 scenarios

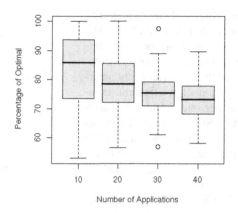

Fig. 8. Percentage of optimality of Greedy Approximation for Greedy Achilles' Heel scenarios *with the initial penalty optimization*

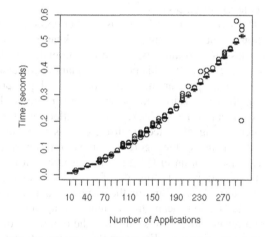

Fig. 9. Runtime of the Greedy Approximation algorithm as the number of applications increase

for each discrete number of resources. Our results indicate that the runtime of Greedy Approximation grows approximately linearly as the number of resources increases, as shown in Figure 10, confirming what we expected from the analysis in Section 2.2.1.

4 Related Work

The information spaces concept has grown out of the *Joint Battlespace Infosphere (JBI)* [2, 10], a US Air Force initiative supporting network centric warfare concepts. It is related to other network centric warfare initiatives, including the *Global Information*

Grid (GIG) and *Net-Centric En-terprise Systems (NCES)*. The GIG will provide the communication, networking, and processing capability to enable the interconnection of warfighters, command personnel, and policymakers [4]. NCES is a set of services (based on Web Services [25]) enabling access to and use of the GIG in warfighting operations [3]. The JBI, as exemplified by the Apollo reference implementation, enables information exchange and management between tactical and enterprise users and is intended to interact with and use NCES services and the GIG as concrete instances emerge.

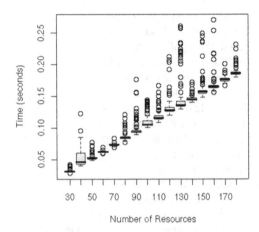

Fig. 10. Runtime of the Greedy Approximation algorithm as the number of resources increases

Dynamic programming [6] is another approach to solving multi-resource QoS allocation problems, treating them as 0-1 knapsack problems. In general, the runtime of this class of algorithms is pseudo-polynomial, or technically an exponential function of their input sizes [9]. This presents a quantization challenge for solving the problem using dynamic programming. A way to develop a polynomial time dynamic programming algorithm is to limit the sizes of the resources by normalizing them and choosing a quantization, i.e., a discrete unit of allocation for each resource. This results in resources being allocated in discrete units (e.g., tenths, hundredths, or thousandths). While this makes the algorithm run much faster, it reduces its effectiveness. For example, a quantization of 0.1 allocates resources in tenths of their total amount available (an application requesting 3% of a resource would get either 0% or 10%). The quantization also places a limit on the number of applications that can share a resource, e.g., a 0.1 quantization means that at most ten applications can share any resource. A finer grain quantization should improve the optimality of the solutions but will increase the runtime significantly. For example, a quantization of 0.01 will allow up to 100 applications to share each resource and will allocate resources in hundredths, but would increase the execution time of the algorithm by at least 10× over that for a 0.1 quantization. For some resources, this would still be a gross quantization. For example, a 100 Mbps link would be allocated in units of 1 Mbps and a 1 Gbps network link would be allocated in units of 10 Mbps. Our experiments showed significantly better efficacy and performance from the Greedy Approximation algorithm.

Einbu provides a method for solving the multi-resource allocation problem by mapping it to the Transportation Problem [5]. The method requires a strictly concave return function, i.e., a utility function in which the additional gain in utility from each additional amount of resources used becomes smaller as the number of resources used increases. While this might be true in many scenarios, it is a limitation that our algorithms do not require. The algorithm is guaranteed to terminate and produce an optimal solution. However, the paper does not analyze the computational complexity of the algorithm.

Xu et al present an algorithm for reserving multiple resources as service requests are made [29]. The algorithm creates a graph for each service request at runtime, with nodes representing QoS levels and edges representing feasible resource requirements. It then runs Dijkstra's shortest path algorithm to determine the suitable resource reservation. The algorithm can run in polynomial time on graphs with no cycles. To handle the more general case, which is NP-complete, the paper presents a two-pass algorithm with heuristics specific to the resource reservation domain. Gopalan and Chiueh present another heuristic algorithm based on tasks with time ordered use of resources [8]. While it is difficult to fully compare just based on the papers, these appear to be viable alternatives to the algorithms we present in this paper.

As an alternative to algorithms based on mathematical foundations or heuristics, Liu et al use a genetic algorithm approach to resource allocation [13]. This approach is based on task scheduling and produces an optimal allocation, but relies on sequential tasks and does not evaluate its runtime performance and suitability to run in-line in a dynamic system.

The work reported in this paper builds upon the authors' previous work in QoS for distributed object and component based middleware [14, 17, 19, 28] and previous work in resource management, such as the Darwin project at CMU [1].

5 Conclusions

For publish-subscribe information spaces to be useful for real-time and critical information exchange, they must include quality of service capabilities. However, traditional QoS mechanisms for resource allocation and differentiated services are not sufficient, unless they include algorithmic means to mediate the conflicting demands for QoS and aggregate QoS control over all the clients and operations of an information space.

In this paper, we have advanced the state of the art in middleware-based multi-resource QoS allocation by defining, evaluating, and prototyping a set of algorithms that allocate QoS levels and resources across large numbers of applications and control points within information spaces. The Optimizing Brute-Force algorithm provides optimal allocations in reasonable execution time for modest numbers of applications (subsecond response up to 40-50 applications in our experiments). The Greedy Approximation algorithm provides approximate solutions, but scales well, with a median of 96% optimality and demonstrated fast execution times to hundreds of applications with subsecond response in our experiments. Greedy Approximation has the fastest runtime, but farther from optimal solutions in highly contentious scenarios (defined by the number of feasible allocations). Conversely, it produces closer to optimal solutions, but takes more time to do so, when contention is low (i.e., there are many feasible solutions).

Under an ongoing effort with the US Air Force Research Laboratory, we are currently prototyping these algorithms as part of a practical application of multi-layered QoS management middleware for information spaces, which will give us the opportunity to evaluate these algorithms in the context of realistic scenarios.

References

1. Chandra, P., Fisher, A., Kosak, C., Ng, T.S., Steenkiste, P., Takahasi, E., Zhang, H.: Darwin: Resource Management for Value-Added Customizable Network Service. In: Sixth IEEE International Conference on Network Protocols (ICNP 1998), Austin, TX (October 1998)
2. Combs, V., Hillman, R., Muccio, M., McKeel, R.: Joint Battlespace Infosphere: Information Management within a C2 Enterprise. In: The Tenth International Command and Control Technology Symposium, ICCRTS (2005)
3. Defense Information Systems Agency, Net-Centric Enterprise Services, http://www.disa.mil/nces/
4. DoD CIO, Department of Defense Global Information Grid Architectural Vision, Vision for a Net-Centric, Service-Oriented DoD Enterprise, Version 1.0 (June 2007), http://www.defenselink.mil/cio-nii/docs/GIGArchVision.pdf
5. Einbu, J.M.: A Finite Method for the Solution of a Multi-Resource Allocation Problem with Concave Return Functions. Mathematics of Operations Research 9(2), 232–243 (1984)
6. Giegerich, R., Meyer, C., Steffen, P.: A Discipline of Dynamic Programming over Sequence Data. Science of Computer Programming 51, 215–263 (2004)
7. Gill, C., Loyall, J., Schantz, R., Schmidt, D.: Experiences Using Adaptive Middleware in Distributed Real-time Embedded Application Contexts: a Dependability Perspective. In: Workshop on Dependable Middleware-Based Systems (WDMS), Part of Dependable Systems and Networks Conference (DSN 2002), Bethesda, Maryland, June 26 (2002)
8. Gopalan, K., Chiueh, T.: Multi-Resource Allocation and Scheduling with Real-Time Constraints. In: Multimedia Computing and Networking (MMCN 2002), San Jose, CA, January 18-25 (2002)
9. Hall, L.: Computational Complexity, The Johns Hopkins University, http://www.esi2.us.es/~mbilbao/complexi.htm
10. The Joint Battlespace Infosphere website, http://www.infospherics.org/
11. Lee, C., Lehoczky, J., Rajkumar, R., Siewiork, D.: On Quality of Service Optimization with Discrete QoS Options. In: Fifth IEEE Real-Time Technology and Applications Symposium (RTAS 1999) (1999)
12. Linderman, M., Siegel, B., Ouellet, D., Brichacek, J., Haines, S., Chase, G., O'May, J.: A Reference Model for Information Management to Support Coalition Information Sharing Needs. In: The Tenth International Command and Control Technology Symposium (ICCRTS) (2005)
13. Liu, Y., Zhao, S.-L., Du, X.-K., Li, S.-Q.: Optimization of Resource Allocation in Construction Using Genetic Algorithms. In: Fourth International Conference on Machine Learning and Cybernetics, Guangzhou, August 18-21 (2005)
14. Loyall, J., Sharma, P., Gillen, M., Schantz, R.: A QoS Management System for Dynamically Interoperating Net-Centric Systems. In: The SPIE Conference on Defense Transformation and Net-Centric Systems, Orlando, FL, April 9-12 (2007)
15. Manghwani, P., Loyall, J., Sharma, P., Gillen, M., Ye, J.: End-to-End Quality of Service Management for Distributed Real-Time Embedded Applications. In: The Thirteenth International Workshop on Parallel and Distributed Real-Time Systems (WPDRTS 2005), Denver, Colorado, April 4-5 (2005)
16. Schantz, R.E., Loyall, J.P., Rodrigues, C., Schmidt, D.C.: Controlling Quality-of-Service in Distributed Real-Time and Embedded Systems via Adaptive Middleware. Software: Practice and Experience 36(11-12), 1189–1208 (2006)

17. Schantz, R.E., Loyall, J.P., Rodrigues, C., Schmidt, D.C., Krishnamurthy, Y., Pyarali, I.: Flexible and Adaptive QoS Control for Distributed Real-Time and Embedded Middleware. In: Endler, M., Schmidt, D.C. (eds.) Middleware 2003. LNCS, vol. 2672, pp. 374–393. Springer, Heidelberg (2003)
18. Sharma, P., Loyall, J., Schantz, R., Ye, J., Manghwani, P., Gillen, M., Heineman, G.T.: Using Composition of QoS Components to Provide Dynamic, End-To-End QoS in Distributed Embedded Applications - a Middleware Approach. IEEE Internet Computing 10(3), 16–23 (2006)
19. Sharma, P.K., Loyall, J.P., Heineman, G.T., Schantz, R.E., Shapiro, R., Duzan, G.: Component-Based Dynamic QoS Adaptations in Distributed Real-Time and Embedded Systems. In: Meersman, R., Tari, Z. (eds.) OTM 2004. LNCS, vol. 3291, pp. 1208–1224. Springer, Heidelberg (2004)
20. Sun Microsystems, Java Message Service, Version 1.1, April 12 (2002), http://java.sun.com/products/jms/docs.html
21. Toyoda, Y.: A Simplified Algorithm for Obtaining Approximate Solution to Zero-One Programming Problems. Management Science 21 (1975)
22. Tukey, J.W.: Exploratory Data Analysis. Addison-Wesley, Reading (1977)
23. U.S. Air Force. A Guide for Communities of Interest (COIs), Implementing the DoD Net-Centric Data Strategy and the Air Force Information and Data Management Strategy, Version 1.0 (April 2005)
24. US Air Force Air Force Research Laboratory, Apollo v.1.0 User's Guide
25. W3C, Web Services Architecture, W3C Working Group Note (February 11, 2004), http://www.w3.org/TR/2004/NOTE-ws-arch-20040211/
26. W3C, XQuery 1.0: An XML Query Language, W3C Recommendation (January 23, 2007), http://www.w3.org/TR/xquery/
27. W3C, Extensible Markup Language (XML) 1.0, W3C Recommendation (August 16, 2006), http://www.w3.org/TR/xml
28. Wang, N., Gill, C., Schmidt, D., Gokhale, A., Natarajan, B., Loyall, J., Schantz, R., Rodrigues, C.: QoS-Enabled Middleware. In: Mahmoud, Q.H. (ed.) Middleware for Communications. Wiley, Chichester (2004)
29. Xu, D., Nahrstedt, K., Wichadakul, D.: QoS and Contention-Aware Multi-Resource Reservation. Cluster Computing 4(2), 95–107 (2001)

Profiling and Modeling Resource Usage of Virtualized Applications

Timothy Wood[1], Ludmila Cherkasova[2], Kivanc Ozonat[2],
and Prashant Shenoy[1]

[1] University of Massachusetts, Amherst
{twood,shenoy}@cs.umass.edu
[2] HP Labs, Palo Alto
{lucy.cherkasova,kivanc.ozonat}@hp.com

Abstract. Next Generation Data Centers are transforming labor-intensive, hard-coded systems into shared, virtualized, automated, and fully managed adaptive infrastructures. Virtualization technologies promise great opportunities for reducing energy and hardware costs through server consolidation. However, to safely transition an application running natively on real hardware to a virtualized environment, one needs to estimate the additional resource requirements incurred by virtualization overheads.

In this work, we design a general approach for estimating the resource requirements of applications when they are transferred to a virtual environment. Our approach has two key components: a set of microbenchmarks to profile the different types of virtualization overhead on a given platform, and a regression-based model that maps the native system usage profile into a virtualized one. This derived model can be used for estimating resource requirements of any application to be virtualized on a given platform. Our approach aims to eliminate error-prone manual processes and presents a fully automated solution. We illustrate the effectiveness of our methodology using Xen virtual machine monitor. Our evaluation shows that our automated model generation procedure effectively characterizes the different virtualization overheads of two diverse hardware platforms and that the models have median prediction error of less than 5% for both the RUBiS and TPC-W benchmarks.

1 Introduction

Virtualization and automation are key capabilities of Next Generation Data Centers (NGDC), promising to create a more agile and dynamic IT infrastructure. Virtualization separates the hardware owner from the application owner – allowing system configuration, monitoring, and management to be homogenized and automated across the data center. While masking the details of server resources from users, virtualization can optimize resource sharing among applications hosted in different virtual machines via the ability to quickly repurpose server capacity on demand, and hence better meet the needs of applications and respond more effectively to changing business conditions.

V. Issarny and R. Schantz (Eds.): Middleware 2008, LNCS 5346, pp. 366–387, 2008.

In NGDC, where server virtualization provides the ability to slice larger, underutilized physical servers into smaller, virtual ones, fast and accurate *performance models* become instrumental for enabling applications to be consolidated, optimally placed and provided with the necessary resources. In order to evaluate which workloads can be consolidated to which servers, some capacity planning and workload analysis must be done. In the simple naive case, the service provider may estimate the peak resource requirements of each workload and then evaluate the combined resource requirements of a group of workloads by using the sum of their peak demands. However, such an approach can lead to significant resource over-provisioning since it does not take into account the benefits of resource sharing to accommodate the complementary workload patterns. A more promising and accurate approach for the design of workload placement services employs *a trace-based approach* that assesses permutations and combinations of workload patterns in order to determine the optimal stacking functions [10, 25, 27]. Under this approach, a representative application resource usage profile is gathered over some time period (typically 3-6 months). Then these traces are used for capacity planning and workload placement in workload consolidation exercises (see existing commercial tools [14, 34]). The general idea behind trace-based methods is that the historic traces that capture past application demands are representative of the future application behavior.

However, capacity planning when transitioning to a virtual environment poses additional challenges due to overheads caused by the virtualization layer. These overheads depend on the type and implementation specifics of the virtualization solution [5, 17, 29, 37]. Often, the "amount" of CPU overhead is directly proportional to the "amount" of performed I/O processing [7, 11]. Current trace-based capacity planning and management solutions have the capability to scale workload traces by a specified CPU-multiplier to account for hardware changes between platforms, but this form of scaling may not be effective when moving to a virtualized platform which can exhibit very different levels of overhead depending on the rate and type of I/O being performed by an application.

In this work, we design a general approach for estimating the CPU requirements of applications when they are transferred to a virtual environment. Our approach has the following key components:

- A selected set of microbenchmarks to profile the different types of virtualization overhead on a given platform. This microbenchmark suite is executed on the native hardware and in a virtualized environment to create two resource usage profiles: *i) native* and *ii) virtualized*;
- Using a regression-based approach we create a model that maps the *native* system usage profile into the *virtualized* one. This model helps to predict the resource requirements of any application on that platform.

The correct execution phase of the microbenchmark suite is a prerequisite for building an accurate model between native and virtualized platforms. If some microbenchmarks have malfunctioned or collected data were corrupted then it can inevitably impact the model outcome. We perform an additional analysis to filter out microbenchmark data with high error against the obtained regression-based model. Then, a more accurate model is created by using the reduced data set. We also can rerun identified "failed" or "malfunctioned" microbenchmarks and repeat the analysis phase. Such an approach aims to eliminate error-prone manual processes in order to support a fully automated solution.

We illustrate the effectiveness of our methodology using Xen virtual machine monitor [5]. The evaluation shows that our automated model generation procedure effectively characterizes the different virtualization overheads of two diverse hardware platforms and that the models have a median prediction error of less than 5% for both the RUBiS [3] and TPC-W [31] benchmarks.

2   Problem Definition

Server consolidation is an approach to reduce the total number of servers in response to the problem of server sprawl, a situation in which multiple, under-utilized servers take up more space and consume more resources than can be justified by their workloads. *Virtual Machine Monitors (VMMs)* enable diverse applications to run in isolated environments on a shared hardware platform, and provide a degree of fault and performance isolation between the applications.

A typical approach for evaluating which workloads can be efficiently consolidated together is based on multi-dimensional "binpacking" of resource usage traces. Under such an approach, each application is characterized by its CPU, I/O and memory usage over time. Then a binpacking algorithm finds a combination of workloads with resource requirements which do not exceed the available server resources. After the initial workload placement, specialized workload management tools are used[13, 15] to dynamically adjust system resources to support the required application performance.

In our work, we are concerned with the initial workload placement phase that requires as an input the application resource usage traces in virtual environment. Resource requirements (in particular, CPU requirements) can increase due to virtualization overheads. It is important to know what an application's resource needs are going to be prior to transitioning it to the virtual environment. If these overheads are not accounted for during initial planning, an application could be deployed to a server with insufficient resources, resulting in unacceptable application performance.

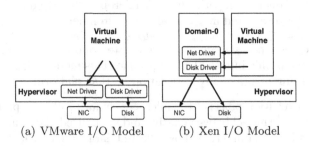

(a) VMware I/O Model   (b) Xen I/O Model

Fig. 1. Two popular I/O models for VMs

Xen and VMware ESX server demonstrate the two popular I/O models for VMs. In ESX (and Xen in its original design [5]), the hypervisor itself contains device driver code and provides safe, shared access for I/O hardware (see Figure 1 a). Later, the Xen team proposed a new architecture [9] that allows unmodified device drivers to be hosted and executed in isolated "driver domains" (see Figure 1 b).

In Xen, the management domain Dom-0 hosts unmodified Linux device drivers and plays the role of the driver domain. This I/O model results in a more complex CPU usage model. For I/O intensive applications, CPU usage has two components: CPU consumed by the guest virtual machine (VM) and CPU consumed by Dom-0 which performs I/O processing on behalf of the guest domain.

In this work, without loss of generality, we demonstrate our approach using Xen running paravirtualized VMs. We believe that our approach can be applied to other virtualization platforms such as VMware ESX Server, but focus on Xen in this work because it presents the additional challenge of modeling both the virtualized application and the driver domain (Dom-0) separately.

Given resource utilization traces of an application running natively, we aim to estimate what its resource requirements would be if the application were transitioned to a virtual environment on a given hardware platform. For example, let a collection of application resource usage profiles (over time) in native system be provided as shown in Figure 2 (top): *i)* CPU utilization, *ii)* transferred and received networking packets, *iii)* read and written disk blocks.

The *goal* is to estimate the CPU requirements of the following two components as shown in Figure 2 (bottom):

- virtual machine (VM) where the application is going to reside and execute;
- Dom-0 which performs I/O processing on behalf of the guest virtual machine.

Intuitively, we expect that CPU utilization of VM is highly correlated and proportional to the native CPU usage profile of the application, while Dom-0 CPU utilization is mostly determined by a combination of I/O profiles (both network and disk).

We focus on estimating only CPU utilization since other metrics (such as disk and network request rates) are not directly impacted by the virtualization

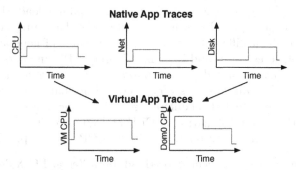

Fig. 2. Using native application traces to predict resource needs in virtual environments

layer–running an application in a virtualized environment will not cause more packets to be sent over the network or more disk requests to be generated. Instead, the virtualization layer incurs additional processing overheads when I/O is performed; it is these overheads which our models seek to capture.[1]

Our Approach: We present an automated model generation system which determines the relationship between the native and virtual platforms being used. The overhead of the virtual platform is characterized by running a series of microbenchmarks on both platforms and building a model that relates the resource requirements on one platform to the other. Although it is created using data from synthetic benchmarks, the result is a general model which can be applied to traces from any other application in order to predict what its resource requirements will be on the virtual platform.

3   Platform Profiling

In this section, we describe the collection of microbenchmarks that are selected for profiling different types of virtualization overhead on a given platform. In order to determine a general relationship between the application resource usage in native and virtual platforms, we first accumulate the samples of such usage profiles by executing a specially selected set of microbenchmarks in both native and virtualized environments.

3.1   Microbenchmark Requirements

The microbenchmark selection for our suite is driven by the following objectives:

- *Microbenchmarks must be able to apply a range of workload intensities.*
There are a large number of benchmarks available which allow you to stress test a system to see how it performs under maximum load. However, a typical enterprise application exhibits variable workloads. A benchmark which simply reports the maximum number of web requests or disk accesses that a system can perform per second is not useful for us since it only provides information about the maximum capacity and corresponding resource usage, not about the utilization under different workloads. In consolidation scenarios, the considered applications are likely to operate at a light or medium load. Therefore, we concentrate on creating a suite of microbenchmarks that can be configured to generate workloads of different *intensities*, i.e., capable of generating different networking/disk access rates and consume different CPU amounts.
- *Microbenchmarks should run nearly-identical in both native and virtual environments.* This requirement is very important for our approach. The application behavior is represented via different resource usage traces over time. When a workload performs a combination of CPU and I/O activities at time interval T on a native system, we correlate it with the CPU usage profile (both VM

---

[1] Virtualization also incurs a memory overhead. Both Xen and ESX Server require a base allocation for Dom-0 or the Service Console, plus a variable amount per VM.

and Dom-0) observed at time interval T in the virtualized environment for the same workload in order to build the model (relationship) between the native and virtualized systems. Thus, the requirement for our microbenchmarks is that the workloads must be *nearly-identical* in both the native and virtual environments we test. While our benchmarks allow some non-determinism in the workload traffic patterns, we carefully design our microbenchmarks to always execute the same set of activities over the same period of time. We avoid benchmarks with a strong feedback loop since virtualization overheads may increase latency and distort the resource usage over time. While our models are primarily designed for open loop applications, such as web servers where the user "think time" is much higher than the average request processing time, they still provide a bound on resource utilization for closed loop systems.[2]

3.2   Microbenchmark Workloads

The selected microbenchmarks have to create a set of workloads that utilize different system resources and have a different range of workload intensities.

We use a client-server style setup in our benchmarks. In general, a client machine issues a set of requests to the benchmark server running on the system being profiled. The clients adjust the rate and type of requests to control the amount of CPU computation and I/O activities performed on the test system. At a high level, our microbenchmarks are comprised of three basic workload patterns that either cause the system to perform CPU intensive computation, send/receive network packets, or read/write to disk.

- Our *computation intensive* workload calculates Fibonacci series when it receives a request. The number of terms in the series is varied to adjust the computation time.
- The *network intensive* workload has two modes depending on the type of request. In transmit mode, each incoming request results in a large file being sent from the system being tested to the client. In receive mode, the clients upload files to the benchmark application. The size of transferred files and the rate of requests is varied to adjust the network utilization rate.
- The *disk intensive* workload has read and write modes. In both cases, a random file is either read from or written to a multilevel directory structure. File size and request rate can be adjusted to control the disk I/O rate.

Each workload is created by adjusting the request type sent to the server from the client machines. We split each of the basic benchmark types, CPU-, network-, and disk-intensive, into five different intensities ranging from 10% load to 90% load. The maximum load that a server can handle is determined by increasing the throughput of benchmark requests until either the virtual machine or Dom-0 CPU becomes saturated during testing. To create more complex and realistic scenarios, we use a *combination* workload that exercises all three of the above

---

[2] Sec. 6 provides a more detailed discussion on the issue of "applications with a feedback loop".

components. The combination workload simultaneously sends requests of all types to the benchmarked server. The relative intensity of each request type is varied in order to provide more realistic training data which does not focus exclusively on a single form of I/O.

The microbenchmarks are implemented as a set of PHP scripts running on an Apache web server at the benchmarked server side. Basing the microbenchmarks on Apache and PHP has the benefit that they can be easily deployed and executed on a wide range of hardware platforms within a software environment which data center administrators are already familiar with. The developed microbenchmark suite allows us to generate a diverse set of simple and more complex workloads that exercise different system components. The full set of PHP scripts, as well as the scripts to create the file structure used in the disk tests, comprise only a few hundred lines of code.

The client workloads are generated using *httperf* [22] and Apache JMeter [4]. These tools provide flexible facilities for generating variable and fixed rate HTTP workloads. The workloads can then be easily "replayed" in different environments. Both tools can emulate an arbitrary number of clients accessing files on a webserver.

3.3   Platform Resource Usage Profiles

We generate *platform profiles* by running a set of microbenchmarks on the systems being tested. While each microbenchmark is running, we gather resource utilization traces to define the platform profile used as the training data for the model. Within the native system, we currently gather information about *eleven* different resource metrics related to CPU utilization, network activity, and disk I/O. The full list of metrics is shown in Table 1. These statistics can all be gathered easily in Linux with the sysstat monitoring package [30]. We focus on this set of resource measurements since they can easily be gathered with low overhead. Since these traces must also be gathered from the live application being transitioned to the virtual environment, it is crucial that a lightweight monitoring system can be used to gather data.

We monitor three CPU related metrics since different types of activities may have different virtualization overheads. For example, user space processing such as simple arithmetic operations performed by an application are unlikely to have much overhead in current virtualization platforms. In contrast, tasks which occur in kernel space, such as context switches, memory management, and I/O processing, are likely to have a higher level of overhead since they can require traps to the hypervisor.

Table 1. Resource Utilization Metrics

CPU	Network	Disk
User Space %	Rx packets/sec	Read req/sec
Kernel %	Tx packets/sec	Write req/sec
IO Wait %	Rx bytes/sec	Read blocks/sec
	TX bytes/sec	Write blocks/sec

We measure both the packet rates and byte rates of the network interfaces since different platforms may handle I/O virtualization in different ways. For example, prior to Xen version 3.0.3, incoming network packets were passed between Dom-0 and the guest domain by flipping ownership of memory pages, thus the overhead associated with receiving each packet was independent of its size [11]. Newer versions of Xen directly copy packets from Dom-0 to the guest domain rather than using page flipping, thus the overhead is also related to the number of bytes received per second, not just the number of packets. We differentiate between sending and receiving since these paths may have different optimizations.

We split disk measurements into four categories based on similar reasoning.

A resource usage trace is gathered for each benchmark set containing values for all metrics listed in Table 1, plus the time interval, and benchmark ID. After the resource metrics have been gathered on the native system, the Dom-0 and VM CPU utilizations are measured for the identical benchmark on the virtualized platform.

4   Model Generation

This section describes how to create models which characterize the relationship between a set of resource utilization metrics gathered from an application running natively on real hardware and the CPU requirements of the application if it were run on a virtual platform. Two models are created: one which predicts the CPU requirement of the virtual machine running the application, and one which predicts the Dom_0 CPU requirements when it performs I/O processing on behalf of the guest domain.

The model creation employs the following *three key components*:

- A *robust linear regression* algorithm that is used to lessen the impact of outliers.
- A *stepwise regression* approach that is employed to include only the most statistically significant metrics in the final model.
- A *model refinement* algorithm that is used for post-processing the training data to eliminate or rerun erroneous benchmarks and to rebuild a more accurate model.

4.1   Model Creation

To find the relationship between the application resource usage in native and virtualized systems we use the resource usage profile gathered from a set of microbenchmarks run in both the virtual and native platforms of interest (see Section 3.3).

Using values from the collected profile, we form a set of equations which calculate the Dom-0 CPU utilization as a linear combination of the different metrics:

$$U_{dom0}^1 = c_0 + c_1 * M_1^1 + c_2 * M_2^1 + \dots + c_{11} * M_{11}^1$$
$$U_{dom0}^2 = c_0 + c_1 * M_1^2 + c_2 * M_2^2 + \dots + c_{11} * M_{11}^2 \tag{1}$$
$$\dots \qquad\qquad \dots$$

where

- M_i^j is a value of metric M_i collected during the time interval j for a benchmark executed in the native environment;
- U_{dom0}^j is a measured CPU utilization for a benchmark executed in virtualized environment with the corresponding time interval j.

Let $c_0^{dom0}, c_1^{dom0}, ..., c_{11}^{dom0}$ denote the approximated solution for the equation set (1). Then, an approximated utilization $\hat{U}_{dom0}^j$ can be calculated as

$$\hat{U}_{dom0}^j = c_0^{dom0} + \sum_{i=1}^{11} M_i^j \cdot c_i^{dom0} \tag{2}$$

To solve for c_i^{dom0} ($0 \leq i \leq 11$), one can choose a regression method from a variety of known methods in the literature. A popular method for solving such a set of equations is Least Squares Regression that minimizes the error:

$$e = \sqrt{\sum_j (\hat{U}_{dom0}^j - U_{dom0}^j)_j^2}$$

The set of coefficients $c_0^{dom0}, c_1^{dom0}, ..., c_n^{dom0}$ is the model that describes the relationship between the application resource usage in the native system and application CPU usage in Dom-0.

We form a set of equations similar to Eq. 1 which characterize the CPU utilization of the VM by replacing U_{dom0}^i with U_{vm}^i. The solution $c_0^{vm}, c_1^{vm}, ..., c_n^{vm}$ defines the model that relates the application resource usage in the native system and application CPU usage in the VM running the application. To deal with outliers and erroneous benchmark executions in collected data and to improve the overall model accuracy, we apply a more advanced variant of the regression technique as described below.

Robust Stepwise Linear Regression: To decrease the impact of occasional bad measurements and outliers, we employ iteratively reweighted least squares [12] from the Robust Regression family. The robust regression technique uses a bisquare weighting function which lessens the weight and the impact of data points with high error.

In order to create a model which utilizes only the statistically significant metrics and avoids "overfitting" the data, we use stepwise linear regression to determine which set of input metrics are the best predictors for the output variable [8]. Step-wise regression starts with an empty model, and iteratively selects a new metric to add based on a significance test. A complete description of the stepwise and robust regression techniques we use is deffered to a separate technical report [38].

Model Refinement: Our use of robust linear regression techniques helps lessen the impact of occasional bad data points, but it may not be effective if all measurements within a microbenchmark are corrupt (this can happen due to unexpected background processes on the server, timing errors at the client, or network issues). If some microbenchmarks have failed or collected data were corrupted then it can inevitably impact the model outcome.

In order to automate the model generation process and eliminate the need for manual analysis of these bad data points, we must automatically detect erroneous microbenchmarks and either rerun them or remove their data points from the training set. At runtime, it can be very difficult to determine whether a benchmark is executed correctly, since the resource utilization cannot be known ahead of time, particularly on the virtual platform which may have unpredictable overheads. Instead, we wait until all benchmarks have been run and an initial model has been created to post process the training set and determine if some benchmarks have anomalous behavior.

First, we compute the mean squared error for all data points (i.e., all microbenchmarks): let us call it e_{mean}, as well as the standard deviation of the squared errors: let us call it e_{std}. Then the model created from the full benchmark set is applied back to each microbenchmark i individually to calculate the mean squared error for that benchmark: let us call it e_i. Microbenchmarks with high error values can then be easily separated so that they can either be rerun or removed from the training set.

4.2 Model Application

Once a model has been created, it can then be applied to resource utilization traces of other applications in order to predict what their CPU requirements would be if transferred to the virtual environment. Resource usage traces of the application are obtained by monitoring the application in its native environment over time. The traces must contain the same resource metrics as presented in Table 1, except that CPU utilizations of VM and Dom-0 are unknown and need to be predicted. Applying the model coefficients $c_0^{dom0}, c_1^{dom0}, ..., c_{11}^{dom0}$ and $c_0^{vm}, c_1^{vm}, ..., c_n^{vm}$ to the application usage traces in native environment (using Equation 1), we obtain two new CPU usage traces that estimate the application CPU requirements in Dom-0 and the virtual machine.

5   Experimental Evaluation

In this section, we first try to justify a set of our choices presented in earlier Sections 3 and 4: why these *metrics*? why these *microbenchmarks*? why this *model creation process*? After that, we evaluate the effectiveness of our models under several realistic web application workloads on two different hardware platforms.

5.1   Implementation Details

Our implementation and evaluation has centered on the Xen virtualization platform. In our evaluation, both the native systems and virtual machines run the Red Hat Enterprise Linux 5 operating system with Linux kernel 2.6.18-8. We use paravirtualized Xen version 3.0.3-rc5.

Monitoring resource utilization in the native environment is done with the sysstat package [30] commonly used in Linux environments. The virtual CPU utilizations are measured using xentop and xenmon, standard resource monitoring tools included with the Xen distribution. Statistics are gathered for 30 second monitoring windows in both environments. We have experimented with both finer grain and longer intervals and found similar results. The system is configured that Dom-0 resides on a separate CPU.

We evaluate our approach using two realistic web applications:

- *RUBiS* [3] is an auction site prototype modeled after eBay.com. A client workload generator emulates the behavior of users browsing and bidding on items. We use the Apache/PHP implementation of RUBiS version 1.4.3 with a MySQL database.
- *TPC-W* [31] represents an e-commerce site (modeled after Amazon.com) implemented with Java servlets running on Tomcat with a MySQL database.

Both applications have an application and a database tier. We profile and predict the resource requirements of the application server tier; the databases are hosted on a separate server which is sufficiently provisioned so that it will not become a bottleneck.

We have tested our approach on two different hardware platforms:

- HP ProLiant DL385, 2 processors: AMD Opteron model 252 2.6GHz with 1MB L2 single-core, 64-bit; 2 x 2GB memory; 2 x 1 Gbit/s NICs, 72 GB 15K U320 Disk.
- HP ProLiant DL580 G2, 4 processors: Intel Xeon 1.6 GHz with 1MB L2 cache, 32-bit; 3 x 2GB memory; 2 x 1 Gbit/s NICs, 72 GB 15K U320 Disk.

5.2 Importance of Modeling I/O

Our system generates models based on up to eleven different resource utilization metrics, here we evaluate whether such complexity is warranted, or if a simple model based solely on scaling CPU requirements is a viable approach. In the simplified approach, a model is created using the same model generation techniques as described in Section 4, except that instead of using all eleven metrics, only a single Total CPU metric is used to predict the CPU needs in virtual environment. We produce a model using each technique to predict the CPU requirements and demonstrate it using the CPU needs of the guest domain, since, intuitively, it is more likely that the simplified model will perform better when predicting VM CPU needs than when predicting Dom-0 since the latter is scheduled almost exclusively for handling I/O.

Since our models are created with stepwise regression, not all of the eleven possible metrics are included in the final model. The Dom-0 model uses five metrics: Kernel CPU, I/O Wait, Rx Packets/sec, Tx Packets/sec, and Disk Write Req/sec. Dom-0's CPU utilization is dominated by I/O costs, so a large number of I/O related metrics are important for an accurate model. In contrast the virtual machine model uses only three metrics: User Space CPU, Kernel CPU,

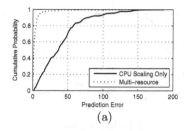

		Test Set Median Error %		
		CPU	Net	Disk
	CPU	0.36	670	13
Training	Net	11	3.4	1
Set	Disk	7.1	1798	1.2
	All	0.66	1.1	2.1

(a)   (b)

Fig. 3. (a) Using CPU as the only prediction metric leads to high error. (b) Using a subset of benchmarks leads to poor accuracy when applied to data sets with different type of I/O.

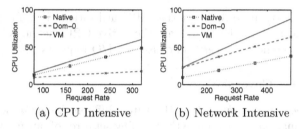

(a) CPU Intensive   (b) Network Intensive

Fig. 4. I/O intensive applications exhibit higher virtualization overheads

and RX Packets. We compare this multi-resource VM model to the CPU-Scaling based model which uses only the Total CPU metric (equal to the sum of User Space and Kernel CPU).

We evaluate the performance of these two models by training them on our microbenchmark set and then comparing the error when the models are applied back to the training data. Figure 3 (a) shows the error CDF for each model, showing the probability that our predictions were within a certain degree of accuracy for the virtual machine.

Our multiple resource model performs significantly better than the CPU scaling approach; the 90th error percentile using our approach is 5% while the scaling approach is 65%. Without information about I/O activities, the simple model cannot effectively distinguish between the different types of benchmarks, each of which has different levels of overhead. Even though the VM model only includes one I/O metric, splitting CPU into User and Kernel time acts as a surrogate for detecting high levels of I/O. Our results suggest that I/O activity can cause significant changes in the CPU requirements of both Dom-0 and the guest domain: Dom-0 since it must process the I/O requests, and the guest because of the increased number of hypercalls required for I/O intensive applications.

Figure 4 presents profiles of some of our CPU and network intensive microbenchmarks. The CPU intensive application exhibits only a small virtualization overhead occurring for the VM CPU requirements and Dom-0 also has relatively low CPU needs. In contrast, the network intensive application has a significantly higher requirement in Dom-0 as well as a much larger increase in VM

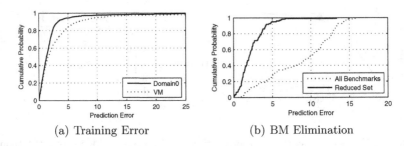

Fig. 5. (a) CDF error of the training set on the Intel 4 -CPU machine. (b) Automatic benchmark elimination can increase model accuracy.

CPU requirements relative to the native CPU utilization. This further demonstrates why creating a model using only the native CPU metric is incapable of capturing the differences in overhead caused by I/O requests.

5.3   Benchmark Coverage

In this experiment we examine how the three different benchmark types each add useful information and examine the training set error of our model. Figure 3 (b) illustrates how using only a single type of microbenchmark to build a model can produce very high error rates when applied to applications with different workload characteristics.

For example, training the model solely with the CPU intensive microbenchmarks provides accuracy within 1% when applied back to the same kind of CPU intensive workloads, but the median error rises to 670% when applied to the network intensive data. This happens because the CPU benchmark includes only very low network rates. When a model based solely on that data tries to predict the CPU needs of the network intensive applications, it must extrapolate well beyond the range of data it was trained with, resulting in wildly inaccurate numbers. The bottom row in the table corresponds to using *all* of the benchmark data to create a model. This provides a high degree of accuracy in all cases – while a specialized model may provide higher accuracy on data sets very similar to it, we seek to build a general model which will be effective on workloads with a range of characteristics.

Figure 5(a) shows the error CDF when *all* of our benchmark data is used to create a model and then the model is validated by applying back to the training set. The error is quite low, with 90% of the predictions being within 3% for Dom-0 and 7% for the virtual machine. This confirms our hypothesis that a single linear model can effectively model the full range of training data.

5.4   Benchmark Error Detection

Our profiling system runs a series of microbenchmarks with identical workloads on both the native and virtual platforms. This experiment tests our anomalous benchmark detection algorithm. To be effective, it should be able to detect which benchmarks did not run correctly so that they can be either rerun or eliminated from the training set. If the detection scheme is too rigorous, it may eliminate too many data points, reducing the effectiveness of the model.

We first gather a set of training data where 10 percent of the benchmarks are corrupted with additional background processes. Figure 5(b) shows the change in model accuracy after the error detection algorithm eliminates the malfunctioning microbenchmarks. We then gather a second training set with no failed benchmarks and run the error detection algorithm on this clean data set. We find that the model performance before and after the error detection algorithm is identical since very few data points are eliminated.

While it is possible for these errors to be manually detected and corrected, our goal is to automate the model creation procedure as much as possible. The error detection algorithm reduces the human interaction required to create high quality models.

5.5 Model Accuracy

To test the accuracy of a model, we use it to predict the CPU requirements of a test application based on a trace of the application running natively. We then run the test application within the virtual environment to determine the prediction error. In this section we evaluate our models on both the RUBiS and TPC-W web applications. These experiments were run on the Intel system described previously.

We create a variable rate workload for RUBiS by incrementally spawning clients over a thirty minute period. The system is loaded by between 150 and 700 simultaneous clients. This workload is repeated twice to evaluate the amount of random variation between experiments. We record measurements and make predictions for 30 second intervals. Figure 6 compares the actual CPU utilization of the RUBiS application to the amount predicted by the model. Note that the virtual machine running RUBiS is allocated two virtual CPUs, so the percent utilization is out of 200.

Figure 7(a) shows a CDF of the models' prediction error. We find that 90% of our predictions for Dom-0 are within 4% accuracy, and within 11% for predicting the virtual machine's CPU utilization. Some of this error is due to model

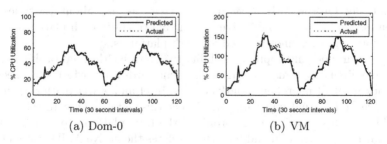

(a) Dom-0   (b) VM

Fig. 6. Prediction accuracy of the RUBiS web application

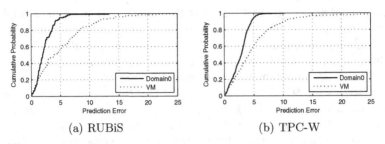

(a) RUBiS   (b) TPC-W

Fig. 7. Error rates on the Intel platform

inaccuracy, but it can also be due to irregularities in the data used as input to the model. For example, there is a spike in the predicted CPU requirements of both Dom-0 and the VM around time interval 10. This spike was caused by a background process running for a short period when RUBiS was run in the native environment. Since the predicted values are based on these native measurements, they mistakenly predict the virtual CPU requirements to spike in the same way.

We have also validated our model on the TPC-W application. We create a changing workload by adjusting the number of emulated clients from 250 to 1100 in a random (but repeatable) pattern. Figure 7(b) presents the error distribution for TPC-W. The error for this application is almost identical to RUBiS, with 90th percentile error rates of 5% and 10% for Dom-0 and the virtual machine respectively.

5.6 Cross Platform Modeling

In many server consolidation scenarios, the transition from a native to a virtual platform is accompanied by a change in the underlying hardware. However, using a single model for multiple hardware platforms may be ineffective if they have different overhead costs. Attempting to apply the model for the Intel system to the AMD system results in high error rates as shown in Figure 9(a). To investigate why these two platforms exhibit such a large difference, we compare the CPU required by the RUBiS application in the native and virtual environments on both platforms in Figure 8. Not including the Dom-0 requirements, the Intel system requires approximately 1.7 times as much CPU in the virtual case as it does natively. On the AMD system, the increase is only about 1.4 times. The different scaling between the native and virtual traces in each platform suggest that a single model cannot be used for both platforms.

We test our modeling approach's ability to determine the relationship between native and virtual systems running on different hardware platforms by executing an identical set of microbenchmarks on the Intel and AMD platforms in both the native and virtual environments. Using this data, we create two models, one which relates a native usage profile of the Intel platform to a virtual usage profile of the AMD system and one which relates the native AMD system to the virtualized Intel system.

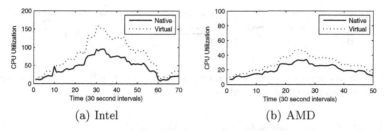

(a) Intel   (b) AMD

Fig. 8. Comparison of CPU overhead on different hardware platforms

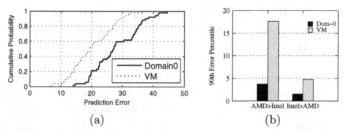

(a)   (b)

Fig. 9. (a) Using a single model for different architectures is ineffective, (b) but cross platform models are feasible

Figure 9(b) presents the 90th error percentiles when these cross platform models are used to predict the CPU needs of both the TPC-W and RUBiS workloads. The cross platform models are very effective at predicting Dom-0 CPU needs, however the VM prediction error is higher, particularly for the AMD to Intel model. We propose two factors which may cause this jump in error. First, the AMD system has a significantly faster CPU than the Intel system, so translating the CPU component from one platform to the other requires a significant scale up factor. As a result, small variations in the CPU needs of the AMD system can result in larger fluctuations in the predicted CPU for the Intel system, leading to higher absolute error values. Secondly, cross platform models for predicting virtual machine CPU are typically more difficult than Dom-0 models. This is because Dom-0 models are predominantly based on I/O metrics such as packet reception rates and disk operations, which have similar costs on both platforms. In contrast, the VM model is primarily based on the CPU related metrics which may not have a linear relationship between the two platforms due to differences in the processor and cache architectures. However, it should be noted that in many cases, the AMD to Intel model performs better than the 90th error percentile indicates; the median error is only 5%, and all of the points with high error occur at the peaks of the RUBiS workload where the virtual CPU consumption exceeds 160%.

6   Discussion

In this section, we discuss the impact of the application behavior on the accuracy of the prediction results and challenges introduced by dynamic frequency scaling.

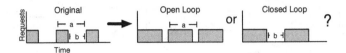

Fig. 10. Resource requirements in different environments is influenced by the amount of feedback in an application's workload

- *Impact of application behavior on resource use.*

The timing for an application's operations in the native and virtualized environments may be slightly different if the application has a strong "feedback loop" behavior. Figure 10 illustrates the difference between an application with (closed loop) and without (open loop) feedback. In the original application trace, a series of requests arrive, with their processing time indicated by the width of the rectangles. The value of a represents the time from the start of one request until the start of the next, while b is the time from the end of one request to the start of the next. When the same application is run on a different platform, the time to process a request may increase due to virtualization overhead. The two figures on the right represent how the trace would appear if the application does or does not exhibit feedback. With an open loop, the time between the start of each request will remain a, even if the request processing time increases. This would occur if the requests are being submitted by a client on another machine sending at a regular rate. For an application with feedback, requests are processed then a constant delay, b, occurs before the next request is processed. The figure illustrates that when request processing times increase, applications with feedback may process fewer requests in a given time interval (due to a slowdown), i.e., its CPU overhead is "spread" across a longer time period, resulting in lower average CPU utilization.

It is impossible to tell if an application's workload has a feedback loop just by looking at resource utilization traces of the original application. So the estimated resource utilization produced by our model for the application with a "feedback loop" might be higher than in reality since such an application might consume CPU resources in virtualized environment "slower" than in native one due to the increased latency on the application's critical path.

- *Understanding Application Performance.*

While our models can accurately predict the changes in resource requirements for a virtualized application, they cannot directly model how application performance (ie. response time) will change. Unfortunately, this is a difficult challenge, akin to making performance predictions under different hardware platforms. Our approach tells system administrators the minimum amount of resources which must be allocated to a VM in order to prevent significantly reduced performance due to resource starvation. The application may still see some performance penalty due to the longer code path as requests go through the virtualization layer. To accurately predict this performance change would necessitate carefully tailored, application specific models.

Our approach helps in estimating the resource requirements that are necessary for the initial application placement in a virtualized environment. After the initial workload placement, specialized workload management tools may be used [13, 15] to dynamically adjust system resources to support the required application performance.

7   Related Work

Virtualization Overheads: Virtualization is gaining popularity in enterprise environments as a software-based solution for building shared hardware infrastructures. VMware and IBM have released benchmarks [33] for quantifying the performance of virtualized environments. These benchmarks aim to provide some basis for comparison of different hardware and virtualization platforms in server consolidation exercises. However, they both are lacking the ability to characterize virtualization overhead compared to a native platform.

Application performance and resource consumption in virtualized environments can be quite different from its performance and usage profile on native hardware because of additional virtualization overheads (typically caused by I/O processing) and interactions with the underlying virtual machine monitor (VMM). Several earlier papers which describe various VMM implementations include performance results that measure the impact of virtualization overhead on microbenchmark or macrobenchmark performance (e.g., [2, 5, 7, 17, 19, 23, 29, 35, 37]). The reported virtualization overhead greatly depends on the hardware platform that is used in such experiments. For example, previously published papers [5, 9] evaluating Xen's performance have used networking benchmarks in systems with limited network bandwidth and high CPU capacity. However, there are cases where throughput degrades because CPU processing is the bottleneck instead of the network [11, 21]. In many virtualization platforms, the "amount" of CPU overhead is directly proportional to the "amount" of performed I/O processing [7, 11]. For example, it has been shown that networking packet rates are highly correlated with the measured CPU overhead [11]. Recent work attempts to reduce the performance penalty of network I/O by bypassing parts of the virtualization layer [18, 36] or optimizing it [24]. However, since these optimizations typically target only one source of virtualization overhead (network I/O), our modeling system can still be employed to provide useful information about the level of overhead incurred by a wider range of activities.

This extensive body of previous work has motivated us to select a set of microbenchmarks that "probe" system resource usage at different I/O traffic rates (both networking and disk) and then employ these usage profiles for predicting variable CPU overhead of virtualized environments.

Trace-based Approaches: In our work, we chose to represent application behavior via resource usage traces. Many research groups have used a similar approach to characterize application behavior and applied trace-based methods to support what-if analysis in the assignment of workloads to consolidated servers [10, 25, 27, 32]. There are a few commercial tools [14, 16, 34] that employ trace-based methods to support server consolidation exercises, load balancing, ongoing capacity planning, and simulating placement of application workloads to help IT administrators improve server utilization. Since many virtualization platforms introduce additional virtualization overhead, the trace-based capacity planning and management solutions provide a capability to scale the resource usage traces of original workloads by a specified CPU-multiplier. For some applications it might be a reasonable approach, however, in general, additional CPU overhead highly depends on system activities and operations performed by the application. Simplistic trace-scaling may result in significant modeling error and resource over-provisioning.

System Profiling: Finally, there is another body of work [6, 20, 26, 28] that is closely related to our thinking and the approach presented in the paper. This body of works goes back to 1995, when L. McVoy and C. Staelin have introduced the *lmbench* – a suite of operating system microbenchmarks that provides a set of portable programs for use in cross-platform comparisons. Each microbenchmark was purposely created to capture some unique performance problem present in one or more important applications. Although such microbenchmarks can be useful in understanding the end-to-end behavior of a system, the results of these microbenchmarks provide little information to indicate how well a particular application will perform on a particular system. In [6, 26], the authors argue for an application-specific approach to benchmarking. The authors suggest a vector-based approach for characterizing an underlying system by a set of microbenchmarks (e.g., *lmbench*) that describe the behavior of the fundamental primitives of the system. The results of these microbenchmarks constitute the *system* vector. Then they suggest to construct an *application* vector that quantifies the way that the application makes use of the various primitives supported by the system. The product of these two vectors yields a relevant performance metric. There is a similar logic in our design: we use a set of microbenchmarks to characterize underlying system and virtualization solution. Then we apply the derived model (analogy to a *system* vector) to the application usage traces (analogy to the *application* vector) and use it for predicting the resource requirements of applications when they are transferred to a virtual environment.

8   Conclusions

Our work is motivated by the need for improved estimates of application resource requirements when they are consolidated to virtual environments. To this end, we designed an automated approach for profiling different types of virtualization overhead on a given platform and a regression-based model that maps the native system profile into a virtualized one. This model can then be used to accurately assess the required resources and make workload placement decisions in virtualized environments.

Although such a model is created using data from synthetic benchmarks, the result is a general model which can be applied to traces from any other application in order to predict what its resource requirements will be on the virtual platform. We profile each platform using open source tools that can be easily deployed and executed on a wide range of hardware platforms within traditional or next generation data centers. We envision that each system in a NGDC will be augmented with a model that reflects the relationship between the *native* and *virtualized* usage profiles.

Our evaluation has shown that our automated model generation procedure effectively characterizes the different virtualization overheads of two diverse hardware platforms and that the models have median prediction error of less than 5% for both RUBiS and TPC-W. In future work we plan to experiment with more diverse application types and different virtualization platforms. We are also interested in how these modeling techniques can be used to predict the aggregate resource requirements of virtual machines collocated on a single host and to determine when an application's resource requirements are likely to exceed the virtual system's capacity.

Acknowledgements. Prashant Shenoy and Timothy Wood were supported in part by NSF grants CNS-0325868, CNS-0720616, CNS-0720271.

References

1. Agostinelli, C.: Robust Stepwise Regression. Journal of Applied Statistics 29(6) (2002)
2. Ahmad, I., Anderson, J., Holler, A., Kambo, R., Makhija, V.: An Analysis of Disk Performance in VMware ESX Server Virtual Machines. In: Proc. of the Sixth Workshop on Workload Characterization (WWC 2003) (October 2003)
3. Amza, C., Cecchet, E., Chanda, A., Cox, A., Elnikety, S., Gil, R., Marguerite, J., Rajamani, K., Zwaenepoel, W.: Specification and implementation of dynamic Web site benchmarks. In: Proc. of WWC-5: IEEE 5th Annual Workshop on Workload Characterization (October 2002)
4. Apache JMeter, http://jakarta.apache.org/jmeter/
5. Barham, P., Dragovic, B., Fraser, K., Hand, S., Harris, T., Ho, A., Neugebauer, R., Pratt, I., Warfield, A.: Xen and the art of virtualization. In: SOSP 2003 (2003)
6. Brown, A., Seltzer, M.: Operating System Benchmarking in the Wake of Lmbenc. In: Sigmetrics 1997 (1997)
7. Cherkasova, L., Gardner, R.: Measuring CPU overhead for I/O processing in the Xen virtual machine monitor. In: Proc. of USENIX AT (April 2005)
8. Draper, N.R., Smith, H.: Applied Regression Analysis. J. Wiley & Sons, Chichester (1998)
9. Fraser, K., Hand, S., Neugebauer, R., Pratt, I., Warfield, A., Williamson, M.: Reconstructing I/O. Technical report (2004)
10. Gmach, D., Rolia, J., Cherkasova, L., Kemper, A.: Capacity Management and Demand Prediction for Next Generation Data Centers. In: Proc. of the International IEEE Conference on Web Services (2007)
11. Gupta, D., Cherkasova, L., Gardner, R., Vahdat, A.: Enforcing Performance Isolation Across Virtual Machines in Xen. In: van Steen, M., Henning, M. (eds.) Middleware 2006. LNCS, vol. 4290, pp. 342–362. Springer, Heidelberg (2006)

12. Holland, P.W., Welsch, R.E.: Robust regression using iteratively reweighted least-squares. In: Communications in Statistics - Theory and Methods 6.9 (October 2007)
13. HP-UX Workload Manager, http://hp.com/products1/unix/operating/wlm/
14. HP Integrity Essentials Capacity Advisor,
    http://h71036.www7.hp.com/enterprise/cache/262379-0-0-0-121.html
15. IBM Enterprise Workload Manager,
    http://www.ibm.com/developerworks/autonomic/ewlm/
16. IBM Tivoli Performance Analyzer,
    http://www.ibm.com/software/tivoli/products/performance-analyzer/
17. King, S., Dunlap, G., Chen, P.: Operating system support for virtual machines. In: Proc. of the USENIX Annual Technical Conference, San Antonio, Texas (2003)
18. Liu, J., Huang, W., Abali, B., Panda, D.: High Performance VMM-Bypass I/O in Virtual Machines. In: Proc. of Usenix AT 2006 (2006)
19. Magenheimer, D., Christian, T.: VBlades: Optimized paravirtualization for the Itanium processor family. In: Proc. of USENIX VM Research and Technology Symposium (May 2004)
20. McVoy, L., Staelin, C.: lmbench: Portable tools for performance analysis. In: Proc. of the 1996 Winter USENIX, San Diego, CA (January 1996)
21. Menon, A., Santos, J.R., Turner, Y., Janakiraman, G.J., Zwaenepoel, W.: Diagnosing performance overheads in the Xen virtual machine environment. In: Proc. of Intl. Conf. on Virtual Execution Environments (VEE) (June 2005)
22. Mosberger, D., Jin, T.: Httperf—A Tool for Measuring Web Server Performance. In: Proc. of Workshop on Internet Server Performance (1998)
23. Padala, P., Zhu, X., Wang, Z., Singhal, S., Shin, K.: Performance Evaluation of Virtualization Technologies for Server Consolidation. HP Labs Tech. Report HPL-2007-59 (2007)
24. Santos, J.R., Turner, Y., Janakiraman, G.J., Pratt, I.: Bridging the Gap between Software and Hardware Techniques for I/O Virtualization. In: Proc. of Usenix (2008)
25. Rolia, J., Cherkasova, L., Arlitt, M., Andrzejak, A.: A Capacity Management Service for Resource Pools. In: Proc. of Intl. Workshop on Software and Performance (2005)
26. Seltzer, M., Krinsky, D., Smith, K., Zhang, X.: The Case for Appliction-Specific Benchmarking. In: Proc. of the 1999 Workshop on Hot Topics in Operating Systems (1999)
27. Seltzsam, S., Gmach, D., Krompass, S., Kemper, A.: AutoGlobe: An Automatic Administration Concept for Service-Oriented Database Applications. In: Proc. of the 22nd Intl. Conf. on Data Engineering (ICDE) (2006)
28. Staelin, C., McVoy, L.: mhz: Anatomy of a microbenchmark. In: Proc. of the USENIX Annual Technical Conference, New Orleans, LA (June 1998)
29. Sugerman, J., Venkitachalam, G., Lim, B.-H.: Virtualizing I/O Devices on VMware Workstation's Hosted Virtual Machine Monitor. In: Proc. of the USENIX AT (2001)
30. Sysstat-7.0.4, http://perso.orange.fr/sebastien.godard/
31. TPC-W Benchmark, http://www.tpc.org
32. Urgaonkar, B., Shenoy, P., Roscoe, T.: Resource overbooking and application profiling in shared hosting platforms. In: Proc. of Operating Systems Design and Implementation (OSDI) (December 2002)
33. VMmark: A Scalable Benchmark for Virtualized Systems,
    www.vmware.com/pdf/vmmark_intro.pdf

34. VMware Capacity Planner,
    http://www.vmware.com/products/capacity_planner/
35. Waldspurger, C.: Memory resource management in VMware ESX server in Operating Systems Design and Implementation. In: Proc. of Operating Systems Design and Implementation (OSDI) (December 2002)
36. Wang, J., Wright, K., Gopalan, K.: XenLoop: A Transparent High Performance Inter-VM Network Loopback. In: Proc. of International Symposium on High Performance Distributed Computing (HPDC), Boston, MA (June 2008)
37. Whitaker, A., Shaw, M., Gribble, S.: Scale and Performance in the Denali isolation kernel. In: Proc. of Operating Systems Design and Implementation (OSDI) (December 2002)
38. Wood, T., Cherkasova, L., Ozonat, K., Shenoy, P.: Profiling and Modeling Resource Usage of Virtualized Applications. UMass Technical Report (September 2008)

Prism: Providing Flexible and Fast Filesystem Cloning Service for Virtual Servers

Xin Zhao[1], Kevin Borders[2], and Atul Prakash[2]

[1] Google Inc.
1600 Amphitheatre Parkway
Mountain View, CA 94043, USA
xinzhao@google.com
[2] University of Michigan
2260 Hayward Street
Ann Arbor, MI 48109-2121, USA
{kborders,aprakash}@eecs.umich.edu

Abstract. This paper describes a prototype virtualized file system, Prism, for supporting hosted servers and utility computing. Prism provides a filesystem service that allows lightweight creation of filesystems for new users from existing filesystems. All users' filesystems are mutable and yet isolated from each other. In our experiments, new filesystems can be created from existing ones in under one-fifth of a second. Prism is also designed to make centralized security-related services across multiple, similar filesystems more efficient. In particular, with Prism, tasks such as virus checking over multiple filesystem clones are much more efficient than scanning each user's filesystem independently. We describe the design of Prism and present performance results.

1 Introduction

One application scenario of hosted services and utility computing is to be able to provide remote users with dedicated data and computing facilities using centralized computing resources. This paper focuses on one aspect of the problem: providing dedicated filesystems to users on demand, as well as common filesystem-related services, such as on centralized virus scanning on users's filesystems in a lightweight way.

This paper describes a prototype virtualized file system, Prism, which supports multiple filesystems, where each filesystem can be assigned to a different user. Each user gets the illusion of having a full-fledged filesystem, which in principle, can include system files, applications, and user files, all under the control of the user. Prism provides an efficient filesystem cloning mechanism to create new filesystems from existing ones. A filesystem clone is semantically similar to a copy of the parent filesystem. Once created, it is independent of the parent filesystem. Subsequent changes to either one are not reflected in the other. Prism's mechanism guarantees isolation of users' filesystems, while providing very fast creation of new filesystems from existing ones. In our tests, new filesystems that are created from existing ones are usable within one-fifth of a second

V. Issarny and R. Schantz (Eds.): Middleware 2008, LNCS 5346, pp. 388–407, 2008.

and provide comparable performance to native `ext3` filesystem when the cloning is complete.

Prism is also designed to make centralized security-related services across multiple, similar filesystems more efficient. In particular, multiple filesystems can often be scanned collectively for tasks such as virus checking much more efficiently than scanning each user's filesystem independently. In our prototype setup, simulating a virus scanning task on all the files for eight cloned filesystems was approximately three times faster than doing eight individual scans.

Prism's mechanism for instantiating a new filesystem from an existing one provides a feature called *selective cloning*. In selective cloning, a user can request a clone of an existing filesystem, while excluding specified directories or files from being cloned (optionally replacing them with default substitutes.) We anticipate that this capability can be a useful feature in specialized scenarios. Consider a user Alice who is given a virtual machine running Linux on a hosted service provider, along with a dedicated filesystem that is provided by Prism. She wants to install a new software application that appears useful, but she is not sure if she should trust it and is not sure if it will be compatible with existing software. She decides to request the Prism's cloning service to provide her a clone of her filesystem, but excluding sensitive files such as her home directory, contents of /tmp and /var/log. This new filesystem can be used to provide her a testing environment that is very close to her current environment, but less susceptible to data theft, all within a few seconds.

Prism's cloning abstraction is semantically similar to making a copy of the entire filesystem, except it appears to be much faster to users. An end-user can get a usable cloned filesystem almost instantaneously, irrespective of the size of the cloned filesystem (either in number of files, depth, or total number of bytes). In addition, the filesystem cloning operation will not interrupt access to the parent filesystem.

Prism makes extensive use of copy-on-write at both file level and for blocks within files so as to use disk space efficiently when providing filesystem services for multiple users. The parent and cloned filesystems share data of unchanged files, which usually occupy a large portion of files. Furthermore, when a shared file is modified, an unchanged blocks continue to be shared.

Prism is currently in prototype stage. It has around 5000 lines of code. We have used Prism to host filesystems for multiple virtual machines. To evaluate Prism's cloning performance, we cloned a standard Fedora Core 4 distribution that consists of over 170K files and over 17K directories. The cloning operation itself was essentially an immediate operation from the perspective of the end-user, taking only 0.18 seconds to complete. After 0.18 seconds, both the parent and the cloned filesystem were completely accessible to end users. In terms of disk space, a clone took up about 1.3% of the space (77MB for the clone versus 6GB for the parent filesystem).

We also measured performance of a Prism-cloned filesystem on several workloads and compared it with solutions based on the `ext3` filesystem. On the Connectathon [1] benchmark and an Apache-build workload, the cloned filesystem's performance was comparable with that of an ext3-based filesystem, with only a minor performance penalty. For scanning multiple cloned filesystems, Prism outperformed an ext3-based solution significantly because it was able to skip over the files that had not been modified since cloning. The performance advantage of Prism over ext3 went up as the number of clones was increased.

The rest of the paper is organized as follows. Section 2 discusses related work. Section 3 illustrates the design of the Prism cloning. Section 4 presents evaluation results. Section 5 concludes this paper.

2   Related Work

Prism borrows ideas from existing filesystems with snapshot and versioning capability, such as WAFL [2], CVFS [13], VersionFS [9] and Ext3cow [10], but also introduces some differences. Like them, it makes extensive use of copy-on-write to help reduce overheads. In versioning filesystems, the notion of providing complete, dedicated filesystems for different users is usually missing. Instead, the assumption is that all versions are under one administrative control. In contrast, filesystem clones in Prism are all writable and isolated from each other; they are designed be exported to different users.

Several recent filesystems, such as Flexclone [4], VMFS [16], Parallax's filesystem [17], and ZFS [7] provide writable snapshots. Prism differs in a few ways in its design. These systems generally use block-level copy-on-write, where the file-level semantics are not available. This would make it difficult to exclude specified files or directories during a snapshot. In contrast, Prism is aware of filesystem structure and uses file-level copy-on-write. It is therefore trivial to selectively exclude directories from a snapshot or even graft part of one filesystem into the clone of another filesystem to compose a new filesystem. As we show later, file-level copy-on-write also permits more efficient central scanning across multiple filesystems.

Some systems, such as UnionFS [19], Ventana [11], Alcatraz [5], IFS [14], and Feather-weight Virtual Machine (FVM) [18], provide efficient cloning-like capability using a metadata manipulation technique. The key idea is to deploy a filesystem virtualization layer to manipulate the pathnames of files when a client or VM requests to access them. As shown in Figure 1, all other VMs are assumed to be created by cloning and sharing the base filesystem. If a user needs to change a shared file, these systems create a new copy in the writing user's

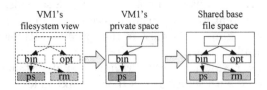

Fig. 1. Cloning via namespace manipulation

private space. Upon receiving a file request, the filesystem virtualization layer first checks the user's private space so that the private copy can override the shared copy.

However, cloning filesystem by manipulating pathnames is not as flexible as the mechanism used by Prism. Prism's design makes it easy to create clones of any user's filesystem, even the parent filesystem is a clone itself. In contrast, systems like FVM assume that only a base filesystem will be cloned. Furthemore, compared with normal filesystems, manipulating pathnames in private and shared spaces incurs higher lookup overhead to locate the right file corresponding to a given pathname. Prism does not introduce another pathname translating layer and thus achieves performance close to a filesystem without cloning support.

3   Prism Design

3.1   Background

Prism was designed by modifying the *ext3* filesystem and adding support for cloning and exporting any part of the filesystem to a user. Currently, Prism's filesystems are simply exported using NFS. In principle, Prism's filesystems could also be made available for access using other protocols such as Samba.

In the most general usage scenario, Prism exports a user's filesystem to the user with full read-write privileges. It is trivial to limit the user to read-only access to selected files that should not be updated by the user, if desired. We have previously proposed a server-side policy engine to do that in [21].

In the rest of the paper, we assume that each user is accessing the filesystem from a standard operating system. In our experiments, we emulated these users' operating systems using guest virtual machines that were hosted by a centralized server. To simplify terminology (since "user" can be an overloaded term), from now on, we will refer to user's operating systems as client virtual machines (VMs), even though users can access Prism filesystems over a network from standard operating systems as well.

As shown in Figure 2, Prism runs a modified ext3 filesystem called *pext3* to manage files for all the users. On the pext3 filesystem, Prism stores each client VM's files in a *fileset*. A Prism fileset is similar to a *volume* in AFS [3,8,12]. It

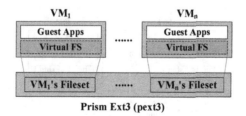

Fig. 2. Cloning via file sharing

is a tree of files and sub-directories on the physical repository managed by the pext3 filesystem. Prism exports a client VM's fileset as a virtual filesystem over NFS. In Prism, cloning a client VM's filesystem is accomplished by cloning the VM's fileset on the pext3 filesystem.

Prism provides three forms of cloning: basic cloning via file sharing, asynchronous cloning, and lazy cloning. We first describe the basic cloning mechanism in which the entire directory hierarchy is cloned. Then, we describe the asynchronous cloning mechanism that allows new filesystems to be usable almost immediately without cloning the directory hierarchy in entirety. After that, we describe lazy cloning, in which directories and files are cloned only as needed.

3.2   Synchronous Cloning Via File Sharing

As Figure 3 shows, Prism avoids copying files that are the same in a clone as in the parent filesystem. To clone a filesystem, Prism always starts from the filesystem's root directory to traverse the entire directory structure and clone the encountered filesystem objects that are not flagged as "nonclonable". For each clonable directory, Prism creates a new directory at the corresponding place in the clone. For a regular file, Prism clones it by creating a hard link to that file in the clone. In fact, all named files can be regarded as hard links in Prism. The name associated with a file is simply a label that refers the operating system to the actual data. More than one name can be associated with the same data. A hard link is essentially a directory entry that associates a file name with the actual data. By creating a hard link to the original file's inode, the cloned file shares the same content with the original copy without physically duplicating the data blocks. Copy-on-write is performed to create a new private copy if either the clone or its parent attempts to change a shared file. All subsequent modifications are applied to the new copy. As such, the isolation between the parent filesystem and its clone is still preserved. This cloning procedure is similar to the copying operation in conventional filesystems and thus very flexible. One can easily clone any selected part of a filesystem to a specified location.

The above solution is inadequate if support for hard links is required in users' filesystems. Figure 4 shows an example that helps illustrate this issue. Suppose a user clones a filesystem FS1 to a new filesystem FS2. We refer to FS1 as the "parent" filesystem and FS2 as the "child" filesystem. In FS1, the file /a/b and /x/y are two hard links pointing to the same file on disk. When cloning FS1 to

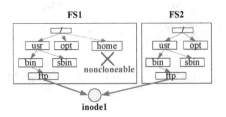

Fig. 3. Cloning via file sharing

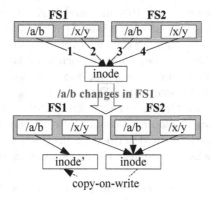

Fig. 4. Copy-on-write on an inode breaks the hard link semantics of a standard filesystem. If both FS1 and FS2 are fully copied filesystems, both /a/b and /x/y should point to the same inode even if the file content is modified.

FS2, Prism creates two hard links in FS2 for /a/b and /x/y, respectively. Now there are four hard links point to a same file. We cannot preserve the Prism cloning semantics and the standard hard link semantics under such a filesystem structure.

Suppose a user writes the file /a/b in FS1. At this time, the file associated with /a/b is being shared by FS2. In order to preserve isolation between FS1 and FS2, Prism duplicates the shared file to a new copy (represented by inode'), and adjusts the /a/b entry in FS1 to point to the new copy. However, /a/b and /x/y in FS1 now point to different files. This breaks the hard link semantics that can be preserved in a fully copied filesystem. According to the standard UNIX hard link semantics, though hard links have different names, data changes made through any hard link will affect the actual data and are immediately visible to other hard links pointing to the same inode. Therefore, /x/y and /a/b should point to the same file even after the file content is modified.

The current implementation of Prism supports hard links, but the description of the solution is beyond the scope of this paper. Zhao's thesis [20] contains the details of the solution.

3.3   Asynchronous Cloning

File sharing technique significantly reduces the cloning overhead, however, the Prism cloning mechanism can still incur nontrivial delay before the cloned filesystem is ready for use. The main reason is that the Prism cloning mechanism needs to traverse the parent filesystems and clone each encountered filesystem object individually, which incurs nontrivial overhead. On the other hand, to achieve selective cloning, Prism has to examine each filesystem object to determine whether the object should be excluded from cloning or not.

To better understand the impact of the filesystem traversal on the cloning performance, we conducted an experiment to clone a Fedora Core 4 system.

The filesystem contains around 170K files and 17K directories. The total size is around 6G bytes. Prism spent approximately 58 seconds to finish the cloning task. More than 70% of the cloning time is devoted to directory traversal. While this latency is acceptable in some scenarios, such as an administrator wishing to create new clones for distribution, it is not good enough for many applications such as testing untrusted applications. From the perspective of end users, they always hope to get a usable filesystem as quick as possible. Aiming at this goal, we developed an *asynchronous cloning* mechanism for Prism. For easy comparison, we call the cloning mechanism described in previous subsection *synchronous cloning*, because it blocks any requests to the cloned filesystem until the cloning procedure is completed.

The asynchronous cloning mechanism provides the same cloning semantics as the synchronous cloning mechanism, but is able to return a usable parent and cloned filesystem almost immediately (less than 1 second in all experiments we have conducted). It presents an illusion that the entire directory hierarchy is completely replicated, as in synchronous cloning, but the replication actually occurs in the background using a kernel thread. The background thread traverses the parent filesystem starting from the root to clone the directory tree, but also aggressively processes a file if it is accessed by the parent or the clone prior to the completion of the filesystem cloning. Eventually, the final state of the directory hierarchies in the fully cloned system is identical to that produced by synchronous cloning.

When a user requests to clone a filesystem, the asynchronous cloning mechanism usually replies to the user that the cloned filesystem is ready for use within a few seconds. A user will reasonably start to access either the clone or the parent filesystem. The asynchronous cloning mechanism must be carefully designed to present the same semantics to users as a fully copied filesystem. In particular, we must properly address the following two situations:

1. *A user in the cloned filesystem may access a file that has not been cloned.*
   Prism should quickly respond to the user, rather than blocking the user until the cloning thread eventually encounters and clones the file. As described earlier, the cloning thread works in the background to recursively traverse the parent filesystem and clone each encountered filesystem object. However, for a large filesystem, it can take a few minutes before the cloning thread encounters the requested file, which can be too long for the user to wait.

2. *A user in the parent filesystem can modify a file that has not been cloned.*
   Under such condition, Prism must ensure that the file is cloned before being modified. According to the cloning semantics, a clone should be identical to the parent filesystem's snapshot taken at the beginning of cloning procedure. Any modification to the parent filesystem afterwards should be transparent to the clone. However, if a file in the parent filesystem is modified before being cloned, the modified content will be exposed to the clone. Therefore, the asynchronous cloning mechanism must ensure that a file in the parent filesystem is cloned prior to modification.

Next, we describe how Prism handles the requests that are issued in the cloned or parent filesystem before the cloning procedure is finished.

Handling Requests in the Cloned Filesystem. When a user in the cloned filesystem issues a request to a file that has not been cloned, Prism aggressively clones the file on demand before processing the user's request. This avoids blocking the user too long.

The Prism on-demand cloning mechanism is based on two observations:

1. Before a process can access a file, Prism first *looks up* the file.
2. Before looking up a directory for a file, Prism must call the *permission* function to check that the requesting process has sufficient rights to access the directory.

Based on these two observations, Prism implements the on-demand cloning mechanism by extending the standard permission checking function.

First, we develop a core function, `pext3_expand_dir()`, that expands a directory at a time. Note that we use the term "expand" instead of "clone", because this function does not recursively go down a directory to clone all filesystem objects. Given a source directory, the `pext3_expand_dir` function only clones the filesystem objects that are directly under this directory. The function clones regular files as described in Section 3.2. However, for each subdirectory under the source directory, the function only creates an empty subdirectory at the corresponding location in the clone. In other words, this function only expands one level of directory hierarchy, and will not go deeper into subdirectories. The function flags each subdirectory as "UNEXPANDED" and associates it with the inode number of the corresponding source directory. To record this information, we add two fields, `i_expanding_flags` and `i_srcino`, to each pext3 inode. For a regular file, these two fields are not used. For a directory, however, these two fields indicate whether the directory is expanded or not. If all filesystem objects directly under a directory are cloned, the directory will be flagged as "EXPANDED". Note that a directory being flagged as "EXPANDED" does not mean that all its subdirectories are expanded. Normally, after running the `pext3_expand_dir()` on a specified directory, this directory is flagged as "EXPANDED", but all its subdirectories are still empty and flagged as "UNEXPANDED".

Next, as shown in Figure 5, Prism combines the core `pext3_expand_dir()` function with the standard permission function to perform asynchronous cloning. Given a directory, Prism first determines whether the directory is expanded or not by checking the directory's `i_expanding_flags` field. If the directory is expanded, Prism jumps to the original permission function. If the directory is not expanded, Prism calls the `pext3_expand_dir()` function to expand the directory, and then calls the original permission function.

With the Prism asynchronous cloning mechanism, a parent filesystem object is cloned by one of the two threads shown in Figure 5. The first thread is the *background cloning thread* that recursively traverses the parent filesystem and clones each encountered filesystem object. The second thread is an *on-demand*

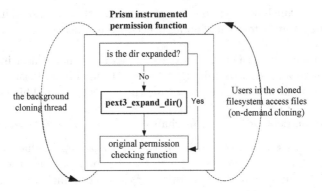

Fig. 5. Prism on-demand cloning

cloning thread that aggressively clones the filesystem objects that are requested by users in the clone.

We first discuss how the background cloning thread works. Upon receiving a request to clone a filesystem, Prism first creates the root directory in the clone. Next, Prism flags the directory as "UNEXPANDED" and associates it with the parent filesystem's root inode. Then, Prism would start the background cloning thread to clone the rest of the filesystem and then returns, presenting the user an illusion that the cloning task is completed immediately. The background cloning thread works as a directory walker that recursively traverses the entire cloned filesystem starting from the root directory. The background cloning thread looks up a file with an arbitrary filename in each encountered directory. The lookup operation is only used to trigger the permission checking function, which in turn expands the directory if it is not expanded. Thus, along with the background cloning procedure recursively traversing the cloned filesystem, the Prism permission checking procedure will be invoked to expand all encountered directories, which clones the parent filesystem in the background.

The on-demand cloning thread works in a similar way to aggressively clone the filesystem objects that are requested by users in the clone. When a user in the cloned filesystem accesses a file, Prism must look up the file before processing the request. This will trigger the permission checking function to expand all directories from the root to the parent directory of the file to be accessed.

To rapidly respond to end users' requests, Prism allow administrators to lower the priority of the background cloning thread with Linux command **nice**. As such, the background cloning thread will not contend with interactive sessions for disk bandwidth. Accordingly, the background cloning time could increase.

We use an example to illustrate the on-demand cloning procedure. Suppose a user accesses a file **/a/b/c**, but only the root directory **/** has been expanded. Prism first looks up the directory "/" for the entry "/a". The permission checking function is invoked to check the access permission of directory "/". Because the "/" directory has been expanded, Prism simply jumps to the normal permission checking procedure. Next, Prism looks up the directory "/a" for the entry

"/a/b". The permission function is invoked again to check the permission of "/a". At this time, the directory "/a" is not expanded yet and flagged as "UN-EXPANDED". Prism then calls the pext3_expand_dir() function to expand the directory "/a". The directory entry "/a/b" is created but flagged as "UN-EXPANDED". By repeating the above procedure, Prism expands the directories from "/" to "/a/b/". Eventually, when Prism looks up the file "/a/b/c", it has been cloned on demand. Note that the user process can run in parallel with the background cloning thread. With the common permission checking function, Prism seamlessly adjusts the cloning order and aggressively clone the directories needed for the file request, which achieves the on-demand cloning.

Handling Requests in the Parent Filesystem. With the asynchronous cloning mechanism, a user can get a command prompt before the parent filesystem is completely cloned. Accordingly, a user can write a file in the parent filesystem before the file is cloned. If the pext3 filesystem were to allow such an operation, it breaks the cloning semantics — the modification in the parent becomes visible to the clone.

One way to preserve the consistency of the parent filesystem is to clone from a snapshot of the parent filesystem. Many filesystems such as WAFL [2] and ZFS [7] provide the snapshot feature. We can adapt an existing mechanism to take a snapshot of the parent filesystem before starting the cloning procedure. This approach, however, requires substantial changes to disk and filesystem structure. As an alternative, Prism preserves the parent filesystem's consistency by detecting and aggressively resolving the consistency issues during background cloning.

Before starting the cloning procedure, Prism flushes the parent filesystem's dirty pages to disk, which eliminates the inconsistency caused by the buffered data. This procedure normally takes less than 1 second. During the period of cloning, Prism monitors the operations on the parent filesystem. If a process attempts to write a file in the parent filesystem that has not been cloned, Prism blocks the process, aggressively clones the file, and then resumes the process to write the file.

An important step in the above procedure is to tell whether the file to be changed is cloned or not. This step must be efficient, because it is critical to the filesystem performance. A naive approach to determine a file's cloning status is to maintain the list of files that have been cloned. By looking up the list, one can determine a file's cloning status. However, it would be slow to look up the file list if the filesystem is large and has a lot of files.

Another way to determine a file's cloning status would be to associate a flag with each parent file indicating whether the file has been cloned or not. However, this solution would require that Prism initialize the cloning status of each file in the parent filesystem before the cloning procedure is started. Otherwise, there would be no easy way to tell whether a specific file is cloned by current or previous cloning procedures. However, the initialization procedure would have taken substantial time for a large parent filesystem, significantly offsetting the benefit of the asynchronous cloning mechanism.

Prism addresses the above problem with three timestamps:

- *The global logical timestamp.* Prism maintains a global logical timestamp to record the occurrence time of cloning events. The logical timestamp is a 32-bit unsigned integer and is initialized to zero. This logical timestamp is incremented at the beginning of each cloning task.
- *The clonestart timestamp.* Prism maintains a `clonestart` timestamp for each filesystem to be cloned. The `clonestart` timestamp is normally equal to zero. When Prism starts to clone a filesystem, it sets the parent filesystem's `clonestart` timestamp to the current value of the global logical timestamp. When the entire cloning task is finished, Prism resets the filesystem's `clonestart` timestamp back to zero.
- *The lastclone timestamp.* Prism maintains a timestamp, called *lastclone timestamp*, for each filesystem object to record the last time when the object is cloned. The `lastclone` timestamp is stored in a 4-byte field, `lastclone`, in the directory entry of the filesystem object. Every time a filesystem object is cloned, Prism updates its `lastclone` timestamp to the current value of the parent filesystem's `clonestart` timestamp.

Prism is able to determine whether an original file has been cloned or not by comparing the parent filesystem's `clonestart` timestamp with the file's `lastclone` timestamp:

- *clonestart* will never be smaller than *lastclone* when the filesystem is being cloned. If a filesystem is not being cloned, its *clonestart* timestamp is 0. Prism can serve any operations to the parent filesystem under such condition.
- If *clonestart* == *lastclone*, the original file has been cloned by current cloning procedure.
- If *clonestart* > *lastclone*, the original file has not been cloned yet.

If a file in the parent filesystem is to be written, Prism first determines whether the file has been cloned or not with the above mechanism. If the file has been cloned, Prism can apply the modification to the file immediately without breaking the consistency of the clone. Otherwise, Prism must first resolve the consistency conflict before applying changes to the parent file. To do so, Prism blocks the writing process, aggressively clones the file, and then unblocks the writing process and serves the write request.

Cloning Open Files. Prism is designed to deliver a clear cloning semantics — the clone is identical to the parent filesystem's snapshot taken at the beginning of the cloning procedure. After a cloning procedure starts, all file modifications made to the parent filesystem are isolated from the cloned filesystems.

The current Prism implementation assumes that there are no open files in the parent filesystem when a cloning command is issued. Based on this assumption, Prism monitors the **open** requests to detect write operations in the parent filesystem. If a process requests to open a file for writing after the cloning procedure begins, Prism will regard the open request as a file modification operation. To preserve cloning semantics, Prism blocks the writing process, aggressively clones the target file to the clone, then unblocks the writing process.

The above assumption could be too strong in real world scenarios. A file in the parent filesystem could be opened *before* the cloning procedure is started. Our current prototype does not address this scenario, but it can be addressed by aggressively cloning all open files before starting the background cloning thread. Upon receiving a clone command, Prism would first suspend the parent filesystem, clone the open files, and then reactivate the parent filesystem. Alternatively, we could have intercepted write operations and cloned at that point. We plan to evaluate these alternatives in the future.

Overall, asychronous cloning has the advantage that both the parent filesystem and the cloned filesystem are usable immediately even before the cloning task is finished. However, the access performance can be lower than normal if one attempts to access a file that is not cloned. Normally, the latency caused by file accesses during cloning should be small in practice because the set of files that are accessed during cloning is usually small compared to the whole filesystem.

3.4 Lazy Cloning

Prism provides another asynchronous cloning mode called *lazy cloning*. The lazy cloning mode is similar to the standard asynchronous cloning mode, except that Prism does not start a background thread to clone the entire parent filesystem. All files are cloned on demand. In other words, it only clones a file when it is accessed.

The major advantage of this mode is that it only consumes little system disk and CPU resource. Prism does not need to pay any cost to clone the files that are never accessed. This is particularly useful for scenarios that only need a ephemeral filesystem. Software testing is a good example. Users often tend to destroy the clone after they test a untrusted application. It is often unnecessary to clone the entire filesystem for such an ephemeral system. The lazy cloning mode is also useful for evaluating the performance impact of the asychronous cloning mechanism on the cloned filesystem. It gives a worst-case bound of cloning penalty incurred by access to a cloned filesystem, because each accessed file is cloned on-the-fly.

However, we do not choose this cloning mode as the default Prism cloning mode. As discussed earlier, if a cloning job is complete, both the parent and cloned filesystems can be accessed as a normal filesystem without incurring additional cloning overhead. In contrast, before the parent filesystem is fully cloned, modifications to the parent filesystem can potentially cause consistency conflicts. When such conflicts are detected, Prism has to temporarily block the modification operations until the conflicts are resolved on-the-fly. The resolving latency would negatively impact end users' experience. To minimize the "impact window", one may want to finish the cloning as soon as possible. Therefore, we choose the standard asynchronous cloning as the default cloning mode in Prism.

3.5   The Prism Copy-on-Write Mechanism

In Prism, copy-on-write (CoW) must be performed if a VM writes a shared file. The CoW operation can be implemented as file copying. However, that can incur unncessary overhead, making operations like "chmod" inefficient. As an alternative, Prism employs a block-level CoW mechanism that is similar to Ext3Cow [10]. In Prism, each file is regarded as an inode associated with data blocks. Prism allows a file's inode and blocks to be shared separately. When performing CoW on a file to be changed, Prism only replicates the modified part, and still shares the unmodified part between the old and new copies. To track the reference counts of blocks, Prism deploys a reference count table for each block device. Each table entry is a one-byte reference count corresponding to a 4KB data block (default block size in pext3). A data block's reference count records how many *files* share the data block. If a block is shared by more than 255 files, it will be duplicated to a new block to avoid reference count overflow. We use the Linux journalling layer (*JBD*) to protect the block reference count table from being corrupted even if the system crashes in the middle of reference count updating.

3.6   Discussion

Prism uses hard links to achieve file sharing between the parent and cloned filesystem. Each hard link of a file will increase the file's reference count by one. In existing Unix-like systems, the maximum value of a reference count is 255. Therefore, if a same file is cloned for many times, the file's reference count can overflow. One solution is to make a physical copy when a file's reference count is about to overflow. This solution has not been implemented due to the time limit. While this solution incurs additional data copying overhead, we do not expect that it will substantially impact the Prism performance, because the reference count overflow issue is rare in a real world system. In addition, hard links are only entries in directory files. These entries are stored in each VM's own directory tree and will not affect other VMs' filesystem operation. Therefore, the increase of the number of hard links will not impact a VM's filesystem performance.

Prism's file sharing mechanism may incur security concerns. For example, one VM may attempt to modify a shared data block to disrupt other VMs. However, in Prism, a guest VM can only modify a file by issuing file system requests, which are subject to the Prism security checking. If a data block is shared by two or more VMs, copy-on-write operation will be performed to ensure the isolation between VMs.

4   Evaluation

Table 1 describes our evaluation platform. To facilitate a quick restoration of the operating system state to a consistent point for all experiments, we ran all the experiments in a DomainU Xen virtual machine, running a Fedora Core 4

Table 1. Experimental platform

Hardware	
CPU	3.00GHz Pentium IV
Memory	512MB(Dom0) 512MB(DomU)
Disk	Maxtor 7200RPM EIDE
Software	
VMM	Xen 3.0.2
Domain0 OS	Linux 2.6.16-xen0
DomainU OS	Linux 2.6.16-xenU
Linux Distribution	Fedora Core 4
Apache	version 2.0.58
Connectathon	version 1.18
Tar	version 1.15.1
GNU gcc	version 4.0.2
GNU ld	version 2.15.94.0.2.2
GNU Autoconf	version 2.59
GNU automake	version 1.9.5

distribution of Linux. The results reported are averages from multiple runs of the experiments. Generally, we found the results to be very consistent across the runs, with low standard deviation as compared to the average values.

4.1 Synchronous and Asynchronous Cloning Latency

We first evaluated the performance of the Prism synchronous and asynchronous cloning mechanisms. For the parent filesystem, we used a filesystem consisting of a Fedora Core 4 system with standard software packages, including around 170K files and over 17K directories. We cloned the filesystem with both mechanisms 32 times and reported the average time elapsed to clone the filesystem.

We first compared the cost of full copying versus synchronous cloning. The full copying of the filesystem took around 10.5 minutes (630 seconds), while synchronous cloning took 58.7 seconds. This clearly demonstrated that the Prism's file sharing technique significantly reduces the cloning overhead.

We then measured the time used by the Prism's asynchronous cloning mechanism to clone the filesystem. With the asynchronous cloning mechanism, the cloning activity largely occurred in the background. Prism instantly presented the users with an accessible filesystem clone. The observed latency was 0.18 seconds. The time spent by the background thread to clone the filesystem is about the same as that used by the synchronous cloning mechanism. This experiment shows that the asynchronous cloning mechanism significantly reduces the latency before the cloned filesystem is ready for use. This helps improve users' experience in filesystem cloning and makes it more practical to perform tasks such as testing untrusted applications in VM clones. While the asynchronous cloning mechanism hides the cloning latency from end users, it does not reduce the cloning overhead. The total time used to clone the filesystem in the background was approximately the same as that of the synchronous cloning mechanism.

We also measured the disk space used by clones after each round of the cloning operation. The experiments showed that the used disk space consistently increased by 77MB each clone. This disk space is used to store a separate directory tree structure for each clone. The size of the fully copied filesystem is around 6GB. The clone size is around 1.3% of the disk space used by the fully copied filesystem before any modification to the clone. We expect that the disk space used by the clone will increase over time but will still be smaller than a fully copied filesystem, because the files that are never written can still be shared without duplication.

4.2   Performance on the Apache Workload

The asynchronous cloning mechanism presents end users a usable filesystem before the cloning procedure is finished. When a user in the cloned filesystem accesses a file that has not been cloned, Prism has to aggressively clone the file before processing the user's file request. Therefore, the asynchronously cloned filesystem could be slower than a fully cloned filesystem before the background cloning procedure is finished.

We used an Apache build task as a representative of typical workloads on a normal development machine to evaluate the performance impact of asynchronous cloning. In our experiment, Apache 2.0.58 was used as the benchmark object. The Apache archive includes 2339 files scattered in 188 directories. The total size of the archive is 6.13MB before being decompressed. After being decompressed, the total size of the Apache directory is 32.9MB. The benchmark first **unpacks** the archive of Apache 2.0.58 into a source directory. Next, it runs **configure** to build the source code dependency, which involves lots of small data read and file lookup operations. During the third phase, it **builds** the Apache binaries from the source files, which is a CPU intensive task, but also generates a lot of object files and temporary files. Finally, it **removes** all Apache files including the Apache source tree, generated configuration files, object files, and Apache executable binaries.

In practice, it is hard to consistently reproduce the dynamics when the benchmark and background cloning procedure run concurrently. The benchmark result can vary with different execution orders and time patterns. For this reason, we used the "lazy" cloning mode described in Section 3.4 — Prism only clones files on-demand and does not run the background thread to clone the unvisited files. As such, all files that are accessed by the benchmark will be cloned at runtime and all cloning penalties related to the benchmark are included into the benchmark result. This provides a stable evaluation on the performance penalty caused by the on-demand cloning mechanism. As another comparison point, to get the best-case performance for Prism, we also ran the benchmark on a fully cloned filesystem, which excludes the cloning overhead from the benchmark results. We compared the ext3, lazily-cloned, and fully-cloned pext3 filesystems on the Apache workload.

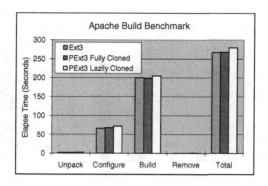

Fig. 6. Performance of Apache build workload. "Ext3" stands for standard Ext3 filesystem; "PExt3" stands for the Prism Ext3 filesystem.

Note that the benchmark needs to use some system tools and libraries such as `tar`, `gunzip`, and `gcc`. In our experiments, the benchmark process used the tools on the cloned filesystem. We guaranteed that by using "chroot" [6] to the cloned filesystem before running the benchmark. As a result, all input and output files needed for the benchmark are accessed from the cloned filesystem. To avoid warm cache effects caused by previous runs, we always ran the experiments right after the filesystem was mounted.

In Figure 6, each bar group shows a phase of the Apache build benchmark, while the "Total" group represents the total time consumed in the four phases of the benchmark. Overall, the Apache build benchmark running on a lazily cloned filesystem was 4.6% slower than on a full copied filesystem. With a fully cloned filesystem, the performance difference with `ext3` was negligible. These results demonstrate that the performance impact of the Prism asynchronous cloning mechanism is not significant. Moreover, once the background cloning procedure is finished, the cloned filesystem can be accessed at the same speed as a fully cloned filesystem.

4.3 Connectathon Test Suite

We used the Connectathon test suite [1] to evaluate operational correctness and performance of the pext3 system. The Connectathon test suite is a standard benchmark widely used by many filesystem projects such as Frangipani [15] and Ext3cow [10] to verify the correctness of filesystems and their interoperability with variety of operating systems.

We modified the Connectathon parameters to invoke more filesystem operations than the default setting. As such, we can better exercise the system and get more accurate performance results. In the experiment, we allocated a dedicated disk partition and used the pext3 and ext3 filesystems to manage this disk partition, respectively. For each setting, we ran the "basic" series of Connectathon benchmark for 10 times. The "basic" series of Connectathon test

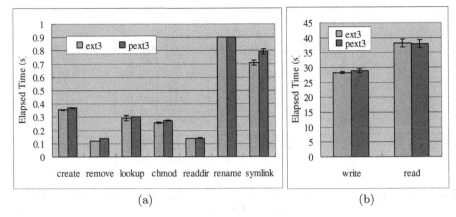

Fig. 7. Connectathon benchmark results. Each block group shows the latency of a step of the Connectathon benchmark.

includes nine steps. Each part tests a separate system call. In order, the nine steps are: (1) create 12400 files 62 directories 5 levels deep, (2) remove these files, (3) 20000 getcwd and stat calls, (4) 80000 chmods and stats, (5) create and write 1000 files. The size of each file is 1MB. Next, we read the 1000 files into 8K buffers sequentially. (6) create 400 files in a directory and read the directory entries for 81000 times using readdir, (7) create 200 files, rename and stat these files for 4000 times, (8) create 200 files, and perform symlinks and readlinks for 8000 times, and, lastly, (9) perform 15000 statfs calls.

The average time elapsed to run the benchmark on the pext3 and ext3 filesystems were measured and compared. The reported results are the average value from ten rounds of benchmark and reflect 95% confidence interval. To avoid warm cache effects caused by previous runs, we rebooted the test VM before each round of benchmark, and conducted the experiments right after the system is started.

The performance comparison is illustrated in Figure 7. Overall, the microbenchmark results indicate that the pext3 filesystem delivers performance comparable to the ext3 filesystem on operations `create`, `lookup`, `chmod`, `readdir`, `rename`, `write`, and `read`. The performance differences between pext3 and ext3 on these operations are at most 6.23%.

Pext3 performs 16.67% and 11.27% slower than ext3 on the `remove` and `symlink` operations, respectively. For the ext3 filesystem, a `remove` operation mainly involves the updates on metadata including directory entries and block bitmaps, which are very efficient. The pext3 filesystem, however, uses the reference count table to track the usage status of data blocks. When removing a file, the filesystem driver must update the reference count (see Section 3.5) for each data blocks used by the file, incurring additional overhead. While the overhead of updating the reference count table is not substantial in term of the absolute value, it can be more pronounced for the filesystem operations that only incur

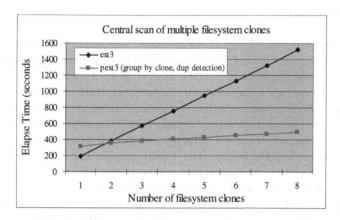

Fig. 8. Performance of central scanning 8 clones of a filesystem. "ext3" stands for fully copied filesystems. "pext3 (group by clone dup detection)" stands for cloned filesystem.

very low overhead. The same reason also explains the performance difference for the `symlink` operations.

4.4 Central Scan of Multiple Clones

Because of the way Prism does cloning (clones via file sharing), it is very easy for applications to identify files that are shared across filesystems. This allows faster versions of centralized applications that scan multiple filesystems (e.g., virus scanning or comparing two filesystems for changes) to be designed. The enhanced central applications can detect the files shared by multiple filesystems and scan them only once. We developed a central virus scanner that can check multiple filesystems (clones) for viruses. To see if Prism provides such performance advantages to the central scanner, we cloned the parent system 8 times. We then sequentially scanned n cloned systems and compared the performance with scanning n copied filesystems. Both the fully copied filesystem and the cloned filesystem have 170K files and 17K directories. The Prism central scanning tool maintained a list of scanned files' inodes (retrieved via the Linux `stat()` call) in a hash table. If it encounters the same inode again from another filesystem, it does not re-scan the file content.

Figure 8 shows the central scanning performance on both pext3 and ext3 filesystems. For $n = 1$, `ext3` outperformed `pext3` because every file had to be scanned in both systems. For small n, a cloned system is not expected to perform as well as a fully-copied system because it may have less spatial locality on the disk. Moreover, when scanning a Prism cloned filesystem, the central scanner needs to build up the hash table, which incurs additional overhead. For larger values of n, scanning cloned systems outperformed scanning copied systems by a significant factor. For `pext3`, there is still some increase in time with n because the directory structure still has to be traversed n times, but the slope is around 10 times lower.

5   Conclusion

This paper describes the design of a virtualized file system for supporting hosted servers and utility computing. Prism provides a file-level cloning mechanism that can clone any selected part of a VM's filesystem to a specified location. Prism is implemented by modifying ext3 with about 5000 lines of code. Prism uses an asynchronous cloning technique that establishes most of the file sharing in the background and also aggressively on demand. This technique allows both systems (parent and clone) to be usable almost immediately, irrespective of the size of the cloned filesystem. On the server side, Prism permits fast centralized scanning. Any files that have not been modified among parent and child filesystems have identical inode numbers and need to be only scanned once.

We implemented and evaluated the Prism cloning mechanism. The Prism cloning mechanism was able to clone a filesystem with around 170K files and 17K directories within 58.7 seconds, and return to the user an usable file system clone within 0.18 seconds. In contrast, copying the same file system takes more than 10 minutes. We also evaluated the performance of Prism's cloned file systems. On the Connectathon benchmark and the Apache build workload, a Prism cloned file system's performance is close to that of a standard ext3 file system. For applications that require scanning or comparing multiple cloned filesystems, Prism was found to be significantly faster.

References

1. Connectathon. Introduction to the Connectathon NFS Testsuite (2007), http://www.connectathon.org/nfstests.html
2. Hitz, D., Lau, J., Malcolm, M.: File system design for an NFS file server appliance. In: WTEC 1994: Proceedings of the USENIX Winter 1994 Technical Conference on USENIX Winter 1994 Technical Conference, Berkeley, CA, USA, p. 19. USENIX Association (1994)
3. Howard, J.H., Kazar, M.L., Menees, S.G., Nichols, D.A., Satyanarayanan, M., Sidebotham, R.N., West, M.J.: Scale and performance in a distributed file system. ACM Transactions on Computer Systems (TOCS) 6(1), 51–81 (1988)
4. Klivansky, M.: A thorough introduction to flexclone[TM]volumes. Technical Report TR3347, Network Appliance Inc. (October 2004)
5. Liang, Z., Venkatakrishnan, V.N., Sekar, R.: Isolated Program Execution: An Application Transparent Approach for Executing Untrusted Programs. In: ACSAC 2003: Proceedings of the 19th Annual Computer Security Applications Conference, pp. 182–191. IEEE Computer Society, Los Alamitos (2003)
6. McGrath, R.: Free Software Foundation. Chroot 5.2.1 - run command or interactive shell with special root directory, The Linux Manual Pages (May 2005)
7. Sun Microsystems. Solaris ZFS - The Most Advanced File System on the Planet (2007), http://www.sun.com/software/solaris/ds/zfs.jsp
8. Morris, J.H., Satyanarayanan, M., Conner, M.H., Howard, J.H., Rosenthal, D.S., Smith, F.D.: Andrew: a distributed personal computing environment. Communications of the ACM 29(3), 184–201 (1986)

9. Muniswamy-Reddy, K., Wright, C.P., Himmer, A., Zadok, E.: A Versatile and User-Oriented Versioning File System. In: Proceedings of the Third USENIX Conference on File and Storage Technologies (FAST 2004), San Francisco, CA, pp. 115–128 (2004)
10. Peterson, Z., Burns, R.: Ext3cow: A time-shifting file system for regulatory compliance. ACM Transcations on Storage 1(2), 190–212 (2005)
11. Pfaff, B., Garfinkel, T., Rosenblum, M.: Virtualization aware file systems: Getting beyond the limitations of virtual disks. In: NSDI 2006: Proceedings of the 3rd Symposium of Networked Systems Design and Implementation, pp. 353–366 (May 2006)
12. Satyanarayanan, M.: Scalable, secure, and highly available distributed file access. Computer 23(5), 9–18, 20–21 (1990)
13. Soules, C.A.N., Goodson, G.R., Strunk, J.D., Ganger, G.R.: Metadata efficiency in versioning file systems. In: FAST 2003: Proceedings of the 2nd USENIX Conference on File and Storage Technologies, Berkeley, CA, USA, pp. 43–58. USENIX Association (2003)
14. Sun, W., Liang, Z., Venkatakrishnan, V.N., Sekar, R.: One-Way Isolation: An Effective Approach for Realizing Safe Execution Environments. In: NDSS 2005: Proceedings of the Network and Distributed System Security Symposium (2005)
15. Thekkath, C.A., Mann, T., Lee, E.K.: Frangipani: a scalable distributed file system. ACM SIGOPS Operating Systems Review 31(5), 224–237 (1997)
16. VMware. VMware VMFS: High-performance cluster file system for storage virtualization (October 2006), http://www.vmware.com/pdf/vmfs_datasheet.pdf
17. Warfield, A., Ross, R., Fraser, K., Limpach, C., Hand, S.: Parallax: Managing storage for a million machines. In: Proceedings of the 10th USENIX Workshop on Hot Topics in Operating Systems (HotOS X), Santa Fe, NM (June 2005)
18. Yu, Y., Guo, F., Nanda, S., Lam, L.c., Chiueh, T.c.: A feather-weight virtual machine for windows applications. In: VEE 2006: Proceedings of the second international conference on Virtual execution environments, pp. 24–34. ACM Press, New York (2006)
19. Zadok, E., Iyer, R., Joukov, N., Sivathanu, G., Wright, C.P.: On incremental file system development. ACM Transactions on Storage (TOS) 2(3) (accepted) (August 2006)
20. Zhao, X.: Improving the storage manageability, flexibility, and security in virtual machine systems, Ph.D thesis, EECS Department, University of Michigan, Ann Arbor (2007),
http://portal.acm.org/citation.cfm?id=1368534&coll=GUIDE&dl=GUIDE
21. Zhao, X., Borders, K., Prakash, A.: Towards protecting sensitive files in a compromised system. In: SISW 2005: Proceedings of the Third IEEE International Security in Storage Workshop, Washington, DC, USA, pp. 21–28. IEEE Computer Society, Los Alamitos (2005)

Moara: Flexible and Scalable Group-Based Querying System

Steven Y. Ko[1], Praveen Yalagandula[2], Indranil Gupta[1],
Vanish Talwar[2], Dejan Milojicic[2], and Subu Iyer[2]

[1] University of Illinois at Urbana-Champaign
[2] HP Labs, Palo Alto

Abstract. Users and administrators of large-scale infrastructures (e.g., datacenters and PlanetLab) are frequently in need of monitoring *groups* of machines in the infrastructure. Though there exist several distributed querying systems for this monitoring purpose, they are not group-based; they mostly focus on querying the entire system. In this paper, we present *Moara*, a new querying system that makes two novel contributions. First, Moara builds aggregation trees for different groups and adaptively maintains the trees to optimize the total message cost. Second, Moara supports a query language allowing groups to be specified implicitly via predicates consisting of arbitrarily nested unions and intersections. Our evaluations on Emulab, on PlanetLab, and with large-scale simulations, demonstrate Moara's ability to answer complex queries within a fraction of a second, to deal with high levels of dynamism in groups, and to incur a low bandwidth overhead per host per query in comparison to existing centralized and distributed aggregation systems.

1 Introduction

Large-scale distributed infrastructures have become increasingly common in various domains. Today's enterprise data centers [1] are equipped with thousands of machines and run thousands of different applications and services. Federated computing infrastructures such as PlanetLab [2], proposed GENI infrastructure [3], and computational grids [4] consist of thousands of hosts providing resources for a number of projects.

A frequent need of the users and the administrators of such infrastructures is monitoring and querying the status of *groups* of machines in the infrastructure, as well as the infrastructure as a whole. These groups may be static or dynamic, e.g., the PlanetLab slices, the machines running a particular service in a datacenter, or the machines with CPU utilization above 50%. Further, users typically desire to express complex criteria for the selection of the host groups to be queried. For example, "find top-3 loaded hosts where (ServiceX = true) and (Apache = true)" is a query that targets two groups - hosts that run service X and hosts that run Apache. Dynamic groups mean that the size and composition of groups vary across different queries as well as time.

In general, users and administrators desire to monitor the performance of these groups, to troubleshoot any failures or performance degradations, and to track usage of allocated resources. These requirements point to the need for a *group-based querying system* that can provide instantaneous answers to queries over in-situ data targeting

V. Issarny and R. Schantz (Eds.): Middleware 2008, LNCS 5346, pp. 408–428, 2008.

one or more groups. In fact, several existing distributed aggregation systems [5, 6, 7] can be considered as a special case of group-based querying systems, as they target querying of only a single group, *i.e.,* the entire system.

Any group-based querying system should satisfy three requirements: *flexibility, efficiency,* and *scalability.* First, the system should be flexible to support expressive queries that deal with multiple groups, such as unions and intersections of different groups. Second, the system should be efficient in query resolution—it should minimize the message overhead while responding quickly with an answer. Third, the system should scale with the number of machines, the number of groups, and the rate of queries.

In this paper, we propose Moara, a new group-based distributed aggregation system that targets all three requirements. A query in Moara has three parts: *(query-attribute, aggregation function, group-predicate)*, e.g., (Mem-Util, Average, Apache = true). Moara returns the resulting value from applying the *aggregation function* over the values of *query-attribute* at the machines that satisfy the *group-predicate.*

Moara makes two novel design contributions over existing systems [5, 6, 7]. First, Moara maintains aggregation trees for different groups adaptively based on the underlying environment and the injected queries to minimize the overall message cost and query response time. Basically, the aggregation tree for a group in Moara is an optimized sub-graph of a global spanning tree, which spans all nodes in the group. By aggregating data over these group-based aggregation trees, Moara achieves lower message cost and response latency for queries compared to other aggregation systems that contact all nodes. Further, we adapt each aggregation tree to deal with dynamism.

Second, Moara's query processor supports *composite* queries that target multiple groups simultaneously. Composite queries supported by Moara are arbitrary nested set expressions built by using logical operators or and and, (respectively set operations ∪ and ∩) over simple group-predicates. Simple group-predicates are of the form *(attribute op value)*, where $op \in \{<, >, \leq, \geq, =, \neq\}$. Consider our previous example "find top-3 loaded hosts where (ServiceX = true) and (Apache = true)", which is a composite query that targets the intersection of two groups - hosts that run service X and hosts that run Apache. Instead of blindly querying all the groups present in a query, Moara's query processor analyzes composite queries and intelligently decides on contacting a set of groups that minimizes the communication overhead.

We implemented a prototype of Moara by leveraging the FreePastry DHT (Distributed Hash Table) [8] and SDIMS [7] systems. Our evaluation consists of experiments on Emulab [9] and PlanetLab, as well as large-scale simulations. Our experimental results indicate that, compared to previous global hierarchical aggregation systems, Moara reduces response latency by up to a factor of 4 and achieves an order of magnitude bandwidth savings. Our scalability experiments confirm that Moara's overhead for answering a query is independent of the total number of nodes in the system, and only grows linearly with the group size. Finally, we show that Moara can answer complex queries within hundreds of milliseconds in systems with hundreds of nodes under high group churn.

In this work, we focus on efficiently supporting one-shot queries (as opposed to repeated continuous queries) over a common set of groups, since we expect this type of queries to be more common in the kind of infrastructures we are targeting at — datacenters and federated computing systems. We expect most users will be performing one-shot queries over common groups (e.g., the same PlanetLab slice, machines in a datacenter, etc) during the time when their service or experiment is running. Further, a user interested in monitoring groups continually can invoke one-shot queries periodically. Our use cases in Section 2 motivate this design decision further.

Any distributed system subjected to dynamism in the environment, suffers from the CAP dilemma [10], which states that it is difficult to provide both strong consistency guarantees and high availability in failure-prone distributed settings. Moara treads this dilemma by preferring to provide high availability and scalability, while providing eventual consistency guarantees on aggregation results. This philosophy is in line with that of existing aggregation systems such as Astrolabe [6] and SDIMS [7]. Moara could also allow the use of metrics proposed by Jain et al. [11, 12] in order to track the imprecision of the query results; however, studying these is beyond the scope of the current paper.

2   Motivation and Use Cases

We highlight the need for on-demand flexible querying and for dealing with dynamism by presenting two motivating scenarios - data centers and federated infrastructures.

Consolidated Data Centers: In the last few years, medium and large-scale enterprises have moved away from maintaining their own clusters, towards subscribing to services offered by consolidated data centers. Such consolidated data centers consist of multiple locations, with each location containing several thousands of servers [1]. Each server runs heterogeneous operating systems including virtual machine hosts. While such consolidation enables running unified management tasks, it also introduces the need to deal with scale.

Workloads on these data centers typically include Terminal Services, SOA-based transaction workloads (e.g., SAP), and Web 2.0 workloads, e.g., searching and collaboration. Figure 1 presents some on-demand one-shot queries that data center managers and service owners typically desire to run on such a virtualized enterprise. Several of these one-shot queries are for aggregating information from a common group of nodes including cases where groups are expressed as unions of groups (e.g., the third query in table), or intersections (e.g., the last query). We would like to generalize this to provide managers with a powerful tool supporting flexible queries using arbitrarily nested

Tasks	Queries
Resource Allocation	Average utilization for servers belonging to (i) floor F, (ii) cluster C, (iii) rack R
	Number of machines/VMs in a given cluster C
VM Migration	Average utilization of VMs running application X version 1 or version 2
	List of all VMs running application X and are VMWare based
Auditing/Security	Count of all VMs/machines running firewall
	Count of all VMs running ESX server and Sygate firewall
Dashboard	Max response time for Service X
	Count of all machines that are up and running Service X
Patch management	List of version numbers being used for service X
	Count of all machines that are in cluster C and running service X.version Y

Fig. 1. Illustrative Queries for Managing the Virtualized Enterprise

unions and intersections of groups. In addition, these workloads vary in intensity over time, causing considerable dynamism in the system, e.g., terminal services facing high user turnaround rates.

Federated Computing Infrastructures: In today's federated computing infrastructures such as PlanetLab [2] and global Grids [4], as well as in proposed infrastructures, e.g., GENI [3], users wish to query current statistics for their distributed applications or experiments. For instance, PlanetLab creates virtual subgroups of nodes called "slices" in order to run individual distributed applications. Monitoring is currently supported by tools such as CoMon [13] and Ganglia [14], which periodically collect CPU, memory, and network data per slice on PlanetLab [2]. Due to their periodic nature, they are not open to on-demand queries that require up-to-date answers. Further, increasing the frequency of data collection is untenable due to storage and communication costs.

In contrast to the above systems, we need a system to answer one-shot queries that seek to obtain up-to-date information over a common group of machines, that can be run on-demand or periodically by an end-host, and are flexibly specified. Some examples of our target queries include: number of slices containing at least one machine with CPU utilization > 90% (basic query), CPU utilization of nodes common to two given slices (intersection query), or free disk space across all slices in a given organization (union query).

Need for Group-based Aggregation: As illustrated by above two target scenarios, we expect that most of the queries are one-shot queries over common groups of machines. Moreover, the predicate in a query specified as a logical expression involves several groups, e.g., some groups in the above examples include the set of nodes in a PlanetLab slice, the set of nodes running a given Grid task, the set of nodes with CPU utilization > 90%, etc. In the worst case, such a group may span the entire system.

In practice though, we expect the group sizes to vary across different queries and with time. In Figure 2(a), we plot the distribution of PlanetLab slice sizes, analyzed from an instance of CoMon [13] data. Notice that there is a considerable spread in the sizes. As many as 50% of the 400 slices have fewer than 10 assigned nodes, thus a monitoring system that contacts all nodes to answer a query for a slice is very inefficient. If we consider only nodes that were actually in use (where a slice has more than one process

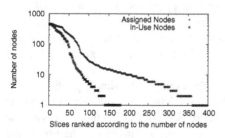
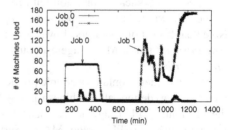

Fig. 2. (a) Usage of PlanetLab nodes by different slices. We show both node assignment to slices and active usage of nodes. Data collected from a CoTop snapshot [15]. (b) Usage of HP's utility computing environment by different animation rendering jobs. We show the number of machines each job uses.

running on a node), as many as 100 out of 170 slices have fewer than 10 active nodes. In another example case, Figure 2(b) presents the behavior of two jobs over a 20-hour period from a real 6-month trace of a utility computing environment at HP with 500 machines receiving animation rendering batch jobs. This plot shows the dynamism in each group over time.

These trace studies indicate that group sizes can be expected to be varying across time in both consolidated centers as well as in federated computing infrastructures. Thus, an efficient querying system has to avoid treating the entire system as a single group and globally broadcasting queries to all nodes.

3   The Basics of Moara

In this section, we first discuss how Moara end-nodes maintain data and how queries are structured. Then we discuss how Moara builds trees for individual groups.

3.1   Data and Query Model

Information at each node is represented and stored as (*attribute, value*) tuples. For example, a machine with CPU capacity of 3Ghz can have an attribute (CPU-Mhz, 3000). Moara has an agent running at each node that monitors the node and populates (*attribute, value*) pairs.

A query in Moara comprises of three parts: (*query-attribute, aggregation function, group-predicate*). The first field specifies the attribute of interest to be aggregated, while the second field specifies the aggregation function to be used on this data. We require this aggregation function to be partially aggregatable. In other words, given two partial aggregates for multiple disjoint sets of nodes, the aggregation function must produce an aggregate that corresponds to the union of these node sets [6,7]. This admits aggregation functions such as enumeration, max, min, sum, count, or top-k. Average can be implemented by aggregating both sum and count.

The third field of the query specifies the group of machines on which the above aggregation is performed. If no group is specified, the default is to aggregate values from all nodes in the system. A *group-predicate* (henceforth called a "predicate") is specified as a boolean expression with and and or operators, over *simple* predicates of the following form: (*group-attribute op value*), where $op \in \{<, >, =, \leq, \geq, \neq\}$. Note that this set of operators allows us to implicitly support not in a group predicate. Any *attribute* that a Moara agent populates can be used as either *query-attribute* or *group-attribute*.

A simple query contains a simple predicate. For example, the simple predicate (ServiceX = true) defines all machines running ServiceX. Thus, a user wishing to compute the maximum CPU usage across machines where ServiceX is running will issue the following query: (CPU-Usage, MAX, (ServiceX = true)). Alternately, the user could use a *composite* predicate, e.g., (ServiceX = true and Apache = true). This composite query is defined with set operators $\cup$ and $\cap$.

Note that the query model can be easily extended so that instead of a *query-attribute*, a querier can specify any arbitrary program that operates upon simple (*attribute, value*) pairs. For example, a querier can specify a program that evaluates (CPU-Available > CPU-Needed-For-App-A) as *query-attribute*, to see how many nodes are available for the application A. Similarly, *group-predicate* can be extended to contain multiple attributes by defining new attributes. For example, we can define a new attribute *att* as (CPU-Available > CPU-Needed-For-App-A), which takes a boolean value of true/false. Then *att* can be used to specify a group. However, for this paper, we mainly focus on the techniques for efficiently answering the queries for given *group-predicates* and hence restrict query model to contain only simple attributes.

3.2   Scalable Aggregation

We describe here how Moara aggregates data for each group.

DHT trees: For scalability with large number of nodes, groups, and queries, Moara employs a peer-to-peer in-network aggregation approach that leverages the computing and network resources of the distributed infrastructure itself to compute results. These trees are used for spreading queries, and aggregating answers back towards the source node. In our architecture, a lightweight Moara agent runs at each server from which data needs to be aggregated. These agents participate in a structured overlay routing algorithm such as Pastry [8], Tapestry [16], or Chord [17]. These systems allow routing within the overlay, from any node to any other node, based on the IDs of these nodes in the system. Moara uses this mechanism for building aggregation trees called DHT trees, akin to existing systems [7, 18, 19]. A DHT tree contains all the nodes in the system, and is rooted at a node that maps to the ID of the group. For instance, Figure 3 shows the tree for an ID with prefix 000 using Pastry's algorithm with one-bit prefix correction. We choose to leverage a DHT, since it handles physical membership churn (such as failures and join/leave) very modularly and efficiently. Also, we can construct aggregation trees clearly, given a group predicate.

Basics of Resolving Queries: Given a simple query with predicate p, Moara uses MD-5 to hash the *group-attribute* field in p and derives a bit-string that stands for the group ID. The DHT tree for this ID is then used to perform aggregation for this query, e.g., Figure 3 shows the DHT tree for an attribute "ServiceX" that hashes to 000.

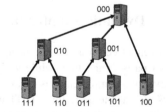

Fig. 3. DHT tree for an ID with prefix 000

When a simple query is generated at any node in Moara, it is first forwarded to the root node of the corresponding DHT tree via the underlying DHT routing mechanism. The root then propagates it downwards along the DHT tree to the leaves. When a leaf receives a query, it evaluates the predicate p in the query (e.g., ServiceX=true). If the result is true, it replies to its parent the local value for the query attribute (e.g., CPU-Usage). Otherwise, it sends a null reply to its parent. An internal node waits to reply to its parent until *all* its children have replied or until a timeout occurs (using values in Section 7). Then, it aggregates the values reported by its children, including its own contribution if the predicate is satisfied locally, and forwards the aggregate to its parent. Finally, the root node replies to the original querying node with the aggregated value.

Moara Mechanisms: The above "global aggregation" approach has every node in the system receive every query. Hence, it is inefficient in resolving queries targeting specific groups. Moara addresses this via three mechanisms.

First, Moara attempts to prune out branches of the tree that do not contain any node satisfying the predicate p. We call this tree a pruned tree or a *group tree* for p. For example, in Figure 3, if nodes 111, 110, and 010 do not satisfy the predicate, then the root does not forward the query to 010. However, this raises a challenge – how do internal nodes know whether any of their descendants satisfy the predicate. For instance, if node 110 decides to install ServiceX and thus satisfies the predicate, the path from the root to this node will need to be added to the tree. Further, if the composition of a group changes rapidly, then the cost for maintaining the group tree can become higher than query resolution costs. Section 4 presents Moara's dynamic adaptation mechanism that addresses this dilemma.

Second, Moara reduces network cost and response latency by short-circuiting the group trees, thus reducing the number of internal tree nodes that do not satisfy the predicate. For instance, in Figure 3, if node 010 does not satisfy the predicate but node 110 does, then the former can be eliminated from the tree by having 110 receive queries directly from the root. Section 5 describes how this reduces the bandwidth cost of aggregating a group with m nodes in a system of N nodes, from $O(m \log N)$ to $O(m)$.

Third, Moara efficiently resolves composite queries involving multiple groups by rewriting the predicate into a more manageable form, and then selecting a minimal set of groups to resolve the query. For example, an intersection query (CPU-Util, avg, (floor=F1 and cluster=C12)) is best resolved by sending the query to only one of the two groups - either (floor=F1) or (cluster=C12) - whichever is cheaper. This design decision of Moara is detailed in Section 6.

4   Dynamic Maintenance

Given a tree for a specific group, Moara reduces bandwidth cost by adaptively pruning out parts of the tree, while still guaranteeing correctness via *eventual completeness*. Eventual completeness is defined as follows - when the set of predicate-satisfying nodes as well as the underlying DHT overlay do not change for a sufficiently long time after a query injection, a query to the group will eventually return answers from all such nodes. For now, we assume that the dynamism in the system is only due to changes in the composition of the groups ("group churn"); we will describe how our system handles node and network reconfigurations (churn in system) later in Section 7.

To resolve queries efficiently, Moara could prune out the branches of the corresponding DHT tree that do not contain any nodes belonging to the group. However, to maintain completeness of the query resolution, Moara can perform such aggressive pruning only if it maintains up-to-date information at each node about the status of branches at that node. For groups with high churn in membership relative to the number of queries (e.g., CPU-Util < 50), maintaining group status at each node for all its branches can consume high bandwidth - broadcasting queries system-wide may be cheaper. For relatively stable groups however (e.g., (sliceX = true) on PlanetLab), proactively maintaining the group trees can reduce bandwidth and response times. Instead of implementing either of these two extreme solution points, Moara uses a distributed adaptation mechanism that, at each node, tracks the queries in the system and group churn events from children for a group predicate and decides whether or not to spend any bandwidth to inform its parent about its status.

Basic Pruning Mechanism: Each Moara node maintains a binary local state variable *prune* for each group predicate. If *prune* for a predicate is true (PRUNE state), then the branch rooted at this node can be pruned from the DHT tree while querying for that predicate. Whenever a node goes from PRUNE to NO-PRUNE state, it sends a NO-PRUNE message to its parent; the reverse transition causes a PRUNE message to be sent. When the root or an internal node receives a query for this predicate, it will forward the query to only those of its children that are in NO-PRUNE state.

Note that it is incorrect for an internal node to set its state for a predicate to PRUNE based merely on whether it satisfies the predicate or not. One or more its descendants may satisfy the predicate, and hence the branch rooted at the node should continue to receive any queries for this predicate. Further, an internal or a leaf node should also consider the churn in the predicate satisfiability before setting the *prune* variable. For example, suppose the predicate is (CPU-Util < 50) and a leaf node's utilization is fluctuating around 50% at a high rate. In this case, the leaf node will be setting and unsetting *prune* variable, leading to a large number of PRUNE/NO-PRUNE messages.

Due to the above reasons, we define the *prune* variable as a variable depending on two additional local state variables—*sat* and *update*. *sat* is a binary variable to track if the subtree rooted at this node should continue receiving queries for the predicate. Thus *sat* is set to 1 (SAT) if either the local node satisfies the predicate or any child node is in NO-PRUNE state.

update is a binary state variable that denotes whether the node will update its *prune* variable or not. So, when *update* = 1 (UPDATE state), the node will update the *prune* variable; but, when *update* = 0 (NO-UPDATE state), the node will cease to perform any updates to the *prune* variable irrespective of any changes in the local satisfiability, or any messages from its children. In other words, a node does not send any PRUNE or NO-PRUNE messages to its parent when it is in NO-UPDATE state. So, to ensure correct operation, a node can move into NO-UPDATE state only after setting *prune* = 0. This guarantees that its parent will always send the queries for the predicate to this node. Formally, we maintain the following invariants:

$$update = 1 \text{ AND } sat = 1 \implies prune = 0$$
$$update = 1 \text{ AND } sat = 0 \implies prune = 1$$
$$update = 0 \implies prune = 0$$

The transition rules for the state machine at each node is illustrated in Figure 4. Note that a node sends a status update message to its parent whenever it moves from PRUNE to NO-PRUNE state or vice-versa. This state machine ensures the following invariant – *each node in the system performs at least one of the following: (a) sends status updates upwards to its parent, or (b) receives all queries from its parent.* This invariant suffices to guarantee eventual completeness because after the group stops changing, any node that satisfies the predicate will be in SAT state. Therefore, the node and its ancestors will all be in NO-PRUNE state, and thus the node will receive the next query. Our technical report [20] elaborates with pseudo-code how Moara evaluates each variable.

Adaptation Policy: To decide the transition rules for the *update* state variable, Moara employs an adaptation mechanism that allows different policies. Our goal is to use a policy that minimizes the overall message cost, *i.e.*, sum of both update and query costs. In Moara, each node tracks the total number of *recent* queries and local changes it has seen (in the tree) - we discuss details of how to keep track of recent queries and local changes in

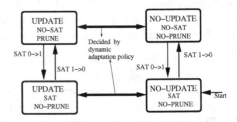

Fig. 4. State machine for dynamic adaptation mechanism

our technical report [20]. Each node keeps two query counts - q_n, the number of queries recently received by the system while the node is in NO-SAT state, and q_s, the number of recent queries received by the system while it was in SAT state. The node also keeps track of the number of times the *sat* variable toggled between 0 and 1, denoted as c.

A node in NO-UPDATE state would exchange a total of $B_{NU} = 2 \times (q_n + q_s)$ messages with its parent (two per query), while a node in UPDATE state would exchange $B_{UP} = c + 2 \times q_s$ messages (one per change, and two per query). Thus, to minimize bandwidth, the transition rules are as follows: (1) a node in UPDATE state moves to NO-UPDATE if $B_{NU} < B_{UP}$, *i.e.*, $2 \times q_n < c$; (2) a node in NO-UPDATE state moves to UPDATE if $B_{NU} > B_{UP}$, *i.e.*, $2 \times q_n > c$. In order to avoid flip-flopping around the threshold, we could add in hysteresis, but our current design performs well without it.

One corner issue with the above approach is that when a node is in the PRUNE state, it does not receive any more queries and thus cannot accurately track q_n. Note that this does not affect the correctness (*i.e.*, eventual completeness) of our protocol but may cause unnecessary status update messages. To address this, the root node of an aggregation tree in Moara assigns a sequence number for each query and sends that number piggybacked along with the queries. Thus, any node that receives a query with sequence number s is able to track q_n using the difference between s and its own last-seen query sequence number.

State Maintenance: By default, each node does not maintain any state, which is considered as being in NO-UPDATE state. A node starts maintaining states only when a query arrives at the node. Without dynamic maintenance, merely maintaining pruned trees for a large number of predicates (e.g., a tree for each slice in the PlanetLab case or a tree for each job in the data center) could consume very high bandwidth in an aggregation system. With dynamic maintenance, pruning is proactively performed for only those predicates that are of interest at that time. Once queries stop, nodes in the aggregation tree start moving into NO-UPDATE state with any new updates from their children and hence stop sending any further updates to their parents.

We note that a node in NO-UPDATE state for a predicate can safely garbage-collect state information (e.g., predicate itself, recent events information, etc) for that predicate without causing any incorrectness in the query resolution. So, once a predicate goes out of interest, eventually no state is maintained at any node and no messages are exchanged between nodes for that predicate. Several policies for deciding when to garbage-collect state information are possible: we could 1) garbage-collect each predicate after a time-out expires, 2) keep only the last k predicates queried, 3) garbage-collect the least frequently queried predicate every time a new query arrives, etc. However, studying these policies is beyond the scope of this paper. We also note that we do not consider DHT maintenance overhead. In addition, note that global aggregation trees are implicit from the DHT routing and hence require no separate maintenance overhead.

Finally, since Moara maintains state information for each predicate, it could be more efficient if we aggregated different predicates. For example, predicates such as CPU-Util > 50, CPU-Util > 60, and CPU-Util > 70 could be aggregated as one predicate, CPU-Util > 50, so that Moara could maintain only one tree. This design choice requires careful study on the tradeoff between the state maintenance overhead and the bandwidth overhead incurred by combining different trees with the same attribute. This is outside of the scope of this paper, since we focus on the tradeoff of the bandwidth overhead based on the query rate and the group churn rate.

5   Separate Query Plane

Given a tree that contains m predicate-satisfying nodes, using the pruned DHT trees of the previous section may lead to $O(m \log N)$ additional nodes being involved in the tree. These extra nodes would typically be internal tree nodes that are forwarding queries down or responses up the tree, but which do not satisfy the predicate themselves. This section proposes modifications to the protocol described in Section 4 in order to reduce the traffic through these internal nodes.

Our idea is to bypass the internal nodes, thus creating a *separate query plane* which involves mostly nodes satisfying the predicate. This optimizes the tree that we built (Section 4) further by eliminating unnecessary internal nodes. This reduces the tree to contain only $O(m)$ nodes, and thus resolves queries with message costs independent of the number of nodes in the system. Note that this technique has similarities to adaptations of multicast trees (e.g., Scribe [18]), but Moara needs to address the challenging interplay between dynamic adaptation and this short-circuiting.

To realize a separate query plane, each node uses the states, constraints and transitions as described in Section 4. In addition, each node runs operations using two locally maintained sets: (i) *updateSet* is a list of nodes that it forwards to its parent; (ii) *qSet* is a list of children or descendant nodes, to which it forwards any received queries. We consider first, for ease of exposition, modified operations only for nodes in the UP-DATE state. When a leaf node in UPDATE state begins to satisfy the tree predicate, it changes to SAT state as described in Section 4 and sets its *UpdateSet* to contain its ID. In addition, when sending a NO-PRUNE message to its parent, it also sends the *up-dateSet*. Each internal node in turn maintains its *qSet* as the union of the latest received *updateSet*s from all its children, adding its own ID (IP and port) if the tree predicate is satisfied locally. The leaf nodes do not need to maintain *qSets* since they do not forward queries.

Finally, each internal node maintains its *updateSet* by continually monitoring if $|qSet|$ < *threshold*, where *threshold* is a system parameter. If so, then *updateSet* is the same as *qSet*, otherwise *updateSet* contains a single element that is the node's own ID regardless of whether the predicate is satisfied locally or not. Whenever the *updateSet* changes at a node and is non-empty, it sends a NO-PRUNE message to its parent along with the new *updateSet* informing the change. Otherwise, it sends a PRUNE message.

The above operations are described assuming that all nodes are in UPDATE state. When a node is NO-UPDATE state, it maintains *qSet* and *updateSet* as described above, but does not send any updates to its parent. For correctness, a node moving from UP-DATE to NO-UPDATE state sends its own ID along with the NO-PRUNE message to its parent so that it receives future queries.

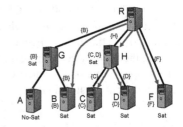

If parameter *threshold*=1, the above mechanisms produce the pruned DHT tree described in Section 4, while *threshold* > 1 gives trees based on a separate query plane. This is because with *threshold*=1, an internal node that receives an *updateSet* from any of its children will pass along its to its parent an *updateSet* containing its own ID, even if the predicate is not satisfied locally. However, with *threshold* > 1, the only internal nodes that do not satisfy the predicate locally but receive queries, are ones that are maintaining a *qSet* of size ≥ *threshold*. Such nodes are required to receive queries so that they can be forwarded to its descendants. However,

Fig. 5. Separate Query Plane for *threshold*=1. We assume all nodes are in UP-DATE mode. Each node's *qSet* is shown next to it, and *updateSet* on the link to its parent.

the tree bypasses several other nodes that do not satisfy the predicate, thus obtaining bandwidth savings. Specifically, an internal node that has $|qSet|$ < *threshold* and does not satisfy the predicate, does not include its own ID in the *updateSet*, and thus does not receive queries.

Having a high value of *threshold* in the system bypasses several internal nodes in the tree. However, this comes at the expense of a higher update traffic since any *updateSet* changes need to be communicated to the parent. Figure 5 shows an example with *threshold*=1. The overhead of forwarding a query in the separate query plane is $O(m)$ for a group with m nodes, independent of system size (details can be found in our technical report [20]).

Our SQP design with *updateSet* and *qSet* variables at nodes, as described above, allow us to easily use the adaptation policy rules described in Section 4. Further details on this can be found in our technical report [20].

6   Composite Queries

So far, we have described how to build and maintain a *single* tree corresponding to one simple predicate. We now describe how a query with a composite predicate is satisfied.

Specifically, we first expand on the multiple possible trees, one tree per simple predicate in the composite query, that such a query entails (Section 6.1). Then, we explain how Moara plans a given query (Section 6.2), and how it selects a low-cost groups of nodes to execute a given composite query (Section 6.3).

6.1 Maintaining Multiple Trees

Section 4 explains the maintenance of trees for simple predicates, starting from the time a predicate is first encountered. If this predicate does not reappear again in subsequent queries in the system, then all nodes in the tree will eventually move to NO-UPDATE state (due to group churn events), and thus there will be no load, either query or update, along the tree. Thus, Moara trees become silent and incurs zero bandwidth cost if not used, obviating the need to explicitly delete trees for simple predicates. Furthermore, Moara does not maintain trees for composite queries, since these might be exponentially large in number - instead, it decides which simple predicate trees (existing or not) will be selected to execute a given composite query. This decision process is described next.

6.2 Composite Query Planning

Consider the following composite query: "find the average free memory across machines where service X and Apache are running". Suppose we have one group tree for (ServiceX=true) and another tree for (Apache=true). A naïve way to resolve the query would be to query both trees in parallel. However, we observe that bandwidth can be saved, without compromising completeness of answers, by (1) sending the query to any *one* of the trees (because it is an intersection query), and (2) choosing the tree that incurs a lower query cost.

Based on this observation, Moara answers arbitrary nested queries involving and and or boolean expressions across simple predicates by selecting a small *cover*. A cover for a given composite query Q is defined as a set of groups (selected from among simple predicates inside Q) which together contain all nodes that satisfy the composite predicate in Q. Thus, we only need to send Q to a cover to obtain a complete answer.

We can compute a cover for a query Q by exploring the boolean expression structure recursively as follows:

- cover(Q="A") = {A} if A is a predefined group.
- cover(Q="A or B") = cover(A) ∪ cover(B).
- cover(Q="A and B") = cover(A), cover(B), or (cover(A) ∪ cover(B)).

For example, for a query with expression ((A and B) or C), the above rules derive {A,C}, {B,C}, and {A,B,C} as possible covers. We call such covers as *structural* covers since we infer them from the structure of the boolean expression.

Once the query originating node calculates the cover for a given query Q, the composite query is forwarded to the roots of trees corresponding to each group in the cover, the answers from these trees are aggregated, and finally returned to the querying node. Notice that it is possible for some node(s) to receive multiple copies of the query, if they are present in multiple trees which appear in the cover for Q. Such nodes reply with the attribute value to only *one* of the trees they are present in, eliminating duplicate answers. This requires nodes to remember the query ids (based on sender IP and sequence number). Such information is cached for 5 minutes in our Moara implementation.

To further save on bandwidth, we would like to select a low-cost cover. This is done by minimizing both the number of groups in the selected cover, as well as the total cost of querying this cover. We explore below three ways of deriving a low-cost cover: (1) *structural optimizations*, which rewrite the nested query to select a low-cost structural cover consisting of simple predicates that already appear within the query, (2) *estimates of query costs* for individual trees, and (3) *semantic optimizations*, which take into account semantic information obtained from users or query attributes.

6.3   Query Optimization: Finding Low-Cost Covers

Given a composite query, Moara first transforms it into a Conjunctive Normal Form (CNF) expression using distributive laws of and and or operators. A CNF form is a two level expression of and's across a series of or terms.

It is important to notice that in the CNF form of a composite predicate for query Q, each series of or terms is a possible cover - this is due to the same reason as our intersection optimization explained earlier. Thus, if Moara can evaluate the query cost of each of these structural covers (as a sum of the query costs for all sets in the cover), then it can select the minimal cost cover for executing the query Q. We will describe query cost calculation soon, but before that we give an example of the query rewriting. The proof of why the CNF form gives the *minimal-cost* cover for a composite predicate can be found in our technical report [20].

Figure 6 shows an example transformation. Consider a query targeting ((A or B) and (A or C)) or D. Moara first transforms the expression to the equivalent CNF: (A or B or D) and (A or C or D). Moara chooses one cover between the two structural covers - either $\{A, B, D\}$ or $\{A, C, D\}$, whichever has a lower cost.

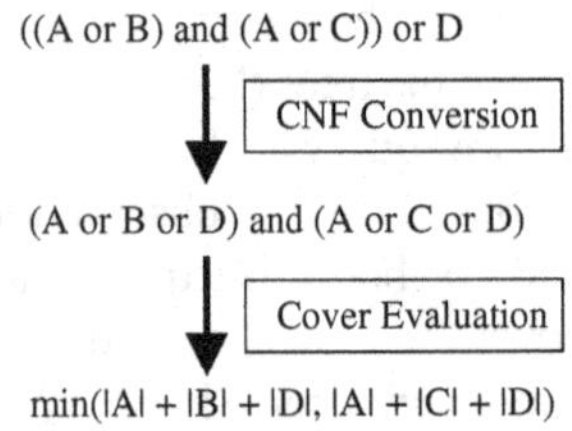

((A or B) and (A or C)) or D

↓ CNF Conversion

(A or B or D) and (A or C or D)

↓ Cover Evaluation

min(|A| + |B| + |D|, |A| + |C| + |D|)

Fig. 6. Example query processing

Estimating Query Costs for Trees: In order to enable low-cost cover calculation, the root node of each tree for a simple predicate continually maintains the query cost for that tree. The query cost is fetched by the querying node and used in the low-cost cover calculation described above. Within the tree, the cost for each query is simply $2 \times np$, where np is the number of nodes in NO-PRUNE state. The values of np are aggregated continually up the tree. Each internal node stores this count for its own subtree, modifies the count according to its own state, and piggybacks this information atop all updates and query responses to its parents. Although this lazy updating of the counts means the query costs may be stale at times, this only affects communication overhead, but not the correctness of the response.

Using Semantic Optimizations: If semantic information is available about the groups, then Moara can further optimize the communication costs by choosing a better cover. We explore two kinds of semantic information in our system: (i) information from description of the group, and (ii) user supplied semantic information. For example, consider two groups A and B defined as follows: $A = \{$nodes with memory $< 2G\}$ and $B = \{$nodes with memory $< 1G\}$. Then, we can infer from these definitions that $B \subseteq A$. In our technical report [20], we detail a variety of semantic relations between two groups Moara exploits and how Moara optimizes further to obtain a low-cost cover.

7 Implementation and Evaluation

We have built a prototype of Moara using SDIMS [7] and FreePastry [8]. All other Moara protocols, described in Section 3 through Section 6, are built atop these systems. Here, we discuss our implementation details and evaluation methodology.

Moara Front-End: The Moara front-end is a client-side interface of Moara. It includes an interactive shell, a query parser, and a query optimizer. Through the interactive shell, a user can submit SQL-like aggregation queries to Moara. The query parser parses the queries, and the query optimizer determines the groups that need to be queried through the algorithm described in Section 6. Once the front-end determines the groups to be queried, it generates a *sub-query* for each group. Each sub-query is resolved exactly the same way as a normal query, except that the front-end waits until it receives all the results from sub-queries, aggregates the results returned by the sub-queries, and returns the final aggregate to the user.

Reconfigurations: To handle reconfigurations, we leverage the underlying FreePastry mechanism for failure detection and neighbor set repair. Further details can be found in our technical report [20].

Evaluation Environments: We use simulation, Emulab, and PlanetLab, and choose a suitable environment to evaluate each of our design choices. We use simulation exclusively for measuring bandwidth consumption in a large-scale environment. We use Emulab and PlanetLab to mainly measure the latency in realistic environments, namely, a medium-scale datacenter (Emulab) and a wide-area infrastructure (PlanetLab).

For each design choice (group-based aggregation, dynamic maintenance, separate query plane, and composite query processor), we choose the evaluation environments that are most suitable. First, we evaluate group-based aggregation on Emulab and PlanetLab, since group-based aggregation is designed to reduce both latency and bandwidth consumption. Second, we evaluate dynamic maintenance and separate query plane using simulation, since both mechanisms are designed for bandwidth optimization and have wide choices of parameters. However, we evaluate the separate query plane on Emulab as well to measure the latency. Lastly, we evaluate our composite query processor on Emulab, since it only affects latency.

Workload: The workload is characterized by two factors - group churn rate and query rate. First, since a group is defined over a particular attribute, the group churn rate depends on how dynamic the attribute is (e.g., a group of (OS = Linux) is likely to be static, while a group of (CPU-util $< 60\%$) is likely to be dynamic). Second, the query rate depends on the usage of Moara and is expected to vary widely. For example, a datacenter operator might typically query a group once an hour on a day, but several times a minute on days with high workloads or unscheduled downtimes. Thus, we parameterize these factors and present the performance of Moara over the parameter range.

7.1   Simulation Results

We perform simulation experiments to measure the bandwith overhead of Moara's dynamic tree maintenance and separate query plane. Our simulations are performed with the FreePastry simulator environment, simulating up to 16,384 nodes. Each node maintains an attribute A with value $\in \{0, 1\}$. All queries are simple queries for (A, SUM, $A = 1$), which counts the number of nodes where A is set to 1.

Dynamic Maintenance: To study the dynamic maintenance mechanism under different workload types, we stress the system by injecting two types of events - query events and group churn events - at different ratios. For example, a query:churn ratio of 0:500 represents an extreme type of workload where there is high group churn, but no queries at all. On the other hand, the query:churn ratio of 500:0 represents the other extreme where there is high query rate, but no group churn. Each group churn event selects m nodes at random, and toggles the value of their attribute A. The value of m determines the "burst size" of attribute churn. We fix the total number of events to 500, and randomly inject query or group churn events at the chosen ratio. All data points are averaged over 3 runs.

Figure 7 shows the average number of messages per node in Moara under various query:churn ratios, in a system of 10,000 nodes with $m = 2000$-sized group churn events. In addition to Moara, we also plot the number of messages generated by two other static approaches that lie at the opposing extremes. These are: 1) the *Global* approach, where no group trees are maintained and queries are sent to all the nodes on the DHT trees, and 2) *Moara (Always-Update)* approach, where a

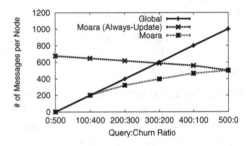

Fig. 7. Bandwidth usage with various query-to-churn ratios

tree is aggressively maintained by having each child send an update to its parent on each attribute churn event.

The Global approach is inexpensive when there are fewer queries in the system, since it avoids the overhead of tree maintenance. On the other hand, with a high-query:low-churn ratio, Moara (Always-Update) performs well because it always maintains group trees and hence incurs lower traffic than Global approach. The plots show that Moara meets or lowers the message overhead in comparison to either of these extreme design choices, at all values of query:churn ratios. When group churn is high, Moara suppresses attribute churn events from propagating to other nodes. With more queries than group churn events, Moara reduces query cost by maintaining trees aggressively. Thus, Moara is able to adapt to various workload patterns.

Separate Query Plane: In Figure 8(a), we plot the query cost against the number of nodes in the system for different threshold values and different group sizes. Note that

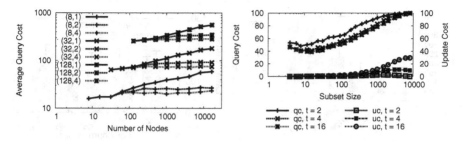

Fig. 8. (a) Bandwidth usage with (threshold > 1) and without the separate query plane (threshold=1) for different group sizes. Each line represents a (group size, threshold) pair (b) Query costs (qc) and update costs (uc) of the separate query plane in a 8192-node system.

the *threshold* value of 1 implies the absence of a separate query plane, while higher threshold values create a separate query plane (refer to Section 5). For this experiment, we do not introduce any group churn during the experiment. We perform 1,000 queries and compute the average of the query cost. Even though there is no group churn, there are updates sent by nodes to their parents as they move into UPDATE state with the first query message. We count those messages as the update cost.

Figure 8(a) shows that without the separate query plane (*threshold*=1), the query cost increases logarithmically as the total system size is raised. However, while maintaining a separate query plane (*threshold*>1), the query cost reaches a constant value and stays flat, independent of the number of nodes in the system. While increasing the value of *threshold* decreases query cost, it can lead to more update messages as discussed in Section 5. In Figure 8(b), we plot the query costs for different *threshold* values as a percentage of the query cost for *threshold*=1 and also plot the percentage increase in the update costs in comparison to *threshold*=1. From these two plots, we observe that (1) with small groups and large total nodes (e.g., 8192 total nodes with group size=8 or 32), using a query plane saves more than 50% bandwidth in query costs, and (2) while using a higher value of threshold does reduce bandwidth, the savings are marginal beyond a threshold of 2 and can incur higher update costs at large group sizes.

7.2 Emulab Experiments

In this section, we study both the latency and communication overhead of Moara under a real deployment scenario in Emulab, that emulates a medium-scale datacenter. Specifically, we evaluate three different workloads. First, we study performance of Moara when querying groups of static attributes (e.g., OS = Linux). We vary the size of groups and show the benefits of using Moara. Second, we study Moara with groups defined over dynamic attributes (e.g., CPU-util < 60%). We stress Moara by varying the frequency of changes. Third, we study composite queries with varying numbers of groups per query.

Methodology: We create a network of 50 machines on a 100 Mbps LAN and instantiate 10 instances of Moara on each machine, thus emulating a 500 node Moara system. Each experimental run is started with one bootstrap node, followed by a batch of 100

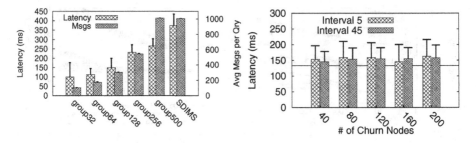

Fig. 9. (a) Latency and bandwidth usage with static groups (b) Average latency of dynamically changing groups. The horizontal line shows the average latency with a static group of the same size.

new instances joining after intervals of 10 seconds each. After the last join, we wait an additional 5 minutes to warm up before initiating queries and group churn from a Moara node. Since we are mainly interested in per-query latency and bandwidth consumption, we fix the query rate and repeat the same query multiple times. As previously, each node maintains one binary attribute A. Our default query is a count, providing the number of nodes with $A=1$. All data points are the average of 3 runs.

Static Groups: Figure 9(a) compares the performance of Moara (with separate query plane) w.r.t. both latency and bandwidth. We vary the group sizes and query 100 times for each experiment. In addition, we compare this performance against an approach where a single global tree is used system-wide - this is labelled as the *SDIMS* approach in the plot. As we can see from the figure, Moara's latency and bandwidth scale with the size of the group. The savings are the most significant for small groups (e.g., set32 which has 32 nodes), where the savings compared to the SDIMS approach are up to 4X in latency and 10X in bandwidth. The latency is reduced due to the use of separate query plane because of short-circuiting long chains of intermediate nodes.

Dynamic Groups: We study the effect of group churn due to attribute-value changes at individual nodes. We considered a group of 100 nodes, with group churn controlled by two parameters *churn* and *interval*. Every *interval* seconds, we randomly select *churn* nodes in the group to leave, and *churn* nodes outside the group to join.

Figure 9(b) shows the effect on query latency, of different *churn* values (x-axis) for two different *interval* values. Queries are inserted at the rate of one query per second, and the data points are averages of 100 queries per run. The plot shows that Moara's query latency is not affected significantly by group churn - (1) even when we increase the group churn rate by a 9-fold factor from *Interval*=45 to *interval*=5, Moara experiences only a small increase in latency, and (2) the latency stays low, and around 150 ms even when the entire group membership changes every 5 seconds.

Figure 10(a) provides an insight into the workings of Moara under the above workload, for *interval*=5, *churn*=160. Notice that the spikes in query latency occur once every 5 seconds, around the time that the group churn batch occurs. However, notice that (1) the peak latency stays within 300 ms, and (2) Moara query latency stabilizes

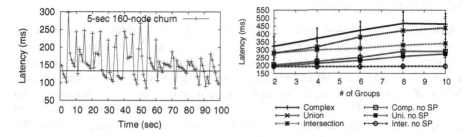

Fig. 10. (a) Latency over time with a dynamically changing group. The horizontal line shows the average latency with a static group of the same size. (b) Latency with composite queries.

very quickly after each group churn batch, typically within 1-2 seconds. Thus Moara shows high resiliency to dynamism due to rapidly occurring attribute-value changes.

Composite Queries: The experiments so far have focused on single groups in Moara. Here, we microbenchmark the performance of Moara on composite queries. Assuming $S_1, S_2, \ldots, S_n$ are simple single predicate groups, we study three types of composite queries: (1) Intersection queries of the form $S_1 \cap S_2 \cap \ldots \cap S_n$, for different values of n; (2) Union queries of the form $S_1 \cup S_2 \cup \ldots \cup S_n$, for different values of n; and (3) Complex queries, which are structured as $T_1 \cap T_2 \cap \ldots \cap T_m$, where each T_i is a union of multiple groups. These experiments suffice to characterize Moara's performance since the query optimization reduces all query expressions to one of the three. Each basic group S_i consists of 50 nodes selected at random. The complex expression we use[1] is $T_1 \cap T_2 \cap T_3$, and each T_i is a union of n basic groups for different values of n. Figure 10(b) plots the latency for above three types of queries with different values of n. For composite queries, recall that Moara first sends size probes to root nodes of group trees, in order to make a query optimization decision. Thus, we plot not only the total latency of a Moara query, but also the latency excluding the time to finish the size probes. Each data point is averaged over 300 queries.

First, notice that the average completion times of all queries, including queries with up to 10 groups, is less than 500 *ms*. For intersection queries, the completion times excluding time for size probes (plot line "Inter. no SP") do not depend on the size of the expression. This is because Moara selects only one of these groups to propagate the query. Although size probes are sent in parallel, the latency for size probes increases slightly since Moara waits until the slowest probe response arrives. For union queries, the total completion time of a query rises gradually with the size of the expression, as Moara needs to contact all groups (two "Union" plots). Finally, the completion time for complex queries is only slightly more than that of union queries, since Moara's query optimization selects only one of T_i's. The additional latency is caused by two factors: (a) the time taken for size probes is higher as we have to query the sizes for larger number of groups, and (b) a complex set expression adds more overhead at each node, because each node evaluates the entire complex expression.

---

[1] We found that the number of T_i's has little effect on latency because Moara queries only one of all T_i's.

7.3 PlanetLab Experiments

Methodology: We deploy Moara atop 200 PlanetLab nodes, which span several continents. Each PlanetLab node runs one instance of Moara. The instances are started sequentially, the system is given 5 minutes to warm up, and then a series of queries is injected from a Moara front-end running on a local machine. In order to study the behavior of Moara's query latency in-depth, we perform experiments on only one group at a time, but for different sizes of this group. Each experiment involves a total of 500 queries injected 5 seconds apart. All plotted data points are the average of 3 runs. We do not timeout on queries, in order to obtain complete answers.

Query Response Latency: Figure 11 plots the cumulative fraction of replies received as a function of time since query injection. The plot shows the responsiveness of Moara in a wide-area setting - even with as many as 100 nodes in the group, the median answer is received back within 1-2 seconds, while 90% of the answers are received within 5 seconds. Our technical report presents more results with different groups [20].

Moara versus Centralized Aggregation: Figure 11 compares Moara against a centralized approach which maintains no trees but has the Moara front-end directly query all nodes in parallel regardless of whether they satisfy the given predicate or not (labelled "Central"). The response for a query from this centralized aggregator is considered complete when the centralized aggregator has received a re-

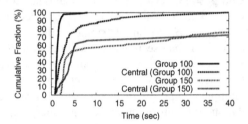

Fig. 11. Moara vs. Centralized Aggregator

sponse from every node regarding the query. The figure plots the cumulative fraction of replies received as a function of time since query injection. This plot illustrates that the comparison between the centralized aggregator and Moara is akin to the comparison of "the tortoise and the hare". For both groups of size 100 and 150, we notice that the centralized aggregator obtains initial replies faster than Moara, but then it slows down waiting for the remainder of the query answers from nodes.

Our analysis reveals that the latency of the centralized aggregator is affected by the slowest node or link in *the whole system*, while the latency of Moara is only affected by the slowest node or link in *the group*. Thus, Moara is faster overall in obtaining a large fraction of replies. Our technical report further discusses this result [20].

8 Related Work

PlanetLab has several management tools in use, such as CoTop, CoMon, etc [15]. However, none of the tools addresses scalability and expressive queries simultaneously. Several distributed systems have been proposed for aggregating data. Astrolabe [6] provides a generic aggregation abstraction, but uses a single static tree and hence has limited scalability with the number of metrics. SDIMS [7] constructs multiple trees for scalability with the number of metrics, but assumes a single group of the entire system. PIER [21] supports recursive SQL-style queries, but does not leverage in-network aggregation. Huebsch *et al.* [22] present a way to optimize global aggregation queries, while Moara optimizes multiple group-based aggregation trees. Seaweed [5] focuses on dealing with data unavailability. MON [23] supports one-shot queries and constructs query trees on-demand, but does not support expressive queries. Finally, Ganglia [14] uses a single hierarchical tree, but collects all data without in-network aggregation.

Structured overlay based multicast systems such as Scribe [18], SAAR [24], and SelectCast [25] bear some similarities with Moara, e.g., path collapsing of Scribe [18], the shared control plane idea of SAAR [24], and predicate-based multicast of SelectCast. However, all these system focus on building efficient trees for multicast where maintenance overhead is assumed to be much smaller than the data plane costs. CUP [26] and Shruti [27], while proposing adaptation techniques to reduce query cost, addresses a different optimization problem than us. In these systems, queries are only spread down to the nodes where updates are also propagated to (rendezvous points). Moara uses updates for pruning the group trees and queries are sent to all predicate-satisfying nodes.

9 Conclusion

In this paper, we have presented the design and evaluation of Moara, a group-based aggregation system. Moara achieves scalability with increasing numbers of machines, injected queries, and groups, by: (1) intelligently resolving composite query expressions, (2) constructing single-attribute aggregation trees that perform in-network aggregation, and (3) dynamically maintaining group trees based on query rates and group churn rates, thus reducing bandwidth consumption. Our experimental evaluations using simulations and deployments atop Emulab and PlanetLab demonstrate the effectiveness of Moara in answering queries accurately within hundreds of milliseconds across hundreds of nodes, and with low per-node bandwidth consumption.

References

1. HP: HP Data Centre Consolidation, http://h20331.www2.hp.com/enterprise/cache/141741-0-0-225-121.html
2. PlanetLab, http://www.planet-lab.org/
3. NSF: The NSF GENI Initiative, http://www.nsf.gov/cise/geni/
4. Foster, I.T.: The Grid 2003 Production Grid: Principles and Practice. In: Proc. HPDC-13 (2004)
5. Narayanan, D., Donnelly, A., Mortier, R., Rowstron, A.: Delay Aware Querying with Seaweed. In: Proc. VLDB (2006)
6. Renesse, R.V., Birman, K.P., Vogels, W.: Astrolabe: A Robust and Scalable Technology for Distributed System Monitoring, Management, and Data Mining. ACM Trans. on Comp. Syst. 21(2), 164–206 (2003)
7. Yalagandula, P., Dahlin, M.: A Scalable Distributed Information Management System. In: Proc. SIGCOMM (2004)
8. Rowstron, A.I.T., Druschel, P.: Pastry: Scalable, Decentralized Object Location, and Routing for Large-Scale Peer-to-Peer Systems. In: Guerraoui, R. (ed.) Middleware 2001. LNCS, vol. 2218, pp. 329–350. Springer, Heidelberg (2001)
9. Emulab, http://www.emulab.net
10. Brewer, E.: Towards Robust Distributed Systems (Invited Talk). In: Proc. PODC (2000)

11. Jain, N., Kit, D., Mahajan, P., Yalagandula, P., Dahlin, M., Zhang, Y.: STAR: Self Tuning Aggregation for Scalable Monitoring. In: Proc. VLDB (2007)
12. Jain, N., Kit, D., Mahajan, P., Yalagandula, P., Dahlin, M., Zhang, Y.: PRISM: Precision-Integrated Scalable Monitoring (extended). In: Proc. OSDI (2008)
13. Park, K., Pai, V.S.: CoMon: a Mostly-scalable Monitoring System for PlanetLab. SIGOPS OSR 40(1), 65–74 (2006)
14. Massie, M.L., Chun, B.N., Culler, D.E.: The Ganglia Distributed Monitoring System: Design, Implementation and Experience. Parallel Computing 30(7) (2004)
15. PlanetLab: Contributed Software, https://wiki.planet-lab.org/twiki/bin/view/Planetlab/ContributedSoftware
16. Zhao, B.Y., Huang, L., Stribling, J., Rhea, S.C., Joseph, A.D., Kubiatowicz, J.: Tapestry: A Resilient Global-scale Overlay for Service Deployment. IEEE JSAC 22(1) (2004)
17. Stoica, I., Morris, R., Karger, D., Kaashoek, F., Balakrishnan, H.: Chord: A Scalable Peer-to-Peer Lookup Service for Internet Applications. In: Proc. SIGCOMM (2001)
18. Castro, M., Druschel, P., Kermarrec, A.M., Rowstron, A.: SCRIBE: A Large-scale and De-centralised Application-level Multicast Infrastructure. IEEE JSAC (2002)
19. Castro, M., Druschel, P., Kermarrec, A.M., Nandi, A., Rowstron, A., Singh, A.: SplitStream: High-bandwidth Multicast in a Cooperative Environment. In: Proc. SOSP (2003)
20. Ko, S.Y., Yalagandula, P., Gupta, I., Talwar, V., Milojicic, D., Iyer, S.: Moara: Flexible and Scalable Group-Based Aggregation System. Technical Report UIUCDCS-R-2008-2989, UIUC (2008)
21. Huebsch, R., Chun, B., Hellerstein, J.M., Loo, B.T., Maniatis, P., Roscoe, T., Shenker, S., Stoica, I., Yumerefendi, A.R.: The Architecture of PIER: an Internet-Scale Query Processor. In: Proc. CIDR (2005)
22. Huebsch, R., Garofalakis, M., Hellerstein, J.M., Stoica, I.: Sharing Aggregate Computation for Distributed Queries. In: Proc. SIGMOD (2007)
23. Liang, J., Ko, S.Y., Gupta, I., Nahrstedt, K.: MON: On-demand Overlays for Distributed System Management. In: Proc. USENIX WORLDS (2005)
24. Nandi, A., Ganjam, A., Druschel, P., Ng, T.S.E., Stoica, I., Zhang, H., Bhattachargee, B.: SAAR: A Shared Control Plane for Overlay Multicast. In: Proc. NSDI (2007)
25. Bozdog, A., van Renesse, R., Dumitriu, D.: SelectCast: A scalable and self-repairing multicast overlay routing facility. In: Proc. SSRS (2003)
26. Roussopoulos, M., Baker, M.: CUP: Controlled Update Propagation in Peer-to-Peer Networks. In: USENIX (2003)
27. Yalagandula, P., Dahlin, M.: Shruti: A Self-Tuning Hierarchical Aggregation System. In: SASO (2007)

Author Index

430   Author Index

Lecture Notes in Computer Science

Sublibrary 2: Programming and Software Engineering

For information about Vols. 1– 4749
please contact your bookseller or Springer